THE BBC TALKS OF
E. M. Forster
1929–1960

A Selected Edition

Edited by
Mary Lago,
Linda K. Hughes, and
Elizabeth MacLeod Walls

Foreword by P. N. Furbank

University of Missouri Press
COLUMBIA AND LONDON

University of Missouri Press, Columbia, Missouri 65201
Printed and bound in the United States of America
5 4 3 2 1   12 11 10 09 08

Library of Congress Cataloging-in-Publication Data

Forster, E. M. (Edward Morgan), 1879–1970.
  The BBC talks of E.M. Forster, 1929–1960 : a selected edition / edited by Mary
Lago, Linda K. Hughes, and Elizabeth MacLeod Walls ; foreword by P. N. Furbank.
      p. cm.
  Summary: "Seventy of Forster's BBC broadcasts trace his evolution from novelist
to skillful cultural critic, revealing his vitality and importance as an astute critic of
contemporary literature—from Joyce to Steinbeck to Tagore—and a political activist
for India. Scripts dating from WWII provide new perspective on the arts during
wartime"—Provided by publisher.
  Includes index.
  ISBN 978–0–8262–1800–1 (alk. paper)
  1. Forster, E. M. (Edward Morgan), 1879–1970. 2. Books—Great Britain—Reviews.
3. Criticism—Great Britain. 4. Radio addresses, debates, etc.—Great Britain. I.
Lago, Mary. II. Hughes, Linda K. III. Walls, Elizabeth MacLeod. IV. Title.
  PR6011.O58A6 2008
  828'.912—dc22
                            2008002934

⊚™This paper meets the requirements of the
American National Standard for Permanence of Paper
for Printed Library Materials, Z39.48, 1984.

Designer: Stephanie Foley
Typesetter: Foley Design
Printer and binder: Integrated Book Technology, Inc.
Typefaces: ITC American Typewriter and Palatino

The publication of this book has been generously assisted by contributions from the
Office of the Dean, College of Arts and Science, University of Missouri–Columbia;
the English Department, University of Missouri–Columbia; the AddRan College of
Humanities and Social Sciences, Texas Christian University; and the English
Department, Texas Christian University.

Contents

The Scripts

Foreword

ERE IS A NICE SURPRISE FOR E. M. FORSTER LOVERS, A VERY generous selection of his radio talks, texts which one might have supposed lost forever. He had delivered occasional talks for the BBC from the late 1920s, and from 1932 onwards, for more than thirty years, he became their book reviewer. He was reporting on New Books to a nonspecialist and, so far as he knew, potentially limitless audience, and how characteristically he does it! He is determined, at all costs, to be helpful to his listeners, indeed bends over backwards to be so. He is the great simplifier, holding the theory that ideas, though they may be complex, may be stated in simple language; and he succeeds in this without the faintest taint of philistinism.

We can do no better than consider the description he gave of his own performance, at the end of his stint: with its fun, its seriousness and its charm it is a perfect sample of his approach. What he has been doing, he asserts, is not criticism, it is the humbler task of recommendation—the most important moment in his talks being the final one, when he offers suggestions for the listener's library list and tells book buyers about prices. "Regard me as a parasite, savoury or unsavoury," he says, "who battens on higher forms of life. And turning my head slightly backward, as a parasite will, I now crane towards the immediate past, I recollect what has nourished me there, and then I turn again to my fellow parasite, the microphone, and continue to address you through it."

This edition was first planned by the late Mary Lago, who died in 2001, but her successors have completed it in admirable style. They provide a long and detailed biographical and critical introduction and very knowledgeable notes, and they present the texts themselves with most exhaustive thoroughness. "For this volume," they say, rather strikingly, "we sought that stage in the life of these texts wherein writer, speaker, editor, bureaucrat, typist, audience member, and larger cultural milieu merged."

P. N. Furbank

Preface
Editorial History of This Project

M ARY LAGO BEGAN THIS PROJECT IN THE 1960S, AFTER SHE HAD completed the two-volume selection of Forster's letters that she coedited with P. N. Furbank. The broadcasts were to have been her solo project. She began reading scripts housed at BBC Written Archives Centre and in the course of her work published the pioneering essay "E. M. Forster and the BBC" in the *Yearbook of English Studies* (1990); the article was succeeded by a chapter devoted to the broadcasts in her biography of 1995, *E. M. Forster: A Literary Life*. By 2000 she had created a tentative list of broadcasts slated for inclusion, obtained permission to reprint them, and secured a contract with the Society of Authors and the University of Missouri Press. Through sheer will and energy she long held metastatic cancer at bay while she continued to develop the edition, but in the early autumn of 2000, when she was still on task in England, her health suddenly deteriorated.

In the 1990s Mary had asked Linda K. Hughes, as her former student, to serve as her literary executor along with her daughter, Jane Lago, an editor with the University of Missouri Press. When Linda visited Mary in January 2001, Mary and Jane both discussed the possibility of Linda's bringing the edition to completion; following Mary's death on 13 February 2001, Jane formally asked Linda to assume responsibility for the edition.

Mary Lago, then, conceived and originated this project, and at the time of her death she had completed the enormous task of reading through all the scripts. She also left behind extensive notes on unpublished letters and memos housed at the BBC Written Archives Centre as well as folders of related material. But she had not yet finalized the contents list or editorial principles for reproducing scripts, annotated any broadcasts, or begun an introduction. The same death that thwarted her completion of an edition of Forster's broadcasts also decreed that the vision behind this volume would be collaborative.

The level of collaboration increased when Linda invited Elizabeth MacLeod Walls to coedit this volume. Together we have finalized the edition's contents and editorial principles, annotated the scripts, and conceived and cowritten the introduction. At the National Sound Archive housed in the British Library, each of us has listened to the recordings that preserve broadcasts included in the edition, independently transcribing Forster's departures from his scripts. Our collaborative research has included visits to the BBC Written Archives Centre and the Forster Archive at King's College, Cambridge, as well as a systematic search of the *Listener* (1929–1960) for materials related to Forster and the history of the BBC.

Acknowledgments

ALL PASSAGES FROM E. M. FORSTER'S UNPUBLISHED WRITINGS, including his locked journal of 1940, 1948, and 1950 and his India journal of 1945, are copyright of King's College Archive Centre, Cambridge, The Papers of Edward Morgan Forster. We acknowledge the kind permission of The Society of Authors as agent for the Provost and Scholars of King's College Cambridge to reproduce unpublished materials authored by E. M. Forster. Forster's published writings are copyright of The Society of Authors, Executors of the E. M. Forster Estate. We thank them for permission to reproduce this material and are grateful for assistance from Rosalind Moad and Elizabeth Pridmore of King's College and Elizabeth Haylett, Literary Estates, Society of Authors.

For permission to quote from official British Broadcasting Corporation memoranda and correspondence, we are grateful to BBC Written Archives Centre (WAC), Caversham Park, Reading. We also acknowledge with warm gratitude the assistance of Trish Hayes, Archives Researcher, during research trips to BBC WAC and in response to requests for information.

In her acknowledgments in *E. M. Forster: A Literary Life* (1995), Mary Lago states, "My first and greatest debt is to Mr P. N. Furbank, authorised biographer of Forster and co-editor with me of Forster's *Selected Letters*, for his unfailing kindness and wise counsel." Mr. Furbank has also graciously responded to queries from the other editors and provided a foreword to this volume. His generosity thus spans the life of this project, for which we are deeply grateful.

This project has been supported by a Texas Christian University TCU/RF Research and Creative Activity Grant (2002). Additionally, we express warm thanks to Dr. Andrew Schoolmaster, Dean of AddRan College of Humanities and Social Sciences at Texas Christian University, and to Dr. Daniel Williams, Chair of the English Department, for contributions toward publication costs of the volume. We likewise thank Dr. Michael J. O'Brien, Dean of the College of Arts and Science at the University of Missouri, Columbia, and Dr. Pat Okker, Chair of the Department of English, for their contributions toward publication costs.

Emma Robinson, Director of the University of London Library, kindly provided access to the Senate House library and its holdings of *The Listener* for a reduced user's fee in 2002. We also thank staff members of the National Sound Archive in the British Library for their assistance during our visits to listen to surviving recordings of Forster's broadcasts. Joyce Martindale, Jill Kendle, and Kay Edmondson in the Interlibrary Loan Department at the Mary Couts Burnett Library, Texas Christian University, and John Montag, Director of the Nebraska Wesleyan University Cochrane-Woods Library, provided invaluable assistance over the course of the project. Our thanks also go to Sarah McNeely, Molly Marten, Amy Milakovic, Courtney Vett, and Jen Meyers for research assistance. In addition we express appreciation to Amy Dooley.

Beverly Jarrett, Director and Editor-in-Chief of the University of Missouri Press, and Jane Lago, Managing Editor, have provided unfailing support and expertise from the time this edition was solely undertaken by Mary Lago to its collaborative completion. Finally, we wish to underscore our appreciation of E. M. Forster—the music of his words and the humanity of his vision—at which we so often found ourselves marveling throughout this project.

The BBC Talks of
E. M. Forster
1929–1960

General Introduction

EFORE MARY LAGO BEGAN THIS PROJECT IN THE LATE 1960S the relationship between E. M. Forster and the BBC was rarely acknowledged by scholars, and it remains something of a surprise today. One might study Forster meticulously, understand his views on the individual and society, enumerate and appraise his life's work without delving into his thirty-year career as a radio broadcaster. Forster's contributions to the wireless previously had been relegated to footnotes, his foray into broadcasting classed as a hobby, little more. Through her research Mary Lago came to recognize the uniqueness of Forster's talks, broadcast throughout the formative years of the twentieth century. These talks were more than avuncular literary advice doled out to pockets of listeners. On the contrary, Forster's talks engaged and helped shape British culture. Though among all of Forster's achievements they have received the least amount of scholarly attention, in their time the broadcasts affected a larger audience than did Forster's fiction and established him as a well-known figure in households across Britain and India. More crucially, the talks enabled Forster to participate in and help direct Britain's cultural influence on the world.

Hilda Matheson, head of the Talks Department under Director-General John Reith, invited E. M. Forster to contribute a series of "talks" on literature and culture in 1928; he became a pioneer of the form. If today the radio talk seems entirely "natural," a given, it first had to be invented—beginning with voice and ethos, as well as content. Matheson, for example, insisted on the importance of the broadcast voice in the talk. As she observed in *Broadcasting*,

1

The most pervasive and the most powerful effects of broadcasting are seen, not in music, but in speech. . . . It has only slowly dawned upon us that the new emphasis and importance given to spoken, as distinct from written, language is likely to have results that were never dreamed of. . . . It is making everybody—throughout the world—more conscious of the sound of language, of pronunciation, cadence, intonation, of larger vocabularies and of larger forms of expression.[1]

She quickly realized that none of the models inherited from the immediate past—the public or classroom lecture, political speeches, sermons, poetry recitations—would engage wireless listeners. Instead, she argued, the key point was for the broadcaster to speak to a single listening individual and to let the broadcaster's own human qualities—his or her personality—suffuse the talk.

For Forster, the mandate to commune with the individual listener was in perfect accord with his own values: namely, the primacy of maintaining individualism and, somewhat paradoxically, the importance of fostering connection among otherwise discrete individuals. This emphasis on personal relationships, always with an eye to the importance of individual freedom, was the philosophy that guided Forster's own life. Thus, while one-on-one connection may have secured Forster's affinity for the medium, Matheson's insistence on a direct, informal approach also made sense given the variety of BBC listeners. Matheson illustrated the importance of broadcasters' ability to connect by telling of H. G. Wells, who, tapped to broadcast on the subject of immortality in 1928, had written out a lecture beforehand. When Wells boarded a train into London on the day of his broadcast, the signalman remarked, "Hullo, Mr. Wells, I'm going to listen to you tonight." Forced to reconceive his audience on the spot, Wells revised his script on the train and presented not a lecture but "an intimate confession of faith to a signal-man"—"a brilliantly effective talk" in Matheson's estimation.[2] The result of talks conceived in these terms was intimacy in the context of distance, impersonality, and mechanical reproduction, and also lively presentation that, consistent with the educative principles undergirding the BBC, stimulated but did not preach. As Matheson concludes, "The good broadcaster does not lecture, he talks in such a way as to evoke response, action, thought and even experiment; skeptics should see for themselves the extent to which the apparent remoteness of the speaker is offset by the intimacy of the microphone."[3]

1. Hilda Matheson, *Broadcasting* (London: Thornton Butterworth, 1933), 59–60.
2. Ibid., 242.
3. Ibid., 185. For further analysis of the ethics of connection and EMF's broadcast career, see Todd Avery, *Radio Modernism: Literature, Ethics, and the BBC, 1922–1938* (Aldershot, Hampshire: Ashgate, 2006), 37–38, 44, 51.

Despite Matheson's emphasis on voice and intimacy in the broadcast medium, the production of radio talks was as artificial as the technology that carried them to listeners. Actual conversation embodied the spontaneity Matheson and her successors sought but also entailed digressions, pauses, and stumbles that were anathema to the tight schedule of a broadcast service intent on engaging, not boring, the listener. The solution was for all broadcasts to be written in advance and submitted to editors, as in the print medium. The approved script then had to be broadcast in a way that sounded spontaneous and "natural," which demanded rehearsal and acquired technique. Matheson identified this hybrid form—part text, part oral performance, part mechanically produced wavelength—in her 1933 book and claimed that most broadcasters welcomed interventions in their scripts and the opportunity to rehearse to achieve optimal rhythms, emphases, and intonations.[4] Forster also recognized the hybridity of the radio talk from the beginning. Two days after making his broadcast debut on 16 July 1928 with a talk entitled "Of Railway Bridges," he wrote to his friend Malcolm Darling: "'What a flow of language!' writes the village schoolmistress to my mother, but . . . everything's organised to the nines, your artless cries written out and typed beforehand.'"[5] Two decades later, the staff critic of talks, Martin Armstrong, confirmed the hybridity of the talk in the BBC magazine, the *Listener:*

Although the innocent listener may not realise it, a talk is not talk but prose. 'But', you may say, 'what about those light, lively, personal and, as they seem, accidental chats that come to us occasionally over the air? Are you going to call them prose?' I am; and prose of the most careful and crafty description. That artless spontaneity and those spur-of-the-moment flashes are the outcome of the most artful deliberation, a put-up job if ever there was one. While composing it, the writer listens critically to each phrase and writes it down only when, to his practised ear, it has the natural flow and phraseology of contemporary speech. With grim deliberation he hammers out the effect of care-free spontaneity. And even then he may spoil it all if he is not an accomplished actor into the bargain, for he must, when broadcasting, endow his carefully wrought prose with exactly the right rhythms and intonations, all the hurryings, delayings and nervous hesitations of natural speech. The result, you may say, is talk, but it is talk purged of the redundance, inaccuracy and flaccidity of any but the rarest talk. It is talk raised to the power of sensitive prose. But as for being what it pretends to be, it is nothing of the kind.[6]

4. Matheson, *Broadcasting*, 76–77.
5. Quoted in Mary Lago, *E. M. Forster: A Literary Life* (New York: St. Martin's, 1995), 96.
6. Martin Armstrong, "The Critic on the Hearth: The Spoken Word," *Listener,* 28 April 1949, p. 731.

Martin's identification of the broadcast talk as a species of prose suggests one of the major reasons Forster found a broadcast career congenial, and why he was so good at it. The talk's status as prose also indicates one rationale for a print edition of this electronic medium.

Forster gave 145 radio talks from 1928 to 1963; additionally, his fiction was adapted for presentation and he participated in numerous interviews and discussions.[7] But he was much more than a performer or unofficial artist-in-residence: he played an active role in giving shape to BBC programming at crucial stages. In the earliest days of the corporation he was one of a trio of literary eminences working with Matheson and her assistant, Lionel Fielden. As Fielden recalls,

> many distinguished people fought shy of risking their reputation on the unfamiliar microphone. Fortunately there were some who did not. I remember best the trinity of E. M. Forster, Desmond MacCarthy and H. G. Wells, who all gave us freely of their time and wise counsels, and would sit round our gas fires at Savoy Hill, talking of the problems and possibilities of broadcasting. Desmond was, of course, a superb broadcaster: the only difficulty with him was to keep him to his script, for he would easily wander, in the Irish way, into a flood of reminiscence. E. M. Forster did not, as a speaker, quite reach the standard of his beautiful prose, but he was a wise and sympathetic counsellor. H. G. was a hopeless speaker with his squeaky voice (we built a special non-echo studio for him, but to no avail) but he was wise, even if, while always preening himself with women, he tended to be offensively rude to men and especially young men.[8]

Fielden pays special tribute to Forster as counselor, suggesting that he had a particularly active role in conceptualizing radio's cultural possibilities. When, upon Fielden's going to India to organize All-India Radio, the British government was unresponsive to his pleas for a selection board to help sift through six thousand job applications, Forster was at the ready: "partly with the assistance of letters from England from E. M. Forster and others, I got a Board together."[9] Forster was also willing to use his stature to defend the India Service, or, as it was called in-house, the Eastern Service. Fielden held a dim view of Forster's friend Malcolm Darling, who headed the service. And when the 5 July 1941 *New Statesman* charged that German propaganda was more appealing to Indians than was the BBC, Fielden in the same paper called for a change in BBC's organization and approach. Forster was one of the first to come to the defense of BBC and

7. Lago, "E. M. Forster and the BBC," *Yearbook of English Studies* 20 (1990): 134.
8. Lionel Fielden, *The Natural Bent* (London: Andre Deutsch, 1960), 105.
9. Ibid., 183.

Darling, who was angered by Fielden's defection; in a letter to the editor Forster declared that "he had found 'no traces of British parochialism in its office' and that he had been much impressed by 'the intelligence and initiative of its Indian staff.'"[10]

Years later, when George Barnes left the Talks Department to organize the more intellectually ambitious Third Programme, Forster again played an active role as counselor during the Third's formative period. Talks producer Jean Rowntree observes Forster's "considerable influence in discussions with Barnes about possibilities, ways, and means, and most particularly whether a general or a specialised audience was the goal." Mary Lago suggests that Forster's 1935 essay "Does Culture Matter?" "was . . . a brief for what would become the Third Programme's reason for being."[11] Yet Forster's influence was not limited to the design or defense of major programs. On 23 July 1947, Donald Stephenson, director of Eastern Services, wrote to Forster inviting him to broadcast a personal message to India on the occasion of Indian independence—included in this edition—in company with a former viceroy, a former secretary of state, an expert on British and Indian economic relations, and "'a man in the street' as representative of those Englishmen who have not been in India and who have taken only a normal discursive interest in Indian affairs."[12] As a 6 August 1947 internal memo confirms, Forster suggested his beloved friend Bob Buckingham as the "man in the street," and Buckingham duly broadcast along with the others.[13] Forster's close involvement with BBC administrators and planning indicates yet another reason that he found broadcasting for BBC congenial: the "wise counsellor" was working within a framework he partially shaped.

Of course, Forster's influence at the BBC took root two decades earlier, when he agreed to affiliate with this new medium—the wireless—precisely because of his interest in speaking about art and ideas to "a man in the street." He simultaneously valued and doubted the wireless for its universality but overcame his distrust of technology and the isolation it caused in order to increase public knowledge and forge connections with others.[14] In 1928, for example, Forster expressed an uneasy truce with this

10. Asa Briggs, *The History of Broadcasting in the United Kingdom*, 5 vols. (London: Oxford University Press, 1961–1995), 3:506–7.

11. Lago, *A Literary Life*, 116, 118.

12. E. M. Forster File 8, 1947–1948 R CONT 1, BBC Written Archives Centre (hereafter WAC).

13. Robin Russell, Eastern Services, 6 August 1947, India Talks Files 2 & 3, 1943–1954, R51/256/2, BBC WAC.

14. EMF's distrust of, and ineptitude with, technology is well documented, but May Buckingham's characterization is perhaps the most telling: "The simplest machine defeated him. I took years to persuade him to have an electric gramophone and he had the greatest

ever-expanding technological force, observing in his *Commonplace Book:* "Wireless etc. abolishes wavings of handkerchiefs, etc. Death the only farewell surviving. We do not get away from each other as we did. . . . But it is puzzling, new. . . . Opposed to wireless etc. are passports etc.—the desperate attempt of humanity to raise new barriers."[15] Forster's first talk occurred around the same time, on 16 July 1928.

Our volume opens with Forster's talk "The Great Frost"—his second— which describes an overwhelming and aberrant winter freeze that crippled London and surrounding areas. This early talk establishes Forster's wit and his eye for the human living within the frozen external world. Yet the talk is also significant for what it does not accomplish. Though literary in parts (Forster contrasts the frost with the Elizabethan scene from Virginia Woolf's *Orlando*), it is also anecdotal and somewhat undeveloped—not at all the compact, if also conversational, literary and cultural analyses he proffers in later talks. Most important, the talk is open, hopeful—innocent. War is behind rather than ahead of his listeners, so they believed. Sharing the new artistic and cultural freedoms of the 1920s, "The Great Frost" equates the unusual with the sublime and finds in nature a profound corollary for human enchantment and curiosity. For these reasons, "The Great Frost" throws into relief the more worldly canon of broadcasts to come, and of course the war broadcasts that changed not only Forster but his listening audience as well.

BBC directors and producers of talks intervened in Forster's broadcasts throughout his radio career, whether by scheduling talks or by proposing subjects for him to develop: George Orwell suggested that Forster address "An Indian on W. B. Yeats" in the 1940s; Harman Grisewood, controller of the Third Programme, first conceived Forster's 1951 broadcast on the service's fifth anniversary; and a public relations director at Heinemann's— Diana, Lady Avebury—provided the impetus for "Recollections of Nassenheide" (1958) when she sent proofs of Leslie de Charmes's biography of Elizabeth von Arnim to BBC.[16] The only surviving evidence of extensive editing of Forster's scripts, however, dates from the 1930s, perhaps an indication that he was still developing as a broadcaster. A 13

---

difficulty with tin openers . . . we were always buying him new ones to try." See G. K. Das, and John Beer, eds., *E. M. Forster: A Human Exploration. Centenary Essays* (New York: New York University Press, 1979), 184.

15. EMF, *Commonplace Book*, ed. Philip Gardner (Stanford: Stanford University Press, 1985), 38.

16. George Orwell to EMF, 18 November 1942, E. M. Forster File 4B, July–December 1942 R CONT 1: Harman Grisewood to EMF, 18 May 1951, E. M. Forster File 9A, 1949–1951 R CONT 1; Diana, Lady Avebury to John Morris, director of the Third Programme, 10 October 1958, E. M. Forster File 10b, 1958–1960 R CONT 1, BBC WAC. Avebury's letter suggested that EMF give a talk on the biography in which he figured.

September 1939 letter from George Barnes outlined several possible themes for "Reading as Usual" (17 September 1939), which Forster gave on short notice. Once Barnes had Forster's script in hand he wrote two pages of detailed suggestions in response, at least one of which Forster adopted.[17]

In general, however, Forster's talks were becoming stronger in both content and delivery during the 1930s. As a frequent contributor to the BBC, Forster generally adhered to literary topics, though he did not eschew social commentary. Perhaps most notable in this regard are Forster's comments on freedom in a world imprisoned by intellectual constraints in "Seven Days Hard" (10 March 1934). His opening query in this talk—"I've been wondering where liberty ends and restraint begins in contemporary society"—articulates more than his philosophical approach to the broadcast; it also encapsulates Forster's approach to life in the 1930s, when his persona moved from novelist to commentator, activist, essayist.

If broadcasting provided an important outlet for Forster's intellectual evolution in the 1930s, it also enabled him to secure a new professional identity, one that the BBC not only encouraged but also took every opportunity to enhance. The BBC valued Forster for his literary stature and compensated him accordingly. In 1939 Forster received the standard fee of ten guineas for a broadcast entitled "The House and the Man" on Clouds Hill, the home of T. E. Lawrence, but by 1941 BBC was paying him twenty guineas per quarter-hour broadcast.[18] By comparison, T. S. Eliot did not receive more than fifteen pounds for a broadcast until after 1945.[19] Forster was also given unusual latitude when it came to rehearsals and recording. If T. S. Eliot welcomed rehearsals, Forster found that his broadcasts succeeded better without them and was exempted from the requirement— though he usually ran through his talks just before broadcasting to get the

17. George Barnes to EMF, 13 September 1939, and Barnes to assistant director of Talks, n.d., E. M. Forster File 2, 1939–1940 R CONT 1, BBC WAC. Barnes's first suggestion was that EMF "Begin with the sentence on p 3. '*We are probably all of us going to have a great deal of time for reading'*"; in the print form of the talk published in the *Listener,* this became the second sentence (21 September 1939, p. 586).

18. Memo of 15 April 1939 from West of England Region Offices to Head Office, E. M. Forster File 2, 1939–40; 4 July 1941 Talks Booking Requisition, E. M. Forster File 3, 1941 R CONT 1, BBC WAC. For a special broadcast such as the half-hour "Fifth Anniversary of the Third Programme" talk, EMF was paid sixty guineas plus travel expenses to London (14 September 1951 Talks Booking Requisition, E. M. Forster File 9A, 1949–1951 R CONT 1, BBC WAC). For the ten-minute "I Speak for Myself" in January 1949, EMF was paid fifteen guineas plus travel expenses (17 December 1948 Talks Booking Requisition, E. M. Forster File 8, 1947–1948 R CONT 1, BBC WAC).

19. Michael Coyle, "T. S. Eliot on the Air: 'Culture' and the Challenges of Mass Communication," in *T. S. Eliot and Our Turning World,* ed. Jewel Spears Brooker (Houndmills, Basingstoke, Hampshire: Macmillan; New York: St. Martin's, 2001), 141.

timing right.[20] Above all, Forster was valued, compensated, respected, and supplicated for his skill as an engaging and persuasive speaker to large, multifarious audiences. As Martin Armstrong comments of Forster's 1949 broadcast "The Raison d'Être of Criticism,"

> Mr. Forster talked for an hour, and an hour's talk is usually, as most listeners know, no picnic. . . . Mr. Forster's was one of the three or four [talks] in my experience which actually ended too soon for me. He has a delightful habit of mixing profundity with strictly apposite flippancy, so that, stimulated alternately by the vinosity and the bubbles, we follow him in a state of intoxicated sobriety which leaves us fresher than when we started.[21]

Armstrong's delight in the intellectual and personal effervescence of Forster's radio talk confirms Mary Lago's assertion that Forster and the BBC were an "ideal match."[22] Their shared commitments to reaching individuals throughout the world while realizing the cultural possibilities of radio enabled them to work in tandem. Yet in doing so they were also subtly shaping each other's developing identities. This "ideal match" also produced an important body of work in the form of broadcast scripts housed at King's College, Cambridge, and the BBC Written Archives Centre at Caversham Park, Reading. The present edition makes this significant archive newly accessible to readers.

As this volume of Forster's BBC talks also reveals, the partnership between Forster and the BBC was anything but simple. The body of work Forster produced for radio was in key respects breath rather than body, live broadcasts that faded away as soon as the broadcast ended, no matter how richly they filled an interval; yet Forster's scripts also compose a significant body of writing. The man who was never comfortable with machines played an important role in shaping a new medium made possible by advanced technology; and Forster used the mass medium of radio to insist on the importance of removing barriers to the interested listener—to foster an intimate broadcast style that invited all audiences to access high culture. Forster's on-air time provided an outlet for his dissident commitment to civil liberties yet also, during World War II, for his participation in state-sponsored propaganda; similarly, his wartime

---

20. Coyle, "'This rather elusory broadcast technique': T. S. Eliot and the Genre of the Radio Talk," *ANQ* 11.4 (Fall 1998): 34. EMF explained his disinclination to rehearse to Mr. Graham, director of talks, in a letter of 20 March 1939 (E. M. Forster File 2, 1939–1940 R CONT 1, BBC WAC); Orwell asked EMF to run through a broadcast for timing in a 3 September 1943 letter (E. M. Forster File 5, 1943 R CONT 1, BBC WAC).

21. Armstrong, "Critic on the Hearth: The Spoken Word," *Listener,* 31 March 1949, p. 551.

22. Lago, "E. M. Forster and the BBC," 132.

broadcasts to India aided British imperial rule even though Forster's deep love of India led him to reject the Empire's legitimacy.

The broadcasts included in this volume are therefore historical artifacts as well as examples of public, intellectual discourse, and we also recognize in Forster's own evolution from novelist to adroit cultural critic a parallel to the BBC's transformation during this time. That is, his changing broadcast style, his persistent challenges to the BBC's policies, and his (sometimes daring) choice of topics reveal not only his sagacity as a broadcaster but also the changing role of the BBC in the midtwentieth century. They also reveal something else: the extent of Forster's effect on British and Indian audiences via the BBC and his magnitude as an intellectual leader for listeners around the globe. Forster, though recognized as a central player in his literary milieu, has been classed by most cultural historians of this period as secondary to Virginia Woolf, James Joyce, or T. S. Eliot. With but five published novels, most of which appeared before the First World War, and an often ignored (though imposing) collection of short stories and essays, Forster has been relegated not quite to the lesser lights of modernism, but perhaps to the "middle lights," if we might invent this term. This characterization is faulty, and not simply because of his prolific creation of talks. Cerebral and autonomous in his Cambridge identity, Forster maintained a certain distance from the London literary set—both literally and in his overall demeanor. Among this group, Forster was known for his Edwardian sensibilities, was sometimes accused of Victorian sympathies, and was believed to harbor unfashionable nostalgia for England itself and for passé humanist values. In a word, Forster appeared effete. Forster himself was aware of these perceptions that barred his participation in the echelon of high modernism. Of Bloomsbury, he wrote in the *Commonplace Book*, "I don't belong automatically"—though he regretted this. He knew that "Cambridge . . . attracts my heart more" than the London crowd, "but [this] depresses me more because as soon as the train slackens at that eel-like platform it's settled who I can know, who not."[23] Broadcasting would in some ways confirm Forster's status as an outsider to modernism; he is nostalgic in his talks, after all, lauding great minds of the past, promoting conservation of the English countryside and national landmarks, and supporting democratic rather than socialist polity.

---

23. EMF, *Commonplace Book*, 23. EMF was also a member of the Reform Club in London—another clue to his intellectual and political tastes. As suggested by its name, the club is devoted to promoting the kinds of social reforms embodied in the 1832 Reform Act. In the nineteenth and twentieth centuries the club boasted important literati among its members (Hilaire Belloc, Sir Arthur Conan Doyle, William Makepeace Thackeray, and, closer to EMF's own period, Henry James and H. G. Wells), but none who might be considered avant garde or affiliated with the modernist elite.

Forster drew upon his public identity as a respected, if somewhat staid, novelist to fortify the reputations of writers whom he admired. While Forster devotes whole talks to authors whose work transcended history and nationality (he is reverent when speaking of Tolstoy, Austen, and Proust) and to contemporaries whose art was widely admired (Woolf, Lawrence, Shaw), he is also deliberate about introducing listeners to little-known or underappreciated writers. Forster was using his cachet as one of the better-known authors of his age to imprint his own artistic judgment on listeners familiar with his profound literary contributions—and there-fore, presumably, more inclined to entertain his views.

If Forster esteems the work of C. S. Lewis, Aldous Huxley, Bertrand Russell, Somerset Maugham, John Dos Passos, John Steinbeck, and Ernest Hemingway, he likewise champions the artistry of lesser-known but in his view equally powerful writers, including William Plomer, Rebecca West, Paul Valéry, Arthur Koestler, and Stefan Zweig. (Forster simultaneously endorses the last two for their courage in speaking out against the Soviet Union and fascism.) Forster also couples adamant honesty with steadfast belief in art for art's sake—for example, he is willing to fight for Joyce's censored and misunderstood prose while, in the same breath, admitting that he does not "take to him." In other talks, Forster exposes his own sin-gularity as an imaginative artist, whether he is praising innovators as prominent as Mark Twain ("Don't you see that river and feel it and sit in it up to your chin and eat that fish? Don't you understand now why I want to visit the Mississippi myself, and why it is one of the rivers of youth?") or as invisible as the now forgotten organizers of an exhibit of Hindu pho-tographs that toured England in 1941 ("Would you have expected that in an industrial town in North England—namely Sunderland—thousands of people would have gone to see that collection and tried to learn from it something of the Indian attitude towards religion and art?"). Forster is, in a word, an egalitarian critic—or rather, connoisseur—of art and literature because he was himself an accomplished author whose ethos allowed him to disseminate a philosophy of understanding, recognition, and connec-tion across the airwaves. Forster's BBC talks are an example of that rare hybrid of homage and invention delivered by an advocate of good art who was himself one of the most important authors of the modern age.

But Forster's talks also underscore his rebellion. His broadcasts refuse the pessimism that defined his age and challenge unjust authority when-ever possible. Forster as broadcaster inhabited an identity apart from that of sentimental novelist, and he used this identity to transform, incite, and empower his listening audience. This volume demonstrates Forster's engagement with ideas that not merely complemented but rather enhanced literary scholarship of his day; the talks also make clear that

Forster carried the greatest influence of any British intellectual on the Indian continent during the last third of his life. Finally, his BBC talks reveal that throughout his life Forster gave primacy neither to novel writing nor to literary criticism. Instead, he upheld as essential an abstruse yet precise philosophy on personal relations that became not only the cornerstone of his existence but also, as these talks show, one of the lasting postulates of his brand of modernism.

Certainly his view of human life was not popular among modernists—and this is another of Forster's unacknowledged contributions to the age. He was, to put it simply, a renegade among his peers. In the desolation of the "long weekend" when *The Waste Land* and *Ulysses* became synonymous with the young intellectual's aimless discontent, Forster broadcast about the inherent hope of literature. In the depressing chasm of the war years when Woolf's suicide and the rise of fascism signaled a new reign of doubt and fear among artists, Forster broadcast about the value of art as a weapon against tyranny. And in the shiftless postwar years when Britain stumbled out of her imperial identity and into an era of economic uncertainty, Forster broadcast about the new—Britten's operas, independent India, P.E.N. and artistic freedom in the age of internationalism. These are not the vague ramblings of an aged novelist or a modernist devalued by a postmodern academy critical of his seemingly naive liberal humanism, his colonial fiction written from a position of privilege, and his relatively staid narrative style. Rather, these talks represent a premier intellectual record of a nation transfigured by war, technology, postimperialism, and American dominance composed by an artist and activist who was consistently evaluating his relationship to this world and his obligation to offer comment on it. Simply put, these broadcasts situate Forster as one of the most poignant voices of the twentieth century.

THE DEVELOPMENT OF BBC RADIO: AN OVERVIEW

Because Forster's late career as a broadcaster cannot be understood apart from the institution that enabled it, an overview of the BBC's development is in order.[24] Since Forster had little to do with the strictly technical side of radio, we focus on the cultural aims of radio and the BBC as a state apparatus before and during World War II. We then turn to Forster's part in these aspects of BBC history and his achievement as a broadcaster, before concluding with our editorial principles.

---

24. For an in-depth account the indispensable source is Asa Briggs's five-volume *History of Broadcasting*.

Brought into being in 1922, when the regulation of wavelengths and of the distribution of wireless sets seemed desirable, the British Broadcasting Company was first funded through a share of Post Office licensing fees. In 1927 the BBC was incorporated and granted monopoly status—a key factor in the direction it took away from American-style commercial radio in favor of commitments to culture and education.[25] John Reith, the corporation's first director-general (1927–1938), who had also served as managing director-general of the British Broadcasting Company (1923–1926), was crucial in forming that policy.

The new medium of radio could not debut in a vacuum; a long media history preceded it, and when Reith implemented BBC policy he was deeply influenced by the vision of Matthew Arnold, poet and critic but also civil servant and journalist. In *Culture and Anarchy*, Arnold conceives culture as the quest for perfection among all human capacities, including not only righteousness but also intellect and sensitivity to beauty.[26] Culture, Arnold contends, has an important social function, for it is civilization's best bulwark against anarchy from the common people and extreme narrowness or rigidity among national leaders. Reith committed himself to a cultural project on similar lines as director-general of the BBC, with lasting effects. As Paddy Scannell and David Cardiff assert, "Victorian ideals of service laced with Arnoldian notions of culture suffused all aspects of the BBC's programme service in the thirty years of its monopoly."[27] Passionately resisting merely popular appeal, Reith also adamantly opposed splintering BBC's listening audience into distinct groups, insisting on a single "great audience" in the interests of achieving national unity through culture and helping inspire interest in the arts and fresh ideas among those who formerly had scant access to them.[28] Reith was not advocating explicit indoctrination or sermonizing; rather, he wanted to advance culture by making it, in his words, "interesting and enjoyable."[29]

25. See ibid., 2:56.

26. Matthew Arnold, *Culture and Anarchy*, ed. Samuel Lipman (New Haven: Yale University Press, 1994), 47, 109. Today his complex project is often evoked in the phrase Arnold applied to criticism's goal rather than to culture, "the best that is known and thought in the world." See Arnold, "The Function of Criticism at the Present Time," in *Lectures and Essays in Criticism*, ed. R. H. Super (Ann Arbor: University of Michigan Press, 1962), 283.

27. Paddy Scannell and David Cardiff, *A Social History of British Broadcasting, Volume I, 1922–1939: Serving the Nation* (Oxford: Basil Blackwell, 1991), 9.

28. Briggs, *History of Broadcasting*, 2:36–37; see also Scannell and Cardiff, *Social History of British Broadcasting*, 227.

29. Briggs, *History of Broadcasting*, 2:185. Avery emphasizes the less democratic elements in Reith's policy, including his early sympathies with Hitler's authoritarianism and attempt to define morality in strict Christian terms. See Avery, *Radio Modernism*, 14–25.

How this was to be done through a broadcast medium was at the time of Reith's accession still an idea-in-the-making, and the adventure of it all inspired a number of talented staff members whom Reith recruited. BBC's mission dictated attention to classical as well as popular music and news broadcasts, and radio talks and discussion also played a significant role from the beginning. The intersection of radio technology and oral performance with prose, as well as Reith's commitment to education in the broadest sense, illuminates not only the Talks Department but also an adjunct to the BBC that debuted almost as early as the corporation itself: the *Listener,* a weekly periodical founded in 1929. Briggs explicitly terms the *Listener* an "educational periodical," later adding, "Of the alternate ways of treating the periodical, the first as a narrowly educational paper, the second as 'a vehicle of general culture,'" founding editor R. S. Lambert "unhesitatingly preferred the second."[30] The *Listener* also figures in the history of Forster's radio talks because it preserved many of them in the form of published essays, saving his prose from the fate of ephemerality.

As Michael Coyle notes, "the standard BBC contract . . . gave the corporation publication [the *Listener*] rights to all talks for twenty-eight days after the original broadcast."[31] Because of her commitment to voice and the talk as a distinct new genre, Hilda Matheson wanted talks to be republished verbatim, as parliamentary debates are in *Hansard.* But Lambert insisted on "editorial tidying up,"[32] with important implications for the differences among scripts, broadcasts, and printed essays. Burton Paulu observes that "the best talks often make poor reading and vice versa, so that praise bestowed on the printed version (seldom changed from the broadcast text) of a program sometimes obscures the fact that it may have been an indifferent broadcast."[33] He makes an important point, but in fact printed versions were not identical with the broadcast in substance *or* in medium. *Listener* essays obviously originated in talks that had first been written out, but in the immediate moment of oral performance broadcasters gave their scripts distinctive inflection and even departed from the text in subtle but substantive ways to achieve a greater sense of spontaneity and intimacy. As well, informalities or colloquialisms in scripts that were apposite to radio talks were often smoothed out into formal prose when the scripts were transformed—"remediated," one might say—as periodical essays. Talks, scripts, and essays were thus never identical. In choosing

30. Briggs, *History of Broadcasting,* 2:219, 290.

31. Coyle, "T. S. Eliot's Radio Broadcasts, 1929–1963: A Chronological Checklist," in *T. S. Eliot and Our Turning World,* ed. Brooker, 206.

32. Briggs, *History of Broadcasting,* 2:291.

33. Burton Paulu, *British Broadcasting: Radio and Television in the United Kingdom* (Minneapolis: University of Minnesota Press, 1956), 177.

BBC scripts as our copy texts, we have deliberately chosen those texts that point at once toward the broadcast medium of mechanically produced voice and toward the world of print and manuscript culture—hence, too, our decision to retain the headings of scripts tied to broadcasts and their technical underpinnings. We have also identified in notes substantive variants between broadcast scripts and *Listener* essays.

We transcribe variants from broadcasts more rarely than we would like, however. What Scannell and Cardiff say of their social history of the BBC from 1922 to 1939 is also true of this edition of Forster's broadcast "texts":

> There is of course an inescapable paradox at the heart of this project of which we have been acutely aware all along—our object of study no longer exists. The early pioneers of radio as an art-form lamented the 'ghastly impermanence' of their medium. . . . although there are recordings of some of the more significant programmes broadcast from the mid-thirties onwards, the vast bulk of output perished in the moment of transmission.[34]

No recordings of talks could be made until the advent of the 1925 Stille electromagnetic machine, which relied on steel wire or magnetic tape. Only during World War II, when scheduled broadcasts might face bombing or other disruptions, and when the need to distribute news worldwide was urgent, did systematic recordings of broadcasts begin; even then recording was seen as a backup rather than as an end in itself.[35] After World War II recordings of broadcasts became standard. Yet the fact of broadcasting was no guarantee of preservation, and of the seventy broadcast scripts collected here (nineteen broadcast after V-E day), only five partial or complete recordings exist.

If the "real" products of Forster's broadcasts have with few exceptions disappeared forever, how should we understand their reception? How many people listened to his or other broadcasters' words, and what effect did they have? It is difficult to tell, a point urged by Gillian Beer in her discussion of literary influence in the age of radio:

> A broadcast is, intimately and fleetingly, part of the mind of the listener, leaving an unwritten trace and the subject of unvoiced dialogue. So when, for example, we are thinking about the interconnections between writers after 1928 . . . we cannot know extensively who tuned into whom or how hard they listened. Arthur Eddington and James Jeans, Virginia Woolf and Vita Sackville-West, E. M. Forster and Bertrand Russell may each have heard any of the others on the airwaves.[36]

34. Scannell and Cardiff, *Social History of British Broadcasting*, xii.
35. See Briggs, *History of Broadcasting*, 3:52, 326–28.
36. Gillian Beer, "'Wireless': Popular Physics, Radio and Modernism," in *Cultural*

Various "Critics on the Hearth" (as the regular review feature of the *Listener* was called) left their responses on record, and occasional letters to the editor also registered reactions. But the letters were often tangential to the broadcast itself or idiosyncratic—as when Henry Edmonds wrote to object as "an artist, an Irishman, and a fellow-citizen of Joyce" to Forster's naming *War and Peace* and *À la recherche du temps perdu*, rather than *Ulysses*, the best novels ever written.[37] Hence the precise impact of talks on listeners is as elusive as are the unrecorded broadcasts themselves.

It is also important to acknowledge that radio talks, though of great interest to literary and cultural historians, played a proportionately small role within BBC radio as a whole. In the corporation's early years broadcasting was fairly limited: until September 1933 no broadcasts were transmitted from 6:15 to 8:00 p.m. on Sundays; in 1934 daily transmissions began at 10:45 a.m. and ceased at midnight. Within this limited broadcasting schedule, not surprisingly, a mere 11.17 hours in 1929 and 6.83 hours in 1930 were devoted to talks and discussion in a given October week.[38] Broadcasting in English comprised an even smaller segment in wartime broadcasts to India: a mere forty-five minutes a day.[39] Ten years after the Third Programme had been founded in 1946, splintering Reith's "great audience" in order to target better-educated listeners, Burton Paulu calculated that each week 18 percent of the Third's programming was devoted to talks and discussions. The Third Programme as a whole, moreover, claimed at most a 1 percent share in the total BBC listening audience.[40] Forster's "Fifth Anniversary of the Third Programme" talk, though of unquestionable cultural importance, reached only 0.2 percent of United Kingdom adults—the same number attracted by T. S. Eliot's "The Three Voices of Poetry," a public lecture broadcast on the Third Programme in 1953.[41]

Babbage: Technology, Time and Invention, ed. Francis Spufford and Jenny Uglow (London: Faber and Faber, 1996), 150.

37. Henry Edmonds, "The Greatest Novel?" (letter), *Listener*, 6 May 1943, p. 541. Briggs reports that most letters were written when someone disliked programming; if such letters had sociological value, they were unreliable as indicators of audience response (*History of Broadcasting*, 2:68).

38. See Briggs, *History of Broadcasting*, 2:26, 35.

39. Review of *Talking to India*, ed. George Orwell, *Listener*, 16 December 1943, p. 701. As John Arlott remarks, the talks portion of the service included a weekly poetry program, a weekly quarter hour devoted to prose writers, and EMF's monthly book review; see "Forster and Broadcasting," in *Aspects of E. M. Forster: Essays and Recollections Written for His Nineteeth Birthday* (New York: Harcourt, Brace, and World, 1969), 87.

40. Paulu, *British Broadcasting*, 153.

41. Listener Research Report, 11 October 1951, LR/51/2147, BBC WAC; Coyle, "'This rather elusory broadcast technique,'" 39. EMF's 1955 Third Programme broadcast on *The Mint* attracted the same audience share (Audience Research Report, 2 March 1955, LR/55/300, BBC WAC). Our thanks to Trish Hayes for providing copies of the two Audience Research reports.

Any notion that Forster and broadcasters such as T. S. Eliot, Desmond MacCarthy, and Harold Nicolson were reaching "the masses" thus needs to be set aside. But neither was this audience insubstantial. When the BBC was composed of a single home service Reith replied to a *Listener* essay complaining that the talks were too "highbrow" and too narrow in appeal by pointing out that 90,000 people were on a permanent list to receive a schedule of talks.[42] As Paulu calculated in 1956, a 1 percent share of the total listening audience could mean as few as 20,000 but as many as 376,000 listeners.[43] Listeners of talks, moreover, included the educated, the intelligent, the curious—those most likely to influence others or to take active roles in society.[44] The same was true of Indian audiences in the 1940s. Forster himself conceded that he knew nothing of Indian peasants (one of the reasons he refused to talk about Indians for the Understanding Other Peoples series aimed at Sixth Form students).[45] The *Listener* cited George Orwell's estimation that only 3 percent of Indians could speak some English and that fewer still had real command of the language; offsetting this limitation was the fact that this elite group (including students) permitted more sophisticated talks than could be given to the Home Service audiences in wartime Britain.[46] Yet it would be a mistake to think of Forster's audience only in terms of an elite, as Wells's signalman might suggest. Working-class listeners in fact composed 35 percent of Third Programme listeners in 1949.[47] As Gillian Beer argues, a radio listening audience was bound to be more "promiscuous" than a targeted book audience, and at their best radio talks provided access to ideas and material on a par with universities but without the exclusiveness of university education.[48]

The impact of radio talks in Britain and India also needs to be gauged in terms of their social and ideological effects. No broadcast, whatever the size of the listening audience or the intent of the broadcaster, was innocent of ideology or divorced from the corporation's function as a state apparatus. To the degree that any medium becomes so interwoven with daily life

42. John Reith, "The New Talks Programme," *Listener*, 30 April 1930, p. 767. Reith was responding to "The Problem of the Talks: A Plea for Popular Treatment," by Norman Edwards, *Listener*, 23 April 1930, pp. 717–18.

43. Paulu, *British Broadcasting*, 369.

44. See Arlott, "Forster and Broadcasting," 87; see also Lago, *E. M. Forster: A Life*, 100.

45. EMF to unknown correspondent ("Dear Sir"), 7 February 1942, E. M. Forster File 4A, January–June 1942 R CONT 1, BBC WAC.

46. Review of *Talking to India*, ed. George Orwell, *Listener*, 16 December 1943, p. 701; see also Arlott, "Forster and Broadcasting," 87. In comparison to the broadcast audiences, the *Listener*, in which broadcast material could be circulated as print, had a circulation of 50,000 in 1934 (Briggs, *History of Broadcasting*, 2:281) and over 133,000 in 1956 (Paulu, *British Broadcasting*, 177).

47. See Briggs, *History of Broadcasting*, 4:83.

48. Beer, "'Wireless,'" 150–51.

that it functions as an "ordinary" feature of the everyday, it helps shape human subjectivity; if it is a mass news medium, it also acquires the power of determining what counts as "real" in the external world. Radio, especially prior to television, quickly became a structural link between individuals within a family and the larger world beyond. Broadcasters spoke directly to the individual, but the peculiar mix of BBC programming devoted to cooking and gardening as well as to music and national culture subtly emphasized family life and so comprised a tacit message about how society ought to be conceived and organized.[49] And of course Reith's Arnoldian policy was inseparable from attempts to construct a national identity for Britons:

> The BBC fulfilled its mandate of service in the national interest by synthesizing a national culture from components that had begun to converge since the late nineteenth century. There was a national education system to inculcate, as part of the curriculum, the achievements of British history and the glories of English literature. The monarchy had been thoroughly revamped and refurbished with a whole new deck of ritual functions and ceremonies. The land itself was reclaimed as the national heritage by the National Trust. . . . A sense of belonging, the 'we-feeling' of the community, has to be continually engendered by opportunities for identification as the nation is being manufactured. Radio and later television were potent means of manufacturing that 'we-feeling'. They made the nation real and tangible through a whole range of images and symbols, events and ceremonies, relayed to audiences direct and live.[50]

Reith may have embraced the opportunity to shape British identity, but in turn he, his staff, and individual broadcasters repeatedly had to fight state political control in the form of governmental attempts to appropriate or silence broadcasts. The corporation's initial charter forbade controversy or partisan political broadcasts, but drawing the line between responsibly informing citizens and engaging in political controversy was often difficult. In 1933, for example, BBC radio planned a series of broadcasts on India to inform listeners of issues at stake in governance. A government then facing civil disobedience campaigns in India led by Gandhi and Nehru was so anxious about the series that the broadcasts were discussed in the House of Commons, and in the end the series was canceled.[51]

49. See Scannell and Cardiff, *Social History of British Broadcasting,* x–xi, 14–15, 278; see also David Cardiff, "The Serious and the Popular: Aspects of the Evolution of Style in the Radio Talk, 1928–1939," *Media, Culture, and Society* 2.1 (1980): 30–31.
50. Scannell and Cardiff, *Social History of British Broadcasting,* 277.
51. See Briggs, *History of Broadcasting,* 2:129, and Scannell and Cardiff, *Social History of British Broadcasting,* 54–55.

Briggs argues that Reith resisted censorship more than is alleged by some of his critics, but the outbreak of World War II in 1939 (by which time Reith had left the corporation) brought a wholesale reorganization of BBC as well as intensified censorship.[52] The Ministry of Information took up residency within the BBC in 1940–1941, in the form of in-house advisers for home and foreign broadcasting; and when a single director-general was replaced by a diarchy in 1942, one of the two leaders, Arthur Foot, had first been brought on board BBC by the minister of information and with Churchill's support.[53] If one important wartime mission was keeping the home audience informed, others besides Britons were listening, and even weather reports had to be censored since Germany could use the details to plan bombing raids. Hence every broadcast during the war had to be submitted to a censor in advance, and anyone departing from the script would be instantly cut off. Sustaining morale became another corporation objective, and herein lay the rub for BBC. The corporation initially stumbled during the "Phoney War"—that phase after war had been declared but before much engagement had taken place. Not only was regular programming canceled and replaced by recorded music punctuated by news bulletins, but a number of those news bulletins also gave overly optimistic accounts of Britain's military. Rather than sustaining morale, this strategy merely created deep cynicism.[54] Where the Home Service was concerned, then, broadcasts were carefully screened to ensure that no comfort or aid was given to Nazi enemies, but corporation officials otherwise decided

---

52. See Briggs, *History of Broadcasting*, 2:129–30.

53. Churchill's connection to BBC policies during wartime—as well as the diarchy created in 1942—affected EMF and prompted several reactions. In 1941, when the government attempted to ban speakers of a questionable nature from broadcasting, EMF and others at the National Council for Civil Liberties protested, and EMF himself boycotted broadcasting for a time. "It was an effective campaign," Furbank notes, for Churchill himself removed the ban (*E. M. Forster: A Life*, 2 vols. [London: Secker and Warburg, 1977–1978], 2:242). EMF wrote to Zulfiqar Bokhari on 23 March 1941, "I have seen V. W. [Vaughan Williams, EMF's partner in these protests] this morning about Mr. Churchill's statement, and we agree that we must examine its wording carefully" (Mary Lago and P. N. Furbank, eds., *Selected Letters of E. M. Forster*, 2 vols. [London: Collins; Cambridge: Harvard University Press, 1983, 1985], 2:192). EMF was right to be circumspect regarding Churchill's statement; it was characteristically vague, and shortly after it was issued the government reorganized the Board of Governors at the BBC—the first step toward a diarchy. EMF's opinion of Churchill was low prior to the war: "Churchill was the one politician whom Forster truly detested" in the 1920s, which was due in large part to Churchill's stint as secretary of state for the colonies and as home secretary in the early part of the century (Furbank, *A Life*, 2:113). Yet in EMF's war broadcasts Churchill always figures positively, if only occasionally. Thus the broadcasts suggest a shift in EMF's attitude.

54. See Briggs, *History of Broadcasting*, 2:646, 3:45, 94–95. Also see Siân Nicholas, *The Echo of War: Home Front Propaganda and the Wartime BBC, 1939–45* (Manchester: Manchester University Press, 1996), 30–32.

that the best way to sustain morale was to provide news that was as accurate as possible.

The BBC nonetheless functioned as an active agent of propaganda to the home and European audiences and to British allies around the world. In part this witting-unwitting collusion with governmental ideology arose from attempts to counter the barrage of German propaganda transmitted to England, but the objective of "morale" was also inseparable from propaganda. As Director-General F. W. Ogilvie declared in an interview published in the 28 August 1941 *Listener,* from the moment of the war's outbreak "we regarded broadcasting, home and overseas, as a new fourth arm, working alongside the fighting services." He also acknowledged that "the B.B.C. has undertaken to accept in war time the directions of the Minister of Information on any matters connected with the national war effort."[55] Part of this "effort" involved broadcasts aimed at bolstering Britons' pride in their democratic form of government in contrast to the totalitarianism of Germany. In this context, promoting broadcasters' freedom of expression also served the ends of propaganda. In contrast to parliamentary nervousness about airing divergent views on Indian governance in 1933, which caused the series to be canceled, the BBC scheduled five Round Table discussions on the political future of India in 1942, with speakers drawn from the Indian National Congress Party and Moslem League and including as well nonaligned Indians and "sympathetic" Englishmen. In addition, each discussion was reprinted in the *Listener* and even illustrated by a photograph of broadcasters depicting Anglo-Saxon and Indian men sitting together on equal terms. As W. E. Williams concluded in "Critic on the Hearth," "these discussions are an unqualified credit to the B.B.C., and the best advertisement for democracy that anyone could devise."[56]

Other designs on the home audience came from attempts to induce friendly feelings toward allies—a challenge since Russia had long been censured as a communist country and Britons generally viewed Americans as self-indulgent materialists. The BBC in tandem with the Ministry of Information responded by scheduling cultural coverage of these two countries.[57] A final strategy directed toward morale undid one

55. "British Broadcasting and the War: Discussion between Sir Frederick Whyte and F. W. Ogilvie, Director-General of the B.B.C.," *Listener,* 28 August 1941, p. 299.

56. W. E. Williams, "Critic on the Hearth: The Spoken Word," *Listener,* 14 May 1942, p. 636.

57. EMF's own November 1941 broadcast to India on Dostoevsky and *The Brothers Karamazov* may need to be seen in this context. The broadcast is not included in this edition, but the *Listener* included extensive quotation and summary in its "What They Are Saying" feature (27 November 1941, p. 720). It quoted EMF's recollection of the only connection he

of Reith's central tenets; rather than retaining one "great" British audience, the BBC in February 1940 divided programming into the Forces Programme, designed to give the armed forces and the home audience sustained light entertainment, and the Home Service.

If Home Service broadcasts were subjected to meticulous oversight by the Ministry of Information, and if many broadcasts to Europe took the form of overt propaganda, wartime broadcasts to India enjoyed greater freedom from the Ministry of Information—even though the Japanese threatened India from Burma, which they had overtaken, and British attempts to negotiate postwar sharing of power in India by means of the 1942 Cripps Mission had failed. What became All-India Radio was initiated in 1935, when Lionel Fielden was appointed to organize a broadcasting system after independent efforts by Indian businessmen had failed. Fielden, who assisted Hilda Matheson in the early days of the corporation and shared her high ideals for radio, considered his results at the end of four years in India a total failure. The British government had never been committed to the new service, and only when Germany began beaming lively programming to India that entertained while mocking the inconsistency between Britain's ostensible democratic ideals and its governance of India did regular broadcasting begin—organized from London. Fielden returned there as editor of the India Service, bringing with him Zulfiqar Bokhari, whom he had recruited shortly after arriving in India; Malcolm Darling, the Indian civil servant who was also a King's College man and longtime friend of Forster's, was appointed to head the India Service. Fielden and Bokhari had it running by May 1940, but Fielden was quickly disillusioned and left BBC in November. Eventually Darling was placed in charge of the Hindustani broadcasts and Bokhari oversaw broadcasts to India in English. In addition to Forster, other English broadcasters on literary subjects were V. S. Pritchett, T. S. Eliot, Louis MacNeice, and George Orwell.

The Hindustani side of the service was given considerable leeway. As Orwell commented, "Most of our broadcasters are Indian left-wing intellectuals, from Liberals to Trotskyists, some of them bitterly anti-British. They don't do it to 'fox the Indian masses' but because they know what a Fascist victory would mean to the chances of India's independence."[58] The English broadcasts enjoyed a similar liberty. Forster himself repeatedly turned down requests to broadcast on the Home Service during World

---

could make with the ruler of an Indian state (clearly the Maharajah of Dewas): EMF's summarizing of the story of Dostoevsky's novel, which made him realize the "natural affinity between the Indian and the Russian outlook." EMF also attested to a similar affinity in music: "Indians so often have a natural appreciation of Russian composers."

58. Quoted in Briggs, *History of Broadcasting*, 3:511.

War II on the grounds that he was freer to say what he liked in talking to India.[59] This enhanced freedom resulted in part from the elite minority to whom Forster and his colleagues spoke—an important link between Forster's India Service and his later Third Programme broadcasts. Sir Richard Maconachie, controller of the Home Service, commented on the distinction between Home and Indian Service talks in a 16 October 1943 memo to Director of Talks George Barnes:

> The broadcasts in English of the Indian Service, judging by the scripts I had seen, e.g., on Proust, etc., were directed—probably quite rightly—to a minority audience of highly educated Indians, who reveled in polysyllabic abstractions. Our problem was very different, and we even had to make it clear that the inhabitants of India were not necessarily Hindus, that there were such things as Indian States, and that the inhabitants of India were not Red Indians, etc. . . . (Life would be a very different affair and a much brighter one for all of us in the Home Service if there was a wavelength available for broadcasting to an intelligent and educated audience.)[60]

India Service broadcasts also enjoyed greater freedom than did Home Service talks, however, because it was Ministry of Information policy to propagate cordial relationships with India's elite and to convince them that British culture was both democratic and universal. Secret Ministry of Information memos authored by the Overseas Planning Committee in 1943 charged the India Department with "projecting" the British war effort to India in appropriate terms; among the required themes were British efficiency and inventiveness, "The *democratic* character of British society," and "The *Universal* character of British civilisation and culture." One "sub-theme," a memo stipulated, was that "The Empire fosters freedom of speech and expression." This same memo likewise encouraged the promulgation of British "Art, music and letters" to India and the castigation of Nazi "Destruction of European culture and values; burning of books, totalitarianisation of art, literature, universities, etc.; suppression of free speech and Press; spoilation of European treasures."[61] Giving Forster,

---

59. See Lago, "E. M. Forster and the BBC," 149.

60. India Talks Files 2 & 3, 1943–1954, R51/256/2, BBC WAC.

61. Paper No. 349, 8 March 1943, and Paper No. 388B, 30 August 1943, Ministry of Information Propaganda files, R34/692/3, BBC WAC. Valerie Holman traces a parallel program of MOI propaganda in print culture and documents the connection between publishing and BBC broadcasts. Sir Stephen Tallents, controller of public relations at the BBC in 1936, was involved in early propaganda efforts before war broke out. See Holman, "Carefully Concealed Connections: The Ministry of Information and British Publishing, 1939–1946," *Book History* 8 (2005): 199. Hilda Matheson conceived the *Britain in Pictures* series of books (including George Orwell's *The English People*), which were marketed as commercial titles but instigated from within MOI ("Carefully Concealed Connections,"

a preeminent representative of English letters among Indians, free rein to say what he liked not only guaranteed that Forster would continue to broadcast for BBC but also demonstrated to the Indian audience the universality of British culture and the free expression deriving from a democratic society. In this context, free speech and propaganda became impossible to separate.

FORSTER'S WAR BROADCASTS

When read together, the talks selected for this volume offer a broad picture of the dominant issues that preoccupied E. M. Forster between the years 1929 and 1960. This picture includes not only large issues of cultural concern—the war, BBC history, or Britain's vexed relationship to India before and after independence—but also smaller, more detailed, and certainly more personal issues for Forster: his practiced (or, indeed, deliberately underpracticed) broadcast style; his celebrity and ideological commitments; his fight against censorship and for the lay reader. The Second World War coalesced overarching national concerns and Forster's personal commitments via a common cultural vehicle: the BBC. Just as the war required the BBC to reconceive its national mission as a nonpartisan, primarily entertaining and educative body, so the war years required Forster to evaluate his broadcasting career and refine and defend his belief in liberal education, artistic freedom, and democratic ideals.

In 1938, after his ten years with the BBC, Forster's previously established ethos as an intellectual yet always informal—and mostly nonpolitical—broadcaster changed. Circumstances in Germany and the rest of the world focused Forster's attention on the threat of war and its incessant companion, censorship. Within this context, he found himself inhabiting the often uncomfortable space between literary critic and political commentator. To say that Forster used his position as a broadcaster and well-known cultural figure to influence British viewpoints on encroaching fascism is to oversimplify his decision to comment on the war as well as his method of delivering this commentary. Forster *was* a propagandist for the British government, but to defuse the power of his propaganda Forster admitted and explained his participation in various talks and writings. He was, foremost, a democrat. In his role as a member of the International P.E.N. Club and as two-time president of the National Council for Civil Liberties,

---

213–14). As Holman points out, print was in key respects superior to broadcasting as a propaganda medium, since broadcasts could be jammed, were restricted by the number of overseas transmitters, and were necessarily diluted by entertainment programming ("Carefully Concealed Connections," 209).

Forster condemned censorship to audiences worldwide. At the microphone and on the printed page, Forster advocated for civic processes in the face of wartime curtailment of democratic rights. He also fought censorship at the BBC, boycotting the talks until communists and others were permitted to speak, for example, and always challenging the administration to think beyond what was "desirable" and promote what was intellectually viable. Above all, during the war years Forster insisted on the significance of the arts as an answer to the monomania and sterility nurtured by the Axis powers.

In fact, when Forster did propagandize, he argued that patriotism meant acknowledging the necessity of art. Forster openly equated support for the arts with British civilization itself, urging listeners and readers to view protection of speech and creativity as tantamount to defense of England's pleasant land. The BBC was not blind to these attitudes, and it even encouraged Forster's campaign against censorship, showing him as an example of Britain's enduring democratic values.[62] Forster ultimately complied with the BBC's barely concealed agenda, but only on his own terms. Forster thus served two roles at the BBC during wartime, one defined by different governmental or administrative authorities and the other crafted and adhered to by him alone. Yet both roles corresponded to Forster's influence over a growing audience at home and especially abroad. For Forster, this influence meant perpetuation and enhancement not only of British civilization but also of liberal values. "He did not choose or want the role of sage," Nicola Beauman argues, yet "his strong sense of loyalty and commitment to liberal values thrust him into political engagement in a way that he once would have thought impossible."[63] Hence Forster transformed during the war years into that creature he once had derisively associated with a Victorian sensibility: the activist litterateur.

In this sense, broadcasting changed Forster. As a broadcaster, Forster was but tangentially a novelist. Primarily he occupied the position of public intellectual, and such an identity carried with it the responsibility of speaking on a range of subjects to wide audiences at home and in India—a profound opportunity for one who cherished books, ideas, and discussions regarding both. Of course, the BBC, influenced by the Ministry of Information, tried to co-opt his public ethos. Time and again, letters to Forster held at the BBC Written Archives Centre exhort him to encourage pro-British sympathy to overseas auditors, as when Marjory Wace, Empire

62. When proposed broadcasts were deemed too politically sensitive by the Ministry of Information, however—including two successive scripts submitted by G. B. Shaw in 1940 and others by J. B. Priestley—they were suppressed altogether (Briggs, *History of Broadcasting*, 3:212, 320–21; Nicholas, *The Echo of War*, 236–37).

63. Nicola Beauman, *E. M. Forster: A Biography* (New York: Alfred A. Knopf, 1994), 355.

Talks organizer, urges Forster "to help convince [an] overseas audience . . . that we really have something worth fighting for in this country" as he is preparing a talk on the freedom of the artist.[64] This request launched a heated exchange among Forster, Wace, and Ormond Wilson, an official in the Overseas Service, regarding artists' true freedom in Britain—but only Wilson acknowledged the value of this talk as "propaganda." In his letter dated 12 March 1940, Wilson congratulates Forster on creating "an excellent propaganda talk" and for sounding "so completely genuine."[65]

In the end, Forster viewed his wartime collaboration with the BBC as both ill-conceived and oddly satisfying.[66] On the one hand, he repudiated furtive propaganda and, of course, the suppression of free speech. Letters from this period underscore Forster's consistent reactions against BBC requests for talks on subjects to which he objected. Forster refused at first to endorse the series on "freedom of the artist," for instance, explaining that he could "not wax enthusiastic . . . either about the libel laws or the blasphemy laws or the laws related to obscenity, or about colour-prejudice encountered by my fellow-writers from India in this country."[67] Yet, on the other hand, Forster willingly joined the government's propaganda effort by speaking against Hitler and for British civilization. His admission of culpability in anti-Hitler rhetoric is tinged with both sarcasm and pride, for example, in his 19 August 1942 broadcast on London theater (included in this edition). Complaining of overt propaganda in *Watch on the Rhine*, he states, "I know that Hitler is trying to do us all in, and I don't want to pay money to hear actors and actresses tell me this: they might just as well listen to me." Forster also felt strongly enough about the philosophy of artistic freedom that he quite ironically propagandized on its behalf. Indeed, that Forster spoke as a propagandist during the war was never, for

64. The talk, not included in this volume, was broadcast on 10 March 1940. Marjory Wace to EMF, 21 February 1940, E. M. Forster File 2, 1939–1940 R CONT 1, BBC WAC.

65. Ormond Wilson to EMF, 12 March 1940, E. M. Forster File 2, 1939–1940 R CONT 1, BBC WAC. Coincidentally, EMF wrote Wace the same day protesting Richard Rendall's use of the word *propaganda* when inviting him to compose a talk for the series. In his letter to Wace, EMF debates the value of announcing that a talk is propagandist at its outset. Rendall, director of Empire Services at the time, acknowledges in his letter that the series is meant to be propagandist, while Wilson's earlier letter to EMF of 4 March 1940 directly contradicts this position. For a more detailed discussion on this exchange and its ramifications, see Lago, "E. M. Forster and the BBC," 136–38.

66. As Furbank has pointed out, EMF's simultaneous distrust and appreciation of BBC preceded the war, which exacerbated his concerns regarding censorship and governmental control. In 1931, EMF published an article entitled "Freedom at the BBC" in the *New Statesman* illuminating what he saw as the BBC's subterranean goals: suppression and control of outspoken broadcasters (*A Life*, 2:171). His criticisms continued throughout the 1930s and intensified during the war years.

67. EMF to Ormond Wilson, 3 March 1940, E. M. Forster File 2, 1939–1940 R CONT 1, BBC WAC.

him, distinct from his intellectual persona. He expresses this relationship in various broadcasts that appear in this volume, though he is perhaps most succinct in *Nordic Twilight,* a compilation of three anti-German broadcasts, commissioned by the Ministry of Information and published as a Macmillan War Pamphlet in September 1940:

> when a culture is genuinely national, as ours has been, it is capable, when the hour strikes, of becoming supernational and contributing to the general good of humanity. . . . it is not confined by political and geographical boundaries, it does not fidget about purity of race. . . . We did not want England to be England for ever, it seemed to us a meagre destiny. We hoped for a world to which, when it had been made one by science, England could contribute.[68]

To save England from Germany was, for Forster, to preserve English culture and, by association, the world's access to Britain's cultural contributions. The first line of *Nordic Twilight* reads, "This pamphlet is propaganda"—a disclaimer issued because he hoped to arm readers against mindless acceptance of his opinions. Yet Forster proceeds to justify his political viewpoint as being essential to the dissemination of English ideals. Privately, he asserted that "[t]he function of the writer in wartime" was "the same as in peacetime. We are fighting for self-preservation, and can't know what we shall be like until we have won."[69] Forster was committed to his anti-German stance because he would not allow any government, German or English or otherwise, to divide him or his listeners from art, and it was this belief that guided his war broadcasts.

This view, tempered as it was by an artist's doubt, did not prevent Forster from despairing about the war and its effect on all Britons. While publicly championing England as a "national culture" consigned by its heritage to be the international hub for artists and writers, privately Forster was anything but sanguine about England's chances of surviving the war. In an entry from his locked journal dated 22 August 1940, Forster bemoans, "WE HAVE LOST THE WAR—but I don't say this abroad." And, in September, Forster articulated a link between his broadcasting and his

68. EMF, *Nordic Twilight* (London: Macmillan, 1940), 9. In the Locked Journal, EMF notes a relationship between *England's Pleasant Land,* a morality play he composed for the Abinger festival about environmental responsibility and England's lasting beauty, and the completion of, presumably, *Nordic Twilight,* which debuted in 1940. The entry dated 3 May 1940 reads, "'England's Pleasant Land' just out. The Ministry of Information have asked me to write a pamphlet." EMF also implies a relationship between *Nordic Twilight* and his broadcasts to India in a letter to Bob Buckingham dated 29 May 1940: "I am to do a pamphlet, as now the B.B.C. (i.e. Malcolm) want me to broadcast regularly to India" (Lago and Furbank, eds., *Letters,* 2:177). Lago and Furbank identify the pamphlet as *Nordic Twilight.*

69. EMF, *Commonplace Book,* 129.

increasing hopelessness over the war. Noting an incident in which
Canadian soldiers cut off the hand of a German prisoner of war, Forster
expresses skepticism about not only the human condition but also the use-
fulness of broadcasting to a lost and ever darkening world: "Until the
Canadian atrocity, I was mildly pursuing broadcasting, but at bottom I
don't belong to this terrible world and all my efforts to take part in it are
half-hearted."[70]

The war broadcasts included in this volume hardly betray the
unnerved, despondent Forster that the journal reveals. On the contrary,
one is struck by the optimism of his London theater talk, for example, in
which Forster revels in the esprit de corps of the city's intellectual existence. "After three years of war," he says, London theater is "still carrying
on—no carrying on's not a good enough phrase: it suggests pluck to the
exclusion of genius, and they are giving performances of genius." After
lamenting the wartime paper shortage and dearth of publishing possibilities for young writers, Forster still manages in his broadcast of 4 July 1941
to uphold the novel, and the novelist, as bulwarks against evil: "But things
aren't nearly as bad as they might be and I feel cheerful," adding, "[b]ooks
are holding their end up and so they ought to, for they are part of the battle against tyranny."

Though Forster's contradictions about the war imply an inharmonious
relationship between what he would call his inner and outer worlds—
thoughtful patriot versus restive citizen—this in fact was not the case.
Forster feared war, certainly. But there was, with Forster, always one pre-
siding resolution to discordant experience, and in the face of doom he
invoked this antidote religiously: personal relations. As he says in the war
broadcast dated 11 November 1942, the values that rest "closest to my
own heart . . . happen to be personal relationships and the human activity
which is vaguely known as 'art.'"

Forster's philosophy of connection, and the primacy he gave to personal relationships, also motivated his specific communication with
Indian audiences. One perceives Forster's sense of affinity with the Indian
people, as well as his respect for the Indian listener as discrete from the
British listener, in various broadcasts included in this volume. In his 15
October 1941 talk, Forster surmises: "In talking to people as far away as
you are—that is to say as far away in space, for it is quite possible that we
may be close together in our hearts: in talking to you overseas, I have to
wonder what subject interests you and whether you can get books on it."
In fact, Forster regularly acknowledges Indians' lack of access to Western

---

70. EMF Locked Journal, vol. 4/4, 22 August, 4 September 1940, King's College,
Cambridge, Archive.

literature and reminds his listeners of his own awareness of their constraints—as well as their opportunities (as, for example, when he recognizes the potential participation of female listeners in his 19 August 1942
talk). In the later war years, Forster (perhaps unsurprisingly) forges commonalities and relationships between anonymous Indian and equally
anonymous British audiences. He suggests to his Indian listeners that his
talks have served "to assure you that we are interested in your culture, in
the culture of the Indian peoples. . . . to some of us . . . [Indian culture]
means what Indians have created through the centuries, what they are creating now, and we wonder too how they are interpreting what we attempt
in the west." This assurance of British investment in Indian culture is an
effective complement to his 14 August 1942 broadcast, "My Debt to
India," that unifies several well-known Anglo-Indians around one aim.
"England is trying to say 'Thank you' to India in this series," Forster, acting as emcee of the series, explains on behalf of his colleagues; he goes on
to assure his listeners that their English counterparts "must express the
warmth in their hearts, the warmth which they hope you reciprocate."

As he did in talking to Home listeners about Nazi Germany, Forster
approached his wartime broadcasts to India with as much subversiveness
as decorous intellectualism. When reading the 19 August 1942 broadcast
on Shakespeare in London, for example, one might well perceive a double
message in his allocating so much attention to *Richard III*, a play interwoven with profound commentary on governance and the inevitable
march forward of history. Even in desperate wartime, Forster implies,
English history is not yet over—and, crucially, neither is Indian history.
Moreover, that Forster should showcase a diabolical English king at such
length, one not fit to rule, seems to underscore his own awareness of the
impact of ineffectual, hard-hearted leadership upon hapless citizens both
at home and in India. This perhaps deliberate focus on the prophetic
Richard (to whom he devotes far more attention than he does to the production of *Hamlet* mentioned later in the broadcast) is reinforced by other
talks that note, and occasionally analyze, books on Indian politics, religion,
and the significance each has on British governance. Indeed, Forster's
maneuvering in the Indian talks always is subtle, always is masterfully
rhetorical. Even in talks seemingly unrelated to Indian politics, such as the
10 December 1941 broadcast on British "Books of 1941" or the 24 February
1942 talk on Thomas Hardy, Forster is careful to respect the cultural differences separating his audience from European society—to point out, in
other words, that these great English authors are not universal and simply
may not export. When the war ended Forster traveled to India for an
International P.E.N. conference and wrote exuberantly in his journal:
"O Lovely World, teach others to expound you as I have not been able

to do so! You remain pure . . . and the imagination of others will [here] converge."[71]

Human connection and creation enabled him to persist with the wartime broadcasts, to make connections between peoples and cultures, and to reconcile his fear with his responsibility—connection, creation, and bald courage, that is. Forster was included on Nazi death lists—a fact of which he was aware—but he did not choose as did some other well-known figures of the age to escape England before the seemingly inevitable invasion. Instead, and despite his private fear, Forster wrote, spoke out—broadcast around the world. Choosing resistance over escape, he remained a public figure, staying on the air and speaking against the Nazis with apparent disregard for his own safety.

Thus, Forster's broadcasts steadily counteracted his private pessimism about contributing to "this terrible world," and they likewise buoyed the morale of his listeners. J. R. Ackerley, Forster's longtime friend and colleague at the BBC, acknowledged that Forster "wept" when Britain entered the war, but also "did much afterwards to help people through it with his broadcasts on tolerance."[72] That Forster's broadcasting on tolerance and especially on the value of democracy was encouraged by the BBC also resulted from the fact that Forster's friends there included some of the most important intellectuals of his time. Ackerley served as book review editor of the *Listener;* Malcolm Darling for a time led the BBC's broadcasting efforts in India and recruited Forster for the India talks; and George Barnes, head of the Talks Department, acted as both friend and manager to Forster, who frequently appealed to Barnes's sense of fairness on issues concerning freedom of speech and the ongoing threat of censorship against contributors to the wireless.[73]

Forster also encountered, and felt assuaged by, persuasive officials at the BBC expert at finessing the links among propaganda, broadcasting, promoting "free speech," and the war effort in India. George Orwell, at one time the Talks Producer for the Indian Section, advised Forster on what not to broadcast to India, for example, citing in essence "big brother" censors as his reason. Regarding Forster's talk dated 29 April 1942, Orwell reminded him that K. S. Shelvankar's *The Problem of India* could not be mentioned in the broadcast—"This has been banned in India," he writes, "and if we refer to it the censor will cut it out." (Notice here the collaborative nature of Orwell's appeal: that "we" must not tempt the censors,

---

71. Indian Journal, 1945, King's College, Cambridge, Archive.
72. J. R. Ackerley, *E. M. Forster: A Portrait* (London: Ian McKelvie, 1970), 19–20.
73. Among EMF's friends and colleagues who broadcast for the BBC during this period were T. S. Eliot, Max Beerbohm, Desmond MacCarthy, Bertrand Russell, Gerald Heard, Rose Macaulay, and, most significantly to him, Goldsworthy Lowes Dickinson.

though it was Forster alone who was implying a challenge.) Orwell continues, suggesting that in lieu of inciting the censor, Forster might "delicately hint" that the English people remain interested in subversive Indian writers, and argues that such insinuations would amount to "a good propaganda point" for listeners abroad and, presumably, at home.[74]

Others at the BBC also persuaded Forster toward one perspective, one text, or one ethos over another—and different tactics spoke to different sides of Forster's personality. While Orwell developed commonalities with Forster as a fellow writer sympathetic to subjects of the Empire, Zulfiqar Bokhari appealed to Forster's desire to connect with Indians, reminding him in various letters that his talks were reaching—and pleasing—a complex but engaged Indian audience. Jean Rowntree used a different tactic. Appealing to Forster's intellect rather than his ego or his cultural sentiments, she matched wits with Forster, a move that often nullified his protests. When Forster balked at participating in a talk celebrating the anniversary of Milton's *Areopagitica,* for example, on the grounds that the BBC's motives for the talk seemed too propagandistic, Rowntree reminded him of Milton's ardent support of free speech and encouraged Forster not only to recognize this strain in Milton's writing but also to emphasize his own link to this equally passionate citizen and writer. Whether appealing to the intellect or to the heart, however, all of these figures approached Forster with the same aim: to convince him of the efficacy of his relationship to the BBC. And all of them knew how difficult this task could at times prove to be.

From the vantage point of readers today, Forster seems to have pivoted between the roles of British loyalist and unbending individualist during the war, while around him the BBC vacillated between acquiescence and resistance to the wartime function imposed on it as a state apparatus. From Forster's own perspective, however, these years must have signified a death of sorts: the free deployment of ideas, and ideals, ended; talks became classified and contained; and audiences soon were parceled out into mutually exclusive categories, a move that delegated book talks to only select listeners.

THE LEGACY OF THE "IDEAL RELATIONSHIP"

Even as wartime broadcasts continued at home and abroad, the BBC was by 1943 beginning to look ahead to postwar Britain and the resumption

---

74. George Orwell to EMF, 14 April 1942, BBC WAC. Orwell's persuasion worked; EMF accepted his advice, as the content of the talk indicates. For more on this letter's influence, see EMF's talk dated 29 April 1942.

of civilian broadcasting. Though television would revolutionize the post-war broadcasting scene, the most important change affecting Forster's broadcasting career was BBC's decision to make wartime divisions among radio audiences permanent (the Forces becoming the Light Programme) and to add a Third Programme, which debuted on 29 September 1946. As Director-General William Haley announced in a supplement to the 26 September *Listener*, the Third was designed to present "the great classical repertoire in music and drama, and—so far as they are broadcastable—in literature and the other arts."[75] It would, moreover, present art and thought without the former compromises entailed by scheduling constraints and the need to generate popular appeal.[76] Instead, the Third would require its audiences to exert themselves. As George Barnes, head of the new service, phrased it, the Third was designed for "the alert and receptive listener, the listener who is willing first of all to make an effort in selection and then to meet the performer half-way by giving his whole attention to what is being broadcast."[77] In keeping with these aims, the service was broadcast only from 6:00 p.m. to midnight, when listeners had free time to attend closely. A third of air time was devoted to music, followed by drama. As well, the program included poetry readings, coverage of the visual arts, book reviews, and literary talks.[78] In deliberately planning a service at the furthest remove possible from commercial radio, the BBC took a principled and courageous stand. The sheer quality of the material it produced, a substantial part of it by Forster, would not have reached so many in Great Britain for so long without such a separation of services. As Asa Briggs asserts, "we have never had ambitious broadcasting of this range in this country—or in any other country—since its demise."[79]

Forster defended the Third's ambitions in his usual ways, by broadcasting and by protesting—sometimes simultaneously. In 1953 he roundly rebuked the Third Programme controller, John Morris, for having, in his view, rejected a broadcast on Chinese prison reform because it was too sympathetic to the Communists. As Forster's letter concludes, "I do hope that the Third [Programme] is not going to be run on these lines. It hasn't been in the past."[80] In his "Fifth Anniversary" broadcast of 1951 Forster

75. William Haley, "Breaking New Ground in Radio," *Listener*, 26 September 1946, supplement i.
76. See Briggs, *History of Broadcasting*, 4:51, 69.
77. George Barnes, "The Aims of the Programme," *Listener*, 26 September 1946, supplement i.
78. "The Programmes in Detail," *Listener*, 26 September 1946, supplement iii–iv.
79. Briggs, *History of Broadcasting*, 4:1012.
80. Lago and Furbank, eds., *Letters*, 2.247–48.

upheld the Third's right to serve only a small minority of listeners, but this defense was accompanied by his complaints about the Audience Research Department, whose quantitative measures threatened to become measures of value, and about recent programming that included music more suited to the Home or Light Programmes. Forster's high standards for the Third meant that, ironically, he thought he was unfit to broadcast for it. As Barnes reported to the director of talks just before the Third debuted, "[Forster] was very doubtful whether his kind of talk and his manner were suitable to the Third Programme. He said that the BBC had trained him well to explain matters in an affable manner; in his opinion neither affability nor explanation were desirable in the Third Programme; a new form of broadcast talk was necessary and what did I propose to do about it?"[81] Despite his doubts he went on to give twenty-two talks on the Third between August 1947 and December 1958,[82] managing in the book talks included here to combine affability with his customary acuteness of critique and luminous explanation of authors' vision and technique.

In this sense, his Third Programme broadcasts were of a piece with themes he had explored throughout his broadcasting career—one of which, unquestionably, was the value of culture itself. Forster shared Reith's high estimation of Matthew Arnold, as the two broadcasts on Arnold in this volume indicate; he too believed, as he expressed in his 1944 broadcast on Matthew Arnold, that the intellectual as well as the poet should approach his or her craft with "the destiny of humanity" in mind. As well, Forster argued that Arnold "of all the great nineteenth century writers . . . is most on the spot today and most in touch with twentieth century troubles," confiding to Indian listeners a year later that "I always read him with a thrill and the famous phrases he uses—such as 'sweetness and light' or 'culture and anarchy' or 'poetry is a criticism of life'—they come with the authority of a creative artist." In 1945 he explicated Arnold's definition of "culture" as "getting to know what is best in human achievements, and trying to pass it on," "a belief in standards and a willingness to submit, in certain ways, to discipline," tenets of his own credo.[83] As in his wartime broadcasts, Forster consistently propounded "literature as a national asset" that should be passed on; to assist in that goal, he developed his talks more in terms of "appreciation" and advocacy than of

81. G. R. Barnes to director of talks, 12 September 1946, E. M. Forster File 7, 1945–1946 R CONT 1, BBC WAC.

82. Lago, *A Literary Life*, 119.

83. Compare "Does Culture Matter?": culture "describe[s] the various beautiful and interesting objects which men have made in the past, and handed down to us, and which some of us are hoping to hand on" (EMF, *Two Cheers for Democracy* [New York: Harcourt, Brace, and Co., 1951], 100).

judgment or skeptical critique.[84] In making the case for D. H. Lawrence's art in 1930, for example, Forster displaced controversy over the sexual content of Lawrence's novels by emphasizing the coherent philosophy underlying Lawrence's writings and its influence on his art. In 1955, when he broadcast on T. E. Lawrence's *The Mint*, he again explained how best to understand and appreciate the other Lawrence's themes, technique, and style just when Lawrence, too, was under attack.

These were defenses of friends but also of high "culture," and the question of whether Forster's advocacy shared the elitism and class politics associated with Arnold and coterie modernism needs to be assessed. In Forster's "Fifth Anniversary" talk, dedicated to the importance of culture, he states unapologetically that culture's adherents form "an aristocracy in the midst of a democracy." In his 1945 broadcast Forster had conceded that in "weaker moments" Matthew Arnold projected a sense of superiority. As might be expected of anyone who read Arnold with a "thrill," Forster did not (perhaps could not) question the fundamental distinction between high and popular culture and the clear superiority of the former. But Forster's defense of this "aristocracy" did not necessarily emerge from the same class politics that underlay *Culture and Anarchy*. In "Fifth Anniversary" a key point was high culture's status as a tiny minority under attack by the majority, liable to be dismissed (as it is by an East Anglian fisherman in the broadcast) as "no good."[85] This judgment was roughly the attitude Forster faced as part of another minority constituency, homosexuals. Forster's passionate advocacy of culture may thus owe something to the suppressed energies he could not publicly direct toward supporting that other minority.

Significantly, Forster linked the two minorities when he could. In a letter to the editor ("André Gide: A Personal Tribute") in the 1 March 1951 *Listener*, Forster identified Gide as a homosexual while memorializing the man and the artist, then immediately inserted the tribute into the 1951 edition of *Two Cheers for Democracy* (following "Gide and George," initially a 1943 broadcast). Even more telling, he found a way to connect his "Fifth Anniversary of the Third Programme" to same-sex desire by recording the talk at Bob Buckingham's house in Shepherd's Bush.[86] Probably only a

84. Lago, *A Literary Life*, 102.
85. Attacks originated from the educated as well as from the untutored. The 27 September 1951 *Listener* reported Lord Reith's attack on the Third Programme as a "waste of a precious wavelength; much of its matter is too limited in appeal" (p. 494).
86. This is confirmed by EMF's 19 September 1951 telegram to P. H. Newby stating a preference for recording at the Buckingham residence and Newby's reply the following day confirming the location of 129 Wendell Rd. (E. M. Forster File 9A, 1949–1951 R CONT 1, BBC WAC).

man of Forster's stature could have secured permission to record this otherwise prestigious broadcast in so informal a setting. The script itself, of course, addresses only the minority interested in high culture, but the recording's audible chime of the Buckingham clock and the sounds heard from without—of children playing, a passerby whistling, trucks rumbling—inscribe along with Forster's words the two great desires of his heart: art at its highest, and love of Bob Buckingham.

Forster's enactment of culture was also linked to his tireless efforts on behalf of civil liberties during and after the war, a commitment that distinguished him from Arnold and most of his modernist compeers. Arnoldian culture and the politics of John Stuart Mill's "On Liberty" (1859) may be strange bedfellows, but Arnoldian criticism is another matter. In addition to pressing for "the best that is known and thought in the world," Arnold assigned criticism the function of creating, through the "free play of the mind on all subjects, for its own sake . . . a current of true and fresh ideas."[87] A current of "fresh ideas" in Forster's talks is one of their most defining and delightful features. In his 3 October 1932 talk on Wordsworth (included in this edition) that inaugurated his "Books of the Week" broadcasts,[88] Forster injects into the idyllic Lake District landscape and peaceful Grasmere cemetery the disruptive figure of Annette Vallon, not to gossip about Wordsworth's hypocrisy but to reassess the spiritual qualities in his poems that stand up to skeptical critique. To take another example, those who expected a sentimental Christmas greeting in "Here's Wishing" encountered instead a curt dismissal of universal goodwill and a plea for the more significant (if colorless) virtue of tolerance.[89] And his appreciation of Samuel Butler in a 1952 talk was based on Butler's independence of mind most of all, which Forster positioned as a still timely riposte to the twin dogmas of religion and communism and their relationship to state control: "Today it is the State that bullies: the State that stifles: not Papa and Mamma." If good literary criticism acted to question cultural practices and assumptions, then so did Forster's talks on civil liberties: yet again high culture and progressive politics were for him kindred practices.

Another defining feature of Forster's broadcasts derived from his commitment to building bridges across classes and cultures. This of course was a raison d'être for his broadcasts to India and the notable cultural exchange they enacted, since Forster relayed not merely the contemporary book scene in London (as well as notices of occasional films, plays, art

87. Arnold, "Function of Criticism," 270.
88. So identified in the 12 October 1932 *Listener* ("The first of Mr. E. M. Forster's talks as a regular broadcast book critic"), which reprinted the script as an essay (p. 536).
89. Broadcast on 26 December 1938; reprinted in the *Listener*, 5 January 1939, p. 18.

exhibits, and musical performances) but also his response to Indian writers and events.[90] His Third Programme broadcast on *The Pelican History of
Art: The Art and Architecture of India* extended the exchange, especially
when he explained his own gradual realization that inside the extraordinary intricacy of the Hindu temple there resides a simple cell in which the
worshipper confronts the eternal: "Hinduism, unlike Christianity and
Buddhism and Islam, does not invite him to meet god congregationally;
and this commends it to me." As G. K. Das observes of the *Listener* version
of the broadcast, Forster here most fully grasps "the quality of complete-
ness in Hindu spiritualism."[91]

Forster's strong identification with working-class men surfaces
throughout his broadcasts—echoing his novels and, more poignantly, love
relationships spanning Forster's life. Most notable among the broadcasts
in this regard are his 1930 broadcast on D. H. Lawrence, his 1932 analysis
of the novel *Egypt's Gold*, or, more compellingly still, the 1949 "I Speak for
Myself." He even found a way to insert his concern for the preservation of
the English countryside into broadcasts, as in "Clouds Hill" in 1939
(reprinted in *Two Cheers*) and his 1958 Third Programme talk, "Recollections of Nassenheide." As this last broadcast also indicates, selected
talks carried an autobiographical impulse, whether detailing his trips to
India, America, or the Lake District in wartime; his stint as a tutor for the
children of Elizabeth von Arnim; his role as author opposite Bob
Buckingham's role as police officer in "Conversations on a Train"; or, more
subtly, his 1931 broadcast on Coleridge, which traced the birth of a critic
from the death of a creative artist.

Forster's Third Programme broadcasts were thus the culmination of his
lifelong commitments to culture, civil liberties, cross-cultural connections,
and personal relationships. But the Third Programme, and by association
Forster's profound contribution to it, did not last. Among the unforeseen
consequences of splitting BBC into three services—"high-brow, middle-
brow, and low-brow" programmes (as the BBC itself termed them in a 26
July 1945 *Listener* editorial)—was the emergence in the late 1950s of internal competition over celebrity and audience appeal.[92] Moreover, the

90. As EMF remarked in his introduction to *Literature and Authorship in India*, published
in 1943 by K. R. Srinivasa, "Our ignorance is disgraceful and is indeed an indictment of our
Empire. We have sent our soldiers and administrators and money-makers to the East, but
few scholars, and fewer artists. . . . It is unwise to suppose that culture is unimportant and
that distance in space and differences in idiom are a sufficient excuse for superciliousness
and obtuseness" (quoted in G. K. Das, *E. M. Forster's India* [Totowa, N.J.: Rowman and
Littlefield, 1977], 111). See also Lago, *A Literary Life*, 108.
91. Das, *E. M. Forster's India*, 111.
92. Tom Burns, *The BBC: Public Institution and Private World* (London: Macmillan, 1977),
48, 92.

fragmenting of audiences was vulnerable to charges of class distinctions. J. Scupham, for example, asserted in 1967, "The formula was coherent and complete: establishment values for the populace at large; indoctrination for the young; and a privileged area of debate for a cultured minority, rather on the principle that held the younger Pitt back from the suppression of Godwin's *Political Justice*. A book costing four guineas was unlikely to do much social harm."[93] Given such criticism at a time when popular culture was becoming a newly dominant force in society, it is not surprising that the Third Programme ended in 1970[94]—the same year Forster died. The convergence seems more than coincidental. With the demise of the Third there would have been no real place for Forster's book talks even had he been alive and able to participate.

THE ACHIEVEMENT OF FORSTER'S BROADCASTS

When Forster inaugurated his broadcasts in 1928, he possessed the celebrity that accompanies a moderately famous novelist. As Forster's broadcasting career lengthened, passing into the postwar decades when he was in his seventies and eighties, his celebrity became palpable. At first blush, Forster's significance to British readers and listeners hardly seems worth mentioning; his notability simply enhanced his audience and thus his stature as a broadcaster. Yet, to both Forster and the BBC, his ascending fame as a broadcaster wielded profound power, which resulted primarily from the following he garnered during the war. Prior to 1939, Forster filled a certain niche in British letters: Edwardian novelist, civil libertarian, essayist, and sometime broadcaster. During the war, however, Forster became much more than a public intellectual; he emerged as a beacon for democratic ideals. Various honors bestowed upon Forster during the postwar decades demonstrate this veneration. In 1946, Forster was invited to give the keynote address at a three-day symposium on music at Harvard University, which only confirmed his growing importance in the United States.[95] This same year Forster accepted the distinguished position of Honorary Fellow at King's—and, once there, discovered that "[h]is daily post was enormous" and that he had become "an object of pilgrimage," particularly for visiting Indians.[96]

93. J. Scupham, *Broadcasting and the Community* (London: C. A. Watts and Co., 1967), 70; see also Kate Whitehead, *The Third Programme: A Literary History* (Oxford: Clarendon Press, 1989), 227–42.
94. See Whitehead, *Third Programme*, 1.
95. "The Raison d'Être of Criticism in the Arts," noted earlier, was subsequently published in *Two Cheers for Democracy*.
96. Furbank, *A Life*, 2:277.

Forster's prestige among Indian listeners was evident as early as 1942, when Zulfiqar Bokhari, Indian Programme organizer, forwarded this Bombay Report on BBC broadcasts: "On the 11th February Mr. E. M. Forster broadcast a review of 'Grey Eminence' by Aldous Huxley. It was a delightful review and created great interest in Mr. Huxley's book. E. M. Forster is most popular in India."[97] Forster's 1945 trip to India for the International P.E.N. conference magnified his fame there. The *Listener* reported on 29 November that "[i]n Jaipur, in Delhi and Lahore his charm of manner" had "won new hearts," and in a 5 December 1945 memo from the director of the New Delhi Office requesting that Forster talk about India on the Home Service after his return, the director added: "he is so respected here—almost alone amongst British literary figures—that it would serve a very real purpose if it were known that his views were being heard by the British home public. . . . Should Forster be talking at all about India to the home audience as a result of his trip, I should be grateful if we could have the earliest information, as the fact itself would constitute a news story here."[98]

At home, meanwhile, "a period of idolization" had begun for him by the 1950s, culminating in his joining, by invitation of the queen, the Companions of Honor in 1951 and, in the following decade, the Order of Merit.[99] Seen in its entirety, then, Forster's work at the BBC did more than help to "set an international standard . . . of excellence in broadcasting."[100] At the end of his career, Forster was profoundly influential and revered.

Yet Forster disliked fame. "He found it a curse," P. N. Furbank wrote; Ackerley noted that "he got more and more bored by the pressure of culture vultures from all over the world, interviewers, biographers, photographers, autograph hunters, sight seers, and young writers who wanted the best free advice on their voluminous typescripts, and had to protect himself from persecution."[101] Forster himself chose a slightly more reserved characterization of his feelings about fame. In his locked journal, he describes replying to fans' letters as "a chore," but he also accepts his lot as inevitable: "Having lived until 70, having moved about a great deal without being unpleasant, and having on top of that become famous, I am naturally inundated."[102]

97. Bokhari to EMF, 27 April 1942, E. M. Forster File 4A, January–June 1942 R CONT 1, BBC WAC.

98. Francis Watson, "What Is Indo-English?" *Listener,* 29 November 1945, p. 624; director, New Delhi Office, to assistant controller, Talks, and assistant controller, Overseas, 5 December 1945, E. M. Forster File 7, 1945–1946 R CONT 1, BBC WAC.

99. Furbank, *A Life,* 2:309. EMF was offered a knighthood but refused it, "prefer[ring] honors that came after his name" (2:288).

100. Lago, *A Literary Life,* 130.

101. Furbank, *A Life,* 2:277; Ackerley, *A Portrait,* 12.

102. EMF Locked Journal, vol. 4/4, 19 June 1948, King's College, Cambridge, Archive.

Though he largely abjured the attention, Forster never dismissed its power. Using it to further causes important to him in broadcasts and behind-the-scenes correspondence,[103] he also became selective about when and where he would broadcast, and on what subjects, as his correspondence with BBC officials in later years reveals.[104]

The BBC, in turn, welcomed Forster's fame and capitalized on it. His renown in India, for example, made him indispensable to Malcolm Darling, who described Forster as "someone whose name would carry special weight amongst . . . our listeners."[105] (It was for this reason that Darling asked Forster to introduce the series "My Debt to India" in August 1942 on behalf of its several weighty participants.) He was cited by other broadcasters and critics as Britain's strongest intellectual—notably by Rose Macaulay in her famous comment, "Forster is our most distinguished living novelist."[106] Portions of *A Passage to India* and some of Forster's short stories, including "The Eternal Moment" and "The Celestial Omnibus," were featured reading on the Third (though Forster fumed when his permission was not sought for the former story). In 1953, he was asked by the controller of the Third Programme, John Morris, to give the annual Reith Lecture, named in honor of the BBC's founder, although Forster refused on the grounds that "I have nothing in my mind on the subject of civilisation that I haven't said before."[107]

Forster himself gave credence to the cultural importance of BBC radio when he published his previously broadcast talks in *Two Cheers for Democracy*, which gained "a particularly enthusiastic and admiring reception," according to Furbank.[108] Indeed, *Two Cheers* arguably may be Forster's best received work; and he most likely enjoyed this reception due to his cadre of listeners and readers after the war. The response to *Two Cheers* presumably pleased Forster, whose real love for egalitarian knowledge

103. Among numerous instances of such interventions, see in particular EMF's letter to John Morris, head of Far Eastern Service, as reprinted in Lago and Furbank, eds., *Letters*, 2:247–48. It should be noted that EMF's largesse for those spurned by the BBC affected more than just those with whom he agreed. In 1956, EMF sketched notes regarding a Mrs. Knight who had been censored by the BBC for broadcasting on her religious views. These notes, possibly "intended for delivery as part of a private speech," according to the catalog at the King's College Archive, are preliminary and hang together only loosely; but they indicate EMF's support of broadcasting religious and nonreligious viewpoints alike.

104. Among other unconventional locales, EMF broadcast from his own home in West Hackhurst, Bob Buckingham's home in London, and Benjamin Britten's cottage in Aldeburgh, where EMF recovered from prostate surgery in 1951.

105. Darling to Programme Copyright Department, 15 July 1942, E. M. Forster File 4B, July–December 1942 R CONT 1, BBC WAC.

106. Third Programme talk, "E. M. Forster: An Appreciation," reprinted in the *Listener*, 12 December 1946, pp. 845–47.

107. Lago and Furbank, eds., *Letters*, 2.251.

108. Furbank, *A Life*, 2:287.

coexisted with his appreciation for the aristocracy of culture. This was also a motive for numerous intellectual exercises, such as writing a morality play for the local pageant at Abinger Hammer, supporting art and performances that were free and open to the public, aiding young writers without substantive income financially—and also broadcasting. That he subsequently republished some of his BBC talks in *Two Cheers*, moreover, indicates that Forster was convinced of the seriousness of his broadcasts and their value to Wells's signalman, and that he wished for such readers to be able to study his broadcasts at length. As he stated in his talk on 19 December 1932, broadcasts detracted from intellectual concentration— "No one's educated who can't concentrate, and it's easier to acquire concentration through a book than through a talk or a film for an obvious reason: if your attention wanders you can go back to the top of the page and start again, whereas in a talk or a film you are carried on."

It may be for this reason that Forster published his talks and lectures and likewise lectured about topics on which he had written. To him, orality and literacy served the same purpose for different audiences: to educate those whose access to ideas and to the arts was sometimes limited.[109] One mode inevitably reinforced understanding of, or indeed concentration on, the other. Note, for example, Forster's easy transference from oral lecture to written criticism and back again in *Aspects of the Novel*. *Aspects* was published in 1927 as a companion to his six Clark Lectures delivered at Trinity College, Cambridge, that same year. In his prefatory note, Forster describes his lectures as "informal, indeed talkative," and argues that it is "safer when presenting them in a book not to mitigate the talk, in case nothing should be left at all."[110] Thus, his lectures became (virtually unaltered) published prose—lectures now put into print upon which readers at large could "concentrate." A portion of these same printed lectures later became the source for his BBC talk "The Art of Fiction," delivered on 24 November 1944. As Mary Lago characterizes it, the talk "has the same easy, colloquial, conversational tone" as *Aspects*, and in it "[h]e neither talked up to the Cambridge audience, nor down to his radio audience."[111]

Two Cheers manifests a similar evolution from orality to literacy. The volume, a thoughtful miscellany of criticism and cultural observations, includes several complete broadcasts and various other essays that stemmed from broadcasts but ultimately developed into something more specialized.[112]

109. This was EMF's basic philosophical position, even though in his 19 December 1932 broadcast he confided, "Between you and me and the ether, I've no great faith in the educational future of broadcasting unalloyed."

110. EMF, *Aspects of the Novel* (London: Edward Arnold, 1927), 7.

111. Lago, *A Literary Life*, 101.

112. "Three Anti-Nazi Broadcasts" ("Culture and Freedom," "What Has Germany Done

That Forster incorporated broadcasts into the book indicates that, in addition to filling the role of "colloquial talk," his comments on the wireless also constituted provocative literary criticism that he wanted to disseminate via another medium. He aimed for accessibility. In this sense, the preserved broadcasts—not to mention the six public lectures and dozens of published and previously unpublished essays that appear in *Two Cheers*—comment in one way or another on the overall theme of the volume. That is, these are *democratic* texts that advance culture on behalf of the individual but require that same individual's contemplative and unique interpretation in order to have meaning. Spontaneous in their transmission (if not in their composition), these originally oral texts are fixed and static in *Two Cheers*—printed for readers of all backgrounds to study, understand, and contemplate.

Certainly, as Gillian Beer has pointed out, "the relations of the written and the oral are rearranged through the often pseudo-orality of radio, invisibly scripted, purportedly dialogic."[113] There is little doubt that Forster polished his thoughts in print, whereas over the airwaves his performance, often punctuated by slight stumbles, seemed a bit disheveled. But to forge a link between the spontaneous and the studied, to make scholars out of listeners and participants out of scholars: that kind of connection is precisely why Forster allowed his orality to metamorphose into literacy, and why he sought a wide audience despite his introversion and disavowal of fame. This transference of the oral to the written in an effort to promote democratic knowledge can be traced to the beginnings of Forster's career as a public intellectual. Forster's beliefs in a liberal education for all people led him to give lectures at the Working Men's College in London for roughly twenty years. Following in the line of eminent lecturers before him—John Ruskin, D. G. Rossetti, and Forster's mentor Goldsworthy Lowes Dickinson, among others—he endorsed the mission of the college "to provide a full liberal education, with . . . teachers and students meeting in fellowship and equality."[114] Here, too, he published in *The Working Men's Journal* such essays as "Dante," "The Beauty of Life," "The Functions of Literature in War-Time" (an interesting correlative to his talks during the Second World War), and, most famously, "Pessimism in Literature." All of these essays "were written to be delivered as talks, and they were intended for a general audience with limited formal education,"

---

for the Germans?" "What Would Germany Do to Us?"), "The Tercentenary of the 'Areopagitica,'" and "The Challenge of Our Time." Other essays that adapted or borrowed from EMF's broadcasts include "George Crabbe and Peter Grimes" and "Clouds Hill." For a complete listing of former broadcasts included in *Two Cheers* see Arlott, "Forster and Broadcasting," 92 n. 1.

113. Beer, "'Wireless,'" 150.
114. Furbank, *A Life*, 1:174.

George Thomson explains.[115] Forster used the media at his disposal—broadcast talk or lecture, scholarly lecture, a book of critical essays, a talk printed in a periodical—for the reason that they allowed him to communicate ideas to all audiences despite the inevitable demarcations of education, class, opportunity, and nationality.

Thus, like his spiritual and intellectual forebear Matthew Arnold, Forster possessed the remarkable talent of being able to extrapolate, both orally and in prose, abstruse concepts into comprehensible ideas for lay audiences. It was this talent that gave Forster his appeal to audiences studying at the Working Men's College, standing at bookstalls, reading weekly magazines, conversing in rural pubs, or indeed sitting around radios in Britain or, more significantly, in India. It was also this talent that drew Forster to the BBC and allied him with Reith's own belief that poetry and everyday life are inseparable. Transcripts of Forster's talks convey this unity of belief; so, too, did Forster's demeanor at the microphone. He addressed all audiences—Indian, British, educated, and uneducated—in the same manner: with the energetic purpose of an academic, the confidence of an artist, and the humility of a student eager, as always, to study and appreciate all that is human.

LISTENING FOR FORSTER:
THE BBC RECORDINGS AT THE NATIONAL SOUND ARCHIVE

From the beginning Forster's talks reflected his ability to convey complex ideas in simple, lucid terms, but he mastered the art of the talk only gradually. In the partial recording of his "Talk for Sixth Forms" of 24 September 1937 (only one of three disks survives), Forster varies noticeably from his script, at one point stumbling through a sentence: "Another example I'll give you—well, of any good novel which you happen to have been reading lately: I've been reading, or rather re-reading, Arnold Bennett's *Old Wives Tale*."[116] Two years later W. E. Williams, the staff "Critic on the Hearth" for the "Spoken Word" in the *Listener*, took a dim view of Forster's talk on wartime reading: "I found him disappointing. He gave us little more than well-worn proverbs like Bacon's exhortation to 'do nothing contrary to your nature'. . . . On such a topic at such a time we wanted

115. EMF, *Albergo Empedocle and Other Writings*, ed. George Thomson (New York: Liveright, 1971), 125.

116. Transcription from National Sound Archive recording, reference 1CS0065404 (BBC reference 1564), "Talks for Sixth Forms. Books—by E. M. Forster," 24 September 1937.

to hear something categorical rather than listen to a literary man's airy nothings."[117]

Williams's "airy nothings" are misplaced where Forster the mature broadcaster is concerned, however. To hear other recordings of his broadcasts is to encounter a thorough professional with an instinctive sense of effective oral communication. His tenor voice, neither too high nor squeaky, was clear and direct—never prissy, pompous, or orotund. He spoke slowly—slower still as he aged—and with deliberate, though not forced, enunciation. Forster also made effective use of auditory effects in broadcasts. In "I Speak for Myself," for example, the repeated "stamp a pointer" recalls not only the mechanical repetition of manufacture but also its noise, given the tiny explosions of the terminal and initial "p" sounds in the words. Even in print the subtle poetry of "The bell pealed, the hound bayed" in "Recollections of Nassenheide" is clear; Forster's command of rhythm and sound effects is even clearer when conveyed through his voice. Forster also approximated the effects of poetry when he unified sections or scripts with recurring images, as when he rounded off his description of the proleptic yet retrospective orientation of the Third Programme with references to Janus, which became a leitmotif of the talk.

Such effects are of course intrinsic to a skilled writer, but only in listening can one discover Forster the actor, capable of impersonating Elizabeth von Arnim, an East Anglian fisherman, or a woman dressed in spinach green from Audience Research—all of which gained distinctive voice through his jovial, though always seemly, interpretation. His humor also emerges more audibly in the broadcasts, as when, in "Recollections of Nassenheide," Forster inserts pauses into the announcement that "spring broke, slow, thematic, teutonic," then shifts the register of his voice in "teutonic" to share a wry moment with his postwar audience. Additionally, Forster maintained a distinction between his own ethos as a broadcaster and the inherent drama of the fiction he was reviewing; in his talk on T. E. Lawrence's *The Mint*, Forster included just a hint of laughter as he recited a passage describing soldiers' frivolity in their huts. His pitch rose; his tone intensified; his otherwise steady broadcast style became slightly theatrical, certainly playful—quite human. Forster everywhere implies a love of spoken language in one who does not so much perform words as pay attention to them. Perhaps it was for this reason that, as Jean Rowntree attested, his talks were easy to remember.[118]

---

117. Williams, "Critic on the Hearth: The Spoken Word," *Listener*, 28 September 1939, p. 639.

118. Lago, "E. M. Forster and the BBC," 133.

Contemporary reviews certainly imply a growth in artistry. W. E. Williams reversed his censure of Forster in 1942: "because he discloses his heart as well as his knowledge he warms us all the more to his opinions. It is a long time since I last heard him, but he seems to be much nimbler in the tricks of wireless speaking than he used to be—more deliberate, more resourceful, more at ease." Williams quickly became an admirer, including Forster among six "outstanding literary critics" who were also "first-class broadcasters" and praising the Samuel Butler broadcast for "so brilliantly" inaugurating the "Books That Have Influenced Me" series, in part through critiquing the negative impact of Carlyle's proto-fascist *Heroes and Hero-Worship*.[119] Martin Armstrong succeeded Williams as spoken-word "Critic on the Hearth," and he, too, frequently lauded Forster's broadcasts. The 1944 talk on Edward Carpenter was "delightful"; the 1945 talk on Romain Rolland added to delight "seriousness spiced with dry humour"; Forster's 1946 broadcast on "The Challenge of Our Time" "was of absorbing interest"; and his 1950 broadcast on Skelton was "full of that humour which is peculiarly his own."[120]

A close look at the four successive versions of the "Fifth Anniversary of the Third Programme"—manuscript, corrected script, transcribed broadcast, and *Listener* essay—also sheds light on Forster's artistry as a broadcaster. In drafting the talk Forster initially employed more opinionated rhetoric than he ultimately broadcast. In this first draft, the Light Programme was nothing more than a "gladgirl"; in the broadcast he balanced condescension with acknowledgment of the powerful reach of the Light Programme: "She is also the dominant partner. She commands a far larger public than Home." Similarly, his regret in the manuscript and initial script that a BBC interlocutor who questioned the value of the Third because of its tiny audience was "more influentially connected with [BBC] than I like to think" was excised in favor of a more neutral stance.

The novelist known for his brilliant dialogue resurfaced when the broadcaster revised passages involving an Audience Research employee. Forster recounts the attempt of a serious young woman dispatched by Audience Research to survey his own listening habits. Forster not only imposed elegant compression on the dialogue as he moved from draft to broadcast, cutting those portions shown here in angle brackets, but also leveled the actors' relative positions when he deleted the researcher's unease ("This rather disconcerted her") and blind obedience to company

119. Williams, "Critic on the Hearth: The Spoken Word," *Listener*, 9 July 1942, p. 60; 16 March 1944, p. 308 (the other "outstanding literary critics" were Desmond MacCarthy, Max Beerbohm, V. S. Pritchett, Raymond Mortimer, and Ivor Brown); 27 April 1944, p. 476.

120. Armstrong, "Critic on the Hearth," *Listener*, 5 October 1944, p. 388; 15 March 1945, p. 304; 18 April 1946, p. 521; 14 December 1950, p. 759.

policy ("'<one has to keep> . . . 'One <must> keeps strictly to the facts'"). The resulting broadcast still mocks the woman and her spinach-green attire, but she is less ridiculous than in earlier drafts. Forster also qualified his acerbity directed at the press ("<a few professional critics work them up and <<pretend>> tell them they are being looked down on>") and at the BBC itself ("<it hasn't and I hope never will have a cultural monopoly—>"). Such revisions reflect an experienced broadcaster who knows how to temper his private opinions (and anger) in order to keep his listeners even as he questions the status quo.

The disparities between his revised script and recorded broadcast also reveal his ability to create a sense of familiar intimacy with listeners. His script's "How do I visualise the Third? Janus-faced, two faces" became, when he talked to actual listeners, "And how do I visualise the Third? Well, as Janus-faced"—slight differences that create the impression of a more informal, casual, and apparently spontaneous conversation rather than a rehearsed lecture. When, in contrast, Forster retooled the script for print, he reimposed formality on his prose, removing contractions and smoothing out any irregularities.

The Audience Research survey of his "Fifth Anniversary" broadcast survives, but most of the panelists' remarks focus on Forster's hostility to the Audience Research Department, which seems to have surprised them. Of greater value is the listener survey of Forster's 1955 talk on T. E. Lawrence's *The Mint*. Many of Forster's signature techniques—his approach to authors in terms of advocacy rather than critique, his ability to craft scripts that his audience found easy to remember, his luminous complexity—as well as Forster's celebrity are reflected in the report's summary paragraph:

> The speaker, E. M. Forster, made a most favourable impression; he was easy to listen to, it was said, and there was appreciation for his urbanity and the tolerance and understanding evident as much in his manner of speaking as in what he said. A number who had no particular interest in Lawrence or in his book appear to have listened purely for the pleasure of hearing Mr. Forster and declared that the talk had held their full attention. In the case of a few, it had apparently stimulated a desire to know more about Lawrence after all.

Individual reactions elaborated on the sources of Forster's success. An educational bookseller singled out the review's balance and thoroughness and Forster's "delightful" on-air manner, which created a broadcast that was "humane and above all sensible." A psychotherapist, not surprisingly, warmed to Forster's "intimate glimpse of the author's complex and tormented personality. Mr. Forster's personal qualities of sympathy and compassionate understanding made this talk particularly attractive." A writer appreciated the sophistication of the book talk and Forster's "reading of some humorous passages," while a biology teacher—perhaps more concerned with modes of presenting information than others—was most specific of all:

> I liked it very much because E. M. Forster gave a reasonable, tolerant, and humane criticism of Lawrence's work whereas so many press comments recently have been either biased by hero-worship or the pleasure of debunking a hero. The fact that Forster knew Lawrence gave him authority, yet he was detached and objective enough to judge the style and content of the book fairly. It was useful, too, that he gave us a clear idea of what the book was about, with examples of the style of each section. I like the ease of Forster's broadcasting manner very much.[121]

These Forster listeners were educated, sophisticated, and therefore able to respond to Forster's content; but they were also simply gratified by his style and approach—his "broadcasting manner," as the biology teacher characterized it.

Yet these reviewers and listeners neglect to mention one of the most significant aspects of Forster's broadcast style: his unflappability. The sounds of clocks striking, horses' hooves in the street, cars driving past, children's voices: none of these distracted Forster in the "Fifth Anniversary" broadcast whose consistent tone and almost methodical tempo never wavered. There were, as well, other elements of tone and delivery that might be imagined by readers of this volume as they peruse individual talks. For example, Forster betrayed trifling idiosyncrasies in his speech patterns— a sibilant "s" and the occasional "r" sounding much like a "w"—but so subtle that a listener must strain to hear them. He also improved with age. In "Talks for Sixth Forms," Forster speaks more quickly than he does in "Recollections of Nassenheide," for example, and his pitch is higher. Is this because he is speaking to young students, or is it because he was younger and less experienced as a broadcaster? In contrast, "Recollections of Nassenheide" resembles a long reminiscence told elegantly, carefully, by a trusted friend. Here Forster is remembering, and his tone matches this mood. He is relaxed and genuine; he is E. M. Forster at the end of his broadcasting career—confident, honest, and complete.

This volume records all stages of Forster's evolution, his eager youth as well as his old age. It also records identities that few readers of his works ever encounter: Forster both as editor and as the edited. The scripts that

---

121. Listener Research Report, 11 October 1951, LR/51/2147; Audience Research Report, 2 March 1955, LR/55/300, BBC WAC.

served as primary documents for this volume present an admixture of Forster's and the BBC's revisions. The original talks metamorphosed into collaborations involving not only Forster but also various figures from the BBC—some well known and others (typists, for example) anonymous. The resulting documents were modified as written text, finessed into oral presentation, and then edited to suit highly specific contexts and audiences. Though challenging, even at times querulous in their multifaceted dimensions, in the end these texts represent the "best of what was thought and said" by E. M. Forster, the reluctant broadcaster turned intellectual guide for the nation.

EDITORIAL CHALLENGES AND DIRECTIONS

A guiding principle of this edition from the beginning has been to exclude any broadcasts that Forster himself reprinted in his books and to minimize the number of scripts reprinted as *Listener* essays. Thus, the body of material presented here is substantially new.

Forster himself found editing the broadcasts "troublesome," as he explains in *Two Cheers for Democracy:*

> There is something cajoling and ingratiating about them which cannot be exorcised by editing, and they have been the devil to reproduce. I have not been consistent over broadcasts. On some special occasions I have taken the microphone by the horns and printed the script as it stood. Elsewhere I have attempted concealments which the reader will probably detect.[122]

Forster's recognition of the implacable nature of his own BBC broadcasts foretells the fate of his editors, who necessarily wrestle the same devils. In addition to posing quandaries over how best to reproduce them—resolvable only through imperfect compromise—Forster's BBC talks repeatedly confound and surprise. Where one might predict denunciation of a cultural practice, Forster embraces it. Where one expects his support, he equivocates, sometimes castigates. Yet for all the broadcasts' "cajoling" difficulty, Forster's idiosyncrasies satisfy far more than they perplex, for who can but enjoy the unpredictable turns of an always superb intellect?

The broadcast texts themselves affirm a close yet often elusive affiliation between technology and meaning. As a result they raise several editorial problems. First, as mentioned earlier, the text itself was malleable. The BBC Written Archives and the Archive at King's College, Cambridge,

---

122. EMF, *Two Cheers for Democracy,* 8.

hold Forster's typescript broadcasts but few handwritten drafts. The typescripts represent a middling stage of Forster's composing process. Forster initially handwrote or typed a draft for each talk and, as his scripts at King's College reveal, usually performed minor edits on such drafts before submitting them to be formally typed and reviewed at the BBC. A typist at the BBC, in turn, typed Forster's original, often misreading and thus misrepresenting his handwriting. Forster then edited these typescripts by hand shortly before broadcasting. (Occasionally, others at the BBC did as well, as evidenced by the presence of handwriting other than Forster's on several transcripts.) Usually he caught the typist's errors; sometimes he did not. In any case, Forster never broadcast precisely what was on the page—not even his own editing—as surviving broadcasts held at the National Sound Archive at the British Library reveal. Frequently, Forster diverged from his text only slightly, emending articles, nouns, the occasional short phrase. But on other occasions his divergences were substantive. Moreover—and finally—several of the broadcasts were reprinted in the *Listener.* These texts, while in one sense definitive, do not re-create the impromptu quality of Forster's talks. They are too polished for that. And they leave no trace of Forster's myriad, often spontaneous revisions.

For this volume, then, we sought that stage in the life of these texts wherein writer, speaker, editor, bureaucrat, typist, audience member, and larger cultural milieu merged—once, and with a good deal of human untidiness. In each of the broadcasts presented here, we re-create this distinct moment as faithfully as possible by choosing as copy text for the edition the corrected scripts Forster took with him to the microphone. In notes to each we identify cancellations (in angle brackets) as well as the odd typographical error and occasional marks evidently inserted to guide pronunciation. Additionally, we track variants between the typed script and broadcast recordings when the latter are available, and between scripts and essays published in the *Listener*—though we omit small or unimportant differences between scripts and *Listener* essays. Our notes also identify references, including the books Forster reviewed, and provide other explanatory material.

The second of our editorial challenges involved the familiar problem of inconsistency. Forster, the typist, and occasional editors of the broadcasts vacillated in their respective uses of punctuation. And as scholars in other editions of Forster's work have likewise noted, Forster often quoted from secondary sources incorrectly and, on occasion, misidentified quotations, authors, or titles throughout his talks. We have let stand the scripts' vagaries of punctuation and the quotations Forster read from scripts, providing references to and pointing out significant departures from his sources in our notes.

Though at one point we considered a diplomatic transcription of the scripts, editorial principle as well as readability forced us to reconsider, since it is not always clear whether emendations are indeed Forster's (though most seem to be). Facing the unresolvable problem of representing anonymous emendations, we decided to emphasize accessibility while also encoding the fundamental hybridity of the broadcast genre. We regularize some simple errors (since they may have resulted from typists' misreading of Forster's handwriting), but we retain the scripts' eclectic punctuation to differentiate them from the polished essays published in the *Listener*. And we approximate an eclectic clear-text edition of Forster's scripts but integrate footnotes that track variants and allusions. Our aim, then, is to enable readers to enjoy the lively prose of Forster's broadcasts or, if they wish, to reconstruct the evolution of his texts through their preproduction, broadcast, and postproduction versions. Either way, the edition expands knowledge of Forster's complete works while gesturing toward that lively, living, but ultimately elusive voice of Forster on the air.

THE SCRIPTS

THE GREAT FROST
by
E. M. FORSTER.

<u>15.2.29. 10.7.</u>[1]

It seems rather impertinent to broadcast on the subject of the great frost, because you are in it as much as I am, and your experiences may have been much more[2] exciting. I have not been snowed up or even fallen down. My gas fire still burns though of course not at all well, and it is still possible, at certain moments, to get enough water to wash in. For me, as for you, those moments always come when they are least expected; sometimes the water is turned off close to the tap, sometimes at the main, sometimes altogether,[3] or, as it is[4] termed, "cut off". Whether it be turned or cut no water comes, and this you too know, and you too have climbed up a ladder into a loft, smashed the ice on the cistern, and carried it down in a pail, or have thawed the gouty joints of a pipe with hot flannel. We have, none of us enough water in our houses now, and[5] when the thermometer rises we shall,[6] most of us, have too much. No one will broadcast to you on the topic of the Great Thaw. He, and you, will be otherwise occupied.

Still, it[7] seems worth while, since we have[8] no domestic duties for the moment, to bring together one or two personal impressions of this remarkable week;[9] you may care to compare mine with your own. I was, until this morning,[10] in Cambridgeshire. This afternoon I have been going about in the Thames Valley, up as far as Staines, so my impressions are confined to those two districts and I don't know what happened between them because the window of the railway carriage was mercifully shut.[11]

Cambridge was wonderful, especially on Wednesday and Thursday. The best kind of fen-weather filled[12] it, bright and exhilarating: the sun shone, and at night the crescent moon hung like a pendant on a chain of which the two clasps were the planets Jupiter and Venus. The old academic city has many beauties, but they are mostly of the recurrent kind. I had never expected to see this new magic of Jupiter and Venus with the moon between them, and beneath them, the Cam frozen solid, and young men walking[13] and skating on the backs from Kings Bridge to Clare. W. H. Davies,[14] in one of his poems, hears a cuckoo and sees a rainbow together, and feels that the experience will never be repeated; but I feel that my experience is still rarer, and if I could write poems on it I would.

Never again, in my life time will those three[15] voyagers of the sky be assembled together[16] to look down on that particular scene; never again will the strangeness of heaven and earth combine into magical fellowship, and a familiar river turn into a corridor of fairyland. And then - the Fountain in the Great Court of Trinity College; if any of you care for the fantastic and are within reach, I do advise you to go and see that fountain with its indescribable mask of icicles, its transparent beard, its curved and crystal whiskers. It stands like a new god in the centre of the city[17] that has already[18] examined and rejected so many - a god who alas will not last for long, not longer than Sunday if the weather prophets are correct, so go and worship him while you can, that spirit of the Fountain, in the Great Court of Trinity; in a day or two, the Great Court will only be the Great Court again, a wonderful place, but a familiar one. You may have read Mrs. Virginia[19] Woolf's exquisite and fantastic novel <u>Orlando</u>, and if you have you will remember her description of the freezing of the Thames in the reign of James I. Well, the fountain at Trinity is at the present moment worthy of that novel, and so are the triple jewels of the evening sky, looking down on the frozen Cam.

What of the Thames to-day though? Is it frozen across? I believe it is above Reading, but did not get so far. The best I saw (if one can speak of the freezing of a navigable river as "good") was a big and rather dirty jam of ice just above Kingston Bridge. It was not beautiful - I don't advise you to go and see it, for you can imagine it from your chairs. It is just a quantity of broken ice that has got jammed, and as for roasting a bullock on it - why, it wouldn't be even safe to roast a chestnut. I am, I may remark at this point, always a little incredulous about those roast bullocks which have figured now and then in our island story. It seems to me that, however thick the ice, the heat of the fire would, after a time, melt a pool in it, and the bullock be, if anything, a boiled one. However, this is captious. Bullocks have been roasted whole, the historians tell us, and the historians know. Looking over Kingston Bridge, I only felt that these half-hearted freezings are rather depressing and hoped that the Thames Authorities would soon return with their poles, and prod the mass until it broke up again and continued its course to the sea. Further up the river, above the lock at Chertsey, I came across another mass of ice, but not a large one, and not extending all across the stream. The barrier at Kingston is the[20] only remarkable manifestation of nature I came across in the London area. Otherwise, mankind had succeeded in keeping the waterway open, and swans and their cygnets are swimming about happily at Staines. The Wey is frozen at Weybridge, but no one slid or skated on it, no doubt for good reasons.

You will see, then, that my impressions of the Great Frost are not on a heroic scale, but like you I have read of wonderful incidents in the newspapers - of ink (not printers ink) that froze into a solid block, of thousands of oysters who died in their beds at Brightlingsea, of a dog[21] who escaped injury from an explosion at Oxted. It is not for me, though it may be for you, to verify the truth of this. One thing is certain: no one will again have the right to bore us with accounts of the Great Frost of[22] the closing years of the[23] last century. We have something to talk about ourselves. "Well do I remember", shall we say in 1950, if 1950 ever comes, "well do I remember how the Thames was blocked at Kingston and how undergraduates skated on the backs." And no one will be the least interested.[24] For these great frosts are all to melt in the imagination as completely as they do in fact, and to mention them is to bore listeners as completely as one does by recalling one's dreams. It is different to-day. You, like me, are involved in it, and you know it is a remarkable experience to have had.

So much of to-day, and what of to-morrow? The plumber will come to-morrow, and I shall wonder, as I have often wondered, why the plumber appears as a humorous object to the middle-class mind, and why, almost every week, there is the same joke about him in our leading comic paper.[25] What we should do without him I don't know, and as for his work, he always seems to do it more efficiently than I do mine. No doubt every profession has its ludicrous side, but jokes on this particular one have become tedious beyond words, tedious and ungenerous, and if we are to make a resolution during the Great Frost, let us agree to show better manners towards the[26] men who will help us through the Great Thaw.

---

1. 15.2.29: date of the broadcast; 10.7: length (10 minutes, 7 seconds). Variants from the handwritten manuscript, BBC Written Archives Centre (hereafter WAC), are given as "MS." The only variant from the broadcast script is given as "SCRIPT." The MS includes a calculation of word length at the bottom of p. 6. For the significance of this broadcast in EMF's BBC career, see the editorial introduction.
2. MS: <quite as exciting>. The cancellations indicated in the notes by angle brackets fall immediately after the note indicators in the scripts. Thus, the script in this instance has "much more ~~quite as exciting~~ exciting."
3. MS: <the result being always the same>
4. MS: <sometimes>
5. MS: <often temperature falls, when the temperature falls>

6. MS: <all>

7. MS: <means well>

8. MS: <nothing to do>

9. MS: <My own confessions>

10. MS: <at 6 am>

11. MS: <shut thank goodness>

12. MS: <the city>

13. MS: <on the Backs>

14. SCRIPT: <Wordsworth> MS: <Wordsworth> "A Great Time," by W. H. Davies, was published in *The Bird of Paradise and Other Poems* (London: Methuen, 1914).

15. MS: <great>

16. MS: <in their position to>

17. MS: <university>

18. MS: <accepted>

19. MS: <exquisite>

20. MS: <largest>

21. MS: <fox terrier>

22. <1896>

23. MS: <19th>

24. MS: interest<ing>

25. MS: <Punch>

26. MS: <work people>

TALK ON D.H. LAWRENCE
By Mr. E.M. Forster.

<u>Wednesday, April 16th at 7.25 p.m.</u> 1930

In one of his recent talks, Mr. Desmond MacCarthy remarked that D.H. Lawrence is a difficult writer.[1] It is a true remark, and I wish that Mr. MacCarthy and not I were speaking to you now. With his subtle insight, mature judgment and charming delivery, he would help you to understand Lawrence, and what is also important, he would persuade you to read him. You can't understand a writer without reading him - an obvious truth yet one that is often forgotten. And the only real reward a writer can have is to be read. There is a vague reward called 'literary reputation' over which critics make a great deal of fuss, but it is an empty and academic affair. To be read is all that matters, and at the time of his death Lawrence was not being read enough or in the right way. He has two publics, neither of them quite satisfactory. There is the general public, who think of him as improper and scarcely read him at all, and there is a special public, who read him, but in too narrow and fanatical way, and thought of him as a sort of god, who had come to change human nature and revolutionise society. His own public - the real public - he hasn't yet found that, and it is in the hope of persuading you to form part of it that I am speaking. I regard him myself as one of the glories of our twentieth century literature. But how am I to persuade you to share this opinion? I wish I was Mr. MacCarthy.

Lawrence belonged to the working classes. He grew up in a collier's cottage on the border of Notts[2] and Derby and he describes that country and the life there in his two early novels "The White Peacock" and "Sons and Lovers", and in a play, "The Widowing of Mrs. Holroyd".[3] He never worked down the mine himself, but was trained as a teacher - probably owing to the influence of his mother: he was devoted to his mother and her death was one of the most terrible things he had to bear. For a time he was a schoolmaster in a London suburb - and perhaps this accounts both for his mistrust of education and for the didactic way in which that dislike is expressed. Then he took to literature, and it was then or about then - that is to say in the Spring of 1915 - that I met him three or four times.[4] I didn't know him well, nor meet him again subsequently, but he leaves an extraordinary impression - so radiant and sensitive, so quick with his fingers and alive in his spirit, so sure that if we all set out at once for one of the South Sea Islands we should found a perfect community there which could regenerate the world. Shelley must have been a little like that, but Lawrence was a rougher tougher proposition than Shelley, there is a vein of cruelty in him, and though he may have beaten his wings against society in vain, he was ineffectual as a bird of prey rather than as an angel. He came to no South Sea Island. The war developed. His health was already very bad, and exempted him from military service, but not from the terrors of the imagination. He suffered acutely, moreover his wife, to whom he was devoted, was German, and they were persecuted by stay-at-home patriots and driven from place to place. He has left a description of this in Kangaroo,[5] and now that war books are fashionable, perhaps this description will be read again; it is to me the most heartrending account of non-fighting conditions that has ever been written; Mr. Wells did something in Mr. Britling,[6] but he is too genial and idealistic. Lawrence is right on it - on it and in it. He escaped from England at last, and never settled down in it again. For the rest of his life he moved from country to country - Germany, Italy, Australia, Mexico, etc. - pursued by good advice from the admirers of his earlier work, and never taking the least notice of it. His later work is less admired and certainly he becomes more mannered and didactic. But his essential qualities - the poetry that broods and flashes, the power to convey to the reader the colour and the weight of objects - that remains. Indeed to my mind his finest novel is a late one - "The Plumed Serpent"[7] - and anyone who is under the illusion that he went to pieces at the end of his life would do well to read it. He died a couple of months ago, in the South of France.

I have already called him both didactic and poetical, and this brings me to the main difficulty about him - that is to say to my main difficulty - I don't know whether it was Mr. MacCarthy's.

Now the difficulty seems to me this. Lawrence felt himself to be a prophet, with a message to humanity. Whether the message is true or not, I don't know; it certainly isn't new. But whether it's true or false, he is certainly a poet, both in prose and verse, and if he hadn't a message his poetry wouldn't have developed. It was his philosophy that liberated his imagination, and that's why it is so idle to blame him for not keeping strictly to literature. Much of his work is tedious, and some of it shocks people, so that we are inclined to say: "What a pity! What a pity to go on about the subconscious and the solar plexus and maleness and femaleness and African darkness and the cosmic battle when you can write with such insight about human beings and so beautifully about flowers." We can't see what he could - namely, that for him all these things were connected, but the magic light that transcends his senses and descriptions is reflected through the prism of a theory. If he didn't preach and prophecy he couldn't see and feel. This seems to me our main difficulty with him; to reckon that he can't be improved. His treatment of sex, for instance, which has raised such protests - I am not going to speak of it here, this is not the place. But it does connect up with things of which I am going to speak and to pretend it doesn't would be to insult his memory. Although he's a creature of moods - you seldom know what's coming next in his novels - he is not a creature of compartments. You can't say, "Let's drop his theories and enjoy his art", because the two are one. Disbelieve his theories, if you like, but never brush them aside. And don't scold him, even when he scolds you. He resembles a natural process much more nearly than do most writers, he writes from his instinct as well as preaching instinct, and one might as well scold a flower for growing on a manure heap, or a manure heap for producing a flower.

I am now going to read a passage from his early novel, "The White Peacock", partly because it is so beautiful, partly because it illustrates what I have been trying to say. It is mainly a description of snowdrops in a Nottinghamshire wood, but towards the end a theory, a mystic philosophy, appears between the familiar flowers.

(p. 196-198)[8]

Here the atmosphere gradually intensifies, till we have moved from an English wood into a lament for vanished wisdom. The lament is not a sentimental addition. Lawrence thought wisdom had vanished with the onrush of civilisation, and his belief had permeated the scene from the beginning, and gives it its magical beauty.

His dislike of civilisation wasn't a pose, as it is with many writers. He hated it fundamentally, because it has made human beings conscious, and society mechanical. Like Blake and other mystics, he condemns the intellect with its barren chains of reasoning and its dead weights of information, he even hates self-sacrifice and love. What does he approve of? Well, the very word approve would make him hiss with rage, it is so smooth and smug, but he is certainly seeking the forgotten wisdom, as he has just called it, he would like instinct to re-arise and connect men by ways now disused. He thinks we have taken a wrong turning. Book after book, he hammers away at this, and strikes many coloured sparks of poetry from it, and sometimes the whole fabric of his mind catches fire, and we get pages and chapters of splendour. He does believe in individuality - his mysticism isn't of the Buddhistic sort - and, illogical as it sounds, he even believes in tenderness. I think here that the memory of his mother counts. Theirs was an attachment which cut across all theories, and which glorified other relationships when she died. Tenderness is waiting behind the pseudo-scientific jargon of his solar plexuses and the savagery of his blood-tests. It is his concession to the civilisation he would destroy and the flaw in the primitive myths he would recreate. It is the Morning Star, the Lord of Both Ways, the star between dawn and dark.

It is obvious, from what I have said, that Lawrence's novels are bound to be unusual. We usually ask of a novel firstly, that its characters shall seem alive, secondly, that it shall have some sort of unity, and if we apply either of these tests to his books, they fail. Are his characters alive? In the earlier books, some of them are, because he was drawing them more on their surroundings than he did later. George Saxton in "The White Peacock" was modelled on a young farmer he knew, and the mother in "Sons and Lovers" is his own mother. And all through his career he was capable of clever malicious thumb-nail sketches - the short story entitled, "Jimmy and the Desperate Woman"[9] contains one of them. But he wasn't a creator of character. He was too irritable and too theoretical for that. His people have to illustrate something, he cannot allow them to wander freely or to indulge in the disinterested humourous by-play that's so characteristic of English fiction. He is in deadly earnest himself, and they have jolly well to be the same, and it is curious to me that with these restrictions they should be as interesting as they are. They are not alive, yet they are filled with the living stuff. The preposterous quartet in "Women in Love"[10] - have you ever met young men and women like that? And one of them is supposed to be in the Board of Education. Yet don't they keep signalling to you despite their arguments and adventures? You cannot class them as dummies or relegate them to the valley of dry bones. And a similar doubt will beset you when you apply the second of the tests suggested above - the test of artistic unity. The plots aren't well made, the books aren't aesthetic wholes, yet there's a satisfied feeling at the close. The sense of life has again swooped in, poetry has taken the place of construction. I have already compared Lawrence to a bird, and when reading his novels I seem to follow a series of short exquisite flights, beginning and ending for no special reason yet linking together all the spots on which the bird has perched.

One novel, though, does I think survive the normal construction-test, and that is the "Plumed Serpent". It is on the face of it a preposterous work about three people who dress up and pretend that the ancient gods of Mexico have returned to earth. But it is beautifully put together, the atmosphere increases with the story, both culminate. We begin in the filth and meanness of Mexico City, which seems to represent the whole country, then there is the hint of something else, of an inland lake of sweet waters, where the filth and meanness are not so much washed away as recomposed; and behind the lake, above thunderclouds of horror and splendour rise the shapes of the returning religion. As the tension grows, hymns are introduced - the finest of Lawrence's prose poems - and bind the narrative emotionally until we can accept what would otherwise seem grotesque. The returning Gods hold dialogue with Christianity. The images of Christ and the Virgin and the Saints are carried with reverence from the village church. They have failed, they are weary, their kingdom of love never came, they must repose. The sweet waters of the lake receive them, they go up to their peace in fire. And the ancient Gods of Mexico enter the church in their place, and receive the worship of men. After that the book concludes rather vaguely, but the general effect has been superb, we have assisted at a great mystical ceremony and all the Mexican landscape has come alive.

The "Plumed Serpent" is the only one of Lawrence's novels that I have time to refer to. I hope you've gathered from the little I've said about him that he is not just an improper writer and a crank. He has been treated stupidly by recent critics, while as for the composers of obituary notices - they have reminded me not so much of guardians of the dead as of a lot of shop-walkers who are so anxious about their personal appearance that they cannot even direct customers to the proper department. They do Lawrence no harm by their superior airs, but they have failed lamentably in their duty to the public. It is the readers, not the writer, who suffer when the writer is undervalued, and it is in the hope of asking you read him as you would any other contemporary author, that I am speaking now. I will conclude with one of his poems. Like the extract from "The White Peacock" it will illustrate one of the points I have been making. It is an early poem on the death of his mother, and it looks forward to the day when he will become great and be able to honour her - a day that is not far off, I think.

("On that Day". Vol. I - p. 229.)[11]

---

1. Former member of the Cambridge Apostles—as well as a journalist and drama critic—MacCarthy described Lawrence in a "book talk" dated 24 March 1930 as easy to "misunderstand."

2. Nottinghamshire.

3. D. H. Lawrence, *The White Peacock* (London: Heinemann, 1911); *Sons and Lovers* (London: Duckworth, 1913); *The Widowing of Mrs. Holroyd* (London: Duckworth, 1913). EMF first met Lawrence in 1915 at a dinner hosted by the Bloomsbury patron Lady Ottoline Morrell; their friendship survived intense disagreements over the purpose and significance of literary art and was punctuated by the famed *Lady Chatterley* obscenity trial, for which EMF served as a witness for the defense.

4. For more on EMF's relationship to Lawrence, see P. N. Furbank, *E. M. Forster: A Life*, 2 vols. (London: Secker and Warburg, 1977–1978), 2:5–13, 132, 164–65, 311–12.

5. Lawrence, *Kangaroo* (London: Martin Secker, 1923).

6. H. G. Wells, *Mr. Britling Sees It Through* (London: Cassell, 1916).

7. Lawrence, *The Plumed Serpent* (London: Martin Secker, 1927).

8. EMF quotes the following passage:

So we went along by the hurrying brook, which fell over little cascades in its haste, never looking once at the primroses that were glimmering all along its banks. We turned aside, and climbed the hill through the woods. Velvety green sprigs of dog-mercury were scattered on the red soil. We came to the top of a slope, where the wood thinned. As I talked to Emily I became dimly aware of a whiteness over the ground. She exclaimed with surprise, and I found that I was walking, in the first shades of twilight, over clumps of snowdrops. The hazels were thin, and only here and there an oak tree uprose. All the ground was white with snowdrops, like drops of manna scattered over the red earth, on the grey-green clusters of leaves. There was a deep little dell, sharp sloping like a cup, and white sprinkling of flowers all the way down, with white flowers showing pale among the first inpouring of shadow at the bottom. The earth was red and warm, pricked with the dark, succulent green of bluebell sheaths, and embroidered with grey-green clusters of spears, and many white flowerets. High above, above the light tracery of hazel, the weird oaks tangled in the sunset. Below, in the first shadows, drooped hosts of little white flowers, so silent and sad; it seemed like a holy communion of pure wild things, numberless, frail, and folded meekly in the evening light. Other flower companies are glad; stately barbaric hordes of bluebells, merry-headed cowslip groups, even light, tossing wood-anemones; but snowdrops are sad and mysterious. We have lost their meaning. They do not belong to us, who ravish them.

9. The story ran originally in the *Criterion* (October 1924) and later was published in *The Best British Short Stories of 1925* (Boston: Small, Maynard, 1925), 88–114.

10. Lawrence, *Women in Love* (London: Heinemann, 1921).

11. "On that Day," from *The Collected Poems of D. H. Lawrence* (London: Martin Secker, 1928):

> On that day
> I shall put roses on roses, and cover your grave
> With multitude of white roses: and, since you were brave,
> One bright red ray.

So people, passing under
The ash-trees of the valley-road, will raise
Their eyes and look at the grave on the hill, in wonder,
    Wondering mount, and put the flowers asunder:

To see whose praise
Is blazoned here so white and so bloodily red.
Then they will say: "'Tis long since she is dead,
    Who has remembered her after many days?"

And standing there
They will consider how you went your ways
Unnoticed among them, a still queen lost in the maze
    Of this earthly affair

A queen, they'll say,
Has slept unnoticed on a forgotten hill.
Sleeps on unknown, unnoticed there, until
    Dawns my insurgent day.

BOOKS

by

E.M. FORSTER

Thursday, 13th August, 1931, 7.0 p.m.

I want to talk partly about Coleridge this evening, and I have a good excuse, as an excellent edition of Coleridge's poems has lately come out. It is quite cheap - only 3/6 - it's well printed and the poems are printed in the order in which they were written, and there are some good notes by Mr. Ernest Hartley Coleridge, a member of the poet's family. This edition is published by the Oxford University Press, in their well-known series, and if you haven't a complete Coleridge I advise you to buy it.

But perhaps you'll say "I don't want a complete Coleridge, I've got 'The Ancient Mariner' in some anthology or other, and that's enough. 'The Ancient Mariner' and 'Kubla Khan' and perhaps the first half of 'Christabel' - that's all in Coleridge that really matters. The rest is rubbish and not even good dry rubbish, it's moist clammy rubbish, it's depressing." So if I tell you that there are 600 pages in this new edition, you'll only reply "I'm sorry to hear it."

Still - 600 pages makes one think. Why did Coleridge produce a little immortal poetry and a mass of decay? And it has made me think of his life as a whole, and that is what I am going to talk about. His life as a whole - the shape of it, for he died a hundred years ago, and we can look back at the shape, just as we can look back at an island when we are sailing away from it on the sea. While we are on the island it hasn't a shape - it is just hills, streams and houses. But when we get away from it we see a special outline which belongs to no other island, and so it is with the lives of certain men.

Now the outline, the shape, of Coleridge's life is most peculiar. Let's compare him to a mountain with two peaks. The first of these peaks rises to an immense height but covers a very small area. It is the peak of his poetry, I think we are all agreed that very little of the poetry is really good. More than this: he wrote all his best poetry when he was a young man - of twenty-five - in a single year, in a particular summer when he was stopping down in Somerset. He wrote a good deal before he was twenty-five, and masses later, but he never reached this summit of inspiration again, and he himself knew this, and that is one of the reasons why he was so unhappy. He felt he'd failed. After he was twenty-five, he either couldn't get his poems done, or there was something dead about them. He seemed, he tells us, to be writing them from the outside instead of from the inside. He <u>saw</u> how beautiful the world was, he couldn't feel it. I don't know whether you follow him here - I think I just can. He writes "The Ancient Mariner", he reaches the peak of poetry, and then there's a rapid descent.

Well, the usual explanation of that descent is that it was drugs. As you know, he took laudanum and opium, and one used to be told that if he hadn't taken them he would have continued to be a great poet, and a moral lesson is drawn from his decline. I don't think this explanation quite works. Because he began to take drugs <u>before</u> his great period, he was taking large doses when he was only twenty-four, we've documentary evidence for it. And earlier than that, when he wasn't taking any drugs, he wrote a quantity of poetry that was worthless. The truth, I suspect, is that the drugs both made him and destroyed him. He was a very odd fellow, he required an abnormal agent to help him to use the material which his previous experience had given, and to turn it into poetry, and he found that agent in laudanum. "Kubla Khan" was actually composed in a narcotic dream and "The Ancient Mariner's" a queer poem as well as a great one. He was playing a perilous game, of course, and he went on too long. In a short time the drugs hindered his creation instead of helping it, and by the time he was thirty they had destroyed him <u>as a poet</u> (I emphasise the words as a poet) - they had destroyed him as a poet, and he wrote little more in this line that's worth reading. If you look at the first two hundred pages of this edition, you'll find the poems won't interest you - they belong to the time when he didn't take laudanum, then about page 200 are the great poems when he'd taken a little, followed by about 300 pages of feeble poems, when he'd taken too much. It's a queer career, and I think we should do well neither to imitate him nor to scold him. He was peculiarly made. The drugs didn't inspire him, they can't inspire anyone, but they did release him: they did enable him to express the poetry he carried in his heart.

They weren't the only help he had, and perhaps some of you have been thinking of his friendship with Wordsworth, and with Dorothy Wordsworth, and wondering whether I was going to mention it. I am - but only in passing - because I haven't much time. That year in Somerset he was stopping close to the Wordsworths; the three young people became devoted to each other, and lived for a few months in a glow of affection and poetry. The glow couldn't last, but before it had vanished Coleridge, with Wordsworth's help, had written "The Ancient Mariner". Wordsworth found work of his own, while Dorothy Wordsworth was keeping her exquisite journal. What a summer it was for him! How the powers of darkness and light contrived to help him, the power of laudanum, the power of sweet human affection and of a fellow poet's sympathy! You see now why what we have called the peak of Coleridge's poetry is so abrupt and of such small extent: he reached it owing to particular conditions which don't recur again.

But remember we've compared him to a mountain with <u>two</u> peaks.

The second peak - perhaps we ought to call it a tableland - he doesn't reach till twenty years later. When he left Somerset he sank into the depths, he lost his will-power, he muddled himself with philosophy in Germany, he suffered remorse, he seemed done for. Then he was cured by a doctor friend, his self-respect is restored, he comes back into the world. But he was back a new creature, a wise, gentle, prematurely aged man. And he is eminent now not as a poet but as a critic - one of the greatest critics in English literature. We have his lectures on Shakespeare and Milton, and the rambling but wonderful Biographia Literaria in which he sketches his own poetical development and Wordsworth's too. The poet is dead, but the critic has been born. And what he couldn't see is that if the poet hadn't died there would have been no critic. We can see it because we stand sufficiently far away. He was complaining, you remember, that he was writing from the outside instead of from the inside - I'll read the actual words of his complaint: they come in a long poem called "Dejection" which he wrote at the age of thirty.

And those thin clouds above, in flakes and bars,
That give away their motion to the stars.
Yon crescent moon, as fixed as if it grew
In its own cloudless starless lake of blue:
I see them all so excellently fair,
I see, not feel, how beautiful they are.[1]
and he goes on:
Though I should gaze for ever
On that green light that lingers in the west
I may not hope from outward forms to win
The passion and the life whose fountains are within.[2]

He was right, he had lost the secret of poetry, he couldn't again win the passion and the life of "The Ancient Mariner", it had gone by him for ever.

But loss brought gain; the feeling of being outside things is a feeling which the critic has or ought to have, he ought to be an imaginative outsider, and that's what Coleridge became at the end of his life, when the fumes of the drugs wore away: that is the second summit of the mountain. If you say poetry is greater than criticism, I agree. But if you say - as is often said - that Coleridge is a failure, because he turned from a poet into a critic, I shall dispute it. He had a double achievement, and he couldn't scale the second peak until he had descended - painfully and with lamentation - from the first.

It is always fascinating when a poet talks about his own work, as Coleridge did in the Biographia Literaria, and it is one of the things that have interested me in another book I want to mention, a book called "The Poet's Progress" by Walter d'Arcy Cresswell. Mr. Cresswell is a young poet from New Zealand. I don't know his poems, and I couldn't guess from this autobiography of his whether they are good or bad, he adds a few specimen sonnets at the end, and as a matter of fact I didn't care for them. But his attitude to poetry interests me, it's vigourous and fresh, he has excellent things to say about the poetic use of experience (Coleridge talked of that too) and about the relation of poetry to philosophy. He writes a charming prose style; he has knocked about a good deal and seen the rougher sides of life, and he is not afraid of speaking his mind on a variety of subjects. Incidentally, he is anti-feminist.[3] He thinks women are inferior to men, and says so. I believe there is a good deal of furtive anti-feminism about to-day, but it seldom comes into the open - partly through gallantry - partly for a less reputable reason: cowardice. People who think women inferior to men often don't say so, because women have become so powerful. Mr. Cresswell has the courage of his opinions. He dares to write passages like this:

"To Poets, Conquerors and Kings it is the love and admiration of men alone that matters, and men have no such deep and lasting love for women as for heroes and poets, but only appear to, in times when heroes and poets no longer exist. For love is like lightning, that for lack of a steeple will strike a tree. Women love men, men love heroes and poets, and these love the Gods; and this upward current is the cause of all glorious periods of faith and power on earth."[4]

You will probably not agree with this, you may be annoyed by it, you might even feel outraged, but you will have to admit that it gives an unusual tang. I don't suggest you should buy this book, unless you specialise on modern poets and their reactions, but if you belong to a library, do put it down on your list, "The Poet's Progress" by Walter d'Arcy Cresswell. Published by Faber and Faber (price 7/6). It will give you some unusual reading. It gave me rather more than that, for I enjoyed it a good deal.[5]

Now both Coleridge the classic and Mr. Cresswell the modern are - to put it mildly - not quite happy. They suffer, both of them, from some sort of strain, which takes the form of remorse or indignation or even violence, and which is enhanced by the fact that they have strong imaginations. I make this comment on them because it conveniently introduces the third book on my list which is a very important book by Mr. Gerald Heard. To Mr. Heard the human race as a whole is not quite happy, it suffers from nervous tension. In the case of the poet, or the revolutionary, or the maniac the tension is obvious; the rest of us conceal it under a mask of convention, but we are none of us quite happy, we all worry more or less. That's the first point I want to make about his book. Now I'll give you its title: it's called "The Social Substance of Religion"; and now I want to say a word about Mr. Heard himself.[6]

Many of you know him as a broadcaster. You have listened, as I always do, to his fortnightly talks on "This Surprising World",[7] and you have probably been thrilled and fascinated by his lucid accounts of scientific progress. And a few of you, but not many, know his books. I say not many, because the books are difficult. He's not nearly as simple when he writes as when he talks, and I'm only recommending "The Social Substance of Religion" to listeners who care for solid, concentrated reading. He seems to me one of the most remarkable thinkers of the younger generation. The British Academy has just awarded a valuable prize to an earlier essay of his, "The Ascent of Humanity",[8] I should say that in five years' time he will be widely recognised. But he's difficult as a writer and for two reasons: he's dealing with profound and subtle subjects, and he doesn't write very clearly. You have to struggle with his books, and you must decide whether it's worth it. I think it is. Most of the books that are written in order to do good - how depressing and useless they are - one feels "I'm sure the chap's nice - oh, but take him away, take him away, he knows nothing about it all and never will."

He is concerned in this one with the fact that the human race is not quite happy, and he tries to trace our uneasiness to its origins, and to suggest a cure. The immediate cause he finds is the growth of individualism. Individualism is a comparatively new force on the earth. The sub-men, from whom the human race has evolved, were unselfconscious, they had a common consciousness, such as one may observe in a herd of animals. Then the individual develops, and is torn by conflicting claims. He wants at times to be "himself" and at other times to "lose" himself in the group consciousness like his remote ancestors. But in what group shall he lose himself? In the family, in the tribe or nation, or in the small secret society? He has tried all, and his various attempts to lose himself constitute the Social Substance of Religion which gives its name to the book. Religion, according to Mr. Heard, is not an individual affair, it does not culminate in personal immortality, though it has often been narrowed down to this. It is a spiritual refreshment which can only be obtained in and through others, and the problem of our society is not political, not economic but psychological: we have to discover how and where that spiritual refreshment can be found, and we must call in Science to help us. Other societies have solved the problem for a moment. Early Christianity solved it by the two or three who were gathered together into the "Agape". But Early Christianity broke up, simply because the communities constituting it became too large for such reunion, and the Agape was transformed into the Mass, with its insistence on individual salvation. Now the problem intrudes anew. A religion of love is indeed necessary - look at the state of Europe, look into your own hearts. But it must not be a sedative, such as Coleridge sought in his opium, and it cannot be generated by individuals working apart, as the ascetics did. We must combine, we must lose ourselves in the group, and modern psychology can teach us how.

My remarks are very sketchy, but they may help you to decide whether you want to tackle Mr. Heard's book or not, and this is all I can hope to do. If you do tackle it, let me give you two pieces of advice. The first is - buy it or leave it. Don't attempt to borrow it, don't think you'll master it in a few days. (Price 10/6, publishers, Allen and Unwin). The second bit of advice is: if you stick in Part I, try Part II. Part II contains the brilliant historical exposition. I've already referred to the section of Early Christianity: it is as brilliant as the famous chapter in Gibbon, and of course infinitely more sympathetic. And it's Mr. Heard's sympathy that I want to stress. He doesn't write because he is learned and clever and fanciful, although he is all these things. He writes because he knows of our troubles from within and wants to help with them. I wish he wrote more simply, because then more of us might be helped. That, really, is my only quarrel with him.

POEMS OF COLERIDGE 3/6 Oxford University Press
THE POET'S PROGRESS, by Walter D'Arcy Cresswell. Faber & Faber 7/6
THE SOCIAL SUBSTANCE OF RELIGION by Mr. Gerald Heard, Allen & Unwin 15/-

---

1. Samuel Taylor Coleridge, "Dejection: An Ode," in *The Poems of Samuel Taylor Coleridge: Including Poems and Versions of Poems Herein Published for the First Time*, ed. Ernest Hartley Coleridge (Oxford: Oxford University Press, 1931), 364.
   2. Ibid., 365.
   3. <pessimist>
   4. Walter D'arcy Cresswell, *The Poet's Progress* (London: Faber and Faber, 1930), 40.
   5. EMF's appreciation for Cresswell's book is at once surprising—given EMF's liberal

social vision—and predictable if one places it in context with his own ambivalence about feminism. For more on EMF's (anti-)feminism, see any of the following of his own writings: *Aspects of the Novel* (1927), his personal correspondence (published in two volumes as *Selected Letters of E. M. Forster*, ed. Mary Lago and P. N. Furbank, 2 vols. [London: Collins; Cambridge, Harvard University Press, 1983, 1985), his various literary portraits (most notably *Virginia Woolf*, given as part of the Clark Lecture Series and published by Cambridge University Press in 1942), and several entries from his *Commonplace Book*, ed. Philip Gardner (Stanford: Stanford University Press, 1985).

6. Gerald Heard, *The Social Substance of Religion* (London: G. Allen and Unwin, 1931).

7. <Amazing> Gerald Heard gave talks on popular science for the BBC throughout the 1930s.

8. Heard was awarded the Hertz Prize by the British Academy in 1929 for his essay "The Ascent of Humanity."

CONVERSATION IN THE TRAIN - VII.[1]

Saturday, 20th February, 1932, at 9.20 p.m.

E. M. Forster
Leonard Brockington   (Fade in terminus noises,
                                then GUARD'S whistle
                                and train starting)

A: (Wait for
     hand signal
     to speak)
     (calling to   I say - Hi, Hi! - You've left your suitcase on
     someone on   the seat . . .
     platform)
     (lower)   I say - He's left his suitcase.

B: No he hasn't. It's mine. Do you mind putting it back
                    where you took it from.

A: I'm awfully sorry, sir.

B: (curt)   All right.

A: I am extremely sorry.

B: (appeased)   That's quite all right. Give it to me - I'll put it up on the
                    rack - then we'll know it's out of harm's way.

A: I often lose my own luggage but I don't generally start
                    on other people's.

B: Perhaps you're a little absent-minded.

A: Perhaps I am a little. I near as could be threw it out.

B: I should have got it back. I'm getting out the next sta-
            tion, I'd have wired. Still it is a bit awkward starting
            one's holiday with nothing - Are these all your papers
            on the floor?

A: Oh yes. Thanks so much.

B: And there goes your pen now.

A: Oh thank you, most kind. It's[2] a bad plan to try to write
            a book in the train; silly of me to try.

B: A book! That's a book you're writing! I wondered what
            you were doing all the time. Then do you mean to say
            you're a writer?

A: Yes. I write novels.

B: (<u>excited</u>)   You a novelist? Why I put you down as some professor.
            I'm sure I'm very pleased to meet you. What sort of
            novels are they? Like Edgar Wallace?[3]

A: No -[4]

B: P. G. Wodehouse?

A: No.[5]

B: Perhaps more the highbrow sort?

A: (<u>reluctant</u>   Well - yes.
    <u>but truthful</u>)
                        (<u>Up train and down again</u>)
B: (<u>retreating</u>   I can't say I get much time for reading. You
    <u>tactfully</u>)   see my work doesn't allow me, at least not novels.

A: What[6] sort of things do you read?

B: Oh, connected with my work.

A: Are you a student?

B: Student! What an idea! No! What put that into your head?

A: Well, you took me for a professor.

B: Well that proves I couldn't be a student, doesn't it? If I
            was a student I'd have known that you weren't a pro-
            fessor. [7]Guess again.

A: I never can guess what people do. You are evidently very much on the spot so perhaps you're in business.

B: [8]Wrong again.

A: Well - an engineer.

B: Isn't an engineer in business?

A: I daresay - I never get the things straight.

B: I should have thought you ought to - being a novelist. Why, novelists should tell who everyone was at the first glance from practice.

A: I'm not that sort of novelist. I try to make up my characters from the inside. I don't bother about getting their outsides "right" as it's called, and I don't try to put the outsides of the people I meet into my novels. They just wouldn't fit round the insides.

B: (losing   Of course I get very little time for reading.
   interest)

A: Or take scenery. That's an easier example. This afternoon, for instance, I've just been trying to describe a view in my novel, but it would have been no good my putting in any of the views we've seen from the train. They wouldn't have fitted in.

A: (Contd.)[9]   I had to make up a view of my[10] - Oh, but never mind all that, I'm getting off the point. I haven't guessed who you are and I never shall. I give it up. Who are you?

B: I'm a policeman.

A: (startled)   Good God!

B: (not pleased) Why? What's wrong with that?

A: That's quite all right. Nothing.

B: I'm glad it's quite all right. I suppose you thought a policeman ought to be with huge feet as they do[11] in the advertisements and a great moustache and a big red nose drinking beer in the area. I suppose you thought if we ever did have a holiday we'd take it -

A: (interrupts) I didn't think anything. You only made me jump.

B: What ever for?

A: Bad conscience.

B: Oh indeed. What was your latest crime?

A: Never you mind. No worse than anyone else's. Everyone has a bad conscience - and meeting a police-man brings it out. It's all right if one has a moment's notice to pull oneself together in, but you did, so to speak, come rather quickly round the corner, didn't you? and that's what we don't enjoy. Nobody's natu-rally law-abiding, also nobody knows what the law is, it's become so complicated. Everybody carries about a little secret load of guilt, and that's why we - well I don't want to annoy you again - but that's why we don't, speaking generally, like the police.

B: (amiable)   That's a pretty stupid remark to make, though I've no personal objection against it. Why, where would you be without us?

A: Where indeed? But that doesn't make me like them - I'm speaking as the general public, you understand.

B: Yes, my brain has got that far - Look here, what's wrong with us from your point of view anyway?

A: You'd be all right if we were all right, but we're not, because we're human beings, and so we have bad con-sciences. For example, just before when I said "Good God", I suppose that, strictly speaking, I could be charged under the Blasphemy Law.

B: Too true.

A: I shan't be - either this time or the next. But there are words which I might say, words which I know perfectly well and won't say, which I might get into trouble for. That's the sort of thing

A: (Contd.)   I mean. Law abiding talk slides into lawless talk which slides into publishable talk, and we wretched public can't be sure where one changes into the other. Similarly, law abiding behaviour slides into unlawful behaviour, and so on. So when we run into someone like you, whose job it is to find us out, no wonder we jump.

B: Ah. You think our job's to find you out.

A: Isn't it?

B: No. Not our principle job. Our principle job is to prevent crime. It's only after an offence has been committed that our job becomes one of detection. We don't slink about trying to catch people out. Our aim is to make things so difficult for people who want to act unlawfully that they just won't. Does that cheer you up at all?

A: Not very much. "Detection is your - er - secondary activity, instead of your primary", as I thought. That's all the difference.

B: I should have thought it was a great difference. I don't think you are being quite fair.

A: You mean that it makes a difference in your attitude towards your work?

B: Yes.

A: You mean you're more inclined to take care of us than to punish us.

B: You can put it like that if you like - though we don't punish the public in any case; that's done by the magistrate when it has to be done.

A: Yes, I see the difference now. Certainly it is better[12] that prevention rather than detection should be uppermost in a policeman's mind, and you have cheered me up a little.

B: I'm relieved at that. Cigarette?

A: Please.
(Strike match)
Though as a matter of fact I suppose you yourself are in the detective branch.

B: No. An ordinary plain policeman who walks about in a uniform. What made you think I wasn't?

A: I don't know.

B: Perhaps you didn't think an ordinary policeman had any education or intelligence.

A: (Slight   Well it was rather that.
     pause)

B: Your mistake is you take your ideas out of books
                    instead of looking about you. You're quite correct that
                    there wasn't much education some years ago, but it isn't
                    beef that gets one into the Police Force, now - it's brains,
                    and study.

A: You have to take your ideas out of books, in fact.

B: Yes. (laughing) No - I mean no. No it's hardly that, but
                    we have to learn the law of England, at least all that law
                    which has to do with police procedure, not to speak of
                    Ju Jitsu and physical training, and that means months
                    and months of hard study. It isn't just a matter of pass-
                    ing the doctor to become a policeman. I don't want to go
                    into details, but -

A: (interrupts)   No don't I shall forget them all - I always forget details -
                    but it will now stick in my mind that the Police are bet-
                    ter educated than I supposed.

B: Yes, and it's the same over promotion. You can't get a
                    sergeant's rank without passing a civil service examina-
                    tion.

A: Oh so! I thought you got promotion for[13] arresting
                    people!

B: Don't bother to apologise. We're accustomed to hearing
                    that said. As a matter of fact, it's even more complicated
                    than I've just been saying. You can't even sit for the pro-
                    motion examination without having first passed the
                    civil service examination. And now are all your troubles
                    at rest?

A: My troubles? Indeed not. The fact that the Police know
                    Ju-Jitsu and can interpret the Law of England doesn't
                    console me in the least. Why should it? I am now going
                    to ask you a very nasty question - and I ask, remember,
                    as typifying the general public. This excellent education
                    they give you, this[14] special training and all the rest of it:
                    does it make you human?

B: Human? I suppose you mean humane?

A: No. Human. Human beings.

B: I should hope not.

A: (scandalised) You should hope not? Well, really!

B: Why, if we were human beings in your sense of the word, we shouldn't be able to do our job, and then where would you be? I don't want to be rude, but you've been dropping bits of writing paper all over the carriage ever since we left London. Well, it wouldn't do for the Police to carry on like that, would it? You'd be the first to complain. The public doesn't want us to be human beings, with human faults. It wants us to be a machine on which it can rely - a machine that will stop the traffic for it when it wants, and pick it up when it faints and show it the way when it's an old lady who's lost and guard its house when it's got one and not be faint when it has an accident or laugh when it treads on a piece of orange peel, but just get on with the job whatever happens.

A: (interrupts) Oh the job, the job! I'm the public and you're not, and it's no use your telling me what the public wants when I know and you don't. We don't want machine-made minds or machine-drilled faces, and if I may say so without offence[15] - that's what the Police tend to develop. I was an official myself for a bit and I've no use for this stereotyped impeccability. I know what it is from the inside.

B: Were you a good official?

A: Not very, but quite good enough. Of course I was always right. I was good enough for that. Officials always are right and I found it a delightful change. Ever since that time, I have never known whether I am right or wrong, but then I was never wrong as far as the public was concerned. Naturally when the public wasn't concerned and I was alone in the office with my superiors, it was a very different story.

B: Exactly. I guessed as much. You were not a good official. Did you get the sack?

A: I did not. I got a little testimonial. But now when I've got to contend with any form of officialdom I realise it's part of its job never to admit a mistake. The telephone people, the post office, the railway companies, the electric light, the water, the gas - I used to be surprised and a little annoyed to find in any correspondence with them that I was always wrong, and they, never. Now I am not surprised. But I am occasionally a little afraid. Institutionalism is all right for the people who are running the institute, it makes for internal loyalty. But to what extent does it benefit the nation as a whole?

B: I don't know about those other institutes you've got your knife into, but I <u>do</u> know, if the Police proved wrong, Law and Order would just break down. It's necessary for the well-being of the public that they should have faith in us.

A: Yes - in your humanity.

B: No - in our efficiency. You can't have it both ways. You can't expect an efficient police constable to act as an ordinary human being.

A: Well well.

B: Oh don't sound so sad! It's not really dreadful. We do introduce some common sense into our efficiency.

A: What sort of common sense? I don't always like common sense. Give me an example.

B: For instance it's common sense not to interfere between a man and his wife when they're scrapping. You stand a very good chance of getting a hat pin stabbed into you if you start touching the old man.

A: I don't mind that sort of common sense - in fact, I call it imagination.

B: I'm glad there's something you don't mind. If I may say so, isn't it rather a pity to keep on grumbling against the Police and everything the way you do? You don't help us nor yourself either.
(Train begins slowing down)

A: [16]It is not a pity, and I shall go on grumbling. I'll try to explain why. You see, I can remember for one thing what happened when I was an official and the letters of complaint rolled into the office.[17] They were never quite on the spot, because the writers hadn't the necessary inside knowledge to criticise us properly. But they often got near the spot and we sometimes altered our ways because of them. I think that's a good thing, don't you? We were always perfect[18] yet we did sometimes pass from one form of perfection to another, gently impelled by the public from behind. Now I'm the public and it's my turn. I shall go on grumbling. They say it's an Englishman's privilege to grumble, well it's certainly his duty, and I'm doing my duty to you. This bickering ungenerous attitude of the public whom I represent: this endless uninformed ungracious criticism of the Police and their ways - it's much more valuable than you think. It keeps you up to the mark -

B: Well I'm[19] -

A: - Our mark, not yours. It counteracts your officialism. It helps you to be human beings and at the bottom of your hearts you should be grateful for it.

B: Well, well! This is my station. Now I must hop out.
    (Door bangs)
    Goodbye - and oh I forgot - I'd like to read one of your novels after meeting you.[20] Will you give me your name?

A: Certainly. I write under my own name. (pause) Here it is -

B: E. M. Forster - I'm afraid I can't say I've ever heard of it.

A: Why should you? [21]Such thousands of novelists.

B: I'll try to get one from the library. Well, goodbye and thank you. I wish we had started arguing earlier.

A: [22]I wish we had. Not that arguing is ever any use. I wish we had argued less and talked more. Mind you enjoy yourself.

B: Rather!
    (GUARD whistles; train begins to move off)
    Well, look after yourself and[23] next time[24] don't be so suspicious of the Police.

A: Goodbye.
(calling)   I say!

B: Hullo!

A: Next time don't be so contemptuous of the general pub-
                   lic. Here! You've left your suitcase up on the rack.

B: Good God! So I have. Chuck it out.
                              (Bang)
                   Thank you!
                       (Fade out on train moving off)
                          (Buzzes out)

ANNOUNCER:
   (wait for
    hand signal
    to speak)[25]

   1. This series, "Conversations in the Train," was produced in the 1930s and involved
scripted, fictional conversations on various subjects written by well-known authors, including Dorothy L. Sayers, Rebecca West, and Rose Macaulay. According to Scannell and Cardiff
in *A Social History of British Broadcasting, Volume I, 1922–1939: Serving the Nation* (Oxford:
Basil Blackwell, 1991), Hilda Matheson launched the series in order to "increase participa-
tion/audience" and cater to "more than a highbrow audience." The series, which employed
everything from witty dialogue to simulated train sounds, ran on and off from 1932 to
1938—often without the authors performing their given parts, since "writers of amusing
dialogue did not necessarily make good performers, so actors were employed in their
place" (173). As Furbank explains, however, EMF did perform this broadcast with his
beloved friend Bob Buckingham, a policeman—identified here, however, as Leonard
Brockington (*A Life*, 2:172–73).
   2. <not the best>
   3. Edgar Wallace, British novelist and playwright, known especially for his detective
novels.
   4. <not at all>
   5. <, alas>
   6. <stuff>
   7. <Better>
   8. <Business?>
   9. "Contd." represents a page break in the script and is retained here to underscore the
state of the text as performers encountered it.
   10. <own>
   11. <them>
   12. <most desirable>
   13. <pinching>
   14. <Peel House>
   15. <to you>
   16. In the margin next to this paragraph is written in a hand other than EMF's:

"Insert - speech on loose page here." The replacement speech, appearing on the final page of the transcript, has accordingly been inserted in the text. Canceled passage: <It is not a pity and I shall go on <<continue>> grumbling. <<And I'll tell you why.>> It's my duty to grumble. This bickering ungenerous attitude of the general public whom I represent: this endless uninformed ungracious criticism of the Police and their ways: <<I suggest to you>> it's much more valuable than you think. It keeps you up to the mark ->

17. <We took no notice of them beyond acknowledging them, oh no of course not, and yet they had an effect.>

18. <- that's inevitable in an official ->

19. <blessed>

20. <Please give me the name you write under.>

21. <There are>

22. <We ought to have done.>

23. <I hope>

24. <you w>

25. The announcer's speech is not given in the transcript.

NEW BOOKS

by

E.M. Forster

October 3rd, 1932, 6.50 p.m.

I have just been for a few days to the English Lakes. I found them as charming as ever. The weather was glorious - that is to say, of course it rained a bit, but rain in the Lakes seems different from elsewhere - in fact one would be almost uncomfortable without it. Grey sheets of rain trailed in front of the mountains, waterfalls slid down them and shone in the sun, and the sky was always sending shafts of light into the valleys. Then - what's so wonderful in the Lakes - the <u>detail</u> was so exquisite. Nothing is careless or shapeless there, it is as if a guiding hand has designed the smallest stream and planted every rock with mosses and flowers. I know no district which is at once so grand and so finished. And on the last day of the tour I came to Grasmere, which lies at the centre of the system, and climbed up Helm Crag. The sun shone everywhere, except for a dark shadow on Easedale Tarn, to the left was the road towards Keswick, and in front was the sacred village Grasmere itself, with the churchyard where Wordsworth lies buried, and close to him lie those whom he loved and trusted - his wife, his sister, and his friends.

Yes - you will have already guessed that my first talk will be mainly about Wordsworth. But I am probably going to talk about him in a way which you will feel unsympathetic. I am going to drop a little book into this grand and romantic scenery, a book on him which I have read with great interest, though scarcely with delight. I don't know whether to recommend it to you or not, because I don't know who 'you' are. It is not a book for the general reader. It will shock some people and bore others. It examines Wordsworth's life and character in rather a merciless way, and

Wordsworth does not come out well. He no longer seems part of the glorious scenery which I have tried to describe. The grandeur of the mountains, the purity of the streams - they get mixed up with something alien - with the psychology of a very complicated and rather unattractive man. Do you care for this sort of book? Anyhow, I'll give you its title: "Wordsworth" by Herbert Read, published by Cape, price 4/6d. Professor Read is one of the most eminent of our younger critics. His main subject is art - he is Professor of Fine Arts at Edinburgh University. But he has also worked at literature, and this book reprints some lectures which he gave at Cambridge.

The trouble with Wordsworth, according to Mr. Read, is that he combined strong passions with great reserve. This sounds like a noble character, but consider a moment: it may result in hypocrisy. Reserve and self-control are not always the same, passions may lead to action, and a situation result which has to be covered up. Wordsworth had a great deal to cover up, and recent scholarship has revealed an episode which he took pains to hide. When he was a young man he went to France and fell in love with a French lady, Annette Vallon, who became his mistress, and by whom he had an illegitimate daughter. He sinned against his own moral code, which was Puritanical, and he brought back to the English Lakes something which is out of harmony with them, and which is forgotten by the pilgrims who visit his shrine to-day. We don't, when we stand in the churchyard of Grasmere, want to remember Annette Vallon. She and her daughter have no part in the Wordsworth legend, and Wordsworth himself took care that they should have no part. He lived to be a respectable and intolerant old man, and when his friend De Quincey, who had also a mistress, married her, he refused to attend the wedding, on the ground that such irregularities can never be condoned.

Now - you will say - Why drag this in? Why scandal-monger? The story of Annette may be true, but what has it to do with the poetry? Why peep and botanise upon the grave? Professor Read has his answer for you. He doesn't write his book in order to serve up an unsavoury tit-bit. He believes that the Annette episode is of the greatest importance in the poet's development, and he works out the theory in a most interesting way. I'll take two of his points. The first is Wordsworth's attitude to France and the French Revolution. He began by wild enthusiasm, then he became cold, and in later years hostile. At first he could write:

Europe at that time was thrilled with joy,
France standing on the top of the golden hours,
And human nature seeming born again.[1]

And then as years went on, he turned completely round, until he would not even admit that the French had genius. He absurdly accuses them of:

> Perpetual emptiness, unceasing change,
> No single volume paramount, no code,
> No master spirit, no determined road;
> But equally a want of books and men.[2]

He moved from being a Bolshie (as we should now call it in modern slang) to being a die-hard, and this change in him has been noted by all his critics. What Professor Read has done is to provide a new explanation of the change. He connects it with the cooling of his passion for Annette. She embodied France for him, they passed into his heart and out of it together, as he grew ashamed of his love he hated the country that had given it birth. That's one of the points. Now for the other one. It is more subtle. Wordsworth wrote no great poetry before he met her, and he wrote nothing after he met her that can be traced to her influence - except perhaps an unimportant poem called Vaudracour and Julia.[3] But as he tired of her - which he did pretty soon - and became ashamed of his weakness, he looked for compensation elsewhere, and he found it in the mountains and streams which he had loved as a boy, and to which he now returned. That's the explanation of the great outburst of nature-poetry. It is a reaction from the French escapade. It is as if the great poet said to himself "Thank God, I have got safe back to my home, here are the places I know Helmeray and Grasmere and Easedale Tarn, and I will never leave them again." And the wonderful outburst of song resulted. It is a paean of deliverance. Then comes another stage. The outburst lasted only about ten years - from the age of 27 to 37; it died out because nothing new came into his life, he felt really safe, and his later verse is conventional and uninspired. His conduct became insensitive too. When he was 50 he went again to France, accompanied by his lawful wife, his sister, and some friends, and they actually all stopped at Paris in the same street as Annette and her daughter, and called upon them. No one seems to have minded. All that Wordsworth cared about by this time was his reputation with the general public, for he had become the poet of conventional morality. He sang of family life, but he was callous in the midst of his own family. No - he isn't attractive.

Well, that will give you an idea of Professor Read's severe and closely reasoned little book, and you will be able to decide whether you want to read it. It's not a gossip book - I must emphasise that: the writer believes the facts, as interpreted by him, do help to the understanding of Wordsworth's poetry. He certainly shatters the Wordsworth legend, and dispels the atmosphere of reverence which some people like to bring to the reading of literature, and which Wordsworth himself was hoping to command. Perhaps where I differ from him - from Professor Read, I mean - is that I do not respond in a sort of religious way to certain scenery, particularly to the scenery of the Lakes, and I find it difficult to prevent my emotion from going further and deifying the poet himself.

> Ah not in vain, ye Beings of the hills,
> And ye that walk the woods and open heaths
> By moon or starlight, thus from my first dawn
> Of childhood, did ye love to intertwine
> The passions that build up our human Soul. . . .[4]

The man who can write like that - it doesn't matter to me whether he had to go first to France or not. I feel grateful to him because he has expressed the mystery of the outer world in words beyond your power, and I shall still go to the churchyard at Grasmere where he is buried.

The next book on my list is also about literature, but it's meant for a very different audience. There's nothing difficult about it, and nothing harsh, and nothing subtle. It calls itself "An Outline of English Literature",[5] it begins with Chaucer and ends with Robert Browning, and it tries to make literature attractive and easy to people who haven't read anything, or who haven't read much. The compilers are Mr. L.A.G. Strong (who has written some good novels) and Miss Monica Redlich, and they've done their job quite well. Most of their book is made up of quotations, it's really more of an anthology rather than an outline, and they hope that when you have read their quotations from - let us say - Ben Jonson's Volpone, you will be so pleased that you insist on reading the whole of Volpone. I hope so too. Yet I have my doubts. I can't help being a little sceptical about this sort of book. Does it really lure the reader on? I should like some statistics. Literature ought to be popularised - Mr. Strong and Miss Redlich are quite right. The problem is - How's it to be done, and I don't think snippets are the best way. I believe that Professor Read - though we may hate his opinions and get choked off by his style - may possibly make us read Wordsworth because he has intense feelings about Wordsworth. Mr. Strong and Miss Redlich may have intense feelings about Wordsworth too, but they give themselves no room to express them, they just talk about him quietly, quote four of his poems, and then pass on. We read the poems, we think "Wordsworth's very good, so was Ben Jonson, so will Jane Austen be, everyone's very good." And then we pass on too. I hope I'm not too pessimistic over this, but I feel that literature is a fire and can only be brought to us by a torch-bearer - unless, best of all, we encounter it by accident ourselves in the coldness and darkness of our mortal night, and comfort our souls at its everlastingness. It doesn't come by nice easy little spoonfuls - at least it didn't come like that to me, I don't know how it may be with you.

So I recommend "An Outline of English Literature" with some reservation, but if you think it will help you, do get hold of it, for it's excellent of its kind. Compiled by Strong and Redlich. Published by Gollancz. Price 5/- and you get nearly 600 pages for your 5/-.[6]

Next week I shall speak of the work of Lowes Dickinson, whose recent death has been such a loss to broadcasting, and to civilisation generally. I shall give you the names of some of his books, and try to convey some idea of the character of his output. He is, to my mind, a most important writer, who has not yet come into his own. Until he broadcast, I don't think many people even knew his name.

"Wordsworth" by Herbert Read	Faber & Faber 4/6d
"An Outline of English Literature" compiled by L.A.G. Strong and Monica Redlich	Gollancz 5/-
"The Pleasures of Poetry"	Edith Sitwell Duckworth 6/-[7]

Addition to E.M. Forster's Talk on "New Books"
3.10.32

The third book on the list also tries to make us like literature. It's astonishing how many people are trying: I think the age in which we live might almost be called "the age of recommendations". This particular attempt is made by Miss Edith Sitwell. She has compiled an anthology called "The Pleasures of Poetry" and she gives in it specimens of Victorian poets, and also a provocative and charming introduction. This book is not the least like the "Outline of English Literature". It's personal. Miss Sitwell is not trying to give good marks all round like Mr. Strong and Miss Redlich, but only to praise enthusiastically certain writers whom she loves such as Swinburne and Christina Rossetti. She writes with passion and delicacy, she is fascinating on the subject of verbal effects, and she knows about poetry from the inside. Is she fair-minded? No, not at all, and I can't see that it matters. She stimulates us instead of being just. Matthew Arnold for instance - she cannot abide Matthew Arnold. She says of him that his verses are only admired by those people who dislike poetry, and as I admire both his work and hers, something must be wrong somewhere. But what does it matter? Literature is an affair of the spirit, and it is a great mistake to think that you <u>ought</u> to like it all, or that anyone ought to like it all. You merely end up not minding any of it, and that is spiritual death. Miss Sitwell will save you from that. All that she writes is a protest against standardisation and stuffiness, and I recommend her little anthology if you are content to take what she gives you.

The Pleasures of Poetry: The Victorian Age. By Edith Sitwell. Published by Duckworth. Price 6/-

1. William Wordsworth (1770–1850), *Prelude* (1799), Book Sixth, lines 339–41.

2. William Wordsworth, "Great men have been among us" (1802, published 1807), lines 11–14.

3. Probably 1804; published in 1820.

4. William Wordsworth, *Prelude*, Book First (1799), lines 405–9.

5. EMF misidentifies the book. The title is *Life in English Literature: An Introduction for Beginners* (1932).

6. <The third book on the list takes us into yet another world. It concerns D.H. Lawrence. There have been a good many books about Lawrence lately - too many in my opinion - and more are coming. People who knew him keep writing about or against him or against one another, and there are psychological and psycho-analytic studies, and little scraps of his work are solemnly served up. We are given him Bowdlerised, non-Bowdlerised, and so on. I think it is time he got a rest, and was left to find his own place - which will be a high place, for he was one of the great writers of our generation. The book I am going to mention is a legitimate publication: it is a big volume of his letters, with an introduction by Mr. Aldous Huxley, and it is quite right that these should have been collected, for they throw light on his development, and will help people who want to know about him in the future. There are a great number of them, they cover 20 years and fill over 800 pages. Many of them are just business notes to publishers, others expound philosophy, others are tragic - there is an appalling description of the way he was persecuted by our military authorities during the war - the episode he introduces into Kangaroo. And others are very amusing: and since I haven't had time to discuss Lawrence seriously here, I'd like to point out how amusing he could be, what fun; it's a side of him that's often forgotten. In these letters you'll every now and then want to laugh. When he's discussing Germany he'll suddenly say: "And these huge German Women sitting round one like mountains that would never even know if they sat <u>on</u> one. . . . . . I want to go somewhere where the women are a bit smaller and where their hats don't sit so menacingly on their heads." Lawrence could be very gay, he was fond of nonsense, and he kept his gaiety to the end of his life. If you pick about in this great volume, you'll find amusement and much else. "The Letters of D.H. Lawrence" is the full title. Published by Heinemann. Price 21/-.> Aldous Huxley, ed. *The Letters of D. H. Lawrence* (1932), 820.

7. <"The Letters of D.H. Lawrence"   Heineman 21/->

BOOK TALK

by

E.M. Forster

<u>Monday, 10 October, 1932, at 6.50 p.m.</u>

A little pamphlet has just been published called <u>The Contribution of Ancient Greece to Modern Life</u>.[1] It is by Lowes Dickinson, who died two months ago,[2] and I am going to make it an excuse for saying something about Dickinson's work as a whole. It's a legitimate excuse because he was to have broadcasted to you this autumn on this very subject. He would have told you in that quiet persuasive voice of his, that the so-called dead civilisations are anything but dead, and that Greece in particular still has valuable things to say to us, even though we go about in aeroplanes[3] and talk, as I am talking to you now, across miles of emptiness and darkness. We know much more than the Greeks, we can press more buttons and levers. Whether we are wiser than they, Dickinson was inclined to doubt. For one thing, he found them more open-minded than we are. They wanted the truth, even if it was unfamiliar,[4] they were better tempered and more honest in discussion, and they weren't so easily shocked or personally offended when they encountered an adverse opinion. For another thing, the Greeks were the first people who looked at the world for the sake of the beauty in it, and so[5] age cannot wither nor custom stale their literature. He brings out these two points in this little pamphlet I've just mentioned, and he would have brought them out in his talks. I'm not specially recommending the pamphlet - it's just a reprint of a[6] lecture, but it's a convenient start for our survey.

[7]First I'll briefly mention his other books about Greece; (and, by the way, while I'm talking you needn't trouble to take down the various books. I'll give them all again at the end, together with the prices). There's <u>"The Greek View of Life"</u>.[8] This is a survey of Greek mental activity, a

86

solid, educational piece of work, but[9] touched with imagination and sympathy, like all that he wrote.[10]

Then there's a book about <u>Plato and his Dialogues</u>[11] reprinting the talks he gave last year over the wireless. The word 'Plato' has rather a boring sound. For some reason or other 'Plato' always suggests to me a man with a large head and a noble face who never stops talking and from whom it is impossible to escape. Dickinson has shown me another Plato - a living attractive person inhabiting a real world.[12] He sets him in his own civilisation. He suggests that the Peloponnesian War, which ravaged Greece, differed only in scale from the Great War which has ravaged Europe, and that both of them resulted in a complete disbelief in progress on the part of the young. Again and again he makes us look at our own age while he speaks of another age. It is a most remarkable book. Instructiveness and imagination are[13] combined, as in the <u>Greek View of Life</u>, and, by the way, Dickinson could do this because he was always thinking of other people when he wrote, and never of himself, and[14] especially of the attitude of the young. Many eminent men have <u>liked</u> young people and sympathised with them: but he did more - he respected the young.[15]

This comes out very strongly in a book which naturally comes next on my list. It is called <u>After 2,000 Years</u>,[16] and Plato again appears, this time as a character in a dialogue, the other speaker being a modern young man. They meet in the Elysian Fields. Once more, and in the most vivid way, the troubles of Ancient Greece and our own troubles are compared, and methods of dealing with them contrasted. Plato believes in Utopia. He hopes that,[17] by organising society under guardians, a perfect state of human life can be evolved. The modern young man is less ambitious. He hopes that the world will become slowly and slightly better,[18] through the resources of science -[19] but he knows that science can do more harm than good, that it endangered civilisation in the Great War and may destroy it in the next war. What is needed is the desire to use science rightly plus the intelligence to use it rightly: that is to say, our[20] real problem to-day is still a human one, as it was two thousand years ago: we are still grappling with the defects in our character, we are still uneducated, and Plato and the modern young man meet on this common ground.[21]

All Dickinson's work is of a piece, and we pass naturally from this Greek section of it, and from the dialogue with Plato, to the dialogues in general. Here's[22] <u>A Modern Symposium</u>,[23] a brilliant little book, at once serious and gay, in which various contrasted characters discuss our civilisation. One character suggests Disraeli, another Gladstone. Another, an amusing journalist, gives a mischievous account of America.[24] As is usual in Dickinson's work the setting is charming and, owing to his fairmindedness, he can throw himself into all types of character. He's not a creator of

character, or a great dramatic artist: I don't want to claim too much for
him, in fact I don't want to use the word 'great' of him at all, it has been
slung about too much to right and left in these days. But he <u>could</u> enter
into people's opinions and state[25] them and this is what he does both in <u>A
Modern Symposium</u> and in two other dialogues <u>The Meaning of Good</u>,[26]
which deals with ethics, and is too philosophic for[27] my taste, and <u>Justice
and Liberty</u>,[28] which is a political dialogue.

Politics! That brings us to the War.

He wrote six or seven books about the War and the secret diplomacy that
led to it, and about the League of Nations of which he was a prominent
originator - it is often forgotten how much he did to start the League. I'm
not going to discuss these books or even to give their names, but I must
emphasise that Dickinson was a pacifist and did become an internationalist, in the broad senses of the words. His attitude towards war colours all
his work. It even comes out in the little book I am going to discuss, the
exquisite fantasy of The Magic Flute;[29] indeed it comes out in it vividly.

I promised last week to talk at length of the <u>Magic Flute</u>, but now that
I put these notes together I find it isn't so easy. It's a lovely book, I implore
you to read it, but rather unluckily it's based on an opera by Mozart. I say
'unluckily' not because the opera is bad, it is Mozart's best, but because
many readers of the book won't have heard the opera, and so won't catch
on to the allusions. You'll have to be prepared for some queer names.
There is Sarastro, the high priest: he, in Dickinson's fantasy, typifies reason, the wish to understand. There is the Queen of Night: she is the creative power, but she destroys while she creates, because she is
uncontrolled emotion, the eternal feminine unchecked, and if Sarastro did
not[30] check her she would destroy the universe. There is Pamina, their
daughter, who is the world's desire: she belongs to both her parents but
she chooses to live with Sarastro, so he and the Queen are at feud. And
fourthly there is Tamino, the young hero ('Everyman' as it were) who is in
love with Pamina, but does not know how she is to be won. All these four
characters come out of Mozart's Magic Flute. Read the book as an allegory,
read it as you would the Pilgrim's Progress, and it too describes a pilgrimage - not from this world to the next, but from this world as it is to the
world as it might be if we used our reason and our emotions properly.
Like all Dickinson's work,[31] it tries to help humanity. Read it as a very profound Fairy Tale. And remember its main point: Pamina, the world's
desire, cannot be won by force nor by fraud. War is useless - so is wickedness. Nor when Tamino does attain her, can he keep her for himself.
Possessiveness is useless. The books ends not with the marriage of the
lovers but with the entry of the hero into the Hall of Sarastro, which is the
home of the followers of truth, and where the true nature of Pamina is

known. And here may I slip in a comment? Dickinson was not a mystic. He had a strain of mysticism in him, but he didn't think reality lay in some other existence. The time to work for humanity is now, the place here, and one of the dangers that Tamino has to escape in his[32] pilgrimage is the danger of the Lotus-Lake of Buddha.

And Buddha brings us to the East.

The last group of books I am mentioning might be called the 'Oriental', though the best known of them was written before he went to the East. This is the Letters from John Chinaman.[33] When this little book came out (thirty years ago now) it made a big sensation, particularly in America. It was published anonymously, and President Bryan[34] actually mistook the author for Chinese, and[35] pitied him publicly for not having had the advantages of a happy Christian home. Certainly it is a detached book. It's a view of western civilisation at the time of the Boxer risings[36] when the west was trying to civilise the east by force. You can't call it a satire - it's too grave - nor an indictment - it's too witty and beautiful. It's rather a contrast.[37] It contrasts Confucianism, which aims at so little and attains that little, with Christianity, which aims at so much and produces the modern industrial state. It contrasts the Family in China which is indissoluble and has its ancestral altar and rites, with the individualism of the West, where everyone tries to rise out of his family and to get on in the social scale. It contrasts a Chinese village and a London slum, the Chinese respect for literature with the Englishman's humorous contempt for it, and so on. No doubt the contrasts are not always fair, but they are never weakened by bitterness, and the little book did, I think, an enormous amount of good, for it shook people here out of their complacency, and made people over in China realise that more than violence can come out of the west. It was the foundation of Dickinson's Chinese reputation, which is still considerable. You must take care not to think of him just as a Cambridge don.

Some years later, he travelled in the East, and two other books resulted: a short Essay on the Civilisations of India, China and Japan and Appearances[38] - a volume of articles. Both of them are worth reading, and it is worth remembering that Dickinson's observations of China when he visited it, confirm the intuitions of it which he had already voiced in the Letters from John Chinaman. I will conclude my account of him by reading an extract from this last-named book. It well illustrates his attitude, and it is an excellent example of his elaborate yet lucid prose style.[39]

He is speaking of the respect for letters, so common among all classes in China, so rare in Europe, and he describes the conditions that produce it.

That's the end of my talk on Lowes Dickinson, and I shan't again be devoting a talk to a single man. There were special reasons for it to-day. For one thing I wanted to pay tribute to a very eminent broadcaster. For another, his books are still not as well known as they might be and I wanted to increase his audience. They are civilising books, they came out of a good life, and the motto which you see on the Radio Times[40] each week "And Nation shall speak peace unto Nation" might well be printed on their covers also.

Here are the names and prices of those I've mentioned:

Greek group
 The Contribution of Ancient Greece to Modern Life. 1/-
 The Greek View of Life.   3/6.
 Plato and his Dialogues.   6/-
 After Two Thousand Years.   6/-

Dialogues
 A Modern Symposium. 4/6
 The Meaning of Good. 6/-
 Justice and Liberty. 6/-

(War Books)
 The Magic Flute. 4/6

Oriental
 Letters from John Chinaman. 1/6
 An Essay on the Civilisation of India, China, and Japan. 2/-
 Appearances. 6/-

All published by Allen and Unwin, except The Greek View of Life, which is Methuen.

1. 1932. EMF provided citations at the conclusion of the talk; publication dates are provided here.

2. 3 August 1932.

3. <and motor cars>

4. <and uncomfortable>

5. <they have a freshness which we have lost, and>

6. <n inaugural>

7. <Well to begin - he wrote several>

8. 1896.

9. <and I believe it's been used a good deal in the upper forms of schools. I hope so, but it is>

10. <and it never forgets that the so-called classics are alive. I wish they had used a book like that at my school. I had instead to learn long passages of the classics by heart without being told what they meant. One of the pieces was thought to be about a dead parrot -

quite appropriate as far as I was concerned. Dickinson had suffered under the same kind of education as myself, and the Greek View of Life is an attempt to save future generations from it.>

11. 1931.

12. <He does this mainly by apt quotations, but also by his own comments. He will point out for example that "To read Plato is to discuss our own problems without the exasperation caused when we are, as it were, embedded in them . . . . . . There is no topic of importance which we discuss that he did not discuss too; and that with an intelligence more profound and elevated than has often been brought to bear on these issues." He brings out Plato's picturesqueness and charm.>

13. <once more>

14. <thinks>

15. <he wanted to know what they thought and felt>

16. *After Two Thousand Years; A Dialogue between Plato and a Modern Young Man* (1931).

17. <by careful breeding, and>

18. <. He commends>

19. <Plato didn't and that's the chief difference between them>

20. <makes>

21. <The dialogue concludes with a wonderful flight of eloquence. Dickinson really lets himself go. But I haven't time to point out his beauties. I want to indicate his general tendency, and I must pass on.>

22. <We come to>

23. 1905.

24. <which we can read with delight, and alas with profit, for the evils of America can now be paralleled here>

25. <fears>

26. 1901.

27. <your>

28. 1907.

29. 1920.

30. <restrain>

31. <it is practical,>

32. <quest>

33. <(or Letters from a Chinese Official as it has also been called)> 1912.

34. Here EMF mistakenly refers to William Jennings Bryan, Democratic congressman from Nebraska (1890–1894) and later secretary of state (1912–1915), as president. Bryan made these remarks in a pamphlet entitled *Letters to a Chinese Official*, aimed at contradicting the anonymous author of *John Chinaman*.

35. <Chinese, and wrote a review in which he>

36. 1898–1900: In response to the increased presence of Japanese and Western European economic and political influence in China at the end of the nineteenth century, a conservative political movement known as Ho Ch'uan (in English, "Boxer") inaugurated violent rebellions against foreign businesses, Chinese Christians, and European expatriates. The uprisings gained such strength that by 1900 the group occupied Beijing for eight weeks. A coalition of European and American forces subdued the Boxer Uprising and subsequently stationed troops in Beijing.

37. To guide emphasis during the broadcast, EMF added accent marks above the first syllable of "contrast" and above the second syllable of "contrasts." He repeated these accent marks later in the paragraph.

38. 1914.

39. No subsequent extract is indicated in the original typescript.

40. The *Radio Times*, launched by the BBC on 28 September 1923, provided a detailed schedule of all radio programs.

BOOK TALK

by

E.M. Forster

Monday, 24 October, 1932, at 6.50 p.m.

This is the third time I have had the honour of speaking to you, and, as I've said, I don't know who 'you' are - except when you are kind enough to write me letters of encouragement or regret. You begin to know who 'I' am, and when my voice starts you can switch off or not as the case may be, but the compliments can't be reciprocated. Still for my own convenience I've made up an imaginary person whom I call 'you' and I'm going to tell you about it. Your age, your sex, your position, your job, your training - I know nothing about all that, but I have formed the notion that you're a person who wants to read new books but doesn't intend to buy them. Now by buying books you help the authors, the publishers and the booksellers - three excellent classes of people - still it can't be helped if you don't want to, and I shan't urge you to do so, except under special circumstances. There are two reasons that stop us from buying books: firstly the economic, everyone's short of cash, and secondly where are we going to put the things? Books take room, and readers in the past generally lived in large houses whereas today we're more and more cramped into little houses and flats. Working people in particular - where on earth are they to put books? For instance, a policeman, a charwoman, a small holder - I take these examples not at random but because I've known people in these jobs who did serious reading - where are they to find shelf-room for their purchases?[1] No, until the housing problem as well as the general economic problem is solved you can't be expected to buy books. You'll have to get them from a library, and this brings me to a little bit of advice I'm venturing to offer.

It's this. Do take a firm line with your library, whether it's a subscription one or a free one. Be polite but be firm, and insist on getting the books you want. Many library assistants are excellent, and will take endless trouble to suit you. Others are what one calls 'merely human' - that is to say, they will follow the line of least resistance and give you any bit of rubbish to get rid of you. Insist on getting what you want, make up a list beforehand when it's possible, don't drift about hoping you'll see something nice, and never listen if the assistant tells you that you won't like the book you've chosen or that it is not suitable for you. You've got to find out all that for yourself.

I feel this is important. It's been said that every country gets the newspapers it deserves. Well, we shall certainly get the libraries we deserve, they will be what we make them, and if we are[2] idle they will become trivial and dull, and triviality and dullness are the two great enemies of literature. Here as elsewhere the consumer has a very real duty to the community.

Now the books I'm talking about today, are none of them books I suggest your buying - unless of course you find some special link with them. But they may well go on your library lists and from that point of view I'm going to say a few words on each. I'm not reviewing them, just indicating their character, and giving you, I hope, enough to decide on.

I've sorted out a batch of memoirs and reminiscences. Here is Sir Henry Newbolt, the poet and man of letters - you'll know his poem of Drake's Drum.[3] Here's Mr. Grant Richards, a publisher and a dillettante - I'm not using dillettante in a hostile sense, not in the sense of trivial. Here's a distinguished actress - Miss Elizabeth Robins. Here's Mr. E.F. Benson, the novelist. All these people are elderly - by which I mean that they are as old as or older than myself. And they will probably appeal to listeners of the same age. It's interesting when a person looks back over the years through which one has lived oneself, and these four people are looking back at much the same period of our social history though through very different pairs of eyes.

I'll take Sir Henry Newbolt first. He calls his memoirs <u>My World as in My Time</u> - but you needn't trouble to take the title down: I'll give it again at the end - I'll always do this.[4] He covers the first forty years of his life, up to the early years of this century, and another volume will probably follow. The key note of the book, and of Newbolt's own character, is loyalty. He is loyal to his country in the first place, he is passionately patriotic, he's loyal to his school (he was at Clifton), loyal to his family, his friends, his profession and to his class - which is the upper middleclass. He has a touch of the mediaeval knight about him, and more than a touch of the sportsman, and one sometimes wonders how he found time to become a writer at all. However he did find time, and to be a scholar and an editor too; he gave up his work at the Bar to run a magazine, The Monthly Review, which you may remember. He will tell you all about this in his memoirs, and his political opinions (he was a liberal imperialist and free trader), and about his boyhood and[5] love of birdsnesting, and the fine gentlemanly life of the English countryside, and his artistic friends, such as Sir William Rothenstein,[6] and his work on the Battle of Trafalgar and much else. His book doesn't happen quite to suit my own taste: I find it a little humourless and rather too self-assured. But it is in good sound English, and in one of the English traditions, and if you care for a quiet piece of reading which will take you among people of the public school type I advise you to put it on your list.

Mr. Grant Richards is a very different story. The title he has given his memoirs proves that: he calls them Memories of a Misspent Youth. He is gay and irresponsible, he loves Paris with a fervour which few Englishmen experience there now-a-days, he likes 'life', and he sometimes puts his foot in it. Like Sir Henry Newbolt he is a friend of Rothenstein and was fond of birdsnesting, but those are the only bond between them, and as for the birdsnests I can't feel sure that Mr. Richards left some of the eggs behind, so that the mother bird shouldn't desert, whereas Sir Henry[7] certainly did. The world of Mr. Richards is not idealistic.[8] It is rather the world of Phil May, Grant Allen, Churton Collins, Sarah Grand and Mrs. Ormiston Chant.[9] I don't know whether these names awake any memories in you - I'm stringing them together on the chance - nor whether you wish to pursue those memories, but you'll certainly be amused and you'll like the little preface by Max Beerbohm. The subject of the memoirs is Mr. Grant Richards' earlier life, and his work as a journalist under W.T. Stead,[10] and we leave him on the threshold of the twentieth century about to set up as a publisher. The atmosphere of the book one might call Bohemian, and if you find yourself in complete sympathy with Sir Henry Newbolt you won't care for Memories of a Misspent Youth, and vice versa.

Mr. E.F. Benson, to whom I now turn, holds as it were a midway position between the other two memoirists. He has a strong feeling towards the country gentleman who has privileges but also has duties - Sir Henry Newbolt's attitude. On the other hand, he's interested in the Bohemian, the bizarre, and the irresponsibility of youth - he even has a good word for the bright young people - Mr. Grant Richards would sympathise here. I don't know what to call his book. He calls it a 'Revue'. Its title is As We Are, and it's a glance back over the last twenty years. A good deal of it is a sort of novel, and then you'll get a series of reflections on the age, and appreciations of various people who have interested Mr. Benson - Sir Ernest Cassel, Archbishop Davidson, and so on - or he will start talking

about the League of Nations, or Grub Street - and then he'll give a piece of
his novel again. The book's uneven - bits of it are perfunctory, but bits are
awfully good, and he is particularly wise on a problem that is important
to some of us - the problem of growing old:

"Unfortunately there comes to the majority of those of middle age an
inelasticity not of physical muscle and sinew alone but of mental fibre.
Experience has its dangers: it may bring wisdom, but it may also bring
stiffness and cause hardened deposits in the mind, and its resulting
inelasticity is crippling. Those who suffer from it, merely sit woodenly
while the days stream past them: the days no longer nourish them or are
digested. Nobody is of any use unless he is still capable of assimilating
new ideas, so that they work that change in him, which is needful for the
due appreciation of changes. Otherwise he does not count, nor is there
the slightest reason why he should. Only those of middle age count who,
though they may not be able to initiate any longer, taste promise in the
new wine of life, though they personally may prefer the old."[11]

It's in this spirit that Mr. Benson glances back, and one can read <u>As We Are</u>
as a sort of spiritual memoir, though he draws very little on the facts of his
own life. He's largely concerned with the decay of a great house and a
great family, which is brought about partly by the war, but mainly by the
changes which followed the war, and by the failure of the great family to
adapt themselves to the new conditions. He calls the great house the
'Parable House'. We enter it when the Earl and Countess - aristocrats of
the best type - are entertaining in all their glory, and we leave it as the Club
House of a golf course, studded with cocktail bars. And what I like about
Mr. Benson is that he sees that this is not wholly a tragedy. It is a tragedy
for the old earl and countess, and they were splendid people. But it is a
tragedy that means compensation elsewhere, for unless the old world
passes away the new cannot be borne. I advise you to get his book. He's
always amusing and clever, as you know, but he's something better
besides - he has worldly wisdom of a very high quality - a very high
quality indeed.

And now I come to Miss Elizabeth Robins. <u>Theatre and Friendship</u> her
reminiscences are called, and they appeal to me because they are mostly
about Henry James, a writer whom I very much admire, and who is much
neglected at the present day. We remember Henry James - if at all - as a
novelist. Miss Robins knew him as a playwright and a critic of plays. He
was passionately, pathetically anxious to succeed on the stage, and in his
letters to her - which she now publishes for the first time - we read how
hard he tried and how bitterly he was disappointed. His delicate reminis-
cent tentative art was not suited to the theatre - at least that is what most

people think, though he did not think so and no more does Miss Robins. It is a charming book and a generous one, and makes me feel again how lucky Henry James was in his friends. I have, alas, never seen Miss Robins act, but she was one of the great exponents of Ibsen in this country, and here we see her trying to embody another and a much less embodiable, dramatist.

[12]Now I leave memoirs and memoirists; now I want to mention the names of three books of another class - three books dealing with our own island, and with the things which may be seen in it today. They are reports of recent travel in this country, and two of them are by a writer well known to listeners, Mr. S.P.B. Mais. Here is The Unknown Island,[13] which actually reprints his broadcasts, and describes seventeen dashes which he made through the country side at the hest of the B.B.C. And here is The Highlands of Britain, a more leisurely work, in which he climbs up various hills,[14] high and low. Mr. Mais enjoys himself everywhere, and goes to many lovely and interesting places; he rightly says that to see England properly one must see it alone, but one never feels lonely in his company, indeed I felt to be the whole time on a motor coach, dashing through village after village, and calling out 'cheerio' to each. Of course he goes too quickly to be always accurate; I don't think there can be 'steep screes rising to nearly 4000 ft. on each side' in the Cairngorms, he must mean 400.[15] Don't read him critically, though: glance at his routes and his anecdotes and the attractive photographs with which both books are illustrated. He is quite right in one contention - we don't know our own country well enough, and in some ways it is a very pleasant country.

In other ways it is not a pleasant country, and last on my list I have put a survey of England which differs acutely from Mr. Mais'. It is by Mr. Fenner Brockway, and is called Hungry England, and it describes a tour he has just taken in the Black Country, and the valleys of South Wales. You can't pass calling out 'Cheerio' here. Here is the house he[16] visited[17]:

> "It would be more suitable for chickens than human beings. The walls and roof are cracked. There are a small scullery and living room on the ground floor, dark damp stuffy places. The wallpaper is peeling off in big patches, as in a disused house. The bricks are falling out. There are steep narrow wooden stairs leading above; a dirty brown stain streaks the wall, where the rain has come through. The two bedrooms are in the same desolate condition, with rotten, falling wallpaper."[18]

Mr. Fenner Brockway holds strong political views, which will commend him to some listeners and discredit him with others. I'm only concerned with his reporting, and he impresses me as a good reporter, and I couldn't in honesty mention Mr. Mais' books unless I mentioned him too, and reminded you that beside the England of pleasure there is an England of pain.

My World as in Time. By Sir Henry Newbolt. Faber & Faber, 18/-
Memories of a Misspent Youth. By Grant Richards. Heinemann, 15/-
As We Are. By E.F. Benson. Longmans, 15/-
Theatre and Friendship. By Elizabeth Robins, Cape, 10/6.
The Unknown Island. By S.P.B. Mais. Putmans, 7/6.
The Highlands of Britain. By S.P.B. Mais. Richards, 7/6.
Hungry England. By A. Fenner Brockway. Gollancz, 2/6.

1. Specifically, EMF maintained a long-standing relationship with police officer Bob Buckingham, who also served as his partner in the 20 February 1932 talk.

2. <inert>

3. Sir Henry Newbolt, "Drake's Drum," in *Admirals All* (New York: Dodd, Mead, 1897).

4. All of the texts EMF cites in this talk were published in 1932.

5. <hours>

6. Sir William Rothenstein, New English Art Club painter and author who came into prominence in the 1890s for his Oxford portraits.

7. <N probably>

8. <and chivalrous>

9. Phil May, path-breaking cartoonist, contributed to *Punch* in the 1890s and founded the *Phil May Annual;* Grant Allen, author and scholar, is best known for his scandalous novel, *The Woman Who Did* (1895); John Churton Collins, literary scholar, urged the study of English alongside Classical literatures at British universities; Sarah Grand (aka Frances Elizabeth McFall), novelist, published several controversial New Woman novels in the 1890s and later served as mayoress of Bath (1922–1928); Laura Ormiston Chant, prominent figure in the Victorian purity campaigns of the 1890s.

10. W(illiam) T(homas) Stead, pioneer of the sensationalized "New Journalism" in the 1880s and 1890s and sometime editor of the *Pall Mall Gazette* and the *Review of Reviews.*

11. E(dward) F(rederick) Benson, *As We Are: A Modern Revue* (New York: Longman's 1932), 39–40.

12. In the margin is the time mark "7.3."

13. *This Unknown Island* (London: Putnam, 1932).

14. <great and small>

15. S(tuart) P(etre) B(rodie) Mais, *The High Lands of Britain* (London: Richards, 1932), 36. "Scree": "A mass of detritus, forming a precipitous, stony slope upon a mountain-side" (*Oxford English Dictionary,* hereafter *OED*).

16. <first> EMF also crossed out "the" preceding "house" in this sentence, though it is doubtful this cancellation remained in the broadcast.

17. <in Bilston - near Birmingham>

18. Fenner Brockway, *Hungry England* (London: Gollancz, 1932), 44–45.

[1]BOOKS OF THE WEEK
by
E.M. FORSTER

Monday, November 7th 1932, at 6.50 p.m.

Just ten years ago there was a disaster at sea. The Egypt, a P. & O. liner, on her way to India,[2] was run into by another boat off the coast of France, and went straight to the bottom.[3] Nearly a hundred people were drowned - a terrible tragedy, yet we shouldn't remember it to-day but for the fact that there was also on the Egypt a quantity of gold and silver - over a million pounds worth - and that went to the bottom of the Atlantic too. Four hundred feet down - and that's a great depth for diving operations; a diver can't go down 400 feet in a rubber suit, the pressure is too great - and for a long time there was no idea of recovering the treasure.[4] Then an Italian salvage company took the matter up, fitted out a steam trawler as a salvage ship, located the wreck of the Egypt, moored the trawler above it to buoys, and started operations.[5] A metal diving suit would resist the pressure all right, but how was the diver to move his arms and legs? The Italians tried suits with joints, like armour, but these were too clumsy. [6]Then they used quite a different type of suit. It was like a steel chrysalis, with windows at the top. The diver didn't try to move his arms and legs any more. He just stood inside the chrysalis and looked, and he telephoned up to the surface, and told the people up in the salvage boat what he saw. His arms and legs were, so to speak, outside him.[7] He could not move, he was only an eye, bobbing up and down at the end of a rope at the bottom of the sea. But he could cause things to move and could see their movements and report on them. In that sense, his arms and legs were outside him. He formed part of a new sort of animal.

Now this million pounds worth of gold was unfortunately stored right down in the hull of the Egypt,[8] and they had to clear away all the upper

99

decks before they could get to it. It was impossible for the steel chrysalis to go down hatchways[9] and along passages, even if it had got fingers to open the bullion room with, when it arrived. Its telephone and other wires would have got broken turning the corners, it would just have got hung up and presently it would have died. All it could do was to direct charges of explosives to be laid and then to retire to the surface while they went off. Then it went down again, reported on the position of the debris, and a steel grab was lowered and removed the debris under its direction. This went on for two years. The chrysalis worked in a half light, often in a quarter light, for artificial illumination was useless - and amid every complexity of weather, currents, and tide. Thirty feet of the Egypt were blasted away, a great crater was formed, and at the bottom of the crater was the bullion room. They wrenched its top off in time, and in the June of this year (1932) they brought the first gold to the surface. And here I'm going to stop.

For what I have been telling you comes out of a book I want you to read, one of the most exciting books I have come across for a long time - The Egypt's Gold, by David Scott.[10] Mr. Scott is a journalist - the only journalist allowed on the salvage boat, and he has really got inside his subject, he puts in his heart as well as his intelligence, and he has produced something quite unique in the way of a sea story. People often complain that the romance of the sea has vanished. I think it is because they look at the sea in an old-fashioned and conventional way, they will keep thinking of sailing ships and pirates, and grumbling when they don't turn up; and they will cling to the old fashioned nautical vocabulary as if it was an incantation which will bring back Nelson and Drake. But the sea's the thing and the sea's still with us and doesn't ask to be spoken of in any special way. The sea is still an immense body of water with problems[11] and perils appropriate to it, and if you will go down to it with Mr. Scott, and look at it through his eyes, and through the eyes of that steel chrysalis as it hovers over the ruined decks of the Egypt, you will be thrilled, and, better still, you will be touched. For inside the steel chrysalis there is a man and Mr. Scott's supreme achievement is that he realises this. He sees that the core of the whole business of the salvage operations, the only thing that matters in the long run, is human courage, combined with human charm. The gold in the Egypt is nothing - unless it reveals the gold that lies buried in man's nature, which in his book it does.

Let me be more precise. I admire the book for two reasons. Firstly, it gives a clear narrative of the salvage operations in untechnical language. I am very stupid over machinery myself, but under Mr. Scott's guidance I could read straight ahead about derricks and grabs and detonating bombs, and even about triple expansion engines. He has all his facts clear in his own mind, and he can use them to build up a story. He will say such illuminating things - will remark for instance that though the Egypt lay four hundred feet under the sea, she was herself five hundred feet long, that is to say she was quite a big object in relation to the surface, and it was possible for a small object like the salvage boat, which was only 150 feet long, to keep more or less above her. I take this as an example - there are others on every page; we move easily through an unfamiliar world because Mr. Scott knows how to tell a story and imparts his knowledge instead of displaying it. He has, as I have said, put all his intelligence into his job.

He has also put in his heart, and that is the second reason why I admire the book. He really cared for the Italians on the boat, especially for the crew. He didn't just chat pleasantly with them and offer them cigarettes like the average journalist, he shared their lives and worked and played with them. One of the stokers said to him in broken English, "Cheerio, plenty work me, you no work, goo' night, goo' night", and Mr. Scott felt ashamed. He determined that he would work, and he started by holding a blow lamp under the stoker's direction. Apparently he did it well, any-how the stoker praised him and it started their friendship. I don't think he gets on so well with the higher command, who are his social equals, he is friendly with them, but his affection and respect really go out to the men, and so from the human point of view, as from the technical point of view, the book comes alive. It is a lyric of the sea. Critics are always talking of epics of the sea - well, The Egypt's Gold strikes me as a lyric, and I'm sad when it ends and they bring the gold to England and land at Plymouth on a dreary Sunday afternoon. I can enter into this part, for I have had to spend Sunday afternoons at Plymouth myself.

I don't know whether I am overpraising the book. Its values happen to coincide with my own, and one does then tend to overpraise.[12] A severe critic would find it smacks of journalese, but it's the sort of book that asks to be judged as a whole, and I do think it carries one on and carries one up. The narrative is so exciting, the men are so real. I do think you will enjoy it. It is, I ought to add, the second book that Mr. Scott has written about these salvage operations. The first was called Seventy Fathoms Deep[13] and deals with the locating of the wreck. I have not read Seventy Fathoms Deep yet, but I mean to.[14]

I have sorted out some other books dealing with the life of action - though none of them are up to The Egypt's Gold. An autobiography, called A Man's a Man, is interesting.[15] It is by Francis Anthony, and it is a queer unusual book. Mr. Anthony's life has been queer. He began in an orphan-school, then he joined the Hussars as a trumpeter and became a trooper, and an infantryman or 'toey' in the war; he was a prisoner in

Germany, travelled in soap, did journalism, visited Hollywood, and now seems to have settled happily down. That's a queer life, but what is queerer are the things that he values in life. Often what a man prizes is more interesting than what he has done, and that is the case with Mr. Anthony. He adores the British aristocracy. He is quite frank about it. The gentleman who is a gentleman, the officer who is an officer, seems to him the finest work of God, and he has done all he can to imitate him. He is not a snob, he is too passionate. The highest desire in his life, which has been a very hard life, is to be 'posh', to talk like Mayfair, to ride like Hurlingham,[16] and to dress like Savile Row, and the apotheosis comes when he visits his former officer, now his friend, at the Cavalry Club. This seems to me queer. But I have to remind myself that nearly everything is queer, and that Mr. Anthony, who wants to be a toff, and has probably succeeded, is exactly paralleled by Mr. Scott, who wanted to be a stoker. Each tried to get outside his own surroundings, and to enter a world for which he wasn't born, and though my own prejudices are with Mr. Scott, I can't deny that the same law is at work. What makes the English like this? - for this romantic desire for an alien environment is extraordinarily English. It is often suppressed, but it is always ready to break out. Perhaps it is the desire which, working through other channels, has produced our literature. Anyhow these two books illustrate it neatly. I ought perhaps to warn you that both of them are about rough men in rough places, and contain swear words. So don't read them if you object to this. The swear words in Mr. Scott's book are veiled in the obscurity of a Mediterranean language which may make things better. Both books will probably suit men readers better than women - though I am quite aware of the folly of this sort of generalisation, and I apologise to the women who are listening to me for making it, and also to the men.

Here is another book about the sea - <u>Bowsprit Ashore</u>, by Alexander Bone.[17] Mr. Bone has been a sailor, and he here gathers together various articles and sketches and reminiscences of his career. They are written in a pleasant informative way, but the writing gets rather too much to the front for my taste. I like the sea and the people to get to the front, as they do with Mr. Scott, and the writing, as it were, to remain in the background and prop it up.

<u>The Din of a Smithy</u>, by J.A.R. Stevenson, is a vigorous, freshly written autobiography.[18] Mr. Stevenson tells us of his work at the forge, the commissions he's had, his opinions about mass-production, and so on. He is an unusual blacksmith, for he was educated at Harrow and Cambridge, and Mr. Walter Runciman[19] is his uncle. He is an artist-craftsman in the William Morris tradition. He longs for an England where people shall [take] pride in their work, and where work shall not be separated from

play. This'll just give you an idea of his book. There are some illustrations of his work, lovely garden gates, grilles and so on, pretty expensive I should imagine, and only within the reach of grandees. He's not a blacksmith of the commercial type. I'd put down <u>The Din of a Smithy</u>, if I were you. It makes a noise of its own.

Then, two books about the English countryside, or rather one about the English country, and the other about the Scottish - <u>The Common Earth</u>, by E.L. Grant Watson, and <u>Memories of the Months</u>, by Sir Herbert Maxwell.[20] If you want to know more about the country, you should read both these books, for however well you think you know it the authors are sure to point out something that you've missed. Mr. Grant Watson will teach you how to squeak like a mouse, and if you squeak properly, sometimes a field mouse will come, and sometimes a weasel. Sir Herbert Maxwell, a landowner in the north, is an antiquarian as well as a naturalist. He will tell you how the larch first came to these islands - at least he told me, I didn't know, and I've a great affection for the larch. And that's how one ought to read these books - picking out things for which one has affection, such as mice or larch, and building up out of them a countryside of one's own.

That's all I have to say - except to thank listeners who have written to me, and particularly those who exclaim with gratifying indignation that they do buy books. I'm glad to hear it. More power to your purse! I've also had nice letters from people, regretting that my talks are above them, and others equally nice regretting that they are below; so hadn't I better pursue the even tenor of my way?[21]

1. <NEW>
2. <was involved in a collision>
3. <of the Atlantic>
4. <gold>
5. <A rubber diving suit was impossible.>
6. <Finally they designed>
7. <That's to say the people up on deck lowered what he wanted - a charge of explosives for instance - and placed it exactly where he told them.>
8. <they knew exactly where, because they had a model of the boat>
9. <ladders>
10. David Scott, *The Egypt's Gold* (London: Faber and Faber, 1932). "I've" became "I have" in EMF's handwritten corrections; numerous other contractions in the script were likewise canceled and replaced by their more formal equivalents.
11. <extraordinary>
12. One of these values with which EMF likely agreed was Scott's affiliation with and affinity for the working-class man. Beginning during the early 1900s as a lecturer at the Working Men's College in London (a post he maintained, on and off, for twenty years) and continuing throughout his life (particularly in his amorous relationships), EMF felt a

connection to working-class men that he did not experience among his "social equals." For more on EMF's experience at the Working Men's College and its impact on his novels, see Furbank, *A Life*, 1:173–76.

13. Scott, *Seven Fathoms Deep* (London: Faber and Faber, 1931).

14. <I want to read about the salvage from the Egypt of the captain's safe. It contained the confidential communications of the late Lord Curzon, and when it was opened one of the crew remarked "Oh! There's never anything but muck in a captain's safe"!>

15. Francis Anthony, *A Man's a Man* (London: Duckworth, 1932).

16. The Hurlingham Polo Association became the premier polo facility in 1875 when the association drew up official rules for English polo.

17. Alexander Bone, *Bowsprit Ashore* (London: Jonathan Cape, 1932).

18. J(ames) A(rthur) R(adford) Stevenson, *The Din of a Smithy* (London: Chapman and Hall, 1932).

19. First Viscount Walter Runciman, shipping magnate and member of Parliament.

20. E(liot) L(ovegood) Grant Watson, *The Common Earth* (London: J. M. Dent, 1932); Sir Herbert Maxwell, *Memories of the Months: Being Pages from the Notebook of a Field-Naturalist and Antiquary* (London: A. Maclehose and Co., 1932).

21. Brackets appear around this final paragraph. Whether or not EMF read it on air is unknown.

NEW BOOKS

by

E. M. FORSTER

[1]In calling these talks side dishes, I'm thinking of English Literature as a banquet. The great masterpieces, the classics as we call them, occupy the chief positions on the table, we cut and come again at them, and stay our hunger. We learn to read for several reasons, but the chief reason is that we may attend the banquet and be able to partake of the best. This was Matthew Arnold's view of literature, and[2] how right he was! Nothing is as good as the best. If we are reading for pleasure it's foolish to keep away from the books that are likely to give us the greatest pleasure. These books I call the main dishes.

But suppose, to speak colloquially, you've had your whack. Or suppose, to use more parliamentary language, you have duly nurtured your aesthetic, intellectual, and ethical capacities upon the English classics - what about it then? What about the side dishes - the dishes which would never be served at all,[3] but for the masterpieces? I see no objection to them, and I am going to talk about a few of them this week. But I want to emphasise that their value is relative. Here are the letters of Jane Austen. Don't read them unless you've read Jane Austen's novels. It's just a waste of time; it's beginning the meal at the wrong end. Read <u>Northanger Abbey</u> and <u>Emma</u> and the other masterpieces, and then try these letters - which are not masterpieces, but profitable in their right place. Here again are some new letters of Edward Fitzgerald's, which are worth glancing at if you know and like the rest of Fitzgerald's letters. Here is a book about Macaulay. If you know the "Lays of Ancient Rome" and some of the <u>History</u>,[4] it will interest you. Here is an anthology. And lastly here is a treatise on words. These five books are all side dishes of various types. They are suitable if one has assimilated something else first, but are not to be taken on an empty stomach.

Jane Austen's letters! The prospect of these may stir you, and you can now read them in a superb edition, edited by Mr. R. W. Chapman, who is a learned, amusing, and human scholar. Let me try to indicate[5] what the letters are like, and let me remind you of what you doubtless know, that Jane Austen was a clergyman's daughter, that she went on living in the country with her mother after her father died, and that her[6] chief correspondent was her sister Cassandra. She belonged to a quiet, cheerful, decent family, and she wrote the kind of letters that people in a quiet, cheerful, decent family like to read - quiet, cheerful, decent letters, in fact. I'm going to read you one of her more exciting letters later on - it's about how she took her nieces to the dentist. We have many of us taken our nieces to the dentist, or even been to him ourselves, and I don't think that Miss Austen's contribution is out of the way thrilling. She wasn't intending to thrill. The great merit of these letters is their absence of affectation and strain. She pops down one thing after another, and Cassandra at the other end must have enjoyed it very much. We shouldn't be so interested, but for the fact that this obscure maiden lady had written novels as well, very great novels.[7]

The social outlook[8] of the letters and the novels is the same, we move in each case among refined middle class people who are living on their own estates in the English countryside, and sometimes they go to Bath, like Catherine Morland, and sometimes to Lyme Regis, like Louisa Musgrove,[9] and just for a little they are in London, and the wars with Napoleon are raging, and they don't notice them, and Wordsworth and Coleridge and Blake and Keats are all writing, and they don't notice them. They are in a backwater[10] - a backwater which has its own charm and calm, and whence we do not hear the murmuring of the weirs of the world. The letters and the novels - they both show this same social outlook. But you won't find, as you do with Charlotte Brontë, that Jane Austen put into her novels the people she met or the things that happened to her, or her own personal emotions.[11] So the novels remain rather a puzzle. How, we ask ourselves, did the little woman do them? Not that she was a little woman, she was a tall one, and Miss Mitford,[12] who did not like her, compared her to a poker. She did them because she had the knack of creating characters, and of arranging them in a suitable frame. Whatever she puts down in fiction makes an immense impression on her readers. What she puts down in her letters only made its impression on the recipient. We may either say that she wasn't a great letter-writer or that she didn't write her letters for us to read. Both statements are true. She wouldn't have been shocked at Mr. Chapman for collecting her correspondence, for there is nothing intimate in it; but she would have been rather surprised, and she would have said in effect, "What is the twentieth century up to?" In effect, but not in words, for her English belongs to a more civilised age than mine. She wrote for her family, and - although she happened to write novels too - it is as family gossip that these letters ought to be judged.

[13]So imagine yourself to be Miss Cassandra Austen, sitting with your mother in a small house in a small village in Hampshire in the autumn of 1813. Your mother has not been well and is perhaps a little contradictious. All your domestic duties have been performed, and you are[14] closeted with mother, who, to be quite precise, has had an application of leeches. But hark! There is the sound of hoofs in the lane. They come nearer and nearer. Can it be the postman? Is he passing through the village? Is he positively stopping at the house? And a servant - for you have got a servant, there was that advantage - comes in with a letter, and it is from your sister Jane, who is on a visit in London. How mother brightens up! And you - with what excitement do you break the seal, and read aloud what I will read aloud now.

"Fanny is very much pleased with the stockings she has bought of Remmington - Silk at 12/s. - Cotton at 4s. 3d. - She thinks them great bargains, but I have not seen them yet - as my hair was dressing when the Man and the stockings came. The poor girls and their teeth! I have not mentioned them yet, but we were a whole hour at Spence's,[15] and Lizzy's were filed and lamented over again and poor Marianne[16] had two taken out after all, the two just beyond the Eye teeth, to make room for those in front. When her doom was fixed, Fanny, Lizzy and I walked into the next room, where we heard each of the two sharp hasty screams. Fanny's teeth were cleaned too, and pretty they are, Spence found something to do to them, putting in gold and talking gravely - and making a considerable point of seeing her again before winter.[17] The little girls' teeth I can suppose in a critical state, but I think he must be a lover of Teeth and Money and Mischief to parade about Fanny's. I would not have had him look at mine for a shilling a tooth and double it. It was a disagreeable hour. We then went to Wedgwood's where my brother and Fanny chose a Dinner Set. I believe the pattern is a small-Lozenge in purple, between lines of narrow gold; and it is to have the crest.

Fanny desires me to tell Martha with her kind love that Birchall assured her there was no second set of Hook's Lessons for Beginners, and that by my advice, she has therefore chosen her a set by another composer.[18] I thought she would rather have something than not. It costs six shillings. With love to you all, including Triggs,[19] I remain,

Yours very affectionately,

J. Austen."[20]

Well, have you been a little bored? I have. Bits were amusing - for instance 'a Lover of Teeth and Money and Mischief' is not a bad description of a dentist. But on the whole it is too tame, because we do not know who Fanny and the rest of them are, unless we turn to Mr. Chapman's notes, and even then we cannot sit down with Cassandra and mother. The letters survive, but the people who received them are dead, and the letters without the recipient mean little. Of course this isn't the case with all letters: those of Edward Fitzgerald, whom I shall mention in a moment, make a wider appeal. But Jane Austen's are only interesting so far as they are from her and about a vanished state of society. You should get hold of these two magnificent volumes if you love the novels, and[21] thousands of people do. But don't expect too much. The quotation I have read you is a fair specimen.

The new Edward Fitzgerald letters needn't detain us a minute.[22] They are not of general interest, and I only recommend them to Fitzgerald enthusiasts.[23] I mention them to get the excuse of praising Fitzgerald's letters as a whole. Do read the main body of them if you haven't - and many people have not read them who know the 'Omar Khayyam'. They are unstudied, like the letters of Jane Austen, but, unlike hers, they manage to reveal a personality. To me the personality is attractive - kind, sensitive, civilised and un-townified. He was sometimes taken in, and he was often lazy, and he has been despised by critics who feel themselves very much on the spot. I like his gentleness. The gentleness of the saint has often been praised, but his was a pagan gentleness, which is rare.

The new little book about Macaulay[24] on the other hand, is of wider appeal,[25] and perhaps I had better drop this metaphor of side dishes while referring to it.[26] It's a learned book, yet it's a light one. Mr. Bryant,[27] who writes it, has read widely and has had access to unpublished material, and he isn't pert and doesn't try to poke fun at his hero. Yet he's amusing and he's critical. The fashion to-day is to think of Macaulay as very middle-class, rather vulgar, and as noisy in his own way as Carlyle. Mr. Bryant wouldn't deny this. But he completes[28] the thin, ungenerous picture with a few lines which transform it, and by the time one finishes the book one loves Macaulay and admires him. This is a book I recommend.

Then an anthology,[29] a collection of passages in prose and poetry. Anthologies are of no use unless the man who does the collecting has an interesting mind. To-day so many dull people are cultivated - there must be more dull cultured people alive to-day than in any stage of the world's history, and dull people are terribly fond of collecting things. If it isn't empty match boxes, it's stamps, and if it isn't[30] stamps it's passages they've read in books. Consequently one fights a little shy of anthologies. But here's a live one, and it's by Mr. Aldous Huxley - <u>Texts and Pretexts</u>. Mr. Huxley has a most interesting mind, and he also feels interestingly, he is sensitive with distinction.[31] And in this anthology he takes you into his company and shows you what he has enjoyed in his reading. Enjoyed? Perhaps that is not the right word. Some of his sections are 'self-torture', 'hypocrisy' and 'misery'. 'What he has found genuine' perhaps. It's a personal book, the fruit of an unusual personality. I'm anxious that you should read it, because I like it myself, still it's my duty to give you a sample. One of the sections is called 'escape'. It starts with quotations from Mrs. Browning, Plato, Shelley, and Mallarmé, all dealing with the horror of the world. Then Mr. Huxley comments, saying, "Yes, there is no remedy save in flight. But whither?"[32] There's death. There's sharing the life of animals: here he quotes Walt Whitman's "I think I will turn and live with animals they are so placid and self-contained."[33] But he quotes only to condemn - the kennel is not an adequate retreat from the world; no more is the cloister, and here he quotes Gregory the Great, and George Gascoigne,[34] Karl Marx, Keats, and Matthew Arnold. This will give you some idea of the originality of his method, the breadth of his reading, and the fastidiousness of his mind, and you will know whether you care to order his book.

The fifth and last of my side dishes is a popular[35] treatise on words by an eminent authority on them, Professor Ernest Weekley. <u>Words and Names</u>[36] he calls his present volume, and it is pleasant to glance through - it is etymology made easy. Did you know for[37] instance that the word 'gun' is derived from a Norse lady called 'Gunhilde'? I didn't, but I scarcely know anything, and that is one of the reasons why this talk must stop.

1. <If it was usual to give titles to these talks, I would call this one 'side dishes'>
2. <in the main>
3. <which would never exist>
4. Thomas Macaulay, *Lays of Ancient Rome* (London: Longman, 1842); *The History of England from the Accession of James II* (London: Longman, 1849).
5. <say very briefly>
6. <great friend and>
7. <and when we look at these letters, it's amusing to observe the connection between them and the novels. It's a connection Mr. Desmond MacCarthy was observing the other day, when he was discussing "Villette". He showed how Charlotte Brontë made use of her own experiences in fiction.
Well, so in certain ways did Jane Austen >
8. <fabric>
9. Catherine Morland: protagonist of *Northanger Abbey*; Louisa Musgrove: secondary character in *Persuasion*.
10. <aesthetically and politically>
11. <It's <u>said</u> that one of her acquaintances suggested Mr. Darcy in "Pride and Prejudice". It's <u>said</u> that an early love of her own irradiates with a distant and gentle glow the latest of her books, "Persuasion." But this, if it is true, doesn't take us far >

12. Mary Russell Mitford, whose mother knew Austen, known for criticizing Austen and her novels to friends.

13. <An experiment>

14. <sitting>

15. Mr. Spence was the family dentist.

16. Fanny, Lizzy, and Marianne were nieces of Austen's.

17. <he had before urged the expediency of Lizzy's and Marianne's being brought to town in the course of a couple of months to be further examined, and continued to the last to press for their all coming to him. My brother would not absolutely promise.>

18. Martha Austen: second wife to Austen's brother Francis; R. Birchall: music seller and publisher. James Hook, *Lessons: Guida de Musica: Being a Complete Book of Instructions for Beginners on the Grand or Small Piano Forte, Entirely on a New Plan, Calculated to Save a Great Deal of Time & Trouble, Both to Master & Scholar. To Which is Added Twenty-Four Progressive Lessons in Various Keys, With Fingering Marked Throughout. Op. 37* (London: Broderip and Wilkinson, 1800).

19. Triggs: gamekeeper at Cassandra Austen's house.

20. R(obert) W(illiam) Chapman, ed., *Jane Austen's Letters to Her Sister Cassandra and Others*, vol. 2. (Oxford: Clarendon Press, 1932), 327–28. EMF placed brackets around the entire quotation and wrote in the margin: "To Printer Please keep capital letters exactly as they are here." EMF emended Chapman's edition for the broadcast, omitting capital letters, ampersands, dashes, and abbreviations.

21. <most>

22. Neilson Campbell Hannay and Catharine Bodham Donne Johnson, eds., *A Fitzgerald Friendship: Being Hitherto Unpublished Letters from Edward Fitzgerald to William Bodham Donne* (New York: W. E. Rudge, 1932).

23. <They are written to his friend, W. B. Donne, and other members of the Donne family.>

24. Arthur Bryant, *Macaulay* (London: P. Davies, 1932).

25. <excellent>

26. <for I think it might have the result of introducing people to Macaulay himself - people who don't read him, and there must be many of them.>

27. <the author>

28. <my>

29. <Anthologies are of two kinds - those which cover a subject, and those which reveal a personality. I like both kinds, but the second kind's no use unless the personality is an interesting one.>

30. In both instances in this sentence, "stamps" replaces "crests."

31. <you may like or dislike him, but you can't deny this.>

32. Aldous Huxley, ed., *Texts and Pretexts: An Anthology with Commentaries* (London: Chatto and Windus, 1932), 288.

33. Ibid., 289. Huxley quotes from Whitman: "Song of Myself" (l. 684) in *Leaves of Grass* (1855).

34. Saint Gregory I, pope from 590 to 604, was a scholar and statesman known for re-organizing the vast holdings of the church into the Papal States; George Gascoigne, member of the court of Elizabeth I, was a playwright and poet.

35. <book about novels>

36. Ernest Weekley, *Words and Names* (London: J. Murray, 1932).

37. <certain>

NEW BOOKS

by

E.M. Forster

<u>Monday, 5th December 1932, at 6.50 p.m.</u>

This evening there are several interesting books to hand, memoirs, records, histories, etc., all bearing on the events of the last twenty years. I looked about, as usual, for some sort of framework in which I could present them to you, for it improves a talk if it can have a framework, and is not a mere library list, and I asked myself what has happened in the last twenty years, what outstanding event. The war, of course. But the war is only part of a longer process which began before 1914 and did not end on Armistice Day. We are too much involved in that process to understand what it means. We only know that it shakes us up and shakes us about, and shakes what we have been accustomed to regard as the solid earth - frontiers, forms of government, standards of conduct and of living, all are shaken by unrest. And unrest is the word I'm looking for to describe this batch of books. Let's call them 'Tales of Unrest'. They are not all unhappy tales, for man is not born to misery, and if the whole of this globe melted, he would, I am sure, up to the last moment, be scampering about and trying to adapt himself to the new conditions, just as his ape-like ancestors did when they first descended from the trees. Men perish, but man keeps smiling. He still carries hope or ignorance about with him in his heart, and unrest is, according to some philosophers, the primal necessity of his being. I am struck how Man thrives in the books I am going to talk about. Here is the singer Chaliapin who has gone through vicissitudes most shattering for an artist, and is now practically excluded from Russia, yet all the time he keeps on singing. Here is the war diary of Arnold Bennett - he writes ahead bravely. Here is a post-war commentary by Messrs. Collier and Lang - they write ahead gaily. Here is Trotsky, who helped to make the

Russian Revolution, and who is now exiled by it and writes a history of it. Here is another book on Russia, by Mr. Kingsley[1] Martin, who describes the chaos and the promise which he saw there last summer. And here are the narratives of various English and German soldiers who escaped from prison camps during the war. These last are indeed Tales of Unrest, but all the books have the same element of instability running through them. And how should we not feel unstable, any of us who have survived the last twenty years? From Trotsky to Arnold Bennett - from the most violent of personalities to the most 'Clubbable' and urbane - all are standing upon a quicksand, so am I and so are you.

Let's take the Chaliapin book first. Chaliapin is a great artist and a great egoist. There are faults in his character which he recognises, but his own faults are more important to him than other people's virtues, and much more important than either Czarism or Bolshevism. He cannot take governments seriously, and it is dangerous not to take a Government seriously today, especially in Russia. He is only serious about his art. He expects the State to support it, and the State is willing to a point, for it's a good advertisement for a government to have a great artist in its shop window - provided he doesn't take up too much room. So Chaliapin was petted by the Imperial regime, and given the title of 'Soloist to His Majesty the Czar'. He likes old Russia, with its splendour and its traditions - an artist will - but then comes the Revolution. He likes the New Russia with its faith in the power of the people - an artist will - and he is made 'Premier Singer to the Soviet People'. But he cannot stand the red tape, and red tape is always tape, whoever ties the knots. An artist and a government are always at loggerheads throughout history, and the tension is worst in an age of unrest like our own. Chaliapin isn't the only recent example. In Italy there is the conductor, Toscanini, who got into trouble by refusing to play the Fascist hymn during an opera.[2] In Spain there is Professor Unamuno, the man of letters, who was imprisoned by the late monarchical government.[3] In India there is Rabindranath Tagore, who disavowed the knighthood which he had accepted from the British government because he wanted to protest politically.[4] All these are examples of the recent friction between the governments and the artists, but Chaliapin is the best example of all, for, poor fellow, he's fallen out both with the old order in Russia and the new. The 'White' Russians regard him as a Red and have deprived him of the title of 'Soloist to His Majesty' and the Bolshevists regard him as a reactionary, and have deprived him of the title of 'Premier Singer of the Soviet People'. He is just plain Chaliapin again, and his voice is the same as ever. (The last point is one which no government will ever grasp.) The book of memoirs - in which he relates this tragi-comedy and much else - is called 'Mask and Man'.[5] There is more man about it than mask. It is a frank unstudied plea for individualism. You can see from Chaliapin's own account what a trial he was to any administration, red, white, or blue, and you can ask yourself which you prefer in a community, discipline or art? In practice, you get, and always will get, a mixture of the two, but which do you prefer? I prefer art.

Trotsky on the other hand, is all for discipline, and he describes in this History the preliminaries which were, in his opinion, necessary for establishing it. They entailed the overthrow of a discipline which already existed; the book forms the first part of his History of the Russian Revolution, and is called 'The Overthrow of Czarism'.[6] Trotsky reviews - from the Bolshevist standpoint - the fast development of Russia, the War, the collapse of autocracy, the revolution of February 1917, the return of Lenin and the episode of Kerensky,[7] and in a second volume he will deal with the October Revolution, which places Bolshevism in power. He writes ably and bitterly, and it's significant that his view of history is the impersonal. I don't mean that he is unprejudiced. Far from it. But he regards the course of events as obeying their own laws (which it is the historian's duty to discover), and not as depending on the characters of individuals. Character doesn't interest him - at least not in theory: in practice he feels its fascination and gives some brilliant and savage sketches of the Imperial Court, and of the liberal leaders who tried to utilise the forces of unrest for their own ends. He regards only general laws as important, and the general law which (he believes) is now at work, ordains that the proletariate shall rule and that the proletariate alone can understand the proletariate. I don't agree with him in that, by the way: observe instead that he is building up a new discipline under which Chaliapin will feel as uncomfortable as ever, and by which he himself will be expelled. Mr. Kingsley Martin (who visited Russia this year) says that Trotsky's name scarcely ever appears. The forces of unrest have proved as fatal to him as they did to his butt Kerensky, and to do him justice, he never complains. I don't know whether to recommend his book to you: it depends as always upon who 'you' are. Communists will already have read it. Noncommunists should read it if they can keep their tempers. It's a work by a big man who has helped to shape the events which he describes.

I recommend Mr. Kingsley Martin's book more confidently. It is called 'Low's Russian Sketchbook' because he accompanied the caricaturist Low,[8] and Low's drawings are amusing and fanciful. Everyone will laugh at them except the Soviet Customs officials - they turned them over without a smile, and tried to confiscate them because some of them depicted soldiers, and a soldier must be a military secret. I'm concerned, though, with Mr. Martin's text. Writing as a tourist, a very intelligent one, he gives a wonderful idea of the mixture of discomfort and hope, brutality and decency, over-organisation and disorganisation, gaiety and determination which exist together in the country to-day. It's often said that the tourist in Russia can only see what he is shown, and there is some truth in that. But it has also been pointed out that there are different types of eyes, and the eyes of Mr. Martin were wide awake. Here is an example of what he sees and of what Low illustrates:

"If the U.S.S.R. is still far from civilised standards in dealing with polit-ical crime, it is equally far in advance of them in its attitude to the ordinary criminal. Low and I stroll into a magistrate's court. There are no lawyers present though a man can employ a lawyer if he wants to. The bench is occupied by a young man who has had some legal training and six years experience of judicial cases. On either side of him sits a factory worker. The young man in the middle, whose place is later on taken by an equally young and considerably more attractive woman, is the magistrate. The two workers are assessors who, in effect, play the part of a jury. One of them looks alert, the other at least as vacant as the average British jury-man. Two men are pleading their case, speaking in turn, respectfully but without any embarrassment. There is a dispute about a horse and cart. Was there money owing by the man who had hired it? After listening for a quarter of an hour and asking questions, the magistrate and his two assessors retired to consider their verdict. If the two assessors write against the magistrate they get their way. They return, however, five min-utes later, and the magistrate announces that the money should be paid. The applicants walk off talking amicably."[9]

The scene is interesting and agreeable, and it would scarcely have been staged by the touring authorities on the chance of Low and Mr. Martin strolling in! It's a genuine peep, and there are many others through the book. Mr. Martin's attitude is sympathetic. He believes that the crudities and stupidities in Russia (which he recognizes) are temporary and that the industrial transformation will succeed and may initiate a new, and a desir-able, form of human activity. To our question this evening - namely what will become of the individual in that new order - he can't give a very sat-isfactory answer, but he may well ask us what is becoming of the individ-ual under Capitalism.

Now we'll leave Russia for England, and for two English chronicles. The first of them is by Arnold Bennett. More extracts from his journals have just been published - the period covering the years 1911–1921: the fatal years which, so to speak, underline the whole age of unrest. Bennett was a calm person outwardly, but his war diaries react to a great variety of events. He was in the Ministry of Information, and he had a good deal of inside knowledge, scraps of which are here revealed, and on one occa-sion he goes to the front. All his life he was blessed - or possibly cursed -

with the gift of holding unpopular opinions and yet not getting into trouble over them, and though he too was a fine artist, he is a great contrast to Chaliapin. Reading his war entries, one is surprised that he fitted into an office, he is so sensible and frank, and so incredulous about the atrocity stories and scare stories which circulated in most patriotic circles. He can write for instance "I agree that Russia is the real enemy and not Germany: and that a rapprochement between England and Germany is a certainty". But then he will, so to speak, save himself by adding "But I doubt whether it is wise, in the actual conduct of affairs, to try to see so far ahead."[10] You should read him and also look at "Just the Other Day" which covers the post-war years. "Just the Other Day" is by Mr. John Collier (who is a brilliant young novelist) and by Mr. Ian Lang.[11] It's a light chronicle which conveys a good deal of seriousness as it discourses on sport, crime, the general strike, brighter London, the fall of the pound, art. It has a limitation, which is shared by the Arnold Bennett diary, and by other books of the sort: it's 'Londony', it doesn't enter much into the feelings of the provinces or the countryside, and the unrest it reveals is a London unrest.

Now for the last book on my list. It is called "Escapers All" and it is mainly a reprint of talks which were given last year over the wireless. The great majority of listeners, I believe, instantly switch off when they hear the human voice, especially when it is raised instructively, but I know of at least one large roomful of men who made an exception over the escape talks. It was something they would stand and understand, and the reprints ought to be popular too - I've certainly much enjoyed them myself. They begin with Mr. Harry Beaumont: Trapped in Belgium - brilliant and amusing and ending with a remark which I find hard to beat as the end of a happy story - "so when I got home I found my wife a widow."[12] Then follow a variety of adventures: Mr. Hugh Durnford's account of the Holzminden Tunnel[13] represents one type, and Herr Justus's 'Unconducted Tour of England'[14] another - a tour which was unfortunately cut short by an attack of influenza, though he managed to get from Yorkshire to Cardiff and visit several music halls in London on the way.

The escaper, like the artist, is an extreme case of individualism: he refuses to fit in, even into the nicest prison, indeed the nicer the prison the more restless he becomes. He won't do what the authorities tell him, disobedience is his life's blood. You can argue that he escapes for patriotic reasons. But most of the prisoners, English and German, escaped because it was their nature, almost for the fun of the thing. Consequently they provide one of the few romantic side-shows that occurred in the war, and as Mr. J.R. Ackerley points out in his introduction, it is a side-show which may not recur. "Perhaps", he writes, "these are the last war-escape stories which will ever be told, for it may not be fanciful to suppose that if ever there is another great war there will be no more prisoners - except so far as nations can be imprisoned in the boundaries of their own lands, and dart about from end to end in their efforts to escape the poisons that fall from the sky."[15]

1. Throughout the script Kingsley is typed as "Kingsly"; unusually, no handwritten corrections by EMF appear on the script.

2. Arturo Toscanini, Italian conductor and recording artist. He was attacked by a fascist gang during a tour of Bologna in 1931 and subsequently refused to conduct in Italy while it remained under fascist rule.

3. Miguel de Unamuno, Spanish philosopher, educator, and novelist. EMF is probably referencing Unamuno's opposition to the dictator Miguel Primo de Rivera, which resulted in his exile from Spain between 1924 and 1930. Unamuno returned to Spain in 1931 and opposed Franco's fascism. He died in 1936.

4. Rabindranath Tagore, Indian novelist and poet, won the Nobel Prize in Literature for his poems collected under the title *English Gitanjali* in 1912. Tagore refused a knighthood in 1919 in protest over the Amritsar Massacre (April 13, 1919), an attack led by Gen. Reginald Dyer against unarmed citizens of Amritsar resulting in the deaths of 379 Indians. See Mary Lago, *Rabindranath Tagore* (Boston: Twayne, 1976).

5. Feodor Ivanovich Chaliapin, *Mask and Man: Forty Years in the Life of a Singer* (London: V. Gollancz, 1932).

6. Leon Trotsky, *The History of the Russian Revolution* (London: V. Gollancz, 1932).

7. Aleksandr Feodorovich Kerensky, Russian revolutionary. Kerensky served for a brief time as premier of the Soviet Union in 1917 but was quickly ousted.

8. New Zealand–born Sir David Alexander Cecil Low was a caricaturist and cartoonist in Britain and New Zealand best known for political cartoons that ran in the *Star, Evening Standard*, and *Manchester Guardian* in the 1920s and 1930s. An outspoken opponent of Winston Churchill, Low developed a reputation, in Churchill's words, as a "green-eyed radical." "Low," as he preferred to be known after 1919, was knighted in 1962.

9. Kingsley Martin, *Low's Russian Sketchbook* (London: V. Gollancz, 1932), 56.

10. Newman Flower, ed., *The Journals of Arnold Bennett: 1911–1921*, 3 vols. (London: Cassell, 1932–1933), 2:94.

11. John Collier and Iain Lang, *Just the Other Day: An Informal History of Great Britain since the War* (New York: Harper, 1932).

12. Harry Beaumont, "Trapped in Belgium," in *Escapers All: Being the Personal Narratives of Fifteen Escapers from War-Time Prison Camps, 1914–1918*, ed. J. R. Ackerley (London: Bodley Head, 1932), 40.

13. Hugh Durnford's tunnel was constructed in 1918 in an effort to free English prisoners of war from an all-British prison camp in Holzminden, Germany.

14. EMF is referring to Heinz Justus, whose "unconducted tour of England" involved using a disguise to slip out of German control and make his way into England undetected.

15. Ackerley, "Introduction," in *Escapers All*, 18.

NEW BOOKS

by

E.M. Forster

<u>Monday, 19th December, 1932, at 6.50 p.m.</u>

[1]It might be called Not New Books, for as it's my last talk I want, with your permission, to be retrospective, and desultory.[2] I say "with your permission", well knowing that you cannot withhold it, and that I am in the position of a preacher who never hears his congregation cough. You can escape my sermons, but cannot interrupt them,[3] and I am going to hold forth for a start on broadcasting generally as it concerns books.

Like everyone else, I speculate a good deal on the future of broadcasting - it's the biggest technical innovation affecting words since the invention of printing, and we don't know at all where it's going to lead, or what effect it will have on literature. It's a mistake to assume that books[4] have come to stay. The human race did without books for thousands of years, and may decide to do without them again. It was thought a century or so back, that the printing press would overthrow the church, and it may be that the microphone in its turn will overthrow[5] those sacred bundles of printed matter called 'books'. [6]I don't want books overthrown, and those who are at present in charge of broadcasting evidently don't want it either. But we are all swept along by something we can't control, science advances mercilessly, and it becomes increasingly difficult for an individual to influence events, and increasingly desirable that he should observe them; so at the close of 1932 we might do well to observe what is happening to printed stuff, also called 'letters' and 'literature'. There's not only the microphone, there's the cinema. Between them are they not turning us from readers into listeners and lookers, and causing us to depend less and less on books?

I think they are, and I'm sorry.[7] For books have an educational value which nothing yet invented will supply. No one's educated who can't concentrate, and it's easier to[8] acquire concentration through a book than through a talk or a film for an obvious reason: if your attention wanders you can go back to the top of the page and start again, whereas in a talk or a film you are carried on. It's[9] more possible to read[10] thoroughly than to listen or look[11] thoroughly, and the habit of concentrating is easiest picked up from books. Between you and me and the ether, I've no great faith in the educational future of broadcasting unalloyed. And between you and me and the screen, I trust in the movies still less. Microphone and screen can both help as long as they are subsidiary only, and are[12] combined with books and refer us to books. They can indicate, but they can't rub anything in. In twenty-four hours all they[13] leave behind is a blur, whereas a book can sink into the mind and strengthen it.

Coming down to my own talks, I haven't tried to rub anything in. The most important moment in each has been the final moment when you have been offered a library list. Criticism is a much subtler job, and it hasn't been attempted. My aim has been rather to recommend and to give reasons for the recommendations, and the reasons I have given have sometimes caused listeners to write and say they wouldn't admit the book in question into their homes at the end of a pair of tongs. That's quite all right. They know where they stand in relation to the book, which is what I wanted. It won't go down on their library list, and that is that. Regard me as a parasite, savoury or unsavoury, who battens on higher forms of life. And turning my head slightly backward, as a parasite will, I now crane towards the immediate past, I recollect what has nourished me there, and then I turn again to my fellow parasite, the microphone, and continue to address you through it.

I want to speak, for three minutes or so, about Lytton Strachey. Lytton Strachey died at the beginning of the year, and the greatness of the loss has not yet been realized. He was so amusing and clever and people like to pretend that these qualities don't matter, and that we only need honour the dead when they have bored us.[14] He could be malicious too, and people won't admit that malice may be sanitary; Strachey's certainly was, and a quantity of festering rubbish as well as a few fine feelings got swept away by him down Eminent Victorian drains. What I want to insist on, though, is a quality which most of his critics have ignored, even his friendly critics. He believed in affection. Look back at the Queen Victoria, the Elizabeth and Essex, the Portraits in Miniature.[15] Forget for a moment the brilliancy of the pictures, and ask instead what Strachey found valuable in the lives portrayed. Not fame or luxury or fun - though he appreciated all three. Affection, extending over many years.

He knows that affection can be ludicrous[16] to the onlooker, and may be tragic in the end, but he never wavers as to its importance, and that such a man should have ever been labelled a cynic and called heartless really fills one with despair.

Let me read the passage in which he[17] speaks of the death of a great Frenchwoman, Madame de Sévigné,[18] and its effect upon those who had loved her. It comes from Portraits in Miniature.

"In the midst of this, the inevitable and unimaginable happened: Madame de Sévigné died. The source of order, light, and heat was no more: the reign of Chaos and Old Night descended. One catches a hurried vision of Madame de Grignan, pale as ashes, elaborating sentences of grief: and she herself and all her belongings - her husband, her son, her castle with its terraces and towers, its Canon, its violins, its Minstrel, its hundred guests - are utterly abolished. For a little longer, through a dim penumbra, Coulange and his wife remain just visible. Madame de Coulange was struck down - overwhelmed with grief and horror. Ever sadder and more solitary she stayed in her room, thinking, hour after hour, over the fire. The world was nothing to her; success and happiness nothing; heaven itself nothing. She pulled her long fur-trimmed taffeta gown more closely around her, and pushed about the embers, wondering for the thousandth time whether it was really possible that Madame de Sévigné was dead."[19]

The dread of death is in this passage, but the[20] preciousness of affection is in it too, and when next you read Lytton Strachey it's worth looking out for[21] his heart. Don't, anyhow, label him as 'highbrow'. And, by the way, since we are being desultory this evening, owing to the approach of Christmas, I wonder if you will join my new league of peace and goodwill, the only condition of membership in which is that neither the words 'highbrow' nor 'Lowbrow' shall ever be used? They are responsible for more unkind feelings and more silly thinking than any other pair of words I know. They attempt to introduce into literature the cleavage which is so[22] lamentable in the world of[23] industrial relations: the cleavage between the brain worker and the manual labourer. I've used them myself in the past, greatly to my[24] regret; now,[25] as penitents will, I want to found a league.

Assuming that everyone has joined, I will now go further into an unexpected region: fiction.

I haven't been talking of novels at all, indeed to do so lies outside my terms of reference. I'm glad in a way, because in the past I've written novels myself, and so may have acquired prejudices which[26] impair the judgment. In a way I'm sorry, because I should have had the pleasure of recommending some of the younger writers. Do you know Rosamund Lehmann's novels, or L.A.G. Strong's?[27] I expect you do, and John

Collier.[28] Have you read William Plomer?[29] Or J. Hampson?[30] Or anything by Christopher Isherwood? Probably not. There! I've mentioned their names, and at the end of the talk I shall venture still further, and name one novel by each. I don't read[31] novels regularly, so my choice will be capricious, and at my age I'm probably not really on to what these younger men and women are[32] attempting in fiction. But there they are, most of them under thirty, and doing things I'd like to have done. They seem to get at poetry so easily, they use realism without getting tied up in it, which was the bother in my generation, they are less flustered by social distinctions, and they are not stupidly hopeful. Generalisations are absurd - the half dozen named above are different from one another, and must seem still more different to one another. But they have all acquired a new freedom of movement which is enviable, and if they are cynical about the world they have good reason to be, working in the nineteen-thirties, and if they still believe[33] in what Keats called the holiness of the heart's imagination, then aren't we with them, and does it make any difference to us that they don't use Keats' words?

Pursuing my mildly wild career, I will next crash on to two books about England - one by a Dutchman, the other by a Czech. The Dutch book came out last year, Miss Sackville West did recommend it, but I am taking a free line this evening, and it'll get recommended again. It is <u>The English are they Human?</u> by G.J. Renier, and Dr. Renier's answer to his own question is "No, the English are not human, but they were human up to the nineteenth century and they will become human again."[34] Here are the makings of a pretty quarrel, on the lines of jam yesterday and jam to-morrow, but margarine to-day, and Dr. Renier is nicely provocative because he dislikes[35] us a little. If he liked us a lot we should say 'How natural! A foreigner must,' and if he hated us we should say 'How natural! A foreigner would!' But to be disliked a little does make one sit up and pay attention to the indictment. He is worth listening to. He knows our habits and writes our language well.

The other book is a translation from the Czech writer Karel Capek, whom you know as the author of the play about Robots. It's a really brilliant little book called <u>Letters from England</u>.[36] It was published seven years ago, and it must not be forgotten. It's again, the work of a man who dislikes England just a trifle.[37] He likes our quietness and hospitality, our great old trees, our great old West end clubs, and the unexpected impishness which lurks both in the trees and the clubs, he likes travelling in a railway train through county after county, in some of which the cows are lying down, in others of which they are standing up. But he dislikes London as a whole, the traffic, the East End, the suburbs, Sunday and the middle classes, and as for Wembley - he visited us under the incubus of poor old Wembley - he feels a mixture of terror and contempt to which only his own prose can do justice. It represents to him the British Empire, minus the four hundred million coloured people who inhabit that Empire, it is a gigantic sample fair where commerce insolently usurps the throne that belongs to Man, and where the statue of the Prince of Wales made of Canadian butter, only inspires a wish that the majority of London monuments could be made of butter too. The machinery he admires, but it frightens him. We can of course retort to this indictment, for machinery and factories are not confined to the British Empire - there is plenty of both in Prague. But it's wiser to listen than to retort, and in Karel Capek's work, as in the novels I have mentioned, and in most of the books that touch my heart,[38] I feel again and again: the importance of man, the sanctity of the individual, and the deceitfulness of riches. He is a most sympathetic writer, and his gay little book against England[39] is not just nationalistic pat-ball. Reading it, we are drawn into the bigger issues which are perhaps best approached incidentally, we are led to what we think valuable in life and perhaps to revise our standards. And when we look at Capek's funny little mischievous sketch of four arm-chairs, all exactly alike, all hideous, all expensive, and labelled respectively "Made in Bermudas, made in Fiji, made in South Africa, and Made in British Guiana", we ask ourselves the same question that Ruskin put to our fathers, namely, is this what we want from our civilization, and will these armchairs help either the men who make them or the men who sit in them, to save their souls. Ruskin's antithesis between body and spirit was perhaps a false one, anyway it is unacceptable to the present generation. But they are with him in seeing that the individual is up against commercialism and up against machinery, and that the blind beggar, covered with scabies who sold Capek a box of matches outside Wembley is a symbol of us all, and is also our brother.

Book List[40]

Lytton Strachey's Works: -

Books and Characters	Chatto & Windus	3/6
Eminent Victorians	" "	"
Queen Victoria	" "	"
Elizabeth and Essex	" "	"
Portraits in Miniature	" "	6/-
Landmarks in French Literature. Thornton Butterworth 2/6		
Pope.	Cambridge University Press 2/-	

Novels of young writers: -

His Monkey Wife. John Collier.	Peter Davis	3/6

A Note in Music. Rosamund Lehmann   Chatto Windus 7/6
The Brothers. L.A.G. Strong.   Gollancz   "
The Case is Altered. William Plomer. Hogarth Press   "
Saturday Night at the Greyhound.   J. Hampson   "   "
The Memorial. Christopher Isherwood   "   "

Two books on England: -
The English are they Human? G.J. Renier.
                                     Williams & Norgate   7/6
Letters from England. Karel Capek. Bles.   3/6

1. <This is the last time I shall be talking this year, and>

2. <and not talk especially about new books at all>

3. <and the fact that listeners cannot interrupt makes these talks a bit unreal>

4. <are cultured necessities>

5. <the press <printed matter> - not only the popular press, whose destruction I should welcome, but also>

6. <I am bookish myself and>

7. <I'm sorry for this. For one thing, books>

8. <learn>

9. <easier>

10. <properly>

11. <properly>

12. <contrived>

13. <convey>

14. EMF placed accent marks above "was" and "matter."

15. Lytton Strachey, *Queen Victoria* (1922); *Elizabeth and Essex* (1928); *Portraits in Miniature* (1931). EMF provided publishing information at the conclusion to the talk.

16. <at moments>

17. <describes>

18. Seventeenth-century French writer and salonnière whose letters to her daughter created a memorable portrait of her world.

19. *Portraits in Miniature*, 56, 58. The broadcast presents a slightly altered version of the original.

20. <importance>

21. <this>

22. <disastrous>

23. <affairs>

24. <shame>

25. <I'm penitent, and>

26. <wouldn't make me a fair judge>

27. Both were British writers and contemporaries with EMF.

28. Author of popular fantasy tales, Collier went on to become a well-known Hollywood screenwriter.

29. <Less likely.>

30. J(ohn) Hampson was the author of such novels as *Saturday Night at the Greyhound* and was a friend to EMF.

31. <at all>

32. <doing>

33. <as I do>

34. Gustaaf Johannes Ranier, *The English: Are They Human?* (1932). EMF is paraphrasing Ranier's overall argument rather than quoting specifically from the text.

35. <the English>

36. Karel Capek, *Letters from England* (1932). The "Robot" play is *R.U.R.* (1920).

37. <whose approval of us is just outweighed by his disapproval.>

38. <this comes out>

39. <contains more than gaiety, nor is it>

40. All citations were handwritten by EMF.

SEVEN DAYS HARD

by

E.M. Forster.

For Saturday, 10th March, 1934 at 9.20-9.40 p.m.

Curious I should have got these seven days hard.[1] I've been thinking a good deal about prisons lately. You remember how Richard II says in Shakespeare:

'I have been studying how I may compare
This prison where I live unto the world'[2]

Well, I've been studying how to compare the world[3] I live in to a prison. I've been wondering where liberty ends and restraint begins in contemporary society. I suppose we're free.[4] But the number of laws, or of conventions which have legal force, is enormous. We're certainly not as free as we were thirty years back, and when people speak of the growth of lawlessness, they don't mean what they say. I rather wish they did: they mean that a new set of lawgivers have arisen, and are driving about in armoured cars trying to impose their particular form of civilisation through the form of the knuckle-duster. I suppose we're still free. But freedom in 1934 is an unfashionable word and maybe even the phrase 'the Laws' is out of date. Plato used it, but he lived a long way back. Perhaps I ought to have spoken of 'the orders'. Certainly in modern Germany or modern Russia or modern Japan you don't live under the laws any more, you live under the orders. You are ordered what to do; the government have instructed the police, the police tell you, and if you disobey or are slow in the uptake - biff! We haven't got to that in England yet, and if we get to it I don't want to be alive; but we are moving in that direction, for the reason that the modern state is so complicated that it can't admit the extra complication of individual freedom. Organisation must lead to standardisation. That's the trouble. People are easier to manage when they are all alike, and if you

124

want people alike you must give up that nineteenth century fad of liberty and[5] pretend you like prison.

Now I don't deny that many restrictions are inevitable, but how they increase! We can't build as we like or drink when we like or dress as we like. We can't even undress[6] as we like, but when we bathe must wear an increasing amount of costume in the combined interest of British modesty and British trade. We can't say what we like - there is this legend of free speech, but you try it on: free speech and saying what you want to say are very different things. We can't read or write what we like. Oh, by the way, some publishers of repute intend to bring out an edition of Joyce's Ulysses in this country: I hope they'll get away with it, for it's an important work - but we'll see.[7] And, finally, we cannot go where we like.[8] Escape is impossible. We can only get out of England on a ticket of leave, issued if our conduct has been satisfactory, and available for a definite period and destination. This ticket of leave is called a passport. Passports have grown in my time from a piece of tissue paper, which you got or not as you chose, in[9] a book of credentials. They are an outstanding instance of the individual's loss of freedom. He has lost the right to lose himself.

What's become of Waring
Since he gave us all the slip?[10]
But it's nearly one hundred years since Browning wrote that. Waring couldn't give us the slip to-day. He would be turned back at Harwich or Croydon. The nearest equivalent to him, Colonel T.E. Lawrence, only conceals himself through the friendly connivance of the authorities, and doesn't always do that successfully.[11] It's impossible really[12] to hide oneself this side of death. It used not to be, and the literature of escape which is so common to-day[13] has come into existence to compensate the modern citizen for the fact that he can't escape in the flesh.[14] His government's got him at the end of a string. My own passport was granted me by one of the kindest and wisest of our statesmen - Mr. Arthur Henderson, then Foreign Secretary.[15] In return for the sum of 7/6d, Uncle Arthur gave me a little book, rather like the butcher's book, only blue, thanks to which I "pass freely without let or hindrance" as he phrases it. Until I lose it, or offend some responsible official here or abroad, I have the illusion of free movement, but of course I am[16] letted and hindered, and so are any foreign objects which I try to introduce inside our tariff walls, and certain domestic objects which I try to send outside them. I[17] must not take[18] Uncle Arthur's promises too seriously.[19]

Such was the trend of my thoughts when I was invited to broadcast. And I had amused myself with an experiment. I imagined a country where freedom has been much more suppressed than is yet the case in England - a totalitarian state like[20] Germany or Turkey. And I imagined that that same country should develop, as it well may, an enlightened and humane prison system, in which everything possible is done for the welfare of the criminal: books, lectures, concerts, sermons, continuation classes, gymnasiums, visits from noble minded women and thoughtful men, - the whole penal reform programme. Might not the point be reached where the inside of such a prison would begin to resemble the outside? Might not the broad arrow turn into a weathercock, and veer about till[21] King Richard II didn't know which way it was pointing? Inside - outside - inside the prison more and more consideration for the individual, outside it less and less, inside it fewer restrictions, outside it more. That's as far as my experiment went but it has been nicely worked out in a French film. This film - it is called[22] A Nous la Liberté. - opens in a prison, a very hygienic and well organised prison.[23] Two of the prisoners escape and get work in a gramophone factory - a very hygienic and well organised gramophone factory. In the prison they make little wooden horses which moved on a continuous belt, in the factory they make gramophone records which move on a continuous belt. Such a difference! One prisoner strikes luck, he gets rich, he takes his friend back to his private house. It is a very hygienic and well organised private house.[24] It's practically the same as the prison, and so's the factory.[25] They haven't escaped at all, because the spirit of the prison is the spirit of modern civilisation. Everything that's spontaneous and personal gets stopped. - That's the theme of[26] A nous la Liberté, though the prisoners do escape in the end. They become tramps. Luckier than Richard II,

> Their vain weak nails
> Do tear a passage through the flinty ribs
> Of this hard world, their ragged prison walls.[27]

Let's look back at the news of the past week and[28] observe a few things which have been stopped. The film of 'Catherine the Great' has been stopped at Berlin, because Miss Elizabeth Bergner is a Jewess.[29] German films have been stopped[30] in Czecho Slovakia. In Paris, a performance of Coriolanus has been stopped because it was made the excuse for political demonstrations. In England - I am sorry to say that a boy named Wilfrid has made a private transmitting set. This is a very serious offence, because the ether belongs to the Post Office. I scarcely like to mention it over the microphone at all - it is like condoning heresy from the pulpit of St. Paul's. The ether belongs to the Post Office - the government has said so, and the Post Office was scandalised by Wilfred's broadcasts, which took the form of the words 'Good luck to the G.P.O.'.[31] He was tracked out: he said he was very sorry but his interest in science had misled him, and he was stopped.[32] Then the town council of Faringdon has tried to stop the butchers of Faringdon from killing animals on Sunday, under an act which dates from the reign of Charles I. The same act makes Sunday worship compulsory, so the butchers have retorted by trying to stop the town council of Faringdon from not going to church. I don't know how this will end, no more does anyone in Faringdon. Finally, here is one thing that was not stopped, and that is a packing case which was sent from Bulawayo to London. It was supposed to contain a bar of gold - the government said so - but when it was opened in the Bank of England, the horrified officials found something even worse than Wilfred: a lump of concrete instead of the gold. Waring had given them the slip for once.

Perhaps I should apologise for my frivolity, for I am really doing this seven days hard in the place of the Reverend Dick Sheppard.[33] I am as it were occupying his cell.[34] Mr. Sheppard would have talked to you very differently, more eloquently much more seriously. But[35] all the same he and I love and hate the same things on this earth. We love individuals - we hate machines. And what I've tried to do this evening[36] is to have a little hit at the machinery which would imprison the spirit of man. Prison is no good. Even if it takes a high sounding name, like the totalitarian state, or patriotism, or united national effort, it is still no good, it is still prison. I'm not giving you any reasons for this statement. It's my faith, and I believe it's Mr. Sheppard's faith too.

But here comes my warder to release me - and to release you.[37]

1. "Seven Days Hard" was a series of talks delivered in 1934 by such notables as Hilaire Belloc, Rose Macaulay, and G. K. Chesterton, who explained the premise of the effort accordingly: "[This series] is not concerned with public life or private life, but with Life. And it seems to me that Life is the one thing that most modern men never think about all their lives. We are asked to consider what has happened in seven days" (*Listener*, 31 January 1934, p. 192). EMF's broadcast was published in the *Listener* on 14 March 1934. There are minor discrepancies between the transcript and its published version, especially formal versions of EMF's contractions in the script. Only substantive variants are noted here.

2. *Richard II*, 5.5.1–2.

3. <we>

4. EMF added accent marks over "I've," the excised "we," and "suppose" in these opening three sentences. He once again emphasizes "suppose" in a later sentence echoing the original: "I suppose we're still free."

5. <put up with prison>

6. EMF added an accent mark over "undress."

7. Random House won the right to publish Joyce's novel in the United States in 1934, prompting a similar effort in the United Kingdom. *Ulysses* was published in Britain two years later. In the margin next to this sentence, EMF placed a question mark next to this statement. He placed an additional question mark next to his subsequent statement about passports. It may be inferred that these markings served as reminders to verify the accuracy of his claims.

8. <This is final.>

9. <an album>

10. Robert Browning, "Waring" (1849), lines 1–2.

11. <and Mrs. Agatha Christie, who ought to know how, was soon detected in a Harrogate hotel.> EMF is referring to Christie's somewhat contrived, and certainly dramatic, disappearance from her home in 1926 after discovering that her husband was in love with another woman. After leaving a series of mysterious clues, Christie was discovered by police at the Harrogate Hydropathic Hotel.

12. EMF added an accent mark above "really."

13. <is of the nature of a compensation and rests on it>

14. The section of text beginning with "The nearest equivalent to him" and ending here is missing from the version of EMF's talk published in the *Listener*.

15. Arthur Henderson was the secretary for foreign affairs from 1929 to 1931 and won the Nobel Peace Prize in 1934 for his leadership of the World Disarmament Conference.

16. EMF added an accent mark above "am."

17. <do>

18. <to>

19. This final sentence is missing from the version of EMF's talk published in the *Listener*.

20. <our Nazi neighbors>

21. <one doesn't>

22. <The Million> It is likely that EMF is mistakenly referring to another film directed by René Claire, *Le Million*, released in 1931.

23. *A Nous la Liberté*, directed by René Claire, starring Raymond Cordy and Henri Marchand, 1931.

24. <What privacy is there?>

25. <the same as the prison too>

26. <The Million>

27. <as far as my experience went, but it has been worked out in that delightful French film 'The Million', and in the light of it I will> 5.5.19–21. EMF wrote by hand the section beginning "That's as far as my experiment went" and ending with the passage from *Richard II* (slightly misquoted).

28. <point out>

29. *Catherine the Great*, directed by Paul Czinner and starring Elisabeth Bergner, Douglas Fairbanks Jr., and Joan Gardner, 1934.

30. <for a week>

31. Ironically, "G.P.O." refers to the General Post Office.

32. EMF added accent marks above "he" and "stopped." He also added an accent mark above "stop" in the next sentence.

33. Rev. Canon HRL (Dick) Sheppard, vicar of St.-Martin-in-the-Fields church and well-known activist on behalf of London's poor. Rev. Sheppard's talk was published in the *Listener* on 11 April 1934.

34. As EMF cancels neither "cell" nor his handwritten phrase "glass of water" at this spot in the transcript, it is unclear which he ultimately chose to read, though the version published in the *Listener* uses "cell."

35. <as far as I know>

36. The phrase "this evening" does not appear in the version of EMF's talk published in the *Listener*.

37. This final sentence does not appear in the version of EMF's talk published in the *Listener*.

TALKS FOR SIXTH FORMS[1]
by E. M. Forster.
Introductory

Friday, 24th September, 1937. 3.35 - 3.55 p.m.

I am going to talk about books. Books are not the only things in the world, and[2] they are not the most important things, but I have had a good deal to do with them, and that is why I'm broadcasting on them. In the course of my life I've read a good many of them, stuck in a good many more - the books I've stuck in would fill a large library - and also written a few - novels chiefly. So whereas some of the speakers in this series are to talk about politics and the art of government, because they know about administration, and others about science because they've worked on that, I am to lead off on books, because I've been a writer and reader. I'm not going to recommend you what to read, or give you the title of anything I've written myself. No, I want to go deeper than that, and ask the question: Are books any use? They take up a lot of room and a lot of time; well, are they worth it? They fill up the shelves - you want to put food or clothes on the shelves but you can't - they're full of books. And they fill up the day - you want to spend the day talking or playing or falling asleep, and cannot do so because you have to read a book. Are they just a ramp which keeps going because of the vested interests behind it, or is there some profound reason for their continued existence? They have been going for about three thousand years, mind. That's not a long time if you measure it against the history of the human race, but it's a long time if you compare it with the life of an individual. [3]Somehow or other, they have managed to tack themselves on, and I'm going to suggest to you three reasons why that is so, and why we find them useful.

The first reason is a very straightforward one. Books are useful because they give us facts. We want to know what's going on in the world and what has gone on in it, and we can very often get the information out of a book. I call this sort of book 'Books That Teach', and we read them in order to learn something - something practical. Take a very simple example. You want to go in a bus from London to Bedford, and you don't know where the bus starts. You look in a book called a timetable, and it tells you. There you are - the bus goes at 3.0 or whatever it is, and the timetable has given you the facts. Take another example. Suppose you want to learn about Mr. Gladstone. You go to the library and ask for a good book on him, and you get given Morley's Life of Gladstone perhaps,[4] and it teaches you the correct facts about Mr. Gladstone. Though it is a big book it is the same sort of book as the little timetable, which taught you the correct facts about the bus. Or again: suppose you are interested in astronomy and want to learn about our earth and its place in the solar system or the stellar universe - then you go to the library and ask for a reliable work on astronomy, and are given something by Edington or Jeans,[5] perhaps, and there you get the facts you want. The book on astronomy is called a scientific treatise, and the book about Gladstone is called a historical biography; but don't you be browbeaten by these grand names. They are both of them the same sort of book as the little timetable; they give us the facts. And of course we expect them to give us them correctly. That goes without saying. If we're told the bus leaves at 3.0 when it really went at 2.34 - well, we miss the bus and that's no good, is it? And if we're told that Mr. Gladstone was a Conservative, or that the sun moves round the earth - well, that's no good, is it, either? The facts are[6] wrong, and so the book is[7] bad. [8]Books that teach us and set out to give us facts must teach us properly.

I think you'll agree that this is straightforward enough, and that books are useful because they tell us about the world in which we live. We want to know about it[9] - in fact we have to know about it, or we shall come to grief - and here is certainly one reason for reading. But it is only one of the reasons; there are two more, and they aren't nearly so easy to explain.

[10]I've got in mind, you see, some such book as Shakespeare's 'Macbeth'. Is Macbeth any use? Does it teach us any facts? [11]Very few. [12]No doubt there is a historical basis to the play, but it is so hidden away that we get[13] no reliable information about Scottish history. We can't learn history from [14]it as we [15]will from Morley's Life of Gladstone. [16]It's quite a different type. [17]It sets out to invent, to create, to make something which didn't exist before; it [18]comes out of Shakespeare's mind, and if [19]he hadn't lived and been what he was, [20]it would never have been written. It's our second sort of[21] book. The first sort was good if[22] it taught us something about life: this[23] sort is good[24] if it seems itself to be alive. It's what the critics call imaginative literature.

[25]Take another example - take any good novel which you have been reading lately: Arnold Bennett's 'Old Wives' Tale'. [26]That splendid novel succeeds not because it gives us facts, but because it [27]creates a picture[28]. It may teach us a little about provincial England[29], but that's[30] by the way, the real point of the book is the characters in it, [31]the sisters Constance and Sophia. It's good because[32] Arnold Bennett [33]makes something up. [34]Or - in case you are a reader of modern poetry[35] - I'll [36]add as another example from that[37] fine poem, [38]T. S. Eliot's Waste Land. The Waste Land is good because of the emotion and the atmosphere in it. [39]There is no such land really, you won't find it on any map, you can't catch any bus to it, or from it; [40]it's good for quite another reason; because the poet has invented it and made it seem real. [41]The timetable, the Life of Gladstone, the handbook to astronomy, are[42] one sort of book. [43]Macbeth, the Old Wives' Tale, and the Waste Land are another sort.[44]

Now this second sort of book - the kind we're discussing - some people like it, others don't. You do or you don't, and really that's all there is to be said. I do. I like it better than any, and if I didn't I shouldn't have taken up literature as a job, or talked this afternoon. But if you think a moment you see it's quite impossible to <u>prove</u> that this sort of book is any use. If you feel that it is a waste of time to read Macbeth, well, it is a waste of time. People like this second sort of book not because they are clever or stupid, not because they are good or bad, but because it happens to call to something inside them. I get called to very easily, and many of you must be the same. You're like me, you would rather read about this sort of book than the first sort; you would rather have novels and plays and poems and even fairy stories than timetables and biographies of Mr. Gladstone. But I also know that some of you are not like that at all, and that you think this second sort of book rubbish. I'm not going to argue with you. It isn't a matter for argument. You're not nicer than we are, and you're not nastier - you're just different. I've only one thing to say to you, and that is that if you're tempted to have a shot at this second type of book, do remember the standards by which it must be judged. They are not the standards of facts. Don't be put off by Macbeth because it begins with the words 'Enter three witches', and you know witches don't exist. They do exist in Shakespeare's mind, and if you can admit this he is calling to you.

Now for the third sort of book. We've had books that teach facts, and books that create. What's the third sort? Or, to put the question more carefully, what is our third reason for reading?

Our third reason for reading is that we need help. The world to-day is becoming a very difficult and dangerous place, and we want all the help we can get in it. When I was young things weren't as bad as they are now. People felt fairly safe. We saw that the world wasn't perfect, but we hoped it would gradually get better, and we were sure it wouldn't get worse. European civilisation - we knew it would have its ups and downs, but we were satisfied that it was[45] a going concern and would never smash up. Wars - we saw that they were wrong, but we thought they would become milder as people got more educated. We were a good deal worried about our own souls but not much about the world. We left foreign affairs and politics generally to experts and occupied ourselves with private matters.

That, as far as I can remember, is how people used to feel when I was young. Well, you know how differently we all feel to-day, whatever our ages. We're frightened and there is every reason we should feel afraid. The world has become more dangerous, instead of safer. European civilisation threatens to blow up, so does Oriental civilisation - [46]the so called 'change- less East' - and as for wars - they have got worse, and owing to the aero- planes civilians get killed in them just as often as soldiers, children just as much as men. This is a very terrible situation, and I am sure that other speakers in this series will be discussing it, and will be advising from their different standpoints what ought to be done. I am keeping to my own standpoint, which is books, and asking the question, Can books help us? For we certainly need all the help we can get. Can they help us <u>in ourselves</u>?

[47]I add 'in ourselves' because I am ruling out books which discuss the political or economic crisis directly and try to help us that way - books which recommend Communism for instance, like Mr. John Strachey's <u>Coming Struggle for Power</u>,[48] or books which recommend Fascism and say Mr. Strachey is wrong, or books which recommend Pacifism and say both Fascism and Communism are wrong, or books which - well there are all sorts of such books, and some of them are useful, but they lie outside my "talk", because I am looking for books that help us in ourselves: in our characters: as individuals: books that teach us to be brave, sensitive and sensible; that work us up so that we see what is happening in the world and strengthen us so that we aren't scared by what we see. Sensitiveness and[49] valour - those are the two virtues we most want today I think. It is no good shutting our eyes to the world - we shall miss what is good as well as what is bad in life if we do that. And it is no good opening our eyes if we are going to be driven mad by terror. What we want is to be able to look at life and at the same time be able to embrace it, and I hold that in this very hard job books will be helpful.

Well, you will say, if you hold this give us a list of them, and we'll get them from the library. - But here we come up against something very queer and[50] rather regrettable. Books that are written in order to be help- ful and to improve the readers' character are never any use. Our ancestors, thought otherwise, but our ancestors were wrong here, in my opinion. They believed in moral treatises, jobations on courage, obedience, etc., but

I doubt such treatises having any practical effect. They believed that we could find moral examples in books, which we could model ourselves upon. You may have read Carlyle's "Heroes and Hero Worship".[51] Well, there is an example of that sort of thing. Carlyle believed that if we read about great and good men and then tried to imitate them, we should[52] improve. Perhaps when one's quite young there is something in this, but as soon as one grows up one finds that imitation won't work. It is no good saying to yourself "What would Alexander the Great or Shakespeare have done[53] in 1937?" because you are not Alexander the Great or Shakespeare. You are probably not as good as they were, you are certainly different, and you must play off your own bat, not try to handle theirs. And in the same way it's no good laying up moral precepts, as our ancestors did. They used to make extracts from books, and learn them by heart with the view of improving their characters. This doesn't work[54]. Suppose you are ill-tempered and revengeful and want to cure yourself - well you'll not do it by memorising Portia's speech in the Merchant of Venice. 'The quality of mercy is not strained.'[55] When the test comes, when the other person is annoying you again and you have the chance of paying him back - you'll forget all about Portia and her impeccable sentiments, and just let go as usual and be sorry for it afterwards. Similarly if you are a coward and want to be braver it is no use memorising Henry V's speech before the battle of Agincourt[56] - you will lose your nerve just the same when the test comes. Read the speeches for their own sakes. Try to get out of them what Shakespeare put into them. Don't read them in the hope of making yourself better.

No - in my experience books help[57] our characters in another and more subtle way: indirectly. For one thing, they wake us up. I was woken up, I remember, by Samuel Butler's fantastic novel Erewhon.[58] I read Erewhon at the beginning of the century, and it started me thinking and feeling in every direction, just as if I had touched something alive - and of course my mind had touched something that was alive: it had touched Samuel Butler's mind. I wonder whether Erewhon has the same effect on people now. I rather doubt it, because each generation wants waking up in a different way. Perhaps Aldous Huxley or Bernard Shaw are doing what Butler did then. - I got so excited, I remember, by the chapters in Erewhon when disease and crime change places. In that topsy-turvey country, you are punished[59] if you are ill, whereas if you steal, your friends sympathise with you and call in a doctor. And that set me thinking. It was a brilliant provocative book, and if you haven't read it you might have a try, in case it has the same exciting effect on you that it had on me. (Erewhon, by Samuel Butler). I don't guarantee it'll have the effect, mind, because different people and different generations have different needs. Still it's worth looking into - and don't miss the chapter on the Machines, when the Erewhonians destroy all their machines, even their watches, in case they are some day destroyed by them. That chapter is[60] terribly to the point today!

[61]And it is not only by waking us up and making us sensitive that books can help us. They can also help by building us up, by depositing strength in us as life goes on. What I mean by this[62] remark is that if you keep on reading good books year after year they will make your minds strong just as your body will become strong if you keep on eating good food. If you eat trash, you will become flabby, and if you read trash[63] you'll become flabby. If you like to have the name of a writer who has deposited a grain of strength in me, I think I'll give you the name of that great and neglected poet, Matthew Arnold, but I give it as an example not as a recommendation. Different readers need different writers, and Matthew Arnold may not be your cup of tea. I've been obliged you see, to generalise all through this talk. I believe that books are useful, but I don't believe in giving lists of useful books. My advice to you is: Read books which give you facts accurately - the books we first talked about, the time-table sort. Read, too, if you can, the books of the[64] Macbeth sort - those which are imaginative and creative. I believe that if you will do this you will find that the two sorts will combine in your mind as the years go on, and will wake you up and strengthen you. To put it in another way and more formally: Study history, economics, science, etc. for their own sake. Enjoy imaginative literature for its own sake. And you will find in the long run that an ethical gain will have resulted[65] from your studies and from your enjoyment.

1. Variants from the recorded broadcast held at the National Sound Archive, the British Library, are labeled "NSA." All other variants derive from the script held at the BBC WAC. The NSA variants are also reproduced using quotation marks to distinguish them from script variants that occasionally appear in the same line of the broadcast.

2. <perhaps>

3. <In that sense literature is an old and a well establish institution,>

4. John Morley, *The Life of William Ewart Gladstone* (London: Macmillan, 1903).

5. Sir Arthur Eddington was an early twentieth-century astrophysicist; perhaps one such work would include *Space, Time and Gravitation: An Outline of the General Relativity Theory* (Cambridge: Cambridge University Press, 1920). EMF was influenced by Eddington's *The Nature of the Physical World* (Cambridge: Cambridge University Press, 1928), which prompted him to consider the relationship between hard science and what he believed to be the "spurious clouds of glory" surrounding the writer and his or her art (EMF, *Commonplace Book*, ed. Gardner, 46). Sir James Hopwood Jeans was a prolific writer and scientist whose chief works published before 1937 include *The Mysterious Universe* (Cambridge: Cambridge University Press, 1930) and *The New Background of Science* (Cambridge: Cambridge University Press, 1934).

6. <all>

7. <worthless>

8. NSA: The surviving recording of this talk begins here.

9. NSA: "the world"

10. NSA: "You see, I've got in mind, you see, what's bothering me is some such book as Shakespeare's *Macbeth*. Where does *Macbeth* come in among the books we've just been discussing?"

11. NSA: EMF excises "Very few."

12. NSA: "It does teach us, perhaps, a few facts. There is a historical basis"

13. NSA: "nothing reliable out of it."

14. NSA: "*Macbeth*"

15. NSA: "could"

16. NSA: "Obviously it's a book of quite a different type."

17. NSA: "The *Macbeth* sort of book"

18. NSA: "indeed"

19. NSA: "Shakespeare"

20. NSA: "*Macbeth*"

21. <good>

22. <because>

23. NSA: "second"

24. <because>

25. NSA: "I'll give you another example—well, of any good novel which you happen to have been reading lately: I've been reading, or rather rereading, Arnold Bennett's *Old Wives' Tale*." Arnold Bennett, *The Old Wives' Tale: A Novel* (London: Chapman and Hall, 1909).

26. <It is>

27. NSA: "makes up"

28. <which seems alive>

29. NSA: "in the last century"

30. NSA: "quite"; <not of>

31. NSA: "particularly those two sisters"

32. <it>

33. NSA: "manages to make something up in a very effective way."

34. NSA: "And"

35. NSA: "I am, in case you are too—"

36. NSA: "give you"

37. NSA: "from that. That fine poem"

38. NSA: "Mr."

39. NSA: "There's"

40. NSA: "the poem's"

41. NSA: "You see,"

42. NSA: "are all"

43. NSA: "And"

44. NSA: The surviving recording of this talk ends here.

45. <established firmly>

46. <it is>

47. <I say>

48. John Strachey, *The Coming Struggle for Power* (London: V. Gollancz, 1932).

49. <courage>

50. <very>

51. Thomas Carlyle, *On Heroes, Hero-Worship and the Heroic* (London: Chapman and Hall, 1840).

52. <be helped>

53. <today>

54. <, surely>

55. *Merchant of Venice,* 4.1.184.

56. *Henry V,* 4.3.34–67.

57. <us usually>

58. Samuel Butler, *Erewhon* (London: J. Cape, 1872). See also EMF's broadcast of 8 June 1952 entirely devoted to Samuel Butler.

59. <, in Erewhon,>

60. <very much>

61. <Still>

62. <last>

63. <it will have a similar effect>

64. <second>

65. <around>

"BOOKSHELF" By E. M. Forster

7:30   26.12.38
R 7.30 - 7.50 pm

The subject of this talk is the health of literature during the past year.[1] My subject is a vague one, but I promise to be definite on one point: I will say before I stop which I think is the best book of the year; I am quite clear in my own mind as to which it is.

[2]My first duty is to record the losses which literature has suffered through death. In this country two names stand out: Lascelles Abercrombie and Aylmer Maude. Abercrombie[3] was a poet, a man of letters, and an educator. He upheld the humanities at a time when many people are denying them; he is a terrible loss. Aylmer Maude,[4] an older man, connects us with the giants, was the friend and the translator of Tolstoy.[5] Then there are other names: E. V. Lucas, the essayist and editor of Charles Lamb; W. B. Maxwell, the novelist, and[6] two writers who were not English: a great Italian, D'Annunzio, and an Indian, Sir Muhammed Iqbal. Everyone has heard of D'Annunzio, but[7] the name of Iqbal is[8] little known over here. He was a poet both in his own language (Urdu) and in Persian, and his reputation in his own[9] There's a great deal of talk in these days about understanding India, but the understanding will not get very far until English readers realise the existence of Indian writers.

To turn from obituaries to a happier topic: to the prizes gained by authors during the past year. Neither the King's Gold Medal for Poetry nor the Benson Medals of the Royal Society of Literature nor the James Tate Black Prize have been awarded, but the Hawthornden[10] went to Mr David Jones for "In Parenthesis",[11] a realistic fantasy on the War, and the Stock Femina Vie Heureuse Prize to Mr Richard Church for his novel "The Porch."[12] As for the prizes outside this country: the Shakespeare Prize, a

137

German award[13] went to our Poet Laureate[14]; the Nobel,[15] which is inter-national,[16] to an American novelist, Pearl Buck.

My next item is what I call fusses - occasions on which there has been a row over a book in the newspapers or elsewhere. Fusses are often very instructive, and two quite interesting ones happened this year. The first of them was a libel case. Now there must be a law of libel. People must[17] be protected from damaging and malicious statements made against them in books and newspapers - there's no doubt of this, and until the last twenty years or so the English Law of Libel worked fairly well. Then people began to abuse it, and to bring actions against books that shouldn't have been brought and they were encouraged to do this because juries nearly always[18] decided in their favour and very often gave thumping damages. The average Englishman tends to feel that if a writer or an artist gets into trouble, it must be the chap's own fault and I think that this feeling some-times influences a jury. Anyhow, the[19] verdicts for libel have been a grow-ing worry not only to authors but to publishers, printers, editors, and to all connected with the book trade: they have actually held up trade. Well, I'm glad to say that this year a libel action was brought that failed. It was over a novel called "People in Cages".[20] There was a villain in the novel and he got arrested in the zoo, and the authoress, Miss Helen Ashton[21] made great efforts not to give the villain the name of any living person. But unfortunately she did not succeed. There did happen to be a very respectable gentleman who bore the same name. This gentleman had some friends of a humorous turn and they used to ring him up at all hours of the night, and make noises of animals at him down the telephone to remind him of his arrest in the zoo - quacking and growling and so on. He got cross; and he brought an action against the publishers, Messrs. Collins, for defamation of character. [22]Well he lost, and I hope that this will be an earnest of saner decisions to come. For in the past, when a plaintiff has brought a case of this type, he has actually won it. The law of libel is not[23] working as it should[24], and it is good news that[25] a bill to amend it[26] is being introduced into Parliament.

[27]The second fuss I want to mention has nothing to do with libel. It con-cerns a biography of Voltaire by Mr. Alfred Noyes.[28] This was published nearly two years back - as a matter of fact, I remember recommending it when I was broadcasting on the books of 1937. It is a serious scholarly work, and since Mr. Noyes is a Roman Catholic, it is of course written from the Catholic point of view. Well, last May, his publishers, who were[29] also Roman Catholic, were informed by an authority in their Church that the book[30] must be withdrawn. No reason was given, no particular pas-sage cited, and Mr. Noyes was, very naturally, surprised and indignant. He took up a strong line, an intricate discussion followed into which I

haven't time to go, and the end of it was that the Voltaire has not been suppressed[31]. Of course, this is a matter that concerns Roman Catholics more particularly, but it also concerns the general public, for in a democracy, an important work ought not to be withdrawn in this arbitrary way, and we may congratulate Mr. Noyes for having won a battle for British freedom, just as we may pat Messrs. Collins on the back over the verdict in that libel case. There's much too much suppression in these days, and it is pleasant to record the occasions when it doesn't come off.[32]

But I must[33] [move] on from these items now to my main subject: the general health of literature during the past year. My report is: literature is doing as well as can be expected. It has not been a good year for books, but how could it be, when the whole world is diseased? [34]The events of the last eight years or so are gradually sinking into the minds of writers, and upsetting them, making them political and spoiling their work. It's absurd to blame the writers for this. They can't help it. How can they keep away from politics when politics won't keep away from them? Some of the critics of the elder generation can't see this, and they indulge in diatribes against the young,[35] sometimes in the columns of the Sunday papers. "Why don't the young give us art?" they complain. To which the young may well reply: "We'll give you art all right if you'll give us safety." They can't be expected to turn out great literature when the world is cracking up under their feet. So[36] they give us poems and plays that are almost pamphlets, and novels that are really written by worried journalists, not by novelists at all. I regret this, but I see it cannot be otherwise. There is plenty of genius about, plenty of energy and integrity. Literature is going as well as can be expected under the circumstances.

It follows from this that the most satisfactory books that have come out are books about the past. There's another volume of Mr. Winston Churchill's life of his ancestor Marlborough, and another of Mr. Arthur Bryant's life of Pepys, and Miss Wedgwood on the Thirty Years War, Mr. Hammond on Gladstone, Miss Finch on Wilfrid Blunt, two books on Jane Austen, two on Turner, Sir Herbert Grierson on Scott, Mr. Lambert on William Whiteley, and so on, and there is my greatest book of the year: the life of Madame Curie, by her daughter. (I'll come back to that later). Then there are the T. E. Lawrence letters, edited by Mr. David Garnett, the Greville Memoirs, edited by the late Lytton Strachey and by Mr. Roger Fulford, and the Kilvert diary, edited by Mr. William Plomer: Kilvert is a clergyman of the 1870's and a delightful discovery. And several good autobiographies - in particular Mr. Siegfried Sassoon's "The Old Century and Seven More Years", and Mr. Somerset Maugham's "The Summing Up." You couldn't have a greater contrast than these two[37] retrospects: Mr. Sassoon, a poet at heart, so sensitive to the countryside and to his happy childhood there, and Mr. Maugham, equally sensitive, but no stay at home, and an acute critic both of himself and of his fellow men. A remarkable pair of books. And there has also been[38] some good minor biographies: Mr. Leslie Halward's "Let Me Tell You,"[39] and Mr. Martin Armstrong's "Victorian Peepshow".[40] And anthologies: "The Oxford Book of Light Verse" selected by Mr. W. H. Auden. And yarns: novels which keep clear of currency-trends and[41] tell a story. Mr. Masefield's "Dead Ned" is one example, Mr. Richard Hughes' "In Hazard" is another.[42]

So much for books about the past. The books depending on the present are less satisfactory, because no one knows what to say. Some are philosophic - Mr. Bertrand Russell's "Power" and Mr. Middleton Murry's "Heaven and Earth" are instances - and most of them are political - Captain Liddell Hart on "The Fog of War", Professor Seton Watson, Mr. Voight[43] and others on the European situation, Miss Elizabeth Monroe on "The Mediterranean", Mr. George Antonius on "The Arab Awakening", Dr. G. C. Allen on "Japan, the Hungry Guest".[44] I seem to be working round the globe, so I'll now mention a book on America which made a very deep impression on me, though no one over here seems to have heard of it. It's a poem by Mr. Archibald MacLeish called "Land of the Free - U.S.A.,"[45] but it's really not so much a poem as an emotional document on the subject of Soil Erosion in the States. On each page is a magnificent photograph, following the rhythm of the verse and collaborating in its meaning. You know what dull dogs most photographers are.[46] But the photographs in "Land of the Free - U.S.A."[47] increase the excitement of the poem. Mr. MacLeish's theme is that America has lost that old freedom of vast fertile expanses, and not yet found the new freedom whose home is the human heart. Like the other writers I've been mentioning, he tries to interpret the present. Indeed, nearly everything one reads does so, in one way or another - I could go on and on; for instance, Mrs. Woolf's treatise, "Three Guineas"[48] blames men for[49] the crisis and puts them in their place, and Mr. H. G. Wells' novel "Apropos of Dolores" blames women and puts them in theirs.[50] Mr. Jack Common - he's a new writer, very vigorous and friendly - he blames the economic system: "The Freedom of the Streets" is the name of his book.[51] Everyone's worried,[52] and many people are offering advice.

There's one book though - it's a novel - which stands out because though it describes a collapsing society it manages itself to[53] remain firm. That is "The Death of the Heart" by Elizabeth Bowen.[54] It's a very quiet book, it is ultra-civilised, and perhaps some readers might find it a bit tame, but it seems to me, from the artistic point of view, the best novel of the year.

I come now to the[55] biography of Madame Curie, which I hold to be the best book. It's very well written by her daughter, but the greatness is in the subject, the character and the achievement of Madame Curie herself. I knew[56] before reading it that she was a genius, who devoted herself to science, and with her husband discovered radium, and I knew that radium unlike most modern discoveries, has done more good than harm, and that Madame Curie is consequently our benefactress[57]. But I had not realised what a grand all round human being she was, nor how she managed to combine the life of the laboratory with family life. Many women are devoted scientists, and very many are devoted mothers and wives. But to keep both passions running at the same time - [58]it means a rare triumph of the human spirit. This is a moment when we particularly need our faith in humanity to be confirmed. On all sides we see people behaving badly and imperfectly, and we are tempted to do the same and to think that the whole adventure of life on earth is a failure. The life of Madame Curie reminds us that it is not. She gives us back true values. It is not only a great book, it is a book that is specially needed in 1938, and that's why I emphasise it. It's an international book. Internationalism is often sneered at as something that is ineffective and feeble. But a good book belongs perforce to the whole world. Madame Curie was a Pole, her biographer is a Frenchwoman, the translator, Mr. Vincent Sheean, is American; yet her life belongs to[59] English people because it belongs to humanity.

That really ends my talk on the health of literature. I'll add a word or two about[60] selling conditions. [61]It has been a bad year. When there is a crisis people stop being ill[62] going to law and[63] reading. During the days before Munich, hardly anything was bought at all (a leading London bookseller tells me) except A.R.P. manuals[64] and political[65] rubbish, of which there is an increasing output; secret lives of dictators, and so on. The number of books published has been as large as ever,[66] but the quality and the response to good quality has been poor. One thing has gone strong - I mentioned it last Christmas too - the sixpenny reprints. But here too there is a disappointment: even when there are good sixpennies it's difficult to find them in the shops. I want to end up with a grumble and a suggestion. The other day, on the railway bookstall at a great London terminus, I tried to buy one of the sixpenny Penguin Shakespeares - an excellent edition, with Mr. G. B. Harrison's notes. "Oh, no, we don't keep Shakespeare", I was told: "he gets so dirty." Poor old Shakespeare! That put him in his place, didn't it? And I imagine that all the rest of the great literature of the past got dirty too, for I could see no traces of it. Our railway bookstalls could, if they chose, be educative centres, because people who never go to a bookshop loiter in front of them considering what to buy for the journey.[67] I know that[68] most people want trash, and it is quite right that trash should be on sale. I'm not taking up a high and mighty line. I only[69] plead that a small corner on bookstalls could be reserved for cheap classical reprints, even if they don't command an immediate sale. We have a great literature. We have enterprising publishers who produce it[70] at a popular price. I do think that booksellers generally and the book-stalls in particular might do more than they do to ensure it being seen by the[71] public.

1. <I shan't have much time to spend on individual books and I shan't try to give you a reading list. You have special talks from Mr. John Brophy and other critics to give guidance here and my job is rather to enquire how books have been feeling during 1938. The world as a whole has been feeling far from well what has been the effect of this on literature? not so much on sales and methods of production as on the quality of the books produced. That is my>

2. <I must begin by chronicling various events, and>

3. EMF added accent marks above the second syllable of "Lascelles," the first syllable of "Aylmer," and the third syllable of "Abercrombie" (in "Abercrombie was a poet").

4. <[a] much>

5. <, and his monumental work was completed before he died.>

6. <I want also to mention>

7. <I expect that>

8. <almost unknown>

9. The text here ends abruptly; it appears that EMF or an editor at the BBC literally pasted new text over the old, eclipsing in the process the remainder of this sentence.

10. <Prize> EMF is referring to the Hawthornden Prize for Imaginative Literature.

11. David Jones, *In Parenthesis: Seinnyessit e Gledyf ym Penn Mameu* (London: Faber and Faber, 1937).

12. <, a novel full of inlets into the Civil Service and the prelude to another work which Mr Church will publish next month.> Richard Church, *The Porch* (London: J. M. Dent and Sons, 1937).

13. <given annually to a British author,>

14. <, John Masefield>

15. <Prize>

16. <went>

17. EMF added accent marks above "must" in both sentences.

18. <convicted>

19. <convictions> In the margin next to emendations of "convicted" and "convictions" is a large "X."

20. Helen Ashton, *People in Cages* (London: Collins, 1937).

21. <took great care>

22. <The jury decided against him>

23. <what>

24. <be>

25. <that Mr. A. P. Herbert has introduced>

26. <into Parliament>

27. In the margin next to this paragraph is the time mark "6 min."

28. Alfred Noyes, *Voltaire* (London: Sheed and Ward, 1936).

29. <suddenly>

30. <was worthy of condemnation and>

31. <, and is still on sale>

32. <There has been one other fuss this year, I remember, but not an important one: over the late Frank Harris' life of Oscar Wilde. This is very readable and very inaccurate work: exceptions were taken to some of the lies in it, brisk controversy arose, and a revised edition has appeared, which is still inaccurate and still readable.> Frank Harris, *Oscar Wilde* (London: Constable, 1938).

33. The transcript is missing a word here; one presumes that EMF would have said "move" or "pass" to his main subject.

34. <I'm not thinking just of the crisis of late September - the crisis didn't affect <<t>>The quality of books. That has been affected by> In the transcript, EMF does not actually cancel the phrase "The quality of books," though its intended omission seems clear.

35. <generally>

36. <you get>

37. <excellent>

38. <a pair>

39. <About It>

40. <: Mr. Halward of the working class and Mr. Armstrong of the employer class, and both putting across very lively stuff.>

41. <try to>

42. Winston Churchill, *Marlborough: His Life and Times* (New York: C. Scribner's and Sons, 1938); Arthur Bryant, *Samuel Pepys: The Saviour of the Navy* (Cambridge: Cambridge University Press, 1938); C. V. Wedgwood, *The Thirty Years War* (London: J. Cape, 1938); J. L. Hammond, *Gladstone and the Irish Nation* (London: Longmans, Green, 1938); Edith Finch, *Wilfred Scawen Blunt, 1840–1922* (London: J. Cape, 1938); Herbert Grierson, *Sir Walter Scott, Bart.: A New Life Supplementary to and Corrective of Lockhart's Biography* (London: Constable, 1938); Richard Lambert, *A Universal Provider: A Study of William Whiteley and the Rise of the London Department Store* (London: G. G. Harrup and Co., 1938); Eve Curie, *Madame Curie: A Biography* (London: W. Heinemann, 1938); David Garnett, ed., *The Letters of T. E. Lawrence* (London: J. Cape, 1938); Lytton Strachey and Roger Fulford, eds., *The Greville Memoirs, 1814–1860* (London: Macmillan, 1938); William Plomer, ed. *Kilvert's Diary: Selections from the Diary of the Reverend Francis Kilvert* (London: J. Cape, 1938); Siegfried Sassoon, *The Old Century and Seven More Years* (London: Faber and Faber, 1938); Somerset Maugham, *The Summing Up* (London: W. Heinemann, 1938); Leslie Halward, *Let Me Tell You* (London: M. Joseph, 1938); Martin Armstrong, *Victorian Peep-show* (London: M. Joseph, 1938); W. H. Auden, *The Oxford Book of Light Verse* (Oxford: Clarendon Press, 1938); John Masefield, *Dead Ned: The Autobiography of a Corpse Who Recovered Life within the Coast of Dead Ned and Came to What Fortune You Shall Hear* (London: W. Heinemann, 1938); Richard Hughes, *In Hazard* (London: Chatto and Windus, 1938). Books on Austen: probably Elizabeth Jenkins, *Jane Austen: A Biography* (London: Gollancz, 1938), and Mona Wilson, *Jane Austen and Some Contemporaries* (London: Cresset Press, 1938). Books on Turner: probably Kenelm Foss, *The Double Life of J. M. W. Turner* (London: M. Secker, 1938), and Bernard Falk, *Turner the Painter: His Hidden Life; A Frank and Revealing Biography* (London: Hitchinson, 1938).

43. EMF is likely referring to F(ritz) A(ugust) Voigt, editor of *Nineteenth Century* and a friend to Sir Hugh Seton Watson. EMF may also be referencing Voigt's *Unto Caesar* (London: Constable, 1938). Several of Seton Watson's books could be viewed as political in scope - though given the date of this broadcast, EMF may well be referring to *Britain and the Dictators: A Survey of Post-War British Policy* (Cambridge: Cambridge University Press, 1938). Our thanks to Sarah McNeely for her assistance with this information.

44. Bertrand Russsell, *Power: A New Social Analysis* (London: G. Allen and Unwin, 1938); John Middleton Murry, *Heaven and Earth* (London: J. Cape, 1938); Liddell Hart, *Through the Fog of War* (London: Faber, 1938); Elizabeth Monroe, *The Mediterranean in Europe* (Oxford:

Oxford University Press, 1938); George Antonius, *The Arab Awakening: The Story of the Arab National Movement* (London: H. Hamilton, 1938); G. C. Allen, *Japan: The Hungry Guest* (London: G. Allen and Unwin, 1938).

45. Archibald MacLeish, *Land of the Free* (New York: Harcourt, Brace, and Co., 1938).

46. <Generally, they made everything so insipid and boring.>

47. <are not illustrations; they are part>

48. Virginia Woolf, *Three Guineas* (London: Hogarth Press, 1938).

49. <our troubles> EMF added an accent mark above "men."

50. EMF added an accent mark above "theirs." H. G. Wells, *Apropos of Dolores* (London: J. Cape, 1938).

51. Jack Common, *The Freedom of the Streets* (London: Secker and Warburg, 1938).

52. <most people are trying to describe the general mess>

53. <stand>

54. Elizabeth Bowen, *The Death of the Heart* (London: V. Gollancz, 1938).

55. <Life>

56. <of course>

57. <, and claims our homage>

58. <both of them intense, both clear, that means reaching a very high pinnacle indeed.>

59. <us>

60. <sales and>

61. <Of course,>

62. <and stop>

63. <stop>

64. Air Raid Patrol manuals.

65. <trash>

66. <since publication was arranged far back in 1937 as a rule,>

67. <But you>

68. <as well as I do what you find on them:>

69. <suggest>

70. <in a popular form>

71. <people>

BOOKS & READING:
BOOKS IN 1941 by
E.M. FORSTER:

FRIDAY JULY 4th 1941. HOME SERVICE FROM LONDON. 6.30-6.45 p.m.

During the past year three well known novelists have died, and I want to refer to them before starting this talk - partly out of respect to their memory, partly because their passing is in a sense symbolic, and marks the end of an epoch. They are James Joyce, Virginia Woolf and Hugh Walpole. They are very different, these three: James Joyce was a writer with a vision of the universe which he expressed through recollections of his early life in Dublin: Virginia Woolf was a poetic writer, whose novels are best understood if they are read as poems: and Hugh Walpole was a story teller, who carried on the tradition of Scott and Trollope. Yet though they are so different they have one quality in common: They are all professionals. Their main job was to sit down and write, and in this sense they mark the end of an epoch, because the professional writer is coming to an end. I think myself that this is a pity, and that civilisation will be the poorer if it happens; however, there it is. The detached artist, who lived - and sometimes starved - in independence, is a vanishing type. The writer today is increasingly drawn into the fabric of society, and his writing is a bye-product of his ordinary work. It's not his main job to sit down and write.[1] The two best novels I've come across this year are novels of action, written by men of action, and I think this is significant of the future. The professionals - whether of the type of Joyce, Mrs Woolf or Walpole, -[2] are, partly for economic reasons, passing away.

Now 1941 is of course being a difficult year for books. What with the paper shortage, what with the bombing of stocks and libraries, what with the general shift into the fighting forces and war industries, publishers, printers, booksellers, readers and writers are all having a poor time. But

145

things aren't nearly as bad as they might be and I feel cheerful. Books are holding their end up and so they ought to, for they are part of the battle against tyranny. You remember those bonfires the Nazis used to make? Well, this war is partly a battle of books against bonfires, and I believe that the books are going to win, and put the bonfires out. Certainly the 1941 lists are much better than could be expected. Most of the books published are, naturally, about the war - why we got into it, what we are doing in it and how we hope to win it.[3] I am not going to talk about such books, important as some of them are: - The Prime Ministers Into Battle,[4] for instance, and John Strachey's Post D[5] for another instance. I want rather to look at literature and scholarship - two of the activities for which we are fighting - and see what they have been doing during the last six months. I'm going to mention about a dozen books - [6]and at the end[7] some of the titles will be read aloud slowly so that listeners can write them down if they want to.[8]

Three novels to start with. For Whom the Bell Tolls by Hemingway. The Ocean by James Hanley, and The Canyon by Peter Viertel.[9] For Whom The Bell Tolls has had a good deal of publicity, and it deserves it. It[10] is a long very serious book about the Spanish War, where Hemingway fought on the Republican side, and it deals with the blowing up of a bridge in the wild mountains[11] and with the Spaniards and the American who are engaged on the work. It is full of courage and brutality and foul language: It is also full of tenderness and decent values, and the idea running through it is that though there must be war in which we must all take part, there will have to be some sort of penance after the war, if the human race is to get straight again. It is a book for grown-up people, like most of the books on my list. The Ocean by James Hanley is another novel of action - very serious, very moving. The scene is a small boat, which is rowing away from a torpedoed liner: only two people on the boat keep their heads - the sailor who is practical, and the priest who sees God - and the situation gradually suggests greater situations: civilisation, rowing its way through the floods of barbarism, torpedoed, machine-gunned but keeping on: and the human race, rowing its way through the hostile universe. It is the finest piece of work Hanley has done I think. Quite a short book.

The third novel I want to mention is a lighter piece of work - The Canyon by Peter Viertel a young American, though it, too, has graver implications. Part of it is a Mark Twain sort of story about boys, a Tom Sawyer story, but The Canyon, where the boys run their little gang, becomes a symbol of the life of youth, which must pass away even though youth wants it to remain.

[12]Now for two collections of short stories, both of them well written and sophisticated, the work of professional artists. The more important of

them is Look At All Those Roses by Elizabeth Bowen;[13] delicate civilised stuff which, by the way, reads aloud extremely well. The other collection is Presenting Moonshine by John Collier[14] - witty, rather satanic[15] unchivalrous to women; an unusual mixture. And before I leave novels altogether, let me mention a translation from the French:[16] Proust's great work Remembrance of Things Past.[17] This translation isn't new, but it now first appears in a cheap and uniform edition.

Now I must rush on to poetry. William Plomer, better known as a novelist, is my favourite contemporary poet and a selection of William Plomer's poems came out a few months back. They are full of colour, feeling, distinction, character-drawing, epigram, and mischievousness: a most[18] attractive selection.[19]

And now I must rush away from poetry. What a way to treat it, but with the time at my disposal, what else can I do?

I must turn to works of learning, and research, and[20] it is very important to emphasise these. Scholarship and biography and philosophy are still being carried on in this country. For instance, there is a definitive edition of the 17th century poet and mystic George Herbert, edited by Robinson.[21] It's an expensive edition and for scholars, and most of us will continue to read Herbert in a cheap form, for instance in the World's Classics. But it shows what is being done and unless we have men of learning like Mr. Robinson constantly labouring in the background, we cannot have the foreground of popular culture. Or take music - here are two volumes of the late Donald Tovey's lectures: A Musician Talks[22] they are called. They[23] don't make easy reading.[24] But they indicate what is being done in serious musical exposition. Or again, take classical scholarship. Here is George Thomson's Aeschylus and Athens:[25] This is a fascinating and challenging work, which re-interprets early Greek history and Greek drama in the light of modern anthropological research. I recommend it to those who already know[26] something about the ancient Greeks - it's not[27] for the general reader. And now - biography. Out of several good biographies here is one which seems to me outstanding: The Life of King George V by John Gore;[28] and this is for the general reader. It is an official biography, but it is not the least sticky or pompous: it realises that the late King, like all human beings, was a human being and it makes him come alive. Two lives of George V have been published in 1941; this one by John Gore is the better of the two, and very good it is.

Finally, here are two books on religion - both of them unorthodox: Hugh Ross Williamson's A.D. 33 and Gerald Heard's The Creed of Christ.[29] A.D. 33 is a striking little essay which attempts to re-interpret the character of Christ: a similar attempt was made by Oscar Wilde in De Profundis, but Ross Williamson's is the more interesting and provocative. Gerald Heard's book The Creed of Christ is a[30] series of sermons which the writer a modernist and a mystic preached in California, and it is provocative too.

Well, that ends my talk. I have had to crowd in more books than the time at my disposal would really carry, but I wanted to counteract the notion that nothing good gets published in war time. The trouble[31] is not that, but that scarcely any of the writers[32] are young. I have only mentioned one young man - Peter Viertel - and he is an American. Over this side young men, and young women, too, are not in a position to write - they have[33] more urgent things to do. That is[34] obvious, but until they are in a position to write one cannot feel confident about the future. For you can't run literature or scholarship either, on a Corps of Veterans. 1941 is an anxious year. It is waiting for youth to come back, and until that happens it must get on as best it can. And when youth does come back, I believe it will be non-professional. It will have post-war jobs, writers will be worked into the general fabric of society. Which brings me back to my opening remarks. I think that the detached artist, the specialised student, are likely to disappear, and I am inclined to regret this. Art for art's sake, study for study's sake, are not the useless undemocratic things which they sometimes appear to be. They are the powers in the background, without which the foreground of popular culture cannot exist.[35]

PAGE 5.

Here are some of the books I've mentioned: Dictation speed.[36]

Three novels:	For Whom the Bell Tolls	Hemingway
	The Ocean	James Hanley
	The Canyon	Peter Viertel.
Two Collections of short stories:		
	Look at all Those Roses	Elizabeth Bowen
	Presenting Moonshine	John Collier
Translation from the French:		Proust's Remembrance of Things Past.[37]
A Book of Poems:	Selected Poems	William Plomer
A work of scholarship:		
	Aeschylus and Athens	George Thomson
A Biography:	Life of King George V	John Gore
A religious Essay:	A.D. 33	Hugh Ross-Williamson

1. Brackets appear around this sentence and subsequent text as noted, perhaps indicating that it should be cut from the broadcast.

2. Brackets appear around "- whether of the type of Joyce, Mrs Woolf or Walpole, -."

3. Brackets appear around "- why we got into it, what we are doing in it and how we hope to win it."

4. Presumably, EMF is referencing Martin Hugh, *Battle: The Life Story of Winston S. Churchill, Prime Minister, Study of a Genius* (London: V. Gollancz, 1940).

5. Evelyn John Strachey, *Post D; Some Experiences of an Air Raid Warden* (London: Victor Gollancz, 1941).

6. <that's all I shall have time for ->

7. <I shall repeat>

8. Brackets appear around this sentence except for the opening phrase: "I'm going to mention about a dozen books."

9. Ernest Hemingway, *For Whom the Bell Tolls* (London: J. Cape, 1941); James Hanley, *The Ocean* (London: Faber and Faber, 1941); Peter Viertel, *The Canyon* (London: Collins, 1941).

10. Brackets appear around "has had a good deal of publicity, and it deserves it. It."

11. At this point there appears a gap in the transcript, followed by "Madrid," which has been excised here for clarity. Brackets appear around "and with the Spaniards and the American who are engaged on the work."

12. <The other two books of fiction on my list are>

13. Elizabeth Bowen, *Look at All Those Roses* (London: V. Gollancz, 1941).

14. John Collier, *Presenting Moonshine: Stories* (London: Macmillan, 1941).

15. <and>

16. <the translation of>

17. Marcel Proust, *Remembrance of Things Past* (London: Chatto and Windus, 1922).

18. <remarkable>

19. <I would also like to mention   by Lillian Bowes Lyon> There is a gap in the transcript where, presumably, EMF was planning on writing in the title of Lilian Bowes-Lyon's *Tomorrow Is a Revealing*, also published in 1941 (London: J. Cape).

20. <I think>

21. There is no record of a book on George Herbert edited by a Robinson. Rather, the book on Herbert released in 1941 was edited by F. E. Hutchinson, *The Works of George Herbert* (Oxford: Clarendon Press, 1941).

22. Sir Donald Tovey, *A Musician Talks*, 2 vols. (London: Oxford University Press, 1941).

23. <make difficult>

24. <and myself I prefer Tovey's brilliant <u>Essays in Musical Analysis</u>> In addition to being crossed out, this phrase is also cordoned off by brackets.

25. George Thomson, *Aeschylus and Athens: A Study in the Social Origins of Drama* (London: Lawrence and Wishart, 1941).

26. <a little about>

27. <exactly>

28. John Gore, *King George V: A Personal Memoir* (London: John Murray, 1941).

29. Hugh Ross Williamson, *A.D. 33: A Tract for the Times* (London: Collins, 1941); Gerald Heard, *The Creed of Christ* (London: Harper, 1940).

30. <collection>

31. <at present>

32. <who do get published scarcely any>

33. <other>

34. <natural and>

35. The final five sentences of the talk were handwritten by EMF.

36. It is not entirely clear what was meant by this notation, but it may have served as a reminder to EMF to read the titles and authors slowly enough that listeners would be able to copy them down. A handwritten line strikes through page 5 and may indicate a deletion.

37. This entry is written in another hand.

WE SPEAK TO INDIA.
"SOME BOOKS"
by
E. M. FORSTER
Red & Green Networks

Wednesday, 15th October, 1941.　　　　　　　Studio S.1. 14.45 GMT

In talking to people as far away as you are - that is to say as far away in space, for it is quite possible that we may be close together in our hearts: in talking to you overseas, I have to wonder what subject interests you and whether you can get books on it. Are you, for instance, interested in the tragedy of France? Of course you recognise its political importance, but does it move you emotionally? It does move me, for the reason that England is only 22 miles from France - much nearer than is Ceylon to India - for the reason that I have often seen France from Dover, seen her cliffs and her fields in the sunshine, and the flashing of her lighthouses at night; and for the further reason that I have often been to France, and think her the light of civilisation and that some of my best friends are French. I can't go there any more, I can seldom get news of my friends. The heavy hand of barbarism has come down with a smack upon that which I love, and consequently I am moved emotionally. Are you? Very likely not. Even if our hearts are close we needn't be moved by the same things. Perhaps France to you is something far away and small and dim in the chaos of Europe and perhaps the two books about her tragedy which I am going to recommend will not interest you and may not even be on sale your end. Still, I will mention their names on the chance. They are accounts of escape: The Road to Bordeaux by Denis Freeman and Douglas Cooper: and Scum of the Earth by Arthur Koestler; I'll say these names again slowly at the end of my talk.[1]

The Road to Bordeaux is by two young Englishmen, cultivated fellows, who knew France well before the war, and loved her civilisation, her cookery, her people. They enlisted as ambulance drivers in the French army in the spring of 1940, they were present at its collapse, and they took part in the terrific and tangled retreat which only ended at the western port of Bordeaux. Here they discovered by chance a British destroyer, which brought them home. If I tell you that this is a pleasant, amusing book, you will scarcely believe me, yet so it is: such is one side of it, anyhow. There is the tragic, heart-rending side. But there is also the good sense and good temper which need not desert an observer even when he is chronicling a catastrophe. In this chronicle, the French - the French people - come out magnificently, and it is indeed to justify the French people against certain critics the author writes. Courage amidst bewilderment, kindness amidst adversity, the courage and the kindness of the common soldier and of the peasant and the workman is what comes out. It coincides with my own observations of France in peace time, and I found it very moving. The idea that the French race is decadent is nonsense, although it is the idea of Hitler. At the end of the book, as the British destroyer slips away from Bordeaux down the estuary, the shores are lined with French people cheering, waving their handkerchiefs and shouting Vive l'Angleterre[2] - the French who had themselves to stay behind and face the Nazis, and Nazi technique.

The second book, dealing with an escape from France, is called "Scum of the Earth", and before I speak of it I want to say a word about its author, Arthur Koestler.[3] He is a Hungarian by nationality, a European in outlook. He was at one time attracted by communism, but disillusion overtook him, and it is expressed in a novel about a Russian revolutionary, called Darkness at Noon.[4] He has travelled in Northern Asia. He fought on the Republican side in Spain, and was in prison there. When war broke out he was living in France and was imprisoned there. He escaped after endless adventures to England, and then he was imprisoned here - in accordance with the misguided treatment which was accorded at one time to friendly aliens. (We have changed in this respect I am glad to say, and our policy is now humane and sensible). And he is doing what he always wanted to do: serving in the British Army. He is evidently an adventurous and tough character, but he is also sensitive and imaginative. You may remember, those of you who listened in to me last month, that I was talking of the Congress of the PEN Club, an international meeting of writers held in London. Many good speeches were made at the Congress, and Koestler's speech was one of the best. He speaks as he writes - forcefully and pictorially - and this last book of his, "Scum of the Earth", is so real and so terrible, that I can't for my own part read much of it at a time. Not that it goes in for physical horrors, but it makes me realise as nothing else does, the break up of Europe, and the slow penetration of the Hitler evil which attacks not only men's bodies but their souls - their way of handling life, if you prefer a less pretentious word than 'soul'. It is full of colour, even of humour: but it is terrifying. Here for instance is a sentence describing the entry of the German tanks into a town in southern France - quite an orderly entry; the Nazi troops are well under control, but listen how terrible.

'I looked at the black procession in the sunshine: there was a tall figure standing immobile in one of the moving turrets; I divined his face, the face of a young peasant lad from Pomerania, with goggling, cretinous eyes and with a vague grin undecided between kindness and brutality, staring at the cathedrals and vineyards of France and licking his pursed lips like a dog in front of a bone'.[5]

Notice that masterly phrase "undecided between kindness and brutality": it describes the useless young barbarism much more effectively than abuse would describe him, and much more devastatingly. The peasant lad from Pomerania, goggling at the Cathedrals and vineyards of France, and incapable of knowing what they mean.

The title Scum of the Earth is ironic. It denotes the refugees who at one time were called the Defenders of Civilisation, but as soon as Hitler turns them out of their homes no government wants them; I have seen a good many refugees over here, and some of them have become my friends and they have made me realise, as nothing else, what sort of war this is, and what the Nazis are after. I never take much notice of what I read in the papers - or of what I hear on the wireless either, though this isn't the moment quite for me to say this - but I do get awfully impressed by talking to people who have suffered, especially when they are the same sort of people as myself. You can't argue them away and say "Oh, Adolf's not so bad really" when there they are before you, ruined, they are what Adolf has done. And when one of them writes a book, as Koestler has and writes it so well and so naturally - it's the best propaganda in the world. So I recommend it to you - with the reminder that it is pretty upsetting, and will make you feel that France is not a far away tragedy, but something which might happen to you. That other book, The Road to Bordeaux, gives the same feeling but Scum of the Earth is more forcible, because it is actually by a refugee. The French by the way, don't come out so well. The author has to do with the small officials and policemen who were ready by temperament to side with the invaders if they will keep their jobs. His comments are scathing.

The next book I want to mention is so different, and belongs to such a different world that I feel I ought to make a two minutes pause before proceeding to it: I cannot do that - the Laws of Broadcasting forbid me and the respectable electric Clock which is embedded in the wall of this Studio would emit a most reproachful tick, if I tried it on. So you must just imagine that there is a pause, that the curtain falls, that it rises again, and shows you - Europe again by a vanished Europe. The book I have in mind is called In Quest of Corvo[6] and it is a study of a crook, a decadent charlatan, a most unworthy and unpleasant character who was at the same time a man of genius and a writer of fine English. He cables[7] himself Baron Corvo, for he loved mystifying people, but he wasn't a Baron and his name was Rolfe. He lived in the early years of this century before Western Europe had been hardened and dulled by the great wars; he scuttled about, now in England, now at Venice, insulting people and cadging on them, sometimes aspiring to become a priest and sometimes denouncing the church. He was a most unusual character, and now here is a life of him which I recommend to people who like something unusual. In Quest of Corvo, by A. J. A. Symons. It is a curious and brilliant piece of investigation - a sort of detective story. Mr. Symons takes us along with him, following clue after clue, until the elusive Corvo is tracked down and gives up all or nearly all the secrets of his shady career. The book was published seven years ago, and I mention it today for one or two reasons. For one thing the author Mr. Symons, died last month, and I wished to pay this tribute to his memory: he was a biographer with an unusual method, and the subject of Baron Corvo suited him well. For another thing, although the book is a strange one, it is easily obtainable. It has come out as a Penguin and you can get it for 6d. I advise you to have a look at it, if you want to get into a world quite unlike the present one.

I'll say the names slowly. "The Road to Bordeaux" by Freeman and Cooper, "Scum of the Earth" by Koestler and "In Quest of Corvo" by Symons. These books are all products of Western European civilisation, and Western Europe only occupies a very small part of the globe. We who live in it sometimes forget this. So next month I hope to move a bit eastward, a little nearer to you on the map and deal with books on Russia.

---

1. Denis Freeman and Douglas Cooper, *The Road to Bordeaux* (London: Cresset, 1940); Arthur Koestler, *Scum of the Earth* (London: J. Cape, 1940).

2. Long live England

3. Koestler at this time was a new acquaintance of EMF's; they corresponded intermittently in the fall of 1941. In his letter to Koestler dated 28 September 1941, EMF commented on *Scum of the Earth:* "It is strange to read, and to know all the time that one may soon have to face such conditions oneself—in my case without much courage, and certainly with no resourcefulness; but if they do come along I think this particular reading will help me" (*Letters,* ed. Lago and Furbank, 2:197).

4. Arthur Koestler, *Darkness at Noon* (London: J. Cape, 1940).

5. Koestler, *Scum of the Earth,* 194.

6. A. J. A. Symons, *The Quest for Corvo: An Experiment in Biography* (Harmondsworth, Middlesex: Penguin, 1940).

7. In the margin, and in a hand other than EMF's, is written the suggestion "calls?" presumably in lieu of "cables," which nonetheless remains in the transcript.

"WE SPEAK TO INDIA"
'SOME BOOKS'
A Backward Glance Over 1941
by
E.M. Forster

Wednesday, 10th December, 1941: 14.45-15.00 GMT: Red Network: Studio S.1.

When I was broadcasting last month, my mind was full - I may say my heart was full of the death of H. W. Nevinson. I wanted to speak about Nevinson, but had not the time, and I will begin with him today.

He was a good man and a good writer. By profession he was a journalist and war correspondent, and by temperament he was a soldier, and he also had, deep within him and very persistent, the outlook of the saint. He was completely unworldly, although he lived in the world and led the life of action. He stood up for the oppressed, the unpopular, and he stood up for them with intelligence - which champions do not always do. Everyone who knew him loved him; he had many friends in India, and if any of them are listening now I apologise to them for not speaking of him more worthily. He was in India back in 1907, as the correspondent of the Manchester Guardian, two of his books are about India and he kept up the connection. For instance, he was broadcasting to India this very year on the subject of Gokhale,[1] whom he got to know well, and whom he admired - he was great at admiring others. I have just been working through the script of his broadcast; it is a brilliant piece of work, and makes those far off times live again, and he composed it when he was 85.

Nevinson published a number of books. You will get the best of him in his reminiscences. There is a volume called "Changes and Chances", and another called "More Changes, More Chances".[2] If you read them you will

155

probably go ahead thinking it all very pleasant and sane and colourful - good simple writing - and then suddenly catch your breath and say "Oh, but this man was a hero!" He was so simple and modest that one only notices his greatness occasionally; there is no pretentiousness about him, no affectation, and no swank.

Coming as it does at the end of the year, Nevinson's death makes me look back upon the year. I'll attempt a retrospect. There have been several other deaths. But I don't want to turn this talk into an obituary catalogue, that's too lugubrious, I shall be more helpful if I remind you of what is good to read in the work of those who have left us, it is the best tribute I can pay them.

I have already recommended Nevinson's "Changes and Chances". Now I'll give you the names of four novels by Virginia Woolf, by Hugh Walpole, by James Joyce, and by the writer who called herself 'Elizabeth'; all four died in 1941. Try "To the Lighthouse" by Virginia Woolf; it is subtle and very lovely, its publisher is Everyman. Try Hugh Walpole's "Mr. Perrin and Mr. Traill" - one of his earlier novels and most exciting: about schoolmasters. That is in Everyman too. Try James Joyce's - no, I'm not going to say what you expect me to say; I'm not going to say "Ulysses". "Ulysses" is great work, but it is difficult to get, and difficult to understand. I'll recommend you a volume of short stories by James Joyce called "The Dubliners". It is early work, and semi-true and lovely, most particularly the short story in it called "The Dead". Finally the lady who wrote under the name of 'Elizabeth' - her actual name was Lady Russell:[3] her best known book is "Elizabeth and her German Garden".[4] This is about the Germany of forty years back - the Germany which still was largely a garden. It's a book that's rather off the oriental beat, if I may use the expression, that is to say removed from your immediate experiences. Still I thought I would include it, for Elizabeth was a graceful writer and a pungent one, and her 'garden' has a few poisonous plants in it, which have grown into the Germany of today.

During 1941, two things have happened in the world of books - one of them rather depressing, the other very heartening. I'll take the depressing one first. It is the paper shortage.

We're short of paper in this country. So probably are you, and so certainly is Germany. Germany was short before the war started, and she was even pulping works by her greatest writer, Goethe, to turn them into objects more useful to the Totalitarian war-machine. We don't pulp our classics in England. We believe in our national heritage and its variety, and our parliament has very rightly exempted books from the tax known as the Purchase Tax. But paper is a bother, new books - especially books by new writers - can't get published, and many old books of value are unobtainable, some of the stocks have been blitzed too. It is stated that since the war began 37,000 books have gone out of print. No doubt many of these books are worthless, and will not be missed, still 37,000 is a large number, and it contains really important works - for instance the other day I couldn't buy G. M. Trevelyan's "History of England",[5] though I believe it is on the market again now.

So that is rather depressing. But now for the cheerful side. It is true that books are more difficult to get. On the other hand people are reading more, and reading good stuff. It is as if the war has brought home to us all the seriousness of existence. We want to find out more about the universe while we still can. We want to know why the world got into this terrible state, and why, in spite of all, it is still a world of the spirit, where the imagination can rove and the senses can respond to beauty. The young men in our fighting forces and the other people who are engaged in civil defence are turning to reading when they have the time and when they can find the books. This cheers me a lot. I'll give you a concrete example - some more figures to set against 37,000 volumes out of print.

My example has to do with the London Library. The London Library is a subscription library of the learned type and it was founded by Thomas Carlyle and has just celebrated its centenary. It caters for the serious student, and it doesn't go in specially for novels. It goes in for solid stuff - literature, history, philosophy - that sort of thing. Well at the outbreak of war its membership decreased, and no one was surprised. But it decreased only to increase enormously, and in the last few months it has had 500 extra members. That shows which way things are going in 1941, and I think that any bookseller, indeed any station bookstall would tell the same story. Serious sixpenny books have an enormous sale. The other day - last Saturday to be precise - I was talking to a young air-mechanic. He had left school at an early age to work in a garage, and he wasn't what you may call well educated, but he asked me if I knew of a cheap book on the Religions of India. "I want to know about them" he said, "I've heard they're great". And later on, talking of knowledge in general, he said "I don't want to condemn anything before I've understood it." That seemed to me the true spirit of civilisation - the spirit the Nazis have missed. Not to condemn until you understand, and books help us to understand. This young airman, looking out for good sixpennies, and the educated people who take out additional subscriptions to the London Library - they are all moving in the same direction. So 1941 is really an encouraging year. There's a dearth of books, but an increasing desire for them. Which is on the whole better than heaps of books and no one wanting to read them.

And then the literary magazines - it was expected they would die off as the war proceeded, but they have not. I don't expect that they have come

out your way much, but I will mention some titles. There's "Horizon" -
perhaps the best known of them and the organ of the younger writers.
There's "Kingdom Come", which started since the war - it represents the
younger writer too. There's the old established "Life and Letters". There's
the scholarly and severely critical "Scrutiny". There is the Penguin series
of New Writings, which may almost be classed as a magazine. And last
but not least, from my own point of view, there is "Indian Writing," an
attractive quarterly edited by and written by Indians.

One more example of cultured activity during 1941, and I have done. It
has more to do with art than with literature, but it well illustrates my
point. There is a wonderful collection of photographs of Hindu temples
which have been collected and annotated by a learned society here, and
now is on tour in the provinces.[6] Would you have expected that in an
industrial town in North England - namely Sunderland - thousands of
people would have gone to see that collection and tried to learn from it
something of the Indian attitude towards religion and art? I confess I was
surprised myself, but I heard it yesterday from the director of the institute
and I pass it on to you. It confirms what that young airman said to me in
the train. We do want to know over here, we are trying to understand. And
though there are many bad things in 1941, this is a good thing.

1. Gopal Krishna Gokhale, educator and nationalist, was a key figure in the Indian
National Congress throughout the early decades of the twentieth century.

2. Henry Woodd Nevinson, *Changes and Chances* (London: Nisbit and Co., 1925) and *More
Changes, More Chances* (London: Nisbit and Co., 1925).

3. Or Elizabeth von Arnim; see EMF's broadcast of 28 December 1958 for a detailed
account of his relationship with Lady Russell.

4. Elizabeth von Arnim, *Elizabeth and Her German Garden* (London: Macmillan, 1898).

5. G(eorge) M(acaulay) Trevelyan, *History of England* (London: Longmans, 1926).

6. For more on EMF's deliberate references to British interest in Indian culture (such as
dance, art, music, and—as here—photography), see chapter 4 of Mary Lago, *E. M. Forster:
A Literary Life* (New York: St. Martin's, 1995).

AS BROADCAST: "We Speak to India"
        Red Network.
        Wed: 11th February, '42
        Studio S.1.
Recording: Stroud's Studio,[1] 55 P.P1
        5-2-42 from 12.0/12.30 p.m.
        DLO:

"SOME BOOKS" - E. M. FORSTER

I want to begin by quoting a couple of remarks which have been made about books by two famous Englishmen, Milton and Mr. Winston Churchill. Milton says: "As good almost kill a man as kill a good book: who kills a man, kills a reasonable creature, God's image; but he who destroys a good book, kills Reason itself."[2] In other words, books may be more important to humanity than the people who wrote them. They may be the very essence of reason. I agree, and I also agree with Mr. Winston Churchill. He says: "Books in all their variety offer the means whereby civilisation may be carried forward."[3] Notice particularly the words . . . . . "in all their variety". They are the words of a democrat who believes that books are and ought to be various. If a Nazi was wanting to praise books, he would have to say this sort of thing: - "Books, when approved by Dr. Goebbels, offer the means by which civilisation may be carried forward on Dr. Goebbels' lines." That is for the moment, the German definition of literature. It is not Milton's definition or Churchill's or yours or mine. We believe in the variety of books. And those who disbelieve in it will sooner or later "destroy good books, and kill Reason itself", as the Nazis have already done, with their bonfires, and their prohibitions.

We, in this war, are not likely to destroy books. Literature and Democracy are natural allies. But we are in danger of starving them - and here I come to another point, and a rather distressing one. There is a paper shortage in this country as elsewhere, and the paper allocated for printing books is a ridiculously small percentage - less than 1.14 percent of the whole. Experts calculate that if it could only be increased a little - up to 11 percent - the situation would be saved, and I hope that this may be done, and that the printers and publishers and writers of[4] England may be able to respond to Mr. Churchill's fine words and "to carry civilisation forward". At present they cannot. Young writers can't get published at all; established writers, and even the classics are going out of print; and broadcasters (this is my own particular little trouble), broadcasters can't ever be sure that the works they recommend will be obtainable by listeners. I think you'll be able to get the book I'm talking about to-day. I hope so, for I'm certain it'll interest you.

It is the latest book by Aldous Huxley - a biography called "Grey Eminence". It is the most important work that has appeared here lately. It is very reasonable and written with Huxley's usual skill, and it should be specially interesting to Indians, and Indians may understand the problem it presents better than can many Europeans. You'll see what I mean by this remark as I get on with the talk, but I'll state straight away what the problem in "Grey Eminence" is: it is the problem of the mystic who goes into politics. In Europe this hasn't happened very often. In India it has happened constantly, from the days of Arjina in the Bhagavad Gita down to the present day, and I think you may comprehend the strange story Mr. Huxley unfolds.

"Grey Eminence" was a monk. His real name was Father Joseph. He lived in France about three hundred years ago, that is to say in the reign of Louis XIII, and he was the friend and assistant of the famous French statesman, Cardinal Richelieu. Richelieu dressed in scarlet, as befitted a Cardinal, and was nicknamed "Scarlet Eminence", and his humble friend who wore the sober habit of his Order got called "Grey Eminence" as a contrast. Father Joseph was of good family, he was extremely intelligent, well-educated and charming, and a brilliant worldly career lay open to him. But he threw everything up and became a monk, so that he might better serve God and know God and do His work on earth. He meditated, he practised asceticism, he fasted, he slept on bare boards, he scarcely ever went in a carriage. He completely subdued the Self.

Now it was the will of God, Father Joseph thought,- that Europe should go to war, and fight the Turks, and free the Holy Places of Christendom. This was, from his point of view, a natural attitude, and however little we agree with it, we must understand it, or we shall not understand its consequences. He wanted a Crusade, and being an ardent Frenchman, he thought the Crusade must be led by France. This again is quite natural. But France cannot lead unless she is united. So he joins with Richelieu to unify France and for many years the Eminences, the Scarlet and the Grey, govern the country together. He attacks the Protestants, who formed a State within the State, he tricks them, he employs spies and fifth-columnists - he helps in the siege of one of their towns. And he succeeds. The mystic has turned politician and been successful - so far. France is ready to lead Europe against the Turks.

Unfortunately, Europe was not ready to be led. Europe was a battlefield of Protestants against Catholics fighting, for the most part, in Germany. It was the beginning of that terrible period of the Thirty Years War - a period from which Mr. Huxley derives many of our troubles in the West to-day. You would have assumed that Father Joseph and Richelieu, who were Christians and desired a Crusade, would have tried to impose peace. They did nothing of the sort, for they wanted Europe to be weak and obedient, so that France should be strong and its unchallenged leader. They deliberately kept the war going until millions of people, mostly poor people, had died. That is bad enough, but worse is to come. Father Joseph and Richelieu - they were Catholics, so you would have thought they would have supported the Catholic side in Europe. They did not. They supported the Protestants. They allied with the very people whom they had been persecuting in their own country. By spies and fifth columnists and assassins and finally by open war, they did all they could to destroy their co-religionists. Did you ever hear such cynicism? Are you surprised that his contemporaries called Father Joseph a demon? Once, when he had gone on a diplomatic mission to the Emperor, and had outwitted him, one of the gentlemen of the Emperor's Court had it out with him as he was descending the steps after an audience, and said to him, "You a monk? You whose profession it is to foster peace in Christendom? And yet you are the man who starts a bloody war between the Catholic sovereigns - between the Emperor, the King of Spain, and the King of France. You ought to blush with shame."[5]

Father Joseph did not blush with shame. On the contrary he had the gentleman who had criticised him, clapped into irons. He did not blush because he was a mystic, and mystics do not heed the judgment of men so long as their consciences are clear. He was a mystic who had gone in for politics. No doubt it was a pity there should be this fratricidal strife, this treachery, this misery and homelessness and cannibalism - but the end of it all would be a Crusade against the Turks. The end of it all was of course Father Joseph's own death. The Thirty Years War, for which he was largely responsible, went on after him and by the time it fizzled out, everyone had quite forgotten about the Crusade.

Well that is the outline of the historical side of Aldous Huxley's fascinating and terrifying study - "Grey Eminence". But it also had a religious side, on which I must venture a few words. Mr. Huxley is deeply interested in religion - not in ecclesiasticism and the Churches - but in the type of mind which desires to know God and to touch the Divine reality. Father

Joseph had a mind of that type. He was completely selfless, he desired no personal advancement or comfort, he was richly endowed with the mystic faculty, and Mr. Huxley sets himself to find out why such a good man should have behaved so badly. It is the stranger, because Father Joseph was not an ignorant fanatic. He was well educated, intelligent, tactful, charming, even humane. He not only went into politics, but he went into them disastrously. Why was that?

Huxley's answer - I don't know that I agree with it but I'll give it you - is that he went wrong because there was something wrong in his mysticism. At a particular point in his spiritual training he took the wrong turning, with the result that his activities were short-sighted and disastrous. And the wrong turning was this: - he believed that you can act and yet abstain from the fruits of action. Now you will remember that this is exactly what Krishna advises Arjina to do in the Bhagavat[6] Gita. In that marvellous poem Arjina shrinks from going into battle and taking life - especially the lives of his relatives. He has the same feeling of horror which we may be sure Father Joseph has in the presence of a starving Europe. But Krishna comforts him and says: "Act - but abstain from the advantages, the fruits of action. Then you will not sin."[7] Mr. Huxley believes this advice is unsound. It is not possible to act and abstain from the results, for the reason that each time you act you alter yourself. You may not gain anything in the worldly sense - you can avoid that - but you will alter your character, and if your action was bad you will become a worse man and do evil on an increasing scale. That certainly was Father Joseph's fate. He passed from the comparatively small matter of Protestant persecution in France to the fermenting of the Thirty Years War. And in Huxley's judgment mystics - whether Oriental or Christian - take a wrong turn when they believe that they can act and abstain from the fruits of action.

It is difficult to broadcast on a subject like this. We ought to be face to face - you and I - while I am talking and able to interrupt each other. This is only a book talk and I mustn't turn it into a sermon. But I do think this book may interest Indians specially, and I thought I would try and show you why. One query occurs to me, as no doubt to you: if the mystic oughtn't to turn politician, how can he help his fellows? Is he just to concentrate on union with God, and to ignore the misery which spreads even more widely around him to-day than it did three hundred years ago? Is he to do nothing for them? Huxley tries to answer this question. If you want to know his answer, you must get his book. It is a humane book and a very wise one. And it reminds us that history is a single process, and that the men who lived hundreds of years ago in India, or three hundred years ago in France, or who live to-day are all in the same storm-tossed boat.

Next month I'll talk of lighter literature. There's not time to do that to-day and I'll end with a curious anecdote about something which happened to Father Joseph when he was a little boy. Very curious - for it is an Oriental anecdote. Some soldiers, who had been pillaging, went[8] past his family house and threw away some of their booty, which they didn't think worth keeping. Among the rubbish was a tattered book, called "Barlaam and Josaphat". The child picked it up and, as he says, "I fell in love with it."[9] It was a story about an Indian Prince, who left the life of pleasure and power by the advice of a hermit. It was in Christian form and he read it as a Christian, but it was really a biography of Buddha. Josaphat is a corrupted form of Bodisatva. The story had been translated from Sanskrit into Arabic, from Arabic into Greek and so had reached mediaeval Europe. Is it not strange to reflect that the mystic, who failed, should at the opening of his life accidentally come across the mystic who succeeded, the great Indian who did not enter politics, who did not clamour for a Crusade, but found other, and bloodless ways of promoting righteousness on earth?

1. <K. M.>

2. John Milton, *Areopagitica and Other Prose Works*, ed. Ernest Rhys (London: J. M. Dent and Sons, 1941), 5.

3. A popular quotation ascribed to Churchill; the source is uncertain.

4. A reading cue indicating the first word of the next page appears at the bottom of the first page in this transcript: "/ England may."

5. Aldous Huxley, *Grey Eminence* (London: Chatto and Windus, 1942), 174. In the original, the first two sentences read as one: "Then you are a Capuchin; that is to say you are obliged by your profession to do what you can to foster peace in Christendom."

6. Sic.

7. In the original Sanskrit, verse 47, chapter 2. For a translation EMF or his contemporaries might have used, see *Gita: The Gospel of the Lord Shri Krishna*, trans. Shri Purohit Swaami (London: Faber and Faber, 1935), 24. This translation reads slightly differently from EMF's reproduction: "But thou hast only the right to work; but none to the fruit thereof; let not then the fruit of thy action be thy motive; nor yet be thou enamoured in inaction."

8. <by>

9. Huxley, *Grey Eminence*, 26.

AS BROADCAST: <u>"We Speak to India"</u>
24th February 1942.
Eastern Transmission - 14.30 - 15.00 GMT.

<u>"MASTERPIECES OF ENGLISH LITERATURE"</u> No. 18 (last in series)
Speaker: <u>E.M. FORSTER</u>
Subject: "THE RETURN OF THE NATIVE" - by Thomas Hardy.

The strange book I am going to talk about is <u>not</u> a masterpiece of English literature. It cannot rank with <u>In Memoriam</u> or <u>The Scholar Gypsy</u> or other works which have come into this series. It is a curious, uneven, dark, difficult book, where the reader may easily lose his way; it is full of imperfections, and it should present special difficulties to an Indian reader. You - or most of you - have not yet been to England, I expect. You have never visited Wessex, as Hardy calls the country of his novels, or wandered on Egdon Heath, where he sets the scene of this one. You have probably never seen a lych gate, and I am certain you don't know what a lynchet is.[1] Hardy is a little corner of England. He is something else as well, and something greater, for he moves in that vast region of ideas which is shared by the whole human race. But geographically, he is merely Dorsetshire and the counties bordering it and those who[2] don't know Dorsetshire naturally get held up when reading him.

I shall start with a sort of experiment with you. Here are half a dozen stanzas from one of his poems. As I read them, see whether you can follow (a) what the poet is saying, (b) what he is feeling. The subject of the poem is a ride across England westward to Exonbury, or Exeter, where the rider seeks tidings of the woman whom he once loved.

"I mounted a steed in the dawning
　　With acheful remembrance,
And made for the ancient west Highway
　　To far Exonb'ry

Passing heaths and the House of Long Sieging
    I neared the thin steeple
That tops the fair fane of Poore's olden
    Episcopal see;

And changing anew my blown bearer
    I traversed the downland
Whereon the bleak hill-graves of Chieftains
    Bulge barren of tree

And still sadly onward I followed
    That highway the Icen,
Which trails its pale riband down Wessex
    By lynchet and lea.

Triple ramparted Maidon gloomed grayly
    Above me from southward
And north the hill fortress of Eggar
    And square Pommerie.

The nine-pillared cromlech, the Bride Streams,
    The Axe, and the Otter,
I passed, to the gates of the city
    Where Exe scents the sea.["]][3]

I don't believe you can have caught much of what Hardy is <u>saying</u> in this poem, because it is full of local details:[4] for instance, the House of Long Sieging is Basing House, which was held by the Royalists in the civil wars. (I passed by Basing myself only last week, and I saw its lovely red brick ruins through memories of the poem.) Similarly

   . . . . the thin steeple
That tops the fair fane of Poore's olden
    Episcopal see

is the spire of Salisbury Cathedral,[5] built by Bishop Poore. You can scarcely follow what Hardy is saying here without a commentator. On the other hand, you can follow what he is <u>feeling</u> if you allow yourself to be sensitive and responsive. You can feel that this is a sad poem and a desolate one, and that the pageant of Wessex unrolling to North and South is the background to a breaking heart.

And still sadly onward I followed
      That Highway the Icen
Which trails its pale riband down Wessex
      By lynchet and lea.

Notice how the word "sadly" is born out by "trails its pale riband", by the
melancholy continuance of the road which seems to go on for ever. Notice
that - and you have gone a long way toward understanding <u>The Return of
the Native</u>. The connections between man and the soil of Wessex - that is
what you must look out for in this novel.

   <u>The Return of the Native</u> appeared in 1878. Hardy, then in his forties,
had already published several novels, but without great success. He
belonged to Dorsetshire and his origin was rustic: I have seen the charming cottage where he was born, and behind it, in summer, still grows the[6]
fern into which he would creep as a little boy, and where he would pray
never to grow up.

"I said: 'I could live on here thus till death'
      And queried in the green rays as I sate
'Why should I have to grow to man's estate
      And this afar-noised world perambulate?'"[7]

He did grow up, he became famous, he was buried in Westminster Abbey,
but to the end of his life it was to scenes like these that his heart went back,
and it was as a gentle country boy that he confronted the irony of circumstances and the cruelty of man. [8]Hardy was never smart or authoritative
or imposing, he had none of the airs of a genius, and when I went to see
him - for I had that honour in his later years - his first thought was to be
hospitable and kind, to see one had plenty of cream in one's tea, for
instance. After[9] that country childhood, he studied as an architect: then he
took to novel-writing and journalism, and after <u>The Return of the Native</u>
he produced several more novels, culminating in the famous <u>Tess of the
d'Urbervilles</u> and in <u>Jude the Obscure</u>.[10] <u>Tess</u> deserves its fame: it is his
best prose work, <u>Jude</u> on the other hand does not deserve the abuse with
which it was greeted. But it marks a turning point in his career. For he was
so upset by the criticisms of[11] his friends - they found it too sordid and
gloomy - that he became disheartened and wrote novels no more. He
turned instead to poetry.

   And here we come to the fundamental truth about[12] Thomas Hardy. He
was by temperament a poet, and not a novelist at all. He had taken up fiction partly because he had to earn a livelihood, partly because he misunderstood his powers. He couldn't manage a plot, he was clumsy at

narrative, and his characters[13] seldom came alive. But he had a poet's intensity of vision - both of great and little things. He had always written poems, and now that he was disgusted with fiction by the ill-success of Jude the Obscure, he took to poetry seriously and produced, in 1907, The Dynasts, that great epic of the Napoleonic Wars by which his name will live. All his work, however remote from it in date, must be considered in relation to The Dynasts. His life - his literary life - lacks all meaning if The Dynasts be forgotten. And in re-reading The Return of the Native to-day, what has interested me most in it are the scenes which forecast the later work - the conversation round the bonfire, on Rainbarrow for instance, and the philosophy which was to develop from the deification of Egdon Heath to the doctrine of the Immanent Will.

Geographically, Egdon Heath is a wild track of land in Dorsetshire. In this novel it is an actor, and the main actor; it wrecks the happiness of Clym and Eustasia, it kills Mrs. Yeobright. The superb opening chapter is dedicated to it: - I'll read: -

"Only in summer days of highest feather did its mood touch the level of gaiety. Intensity was more usually reached by way of the solemn than by way of the brilliant, and such a sort of intensity was often arrived at during winter darkness, tempests and mists. Then Egdon was aroused to reciprocity: for the storm was its lover and the wind its friend. Then it became the home of strange phantoms: and it was found to be the hitherto unrecognised original of those wild regions of obscurity which are vaguely felt to be compassing us about in midnight dreams of flight and disaster, and are never thought of after the dream, till revived by scenes like this."[14]

In The Dynasts there is also a power behind men[15] - the Immanent Will, which sometimes appears visibly in the drama as a sort of ganglion, working, it knows not for what, and causing Napoleon, Nelson, Wellington, whole nations to twitch into action. Egdon Heath is an earlier sketch for this; it is the conception of a poet and a brooder, who[16] looked through the smooth surface of civilisation into something disquieting. He sees little grounds for hope, but at moments he hopes. There is a famous Choric passage at the end of The Dynasts which I will quote: all through this talk I am deliberately quoting poetry, because it is only through poetry that this queer novel can be[17] grasped. Here, after the chaos of the Napoleonic Wars, the chorus of the Pities speak:

"But - a stirring thrills the air
Like to sounds of joyance there,
    That the rages
    Of the ages

Shall be cancelled, and deliverance offered from the darts that were,
Consciousness the Will informing, till it fashion all things
fair!"[18]

That is to say, perhaps some day the blind force behind the universe will
become aware of itself, and creative, and loving.

So philosophically <u>The Return of the Native</u> gives us much to think
about, and poetically much to enjoy. But philosophy and poetry cannot
make a novel. A novel requires human action and human characters: and
now for our disappointment. What is the action? The tragic marriage of
Clym Yeobright and Eustasia Vye. What is Hardy's aim? To link the action
with the sombre background of the Heath. With this intention, he gives
Eustasia Vye a superb entry in the second chapter, and shows her standing alone on the summit of Rainbarrow in the November twilight,[19] hating
the Heath and[20] feeling it will kill her. With this same intention he introduces with magnificence Clym, the native who returns, who is akin to the
Heath, who is the man of the future, too grave for beauty, too thoughtful
for joy. But when Eustasia and Clym speak and act, they do not live up to
the high descriptions of them, in fact they do not live at all. They are
stagey, stilted, Eustasia is the worst. She behaves as a silly flirt, who longs
for a seaside esplanade, she is a snob, who takes against her husband as
soon as he does manual labour, she is hateful to her mother in law, she
does not make one remark which shows a good heart or good sense, or
even good taste. Yet Hardy requires us - if not to adore this creaking doll,
at all events to be deeply moved by her fate. He endows her with beauty
and tells her she is a heroine. No, - Eustasia will not do. And Clym is
nearly as unsatisfactory. He turns out to be a worried young man who
believes in raising people,[21] a prig who cannot even talk naturally to his
own mother. This is the sort of thing he says to her when he thinks of
becoming a schoolmaster: -

"'I no longer adhere to my original intention of giving with my own
mouth rudimentary instruction to the lowest class.'"[22] What pomposity!
No, Clym will not do. The truth is that Hardy is not a natural novelist, and
is a natural poet, and he is here working in a medium which does not suit
him.[23] Another instance. Count up the number of times the various characters eavesdrop or overhear one another accidentally. I should think it
happens at least a dozen times and one of them, the Reddleman, spends
half his[24] life holding his hand to his ear. The result is extreme artificiality
and remoteness from ordinary existence - and a true novelist keeps in
touch with ordinary existence, I think.

I don't want to labour this point, it seems ungenerous, but you will
understand now what I meant when I said at the beginning of this talk

that <u>The Return of the Native</u> is full of imperfections. If you judge it as a novel of human contact and human character you cannot rank it high. Read it rather as the work of a poet, who had a magnificent conception which, as a novelist, he could not execute. Forget the technical fumblings and the strained use of coincidence, and concentrate on the bleak background of Egdon;[25] also on some of the rustic scenes.

These rustic scenes are characteristic of Hardy, and[26] have rightly made him popular. He has a deep feeling for old-fashioned characters, and local customs which were dying out. He remembered his boyhood in the cottage and what he had seen and heard[27] there, and he[28] loves to introduce some quaint individual, some charming or perhaps sinister incident. His early novel <u>Under the Greenwood Tree</u>[29] is completely rustic, and a delightful little book it is. <u>The Return of the Native</u> has likewise its group of worthies - Granfer Cantle and the rest: ([30]the Granfer[31] reappears as a young militiaman in <u>The Dynasts</u>). It also has its rustic scenes - for example, the jolly scene of the mumming where Eustasia dresses up as a Turk: and for an uncanny example, the terrible scene where the adders are fried in a pan to cure Mrs. Yeobright of snake bite. (This is by the way the finest human moment in the book - the relations between Clym and his mother, which have always seemed unconvincing, gain reality at the moment of her agony.) The waxen image Susan makes of Eustasia, the pin she drives into Eustasia at church, the Sunday hair-cutting in the village street - these are other examples, relics, good and evil, of a time that has gone, and only survives in the writer's meditative mind.

When you study this novel do get hold of a copy of that poem <u>The Dynasts</u>. Don't read it through - that would take you too long - but look about in it for half an hour, and see the direction which Hardy's genius finally took. You will then, as it were, get <u>The Return of the Native</u> into perspective and understand the emotional importance of Egdon Heath.

"The great inviolate place had an ancient permanence which the sea cannot claim. Who can say of a particular sea that it is old? Distilled by the sun, kneaded by the moon, it is renewed in a year, in a day, or in an hour. The sea changed, the fields changed, the rivers, the villages, and the people changed: but Egdon remained."[32]

A good book on Hardy has just been written by Edmund Blunden, who was speaking to you in this series[33] recently.[34] Another book you[35] should look at is the charming Life[36] by his widow. You will get his gentleness there, and his integrity and his touches of shrewdness, and you will realise that he was part of the country he loved, and of an age that has gone for ever. One of his poems is called <u>Friends Beyond</u>. This is how it opens: -

"William Dewy, Tranter Reuben, Farmer Ledlow, late at plough,
    Robert's kin, and John's, and Ned's,
And the Squire, and Lady Susan, lie in Melstock churchyard now!
"Gone!" I call them, gone for good, that group of local hearts and
Yet at mothy curfew tide,   heads:
And at midnight when the moon-heat breathes it back from walls
                                  and leads,
They've a way of whispering to me . . . . ."[37]

It is[38] this whisper as well as the great voice of the Universe that he transmits.

1. A lych-gate is a small, gated opening demarcating a churchyard from the surrounding community. It is distinguished by a small, A-frame roof overhanging an entryway or door leading into the churchyard. A lynchet is a gathering of earth that forms around heavily plowed fields. These agricultural phenomena are ancient landmarks in the rural areas of Britain, dating from centuries-old Celtic field systems.

2. <have not inhabited that corner of this island find obstacles in>

3. Thomas Hardy, "My Cicely," lines 21–56, in *Wessex Poems and Other Verses* (London: Harper and Brothers, 1898). EMF added accent marks over "heaths," "blown," and "bearer."

4. <which only appeal to an Englishman>

5. <which was>

6. <bracken>

7. Hardy, "Childhood Among the Ferns," lines 12–15, in *Wessex Poems and Other Verses*. EMF added accent marks over "could" and "thus" in the first line of this excerpt.

8. <He>

9. <a>

10. Thomas Hardy, *Tess of the d'Urbervilles* (London: Osgood, 1892), and *Jude the Obscure* (London: Osgood, 1895).

11. <it by>

12. <him>

13. < - except perhaps Tess - never>

14. Thomas Hardy, *The Return of the Native*, book 1 (London: Smith, Elder, 1878), 1. EMF added an accent mark over "obscurity."

15. <, and through them>

16. <all his life>

17. <understood>

18. Thomas Hardy, *The Dynasts: An Epic-Drama of the War with Napoleon, in Three Parts, Nineteen Acts, and One Hundred and Thirty Scenes, the Time Being Covered by the Action Being About Ten Years*, part 3 (London: Macmillan and Co., 1910), 525.

19. <and he tells us that she hates>

20. <feels>

21. <and>

22. Hardy, *The Return of the Native*, book 3, p. 173.

23. <, and working as it were in a trance>

24. <time>

25. <and>

26. <they>

27. <of>

28. <is always introducing>

29. Thomas Hardy, *Under a Greenwood Tree: A Rural Painting of the Dutch School* (London: Tinsley, 1874).

30. <And>

31. <by the way>

32. Hardy, *The Return of the Native*, book 1, p. 6. Brackets appear around this quotation, perhaps indicating that this excerpt could be cut from the broadcast.

33. <last week>

34. Edmund Blunden, *Thomas Hardy* (London: Macmillan, 1942). This statement about Edmund Blunden was handwritten by EMF at the conclusion to the talk; he indicated its placement here.

35. <might>

36. <of Thomas Hardy> Florence Hardy, *The Early Life of Thomas Hardy, 1840–1891; The Later Years, 1892–1928* (New York: Macmillan, 1928).

37. Thomas Hardy, "Friends Beyond," in *The Poetical Works of Thomas Hardy in Two Volumes* (London: Macmillan, 1923), 1:52–53. EMF added accent marks above both syllables of "churchyard."

38. <the>

Last week there died in Brazil an exiled German writer, called Stefan
Zweig, about whom I want to talk. Zweig was a man of letters and a novelist, and he not only had talent but he was typical of our age and of its
troubles. He was sensitive and humane, he could see both sides of a question, he had a detailed, analytic intelligence, he was cultured and loathed
violence. Such a man is bound to have a rough time. He is not the Happy
Warrior type because his heart is not in the fight, and he is not the Saint,
who can see beyond the fight. He is the humanist who hopes for the continuance of civilisation, and civilisation to-day is a far from encouraging
spectacle.

Zweig was Austrian by nationality, and in 1938, when Hitler brought
the blessings of Nazism to Vienna, he went into exile. He shared the fate
of dozens of other writers, for wherever Hitler arrives with his Strength
through Joy rubbish, true joy has to depart, the free exercise of the mind
has to stop, sensitiveness and independence have to find other quarters,
the torch of human hope has either to be extinguished or to be carried
overseas. Zweig came to England. He made many friends in this country,
and he became a British citizen. Then he went to America, which seemed
to offer better facilities for the work which a man of his temperament is
able to do, and then the war and violence spread to the New World, and
we hear of his death by suicide in Rio de Janeiro. This catastrophe is typical of our age, which is a brutal one. It is no respecter of individuals, and
I believe that in the future it will pay the penalty for this, and will receive
no respect from historians.

However, this is speculation. Let us get back to Stefan Zweig's books - don't by the way confuse him with his namesake, Arnold Zweig, also a writer of eminence and the author of <u>The Case of Sergeant Grischa</u>.[1] Stefan Zweig's chief work is a study of Queen Marie Antoinette. It is a subtle and exciting reconstruction of history; subtle because Zweig was a bit of a pathologist, who understood queer morbid states and could analyse both Marie Antoinette and the King: and exciting because he was a bit of a dramatist and could make the terrific drama come alive. It also has nobility in it; for he emphasises the gradual improvement of Marie Antoinette's character under her sufferings, and shows her developing from a silly little princess into a great heroine. I advise you to get hold of the book if the French Revolution interests you, for it's first class of its kind. And I'll also recommend a long novel by him called <u>Beware of Pity</u>, and a volume of short stories called <u>Kaleidoscope</u>.[2] <u>Beware of Pity</u> is described by its title: it is the story of a young Austrian officer who becomes engaged to a cripple, not through love, but because he had a feeling of compassion for her, which enervated his judgement and impaired his power of decision. The consequences of his weakness were tragic, and Zweig analyses them well with that clinical power which he possessed, and he also gives an interesting picture of Austrian military life under the old régime. <u>Kaleidoscope</u>, the short story volume, has the same sensitiveness, the same psychological pertinacity and interest in dark corners: some of the best stories concern children.

But the book I most recommend is another historical study: much shorter than the <u>Marie Antoinette</u>, indeed quite a little book: a study of the humanist Erasmus.[3] Erasmus lived at the time of the German Reformation - that is to say about four hundred years ago. He was a scholar, a wit, and a man of culture. He believed in kindness and tolerance and urbanity. Cultured men had then a prestige which they have since lost, and both parties - Catholic and Protestant - wanted the support of Erasmus in the religious controversy which tore Europe asunder: but Erasmus refused: he would not take sides: he believed it was not his job to take sides and in the end he was repudiated by both parties, and died unhappily. You see why this theme should be congenial to Stefan Zweig. He and Erasmus had a great deal in common, and the Germany of Erasmus' day, with its appeal to force, and its belief in theories, had much in common with the Germany of Hitler. Very delicately the biographer brings this out; so delicately that although the book is really an indictment of Nazi mentality, it has quite a large sale in Germany. It is a very fair-minded book. Erasmus has faults - he was not brave, he disliked defining his attitude, he wouldn't join either side yet he tried to keep in with both. Stefan Zweig does not shirk the faults, and he does justice to the merits of his opponent, Luther, who took sides and condemned all who did not, and loved hating his enemies and being violent. But there is no doubt where his sympathies lie: Erasmus, with all his weaknesses, is better than Luther with all his strength; Erasmus is the power which tries to understand people instead of smashing them, and has raised mankind out of animal darkness. Judged by any single life, tolerance is a failure, tolerance does not seem to pay, only passion and brutality deliver the goods. But this is the short-term view. Take the long-term view. Look back at the slow ascent of human history, from the abyss, and tolerance appears as the major instrument in the upward movement of our race: it is the desire to understand people, not the power to boss them, that distinguishes us from the apes. Stefan Zweig had this desire, and he found a classic example of it - with all its attendant weaknesses - in Erasmus. The biography is not only brilliant and true to the faith: it is a personal meditation upon a theme which concerns you and me; it raises for the twentieth century, a question which troubled the sixteenth century and is likely to be eternal: namely, which is the better. Thought and understanding? or Passion and Power?

I said last month that I would talk of lighter books to-day. I can't say I'm keeping my promise very well, for neither Erasmus nor Marie Antoinette nor even Beware of Pity or Kaleidoscope can be classed as light. They are well written and well translated and readable, but they are distinctly on the serious side. I felt, though, that the death of Stefan Zweig was an event I couldn't ignore - partly because I knew and respected him, partly because it allowed me to talk about general tendencies in European thought.[4] I don't expect Europe means very much to you; I don't see that it can or indeed that it should. When I went out East myself, many years ago, it was extraordinary how Europe, including my own particular island, receded, until I could recall it by an effort of the imagination. To-day its just my voice that goes East and reached India: the rest of me stays sitting in a London Studio - worse luck - and it's only by an effort of the imagination that I can guess where you're sitting and what thoughts are in your minds. I often wish you could answer me back: and so perhaps do you! But since you can't, I try to make remarks which, though they are coloured by my surroundings, may perhaps be applicable to yours. I talk of Erasmus and mention Luther: we'll try to translate these two figures and their problems into terms which are familiar to you: think of tolerance and hesitancy: think of narrowness and violence: and with the help of European difficulties try to solve your own.

Well, so much for that, and now for the list of light books. There is a nice series called the Vintage Books. They cost 1/-d. each in this country, and I'm told they are on sale in India. I pick out two of them - Hilaire

Belloc's <u>Hills and the Sea</u>, and Kenneth Graham's <u>The Wind in the Willows</u>.[5] <u>Hills and the Sea</u> is a little collection of essays - short, well written, and charming. Mr. Belloc, who is one of our most distinguished writers, here lets his learning and imagination loose: the theme is again - Europe, and European unity, but the essays are on all sorts of subjects. <u>The Wind in the Willows</u> is the lightest of the light; indeed it is a children's book about animals, but I rank it very high in its class - up in the region of <u>Alice in Wonderland</u> almost, - and much higher than the efforts of Micky Mouse. There are so many good stories about animals in the literature of India that Indians should be good judges of the merits of this fanciful tender little book: do have a look at it: <u>The Wind in the Willows</u>, by Kenneth Graham.

And now for some sixpennies chosen from the ever-useful Penguin's series. Do you like Ghost Stories? Here is <u>And Still She Wished for Company</u> by Margaret Irwin[6] - a subtle, entrancing novel. Here are <u>Ghost Stories of an Antiquary</u>: their title describes them, and they are by an eminent antiquary, the late Dr. M. R. James:[7] they are calculated to make you think twice before you meddle with a wicked bishop's tomb, or blow a whistle which has a latin inscription on it. Do you like Detective stories? I don't as a rule - detective plays, yes; detective stories, no - so I am an unsatisfactory guide. But I did enjoy <u>The Unpleasantness at the Bellona Club</u> - one of the earlier books of Dorothy Sayers.[8] I belong to a sort of Bellona Club myself,[9] and I know how very unpleasant any unpleasantness there would seem and what a sensation a retired colonel would cause if he were found dead in a telephone box. See how Miss Sayers solves this. For solve it you may be sure she will. <u>Ten Minutes Alibi</u> by Antony Armstrong is a story which I enjoyed very much on the stage some years ago.[10] Here it is a book, and perhaps when you read it, you will be able to discover what I couldn't discover: namely whether the answer which the hero makes to the policeman was the right answer. Was he right in thinking it the wrong answer or was the policeman wrong in thinking it the right one? I became completely muddled at this point and determined never to alter a clock myself, even by Ten Minutes, either forwards or backwards.

Turning to straight novels, here - also in the Penguins - are <u>Saturday Night at the Greyhound</u> by John Hampson, and <u>Mr. Perrin and Mr. Traill</u> by Hugh Walpole.[11] John Hampson, whom one might describe as a sensitive realist - gives in <u>Saturday Night at the Greyhound</u> a tense picture of an English pub at a moment of catastrophe. <u>Mr. Perrin and Mr. Traill</u> is about schoolmasters. It is - in my judgement - the best of the late Sir Hugh Walpole's novels, and it should be read as a warning by all who have ventured into the teaching profession. Finally - a very different book from all I have mentioned, though perhaps it has a distant poetic kinship with <u>The</u>

<u>Wind in the Willows</u> - finally, W. H. Hudson's romantic remote novel - <u>The Purple Land</u>, in which you can rest yourselves and dream.[12]

1. Arnold Zweig, *The Case of Sergeant Grischa* (London: M. Secker, 1928).

2. Stefan Zweig, *Beware of Pity* (New York: Viking Press, 1939) and *Kaleidoscope* (London: Cassell, 1934).

3. Stefan Zweig, *Marie Antoinette* (New York: Viking Press, 1933) and *Erasmus of Rotterdam* (London: Cassell, 1934).

4. Though EMF does not specifically refer to Zweig in his letters, it is likely that they interacted due to their membership in P.E.N. and their mutual commitment to speaking out against the Nazis' attack on culture and free thought.

5. Hilaire Belloc, *Hills and the Sea* (London: Methuen, 1906); Kenneth Graham, *The Wind in the Willows* (London: Methuen, 1923).

6. Margaret Irwin, *Still She Wished for Company* (London: Chatto and Windus, 1924).

7. M. R. James, *Ghost-Stories of an Antiquary* (London: Edward Arnold, 1904).

8. Dorothy Sayers, *The Unpleasantness at the Bellona Club* (London: Ernest Benn, 1928).

9. EMF was a member of the Reform Club in London, founded in 1836 and dedicated to promoting the principles inherent to the Reform Act of 1832 and subsequent measures promoting civic rights for Britons.

10. Anthony Armstrong, *Ten Minute Alibi* (London: Methuen, 1934). Armstrong's play debuted at the Haymarket Theatre, London, in 1933, when EMF presumably saw it performed. Two years later, it was made into a film directed by Bernard Vorhaus.

11. John Hampson, *Saturday Night at the Greyhound* (London: Hogarth Press, 1931); Hugh Walpole, *Mr. Perrin and Mr. Traill: A Tragi-Comedy* (London: Mills and Boon, 1911). See EMF's broadcast dated 10 December 1941 for a more detailed discussion of Walpole's text.

12. W. H. Hudson, *The Purple Land: Being the Narrative of One Richard Lamb's Adventures in the Banda Oriental in South America* (New York: Three Sirens Press, 1900).

<LIST OF BOOKS MENTIONED:

Stefan Zweig	. . .	Beware of Pity
		Kaleidoscope
		Marie Antoinette
		Erasmus
H. Belloc	. . .	Hills and the Sea
Kenneth Graham	. . .	The Wind in the Willows
Margaret Irwin	. . .	And Still She Wished for Company.
M. R. James	. . .	Ghost Stories of an Antiquary
Dorothy Sayers	. . .	The Unpleasantness at the Bellona Club.
Antony Armstrong	. . .	Ten Minutes Alibi
John Hampson	. . .	Saturday Night at the Greyhound.
Hugh Walpole	. . .	Mr. Perrin and Mr. Traill
W. H. Hudson	. . .	The Purple Land.>

BROADCAST: 1st April 1942.
                    WE SPEAK TO INDIA
                    Red Network
                    14.45 - 15.00 GMT.
                    Eastern Transmission.

"SOME BOOKS" - by E.M. Forster.

Today I'm going to desert my proper subject, which is prose, and speak instead of poetry, and on contemporary poetry. Anyhow I have one qualification for doing this: I believe in poetry: I hold that those who write it to-day ought to be respected and cherished, so that the future may judge them.

I believe in poetry because it is a special human product, for which no substitute has yet been found. It employs rhythm - a rhythm more regular than that of prose and nearer to the dance - and it sometimes employs rhyme and sometimes assonance. Rhythm, rhyme and assonance are not in themselves remarkable devices - anyone can work them - but they may release intensities and delicacies of the human mind of which we shouldn't otherwise be aware. That, condensed into a single sentence is my defence of poetry.

My subject is a large one and I shall divide it into five sections. Five generations - poetic generations that is to say - are creative in this island at the present moment. I will enumerate them in turn.

Firstly there is the generation of poets who matured in the period before 1914 - the period of the primaeval peace one might almost call it, so far away does it now seem. These poets are rooted in stability, and in what is politically called liberalism. They have been disillusioned since and have experienced much, but no one ever quite forgets the soil which nourished him. Some of them are still active and doing good work - de la Mare, for instance, and Laurence Binyon, and I would mention others.

Secondly, there is the generation which grew up during the 1914-1918 war. This, as you may have heard, was the war which was to end war, and the poets who fought in it had the faith that however beastly it was, it would not recur. That was their soil, and they have never forgotten it, despite later experiences and disillusionment. Several of them are writing to-day - Robert Graves and Edmund Blunden among them.

Thirdly, the post-war generation, the poets of the 1920[s], dominated by the great name of T. S. Eliot. The 1920's were a decade of disillusion. Hard things are often said of it, but I admire it myself, because people were trying to look at the truth, instead of sailing on hopefully with a favouring wind behind them and the rocks in front. They were also desirous of refinement, which I also admire, and the decade gives birth to the sensitive work of Edith Sitwell. But Eliot's "Waste Land" 1922 is the typical poem in it. Here he expressed his disappointment with a war which did not end war, and hence dates his progress to the religious mysticism which has just given us that lovely meditation - The Dry Salvages.[1]

Fourthly, the generation of the 1930's marked by the growth of a social and political conscience and by the recognition that England is part of Europe. Poetry looks outward again, and the poets read the newspapers and attend conferences - and fight. The great event in this decade is the Spanish Civil War. Vaster catastrophes have happened since, but the Spanish Civil War got home first, so to speak, and got home to the heart. W. H. Auden, Stephen Spender, Day Lewis, George Barker and - from his different angle - Roy Campbell - here are some of the poets it inspired. To the politician or the strategist it may be a trifling incident; to the men I have mentioned it was tremendous, it was a symbol, and the death of the Spanish colleague, the poet Lorca,[2] affected some of them like the defeat of an army. There hasn't, at least in my day, been such mobilising of the imagination, and the mobilisation was led by Auden; he is, in my judgment, another great poet, and he typifies for this decade just as Eliot typifies the previous one.

And now for my fifth and last. Fifthly, the young people who want to write poetry and have been caught by this war and by the world collapse of the civilisation of prose. I will return to them in a minute, but you can see now that when we speak of contemporary poetry in England, we mean something very composite to which five poetic generations contribute: poets dating from the primaeval peace, poets who found their inspiration in the war that was to end war, poets of the post-war disillusionment, poets of the European awakening, poets whose first imaginative impression is of this crashing, swaying movement - specimens from all these five classes are creative today. Some of them are over seventy years old: others are barely twenty, so you will appreciate how impossible it is to generalise about them. I do feel, though, that as a body, they are our standard bearers. Through the devices of their art, they express profundities and delicacies of the human spirit which would otherwise remain hid. They are leading us out of the darkness. Toward happiness and justice? I don't know. But towards greater sensibility. They are part of a movement which began before this war was thought of, and which will continue when it has shrunk to half a sentence in a text book.

Before I speak of the younger people - and it is on them that I shall spend the few minutes that remain to me - I'll tell you where you are likely to find them. Several of them have published books, but there is not much chance of your getting hold of the books in the present upheaval. Your best hope of reading them is in anthologies. So here are the titles of four anthologies.

"The Little Book of Modern Verse" with a preface by T. S. Eliot.[3] Here are good specimens of the poetic output of the present century, and full justice is done to the young. "The Little Book of Modern Verse" published by Faber and Faber.

"Modern Verse" covering the same period and chosen by Phyllis Jones.[4] The Oxford University Press are the publishers of "Modern Verse".

Then "The Best Poems of 1941" edited by Thomas Moult.[5] This is an anthology which Mr. Moult brings out yearly, and he includes American as well as English writers. Publisher - Jonathan Cape. The selections are on traditional lines. As a counterweight to it, I'll give you "Poems from the Forces", edited by Keidrych[6] Rhys,[7] himself a poet, which is experimental and iconoclastic, and the work of the youngest generation - the generation for whom Auden and Spender are already back numbers. "Poems from the Forces" is published by Routledge.

If you can get hold of these anthologies, and in particular "The Little Book of Modern Verse" and Modern Verse, you should get some idea of what is happening, and if you take in the BBC periodical "The Listener,["] be sure you read the poems which appear in its pages: they are usually poems by the youngest generation, and I[8] shall quote from one of them - Henry Reed's "Map of Verona"[9] in a moment.

Now this youngest generation. Their work is often obscure and hasty, it is full of indignation and disgust, and there is no "Ho, my shining amour" stuff. How should there be? These young people come into a world which ought to have been fit for poets to work in, and they find death and dirt. But, oddly enough, they seem to believe in love, and to hold that it provides the most favourable solution of our difficulties. Love is an unfashionable word in the world today. I can't remember any statesman using it in the last few months, and clergymen[10] only employ it after due precautions - so it is all the more moving to find love explicit or implicit in the work of these modern writers - in A.J. Tessimond and Francis Scarfe and A.L. Rowse[11] and Vernon Watkins and Adam Drinan.[12] Which brings me back to what I was saying earlier, namely that the poet, through his peculiar technique, expresses delicacies and profundities which lie beyond the speech of the rest of us. And there is nothing more delicate than love. Nor more profound.

I must end with two specimens of modern work. Here is a short poem by George Barker, entitled "To Robert Owen." I have already mentioned Barker in connection with Spain, and he shares the social awareness of the pre-war years, though he is younger than Auden - only 29. The Robert Owen of his poem was a British mill-owner and philanthropist of a century back, who hoped to bring on a revolution, which would leave the poor richer, and the rich[13] poorer. The poem is a vision, rather in the style of William Blake, and cutting, like Blake's visions, deep into contemporary life.

"TO ROBERT OWEN".

I walk under the winter tree,
It scatters heavy drops on me,
I lift my left hand and look,
It is the blood of the folk,
I turn, and the tree turns and cries,
I have wept out my eyes.

I feel the burning of that blood[14]
Penetrate my sense of good;
And where the weal shows on my hand
The figure of Robert Owen stands.
I did mine, he says, you
Do what you can do.

I walk near the summer sun,
Among the plethora of plenty,
Calcutta roses suffocating;
I see the many have none,
I see two rise on twenty,
I know the way they suffer.

In the plenitude of rot,
Like Pearl and like spirit,
I again recognise his spirit
Rising like a whirlwind at
The summer tree that has too much,
And blows it on the winter branch.[15]

I chose this poem partly for its intensity and social compassion, and partly because its technique is modernistic, but not puzzling. For instance in the last verse, there is not a single rhyme which Tennyson, or for that matter Blake, would have admitted, yet we have the impression of melody.

In the plenitude of rot,
Like pearl and like spirit,
I again recognise his spirit
Rising like a whirlwind at
The summer tree that has too much,
And blows it on the winter branch.

Next, part of a poem by Henry Reed - to be distinguished from the critic Herbert Read, who is also a poet. Henry Reed's poem is called "A Map of Verona". It is a subtle haunting dream which has nothing to do with the war or with any practicable peace. It plays with the idea of a map of an unvisited city, which we brood over, and upon which our imagination feeds.

"A map of Verona is open, the small strange city:
With its river running round and through, it is river-embraced.
And with this city for a whole long winter season,
With streets on a map, my thoughts have been interlaced.["]

He has visited Naples once, after similar brooding, and knows that a map of a city cannot reveal a city, but his thoughts are of Verona now, and all his talk envisages her, and leads towards her.

Again, it is strange to lead a conversation
Round to a name, to a cautious questioning
Of travellers, who talk of parasols and fountains
And a shining smile of snowfall late in Spring.
Their memories calm this winter of expectation,
Their talk restrains me, for I cannot flow
Like your impetuous river to embrace you;
Yet you are there, and one day I shall go.

The train will bring me perhaps in utter darkness
And drop me where you are blooming, unaware
That a stranger has entered your gates, and a new devotion
Is about to attend and haunt you everywhere.

The flutes are warm: in to-morrow's cave the music
Trembles and forms inside the musician's mind.
The lights being, and the shifting crowds[16] in the causeways
Are discerned through the dusk, and the rolling river behind.

Ah! in what hour of beauty, in what good arms,
Shall I those regions and that city attain
From whence my dreams and slightest movements rise?
And what good Arms shall take them away again?[17]

The Verona of this poem is not an enemy town, in Mussolini's possession, but a city of the heart, a possession of the imagination. The poem is
personal, and since poetry, whether written by the old or by the young,
should be an individual expression, I am glad to conclude with it.

Next month I shall return to prose.[18]

1. "The Dry Salvages" is movement three in Eliot's *The Four Quartets* (New York: Harcourt, Brace, Jovanovich, 1942).

2. Federico García Lorca, Spanish poet and dramatist, murdered by the Nationalists at the start of the Spanish Civil War.

3. Anne Ridler, ed., *The Little Book of Modern Verse* (1941). Publishing information is given in the broadcast for this and subsequent works.

4. Phyllis Jones, ed., *Modern Verse, 1900–1940* (1941).

5. Thomas Moult, ed., *The Best Poems of 1941* (1942).

6. <l> The correction, written in EMF's hand, is also indicated in the margin next to the reference to Rhys.

7. Keidrych Rhys, ed., *Poems from the Forces: A Collection of Verses by Serving Members of the Navy, Army, and Air Force* (1941).

8. <hope I>

9. In the typescript, the name is written "Henry Green." Reed's "The Map of Verona" was published in the *Listener* on 12 March 1942. It was later anthologized in *The Map of Verona and Other Poems* (London: J. Cape, 1946). EMF may have been confusing Reed with the novelist Henry Green (aka Henry Vincent Yorke), author of numerous novels, four of which EMF would have known by the time this broadcast aired: *Blindness* (London: Dent, 1926), *Living* (London: Hogarth Press, 1929), *Party Going* (London: Hogarth Press, 1939), and *Pack My Bag* (London: Hogarth Press, 1940).

10. <t>

11. <wes> Once again, the correction "Rowse," which also appears to be written in EMF's hand, is indicated in the margin next to the reference.

12. A(rthur) S(eymour) J(ohn) Tessimond, Francis Scarfe, A(lfred) L(eslie) Rowse, Vernon Watkind, and Adam Drinan. All were British poets and critics.

13. <er>

14. <,>

15. George Barker's poem "To Robert Owen" appeared in the magazine *Wales* (issue 10, October 1939, p. 261). Our thanks go to Dr. Robert Fraser of the Open University for his help

with this reference. The typist made two errors while reproducing the poem for the broadcast. The word "blood" in the first stanza was mistyped as "blook," and "suffocating" in the third stanza was mistyped as "succucating."

16. The original transcript reads "crods," though the typist surely meant "crowds," matching Reed's poem.

17. Reed, *A Map of Verona and Other Poems*, 14. The typist once again made two errors in reproducing Reed's poem for the broadcast. The word "conversation" in the second stanza was mistyped as "vonversation," and "darkness" in the third stanza was mistyped as "darkeess."

18. Brackets appear around this phrase.

Red Network

SOME BOOKS - by E.M. Forster[1]

Kipling! How that name does excite people! If you suddenly say "Kipling" you are sure to arouse passions and contradictory reactions. One listener will exclaim "Kipling! the British character at its best - noble, courageous, stern but just, and merciful in the hour of victory. A great writer, teacher and prophet." Another will retort - "Kipling! - the British character at its worst - arrogant, complacent, uncultivated. A mere journalist, a political hack, a writer of music-hall doggerel and magazine stories". Both speakers will be excited. For Kipling is an exciting person. On this point we can agree. He is incisive and unusual and independent. You may worship him or detest him. But you cannot neglect him.

I mention him today because he had an Indian connection - and I am devoting this talk to Indian connections of various types - also because of a book which has come out over here. It is a selection from his verse, with a preface by Mr. T. S. Eliot; and it has again been rousing people to say "Kipling - how glorious" or "Kipling - how loathsome", as the case may be.[2] Mr. Eliot, I need scarcely say, is guilty of neither expletive. He brings his delicately poised and highly critical mind to the interpretation of a writer whose temperament and opinion are different from his own. The result is very interesting, and he makes some admirable remarks about Kipling as a writer. He points out that he knew his job, that he is never slap-dash in spite of his lilting and slang, and that he is a craftsman of the school of William Morris. This is very true, and anyone who is a writer must admire Kipling because of his technique - I do myself - and I admire his magical quality. Mr. Eliot also points out that the verse[3] was written as verse, not as poetry and that we must not blame Kipling for not doing something he never tried to do. He was a verse-maker, a ballad monger, a writer of hymns and epitaphs - a producer of stuff which is planned to release its full effect the first hearing, whereas poetry only yields itself after repeated readings. All this is wisely and generously said. But when Mr. Eliot goes further and tries to ennoble Kipling's opinions and make out that he is an estimable character, he goes rather too far for me. No amount of sympathetic pleading will conceal the fact that[4] the man was a bully and a vulgarian, and rotten with racial-consciousness. I don't say "racial arrogance": he hadn't that, he could be scathing about his own people of "the flanneled fool at the wicket and the muddled oaf at the goal".[5] But he saw everything and everyone in terms of race, which is to me[6] lamentable. He had no conception of economics beyond something which he called "the mart", no interest in science except in the form of machinery, and no belief in any future for which I want to die. And the vulgarity - I don't mean coarseness by that word: I mean a certain commonness of mind.[7]

I am getting excited myself - it is the fault of the subject. It will cool me down if I turn to a very different sort of book which has also come out during the last few weeks - a little book called Ethical Ideals in India To-day by Edward Thompson.[8] This is a reprint of a lecture which Mr. Thompson gave last month in London. I went to the lecture. There was a large and attentive audience, and we came away a little less ignorant about contemporary India than we had been. (We are ignorant - not so much politically as culturally.) Mr. Thompson spoke of Tagore, Gandhi, Iqbal and Nehru, all of whom he has known personally; he analysed the mental outlook of each, and indicated the public activity which proceeded in each case from the outlook. I was particularly interested in what he said about Iqbal and his eclecticism. I know Sir Mohammed Iqbal slightly myself, and I have always felt that of all great contemporary Indian thinkers he has received the least attention over here. I was interested too when Mr. Thompson prophesied that the immediate spiritual future of India would be atheism. The India I remember didn't give me that impression, but it is years since I was there. You are better placed and you can judge. The book Ethical Ideals in India Today will certainly make you think.

Thompson and Kipling are both Englishmen. The rest of my time I'll devote to Indian writers - Indians who are over here, and are helping us to understand their land. There are not a great many of them, and they have a limitation which they frankly recognise: namely that because they live over here, they cannot be in close touch with you. Still they are doing valuable work, both as creators and interpreters.

Do you remember how, about a year ago, I spoke of four Indian novelists who were writing in English - Ahmed Ali, Raja Rao, R.K. Narayan, and Mulk Raj Anand?[9] The first three are in India now, but Anand is still in this country and he has just completed his trilogy of Sikh peasant life. The new volume is called The Sword and the Sickle. The first book of the series, The Village, described the emancipation of a Punjab country lad, Lal Singh. In Across the Black Waters, Lal Singh went as a soldier to France in the 1914 war, and was taken prisoner.[10] In The Sword and the Sickle he returns to India and to the economic upheavals of the early twenties, and we leave him again in prison. It is a long diffuse book with many characters in it, and many episodes. The episode which struck me most was the interview of Lal Singh with Gandhi. I have read many accounts, fictitious and otherwise, of interviews with Gandhi, but this one is by far the most vivid, and gives us a picture of the Mahatma and his entourage which is partly admiring and partly critical. I can't tell you whether the picture is a true one, because I have never seen Mr. Gandhi, myself, but I can tell you that it is life-like, with a spice of malice in it, and that you will feel that you are reading about a real person. The Sword and the Sickle is certainly the most considerable literary work which has been published by an Indian over here during the last few weeks, and it is being widely read. Its title by the way comes from a poem by William Blake.[11]

Turning to the Magazines, one of our periodicals, Life and Letters, published in March a special India number - that's to say a number written by Indians. It contains, among other articles, a careful examination of Tagore by Iqbal Singh, something on Indian Music by Narayana Menon, and something on Indian Folk Art by Ajit Mookerjee - I believe by the way that Mr. Mookerjee is about to publish a longer article on this same subject, in Horizon, an article dealing more particularly with eighteenth century Bengal.

Then there is a Magazine which I have mentioned to you before - Indian Writing, which is edited by, and written in English, by Indians. The new number of Indian Writing is not out yet, but I have had the advantage of seeing the proofs. I note an article on Science in India by Shelvankar (who was speaking to you about Russia when I was in this studio last), and a touching and well constructed story by S. Raja Ratnam, called "A Practical Joke".[12] - Then, though it doesn't come under the heading of books, I want to mention a cultural entertainment which was given by Indians last week in a London theatre; it was organised by the Indian Committee for aid to the Soviet Peoples, and the Soviet Ambassador and Madame Maisky attended it. There was singing, dancing, solos[13] on the Veena, and scenes from Rabindranath Tagore's play Chitra. The entertainment was a success, and there are plans for repeating it.[14]

Well, that ends my list of the Indian connections to which I have devoted this talk. With Kipling at one end and dramatic performances at the other, they cover a wide range, and suggest that there are several

Englands as well as several Indias. It seemed worth assembling them in order to point out the growing interest there is over here in Indian civilisation. I don't want to exaggerate; there isn't the interest there ought to be - indeed our ignorance of the Orient after three hundred years of material connection with it is most remarkable. What has been lacking, I think, is contact between writers and artists and musicians and people who (generally speaking) care about what is intangible and delicate and harmonious in life. East isn't East and West isn't West when two such people meet,[15] though they come from the ends of the earth. I am one of those people, and you must be another, or you would not have switched on to a talk entitled "Some Books". And I say to you that our job is to understand one another and to interpret to one another the communities in which we are mutually planted. People like ourselves are in the long run the only reliable interpreters. We don't issue statistics, we don't preach sermons, we don't even formulate creeds. Ours is ordinary human intercourse, but it is touched and heightened by our belief in the potential greatness of man, which includes aesthetic greatness and consequently we stumble upon truths which are missed by the so-called practical observer.

Next month, I shall return to my normal duty of keeping you in touch with English literature and Western literature as well as I can. My home is in England and I am conditioned by the West. But I shall retain the notion of connection with India, and shall continue to speculate where you are sitting and what you are thinking about. You know my thoughts, and that I am sitting in a studio. I have popped on to a seat lately occupied by a previous speaker, and now I must vacate it in my turn, so that you may be addressed by someone else. On the wall of the studio is an electric clock looking very scientific and authoritative and pretending to tell me the time. The clock says it's a quarter to two, and that I must stop. I will do so, but I must observe that your clock does not indicate a quarter to two or anything like it. It points to some other hour, which prompts in me the fancy that the connection between us is a connection outside time.

1. The date, stamped on the heading of this broadcast, is 29 April 1942.

2. George Orwell suggested a variety of texts for this talk, among them Eliot's edition of Kipling's verse. Orwell restricted mention of Shelvankar's book; EMF sidestepped Orwell's stricture by alluding to another of Shelvankar's works later in the talk. In a letter to EMF, Orwell wrote: "I think it would be a good idea to more or less wrap your talk round Anand's novel and the Indian number of 'Life & Letters'. 'Indian Writing' could be mentioned in the same connection, and perhaps also the recent selection of Kipling's poems with Eliot's introduction. A book which is more or less apropos but unfortunately must not be mentioned is K. S. Shelvankar's 'The Problem of India'" (14 April 1942, E. M. Forster File 4A, January–June 1942 R CONT 1, BBC WAC). Presumably, Orwell felt that Shelvankar's book was too nationalistic to be mentioned in EMF's wartime talk.

3. \<here selected\>

4. \<Mr. Kipling\>

5. Rudyard Kipling, "The Islanders," in *A Choice of Kipling's Verse Made by T. S. Eliot*, ed. T. S. Eliot (New York: Doubleday, 1941), 137.

6. \<unpardonable\>

7. This final sentence was written in a hand other than EMF's.

8. Edward Thompson, *Ethical Ideals in India Today: Delivered at Conway Hall, Red Lion Square, W. C. I., on March 22, 1942* (London: Watts and Co., 1942). EMF presided over this talks series.

9. Talk of 9 June 1941, entitled "Turning Over a New Leaf," not included in this volume.

10. Mulk Raj Anand, *The Sword and the Sickle* (London: J. Cape, 1942), *The Village* (London: J. Cape, 1939), and *Across the Black Waters* (London: J. Cape, 1940).

11. From a fragment, entitled "The Sword Sung," from William Blake's *Notebook*, 1791.

12. Ratnam's story was in fact entitled "Famine." It concerns a rural community that must choose between the rules of its religion and survival—which ultimately depends upon eating cattle. This is the only story Ratnam published in the journal, which ran to just five numbers. See S. Raja Ratnam, "Famine," *Indian Writing* (Summer 1941): 211–16. Our thanks to Eric Frierson at the Graduate Library of the University of Michigan for his assistance with this reference.

13. Given as "sols" in the script.

14. Rabindranath Tagore, *Chitra* (London: India Society, 1913). The specific event cannot be traced.

15. EMF alludes to the opening line of Kipling's "The Ballad of East and West": *"Oh, East is East, and West is West, and never the twain shall meet."*

SOME BOOKS

- by -

E.M. Forster

Eastern Transmission
27th May 1942

A book which has attracted a good deal of attention over here lately is a book on Yugoslavia by Rebecca West. It is called <u>Black Lamb and Grey Falcon</u>. Yugoslavia is quite off my beat and probably off yours, and I don't suggest that this book touches us intimately. Still, you might like to hear of it, for Miss West is an intelligent, warm-hearted, original and able writer, also a provocative one, so that one is constantly agreeing or disagreeing with what she says: she never lets the reader go to sleep. By the way she has been speaking in this service to you. I think too that it is good occasionally to go off one's beat: it reminds us of our limitations, and of the greatness of the earth. So I suggest that I in England and you in India turn our thoughts to Yugoslavia for ten minutes, and open these two volumes of <u>Black Lamb and Grey Falcon</u>.

Yugoslavia, as you know, is one of the Balkan States; it used to be called Serbia, it is largely inhabited by the southern Slavs, who are as it were the cousins of our Russian allies, it fought against Hitler, and its young king is at present an exile in this country. Its previous king, Alexander, was murdered in Marseilles in 1934 and this, Miss West thinks,[1] led up to the present war. And back in 1914 there was another murder. Some Yugoslavs killed the Arch-Duke Franz Ferdinand of Austria, and this was certainly the immediate cause of the so-called great war. I mention these two deeds of violence because they[2] figure a good deal in what may be called the philosophy of the book. Miss West believes that Yugoslavia is the centre and the symbol of the European tragedy, and that things have gone wrong with us ever since it was over-run by the Turks in the fourteenth century.

I will come back to this in a moment - merely remarking here that it isn't[3] my own belief. Now for the book.

It's a travel book. It's a lively, readable and[4] chatty diary of a tour which she made[5] five years ago with her husband (Rebecca West is a pen name) and some Yugoslav friends. They visit Croatia, Dalmatia, Herzegovina, Bosnia (where the Arch-Duke was murdered), Serbia proper, Macedonia, Montenegro - all of which were part of the[6] country. They have a thrilling time, visiting monasteries, castles, peasants, getting stuck in the snow or baked in the sun, drinking plum brandy, eating sucking pig which is so deliciously tender that it spreads on bread as if it were butter, seeing the crumbling relics of Turkish dominion, talking to wild little girls above the lake of Janina. And there is plenty of fun. The writer pokes fun at her excellent husband, whose favourite pastime, she tells us, is inattention, and she takes a lively dislike to the wife of one of their Yugoslav friends, a German lady called Gerda. Gerda is all nobility and stolidity, and whenever she appears on the scene we may be sure of sparks. Dress too - Miss West has a frank and feminine delight in finery, and more fun is poked at earnest left-winged women who look like sacks.

But beneath all the tourism and the smart chatter, there run some very serious considerations - considerations implicit in the title of the book. Why <u>Black Lamb and Grey Flacon</u>, you may have been wondering? Why give such a fanciful name to a travel diary?

Black Lamb refers to a blood sacrifice, a pagan fertility rite, which is still practiced on a stone on a mountain near the southern frontier. Lambs are slaughtered, also poultry, their blood is spattered on the rock and on the worshippers, is carried away in phials to promote childbirth. Miss West attends the[7] sacrifice. She is disgusted, for she loathes cruelty, and she notes how "under the opening glory of the morning the stench from the rock mounted more strongly and became sickening."[8] It is a vivid description, and reminded me of the accounts which D. H. Lawrence has given of sacrifices in Mexico. Then she goes on to meditate "I knew this rock well, I had lived under the shadow of it all my life. All our Western thought is founded on this repulsive pretence that pain is the price of any good thing."[9] Here you see what I have called the philosophy of the book coming out. Pain does not pay, she tells us. The idea of the sacrifice, the atonement, is wrong. And then she links this bloodshed of the black lamb to those other useless sheddings of blood which have characterised Yugoslav history - the murders of King Alexander, of the Archduke Franz Ferdinand - and so brings the country into the centre of our European shambles.

That is the Black Lamb. The Grey Falcon is the title of an old Serbian folk-poem. This poem - she gives a translation of it from which I'll quote - is deeply interesting. It's a legendary account of the defeat of the Serbians by the Turks back in the fourteenth century - that defeat to which she attributes our miseries in Europe because it led to the weakening of the Balkans, the rise of the Austro-Hungarian Empire and the opportunity of Germany. The Poem also raises a profound problem in human conduct - the problem of non-intervention or half-hearted intervention. The grey falcon - a magic bird - flies to the ruler of the Serbs - the Tsar as he is called - bearing to him a message from the Mother of God. The Tsar reads the message. He is asked whether he wants an earthly kingdom. If so,[10] let him drive out the Turks. Or does he want a heavenly kingdom? If so, let him build a church. The poem goes on: -

The Tsar pondered and he pondered thus:
"Dear God, what kingdom shall I choose?
Shall I choose a heavenly kingdom?
Shall I choose an earthly kingdom?
If I choose an earthly kingdom
An earthly kingdom lasts only a little time
But a heavenly kingdom will last for eternity.["]

The Tsar chose a heavenly kingdom
And not an earthly kingdom.
He built a church. . . .
And in the same hour the Turks attacked . . .
And the Tsar was destroyed
And his army was destroyed with him
Or seven and seventy thousand soldiers.
All was holy, all was honourable.
And the goodness of God was fulfilled.[11]

Reading more into this old ballad than it will bear perhaps, Miss West proceeds to analyse the pacifist spirit. Shall we save our own souls, when by so doing we destroy the souls of our friends - "of seven and seventy thousand soldiers"? She also asks herself why righteousness has made so little progress down here. She believes that it fails because it is tainted by defeatism and chooses heaven because it fears at the bottom of its heart that it is going to lose the earth. And here again she finds in the tragedies of Yugoslavia the seeds of the European tragedy. The Black Lamb - which attempts to procure blessings through cruelty - was a mistake. The Grey Falcon - which attempts to avoid evils through non-resistance - is a mistake too. The gifted country where Lamb and Falcon occur is (to her mind) the key to the European pattern, and until we understand it we cannot understand ourselves, or our faults.

Before commenting on this, may I remind you of another book which I talked about some months ago - Aldous Huxley's <u>Grey Eminence</u>,[12] a study of France in the days of Cardinal Richelieu.[13] Although the two books are so different - Mr. Huxley's being the more important of the two[14] - they have one feature in common: they both seek for a pattern in European politics and for an explanation of our present disasters. Mr. Huxley finds the explanation 300 years ago in the policy of Richelieu, who entered the Thirty Years' War and created misery and revengefulness in Germany. Miss West finds it 500 years ago, when the Serbians went down before the Turks. They cannot both of them be right. And I am tempted to think they are both wrong. Anyhow, I would like here to quote from a third writer, the famous historian H.A.L. Fisher, and hear what he has to say on that fascinating question whether there is a pattern in history. H.A.L. Fisher says (in his preface to his History of Europe):-

["]Men wiser and more learned than I discern in history a plot, a rhythm, a predetermined pattern. These harmonies are concealed from me. I can only see one emergency following on another as wave follows wave, only one great fact with respect to which, since it is unique, there can be no generalisation, only our safe rule for the historian: that he should recognise in the development of human destinies the play of the contingent and the unseen."[15]

By the way if you will try this passage which I've just read upon a Marxist, you will see more sparks. For the Marxist does detect a pattern in history, though it is not Mr. Huxley's pattern, nor is it Miss West's. [16]Do you see a pattern? Ask yourself that question. I don't, and I follow very humbly, H.A.L. Fisher as my guide here.[17] It seems to me that the human experiment is so unique, so governed by the "contingent and the unseen" that we cannot discern a pattern in it. And I don't think we can ever explain the present by the past, for the simple reason that we don't know enough about the past.

However, this is taking us too far away from a book which is first and foremost a good travel diary, though it has the extra merit of making us think. If you can get hold of it you will learn about Yugoslavia, and you will also be exercising your brains. <u>If</u> you can get hold of it. <u>If</u>. That little word "if" falls like a shadow across all these book talks. For we in England find it difficult enough to get the books we want, so what must it be for you, when you want to get a particular English book in India? Moreover, <u>Black Lamb and Grey Falcon</u> is lengthy, and therefore expensive. Perhaps your best plan is to ask for it in a public library. And if the assistant replies "Never heard of it"[18] then ask for something else by this gifted author. She has written novels <u>The Judge</u> and others.[19] She has written a life of St. Augustine. She has written a good critical study of Henry James.[20] She has above all written short stories, one of which <u>The Salt of the Earth</u>[21] I would place among the most brilliant and disquieting short stories I have ever read. <u>The Salt of the Earth</u> is about a woman who was poisoned by her husband because she was always in the right. Whatever he did, whatever anyone else did, she always knew better. She was the salt of the earth but she was too much for him, and he bethought him of another salt, whose name is - arsenic. This story comes in a volume called The Harsh Voice. Get hold of it if you can.

1. <was a premonition of>

2. <bulk largely>

3. <a belief which I share>

4. <discursive>

5. <in the late thirties>

6. <Yugoslav state>

7. <rite which takes place on the eve of St. George>

8. Rebecca West, *Black Lamb and Grey Falcon: The Record of a Journey through Yugoslavia in 1937*, 2 vols. (London: Macmillan, 1941), 2:824.

9. Ibid., 2:827.

10. <he must>

11. West, *Black Lamb and Grey Falcon*, 2:910–11.

12. <which dealt with>

13. For more on Huxley's study, see EMF's broadcast dated 11 February 1942.

14. <to my mind>

15. H(erbert) A(lbert) L(aurens) Fisher, *A History of Europe* (Oxford: Clarendon Press, 1920), v.

16. <What is the truth, and>

17. <rather than Miss West>

18. <perhaps you may care to>

19. West, *The Judge* (London: Hutchinson, 1922).

20. West, *Henry James* (London: Nisbit, 1916).

21. West's *The Salt of the Earth* appeared in *The Harsh Voice: Four Short Novels* (London: J. Cape, 1935). EMF discusses this story at greater length in the broadcast dated 15 December 1944.

SOME BOOKS

- by -

E. M. Forster

Eastern Trans: 24th June 1942

Several books on America or connected with America have come my way lately. They'll provide the subject of to-day's talk. They are all new books, and it may be a long time before you see them. Here's a study of Walt Whitman. Here's the diary which Mr. Joseph Davies, a United States ambassador kept in Moscow. Here's a re-interpretation of American history by John Dos Passos. Here's a story by John Steinbeck, a fine novelist of the younger generation. These four books will give us something to think about for a few minutes. I assume that, like myself, you do think about America just now. She touches your fortunes, and perhaps your hearts, in a way which western Europe can't. I don't know whether American books and American magazines circulate widely in India. I hope they do. American films do, but America isn't all film; with all respect to Hollywood, there are other places in the continent whose existence it is well to remember. These four books are about those other places. That's to say, they show us an America which isn't all cow-boys and glamour girls and wise-cracks, and dollars; an America which has experimented and meditated and is now trying to understand the world, and to help mankind. Listen for instance to this remark by their poet, Walt Whitman. "I have imagined a life which should be that of the average man in average circumstances and still grand and heroic".[1] Listen again to the following remark: you may disagree with it, but listen. It's made by Ambassador Davies in his Moscow Diary, when he is bidding farewell to his staff. He says "I don't care how much totalitarian states or dictatorships may provide in material benefits or social benefits to childhood or old age. If liberty and freedom have to be sacrificed, the price is too high to pay".[2] There's a big question, but it is one which America is considering, and leading us to consider.

I mentioned just now the name of John Dos Passos. He is a man of letters, a democrat, a believer in the Anglo-Saxon middle classes and their puritan tradition, an upholder of religious tolerance. Repelled, like all of us, by the new values which the Nazis are advertising, he has written this book called "The Ground We Stand On",[3] where he re-examines American history in the light of modern events. It's a loosely connected series of essays. For example there is an essay on Roger Williams, the founder of the state of Rhode Island. Williams came from this country, he knew Milton, and like Milton he believed in tolerance and in free speech. He also believed in unified Government, and he was a sound man of business, who made money by trading with the Red Indians - at the same time behaving very well to them. Living three hundred years ago, he was able to combine these rather contradictory qualities. Can they be combined today? Can you harness tolerance and centralisation? Commercialism and sympathy? That is the sort of question Mr. Dos Passos raises. He thinks that you can, though he appreciates the difficulties. He holds, with all its implications, the democratic faith, the "ground we stand on".

I'll take next, out of these American books a story The Moon is Down by John Steinbeck.[4] You probably know John Steinbeck's name. He wrote a magnificent novel called The Grapes of Wrath, which was made into a film, and a play Of Mice and Men - also filmed. He is on the side of the underdog, the insulted, the unsuccessful, and there are moments when he has reminded me of Maxim Gorki.[5] This particular story, The Moon is Down, is of a different type. It's the story of an invasion - the invasion of a little European town - locality unnamed. The town is easily taken - with the help of the local Quisling[6] - the invaders are polite, even humane, and only want the inhabitants to collaborate and go on working the local coal mine. The inhabitants refuse - there are incidents, executions, a reign of terror. The invaders have the town, they have the mine, they win the battle, they have everything. But they lose the war, because no one can invade the human soul. John Steinbeck here has turned against national injustice the wrath he turned against social injustice in his other work. He believes that the soul can stand firm and - to echo Walt Whitman - that the life of the average man can be grand and heroic. The Moon is Down is quite short - you can read it in an hour, and it hasn't the majesty and weight of Steinbeck's longer works. But it is very moving and it contains a terribly practical lesson for us all.

Mission to Moscow is testimony of another type. It contains the confidential dispatches and the correspondence both official and personal of Ambassador Davies during the fateful years 1936 to 1938, and includes various notes and comments up to the autumn of 1941. One is reminded of the diary of Ambassador Dodd, who was during the same period representing his country in Berlin.[7] Mr. Davies, like Mr. Dodd, is quiet, simple, unassuming, friendly, but independent and shrewd, and not to be intimidated by European blusterers. He has an open mind, he is sympathetic to the Soviet Union, but he is a western democrat, and occasionally critical. These criticisms have been taken in good part by the Soviet authorities, and the Diary has an appreciative foreword by M. Litvinoff.[8] Mr. Davies arrived in Moscow at the time of the Trials, which he attended, and he ends with the Russo-German pact, and the outbreak of the war. If you are trying to understand contemporary politics, you should certainly get hold of his record.

I have left till the last the book on Walt Whitman. It is by an Englishman, Mr. I'Anson Fausset,[9] and before mentioning it I should like to speak of Whitman himself. I don't know whether he is much read in India. I certainly advise you to try him, and his vastness, his warmth, and his fearlessness might very well knock you over. On the other hand you might remain quite unmoved. Whitman either succeeds with a reader or fails. I used to love him unreservedly myself, and one of his poems "Passage to India" supplied me with the title of a novel which I wrote about your country. There is certainly no one like him (if we except his disciple Edward Carpenter), and no one who can so suddenly ravish us into communion with all humanity or with death. He calls himself the poet of democracy and his colouring is distinctively American. But his appeal is to all mankind, apart from politics or creed. Get if you can a complete edition of his Leaves of Grass; one has been published in Everyman and you should be able to find it in any large town. There is also a selection of his poetry and prose in the World Classics, but the complete Leaves of Grass is preferable.

When you have read the poems or some of them, you will be able to appreciate Mr. Fausset's study of the poet. It is a well-informed account of Whitman's life, and of his strange character; he was not the reckless hero of his poems, but cautious and prudent, and not always straightforward. Mr. Fausset is critical of him, is indeed inclined to be pernickety. He doesn't like Whitman's praise of the human body and of its functionings. He thinks that he is finer and truer as a poet of death than as a poet of life, and gives his highest praise to the Ode on the Death of President Lincoln.[10] I'm not sure that I agree. However, it doesn't matter what I say or what Mr. Fausset says. The important thing is that you should get hold of Whitman's poems and see whether you respond to them, whether you find in their strange mixture of the mystic and the physical, something which corresponds to your own view of life. If we can care for poetry, we ought to go on reading it now, even in this, the worst of wars. It is not just a peace time adornment. It is something which lies deeper than either war or peace, and testifies to the persistency of the human spirit. Walt Whitman mayn't be the greatest poet that ever was, still, he's great enough to get down to those depths and to remind us that we too have a share in them.

Here then are four - or rather five - American books.

The Ground we Stand On, by John Dos Passos (spell)

The Moon is down, a novel by John Steinbeck

Mission to Moscow, by Ambassador Davies.

Walt Whitman - a study[11] by Hugh I'Anson Fausset (spell)

But - more important than all - Leaves of Grass by Walt Whitman himself.

1. EMF evidently quotes from a secondary source: *Cosmic Consciousness: A Study of the Evolution of the Human Mind,* by Richard Maurice Bucke (Philadelphia: Innes and Sons, 1901), 219. Our thanks to Dr. Ken Price, director of the Whitman Archive at the University of Nebraska–Lincoln, for his assistance with this reference.

2. Joseph E. Davies, *Mission to Moscow* (New York: Simon and Schuster, 1941), xvii. Davies was ambassador to the Soviet Union from 1936 to 1938.

3. John Dos Passos, *The Ground We Stand On* (New York: Harcourt, Brace, and Co., 1941).

4. John Steinbeck, *The Moon Is Down* (New York: Viking Press, 1942).

5. Maxim Gorki (Aleksey Maksimovich Peshkov) was a Russian socialist and dramatist, known for *The Enemies* (1906), *The Last Ones* (1908), *The Zykovs* (1914), and *Counterfeit Coin* (1926).

6. "A traitor to one's country, a collaborationist, esp. during the war of 1939–45" (*OED*). The etymology of the word stems from Major Vidkun Quisling (1887–1945), a Norwegian officer and diplomatist who collaborated with the Germans during their occupation of Norway from 1940 to 1945.

7. Ambassador William Edward Dodd, professor of history at Randolph Macon College and the University of Chicago, was a statesman and professional historian. Dodd served as ambassador to Germany from 1933 to 1937. *Ambassador Dodd's Diaries, 1933–1938*, edited by his son, William Dodd Jr., and his daughter, Martha Dodd, chronicles this fascinating period in Dodd's public career (London: Victor Gollancz, 1941).

8. M. Litvinoff, soviet foreign minister during the war.

9. I'Anson Fausset, *Walt Whitman: Poet of Democracy* (New Haven: Yale University Press, 1942).

10. EMF refers to "When Lilacs Last in the Dooryard Bloom'd" but perhaps conflates Whitman's elegy with Alfred, Lord Tennyson's "Ode on the Death of the Duke of Wellington" (1852).

11. <of>

"MY DEBT TO INDIA"

As broadcast
   Introductory talk by <u>E.M. Forster</u>
   10 mins
<u>Hindustani Service, 13th August 1942</u>
<u>In English, 14th August 1942</u>

During the next few weeks seven English people will be coming to the microphone in order[1] to express the gratitude they feel towards[2] India. Some of these people are well known, are indeed of the highest public distinction. Others are not well known, and their names will only be familiar to their own circle. This mixture of celebrities and non-celebrities - of big people and small people, if I may use that expression without offence - is intentional. England is trying to say "Thank you" to India in this series, and the "thank you" wouldn't be representative if it were only voiced by the eminent. The non-eminent must say it too. They, equally, must express the warmth in their hearts, the warmth which they hope you reciprocate. They must join with their better-known colleagues in holding out, in this distant London studio, a garland of affection.

I don't know in what order the speakers will come to the microphone, but in introducing them now, as I have been asked to do, I shall give their names in alphabetical order. I shall speak of each in turn very briefly, and shall indicate the line which he or she[3] is likely to take. He or she - for some of the speakers will be women; it would be a poor "thank you" if it were voiced by men alone.

Firstly then comes the name of Field Marshal Lord Birdwood.[4] Lord Birdwood was born in the Mahratta country, and his family has served in India for three generations, his father[5] was a High Court Judge.

Second in this alphabetical list is Mr. A.P. Blair.[6] Mr. Blair is a business man - in[7] the Shell Oil Company - and he worked in India for twelve years, chiefly in Karachi, the Punjab and Calcutta.

Thirdly Miss April Darling;[8] I shall indicate Miss Darling's contribution, and the contributions of the other speakers in a minute; just now I want to run through their names.

Fourthly, Lady Hartog, who lived for over twenty years at Dacca where her husband, Sir Philip Hartog, was Vice Chancellor of the University.[9]

Fifthly, Mr. Gerard Wathen of the educational service.[10] Mr. Wathen served in the Punjab for nineteen years, retiring as the Principal of the Khalsa College, Amritsar.

Sixthly, Major Yeats Brown, soldier, student of mysticism, and man of letters; among Major Yeats Brown's writings "Bengal Lancer" is the best known.[11]

And lastly, - in alphabetical order - comes the name of Sir Francis Younghusband, soldier, explorer, and author of many books.[12] I add his name because his talk is going to form part of this series, but I am very sorry to have to report to you that he has recently died. Sir Francis Younghusband was born in Murree, and here again is a record of English family connection, for his father went out to India exactly 100 years ago.

That is the list of speakers. They are people of most varied experience and eminence. And yet it is possible to generalise about them. For there is one aspect which they will share. They all lay stress upon friendship - Lord Birdwood, Major Yeats Brown and Sir Francis Younghusband speak of comradeship in the Indian army - and outside it - Mr. Wathen of the links which bound him to his colleagues and his pupils, in a happy atmosphere of laughter and sunshine. Miss Darling - happiness again - speaks for the thousands who have been happy as children in India, and she speaks with youth's freshness and ardour; Mr. Blair tells of the many friends he has made in the course of his work and his leisure. Lady Hartog of her intimacy with Indian women. All are agreed that their main debt to India is a debt of love.

Beyond that, they find different things to praise; there is scenery, there is sport; the spiritual message of India moves Sir Francis Younghusband and Major Yeats Brown; and Mr. Blair, who also feels her cultural beauty; and Lady Hartog, who believes that through the co-operation of Indian women peace may come to the woes of the world. It is not for me to discriminate between the talks. But I think Lady Hartog's may prove specially interesting because she develops the theme of womanhood which is scarcely touched on by the other speakers.

That concludes my task of introduction. I have been, you see, in the position of a servant who has announced to you the names of your approaching guests. Having told you their qualifications and their titles I ought to retire. But servants too have their feelings, and I should like to seize this opportunity of expressing mine. I should like, as it were, to linger in your doorway and praise what I have seen in your house. I have been to India in the flesh, but my affection for her began long before my visit, in England, when I gained my first Indian friend. He was Masood - Sir Syed Ross Masood he became afterwards - and perhaps I owe more to him than to any one individual, for he shook me out of my rather narrow academic and suburban outlook, and revealed to me another way of looking at life - the Oriental, and, within the Oriental, the Moslem.[13] He prepared me for one aspect of India. When I first came East in 1912 and visited him I made another great Indian friend. I knew this friend as Bapu Sahib - officially he was H.H. the Maharaja of Dewas State Senior.[14] Bapu Sahib revealed another aspect of India to me - the Hindu - and through it another aspect of life, and he had a deeper sense of the nobilities and the delicacies of personal intercourse than anyone whom I have ever met, whether English or Indian. And to these two friends, Sir Ross Masood and the Maharaja of Dewas Senior, I had the immense privilege of adding a third, a woman friend, Lady Hydari of Hyderabad Deccan; to her and to Sir Akbar Hydari my debt is tremendous.[15] You will see from this why I too am grateful to India, and how, round these friendships, there gathered opportunities for insight and for vision and for work. I am not so foolish as to say that I understand your country. But I have good grounds for saying that I love it.

And now I must withdraw from your doorway and make way for your guests - who will begin to arrive next week. I give, as it were, a last look round at your house. There has been no house quite like it since the formation of the world. I thank you for what I have seen in it, and I wish you happiness in it.[16]

1. <to speak of their debt to India and>

2. <her>

3. EMF added accent marks above "he" and "she."

4. In the subsequent list, EMF added accent marks above both syllables in "Birdwood," above "A.P." and "Blair," and above the first syllable of each word in the names "April Darling," "Lady Hartog," and "Gerald Wathen." Finally, EMF added accent marks above the first syllable in "Major" and above both the Christian and surname "Yeats Brown." Field Marshal Lord Birdwood (William Riddle Birdwood) served in India in his youth as a cavalry officer and later in South Africa under the leadership of Lord Kitchener. Birdwood went on to serve as secretary of the Indian Army Department (1912–1914) and during WWI commanded Australian and New Zealand corps in Egypt, Gallipoli, and France. He ended his military career in India as commander in chief.

5. <being>

6. No information beyond EMF's details is available on A. P. Blair.

7. <Burmah>

8. April Darling was the daughter of Sir Malcolm Darling, writer, Indian talks producer,

and friend to EMF. She and her husband, Pierre van Biervliet d'Oeuverbroek, traveled through India with her father on a riding tour that he made from Peshawar to Jubbulpore from 25 November 1946 to 15 March 1947; during this tour, Malcolm Darling gathered information on what village people thought of Independence. April Darling kept a thorough diary of her experiences—and it was from this diary that Malcolm Darling drew while writing his well-known work, *At Freedom's Door* (London: G. Cumberledge, 1949).

9. Lady Mabel Hélène Kisch Hartog, author, published three works on India in her lifetime: *Living India* (Glasgow: Blackie and Son, 1935), *India in Outline* (Cambridge: Cambridge University Press, 1944), and *India: A New Pattern* (London: Allen and Unwin, 1955). Sir Philip Joseph Hartog, educator and statesman, served on several important boards and committees concerned with Indian education, including the Calcutta University Commission and the Indian Public Service Commission. He also served as chair of the Indian Education Committee from 1927 to 1929. The author of several books on examination and writing, Hartog helped found the London School of Oriental Studies in 1916, was named the vice chancellor of Dacca University in India in 1920, and was knighted in 1926 for his dedicated service to education at home and abroad.

10. Gerard Wathen was at one time the principal of Khalsa College in Amritsar. He was best known for initiating the "coats off movement" through which he urged students to perform manual work for the institution as part of their education.

11. Francis Yeats-Brown, soldier and author, is best known for *The Lives of a Bengal Lancer* (New York: Viking, 1930), which was made into an Academy Award–winning film. Yeats-Brown was a prolific author of eclectic works; he specialized in accounts and analyses of wartime India and Germany.

12. Sir Francis Younghusband, soldier, diplomat, and adventurer, is known for his extraordinary expeditions through Asia and India. Younghusband was the first European to cross the Gobi Desert on foot. A prolific author, devout Christian, and self-described mystic, Younghusband was active in the Royal Geographic Society, led expeditions to climb Mount Everest, and founded the World Congress of Faiths in 1936.

13. Syed Ross Masood was among EMF's closest friends. Born to Indian Muslims who could not care for him and raised in Britain by a white British family, Syed Ross Masood was a gregarious, intelligent, Oxford-educated lawyer who later in his life served as vice chancellor of the Muslim Anglo-Oriental University at Aligarh.

14. The Maharaja of Dewas (Dewas State Senior, Tukoji Rao III) was a longtime friend and onetime employer of EMF's. EMF met the maharaja during his first trip to India in 1912 and later accepted the maharaja's invitation to become his personal secretary, a post that EMF held briefly in 1921.

15. Lady Amina Bibi and Sir Akbar Hydari were friends of Syed Ross Masood's; EMF quickly accepted them as his own friends as well. Both were powerful political figures, instrumental in establishing Osmania University and fighting the purdah system for women.

16. EMF handwrote the following sentence, which appears earlier in the talk, at the conclusion of the transcript: "I add his name because his talk is going to form part of this series, but I am very sorry to have to report to you that he has recently died." It is not clear where EMF ultimately included the sentence in his broadcast.

NOT CHECKED WITH BROADCAST:
19th August 1942
1145-1200 GMT
Eastern Transmission
Red Network

As broadcast
13'30"

SOME BOOKS

- by -

E.M. Forster

You know how fond broadcasters are of employing the word "you". It's "you" this and "you" that, and it's often "you" ought to do this or that. ("You" generally seems to be in need of good advice.) When I switch on myself, and become a listener instead of a speaker, I get heaps of good advice, most of which is no use whatever to me. The ether, as it were, crackles with invisible uncles and aunts, who assume that they know what I'm like and how I shall react to their admonitions. They don't know, and can't know. And I don't know what you're like, you, my unknown listener.[1] As I write this script down in the country - and the country is charming now: the trees, the sunlight and the clouds have never seemed more indifferent to the conduct of man - or as I walk to deliver it through the battered London streets which have a wartime strangeness not wholly depressing -: or as I sit perched in the studio pretending to improvise it whereas it is actually all written out -: I keep speculating where you are sitting or standing, what are you like. And today I am going to draw a bow at a venture and tell you what you're like. I'm going to describe you.

I think, in the first place, that you're Indian. You mayn't be - I know that many who are not Indians tune in to this particular wavelength. Still that is always my assumption when talking: that the unknown listener is Indian. Secondly I assume that you are a man - although I believe and hope that I may have women-listeners also. And my third assumption is that you are about thirty years of age. You may be much older and have high dignities and influence. Or you may be a student or a schoolboy. But I think of you as about thirty. To what community in India do you belong? I don't know. My imagination doesn't reach to that. Where were you educated? In India. You may have visited Europe, and you are certainly curious about Western culture, or you wouldn't have switched on to this talk, but by education and in outlook you are oriental.

So that's the unknown listener in my mind. That's what I think of when I say "you". An Indian, aged about thirty, educated in India but interested in Western civilisation. And I propose today that "you" as above defined shall come with me to one or two London theatres. Yes - I know that this talk is entitled "Some Books", but no matter. It is going to be "Some Plays" instead. I have got tickets for Macbeth, which is being performed close to Piccadilly Circus, for The Merry Wives of Windsor, which is being given by the Old Vic company, though not in their own house, as it has been bombed; and for The Watch on the Rhine - a modern play at a theatre near the Strand.[2] We must be in our seats by about half-past six. The seats are rather expensive, owing to the high entertainment tax: they range from about 12/6 for a stall to 1/6 for the gallery. The music is mostly on gramophone records. We get out somewhere after 9.0, as the blackout starts and the west end streets are crammed with pedestrians queuing up for buses to go home or plunging into pubs for a drink, or into milk bars for a sandwich or a plate of soup. That's the sort of scene. After three years of war the London theatres are still carrying on - no: carrying on's not a good enough phrase: it suggests pluck to the exclusion of genius, and they are giving performances of genius.

The Macbeth is quite wonderful. You'll be thrilled by it. It's wonderful to look at - the grey-storm-laden landscape of the witches' heath, the grey courtyard of the hateful castle with interior staircases up and down which the murderers creep, their hands crimsoned with blood. Wonderful to listen to: the words of Shakespeare come as freshly at us, as if they were being spoken for the first time. Wonderful, above all, because its action grows up to the very end. You know as a rule how Macbeth rather falls to pieces after the murder of Duncan. Here all is knit together and worked up, one crime leads to another, the whole universe has to be criminal, until the tyrant is caught like a rat in his own castle and raves and rushes around and his head's cut off. John Gielgud acts Macbeth, and produces the play: it's a great triumph for him and triumph for wartime London. The Lady Macbeth doesn't please me equally: the actress[3] who took the part isn't suited to it, though she is a very good actress when properly cast, and even here she did well in the sleep-walking scene.

And now we're off to a very different Shakespeare: The Merry Wives of Windsor, at the New Theatre. Up goes the curtain and here is a very clever adaptation of the Elizabethan stage. A semi-circle of houses. To the left, the house of the jealous Ford, and the Garter Inn. To the right the house of Dr. Caius and the house of Page. And in the middle - a back stage, which can be used when needed to represent the interior of any of the houses or a peep into the country. Comedy and farce must be played quickly or we shall get bored, and this arrangement of the scenery allows the actors to rattle us through the Merry Wives at a good pace. Do you like Shakespeare when he does slap-stick? I like to see Falstaff carried away in a dirty linen basket, and catching an awful cold because he's been tipped into the Thames. He's pleasantly acted, and the two Merry Wives, particularly Mrs. Page, are excellent. Over the back stage is a date, 1598, the date of the original performance, and "yes, we're keeping on", I thought. "We're bearing up. Shakespeare's still with us, playing the fool". It's a cheerful performance - not a great one like the Macbeth, but The Merry Wives of Windsor doesn't set out to be great. It's just a provincial romp - touched here and there with gleams of woodland poetry.

The third play I'm taking you to is The Watch on the Rhine.[4] In the case of Shakespeare, I hadn't to describe the plots, because you know them, but The Watch on the Rhine requires a word of introduction. It's propaganda. As a rule, I fight shy of propaganda plays. I know that Hitler is trying to do us all in, and I don't want to pay money to hear actors and actresses tell me this: they might just as well listen to me. But sometimes propaganda has humanity and intelligence attached to it, and that is the case here. It takes place in the drawing room of a rich and temperamental elderly lady. Her son lives with her, they are decent civilised people, intelligent, kind, and permeated with the sense of security. Europe is starting its troubles - it's the late thirties - and they are putting up a couple of refugees - a Rumanian count and his wife. When the play starts, the old lady is in a great state of excitement. Her daughter, who has married a German, is about to pay her a visit. We soon gather that the Rumanian count is a bad lot. He has friends in the Nazi Embassy at Washington, and is in need of money. The family from Germany arrive. The daughter is charming, the quaint children soon win their grandmother's heart: and the German husband? Why has he come to America? He is reserved and cautious, and the Rumanian watches him narrowly, and sees in him a possible victim for blackmail. Sure enough, he turns out to be head of an anti-Nazi organisation, and he has come to America to collect funds to be used against Hitler inside Germany. The Rumanian duly blackmails him, there is a series of tense scenes into which the whole household is drawn, and finally the anti-Nazi German kills the villain behind the drawing room sofa. America has been drawn into Europe's troubles after all. The old lady turns out a trump, she approves of her son-in-law's action, although it is so uncivilised, she helps him to escape to Germany with his funds, and she prepares to face the music, and to explain to the police how it is that the corpse of her Rumanian guest should be found in her motor car - to which it has been dragged.

That's the barest outline of The Watch on the Rhine. It's an intricate play, very exciting and often very amusing. The acting is first rate - particularly Miss Athene Seyler[5] as the temperamental old lady. Although it's not a great work, it does clothe the problems of the day with flesh and blood. The Rumanian count for instance - he's not a hundred per cent villain or anything like it. He is just one of the weak needy pretentious people who are being used by the Nazis as their agents all over the world, and aren't even being properly paid by them. I think you'll be held by this play. I know you'll be charmed by the German grandchildren. You won't always follow what they say, but the characters on the stage can't always understand them either.

As we come out, though, as we jostle through the darkling streets of London, a city at war, let us turn into Macbeth at the Piccadilly Theatre again - for even if the performance there has ended by the clock it is going on in our minds. John Gielgud, as Macbeth, is alone on the stage, in the huge trap of his castle, and he is beginning his famous monologue "Is it a dagger that I see before me?".[6] How we've all tried to recite that at school - or have played the fool with it. It has become almost meaningless. But listen! Gielgud takes it quietly. He is thinking the words out, he is thinking the dagger out, he stretches out his hand, we almost see the instrument of death slipping itself into his grasp, and we know that it is of the same substance as the witches.

Well, it is time for us to part now. The entrance to the Piccadilly underground station glimmers like a glow worm, and I must descend into it and go home. And you - you must return by an even quicker route to India. We shall meet again next month, all being well.[7]

1. EMF added accent marks over "you're" and "you."

2. As Mary Lago explains, Macbeth, at the Piccadilly Theatre, was the famous production with John Gielgud and Gwen Ffrangcon-Davies. The Merry Wives of Windsor was at the New Theatre, while Watch on the Rhine, by Lillian Hellman, was at the Aldwych. See "E. M. Forster and the BBC," Yearbook of English Studies 20 (1990): 133, n. 5.

3. EMF is presumably referring to Gwen Ffrangcon-Davies.

4. Watch on the Rhine, by Lillian Hellman, debuted in New York on 1 April 1941 and was published by Random House the same year. Dashiell Hammett wrote the screenplay for the Warner Brothers film adaptation released in 1943.

5. Athene Seyler (1889–1990) specialized in classic and light comedy.

6. Macbeth, 2.1.33.

7. A bracket appears around this final paragraph. Next to the bracket is a large, hand-

written asterisk. This transcript then concludes with the statement, "*This is the cue. Please stick to it word for word." It is written in a hand other than EMF's; the direction apparently refers to a corresponding asterisk adjacent to the bracketed final paragraph.

CHECKED WITH BROADCAST
EASTERN TRANSMISSION
RED NETWORK
11th NOVEMBER, 1942
1130-1145 GMT
"SOME BOOKS"
STUDIO:

NEW BOOKS
by E. M. Forster

I have just had the pleasure of receiving a new book from India, published in Lahore. It is in the form of a novel, its title is "Scented Earth", and its author is Sir Firozkhan Noon,[1] who was High Commissioner here for some years, and who is now Defence Member of the Government of India.

Although in the form of fiction, it is really a document about conditions in a Punjab village, and I found a good deal of it most interesting. It occurred to me, as I finished it, how well supplied we are in England with books about Punjab country life. The Punjab, like Bengal, is a Province which has found favour with authors. There are the accomplished and widely read novels of Mulk Raj Anand, who takes the standpoint of the peasant and whose theme is social unrest and economic change. There are the fascinating rival studies of Sir Malcolm Darling, who writes as a Civil Servant, and now we have a third type of commentator, a great landowner, Sir Firozkhan Noon. As I have implied, "Scented Earth" is not really a novel, and should not be criticised as if it were. The author uses his characters, the headman, the money-lender, etc. - as types to illustrate local conditions and the construction of the village polity. The chief event is the arrival of the Settlement Officer with his wife and daughter and the widespread upheaval it causes. I enjoyed this. I liked too the shrewdness and bluntness of Sir Firozkhan Noon's personal comments, and there are some entertaining anecdotes. One for instance about a God who is sitting on the summit of the Himalayas and sees a Scotsman pass before him. "What do you want?" he asks. The Scotsman answers: "Money". "Very well", says the God, "go on: you shall have plenty of money in India". Then an Englishman passes. "What do you want?" he asks. The Englishman says: "Power". "Very well, go on, you shall have plenty of power in India". Then an Indian follows. "What do you want?" "Religion". "Very well - go on, you shall have plenty of religion in India".[2] This anecdote - I scarcely know why - gave me a queer sense of the vastness of your country and of her destiny. India may in the end give neither the Scotch, nor the English nor the Indians what they want, but she may have some gift of a value passing conception for the world, I felt. However, this leads us rather far from "Scented Earth", and I must pass on to mention another work by an Indian writer.

This is "Constituent Assembly for India" by Professor N. Gangulee, formerly at the University of Calcutta, and who is at present living over here.[3] It is a work of politics and statesmancraft, and deals with matters outside my competence, but I want just to allude to it. It gives an account of the formation and the functioning of constituent assemblies in England, Europe and the U.S.A. from the 17th Century, right down to the Assembly of the Spanish Republic in 1931. Professor Gangulee then turns to India, criticises the Government of India Act of 1935,[4] discusses the Indian demand for a constituent assembly, and makes some practical suggestions as to how such an assembly could be summoned. He writes with learning and restraint, but his convictions shine out clearly and are expressed in the book's sub-title, "Freedom to achieve Freedom".

A book which has attracted a good deal of interest over here lately is "The Managerial Revolution" by James Burnham.[5] No one likes it, and if you can get hold of it and read it you won't like it either, for it is certain to contradict your hopes for the future, whatever those hopes may be. It is about what is going to happen to the world immediately after the war. Mr. Burnham's idea is that a new type of society is evolving, and is indeed already in existence for those who have eyes to see. It won't be capitalism - he agrees with the Socialists that the age of Capitalism is over. But it won't be Socialism either; Socialism will never come into being. It is what he calls 'Managerialism'; the control of society by Managers. That's why he entitles his book "The Managerial Revolution". He argues that in any society power is possessed by those who control the instruments of production, and the distribution of the products. Who possess that power today? Not the financiers and shareholders - it has passed from their hands. Not the workers as is sometimes alleged - they haven't and can't have the necessary technical knowledge, and are obliged to delegate it. Neither of these classes;-but the Managers, who are rapidly annexing the machinery of the State, and creating ideologies favourable to themselves. He traces the growth of the process in Russia and in Germany - these chapters are particularly provocative - and also in America, where it takes the milder form of the New Deal. He goes on to prophesy - and this is what is so unwelcome and so depressing - that after the war, whoever wins it, we shall have three large managerial areas - the European, the Far Eastern, and the American, and that between these three areas we must expect further and even greater wars. I don't like this. You won't like it. And Mr. Burnham doesn't like it himself. But he writes as an enquirer after the truth, and that is the direction in which he concludes the truth is to be found. It is no good getting angry with his conclusions, as some critics over here have done. What you have to do is to find an argument which proves[6] them wrong. He writes dispassionately and bleakly, and I had the feeling when reading him that he was very sincere. He is an American,[7] he was at one time connected with Trotsky, though he writes now as an independent.

My own reaction to such a book is that it may be right, it may be wrong, but it doesn't deal with the subjects which lie closest to my own heart. Those subjects happen to be personal relationships and the human activity which is vaguely known as 'art'. Whether art is going to have any future I don't know; the prospects aren't too favourable, and the people who rise into eminence and control our destinies seem quite devoid of the aesthetic sense, if one may judge from their public pronouncements. But that's where my own feelings lie - towards art - and that's why I have found pleasure in a volume of reminiscences by Siegfried Sassoon called "The Weald of Youth".[8] It is one of several volumes. Mr. Sassoon - eminent in the last war as a poet - has lately been recalling his own boyhood and early manhood: and presenting them with the skill of an artist. One might say 'the artist in water colour', for he writes gently, and does not seek broad or dramatic effects. He believes in taste, and he possesses taste and exercises it. "The Weald of Youth" is not a great creative autobiography, nor does it set out to be one. It is rather a tender evocation of the years when he began to write, and to meet other writers, writers of the generation and the calibre of Edmund Gosse and Charles Doughty,[9] and it contains some charming sporting episodes - of the type he has already given us in "The Diary of a Fox Hunting Man".[10]

It's amusing to be mentioning "The Weald of Youth" and "The Managerial Revolution" in the same broadcast. If you get these two books and place them side by side on your library shelf, I do believe they will blow each other to pieces. Two more dissimilar examples of printed activity cannot be imagined. Yet both of them are written by men and are about men. I think again of that God in Sir Firozkhan Noon's anecdote who sits on the Himalayas and says to one man 'go on, you shall have plenty of money', and to another 'go on, you shall have plenty of power', and to a third 'go on, you shall have plenty of religion', and to a fourth 'go on, you shall have plenty of beauty'. Numerous and incompatible are the desires of men.

[11]"I will end with beauty. I want to mention, not a book, but a pleasant little entertainment of Indian Dancing which was given in London last month. It was organised by Mr. Rafiq Anwar, who danced, or rather mimed, the withdrawal from earthly pleasures of the Buddha, and who also performed traditional dances with other members of the company.[12] There was some excellent music. I particularly enjoyed the solos upon the sarode by Dr. Bhupin Mukerjee, and also his playing on the drum. The performance ran for a week, and the hall was well filled. Indian dancing and music aren't really understood by our general public, and it is not likely that they ever will be, for their technique and their tradition are so remote from their Western equivalents. But they are no longer dismissed as 'something odd'. I remember so well, years back, meeting on a boat an Englishman who was very musical and had been in India for years, and he assured me that there was no Indian music. "Why they have no solo instrument" he said. I timidly mentioned the Vina. But my compatriot shook his head, said he had[13] never heard of the thing, and continued to play upon the piano, which he did quite well. I don't think that could happen today. Several good artists have come to England and educated us, and there was certainly an appreciative audience for Mr. Rafiq Anwar's show.[14]

1. EMF refers to the title of Noon's novel, *Scented Dust*, incorrectly throughout this talk. Originally from Pakistan and active in the Pakistan Movement, Noon served as high commissioner of India to the United Kingdom between 1936 and 1941.

2. Malik Firozkahn Noon, *Scented Dust* (Lahore: R. S. M. Gulab Singh, 1942), 342. EMF paraphrases the quotation, which is as follows: "'Who are you, my man?' enquired the god. 'I am a Scotch missionary, Sir.' 'What do you want?' 'I want money, Sir.' 'Money you shall have. Pass on.' Later on this god saw another man, and put the same questions to him. The man replied that he was an Englishman and that he wanted power. 'Power you shall have. Pass along.' Then this god noticed another human creature sneaking behind him. 'Who are you?' enquired the deity. 'I am an Indian, Sir.' 'What do you want?' 'I want religion, Sir.' 'Religion you shall have in plenty, my man. Pass along.'"

3. Nagendranath Gangulee, *Constituent Assembly for India* (London: Allen and Unwin, 1942).

4. The act gave more autonomy to Indian governing bodies and redefined the role of the princely states in Indian governance.

5. James Burnham, *The Managerial Revolution, Or What Is Happening in the World Now* (London: Putnam, 1941).

6. <their irony>

7. <and>

8. Siegfried Sassoon, *The Weald of Youth* (London: Faber and Faber, 1940).

9. Charles Montagu Doughty (1843–1926), English poet and author of travel books, including *Travels in Arabia Deserta* (Cambridge: Cambridge University Press, 1888), resurrected with the help of EMF's friend T. E. Lawrence in the 1920s.

10. Siegfried Sassoon, *The Memoirs of George Sherston: Memoirs of a Fox-Hunting Man, Memoirs of an Infantry Official, Sherston's Progress* (London: Faber and Faber, 1937).

11. In the margin next to this paragraph, EMF wrote: "omit."

12. Of this performance, EMF wrote to George Orwell in October 1942: "not much of a show I am sorry to say," adding, "I don't see why the B.B.C. shouldn't refund the money [for the show] if they would like to, but do not put yourself to trouble over this" (n.d., BBC WAC).

13. <heard>

14. "/End." appears at the bottom right corner of this page.

NOT CHECKED WITH BROADCAST
9th December, 1942
EASTERN TRANSMISSION
RED NETWORK:
1130-1145 GMT:
Studio: O.S.1.

SOME BOOKS

by

E. M. FORSTER

Does poetry play any part in your life? In my life it doesn't. This is odd, since I enjoy the stuff when I read it, or listen to it being read, and I should mention in any event that it is one of the highest achievements of the human spirit. Yet I don't seem to think of it between times, in the way I think of music. It's only present on special occasions, and when a thing is only present on special occasions it can't be said to play much part in one's life can it? What's your own experience? Perhaps it's different, for I remember in the old days how easily some of my Indian friends used to slip into verse. It seemed nearer to the surface with them than it is in the West.

We are busy working and planning, or resting from work and amusing ourselves. We feel, 'I'm too busy now to think about poetry - or too tired. There's the book on the shelf, anyhow, it'll keep. When I'm more in the mood, I'll take it down'. And we do take it down now and then, and enjoy its marvels, and then we put it back again. We don't think of it between times - as the Elizabethans did, and as the Orientals possibly do.

These ideas occur to me because I've just been reading a poet who did think of poetry between times. He never stopped thinking of it, he lived it as well as wrote it, and he was indignant with people who wouldn't live it too. He's the Irishman, W. B. Yeats. Yeats died not four years ago, he lived through stirring times in his own country and elsewhere, he didn't shrink into retirement and often entered into affairs - for example he

212

became Senator in the Irish Parliament - but he never stopped thinking of poetry or denouncing those who wouldn't or couldn't. Though an extremely complicated character, he is in this respect simple. We know where we are with him just here.

I've been reading Yeats because I've been led to do so by an admirable study on him which has just come out. "The Development of William Butler Yeats" is the name of the book, and the author is an Indian, V. K. Narayana Menon.[1] I referred to Mr. Narayana Menon in my talk last month; I was speaking of Indian music at an entertainment here, and Mr. Menon was as a matter of fact one of the musicians; he was playing the vina.[2] He is also a literary scholar of distinction, and this study of Yeats is first class: well written, well informed and cool in its judgements. Now you have to be cool over Yeats. He was a great poet, he lived poetry, but there was an element of bunkum in him. At various periods of his life he believed or half believed in astrology, Rosicrucianism, magic, incantation, séances, fairies, and a private invention of his own called the Great Wheel. He also sought wisdom in the East, invited an Oriental seer to Dublin, and declared that the sculptures of Elephanta contain a profound answer to the riddle of the universe. Perhaps they do, but Yeats went on to say that an equally profound answer is to be found in the markings on a sea-shell which a gypsy carries about for good luck in his pocket. The shell and the marvels of Elephanta were bracketed by him as equally important. He had no discrimination, and more enthusiasm than knowledge, and though he could say very sharp things about his opponents, he had no critical sense. Mr. Menon realises this and exposes the bunkum - not unkindly but firmly. Though he is certain that Yeats is a great poet, he knows he was a bit of a poseur, and he dares - in language more scholarly than mine - to say so. I like this about the book. And I like still more his realisation that a little bunkum was necessary to Yeats, that it upheld his genius, that the arbitrary contraption of the Great Wheel, for example, in which he only half believed, did inspire some of his finest work. Mr. Menon probes deep here into the complexities of human nature. The simple view is that creation can only proceed from sincerity. But the facts don't always bear this out. The insincere, the half sincere, may on occasion contribute. And they contributed in the curious case of Yeats.

Let me, with Mr. Menon's help, try to illustrate this. I'll read out a short poem of Yeats called "The Second Coming". It is a grim violent poem, and has nothing of the Celtic Twilight about it. Written back in the twenties, it contains a prophecy of the evils which Nazism and Fascism have since brought to Europe. In itself, it's sincere. It is a creation. But when I've read it I'll go back and examine the mental state which produced it, and in that we shan't find the same sincerity. "The Second Coming" - the First

Coming was that of Christ - whose cradle at Bethlehem is referred to at the close. It opens with the idea that civilisation is getting out of hand, like an escaping falcon.

Turning and turning in the widening gyre
The falcon cannot hear the falconer;
Things fall apart; the centre cannot hold;
Mere anarchy is loosed upon the world,
The blood dimmed tide is loosed, and everywhere
The ceremony of innocence is drowned;
The best lack all conviction, while the worst
Are full of passionate intensity.[3]

Isn't that an imaginative picture of the world flying to pieces under the centrifugal forces of evil - the world which failed to solidify after the 1914 war! And a more sinister image follows: -

Surely some revelation is at hand:
Surely the Second Coming is at hand.
The Second Coming! Hardly are those words out
When a vast image out of <u>Spiritus Mundi</u>
Troubles my sight: somewhere in sands of the desert
A shape with lion-body and head of a man.
A gaze blank and pitiless as the sun,
Is moving its slow thighs, while all about it
Reel shadows of the indignant desert birds.
The darkness drops again: but now I know
That twenty centuries of[4] stony sleep
Were vexed to nightmare by a rocking cradle,
And what rough beast, its hour come round at last,
Slouches toward Bethlehem to be born?[5]

The epoch of Christianity and the rocking cradle is to be succeeded by the epoch of mercilessness and roughness, slouching in their turn towards their incarnation. That is the conception, and it's a fine one. But did you notice, as I read, the words 'Spiritus Mundi'?

a vast image out of Spiritus Mundi
Troubles my sight;

'Spiritus Mundi' is an example of what I have ventured to call Yeats' bunkum. It alludes to a theory of the universe and of history which he worked out elsewhere in detail, the theory or rather the doctrine of the Great Wheel. This doctrine, he asserted, he discovered in a book which he never produced, and it was confirmed by a medium. It entailed 28 cycles, each for one day of the lunar month and people took their characteristics from the cycle in which they were born. It is full of hocus-pocus and arbitrary statements - yet it inspired his poetry, and unless we know of its existence many of his later poems are unintelligible. The one that I have quoted, "The Second Coming", stands by its own imaginative force, but the creature it pictures, the shape with the lion's body slouching towards Bethlehem to be born, comes out of the Great Wheel.

I hope that what I have said may lead you to re-read Yeats and to read what Mr. Menon says about him. Yeats is many sided, and I haven't the time to speak of the Celtic Yeats, or of Yeats the dramatist who founded the Abbey Theatre, or of Yeats the aristocrat, who admired kings and peasants and despised the middle classes, or of Yeats the Irish Nationalist who could say such bitter things about Irish Nationalism, and I haven't spoken of the development of Yeats which is Mr. Menon's main theme. I wanted just to make the point that here's the man who - unlike the rest of us - lived continuously in poetry, a man whose make-up was so strange that a certain amount of mystification and faking seemed to help the action of his genius. Yeats is worth thinking about as well as well worth reading. He will enlarge your ideas about the human mind.

I turn from him to another poet who is as a matter of fact much more sympathetic to me: T. S. Eliot. I don't always agree with Mr. Eliot as a critic, nor do I share his Christian mysticism or his belief in the value of suffering, but when I read him I feel that here is someone authentic, someone who rings true through and through. He has increased in stature and authority since he wrote the "Waste Land". He is master of his medium now he knows what he wants to say, and is only difficult because what he communicates is difficult. His latest poem - it only came out last week - is called "Little Gidding". It is the conclusion of a series of four, all named after places - Burnt Norton, East Coker, and The Dry Salvages were the others. Little Gidding is a village in Eastern England where, in the reign of King Charles 1st, a group of religious enthusiasts met and built a chapel. I have been there myself. It is a remote, abandoned place, a husk, an empty shell, and I remember experiencing there, prosaically, the emotions which Mr. Eliot touches into fire.

> You are not here to verify,
> Instruct yourself, or inform curiosity
> Or carry report. You are here to kneel
> Where prayer has been valid. And prayer is more
> Than an order of words, the conscious occupation
> Of the praying mind, or the sound of the voice praying.
> And what the dead had no speech for, when living,
> They can tell you, being dead: the communication
> Of the dead is tongued with fire beyond the language of
> the living.[6]

The reference 'tongued with fire' is to the main motive of the poem; to the Christian mystery of Pentecost when the tongues of fire descended on the Twelve Apostles. And when we have accepted this mystery and realised that the burning of pain and the burning of love are inseparable, then we shall have gained a condition of complete simplicity and all will be well.

And all shall be well and
All manner of things shall be well
When the tongues of flame are in-folded
Into the crowned knot of fire
And the fire and the rose are one.[7]

This mystery is embodied by Eliot at Little Gidding, the forgotten village where emotion was once aflame, and

While the light fails
On a writer's afternoon, in a secluded chapel
History is now and England.[8]

Now here is a voice more authentic than Yeats' and his slouching monster: we may not agree with the voice but we can trust it, it is speaking what it knows to be true. I hope that some day this wonderful poem will come your way. It seems to me the crown of Mr. Eliot's achievement.

Now here are the names of those books again:-

THE DEVELOPMENT OF WILLIAM BUTLER YEATS by V. K. Narayana Menon

LITTLE GIDDING by T.S. Eliot and Yeats own poems published by the Oxford press.

1. V. K. Narayana Menon, *The Development of William Butler Yeats* (Edinburgh: Oliver and Boyd, 1942).

2. See EMF's broadcast dated 11 November 1942.

3. William Butler Yeats, "The Second Coming," lines 1–8, in *The Poems of William Butler Yeats: A New Edition*, ed. Richard J. Finneran (London: Macmillan, 1924).

4.

5. Yeats, "The Second Coming," lines 9–22.

6. T. S. Eliot, *Little Gidding* (London: Faber and Faber, 1942), 8.

7. Ibid., 16.

8. Ibid., 15.

NOT CHECKED WITH BROADCAST
EASTERN SERVICE
RED NETWORK
6th JANUARY, 1943
1130-1145 GMT
"SOME BOOKS"
Studio: Mixer 2

"NEW YEAR'S GREETING"

by

E. M. Forster

A Happy New Year! My terms of reference are books, and generally speaking culture, and in that reference I wish you happiness. The world of 1942 was convulsed with[1] military operations,[2] the convulsions will continue into 1943, bringing death and sorrow,[3] so the happiness which books and culture can bring may appear in such times as a[4] trivial blessing, hardly worth mentioning. Yet I mention it. I believe that "books" represent something much deeper than the mere word "books". They are not only a solace, not only a source of information and a means of interpretation; they are one of the proofs that the human spirit is profound and is anchored to something far beneath those surface storms that ruin our physical lives. That something I call Art, and that is why I send you these New Year Greetings from the portico of the National Gallery, Trafalgar Square, London. I don't mean that I am actually standing in the portico. I am not standing anywhere. I am sitting in a studio, reading from a prepared script, and a BBC studio, though decently upholstered, does not inspire to thoughts of art. The National Gallery does, so[5] imagine me as standing in the portico. On my left as I look out is one of the most distinguished of our London churches, St. Martin-in-the-Fields, impressive to look at and memorable for its spirited enterprise and for its championship of the poor. Straight ahead beyond Trafalgar Square rise the towers of Westminster, representing democracy. They do not represent it properly, democracy has not yet found adequate outward expression anywhere. But they represent a move in the right direction, and believing as I do that without freedom art is sterile, I am thankful to see them. Meanwhile, the pigeons are whirling about, and if I add that the January sun is shining you are in no position to contradict me. And behind me is the Gallery itself. Let us go into it.

The first thing you will notice, if the hour is midday, is a smell of coffee.[6] Yes, coffee in the National Gallery![7] provided for the people who come in their hundreds to the lunch-hour concerts.[8] They can get excellent coffee and sandwiches cheaply, and then listen to first-class music for 1/-s. This has been going on five days a week since the beginning of the war, and will continue through 1943, all being well. That's part of my Happy New Year to you; the thought that in the heart of a war and close to destruction, great music is being upheld: for instance, all the Beethoven Quartets have been performed and all the chamber music of Brahms, and the songs of Schumann, and modern stuff, like Benjamin Britten's settings of the sonnets of Michael Angelo.[9] The enterprise is due to two individuals; to the pianist, Dame Myra Hess, who organised the concerts and often performs at them; and to the director of the National Gallery, Sir Kenneth Clark, who found them a home in the empty rooms. When the war threatened, the pictures were taken down and stored in safety, but Sir Kenneth Clark has not allowed the gallery to be wasted; he believed that the public ought to get pleasure out of public buildings, that they ought to be allowed to[10] drink coffee in them and even to drop crumbs on the floor. As a rule, Government officials have a horror of crumbs - a horror which almost demands the attention of the psychoanalyst - [11]they dread the public, and would like to exclude it, if they dared. Kenneth Clark[12] wants the public to feel at home, and,[13] he has got them happily listening to music for over three years. Note by the way that much of the music is German: Beethoven, Brahms, Bach. And note here a difference between this war and the last; in the last war there was a tendency to bar German music; in this war we all realise that this would be foolish, especially since the Nazis themselves are not and don't want to be the inheritors of their own national culture. They ban some German music. They won't listen to Mendelssohn or Bloch because those composers are Jewish, they won't read the poet Heinrich Heine for the same reason, nor Goethe because he is cosmopolitan. They ban German culture. We don't.

Now as we go up to the concert we shall encounter on a landing to the left another treasure, and that is a single picture, a solitary masterpiece chosen from the National Gallery collection (which is[14] concealed somewhere or other until the end of the war). This picture rises up like a flower from the earth, like a pledge of hidden richness and beauty. It changes every few weeks: at present the picture on view is Andrea del Sarto's portrait of himself, and previously there have been works by Rembrandt, Turner, and so on. I believe that this exhibition of a single masterpiece has had a good effect on the public. It is so much easier for an ordinary man to enjoy a work of art when it is alone, and he can concentrate on it. In a gallery he gets mesmerised - at least I do - and drifts weakly about from frame to frame, without really seeing what's inside the frames. For instance, Tintoretto's St. George and the Dragon,[15] though I had often seen it before, has become definite to me, and even while I talk in this studio I can visualise the lovely sumptuous princess, crumpling forward out of the canvas, and behind her the spectral combat, and behind that again the high romantic castle. If I could thank the war for anything, it would be for these extra visions of beauty, these sharpenings of perception which, but for the war would not have been granted. And this too comes into my New Year's Greeting. Tintoretto's St. George and the Dragon has been withdrawn now, and we shall not see it again till the peace. When that happy day comes, when it rises again with its fellow pictures, when the vaults of all the tortured galleries of Europe give up what is buried in them - what a renaissance, what a resurrection that will be! During the last three years, nothing has been so much impaired as visual beauty. Music and books remain; it is the eye of man that has been starved. And the exhibition by the National Gallery of a single picture from its store both reminds us of our loss and teaches us how to repair it.

This isn't the only exhibition in the Gallery. There are war pictures, up to the right, and in another part of the building there is a show of French pictures of the 19th century. These pictures are[16] lent by private owners. It is a charming show and a timely one, for it comes at a moment when some people here have been tempted to forget the great cultural message of France - France who has been the light of Europe, and who will be that light again. There are canvases by Degas and Monet, Van Gogh and Cezanne, Sisley, Pissarro.[17] They are mostly landscapes, and if I had to describe them in a single phrase I should say that they desired to please, and to extend the boundaries of pleasure. While full of technical experiments, they try to convey joy. In a foreword to the catalogue,[18] it is suggested that they may help to counteract the provincialism into which we in England are falling owing to our wartime isolation. The remark is just. We are getting provincial here, and so I hasten to add are you in India. People are becoming provincial all over the world - they can't help it, it is part of the trend of events. But let us keep an eye on ourselves, and let us correct the trend as soon as we have the power to do so. In England, these French pictures are a little help, for they recall us to another tradition of art.

As I walked round the shops I thought of a painter - an Englishman - who practised that tradition and who died during 1942, the painter W. R. Sickert. Sickert, according to the best critics, was the greatest English painter of his generation. I don't know how widely his fame extends or how well you know his name. If you are an artist yourself you will certainly know it, for he is[19] a painter's painter.[20] He studied in France and was in close touch with his French impressionist colleagues, but some of his subjects are English - for instance his famous interiors of Music Halls; Music Halls of the old type, lavish and not too patrolled. I remember particularly one of the interior of the Old Bedford, a splendid purple oblong. In mentioning him, and painting generally, I'm really talking upon a subject for which I have poor qualifications. I understand but[21] little about the visual arts, and I couldn't make a sketch of the simplest object - not to save my life. But particularly since the war, I have realised how wonderful painting and sculpture and architecture are, and how limited must be the civilisation that does not practise them, so I thought you would pardon me for introducing these references into what is technically a book talk; references to the isolated masterpieces which the National Gallery exhibits; to the show of 19th century French pictures there; and to the English painter Sickert who died during the past year.

His death reminds me of a general duty, the recording of obituaries. I have looked up the names of writers who have died in 1942 and I am glad to say I have very little to report. The most important writer who has died is an exiled Austrian, Stefan Zweig, and you may remember that I devoted a talk to his work at the time.[22] If you didn't happen to be listening then, do make a note of his name, Stefan Zweig, and do try to get hold of his book on the 16th century humanist, Erasmus, for it is his best work. Zweig himself was a humanist. He belonged to the cosmopolitan European civilisation which is at present broken, he hated fanaticism, he believed in reason, in tolerance and in the production of beauty. Being very fair-minded, he saw that humanism has its[23] dangers; the humanist[24] shirks responsibility, dislikes making decisions, and is sometimes a coward. He notes this in the case of Erasmus, and I think he felt difficulties himself, that the world of 1942 became too much for him, and perhaps that was why, to the grief of his many friends, he committed suicide[25] over in Brazil. Zweig is a great loss. Not only was he an excellent historian and a readable novelist, but he stated very clearly and fairly a problem which confronts us all. Do we, in these terrible times, want to be humanists or fanatics? I have no doubt as to my own wish, I would rather be a humanist with all his faults, than a fanatic with all his virtues[26] and in that spirit I wish you, I know not how acceptably, a Happy New Year.

1. <vast>
2. <by air, sea and land>
3. <and>
4. <very>
5. <please>
6. <Coffee?>
7. <It is>

8. These lunchtime concerts were later taken up by St. Martin-in-the-Fields church and continue there—free and open to the public—today. The concerts also yielded an important personal result for EMF: his first meeting with Elizabeth Poston, the musician who came to occupy his childhood home, Rooksnest. EMF met Poston while she was performing in one of Hess's concerts. (Incidentally, Poston worked for the BBC at the time and was urged by the network not to perform publicly—a warning she ignored.) After EMF's meeting with Poston, he happily returned to Rooksnest and enjoyed many subsequent visits there at her invitation.

9. Britten completed *The Michelangelo Sonnets*, honoring Michelangelo's seven metaphysical love sonnets, in 1940 while he was residing in the United States.

10. <eat sandwiches>
11. <and generally speaking>
12. <has a different reaction; he>
13. <with the assistance of Myra Hess and her colleagues,>
14. <stored away in safety>

15. Tintoretto (born Jacopo Robusti) completed *St. George and the Dragon* between 1555 and 1558.

16. <not national property. They are>

17. The parenthetical note (? Picasso) is typed here, though presumably this note served as a prompt for further inquiry rather than as text to be read in the final broadcast.

18. <of the French Pictures>
19. <above all>

20. EMF, however, did not enjoy Sickert, as a diary entry of 6 June 1950 reveals: "Disliked painters: Sickert, Matthew Smitte, Starkey Spencer" (Diary of 1950, King's College, Cambridge, Archive).

21. <very>
22. See EMF's broadcast dated 4 March 1942.
23. <defects>
24. <often>
25. <at Rio de Janeiro>
26. <of will power and courage,>

EASTERN SERVICE
RED NETWORK
WEDNESDAY, 3rd FEBRUARY, 1943
1130-1145 GMT
STUDIO: Mixer 2

SOME BOOKS

by

E. M. FORSTER.

What's wrong with the world? Three out of four books I'm mentioning try to answer this question. Something is wrong with a war every twenty-five years, national and communal and racial hatred, frightened individuals, people starving in one place while food is being destroyed in another.[1] If we listen to the past we can, as it were, hear that same ugly tune of human failure played quietly. Today it is being played fortissimo, and it is often difficult to listen to anything else. So it is natural that three out of these four books should deal with the question[2].

You've probably noticed in books - and in yourself - two tendencies. Sometimes when you ask yourself what's wrong with the world, you answer 'It wants reorganising economically. When a basic standard of physical comfort has been achieved, the rest will follow'. And this is the[3] attitude of Mr. Mulk Raj Anand in his "Letters on India",[4] one of the books on my list. At other times you'll answer, 'No it wants a change of heart. When we[5] become different - and better - as individuals, then the rest will follow[']. That is the[6] attitude of Mr. Gerald Heard, a practising mystic, and a pacifist, in his new book "Man the Master".[7] And a change of heart is also demanded by an orthodox Christian writer, Mr. C. S. Lewis, in his "Screwtape Letters".[8] Mr. Heard and Mr. Lewis have very little in common. But they both take hold of the psychological end of the stick, as opposed to Mr. Anand who takes hold of the economic end. Which end do you take hold of yourself?

I will take Mr. C. S. Lewis first. He is an Oxford don, and a layman of the Church of England, and he writes to justify the Christian point of view, and to give the Christian interpretation of what's wrong with the world. Sin is what's wrong, wars and starvation being only a consequence, and although the Creator of mankind is good and omnipotent, men sin because he chose to give them free will, and because they choose to make a wrong use of that will. Mr. Lewis attacks these mysteries in an interesting book called "The Problem of Pain"[9] which I've also been reading, but I won't talk about it here. I will confine myself to a much livelier work, "The Screwtape Letters".[10] But, besides being a theologian, Mr. Lewis is as clever as they make 'em, if I may use the expression. He is witty and ingenious, and sometimes recalls the late G. K. Chesterton, though he hasn't Chesterton's robustness. Here is a book of his "The Screwtape Letters" which purport to be written by a devil called Screwtape who has rather a good position in an underground office, and writes weekly to his nephew Wormwood. Wormwood is on earth, in charge of a mortal, and being young and inexperienced is constantly making mistakes, and driving his patient toward righteousness instead of the reverse direction. Screwtape advises him on each occasion, for instance what to do when the patient quarrels with his mother or falls in love or is converted to a religion.[11] Unfortunately the patient dies in an air raid, when he behaves heroically, and is saved. Wormwood loses his prey and returns to Hell where his affectionate uncle eats him up.

[12]A couple of sentences which [13]will give you the taste of the book. Screwtape is writing about the Future,[14] and says, it is of all things the least like eternity:

"Hence the encouragement we have given to all those
"schemes of thought such as Creative Evolution, Scientific
"Humanism, or Communism which fix men's affections on the
"Future. Hence nearly all vices are rooted in the future.
"Gratitude looks to the past and love to the present: fear,
"avarice, lust, and ambition to the Future".[15]

I should have thought that Hope looked to the Future too, and that it was a virtue. However I am not here to criticise either Mr. Lewis or Screwtape, but to indicate the provocative little book which they have collaborated to produce. Mr. Lewis does not believe in progress or that the world will be put right by humanism or by planning. It is wrong because men have sinned, and they have sinned because God has left them free to choose between good and evil, and, tempted by the devil, they have chosen evil. The world, indeed, is not a place to put right. It is a place to do right in.

Compare with this view the view of Mr. Gerald Heard. Mr. Heard also begins with the unseen. Like Mr. Lewis he believes that the world has gone wrong for psychological reasons. But there the resemblance between them ends, for he believes that the miseries with which we are all surrounded - the war, the starvation, the mutual hatred - can be averted if we like, and that now is the moment. He calls his book "Man the Master". Man can be master if he will. But how? I can only indicate briefly. He holds on the evidence of anthropology, that men were once in touch with each other instinctively like a herd of animals, that[16] they have lost touch, through the development of individuality, and that[17] they must re-establish it or perish. At this point he has recourse to Indian thought - he has studied the Upanishads - and to the conception of an enlightened clan of people, seers, Brahmins, who will reintegrate mankind and, having no power of themselves, will be obeyed by[18] rulers. He thinks that the seer-type is being produced today and that a fourfold society (as in Ancient India) can be constituted under it.

I always feel when reading Mr. Heard's books - and I think I've read them all - that his analysis of our troubles is convincing, but that his remedies are not. I believe with him that there is this 'seer' type with enhanced spiritual powers, but I don't believe that Hitler, or indeed a Cabinet Minister, or indeed a Civil servant, would take the least notice of anything a seer said. They haven't in the past.[19] "Man the Master" will, however, give you plenty to think about if you tackle it. It faces up to our troubles and it takes hold of what I have called the psychological end of the stick.

Now for the materialistic[20] end of the stick. Mr. Mulk Raj Anand's little book, "Letters on India", provides an example of this. Mr. Anand lives over here. He is an important writer who, through his novels, has kept us in touch with contemporary tendencies out your way. "Letters of India" are really a series of articles, thrown into the form of letters to an imaginary British Working Man. They discuss Indian problems, Indian land tenure for instance from the Congress standpoint, and they rest on the assumption that Indian problems, like all problems, are fundamentally economic. He knows that psychology comes in of course. But his general attitude is "Make people comfortable and then they'll be[21] good". Whereas Mr. Heard's attitude is "Make people good and then they'll be[22] comfortable". And Mr. Lewis's is "Make people good and it doesn't much matter whether they're comfortable or not".[23]

By way of contrast I will end with a book of another type: the entertaining letters of Sir Henry Ponsonby, who was Private Secretary to Queen Victoria from the year 1870.[24] This takes us into a world which is today almost inconceivable, and seemingly trivial, though it did not so seem to itself. Sir Henry Ponsonby was a court official who had a difficult job, namely the Queen herself, and he managed her so far as she was manageable, with great tact and skill. He admired her fine qualities, her industry, her integrity, but he was well aware of her obstinacy and touchiness and narrow-mindedness and he lets himself go about them when writing to his wife. Most of these letters are to his wife - who was suspected of being "clever", highbrow, as it is now called, and so was not often invited to court. Here is a good deal of new information, personal and political, and some brilliant character-sketches and descriptions of scenes. For instance, an extraordinary account of Balmoral, where Sir Henry was condemned to spend much of his time; its isolation, its chilliness - for Queen Victoria disapproved of fires; and the habit that prevailed there of communicating by letter rather than by word of mouth. The habit was set by the Queen, who did not like seeing people[25] unless she was sure they were going to agree with her, so wrote notes even to her own children. On one occasion Sir Henry Ponsonby left the Castle at too early an hour, and although his destination was church, he was reprimanded afterwards in a note. The members of the Royal household wrote to each other too, and the idea of all those bits of paper, mostly about nothing, being carried up and down the gloomy passages of Balmoral gives one a curious feeling.

The letters are edited and presented by Sir Henry's son, Lord Ponsonby. Lord Ponsonby is a distinguished man of letters and a free-lance, whose temperament has carried him away from official circles. Consequently he presents his subject vividly and freshly. His judgment on his father's work is a balanced one, nor does he idealise the Queen. The Queen doesn't indeed come out very attractively, but you must remember that the period[26] which Sir Henry's secretaryship covered, was very difficult for her. She began her reign a gay and popular princess, and she ended it as a revered Empress, mellowed by age and prosperity. But there was an intermediate period, when she was an unhappy widow, who dreaded personal relationships and public functions, and it was during this period that she was Sir Henry Ponsonby's "job".[27]

It was a strange job and a strange age - though I suppose a philosophic observer, or an economic expert for that matter, can see latent in it the evils which have risen to the surface and occupy Mr. Heard and Mr. Lewis and Mr. Anand today. Even in these days the evil melody of war is already being played - but softly, a sinister undertone. We today are much more conscious than the rulers and the people of the Victorian era. We know much better what the human race is up against. And it may be that our successors, fifty years hence, will know much better than we do, and will consequently discover solutions.

1. <Such evils have always occurred, but during the present century they occur much more dramatically, and they attract the attention of any serious writer.>
2. <and that two of them should offer a remedy>

3. <tendency>

4. Mulk Raj Anand, *Letters on India* (London: G. Routledge, 1942).

5. <are becoming>

6. <tendency>

7. Gerald Heard, *Man the Master* (New York: Harper, 1941).

8. C(live) S(taples) Lewis, *The Screwtape Letters* (London: G. Bles, 1942).

9. Lewis, *The Problem of Pain* (London: G. Bles, 1942).

10. Brackets appear around the two sentences beginning with the phrase "Sin is what's wrong."

11. <a most favourable opportunity for a devil, this last one: it is very (?) naif of Wormwood to despair>

12. <Here are>

13. <A short quotation>

14. <which is, he>

15. Lewis, *The Screwtape Letters*, 77. Lewis's quotation in fact ends, "fear, avarice, lust, and ambition look ahead."

16. <we>

17. <we>

18. <its temporal>

19. <And there is a further difficulty in reading him: he doesn't, as a writer, express himself easily. He is a natural talker, and in the old days of broadcasting in this country, he was a superb populariser of science. He is not a natural writer.>

20. <the economic>

21. <come>

22. <come>

23. <I can't here go into the particular points Mr. Anand raises - I was specially interested in his account of Indian land tenure - I want really to emphasise his answer to 'What's wrong with the world?' - the question which concerns us all today, English, Indians, everyone, and with which I began my talk.> Following this crossed out and bracketed passage, EMF inserted a fragment that is somewhat indecipherable: "that is in his spiritual [?] searching [?]"

24. Lord Arthur Ponsonby, *Henry Ponsonby, Queen Victoria's Private Secretary: His Life from His Letters* (London: Macmillan, 1943).

25. <when>

26. <of the seventies and eighties>

27. <He had to soften impacts, to act as a buffer, to modify intolerance, and he seems to have done his job well.>

[1]BROADCAST   Dox 16261
EASTERN SERVICE - (PURPLE NETWORK)
Sunday 20th June 1943   13'11"
1515-1530 GMT

                                                  PLAYS

SOME BOOKS

by

E.M. FORSTER

These monthly talks are now to be on Sundays instead of Wednesdays. Travelling up to London on a Sunday isn't easy in wartime, so in the future I expect to be making a record for each talk beforehand. I don't like recording. It seems to me to interpose an extra piece of machinery between us, between you and me, and there's machinery enough already, in all conscience, both at this end and in India, without having a spinning black gramophone disc as well. If you hear my voice now, and want to visualise me, don't think of a human face. My face, such as it is, is away down in the country somewhere. Think instead of a needle moving down a groove, in a studio, for that's what's making the noise. And through that extra impediment I salute you. I salute you, and would remind you that civilisation rests upon direct personal intercourse, that there is no substitute for personal intercourse, and that broadcasting, even at its best and most intimate, is only a makeshift which will never be taken seriously by friends.[2]

What I'd like all these scientific contraptions to put across to you this time if they can, is: a few remarks on the subject of our London theatres. I've been to several theatres in the past month. The play I've enjoyed most, and to which I shall keep returning while I talk, is Congreve's <u>Love for Love</u>.[3] <u>Love for Love</u> is an old play - and it was first performed in the year 1695. It is also a young play, for Congreve was only 25 when he wrote it. He wrote it for a theatre in Lincoln's Inn Fields, where it had a terrific success, and now it's being done at a theatre about half a mile distant, and again the success is terrific. This makes me think of the continuity and of the smallness of London. 250 years in time, half a mile in space, and the same comedy being performed and causing delight and intelligent

227

laughter. Congreve a handful of dust now in Westminster Abbey, but his youthfulness living, and likely to go on living when heavier propositions are dead. He's brilliant and witty and naughty: he's subtle and distinguished and cynical; he has got odd touches of poetry which belong to the age of Elizabeth rather than to that of William and Mary; and above all he can create human beings suitable to his theme.

The plot of <u>Love for Love</u> is complicated, and awakes no special interest in the fortunes of the heroine and hero. What matters is the dialogue and the characters. The hero himself - Valentine - is an entertaining if undeserving man about town, who has been disinherited by his father for riotous living. When the curtain rises, he's reading a book - for he's studious and intelligent too - but he's soon diverted to gossip, and to dodging his creditors. Later in the play there's a curious scene in which he simulates madness, and here Congreve's feeling for poetry comes out, and he recalls the Elizabethans, and Hamlet. "Do you know me, Valentine?" asks the woman who loves him, "Oh, very well." - "Who am I?" - "You're a woman - one to whom Heaven gave beauty, when it grafted roses on a briar. You are the reflection of Heaven in a pond, and he that leaps at you is sunk. You are all white - a sheet of lovely spotless paper when first you are born: but you are to be scrawled and blotted by every goose's quill. I know you: for I loved a woman, and loved her so long, that I found out a strange thing: I found out what a woman was good for." - "Ay, prithee, what's that?" - "Why, to keep a secret."[4] This strange and beautiful episode isn't indeed typical of the play: more typical is Valentine's sailor brother, Ben, a rough and hot-tempered chap, who asks the ladies to marry him at sight; and rounds on them when they decline; and the ladies themselves, a delicious pair of sisters called Mrs. Foresight and Mrs. Frail, and an absurd astrologer, Mr. Foresight, who regulates his life by the stars. These characters are not drawn in great detail, they are not solid comic creations like Falstaff or Malvolio (who seem to exist outside the plays in which they occur), but they fit their surroundings perfectly, and this is one of Congreve's triumphs. His other triumph - as I've just said - is his dialogue, his English. Not a word, not a jest, not an oath out of place. The play delights our taste and our intelligence from start to finish. Earlier, I used the phrase "intelligent laughter". Yes, that <u>is</u> what Congreve gives us. Intelligent laughter. In a modern farce you are invited to "laugh your head off". In Congreve you laugh your head on, and the sensation is a civilised one.

I enjoyed <u>Love for Love</u> so much that I looked around London for the play most likely to resemble it, and I found that down in Westminster one of Molière's comedies was being performed, and I went to that on the following evening. The comedy in question is <u>Le Malade Imaginaire</u>, translated from the French as <u>The Imaginary Invalid</u>, and Mr. Donald Wolfit, as the Invalid, gave an entertaining performance.[5] This play was originally written to amuse King Louis XIV, in 1675 - that is to say, exactly twenty years before <u>Love for Love</u> came out in England. I felt it great luck to see two masterpieces of that period on successive nights, and one of the proofs that London today is not a barbarous city, even after its four years of war. <u>The Imaginary Invalid</u> is a satire on doctors; Molière had a down on doctors, as at one time had Mr. Bernard Shaw. He introduces some ridiculous specimens on the stage - particularly the dreary young surgeon who tries to ingratiate himself with a lady by offering to take her to his dissection of a corpse. And his satire is the keener because he does not present his doctors as characters: they are merely stupid and pompous, and when they consider themselves insulted professionally, oh, how they storm. I have witnessed such storms myself, even in Harley Street, and I couldn't but smile at them on the stage, and could not but be pleased when the Imaginary Invalid was cured rather farcically and blessed the union of his daughter with a fashionable young man. I didn't however enjoy the play as much as the Congreve, no doubt because I am English and Molière is of all great French writers the most French.

Talking of Bernard Shaw, I've been to a play by him too - <u>Heartbreak House</u>.[6] I wish you'd read it - all the plays I'm mentioning today are easily obtainable in book form, both the Congreve and the Moliere - but Shaw's <u>Heartbreak House</u> is the sort of play that is specially suitable for the study. He wrote it in 1919 - that is to say, just after the so called great war - he calls it a fantasy in the Russian style, and he attempts to depict the disillusioned generation which has somehow broken its heart - either through a love affair or through other failures - and which just will not buckle to and help to pull the world together. In Heartbreak House they dwell. The profoundest of them - mad old Captain Shotover - invents death-dealing gadgets, invents to make money in the dark. And the most energetic of them, the financier and the burglar, are killed by a bomb from a German aeroplane. The outline of the play is poetic and shows the influence of Tchehov and Ibsen, but Mr. Shaw, though he has many gifts, is no poet, and he has filled in the outline with wisecracks and scraps of farce, nor has he enough respect for his characters to make them convincing - or even consistent. At least that was my impression, and I came away disappointed. Other critics have felt differently though - have praised <u>Heartbreak House</u> highly. Read it for yourself and read Mr. Shaw's preface to it - he says much that is wise and stimulating there.

Talking of Russia - I seem to stray on from point to point talking but the theatres of London do link up when one looks round them - talking of Russia, there are actually two Russian plays being done. I haven't managed to go to either of them yet. One of them is a nineteenth century comedy of serious type, "A Month in the Country" by Ivan Tourgeniev.[7] The other is a product of the present war - a Soviet play by Siminov, called The Russians;[8] its date is 1941, and it exhibits the life and death struggle in which our allies are still engaged. In such a struggle there is no place for subtlety or fastidiousness, or cynicism or wit, or the other civilised qualities which I have been describing. In such a struggle black is black and white is white and heroism is the only virtue. In such a struggle men live or die not for their own sakes but for their country. In such a struggle war is not a topic to think about fancifully: it is war and it requires action. I wish I had seen The Russians before broadcasting to you - partly because it is said to be powerful, partly because it must be a complete contrast to the other works I've mentioned. It would have indicated the wide range of the drama's action, and also the variety of experiences which we human beings encounter.

I'll return, instead, to Congreve, for I haven't yet said how Love for Love was performed. Admirably. The scenery was charming to look at. The first scene was in the rooms of the hero Valentine, the second in the house of Mr. Foresight, the astrologer. Here there was a union of superstition, opulence and good taste which I found unusual and intriguing. Behind comfortable chairs and sofas was a wall painting, in the style of the period, representing King David consulting the Witch of Endor.[9] In the middle of the stage stood an enormous celestial globe, which the more frivolous characters twirled around with scant ceremony. And around the ceiling ran, in exquisite lettering, a Latin inscription announcing that the stars rule us all, but that God rules the stars. Poor Mr. Foresight (well played by Miles Malleson) seemed very little at home in his home. What with his wife, what with Miss Prue his hoyden of a daughter, what with his sister-in-law, Mrs. Frail, and his boisterous neighbour and his niece, and what with the stars, he was nearly demented. The old nurse was his only comfort. In the end Mr. Foresight was drawn into a dance, and the curtain rose and fell amidst our applause, upon a dance in which all the characters took part, and in which, at the final curtain, Ben the Sailor was sent sprawling by a well-directed blow on the part of Miss Prue.

So young Congreve and his comedy still live, although they are 250 years old, and they are enjoyed by people who differ entirely in their outlook and circumstances from the aristocrats for whom he originally wrote. This is earthly immortality, I think. When the play was over, I hurried out, together with other members of the bourgeoisie and proletariat, to get some food. A pleasant evening ended, and ended in daylight, for we now have double summertime over here.

But I am recording: the needle is sliding towards the centre of the disc, and I must stop. Through the microphone, through the gramophone, through the BBC transmission station and through your own receiving set, I bid you au revoir, and I hope in a month's time to be talking again.

1. <NOT CHECKED WITH>

2. In the margin next to each paragraph, time marks appear in the following order: 1', 2', 3', 4', 5', 6', 6.30, 7' (appearing next to the paragraph beginning "I enjoyed Love for Love"); 8', 9, 9.30, 9.25 (appearing next to the paragraph beginning "Talking of Bernard Shaw"); 10', 11', 12, 12.30 (appearing next to the paragraph beginning "I'll return, instead, to Congreve"); 13', 13.25.

3. *Love for Love*, starring Sir John Gielgud, was performed at the Phoenix Theatre in London; the production ran from 1942 to 1944.

4. William Congreve, *Love for Love*, act 4, scene 16 (New York: Scribner's, 1940), 68–69.

5. *The Imaginary Invalid*, starring Donald Wolfit, was performed at the Westminster Theatre in London in June 1943. Our thanks to Sarah McNeely for her assistance with this information.

6. *Heartbreak House: A Dramatic Fantasia* was performed at the Cambridge Theatre, London, 1942–1943.

7. Ivan Sergeevich Turgenev, *A Month in the Country* (New York: Rialto Service Bureau, 1930). Performed at the Royalty Theatre, London, starring Valerie Taylor and Michael Redgrave, 1943.

8. Konstantin Mikhailovich Simonov, *The Russians* (Southport, Eng.: A to Z Publishers, 1943). The play is set in the year 1941; it was first published in 1943 and was performed at The Playhouse in London in June 1943. Our thanks to Sarah McNeely for her assistance with this information.

9. 1 Samuel 28. It is Saul, and not David, who meets with the medium at Endor.

[1]AS BROADCAST
EASTERN SERVICE (PURPLE NETWORK)
Sunday 18th July 1943
1515-1530 GMT
Studio:

"SOME BOOKS"

by

E.M. FORSTER

I have had the honour now of giving these monthly book talks for a couple of years. They have had two aims. Firstly, they have tried to show you in India that there is such a thing as culture over here, even in war-time; that we still read books and write them and even write poetry; that we go to good plays and listen to music and look at pictures; that we study and discuss: that the blitz didn't stop us and won't stop us if it should return. We're well aware that this war against the dictators is a war of life and death, but we are not obsessed by it, and desire to uphold the values of life and to keep the many coloured flags of the spirit flying. Culture is a greatly-abused word, and I used to fight shy of it but I just bawl it into the microphone today. I believe in culture, and in art, and in the many coloured flags of the spirit. And I've tried in these broadcasts to show that they are still flying in these islands.

That's been my first aim. My second aim has been to assure you that we are interested in your culture, in the culture[2] of the Indian peoples. We don't know much about it, not nearly as much as we should considering our past advantages - and[3] we're not very influential officially; Indian culture wouldn't appeal to Colonel Blimp, I imagine, and indeed I can almost hear that estimable gentlemen saying, "Indian culture? Gad, sir, nothing but a few old curios."[4] But to[5] some of us it means much more: it means what Indians have created through the centuries, what they are creating now, and we wonder too how they are interpreting what we attempt[6] in the west. I've tried to bring this out in my monthly talks, and to be not just the Englishman advertising European civilisation, but the Englishman asking for knowledge.

My homage to culture, this afternoon, is the prelude to a talk which is going to be non-cultural, and rather off my beat. Several books have come in dealing with the present Indian crisis, and you'll want to hear about them, and I felt they ought to be mentioned.

They are controversial books. That goes without saying. Some of them support British rule, others are violently critical of it, and of the British record. Some of them believe in India as a united nation: others, in India as an independent association of loosely knit communities. In mentioning such books I am bound to tread on somebody's toes - probably upon everybody's toes, so will you please either switch off or else[7] keep calm.

To begin with, the point of view of the British Government. This is expressed in an important work by Professor Coupland, who teaches colonial history at Oxford and was unofficially attached to the Cripps mission.[8] Its title is 'A report on the constitutional problem in India', and as the title implies it concentrates on politics, and[9] not on economic or[10] social questions. It is in three volumes. The first covers the period 1833-1935, when the problem was developing, the second the years of the present crisis (1936-1942); and the third volume has not yet come out: it will discuss the possibilities of an ultimate constitutional settlement. Professor Coupland writes moderately, and lucidly, and learnedly. His conclusion, after the failure of the Cripps mission is that "the Indian problem" (I quote him)[11] "is no longer a political problem in the wider sense. The relationship between Britain and India has ceased to be the major question, since it has been shown that the final transfer of power presents no insuperable difficulties. The major question now is, the relationship between Indians and Indians . . . . whether a system can be devised under which the different sections and communities of India . . . . can agree to live together."[12] I quote these words to indicate Professor Coupland's attitude. It can be challenged, but whether you share it or not you will benefit by reading his book. "A Report on the Constitutional Problems in India" is invaluable for the political student. It contains,[13] to take an example, separate histories of the fortunes of the various Provincial governments, both Congress and non-Congress, which were set up as a result of the Act of 1935. He has also produced some pamphlets which express the British attitude more briefly: one is called Britain and India 1600-1941, and the other is on the Cripps Mission.[14]

To turn from Professor Coupland to Mr. H. N. Brailsford is to turn to an India where the shadows fall in a different direction and fall very darkly.[15] Mr. Brailsford has written a tragic and a compassionate book, which has attracted much attention over here. Even those who dislike it realise it has to be answered. Its title is Subject India - and those two words epitomise the writer's attitude and define his theme. Subject India. He believes that the British connection has been a failure, and the failure has been even more disastrous in the economic than in the political sphere. I will quote from him, just as I have been quoting from Professor Coupland: it is the fairest way to present the highly provocative matters which come into today's talk. Mr. Brailsford, in his summing-up, says: "The fact which for me overshadows every other is the immeasurable, the inhuman poverty of the Indian masses. To grasp it, to analyse its causes, to discover the beginnings of a remedy - that is the Indian problem. If politics rather than economics have filled the greater part of this book, the reason is that the solution of this complicated evil is and for long has been hopelessly beyond the competence of India's British rulers. Our day in India is over. We have no creative part to play. India's poverty has its psychological aspects, which we can only complicate."[16] Here again the conclusion can be challenged. But whether you share it or not, you had better consider it.[17] Brailsford's[18] book[19] attempts a wider survey than Professor Coupand's. It deals not only with the constitutional problem, but with poverty, and with social[20] friction. "We must proceed on the assumption that Indians distrust us and dislike us", he says, "there are exceptions to this rule, but such men are not typical; their motives are often interested and their advice may mislead us."[21] He dismisses the Cripps offer as disingenuous and makes in its place some drastic suggestions which include a Pacific Charter and the transference of Indian business from the India Office to the Dominions Office. He has not, he admits, any recent knowledge of what is happening on the spot, for the reason that India is at present inaccessible to non-official visitors.[22] I have been[23] deeply moved by Subject India. If you read it, and the Coupland report, you may get the problem into perspective.

[24]Passing on, let me mention Beggar My Neighbour by Lionel Fielden and Hell in the Sunshine by Cedric Dover.[25] Here again by their titles shall you know them. They are both of them highly critical of British rule. As for their authors, Mr. Fielden, an Englishman, was from 1935 to 1940 controller of broadcasting in India,[26] and Mr. Cedric Dover is a coloured man, a member of the Eurasian community; I use the word "Eurasian" of him rather than the authorised Anglo-Indian because he himself prefers it.

Mr. Fielden's Begger My Neighbour is a personal book. All books are personal, even when they are stuffed with statistics, but he seems to react to the Indian tragedy as it were sentence by sentence, and to pass abruptly from journalistic cynicism into deep emotion. He loves India - while realising that nothing so vast or shapeless can be loved. He loves her - a feeling which would scarcely occur to Professor Coupland. And he hates industrialism - an attitude which would not commend itself to Mr. Brailsford. He too has his practical suggestions to make - about the India Office, the Princes, Pakistan, and so forth - but his most striking remarks are emotional. "Damn Logic!" he exclaims, "because it leads us nowhere."[27] And he dreams of "an Indian culture differing widely from that of the West. . . . an Indian culture which might give to the West a wisdom other than the wisdom of expediency and wealth."[28]

Mr. Cedric Dover's work is of another type - though equally[29] anti-official. In Hell in the Sunshine he surveys the colour-question all over the world in connection with the menace of Japan. He believes that Japan is exploiting it,[30] and trying to lead the coloured peoples against the whites, and that she can only be checked if the West abandons its racial snobbery - snobbery which did not exist a couple of hundred of years back. India only comes into Mr. Dover's picture incidentally, but he gives an interesting account of the growth of his own community there, and he regrets that it is not in close touch politically with the Congress party. He writes very well, and movingly.

Finally, here is a book by a Christian social worker: Indian Crisis by John Hoyland.[31] This has only just arrived, and I have merely glanced into it. Like the previous writers, Mr. Hoyland is critical of the British government, but he differs from them in his conception of what the new India should be. His[32] sympathies incline to Hinduism - particularly to a[33] reformed Hinduism. Like Mr. Fielden, he believes in love, in affection, but unlike him, he hopes for collectivization, and he has no use for Pakistan. Mr. Hoyland has been for many years in touch with Indian students: his account of them is sympathetic and indeed respectful - he considers that they are superior to students[34] in the West.

I have now mentioned five authors - Professor Coupland, Messrs. Brailsford, Fielden, Dover and Hoyland. I wish that I could have mentioned a sixth. I wish that our old friend Colonel Blimp had also written a book. Something on the lines of, "Gad, sir, the Indian question? Dammit, sir,[35] there is no Indian question." I want a book of this type, to balance off our survey. But it is not forthcoming. The colonel is not [to] be drawn. And speaking more seriously, I would remind you that all our five writers, including Professor Coupland, know that there is an Indian question, and that Professor Coupland is[36] quite as desirous as the others to solve it.

1. <NOT CHECKED WITH>

2. EMF added accent marks above "your" and the first syllable of "culture."

3. <I grant>

4. EMF is alluding to the popular and controversial film of 1942, *The Life and Death of Colonel Blimp*, directed by Michael Powell and Emeric Pressburger and starring Roger Lindsay, Deborah Kerr, and Anton Walbrook. The film popularized the ridiculous ideologies of a fictional military buffoon, Colonel Blimp.

5. <a few>

6. <ed>

7. <sit tight>

8. "Cripps Mission" refers to the British government's dispatch of Sir Stafford Cripps in March 1942 to negotiate the cooperation of Hindu and Muslim congressional factions in the interests of the British war effort. The mission was a failure insofar as the Indian National Congress objected to various elements of Cripps's proposal, which offered a degree of Indian independence in return for Indian support during the war.

9. <is only incidentally concerned with>

10. <with>

11. In the margin next to the early section of this quotation, EMF wrote "slow."

12. Reginald Coupland, *A Report on the Constitutional Problem in India Submitted to the Warden and Fellows of Nuffield College, Oxford*, 3 vols. (London: Clarendon, 1942–1943), 1:307. The quotation is not exact, though EMF's deviations from Coupland's text are minor. EMF added accent marks above each word in the phrase "major question now." In the margin next to this latter portion of the quotation, EMF wrote "slower."

13. <for instance>

14. Reginald Coupland, *Britain and India, 1600–1941* (London: Longman's, 1941) and *The Cripps Mission* (Oxford: Oxford University Press, 1942). EMF wrote "on the Cripps Mission" at the bottom of the page and excised the typed version at the top of the next, presumably to aid in reading.

15. In a letter to EMF dated 1 July 1943, George Orwell "approved" of EMF's use of Brailsford's book in his talk - but only if it would be balanced by a reference to Coupland's text. "I have seen Mr. Rushbrook Williams about Brailsford's book," he wrote. "He says that it is not officially banned in India and that it will be all right to talk about it on the air but that to balance it one should have some book giving the opposite view-point. He suggests Professor Coupland's book called, I think, INDIAN CONSTITUTIONAL PROBLEMS, and issued by the Nuffield Trust" (E. M. Forster File 5, 1943 R CONT 1, BBC WAC).

16. Henry Noel Brailsford, *Subject India* (New York: John Day Co., 1943), 200. In the margin next to this quotation, EMF wrote "slow." EMF added accent marks above "is" and "has," above the first syllable in "hopelessly," above the second syllable in "beyond," and above the first syllables in "competence," "India's," "British," and "rulers" in the third sentence of the quotation.

17. <, and the arguments on which>

18. <founds it. His>

19. <, you see,>

20. <position>

21. Brailsford, *Subject India*, 204.

22. <But he introduces some of his past experiences there, and they are brilliantly and sincerely expressed.>

23. <much>

24. In the margin next to this paragraph, EMF wrote "4 minutes to go."

25. Lionel Fielden, *Beggar My Neighbour* (London: Secker and Warburg, 1943); Cedric Dover, *Hell in the Sunshine* (London: Secker and Warburg, 1943).

26. Fielden dedicates the book to the Indian Programme organizer at the BBC, Zulfiqar Bokhari, with whom he worked "through the blitzes and broadcasts and bafflements of London" and had talked "incessantly about the problems of your country and mine."

27. Fielden, *Beggar My Neighbour*, 113. The exclamation mark is EMF's addition.

28. Ibid., 108. The original reads "widely differing." EMF added an accent mark above "to."

29. <critical of British officialism>

30. EMF added accent marks above the first syllables in "believes" and "exploiting."
31. John Hoyland, *Indian Crisis* (London: Allen and Unwin, 1943).
32. EMF added an accent mark above "His."
33. <refined>
34. <of>
35. <they ought to be more grateful to us and not have a question at all>
36. <as anxious as anyone>

PURPLE NETWORK   3.0-3.30 p.m.
Sunday, 12th September, 1943
O.S.2.1515-1550 GMT   DOX 20279

SOME BOOKS

by

E.M. FORSTER

Rabindranath Tagore died a little over[1] two years ago, and there has lately been a meeting in memory of him, held at the Queen Mary Hall in the middle of London. I was able to attend the earlier part of the meeting, and was impressed by two circumstances. Firstly, the commemoration had been organised by the younger Indians resident over here; it was due to the joint efforts of the London Kajlis of Students, the Bengali Literary Society, the Indian Progressive Writers' Association, and the Hindustani Speaking Union. These younger Indians - few in number - are doing a good deal to interpret you to us, and to lighten our darkness on the subject of your culture, which still is extreme. They do well - if I may express myself colloquially - to plug Tagore, for Tagore has already touched the imagination of the west. He is a channel through which other influences can flow. On this occasion there were readings from his works, in prose and verse, in Bengali and English, and songs and homages. That's one point: the Tagore meeting was organised by the young. And the second point is that it was of an international character. Representatives of China, Czecho-Slovakia - and England were on the platform, and the considerable audience appeared to be mainly English. That was in accordance with Tagore's fame, and with his temperament. For - like other great men - he was an internationalist rooted in the soil of his own nation. He was an Indian who felt beyond India. And one of the items in the programme was his famous letter of criticism to the Japanese poet Yone Noguchi, who failed to feel anything outside Japan.[2]

This meeting started me thinking about Indian products. What has come out here lately? I have been reading an Essay on the Indian literatures by an Indian, a little book of poems by an Indian, and a treatise by an English historian on the rise of the Indian princes. These three books - so different in their character - shall now occupy us for a few minutes.

To begin with the essay. Its title is <u>Literature and Authorship in India</u> and its author is Professor Srinivasa Ivengar, of the University of Bombay, who is Professor of English at Belgaum. I don't know whether Professor Ivengar has ever been to this country, but he understands the English mentality and knows our difficulties - knows for instance that we easily get bogged by a lot of Indian names. So he divides his essay - there are only forty pages of it - into well-defined chapters, writes very clearly, and succeeds in giving us some idea of the achievements of the various Indian languages. He describes the early and rather promising impact of western culture on the East, and traces its unexpected reverberations down to the present day, when "India can neither do with English nor without it.["][3] He speaks of the 19th century and the Brahmo-Samaj.[4] A Madrassi himself, he speaks with enthusiasm and generosity of the 20th century Bengali renaissance, and connects it with similar movements in other parts of the peninsular. He is amusing and wise on the subject of purism in literature. He complains that during the last twenty years "Urdu is being deliberately Persianised and Hindi deliberately Sanskritized" until the two languages are "glaring at each other like angry cats, and neither is the language of the people."[5] Meanwhile Tamil is being Dravidianised. He hopes all this puristic nonsense will fail in India: it has already failed in England, where, an attempt was once made to Anglo-Saxonize English. I oughtn't strictly speaking to be praising this book, for the reason that I have contributed a foreword to it over here, and professional etiquette demands silence. But perhaps you will pardon the lapse, and allow me to repeat that I think it a good book. It has also been published in India.

The little volume of poems now briefly to be mentioned is called <u>Monsoon</u> and the author, Mr. B. Rajan, is studying at Cambridge. [6]their rhythmic repetition of such monosyllables as "sea" "lone" "dust" "sand" suggest the influence sometimes of Eliot, sometimes of Auden. They are obscure, they are declamatory, but one of the notions underlying them appears to be the upholding of personality - a notion congenial to me. Here are half a dozen lines from Monsoon which may enable you to judge the quality of this young Indian poet, B. Rajan.

Oh warm west wind of melting modulation,
On the breath of the bride recall your sifted music!
We who have built the cities of the bone,
From the scarred earth convulsed the citadel,
We of the prison, and the lamps restraint,
Have preserved identity. We shall not surrender.[7]

To turn from Indian writers to an Englishman writing on India. You are certain to know the name of Edward Thompson. You are familiar with his integrity, his independence of outlook, and the width of his interests. He has written novels: and poems, and treatises and histories: and now he presents a historical study about India in the early years of the 19th century. The exact title is <u>The Making of the Indian Princes</u>[8] and the origins of several reigning dynasties are indeed described not always in flattering terms. But the main subject of the book is the three Mahratta Wars, and the war against Nepal. [9]And we get much detailed information about this confused period. From about 1800 to 1820 everything in India was confused - not merely the military operations, not merely the composition of the armies when soldiers and camp followers were often indistinguishable, not merely the political settlements which settled nothing, but the psychology of the actors - that too was confused. And Dr. Thompson believes that during the period the English under went a psychological change. They cleared up the confusion in their minds. Before the Mahratta wars they felt themselves to be traders; after the wars they realised that India was too great and too grand to be plundered, and that they had become its overlords. He is very sympathetic to the Englishmen of the period - to Malcolm and Metcalfe and Klahinstone and Ochterlony and Lake: he even gives praise to Lord Wellesley, the stiff necked little governor-general. They were for the most part cultivated men who had no inhibitions or prejudices, men who came out to India in their teens and made it their home and thoroughly enjoyed themselves in Indian society. And he contrasts these with their successors, the men of the so called 'Mutiny' period who may have had higher principles, but were prim and self righteous, and too obviously the product of public schools. The earlier people were humanists, their successors were moralists. And Dr. Thompson, who began life himself as a moralist, has come to believe, he tells us, that humanism is what is most needed for the healing of wounds, and he recommends both English and Indians to study these earlier times, when hearts were warm.

<u>The Making of the Indian Princes</u> I must add is a work of research, most of which can only be appreciated or criticised by the expert. To the beginner I would rather recommend an earlier book of Dr. Thompson's which he produced in collaboration with Mr. Garrat - <u>Rise and Fulfilment of British Rule in India</u> by Thompson and Garratt.[10] There you will find in simpler form the matters here elaborated in detail.

A few minutes remain. Let us leave India and all connected with it, and let me just mention an English writer who has just died: the novelist and story teller W.W. Jacobs. Jacobs was born in the East End of London, at Wapping. He was familiar with life on the Thames and the docks, and their surroundings, and the types who frequent them, and he utilised this in his work. He had two lines. He is best known as a writer of humorous short stories about sailors, longshoremen, etc. These stories were collected into volumes with such titles as Many Cargoes, Odd Craft, Light Freights,[11] and won him an extensive[12] popularity. They are ingeniously constructed and usually on the theme of the biter bit. The bosun or the stevedore or the pub owner or the pub-crawler, whoever it may be lays a plot often to win the hand of a young lady, and is caught in his own toils and laughably dis-comforted. The incidents are unexpected and there is plenty of lively dia-logue and dialect. The characters are all working class, and W.W. Jacobs rather tends to regard the working classes as in themselves funny. They are not so regarded today, and consequently these short stories of his begin to date, and I don't think they are much read by the present gener-ation. However, that is only one of his lines. The other line - he did not often practise it - is the supernatural and the gruesome.[13] He can make your flesh creep. I've just read a powerful little yarn called The Brown Man's Servant (a snake is the servant), and then there is the Monkey's Paw - a variant on the old legend of the three wishes.[14] The Monkey's Paw has been adapted for broadcasting, and if you are at all sensitive or nervous don't listen in when it's being done. It is by his sinister stories rather than by his humorous work that W.W. Jacobs will probably be remembered.

1. <a>

2. Tagore corresponded with Noguchi in 1938 on the subject of Japanese nationalism, of which he disapproved strongly. At the end of EMF's sentence the time mark 2:00" is can-celed and 2'30" is inserted. Other time marks appear at intervals throughout the script, end-ing at 11'40" (a time mark inserted and then excised).

3. Srinivasa Ivengar, *Literature and Authorship in India* (London: G. Allen and Unwin, 1943), 25.

4. Brahmo-Samaj was an Indian religious movement dating from the nineteenth century that promoted reformed Hinduism with an emphasis on women's rights and opposition to idolatry and animal sacrifice.

5. Ivengar, *Literature and Authorship*, 41.

6. The surviving script cuts off the last line on the second page, and the first few words of this sentence cannot be recovered.

7. B. Rajan, *Monsoon* (Cambridge: Cambridge University Press, 1943), 2.

8. Edward Thompson, *The Making of the Indian Princes* (London: Oxford University Press, 1943).

9. <There is>

10. Edward Thompson and G. T. Garratt, *Rise and Fulfilment of British Rule in India* (London: Macmillan, 1934).

11. W. W. Jacobs, *Many Cargoes* (London: Lawrence and Bullen, 1896); *Odd Craft* (London: George Newnes, 1900); *Light Freights* (London: Methuen, 1901).

12. <reputation>

13. <macabre>

14. W. W. Jacobs, *The Skipper's Wrong and The Brown Man's Servant* (London: C. A. Pearson, 1897) and *The Monkey's Paw: A Story in Three Scenes* (New York: S. French, 1903).

[1]AS BROADCAST
EASTERN SERVICE
PURPLE NETWORK
Sunday, 3rd October, 1943
1515-1530 GMT
MODERN MEN OF LETTERS No. 6.[2]

LYTTON STRACHEY

by

E.M. Forster

Lytton Strachey was the author of two great books - <u>Queen Victoria</u> and <u>Elizabeth and Essex</u>. From the artistic point of view <u>Elizabeth and Essex</u> is the greater: it has action and passion and colour and form: it is written with intense and continuous emotion, and after reading it one has the sense of having witnessed a tragic and sumptuous drama.[3] But from the historical point of view <u>Elizabeth and Essex</u> can be criticised. Strachey did not know his period very well (it was the late sixteenth century) and he had not the natural sympathy with it which sometimes helps an amateur to guess correctly. He made some blunders, he guessed wrongly, and the pundits have pounced on him. They have not been able to pounce on his <u>Queen Victoria</u>. Here[4] he knew his facts, he had mastered his documents, and he understood the Victorian tradition, and the 19th century way of looking at things. He laughed at it, but he could get inside it, and could[5] make its personages live from the Queen and Prince Albert and Lord Palmerston at one end of the social scale down to the gillie John Brown and the chimney-sweep Boy Jones at the other. <u>Elizabeth and Essex</u> is a masterpiece, but a tour de force. <u>Queen Victoria</u> is a natural[6] masterpiece. Published as long ago as 1921, it is standing the test of time, and though prophecies are dangerous I should say that in the year 2021 it will still be read with profit and delight; and laughter.

Now, it is a book of a new type, which has revolutionised the art of biography. I'm not thinking of its celebrated debunking: Strachey did de-bunk of course: he hated pomposity, hypocrisy and muddled headedness,

243

he mistrusted inflated reputations and was clever at puncturing them, and he found in the Victorian age, which had taken itself very seriously, a tempting target for his barbed arrows. But he was much more than a debunker. He was a creator, who got inside his characters. Earlier biographers, like Macaulay and Carlyle, had got close up[7] to their characters, and had given convincing pictures of them. Strachey gets inside[8] them, with the result that they live like the characters in a novel. He had already done this in his brilliant essays, Eminent Victorians.[9] Now he does it in a full length work. He presents a pageant in the historical style and shows with dignity a famous queen proceeding from her birth to her death through many vicissitudes of fortunes, but as the grand procession passes we - you and I - we little readers - are somehow part of the procession, we mingle unobserved with royalty and statesmen and courtiers and underlings, and hear their unspoken thoughts. That is new in biography. No one had tried to do it before, though many have tried since. And I am inclined to ascribe his success - mainly of course to[10] his genius, but partly to the moment of time in which he wrote. It was a moment for psychology. People were interested in motives, in the subconscious, in the view of human-nature suggested by the speculations of Freud. Strachey wasn't a scientist, but he was sensitive to what was going on around him, he breathed it in and breathed it out in his art. Psychology helped him to make his people real. He excels with complicated and subtle characters, like Lord Melbourne or Disraeli. And he is even more successful with characters who appear not to be complicated but are, like the queen herself. Patiently if mischievously does he unravel her contradictions, and explore the debatable ground where the ruler ended and the woman began - the ground where Mr. Gladstone came so dreadfully to grief, Mr. Gladstone who would[11] address the queen as if she was a public meeting. The queen did not like Mr. Gladstone.[12] Would she have liked Lytton Strachey? I am inclined to think she would have, despite his irony and his irreverence. She would have liked him for detecting that there was so much in her. This homage he does pay her as she progresses across the crowded stage.

So in reading this book - which is a history and a reliable one - you will get in addition the pleasure which comes from reading a novel. You will feel you are right amongst the characters and overhearing what they say. The queen in particular - you will get to know her as she certainly never knew herself, for she had not a detached or an introspective mind. Lytton Strachey has written a new sort of biography, and one accordant with the spirit of his age.[13]

What is he serious about, though? That question is sometimes asked, and in querulous tones. Is he ever serious? Is he just an analyst and a mocker, who examines human effort only to be satirical? Certainly he was not interested in social reconstruction[14] and for many people today this is the only subject about which it is possible to be serious. He believed, however, in wit, in aristocratic good manners, and in good taste, and he was implacable in his pursuit of truth.[15] And if this does not satisfy you, let me add that he also believed in fidelity between human beings. Constant affection never fails to move him. When people are devoted to each other for years, the warmth of his heart comes out. Now the great thing in the queen's private life was[16] her devotion for the Prince Consort and for his memory. She loved him when he was a handsome young man, and through all the happy years of her marriage, and through the desolations of her widowhood, she possessed, to a supreme degree the quality of faithfulness. Lytton Strachey realised this, it preserves his biography from frigidity, and makes it glow. Here he is[17] serious. I want to emphasise his belief in human fidelity, for it is easily missed. And I want to emphasise the helpful part it plays in the construction of this particular book. The great emotion which dominated Queen Victoria's inner life is an emotion which he understands. It led her into absurdities, especially during her mourning, and these are duly exhibited, but the central feeling commands his respect.

As a stylist, he has a wonderful range. He can chronicle solemnly, he can tell funny stories, he can at need make high poetic flights, and yet he is always himself, he and no one else is holding the pen.[18] You may remember[19] one of the poetic flights, the famous paragraph at the end of the book describing the death of the queen. He has just described the event in grave official language and stated the facts and the date - January 22nd, 1901. Then he dismisses with tenderness the subject that has occupied him so long, and launches the Queen as it were on an ebbing tide which carries her in reverse direction through time till she vanishes in the mists of her birth. I'll read you the paragraph as well as I can.[20]

"When, two days previously, the news of the approaching end had been made public, astonished grief had swept over the country. It appeared as if some monstrous reversal of the course of nature was about to take place. The vast majority of her subjects had never known a time when Queen Victoria had not been reigning over them. She had become an indissoluble part of their own scheme of things, and that they were about to lose her appeared a scarcely possible thought. She herself, as she lay blind and silent, seemed to those who watched her to be divested of all thinking - to have glided already, unawares, into oblivion. Yet, perhaps, in the secret chambers of consciousness, she had her thoughts, too. Perhaps her fading mind called up once more the shadows of the past to float before it, and retraced, for the last time, the vanished visions of that long history - passing back and back, through the cloud of years, to older and ever older memories - to the spring woods at Osborne, so full of primroses for Lord Beaconsfield - to Lord Palmerston's queer clothes and high demeanour, and Albert's face under the green lamp, and Albert's first stag at Balmoral, and Albert in his blue and silver uniform, and the Baron coming in through a doorway, and Lord[21] Melbourne dreaming at Windsor with the rooks cawing in the elm-trees, and the Archbishop of Canterbury on his knees in the dawn, and the old King's turkey-cock ejaculations, and Uncle Leopold's soft voice at Claremont, and Lehzen with the globes, and her mother's feathers sweeping down towards her, and a great old repeater-watch of her father's in its tortoise-shell case, and a yellow rug, and some friendly flounces of sprigged muslin, and the trees and the grass at Kensington.["]"[22]

Thus does he[23] bid farewell, and it is not the farewell of a cynic. He believes in the importance of human life, though not in a way which commends itself to the ordinary or even to the earnest man. By temperament he was aristocratic, and his spiritual century was the 18th, the century of Voltaire. Voltaire - whom he greatly admired - resembles him in many ways. They both had intellectual integrity, were witty, fastidious, learned and mischievous, and believed in personal friendship.[24] In[25] one way, Voltaire was his inferior, for he wasn't a poet, although he wrote poetry, whereas Strachey, though he didn't write poetry, was a poet. The paragraph I've just read shows that. It is moreover a paragraph which could not have been written before the year 1921. The last long lovely drifting sentence, with its imaginings of the subconscious, belongs to our time, and to our psychology. It is a reminder that the biography of <u>Queen Victoria</u> is a product of our age, and perhaps in the year 2021 we shall be congratulated on it by historians, when our other achievements are forgotten, or are condemned.

You should easily be able to get this book in India. There is a cheap edition of it in the Phoenix Library.[26]

1. <NOT CHECKED WITH>

2. Handwritten beneath the heading is: "Censored by C. Lawson Reece." Lawson-Reece was the Eastern Services organizer for the BBC.

3. Lytton Strachey, *Elizabeth and Essex: A Tragic History* (London: Chatto and Windus, 1928).

4. EMF added an accent mark above "Here."

5. <without great effort,>

6. EMF added an accent mark above "natural."

7. EMF added an accent mark above "up."

8. EMF added an accent mark above the first syllable of "inside."

9. Lytton Strachey, *Eminent Victorians: Cardinal Manning, Florence Nightingale, Dr. Arnold, General Gordon* (London: Chatto and Windus, 1921).

10. <Strachey's>

11. EMF added an accent mark above "would."

12. EMF added accent marks above "not," "like," and the first syllable of "Gladstone."

13. EMF handwrote a mark indicating a paragraph break here and in the margin.

14. <reform>

15. EMF added accent marks above "wit," the first syllable of both "aristocratic" and "manners," as well as above both "good" and "taste."

16. EMF added an accent mark above "was."

17. EMF added an accent mark above "is."

18. <throughout>

19. <the most famous>

20. <though it requires a better reader than myself to do it justice - >

21. <M.> Strachey's text reads "M."; EMF excised the initial in favor of the more explanatory "Melbourne."

22. Lytton Strachey, *Queen Victoria* (London: Chatto and Windus, 1921), 269.

23. <bade>

24. <In one way, indeed, Voltaire was Strachey's superior; he has a burning passion for justice and would risk his life and position in order to rescue the innocent and the downtrodden.>

25. <another>

26. This last sentence is handwritten by EMF.

AS BROADCAST   Recorded 8.10.43
EASTERN SERVICE
PURPLE NETWORK   14(approx.
Sunday, 10th October, 1943
1515-1530 GMT   CENSORED BY Z. A. BOKHARI

SOME BOOKS

by

E.M. Forster

Japan is a country that I have never visited - indeed I have only once conversed with a Japanese, and then it was about the poetry of Mr. T. S. Eliot. So there will be nothing authoritative in today's broadcast. Three books on Japan have come my way and I want to indicate their contents - that is all - and to say why they have interested me. They all deal with modern Japan, and cover that fatal night of December 7th, 1941, the night of Pearl Harbour. One of them is by the American ambassador, Mr. Grew, the second is by Mr. Tolischus, an American journalist, who was correspondent to the New York Times and to the Times of London, and the third is by an Englishman, Mr. John Morris. The titles of these three books happen to be so similar that I shan't give them until the end of the talk - otherwise we shall keep getting muddled. I shall just refer to the names of the authors - Ambassador Grew, Mr. Tolischus and Mr. Morris. The last named went out to lecture in English, and I think got most out of his book - anyhow he helped me most with my difficulties.

What exactly are my difficulties? Two. In the first place Japan is so far away. I know that she is my enemy, but I cannot think vividly or angrily of her as I do of the Nazis. If I went to Dover, as I often did in peace time, and looked across the channel, I should see Nazis - occupied France. But I can't see Japan. She and her misdeeds are on the other side of the globe - nearer to you. Our minds tend to dwell on what we're near to, and perhaps you can realise her, down in Burma, and cannot realise the Nazis, over the straits of Dover.

My second difficulty with Japan is that she is so contradictory. Like most Englishmen I have heard of her charm and courtesy and chivalry, of her chrysanthemums, her geishas. I have admired specimens of her art and have read a wonderful novel called The Tale of Genji which has been translated into my language.[1] Yet I know that she is treacherous and pitiless and insolent - and commercial and vulgar - and obscurantist - and generally speaking a totalitarian terror, by the side of which Germany looks almost human. How are these discrepancies to be reconciled? All the three authors help us here, Ambassador Grew, Mr. Tolischus, Mr. Morris all tackle the profound problem of the contradictory Japans. After reading them, I feel that I'm up against not merely a dangerous enemy but a queer one.

The Ambassador's book, a short one, is addressed to his own people. He warns them what they are up against, and against the delusion that Japan will 'crack'. He contrasts the Japanese make up with the German. Germany may crack. But the Japanese "will pull in their belts another notch, reduce their rations from a bowl to a half bowl of rice, and fight to the bitter end. Only by utter physical destruction or utter exhaustion of their men and material can they be defeated."[2] He speaks of their spiritual resources, and of the "ancient dreams and traditional ambitions which they are unable to shake off" and which inspire them to fight and to die and of their unscientific belief in Race and in their divine origin.[3] He does not go far into these matters - not so far as Mr. Tolischus or Mr. Morris - for his main concern is to shake up public opinion in America and the Anglo-Saxon world generally, and to scare it out of its self-complacency; incidentally he emphasises the importance and the intelligent heroism of China. His book opens with an account of that night - December the 7th, 1941. He had received a telegram containing a peace-appeal from President Roosevelt to the Emperor, and went round to the Japanese Foreign office to ask for an audience. He was told nothing there, and only learnt, two hours later, from a press bulletin, of the attack on Pearl Harbour. Soon afterwards, the Embassy's gates were locked by the police and he was treated as a prisoner. So much for Japanese methods. Ambassador Grew did not reach his native shores until nine months later and we can well believe him when he says he was pleased to see them.

The book of Mr. Tolischus takes the form of a reconstructed diary.[4] An experienced journalist, he went out in January 1941 and returned to America on the same boat as the Ambassador. It was his first visit to the mysterious East, and I expect he hopes it will be his last. His chief aim, in writing, is to recount the events that led up to Pearl Harbour, the ups and downs and ins and outs, the speeches and counter-speeches, the bluffs and rebuffs and appeasements, the shiftings of power inside the Japanese fabric from the government and the Foreign Office to the army. He does it very well, and if it doesn't happen to be the sort of thing that interests me, that is no doubt my loss. I think that accounts after a war has broken out, of the events which immediately led up to that war, make uncongenial reading - except on the rare occasions when they have philosophical depth, as they have, in such a book as Lowes Dickinson's International Anarchy.[5] But many people are fascinated by such accounts and if you want to know who said what at Tokyo in 1941, and who reacted to what and what to whom, you cannot have a better guide than Mr. Tolischus. He is a news man and here is the news.

He has another aim, and that is to interpret the Japanese mentality. He describes a booklet, called The Way of Subjects which lays down the new ethical code for the nation, and informs it that it is its duty to exterminate European and American thought, and to conquer the world.[6] This task, the booklet continues, has been imposed on the Japanese by the Sun Goddess and the other gods, from whom they are descended, and this statement so startling to a democrat leads Mr. Tolischus to look at Japanese mythology. He finds it queer and barbaric, and he is puzzled, as to how far the Japanese take it seriously. Here is one of the problems of the 'two Japans' which I mentioned before. Do they, or don't they, feel that they are descended from the gods? If we could answer that question we should come nearer to understanding them. Mr. Tolischus holds that they have been drilled into having the feeling during the last ten years. He holds too that there has been no interruption between them and their barbaric past - such as has inter- rupted the barbarisms of Europe - and that this is a great misfortune for them and for the world. He is not a scholar, and how deep he goes into these important matters I can't judge. But he starts one thinking.

What interests me most in his book though is when he describes what happened to him when the news of Pearl Harbour arrived. He was thrown into prison. He was examined and reexamined, accused of being a spy, he was starved, stamped upon and slapped. He tells it all without self pity, and it makes a terrible story. The strangest incident came when he was released and awaiting repatriation to America. He and other newspaper men were invited to a lunch by a Japanese organisation - called the Pacific War Relief Committee. It was an excellent lunch at a good hotel, and there were courteous speeches. The guests were then invited to broadcast to America and say how nice everything was. They declined, and some of them were man-handled by their hosts. One of them was punched on the jaw in the hotel lounge and his dental plate was broken, another was half choked by his necktie. They were then reassembled, served with beer, and promptly dismissed. What a party! Don't you agree that the Japanese are odd?

Now for Mr. Morris' book. It provides me with my favourite generalisation - namely that you cannot generalise. As soon as you have got your facts marshalled, another fact comes along and upsets them. Mr. Morris' experiences are different from those of the other two, and largely because he is a different person. Different people are different, and there is the trouble. He went out to Japan not to represent his country or to gather news, but to make human contacts through his work. Human contacts being an aspect of life which appeals to me, I have got a good deal out of this book. I thought I should as soon as I read a sentence in which he complains that Englishmen in India (where he has seen service) too often accept their status there without question. He goes on: "It is indeed difficult to refuse the greatness that is thrust upon one, especially as one becomes older, but it is vital to do so if one is to remain a civilised being."[7] That sentence struck me as a wise one. And the whole book is wise and sane, and quietly unravels Japan or part of it and makes it intelligible. How do you get a telephone in Tokyo? How are the houses numbered? Why is Japanese easy to talk and difficult to read? What kinds of plays can one go to? What are the facts about the Geisha systems? Answers to such questions are given and from the point of view of a resident. He went out in 1938, soon settled down to his teaching and literary work, made many Japanese friends, and felt at home. As regards his private life, his picture is favourable. But he does not lose sight of the trend of events outside. He is alarmed and disgusted by them, and the general effect of his book is quite as sinister as the American ambassador's or Mr. Tolischus'. For all the good qualities of Japan - the charm, the fidelity etc. - are ineffective as long as militarism and racialism are on top. When 1941 came and trouble was beating up British people were advised to go.

"I decided to stay (he says), I was extremely interested to see how the situation was going to develop and I wanted to see things through to the end. There was also another fact which the reader may find difficult to comprehend: I had grown extremely fond of the Japanese people. But I do not wish this statement to be misinterpreted. The majority of my friends were intellectuals, many of whom would have done anything to prevent this war, and were profoundly shocked when it came. That they had been, in point of fact, ineffectual is beside the point . . . I desire most earnestly to see Japan's military might utterly destroyed. This, in my opinion, is necessary not only for the well being of the world at large, but also for that of the Japanese people themselves. They cannot display themselves as they truly are when their country is ordered by its present band of military gangsters."[8]

On Mr. Morris too came December 7th and Pearl Harbour. And here again one cannot generalise. Although he was visited by the police, who confiscated some x ray photographs of his lungs under the belief that they represented secret fortifications, he was not thrown into prison, he taught as usual, and his students came freely to his house. Although he too was invited to broadcast, and refused, he was not punched on the jaw or throttled with his neck-tie. He was left at large, his servant was faithful to him and declined to hang out a flag when Singapore fell, and he was only once insulted in the street. In July 1942 (eight months after Pearl Harbour) he was allowed to leave the country. His book is valuable as a document as well as for its tolerance and humanity, for he was the only Englishman left free to observe during those months. It seemed to me a good book, it helps to interpret what I have called the two Japans, and their interactions, and to make them less strange.

Now for the promised titles. Ambassador Grew's book: <u>Report from Tokyo</u>. Mr. Tolischus' book: <u>Tokyo Record</u>. Mr. John Morris': <u>Traveller from Tokyo</u>.

1. Murasaki Shikibu, *The Tale of Genji: A Novel in Six Parts,* trans. Arthur Waley (London: Allen and Unwin, 1935).

2. Ambassador Joseph C. Grew, *Report from Tokyo: A Message to the American People* (New York: Simon and Schuster, 1942), 29.

3. Ibid., 42.

4. Otto Tolischus, *Tokyo Record* (London: H. Hamilton, 1943).

5. Goldsworthy Lowes Dickinson, *The International Anarchy* (London: Allen and Unwin, 1926).

6. The booklet, released in Japan, was underwritten by the World Future Fund.

7. John Morris, *Traveller from Tokyo* (London: Cresset Press, 1943), 155.

8. Ibid.

[1]EASTERN SERVICE
PURPLE NETWORK
Thursday, 4th November, 1943
1515-1530 GMT

SOME BOOKS

by

E.M. Forster

I have only seen three of the great rivers of the world - the Nile, the Danube, and the Ganges. I should dearly like to see a fourth, and that is the Mississippi. No doubt if I ever reached the banks of the Mississippi I should be disillusioned, and find it dull and standardised. But it remains a romantic river to me, because I have read about it in the pages of a famous American writer Mark Twain. Mark Twain made his name as a humourist and a rather bitter commentator on society but he is best remembered now because he immortalised the Mississippi. Just a hundred years ago he played by the river and swam in it and fished in it, and floated on it in canoes and rafts as a rough little boy, and as a young man he became for a time a pilot on a Mississippi steamer. These early experiences sank deep into his mind. And his best books are those in which he goes back to his youth and recreates the days when he was obstreperous and naughty.[2] He is the type of writer who does best when he remembers his boyhood. Wordsworth - so different to him otherwise - belongs to the same type. They feel when they remember. His very name - Mark Twain - belongs to the river and the past. His real name was Clemens, Samuel Clemens, but he adopted as a pseudonym a cry of the Mississippi pilots - "Mark Twain" meaning that the sounds were deep enough for the steamer to proceed in safety. Broadcasting about him today, I should like to pronounce his name as 'Mark Twain' a cry from the untamed enormous river, rather than as Mark-Twain the international joker and lecturer who took the Anglo-Saxon world by storm and sent thousands of half educated people into peals of[3] ungovernable laughter. His jokes are wearing badly.

They date and grate. His philosophy of life is crude. But the river flows on. The immediate excuse for this broadcast is a reprint of the two most famous of the Mississippi books - the tales of <u>Tom Sawyer</u> and <u>Huckleberry Finn</u>. These are coming out shortly in a single volume of the Everyman edition, accompanied by a useful introduction, and a useful map of the river. They are very much products of the western hemisphere. I don't expect they are well known in India[4], but they should interest you. <u>Tom Sawyer</u> is the better. It's a book about boys which isn't a boy's book. It's an evocation of eternal youth fooling about by an eternal stream. You'll enjoy it if you have, as I have, a soft spot for literature that isn't technically great, literature that is full of flaws and weaknesses, but somehow or other it gets going and it gets home.

There's murder and detection and hidden treasure in <u>Tom Sawyer</u>, there's truancy on an island, and naughtiness in a Sunday School, and a scene in church when Tom and his friend Huckleberry Finn attend their own funeral service, and a thrilling scene - at the close when Tom and the little girl Becky are lost in a gigantic cave. There are negro slaves and wicked half breeds, and forgotten superstitions. How to cure warts on the hand, for instance. "I play so much with frogs that I've always got considerable many warts", says Tom. "Sometimes I take 'em off with a bean." "Yes, bean's good. I've done that" says Huck. But Huck prefers a dead cat - indeed he is swinging one by its tail as the boys talk. Here is Huck's recipe for curing warts:-

'Why you take your cat and go and get in the grave-yard, long before midnight where somebody that was wicked has been buried; and when it's midnight a devil will come, or maybe two or three but you can't see 'em you can only hear something like the wind or may be hear 'em talk: and when they're taking that feller away you heave your cat after 'em and say "Devil follow corpse, cat follow devil, warts follow cat, <u>I'm</u> done with ye!" That'll fetch <u>any</u> wart.'[5]

So the boys take this particular cat to a graveyard: with melodramatic result. And at the end of the book they become melodramatically rich, as little American boys should. But it's fairy gold, as all gold should be, and they are soon poor and happy and dirty and naughty again. They never grow up, and it has been complained of Mark Twain that he never grew up. He remained immature. Consequently the psychoanalysts have got going at him. They would. [6]Let us listen for a minute to what they have to say.

I am all for the psychoanalysts having a go at everyone. They can often explain why a writer writes as he does, and there is in existence an interesting book[7] entitled 'The Ordeal of Mark Twain'.[8] The author of the book

Van Wyck Brooks took as his thesis that Mark Twain never developed, that after a brief period of 'finding himself' as a pilot on a steamer he shrank from the responsibilities of life and from the training requisite to face them, and relapsed into boyish[9] prospecting for gold, and later into a marriage where his wife's relationship to him was maternal and possessive. Neither as pioneer or as husband did Mark Twain grow up, and he harks back emotionally to childhood until he dies. I think that's true, and The Ordeal of Mark Twain is a sound study in inhibitions the Oedipus complex and all that. But why do these psychoanalysts nag so? Why do they sound so cross? Mr. Van Wyck Brooks is so irritated with his victim the whole time. And although he explains why Mark Twain wrote <u>Tom Sawyer</u> and <u>Huckleberry Finn</u>, he doesn't and can't explain why the books are good. As soon as we[10] cease to consider[11] the causes of a book and start to assess its <u>merit</u> psychoanalysis becomes[12] useless and we need another more old fashioned set of tools.

I'm[13] about to read you a longish passage from <u>Huckleberry Finn</u>, and while listening to it you will be instinctively using those tools and deciding whether the passage is good or bad. Huckleberry Finn, the sequel to Tom Sawyer, was written several years later and it is rather journalistic and uneven. Huck (who cured warts with a cat) has become a voluble author. However,[14] the middle of the book, where he is drifting down the river on a raft with an escaping negro slave, is gay, natural, gentle, humane. Here's the passage - and if you are a student of James Joyce you may be amused to detect in its artless prose an occasional premonition of the cadences of Ulysses.

"Two or three days and nights went by; I reckon I might say they swum by, they slid along so quiet and smooth and lovely. Here is the way we put in the time. It was a monstrous big river down there - sometimes a mile and a half wide; we run nights, and laid up and hid day-times; soon as night was most gone, we stopped navigating and tied up - nearly always in the dead water under a tow-head; and then cut young cotton-wood and willows and hid the raft with them. Then we set out the lines. Next we slid into the river and had a swim, so as to freshen up and cool off; then we set down on the sandy bottom where the water was about knee-deep, and watched the daylight come. Not a sound anywheres - perfectly still - just like the whole world was asleep, only sometimes the bull frogs a-clattering, maybe. The first thing to see, looking away over the water, was a kind of dull line - that was the woods on t'other side - you couldn't make nothing else out; then a pale place in the sky; then more paleness, spreading around; then the river softened up, away off, and warn't black any more, but gray; you could see little dark spots drifting along, ever so far away - trading scows, and

such things; and long black streaks - rafts; sometimes you could hear a
sweep screaking; or jumbled up voices, it was so still and sounds come
so far; and by-and-by you could see a streak on the water which you
know by the look of the streak that there's a snag there in a swift current which breaks on it and makes that streak look that way; and you
see the mist curl up off the water, and the east reddens up, and the river,
and you make out a log cabin in the edge of the woods, away on the
bank on t'other side of the river, being a woodyard, likely, and piled by
them cheats so you can throw a dog through it anywheres; then the nice
breeze springs up, and comes fanning you from over there, so cool and
fresh, and sweet to smell, on account of the woods and the flowers: but
sometimes not that way, because they've left dead fish laying around,
gars, and such, and they do get pretty rank; and next you've got the full
day, and everything smiling in the sun, and the song-birds just going it!

A little smoke couldn't be noticed, now, so we would take some fish
off the lines and cook up a hot breakfast. And afterwards we would
watch the lonesomeness of the river, and kind of lazy along, and by-
and-by lazy off to sleep. Wake up, by-and-by, and look to see what done
it, and maybe see a steamboat, coughing along up stream, so far off
towards the other side you couldn't tell nothing about her only whether
she was stern-wheel or side-wheel; then for about an hour there
wouldn't be nothing to hear nor nothing to see - just solid lonesomeness.["]^{15}

This passage doesn't contain anything specially striking or poetic or
smart. But doesn't it get you there! Don't you see that river and feel it and
sit in it up to your chin and eat that fish? Don't you understand now why
I want to visit the Mississippi myself, and why it is one of the rivers of
youth?

Remember the Everyman edition, then, Tom Sawyer and Huckleberry
Finn are coming out in it shortly.[16]

1. <NOT CHECKED WITH BROADCAST>

2. <, and stole>

3. <uncontrolled>

4. <and they have no special Indian appeal.>

5. Mark Twain, *The Adventures of Tom Sawyer and Huckleberry Finn* (London: J. M. Dent,
1943), 37.

6. <Suppose we>

7. <published some twenty years ago>

8. Van Wyck Brooks, *The Ordeal of Mark Twain* (New York: Dutton and Co., 1933).

9. <digging>

10. <stop>

11. <only>

12. <completely>
13. <just going>
14. <in>
15. Twain, *Tom Sawyer and Huckleberry Finn*, 285–86.
16. This final sentence is written in a hand other than EMF's.

AS BROADCAST
EASTERN SERVICE
PURPLE NETWORK
Thursday, 2nd December, 1943
1515-1530 GMT

SOME BOOKS

by

E.M. FORSTER

New books. I have had the pleasure of receiving some new books from India, and will mention them first. Here is Echo and Ego by Roop and Mary Krishna,[1] two artists. Here is a critical study of T. S. Eliot by Ahmed Ali[2] - already known to many English writers as a novelist,[3] and finally here's a play The Well of the People by Bharati Sarabhai.[4] Before I say more, let me thank those who have sent me these books, and[5] say that I am glad to mention in my broadcasts books published in India, whenever they are suitable. I can't make a definite promise, because I only talk once a month and then for under a quarter of an hour, and there's a great deal of ground to be covered. But if I can include books published in India I will. And I am grateful for them personally. They make me feel less lonely. They remind me that[6] links between culture here and culture your end do exist, and that the microphone, which hangs before me now like a petrified pineapple, is capable of evoking a human response.

Echo and Ego is a miscellany. The authors, Roop and Mary Krishna, have collected together some of their articles, satirical and serious, essays, reviews, poems, etc. and have included some reproductions of their paintings and drawings. They are in touch with European art and literature - Picasso, Joyce, - and they dedicate their volume to the artist Dr. Rabindranath Tagore. And they have the artist's outlook: that's to say they believe in communion and disbelieve in propaganda. That is my own outlook, and I find the same outlook in Mr. Ahmed Ali's study on T. S. Eliot. Mr. Ahmed Ali holds that when a poet preaches[7] his poetry suffers, and illustrates this from Eliot's poems. I advise you to get hold of his book, - which being in India you can easily do - and see whether you agree with his judgements. He regrets Eliot's increasing Christian orthodoxy and his neglect of economic[8] poverty and material misery and he argues that his poetry is deteriorating in consequence. Mr. Ahmed Ali doesn't and can't consider Eliot's latest poems - they had not reached him in time - and I wonder whether they would affect his conclusions, for I do think these latest poems very fine. One of them, by the way, Little Gidding, will be broadcast this day week: Mr. Eliot himself will be reading it.

Let's turn from criticism to creation. Do read <u>The Well of the People</u>, a poetic drama by Miss Bharati Sarabhai. This is an attempt to combine ancient Indian tradition with contemporary Indian troubles, political and economic, and to present the whole in a western literary form. The action opens at Haridwar, but it is the Haridwar of a vision, and continues in an Indian village - a stylised village where the hopes and sufferings of the epoch are epitomised. The chief character is an old woman. She represents the past, she is the future too. She is the source of the national life, the sacred river, the Well of the People which gives the play its title. In her interesting introduction Miss Sarabhai explains how the idea came to her. She read a story of an aged Brahmin woman who earned four annas a day spinning, and saved up the money to go on a pilgrimage to Benares. But when the time came no one would carry her there. So she spent the money instead on building a well in her own village for the outcasts, and the well still exists.

A few verses from the play may indicate its atmosphere:

<u>Old Woman</u>   I could not go. All I have is not enough.

<u>Peasant</u>   When Haridwar receded, leaving her
<u>Chorus</u>   Dry on the shore, she floated all her vows
                   Like earthen lamps nearer Benares.
                   One word Benares, only say Benares,
                   Benares and she stares - her eyes, their light,
                   Beating like a gong [on] those golden walls.
                                                        Benares

<u>Old Woman</u>   Who will carry me to Benares.[9]

In the end she is not carried - she carries. She[10] bears the suffering myriads of India to their refreshment and salvation. Benares lies within.[11]

Miss Sarabhai's work has attracted much notice in India. She belongs to the younger generation of writers, who sought to be better known in England. The play is often difficult to follow, and that's partly because her subject is difficult - she is contrasting the contemplative mystic and the practical mystic - and partly because the technique she adopts (the technique of Eliot and Auden) doesn't make for clarity. The play reads like a dream: seen on the stage it might acquire a dream's intensity.

[12]I come now to new books published in England. I'll keep to those which have a specific Indian bearing, and I have been reading two excellent accounts of the Japanese invasion of Burma - tragic accounts, I needn't add. Both are by American journalists - Jack Belden and George Rodger. Mr. Belden's book is called <u>Retreat With Stilwell</u> and its title describes it. Having witnessed the destruction of Mandalay and the battle of the Yenangyaung[13] oil fields, he accompanied General Stilwell, the American who had commanded the Chinese in Burma, on his retreat into India.[14] It's a fine book and an honest one, and there's something epic about it. The earlier part is haunted by the Japanese, infiltrating through the trees and swamps, burning, sniping, stealing up the rivers, always nearer than is expected, and seldom seen. The latter part describes the amazing march. General Stilwell led one of the little groups that struggled northward out of the doomed country. This particular group got through, crossed the upper waters of the Chindwin and arrived, on foot, at Manipur. Other groups failed,

> 'These (says Mr. Belden) were the heroes of the retreat from Burma. These, the unnamed and the unsung, were the glorious, the martyred, and the damned. And not we, who thought we suffered, but didn't: who talked glibly of courage and adventure when there wasn't any: who paled at dangers that were never there. These are the people whose pictures should be in the magazines, but aren't; these are the people this book should be about, but isn't, these are the lost children of Burma who got killed.'[15]

There were about 115 people in his group, 21 of them being women. Nationalities included American, English, Chinese, Burman, Indian, Chin, Karen, Kachin, Malaysian, Anglo-Indian, Anglo-Burman, half breeds from all Asia. They went by truck or jeep at first, then they abandoned their transport, threw away their possessions and walked. And what a walk.

> 'Clambering down the rocks, without a moment's hesitation Stilwell plunged into the water. With his tommy gun moving back and forth in rhythm with his stride, he led us directly up the middle of the stream. Behind us like a coloured dragon our column uncoiled from the bank and slid into the water. Between the drab khaki of the men the coloured skirts of the girls flared like an oriental banner. Blue, yellow, purple, red, magenta, green and orange skirts bounced up and down over the surface of the stream. Bare legs glistened in the pale water. The girls were laughing, singing, dancing, jumping up and down in childish

ecstacy, and it seemed as if a chorus troupe was on a holiday excursion. Obstinately scrutinizing his watch and counting 105 steps to the minute, the bow-legged general slogged steadily onward through the shallow water, and the long column of men and girls stretched out in single file behind him as far as the eye would see - a marvellous sight.'[16]

Well, it arrived that column. Through enormous forests, by elephant paths, up mountains, through clouds, it reached India. Others perished, and Mr. Belden doesn't gloss over the gravity of our defeat. Retreat with Stilwell is indeed one of those clever censorious books that appear in the wake of every military disaster. There is a good deal of "surely any one might have foreseen" stuff about it, and the authorities at London and New Delhi, at Washington and Chungking, are liberally blamed. If it was only a clever censorious book I wouldn't recommend it to you as strongly as I do. But it has also power, observation, and humanity. It testifies to the sufferings and courage of men, and to the brilliancy that sometimes attends them, even in their misfortunes. Think of those 115 men and women from Asia, Europe and America walking up a stream in Burma. You get there the richness as well as the horror of the world.

The other book Red Moon Rising is not so remarkable, but it has mar-vellous photographs of the same or similar scenes.[17] The author, George Rodger, is a photographer, and here is Rangoon deserted, Mandalay burn-ing, Sikhs fighting, Indian Refugees, the Burma road seen across the Salween and the swamps and jungles of the north. Mr. Rodger escaped by a route through the Naga country - to the north of the route taken by General Stilwell and his little party. He has the same tale to tell of bureau-cratic incompetence and individual heroism, and he has the same creep-ing dislike of the Japanese. Over here we don't think of the Japanese enough. We are too apt to think of the war as a European one, and to assume that if Hitler is smashed the millennium will start. These books on Burma will help us to adjust our ideas. And by the way - there is an exhi-bition of pictures on in London now at the National Gallery about that part of the world. The pictures are by Mr. Antony Gross, an official artist - sketches of the Arakan operations and of Chin tribesmen.

My quarter of an hour is almost up. One other book to mention, and that is the third and last volume of Professor Coupland's report on the Indian Constitutional Problem.[18] I discussed the preceding volumes a few months ago.[19] They dealt with the past and with the present. Here he examines the prospects of a solution in the future. He writes temperately, learnedly, and from the government point of view, and if you are inter-ested in politics you should read him, whatever your politics may be.

Here's a list of the new books I've mentioned.

Published in India: Echo and Ego by Roop and Mary Krishna. The Poetry of T. S. Eliot by Ahmed Ali. The Well of the People, a play by Bharati Sarabhai.[20]

Published in England: Retreat with Stilwell by Jack Belden, Red Moon Rising by George Rodger, and the final volume of Professor Coupland's constitutional study. The Future of India is its name.[21]

1. Mary Krishna and Roop Krishna, *Echo and Ego* (Lahore: Krishna, 1943).

2. Ahmed Ali, *Mr. Eliot's Penny World of Dreams: An Essay in the Interpretation of T. S. Eliot's Poetry* (Bombay: Lucknow University Press, 1942).

3. <. Here is a theosophical work on Human Nature by Arthur Robson,> Arthur Robson, *Human Nature* (Adyar, Madras, India: Theosophical Publishing House, 1940).

4. Bharati Sarabhai, *The Well of the People* (Calcutta: Visva-Bharati, 1943).

5. <let me>

6. <, though the>

7. EMF added accent marks above "poet" and the first syllable of "preaches."

8. <power>

9. Sarabhai, *The Well of the People*, 30. The quotation is not reproduced exactly. For example, in the transcript, EMF does not distinguish among different peasant speakers but refers to the parts labeled "First Peasant" and "Second Peasant" in Sarabhai's text as "Peasant Chorus."

10. <leaves>

11. EMF originally offered another quotation from the play, which he or a BBC editor crossed out before the talk was broadcast: <"He who thinks he kills was never alive / But he who wills to concentrate on life / For him I promise a world come to drink.">

12. <Having mentioned again Mr. Arthur Robson's book, Human Nature, which is a theosophical exposition of a somewhat specialised character,>

13. EMF added an accent mark above the second syllable of "Yenangyaung."

14. General Joseph Stilwell was commander of the American forces in the China/Burma/India theater during World War II. He served as Chiang Kai-shek's chief of staff in China. Stilwell is best known for his rescue in 1942 of the Chinese Fifth and Sixth Armies, encircled by the Japanese. They marched into India on foot via the Burma Road.

15. Jack Belden, *Retreat with Stilwell* (New York: Knopf, 1943), 307–8.

16. Ibid., 310–11.

17. George Rodger, *Red Moon Rising* (London: Cresset Press, 1943).

18. Sir Reginald Coupland, *The Future of India: The Third Part of a Report on the Constitutional Problem in India Submitted to the Warden and Fellows of Nuffield College, Oxford* (London: Oxford University Press, 1944).

19. 18 July 1943.

20. <Human Nature by Arthur Robson.>

21. EMF handwrote this final sentence at the bottom of the penultimate page, presumably to save needing to turn the page at the conclusion to his talk.

[1]AS BROADCAST
EASTERN SERVICE - PURPLE NETWORK
THURSDAY 6th JANUARY 1944.
1515-1545 GMT.

<u>UNWILLINGLY TO SCHOOL</u>

<u>MATTHEW ARNOLD</u>

<u>By E.M. Forster</u>[2]

Matthew Arnold was born in 1822 and died in 1888, so he is what we call a Victorian. He was the son of a famous schoolmaster Arnold of Rugby, he was well educated in Greek, Latin, French, German and his own language, became inspector of elementary schools, lectured in America, and at home, and became at the end of his life Professor of Poetry at his old university, Oxford. So he is what we call academic, Academic, Victorian, educationist. These are depressing words, and you may feel that Matthew Arnold is only too suitable a subject for the first of a series of talks to schools, and that never never will you read a line of his poetry if you can help it. But of all the great nineteenth century writers he is most on the spot today and most in touch with twentieth century troubles. Carlyle is on the spot too, but it's the wrong spot. Carlyle, with his hysterical hero worship and his denunciations of Parliament foreshadows only too clearly the Nazis. Arnold who disliked Carlyle, believed in sweetness and light, and he is an inspirer of all who long for the light now. He is not only a great poet, he is a person who can help us.

Before I start, I want to recommend a book on him, by a young American scholar, Matthew Arnold by Lionel Trilling.[3] It is a splendid bit of work, a standard biography.

We'll begin with an early poem, Resignation. Arnold was not well satisfied with this poem, and with reason, for it is uneven and it starts badly. He was a bad starter - he takes a little time to warm up. One of the most famous of his sonnets begins with an appalling line 'Who prop, thou ask'st, in these bad days, my mind?' What a line! and 'ask'st'! what a word! Yet the sonnet develops melodiously and contains the famous

phrase 'Who saw life steadily and saw it whole'.[4] And so with this poem
Resignation, listen to its opening stanza, so that you may know what
Arnold is like before he has realised emotionally what he wants to do.

> To die be given us, or attain!
> Fierce work it were, to do again.
> So pilgrims, bound for Mecca, pray'd
> At burning noon; so warriors said,
> Scarf'd with the cross, who watch'd the miles
> Of dust which wreathed their struggling files
> Down Lydian mountains; so, when snows
> Round Alpine summits, eddying, rose,
> The Goth, bound Rome-wards; so the Hun
> Crouch'd on his saddle, while the sun
> Went lurid down o'er flooded plains
> Through which the groaning Danube strains
> To the drear Euxino; — so pray all,
> Whom labours, self-ordain'd, enthrall;
> Because they to themselves propose
> On this side the all-common close
> A goal which, gain'd, may give repose.
> So pray they; and to stand again
> Where they stood once, to them were pain;
> Pain to thread back and to renew
> Past straits, and currents long steer'd through.[5]

We aren't getting much forrader, are we, Academic poetry. The chilly
don, eking out his lack of inspiration with classical references. But now let
us dip into the poem further on. We shall find ourselves in a very different region. Arnold has found his central theme, Resignation. Not the resignation that folds its hands and says "Oh, I can do nothing, oh life is too
awful". But the resignation which enters into life not to possess it but to
comprehend, and thus lives more intensely than the mere possessor.
Listen to this sensitive passage about the poet and note the lines at the
beginning which "subdues his energy to scan Not his own course but that
of man", for they will give you the key to what follows. Resignation is not
introspection, it is rather emotional understanding. If I, in this studio,
could enter into your life in India without appropriating it or exploiting it,
I shall be, in Arnold's sense, a poet.

> The poet, to whose mighty heart
> Heaven doth a quicker pulse impart,
> Subdues that energy to scan
> Not his own course, but that of man.

Though he move mountains, though his day
Be pass'd on the proud heights of sway,
Though he hath loosed a thousand chains,
Though he hath borne immortal pains,
Action and suffering though he know -
He hath not lived, if he lives so.
He sees, in some great-historied land,
A ruler of the people stand,
Sees his strong thought in fiery flood
Roll through the heaving multitude
Exults - yet for no moment's space
Envies the all-regarded place.
Beautiful eyes meet his - and he
Bears to admire uncravingly;
They pass - he, mingled with the crowd,
Is in their far-off triumphs proud.
From some high station he looks down,
At sunset, on a populous town;
Surveys each happy group, which fleets,
Toil ended, through the shining streets,
Each with some errand of its own -
And does not say: I am alone.
He sees the gentle stir of birth
When morning purifies the earth;
He leans upon a gate and sees
The pastures, and the quiet trees.
Low, woody hill, with gracious bound,
Folds the still valley almost round;
The cuckoo, loud on some high lawn,
Is answered from the depth of dawn;
In the hedge straggling to the stream,
Pale, dew-drench'd, half-shut roses gleam;
But, where the farther side slopes down,
He sees the drowsy now-waked clown
In his white quaint-embroider'd frock
Make, whistling, tow'rd his mist-wreathed flock -
Slowly, behind his heavy tread,
The wet, flower'd grass heaves up its head.
Lean'd on his gate, he gazes - tears
Are in his eyes, and in his ears
The murmur of a thousand years.
Before him he sees life unroll,

A placid and continuous whole
That general life, which does not cease,
Whose secret is not joy, but peace;
That life, whose dumb wish is not miss'd
If birth proceeds, if things subsist;
The life of plants, and stones, and rain,
The life he craves - if not in vain
Fate gave, what chance shall not control,
His sad lucidity of soul.[6]

Arnold has no particular feeling for India, and was not influenced by Indian thought. Nevertheless one could draw a parallel between the above passage and some of the teaching of the Bhagavad Gita. There too we are enjoined to resign - not from action but from the fruits of action. There too we catch a glimpse of 'That general life . . . . Whose secret is not joy but peace.'

The poem now shoots up into the sublime. In the last quotation it was English - the imagery recalled the England of Milton's L'Allegro - now it attains the lofty region where all countries commingle and national colourings fade. I should add Arnold addresses the poem to his sister: she is the 'Fausta' who occurs in the forth-coming quotation.

The world in which we live and move
Outlasts aversion, outlasts love,
Outlasts each effort, interest, hope,
Remorse, grief, joy; - and were the scope
Of these affections wider made,
Man still would see, and see dismay'd,
Beyond his passion's widest range,
Far regions of eternal change.
Nay, and since death, which wipes out man,
Finds him with many an unsolved plan,
With much unknown, and much untried,
Wonder not dead, and thirst not dried,
Still gazing on the ever full
Eternal mundane spectacle -
This world in which we draw our breath,
In some sense, Fausta, outlasts death.[7]

The greatness of the universe is too great for man. It will outlast him - and isn't there something deeply wrong with it? I put this in question-form, because Arnold alters his feelings about the universe at different times of his life. In Resignation he concludes that there is something wrong, he is pessimistic, and he warns us not to delude ourselves by supposing that if we go in for action, for practical life, we shall put right this wrong.

Enough, we live! - and if a life,
With large results so little rife,
Though bearable seem hardly worth
This pomp of worlds, this pain of birth;
Yet, Fausta, the mute turf we tread,
The solemn hills around us spread,
This stream which falls incessantly,
The strange-scrawl'd rocks, the lonely sky,
If I might lend their life a voice,
Seem to bear rather than rejoice.
And even could the intemperate prayer
Man iterates, while these forbear,
For movements, for an ampler sphere,
Pierce Fate's impenetrable ear;
Not milder is the general lot
Because our spirits have forgot,
In action's dizzying eddy whirl'd,
The something that infects the world.[8]

Thus the poem ends. What a change from the chill academic, with which it started! The cold at the close is the cold of eternity, and its consummation is not action, not joy, but peace.

I have suggested to you that of all the great Victorians Arnold is most on the spot today. His troubles seem to be ours, and his remedies practicable. For one thing he desired peace - and how do we! For another, he had not the childish Victorian faith in the beneficence of science. He knew that human destiny depends not upon what men make but upon what they think and feel. Again he was absolutely sincere so his voice reaches us free from overtones. He was moreover compassionate. That great virtue he shared with his contemporaries. They were horrified by human death and suffering; we are not. In the catastrophe that has befallen our civilisation, we have all become callous as an alternative to going mad. Matthew Arnold reminds us that it is possible to be sensitive as well as sane, and that the possibility may recur. He reminds us - to come to lesser things, of the importance of great literature, of culture. He warns us against Philistinism, against saying 'I know what I know and I like what I like and that is enough for me.' He hates pedantry. He has a sense of history. For these reasons we keep meeting him on our steep path through the 1940's, even as he in his century, kept meeting his guide, the author of Obermann. You shall hear some verses presently from one of the

Obermann poems. But our next quotation is a poem called The Future. It is a sustained work, based upon a single image, that of a river, and I shall not interrupt with any comment. It is a general survey of the destiny of man, and the conclusion, unlike that of Resignation, admits hope.

A wanderer is man from his birth.
He was born in a ship
On the breast of the river of Time;
Brimming with wonder and joy
He spreads out his arms to the light,
Rivets his gaze on the banks of the stream.

As what he sees is, so have his thoughts been.
Whether he wakes,
Where the snowy mountainous pass,
Echoing the screams of the eagles,
Hems in its gorges the bed
Of the new-born clear-flowing stream;
Whether he first sees light
Where the river in gleaming rings
Sluggishly winds through the plain;
Whether in sound of the swallowing sea -
As is the world on the banks,
So is the mind of the man.

Vainly does each, as he glides,
Fable and dream
Of the lands which the river of Time
Had left ere he woke on its breast,
Or shall reach when his eyes have been closed.
Only the tract where he sails
He wots of; only the thoughts,
Raised by the objects he passes, are his.

This tract which the river of Time
Now flows through with us, is the plain.
Gone is the calm of its earlier shore.
Border'd by cities and hoarse
With a thousand cries is its stream.
And we on its breast, our minds
Are confused as the cries which we hear,
Changing and shot as the sights which we see.

And we say that repose has fled
For ever the course of the river of Time.
That cities will crowd to its edge
In a blacker, incessanter line;
That the din will be more on its banks,
Denser the trade on its stream,
Flatter the plain where it flows,
Fiercer the sun overhead.
That never will those on its breast
See an ennobling sight,
Drink of the feeling of quiet again.

But what was before us we know not,
And we know not what shall succeed.

Haply, the river of Time -
As it grows, as the towns on its marge
Fling their wavering lights
On a wider, statelier stream -
May acquire, if not the calm
Of its early mountainous shore,
Yet a solemn peace of its own.

And the width of the waters, the hush
Of the grey expanse where he floats,
Freshening its current and spotted with foam
As it draws to the Ocean, may strike
Peace to the soul of the man on its breast -
As the pale waste widens around him,
As the banks fade dimmer away,
As the stars come out, and the night-wind
Brings up the stream
Murmurs and scents of the infinite sea.[9]

This is a wonderful survey of the future - though as a friend of mine said the other day it misses out the terrible cataracts down which the River of Time had yet to crash; it misses out the 20th century wars. It is a philosophic poem, not a historical one. Philosophy, thoughtfulness, dominates most of Arnold's work. Even when he is personal, the destiny of humanity recurs. There is a famous group of love-lyrics - and they too pass to the topic of the 'general lot'. The group is connected with Switzerland and with a girl there called Marguerite. There was a good deal of hush-hush over Marguerite, of a kind that seems foolish today, and we don't know

much about her. She was probably of humble birth, he was for a time
deeply in love with her, and she inspired him, then their ways parted, and
later on he fell in love with an English woman of his own rank, married
and was happy, and Marguerite was forgotten - except in the immortality
of verse.

> Like driftwood spars, which meet and pass[10]
> Upon the boundless ocean-plain,
> So on the sea of life, Alas!
> Man meets man - meets and quits again.
>
> I knew it when my life was young;
> I feel it still, now youth is O'er.
> - The mists are on the mountain hung
> And Marguerite I shall see no more.[11]

Thus does he look back, with tenderness and without bitterness. Here
is another of the poems, composed ten years earlier.

> Yes! in the sea of life enisled,
> With echoing straits between us thrown,
> Dotting the shoreless watery wild
> We mortal millions live alone.
> The islands feel the enclasping flow,
> And then their endless bounds they know.
>
> But when the moon their hollows lights,
> And they are swept by balms of spring,
> And in their glens, on starry nights,
> The nightingales divinely sing;
> And lovely notes, from shore to shore,
> Across the sounds and channels pour -
>
> Oh! then a longing like despair
> Is to their farthest caverns sent;
> For surely once, they feel, we were
> Parts of a single continent!
> Now round us spreads the watery plain -
> Oh might our marges meet again!
>
> Who order'd that their longing's fire
> Should be, as soon as kindled, cool'd?
> Who renders vain their deep desire? -
> A God, a God their severance ruled!

And bade betwixt their shores to be
The unplumb'd salt, estranging sea.[12]

The Marguerite poems have always moved me deeply, and do so more than ever now, for the scenery where they occur - the lake of Thun, the Terrace at Berne - happens to be the last which I saw before Hitler pulled down his shutters of steel on to Europe. Here are two more from the series that speak to my heart, and may touch yours.

Yet we shall one day gain, life past,
Clear prospect o'er our beings whole;
Shall see ourselves, and learn at last
Our true affinities of soul.

We shall not then deny a course
To every thought the mass ignore;
We shall not then call hardness force
Nor lightness wisdom any more.[13]

Not to mistake hardness for force. Yes, Matthew Arnold is on the spot.

Now I must make some reference to his Oxford poems - to The Scholar Gypsy and to Thyrsis. They too are personal and they too pass from the personal to the general. They are full of delicate and opulent references to the Oxfordshire countryside, exhale a nostalgia which Oxford men appreciate best. The second of them is an elegy on the poet's friend, Arthur Hugh Clough.[14] Arnold had once been very fond of Clough, who had himself shown high promise as a poet. But the promise had not matured. Clough had found life too painful; his sensitiveness was not strengthened, as Arnold's was, by virility, his resignation had taken the form of 'Oh I can do nothing', and he had faded away. Arnold had seen little of him in later years and Thyrsis is more an elegy on vanished youth than on Clough. Contrast it with Tennyson's In Memoriam, which is, first and foremost a lament for a friend. Here are the opening stanzas of Thyrsis.

How changed is here each spot man makes or fills!
 In the two Hinkseys nothing keeps the same;
The village street its haunted mansion lacks,
 And from the sign is gone Sibylla's name,
And from the roofs the twisted chimney-stacks -
 Are ye too changed, ye hills?
See, 'tis no foot of unfamiliar men
 Tonight from Oxford up your pathway strays!
 Here came I often, often, in old days -
Thyrsis and I; we still had Thyrsis then.

Runs it not here, the track by Childsworth Farm,
 Past the high wood, to where the elm-tree crowns
The hill behind whose ridge the sunset flames?
 The signal-elm, that looks on Ilsley Downs,
The Vale, the three lone weirs, the youthful Thames?
 This winter-eve is warm,
Humid the air! leafless, yet soft as spring,
 The tender purple spray on copse and briers!
 And that sweet city with her dreaming spires,
She needs not June for beauty's heightening.

Lovely all times she lies, lovely to-night! -
 Only, methinks, some loss of habit's power
Befalls me wandering through this upland dim.
 Once pass'd I blindfold here, at any hour;
Now seldom come I, since I came with him.
 That single elm-tree bright
Against the west - I miss it! is it gone?
 We prized it dearly; while it stood, we said,
Our friend, the Gypsy-Scholar, was not dead;
While the tree lived, he in these fields lived on.

Too rare, too rare, grow now my visits here,
 But once I knew each field, each flower, each stick;
And with the country-folk acquaintance made
 By barn in threshing-time, by new-built rick.
Here, too, our shepherd-pipes we first assay'd.
 Ah me! this many a year
My pipe is lost, my shepherd's holiday!
 Needs must I lose them, needs with heavy heart
 Into the world and wave of men depart;
But Thyrsis of his own will went away.

It irk'd him to be here, he could not rest.
 He loved each simple joy the country yields,
 He loved his mates; but yet he could not keep,
For that a shadow lour'd on the fields,
 Here with the shepherds and the silly sheep.
 Some life of men unblest
He knew, which made him droop, and fill'd his head.
 He went; his piping took a troubled sound

Of storms that rage outside our happy ground;
He could not wait their passing, he is dead.

So, some tempestuous morn in early June,
 When the year's primal burst of bloom is o'er,
 Before the roses and the longest day -
When garden-walks and all the grassy floor
 With blossoms red and white of fallen May
 And chestnut-flowers are strewn -
So have I heard the cuckoo's parting cry,
 From the wet field, through the vext garden-trees,
 Come with the volleying rain and tossing breeze:
The bloom is gone, and with the bloom go I!

Too quick despairer, wherefore wilt thou go?
 Soon will the high Midsummer pomps come on,
 Soon will the musk carnations break and swell,
Soon shall we have gold-dusted snapdragon,
 Sweet-William with his homely cottage smell,
 And stocks in fragrant blow;
Roses that down the alleys shine afar,
 And open, jasmine-muffled lattices,
 And groups under the dreaming garden-trees,
And the full moon, and the white evening-star.

He hearkens not: light comer, he is flown!
 What matters it? next year he will return,
 And we shall have him in the sweet spring-days,
With whitening hedges, and uncrumpling fern,
 And blue-bells trembling by the forest-ways,
 And scent of hay new-mown.
But Thyrsis never more we swains shall see;
 See him come back, and cut a smoother reed,
 And blow a strain the world at last shall heed -
For Time, not Corydon, hath conquer'd thee![15]

You will perhaps complain that Arnold is always worrying about something, that he is a poet who thinks too much, and he would agree. Once in a way he got free, and gave us The Forsaken Merman; justly famous, this poem is not only colourful and fanciful, but it has a music which is rare in his work. Arnold, as a rule, hadn't much of an ear, and knew it; here are the final stanzas. You are sure to have read the poem, and will remember that the mortal maiden (named Margaret by the way) has married a Merman and deserted him for her own people.

> Down, down, down!
> Down to the depths of the sea!
> She sits at her wheel in the humming town,
> Singing most joyfully.
> Hark what she sings: "O joy, O joy,
> For the humming street, and the child with its toy!
> For the priest, and the bell, and the holy well;
> For the wheel where I spun,
> And the blessed light of the sun!"
> And so she sings her fill,
> Singing most joyfully,
> Till the spindle drops from her hand,
> And the whizzing wheel stands still.
> She steals to the window, and looks at the sand,
> And over the sand at the sea;
> And her eyes are set in a stare;
> And anon there breaks a sigh,
> And anon there drops a tear,
> From a sorrow-clouded eye,
> And a heart sorrow-laden,
> A long, long sigh;
> For the cold strange eyes of a little Mermaiden
> And the gleam of her golden hair.
>
> Come away, away children;
> Come children, come down!
> The hoarse wind blows coldly;
> Lights shine in the town.
> She will start from her slumber
> When gusts shake the door;
> She will hear the winds howling,
> Will hear the waves roar.
> We shall see, while above us
> The waves roar and whirl,
> A ceiling of amber,
> A pavement of pearl.
> Singing: "Here came a mortal,
> But faithless was she!

And alone dwell for ever
The kings of the sea."

But, children, at midnight,
When soft the winds blow,
When clear falls the moonlight,
When spring-tides are low;
When sweet airs come seaward
From heaths starr'd with broom,
And high rocks throw mildly
On the blanch'd sands a gloom;
  Up the still, glistening beaches,
Up the creeks we will hie,
Over banks of bright seaweed
The ebb-tide leaves dry.
We will gaze, from the sand-hills,
At the white, sleeping town;
At the church on the hill-side -
And then come back down.
Singing "There dwells a loved one,
But cruel is she!
She left lonely for ever
The kings of the sea."[16]

Two more quotations, and then we will leave you to the enjoyment of this very great and poignantly 'actual' poet, and to the study, if you can get hold of it - of Lionel Trilling's book on him. The first is from "Obermann Once More". There are two Obermann poems, and Obermann, whom I have already mentioned as Arnold's spiritual guide, occurs in a book of a little known writer called Senancour, a book inspired by nature and the Alpine solitudes.[17] We are in Switzerland again, and it is along the Lake of Geneva that Arnold imagines them meeting. The poem, besides lovely descriptions of scenery, contains a famous survey of European civilisation - the survey of one who is not duped[18] by material triumphs, and does not mistake hardness for force. Here are some stanzas describing the coming and the failure of Christianity - for though Arnold was outwardly orthodox he believed that Christianity had failed, and he delegates Obermann to say so.

"Oh, had I lived in that great day,
How had its glory new
Fill'd earth and heaven, and caught away
My ravish'd spirit too!

"No lonely life had pass'd too slow,
When I could hourly scan
Upon his Cross, with head sunk low,
That nail'd, thorn-crowned Man!

"Could see the Mother with her Child
Whose tender winning arts
Have to his little arms beguiled
So many wounded hearts!

"And centuries came and ran their course,
And unspent all that time
Still, still went forth that Child's dear force,
And still was at its prime.

"Ay, ages long endured his span
Of life - 'tis true received -
That gracious Child, that thorn-crown'd Man!
 He lived while we believed.

"While we believed, on earth he went,
And open stood his grave.
Men call'd from chamber, church, and tent;
And Christ was by to save.

"Now he is dead! Far hence he lies
In the lorn Syrian town;
And on his grave, with shining eyes,
The Syrian stars look down.["]¹⁹

Finally, here is the greatest of Arnold's sonnets - the one on Shakespeare. To compare Arnold to Shakespeare would be ridiculous, and would cause his ghost to smile sardonically. But he was near enough to him to pay a homage which most of us are too small to give.

Others abide our question. Thou art free.
We ask and ask - Thou smilest and art still,
Out-topping knowledge. For the loftiest hill,
Who to the stars uncrowns his majesty,

Planting his steadfast footsteps in the sea,
Making the heaven of heavens his dwelling-place,
Spares but the cloudy border of his base

To the foil'd searching of mortality;
And thou, who didst the stars and sunbeams know,
Self-school'd, self-scann'd, self-honour'd, self-secure,
Didst tread on earth unguess'd at. - Better so!

All pains the immortal spirit must endure,
All weakness which impairs, all griefs which bow,
Find their sole speech in that victorious brow.[20]

1. <NOT CHECKED WITH>

2. Edward Sackville-West, who produced this talk for the Features and Drama Department, requested that EMF "include 14 minutes of Arnold's poetry, to be read at intervals in the course of the talk - as examples of the points you make . . . this will make a more acceptable broadcast than 15 minutes solid talk followed by a 14 minute wedge of poetry. It will also be (1) less tiring for both readers, and (2) have the additional advantage of being more homogeneous, since otherwise I should have to choose the poems and might not choose what you would like" (Sackville-West to EMF, 20 December 1943, E. M. Forster File 5, 1943 R CONT 1, BBC WAC).

3. Lionel Trilling, *Matthew Arnold* (London: Allen and Unwin, 1939).

4. "To a Friend," *The Poems, 1840–1867* (London: Oxford University Press, 1937), lines 1, 12.

5. "Resignation," lines 1–21.

6. Ibid., lines 144–98.

7. Ibid., lines 215–30.

8. Ibid., lines 261–78.

9. EMF quotes "The Future" in its entirety.

10. Due to an apparent typing error, "meet and pass" is reproduced as "sweetened" in the transcript.

11. "The Terrace at Berne," lines 45–52.

12. EMF quotes "To Marguerite" in its entirety.

13. "A Farewell," lines 53–60.

14. Arthur Hugh Clough (1819–1961), poet and an Oxford associate of Arnold's.

15. "Thyrsis," lines 1–80.

16. "The Forsaken Merman," lines 85–143.

17. Étienne Pivert de Senancour, *Obermann* (Paris: Cérioux, 1804).

18. EMF likely meant "duped," though the transcript reads "doped."

19. "Obermann Once More," lines 141–44, 152–76.

20. EMF quotes "Shakespeare" in its entirety.

SOME BOOKS

by

E.M. FORSTER

I've read two new books which have impressed me and I hope they may come your way some time. One is a novel, the other is an autobiography. I shall concentrate in my[2] talk this evening on these two books, and give most of the time to the novel. Its title is <u>Arrival and Departure</u> and it is by a refugee, Arthur Koestler.[3] Mr. Koestler comes from central Europe, and now he is continuing his fight against the Nazis over here. He is a brilliant writer, and a man of courage and generosity with a strong and strange bent of mind. Hitler's folly has been our gain, for if circumstances had been normal, Mr. Koestler would have certainly remained on the continent, writing in German and carrying on the tradition of continental culture. But he has had to[4] escape to England and write in English, and the horrors through which he has passed give him a driving force and an authority which are unique and sometimes scaring. It is well we should be scared for we are too prone to believe that the worst that can happen to a civilian in a war is to be blitzed and then buried by his own people. Mr. Koestler shows that there are worse fates: scientific torture: air raids on the soul.

I broadcast about a year ago on a book by him called <u>Scum of the Earth</u> where he described his escape from France.[5] Though <u>Arrival and Departure</u> is fiction parts of it may be biography. I'll give you an account of it. The scene is laid in a European country called Neutralia which has kept out of the war - evidently Portugal is intended - and it opens with the arrival of the hero, Peter Slavec. Peter arrives as a stowaway, slips over board into the harbour where his boat anchors, and swims ashore in the dark. He is a student from the Balkan area: we don't know more of him than that - he has been connected with the communist party and been badly beaten up by his local Gestapo, and now he wants to get away from it all and go to America. He has lost all faith in communism, though he behaved heroically under torture and betrayed none of his late associates. "Behaved heroically?" Well, has he? The world thinks so, but he himself has a profound feeling of guilt and is haunted by an evil dream: He believes that he has been a traitor. But when? and to whom? He can't say, no more can we, but as he creeps out of the darkness and enters the sunny capital of Neutralia, we realise that the book's theme won't be adventure or politics, but individual psychology, and that the upheaval of war has accelerated the break up of a soul.

Peter - who has brought some money with him and a bundle[6] of clothes - trails round the restaurants and up to the allied consulates and tries to book a passage to the New World. There are difficulties, delays. The city is full of refugees, some of whom know his fine record and would like to be friendly. He shrinks from them and he is not grateful when a compatriot and old friend of his family, a woman doctor called Sonia, receives him into her flat. His evil dream pursues him there. It is about a flower pot. A flower pot? Things improve when he falls in love with a friend of Sonia's, Odette. He is happy for a little while. Then he gets a note from Odette saying that she has got her passage and is off to America, and hopes he will follow her there if he can. The loss of his mistress upsets him, as is natural, but the upset assumes supernatural proportions. He falls ill. His left leg is paralysed, he tumbles about Sonia's flat and has to be put to bed, another doctor is[7] called in, pins are driven into him and he cannot feel them. Something is deeply wrong - something deeper than Odette or the sadistic police; they are the occasions by which evil is raised into the light of day.

In the next chapters we learn what the deep experience was, and Mr. Koestler presents it with such skill that we seem to be implicated. Peter Slovac went wrong at the age of five when a baby brother whom he hated was killed. He wasn't guilty but then was confirmed a fantasy of guilt which had already hovered round the person of a stern judging father. His father and the chief of police who later on had him tortured - are part of the same morbid sequence. And the fatal and grotesque dream of the flower pot - it was connected with the fantasy that he had caused his mother's death, caused it by the catastrophe of his baby brother, caused it again recently when the police arrested him in her flat. Sonia, who is a psycho-analyst makes him face his past and put its pieces together. She frees him from his sense of guilt. He has never been a traitor.[8] Nor a hero either. In both roles he has been posing and mistaking the inhibitions of childhood for the decisions of an adult. He recovers his health and can walk properly, and there is no reason why he should not follow Odette to America.

I can't, in this summary, do justice to the literary merits[9] of the book. I'm making it sound too like a clinical report. Believe me it is vivid as well as profound and it implies a terrific indictment of Hitler and all who imitate the methods of Hitler. The climax of horror is a description of the little trains which go about Nazi Europe in the night, taking Jews to be massacred and women into prostitution, and these trains pass behind the sunlit restaurants and the loafing crowds of Neutralia. The book isn't perfect as a work of art. A writer who penetrates as deeply into motive as Mr. Koestler, often has to sacrifice verisimilitude of surface, and I don't think that the three chief characters of <u>Arrival and Departure</u> have the reality: well of Charlotte Bronte's Jane Eyre: Jane Eyre[10] pops into my mind because I've just seen a film on her. We know all about them. But we don't know[11] them.

This remark - it sounds cryptic - leads us to the final section of the novel. Peter knows all about[12] himself. But does he know[13] himself? Sonia has cleaned[14] him up, and all he has to do is to go to America and live logically. But does he want[15] to live logically? Granted that his reasons for heroism were wrong - do reasons matter? Isn't it better at a moment of history like this to go on being brave if you can? He gets his permit, takes his ticket, goes on board. He sees there his fellow refugees escaping with him, and Nazi agents, setting out to poison the New World, and he revolts. Just as the boat is moving off, he leaps back on to shore, returns to the bewildered allied consulate, and volunteers for active service. The last we see of him is - Departure. A trained parachutist, he leaps out of a plane and floats down on a secret mission into Europe. From a previous hint in the book we know that he succeeds, and becomes a hero to his generation. But his success isn't our concern.

Don't read <u>Arrival and Departure</u> if you are squeamish or if you dislike mysticism. Its solution is[16] mystic. The findings of science are accepted, but the consequences of those findings are rejected. Peter believes, against reason, that a new god is going to be born, and that he must not speak about this yet, must not even think of it often. For my own part I don't share Peter's solution but then I have not had to share his sufferings.

[17]To turn from this novel to the autobiography I want to mention, its title is <u>Double Lives</u> and it is by William Plomer. Double Lives I recommend to every one. You are certain to enjoy it and you may love it. It's charmingly written,[18] amusing and witty, and brilliant in its descriptions of England, South Africa, and Japan, and it's civilised and mature without

being sedate. I love it, because its values are my own, and to read it after Arrival and Departure is to escape from subterranean night-mares into the upper air. The one book is not "better" than the other - that would be a crude judgement to pass; and when we say "the upper air" we mustn't forget that there, too, flames and storms can burst out. There too Mr. Plomer hints at some of these - for example when he speaks of racial prejudice, or of militarism in Japan. But Double Lives is on the whole equable and happy: it is the record of a sensitive yet efficient young man who has managed to harmonise reason with emotion, and to meet adventure rather than cruelty as he bumps about the world.

Mr. Plomer was born in South Africa, and until he was 22 lived partly there, partly in England: hence the Double Lives of the title. His book begins with an account of his ancestry. It gets better and better as it goes on, towards the end where he helps his parents to keep a store up in Zululand, where he enjoyed the work and admired the inhabitants, and adored the scenery. Devoid of all prejudices, whether racial or social, he starts to be a[19] novelist. Then he has a romantic adventure. He meets a Japanese captain who takes him on his cargo-ship to Japan, and he settles in that country for a time, supports himself by teaching English, and learns much. In the 1920's Japan was still comparatively liberal, the suppression of "dangerous thoughts" had not begun, and William Plomer found much to admire there and even to love. I will quote the final paragraph of his book. It will show the charm of his style and the enlightenment of his mind: -

> It seems to me that I have been very fortunate to have known and enjoyed, in youth and in time of peace, spells of existence in Africa and Asia, and later to have seen something of immeasurable Russia, of independent Poland, of Germany before Hitler, of Italy before she was brought to ruin by the ridiculous Mussolini, of France before the collapse, and above all Greece. Civilisation has many dialects but only one language, and its Japanese voice will always be present to my ear, like the pure and liquid notes of the bamboo flute in those tropical evenings on the Indian Ocean, when I heard it for the first time, speaking of things far more important than war, trade and empires - of unworldliness, lucidity and love.[20]

That's the lesson William Plomer has learnt from this age of upheaval: the need of unworldliness, lucidity, and love. It's a good lesson, and without condemning the conclusions of Arthur Koestler one may say that it would be difficult to find two contemporary writers who were more unlike.

1. <NOT CHECKED WITH BROADCAST>
2. <today's>
3. Arthur Koestler, *Arrival and Departure* (London: Jonathan Cape, 1943).
4. <come>
5. See EMF's broadcast dated 15 October 1941.
6. EMF added an accent mark above the first syllable of "bundle."
7. <summoned>
8. EMF added accent marks above "never" and "been" and the first syllable of "traitor."
9. <power>
10. <comes>
11. EMF added an accent mark above "know."
12. EMF added an accent mark above the second syllable of "about."
13. EMF added an accent mark above "know."
14. EMF added an accent mark above "cleaned."
15. EMF added an accent mark above "want."
16. EMF added an accent mark above "is."
17. In the margin next to this paragraph is the time mark "4 - 4 1/2 to go."
18. <most>
19. <writer>
20. William Plomer, *Double Lives: An Autobiography* (London: Jonathan Cape, 1943), 216. EMF added accent marks above "above" and "Greece" in the first sentence of this quotation.

[1]Eastern Service
Purple Network
Thursday, 24th February, 1944
1515-1530 GMT

SOME BOOKS

by

E.M. Forster

A new book on James Joyce has come along.[2] Joyce is so difficult to get, and when one has got him so difficult to understand that a good book on him is a godsend, and I can recommend this one. It's by a young American, Harry Levin.[3] The Americans have been doing excellent criticism - sensitive, thorough, and detailed. I was mentioning the other day that study of Matthew Arnold by another young American, Lionel Trilling, and[4] suggesting that it was the authoritative work on Arnold. And now here's Mr. Harry Levin on Joyce. It may not be the last word on Joyce: he wouldn't claim that it was himself. But it has certainly helped me enormously, and I need a good deal of help.

Why? Because - to be honest - I don't really[5] take to Joyce. I can[6] admire him but I don't[7] take to him. He doesn't display, in his writings, the sort of character I care for; he is vindictive and he is soured. That's no hindrance to him as an artist any more than snobbery and neurosis were hindrances to the artist in Proust. But if you happen to dislike vindictiveness and sourness the artist who displays[8] them slows you up, and when you find that he is also obscure and uncompromising,[9] may stick altogether. That has been my case. I have sometimes stuck in James Joyce. And though I get on better with him now, I shall never take him to my heart, nor would he wish me or any one to do so.

He produced four major works - Dubliners, which is a volume of short stories. Portrait of the Artist as a Young Man, an autobiographical novel; the famous Ulysses; and finally Finnegan's Wake. This last I haven't tackled yet, though Mr. Harry Levin encourages one to have a shot. On these four works his reputation rests. And in my talk to day I am going - not to criticise them: I haven't the time or the apparatus - but to give you or rather hand on to you a tip.

The tip is that Joyce was an Exile. We are familiar with exiles today, it is the tragic age of refugees, there are millions of them, but he wasn't an exile in that sense. He wasn't driven out. He drove himself out. He deliberately abandoned his triple heritage of a country, a religion, and a language. His country: he was born Irish, a Dubliner. And he abandoned Ireland. He left her at the age of 22 to live abroad. Ten years later he visited her for the last time, in a futile attempt to get his short stories printed there, then[10] retired in bitterness and never ceased jeering at his native land. He calls her, in an early[11] satire,

> This lovely land that always sent
> Her writers and artists to banishment
> And in a spirit of Irish fun
> Betrayed her own leaders one by one.[12]

And he didn't just abuse Irish Philistinism and intolerance. He was also bitter against the Irish literary movement. He attacked Yeats ('You are too old for me to help you' he wrote), he called Irish art 'the cracked looking glass of a servant', and reserved his sharpest knives for the Celtic Twilight.[13] The Irish would not have been human if they hadn't resented this, and to say that Joyce is unpopular in his native country is to put it mildly.[14] Difficult to obtain any where, his books can't be got in Ireland at all, I believe. She has deprived herself of his[15] genius.

He rejected his country, and his religion. He was born into the Catholic Church, and trained by the Jesuits. He exiled himself from that also. He abandoned the faith of his ancestors and was excommunicated. Of that I shall say more in a moment. Here I want to point out that, thirdly, he abandoned his language. He was born into the use of the English language, and his earlier books are written in it. But in Ulysses he is breaking down the normal idiom of English, and in Finnegan's Wake the process has gone much further. Many of the words in Finnegan's Wake aren't in the dictionary at all. They are made up out of other words, and sometimes not out of English words, for he was a learned linguist. It is, as Mr. Levin calls it, the language of the outlaw. Away from his country, away from his faith, he has also tended to exile himself from his speech. And he suffered a fourth form of exile, which was not of his seeking. Towards the end of his life, he became blind. Consider all this, and you will realise what an unusual writer he must be, and how likely we are to misjudge him.

For if we consider him, as I've so far been doing, in terms of his deprivations, we shall go quite wrong. He abandoned a great deal, but what did he gain? Nothing by the world's judgement. A great deal, if we seek the subtler judgement of art. Joyce managed to build up something that was unique, something which represents our troubled age more than our age likes to confess - something very disquieting, very unsatisfying, something which lacks the milk of kindness and even dramatic movement, but it expresses our inmost writhings with an appropriateness that achieves beauty. Mr. Levin illustrates it thus:

> Joyce's characters move in space but they do not develop in time. They only look forward to the ruin of all space, to Time's livid final flame, to doomsday. Ulysses is not so rich in psychological insight as in technical brilliance. The burning intensity of Joyce's own creative effort animates the statuesque coldness of his creations. It beats down, like an aroused volcano upon an ancient city, overtaking the doomed inhabitants in forum or temple, at home or at brothel, and petrifying them in the insensate agonies of paralysis.[16]

With all his[17] resentment, Joyce loved play. It amused him to write and to exercise that technical brilliance, he enjoyed handling words, and it's here that his central impulse is to be found. He was an artificer of words, and he calls himself in his books Stephen Dedalus, because Dedalus in Greek mythology was the first craftsman. Stephen Dedalus is the hero of Portrait of the Artist as a Young Man, and also appears as a character in Ulysses; he is interested in events, and people it is true, but still more in the words which express them and[18] even in words for their own sake. To put it another way Joyce's work tends to twist away from fiction towards music, and that's one of the reasons why I get stuck in it. I like a novel to be a novel. I expect it to be about something or someone. And when I realise that even his condemnation of the human race is incidental, and that what really interests him is words, their overtones, their undertones. I get annoyed. It is[19] foolish to get annoyed. One can cure oneself, and should. It is foolish to insist that a novel must be a novel. One must take what comes along, and see if it's good. I'll read now a few sentences out of Finnegan's Wake. Two old washerwomen are on the bank of the Liffey, the river that flows through Dublin, and the night is about to change them into an elm tree and into a stone. But the words aren't trying to say that. The words are - so to speak - starting from that and trying to become music.

> Can't hear with the waters of. The chittering waters of. Flittering bats, fieldmice bawk talk. Ho! Are you not gone a home? What Thom Malone? Can't hear with bawk of bats, all them liffeying waters of. Ho, talk save us! My fous won't mous. I feel as old as yonder elm. . . . Night night. My ho head halls. I feel as heavy as yonder stone. Tell me of John or Shaum? Who were Shem and Shaun the living sons or daughters of? Night now! Tell me, tell me, tell me, elm! Night, night! Telmetale of

stem or stone. Beside the rivering waters, of, hitherand-thithering waters of. Night.[20]

Most of the above words happen to be English. But the whole passage isn't English. Literature isn't playing the game. It's playing some other game. It's verging towards music. And why shouldn't it? Don't let's lose our tempers.

That's what many people do about Joyce. They turn cross. Comments about him are usually abusive, and when they are not they proceed from highly trained critics who are sympathetic to him and rather above the general public's head. I believe that there are a good many readers who are in the same boat as myself - that's to say muddled and vexed by the uncomfortable fellow but certain that he's not a fake, and it's to them I'm now speaking. Let me return for a minute to two of his exiles - his exile from his country, Ireland, and from his religion. Here again Mr. Harry Levin brings first aid. He points out that though Joyce left Dublin as a city and Catholicism as a faith, they both remained with him as ingredients for his art. The action of all his books takes place in or around Dublin. He never visualised any other city, although he lived for years on the continent, Paris, Trieste, Zurich, etc., and rightly called himself a European. After leaving Dublin, he picked up thousands of new words but no new impressions. The shutters of his observation closed down. This has been ascribed to his increasing blindness, but he was probably of the type of which Wordsworth, among others belong: the type which experiences acutely in youth, and is afterwards dependent on memories and combinations. He never got away from the city he hated, and he didn't want to get away from it. He found in it a target for his art. Nor did he get away from his religion. He rejected the doctrines of his Jesuit teachers, he could not throw off their methods, nor again did he wish to. He protested against Catholicism by inverting it - and this accounts for the blasphemies in him which naturally shock the believer, and which appear to the outsider like myself, as bad manners. The rejected country, the rejected creed - they remain in other forms in the exile's soul and he makes use of them in his writing. His writing is what mattered to him. The words. The words. And he compared the mystery of esthetic to the mystery of material creation. He believed in art for art's sake, though he was anything but arty, and we must remember this when we try to read him: it has just carried me through my second reading of Ulysses.

Mr. T.S. Eliot was talking to India about Joyce a few months ago. His admirable broadcast was printed in the listener.[21] Do get hold of it if you can. He advised us to begin with the Dubliners, then to read Portrait of an Artist, then and not till then to attempt Ulysses, and to leave Finnegan's Wake till the last. With Mr. Eliot's talk and this book of Mr. Harry Levin's, you'll have the necessary preparation, and in the case of Joyce, preparation is necessary. If we plunge into him by the light of nature, we shall just gasp "I never saw such stuff in my life, ridiculous stuff, disgraceful stuff", scramble out of him again, and so miss a great deal.

1. <NOT CHECKED WITH BROADCAST> Z. A. Bokhari signed off on the script.

2. EMF wrote to Indian Section Talks producer Charlotte Haldane, "Have just read a good new book on James Joyce by Harry Levin, and have also finished rereading Ulysses. So suggest a talk on Joyce on the 24th. T. S. Eliot gave an excellent one last year, but I could probably manage some remarks from another angle. - Should not have to trouble you about books in this case, as I have what is necessary" (EMF to Haldane, n.d., received 14 February 1944, E. M. Forster File 6, 1944 R CONT 1, BBC WAC).

3. Harry Levin, *James Joyce: A Critical Introduction* (London: Faber and Faber, 1941).

4. <saying> EMF discussed Trilling in his 6 January 1944 broadcast.

5. <cotton to>

6. <swallow>

7. <cotton>

8. <it then>

9. <you are inclined to>

10. <returned>

11. <lampoon>

12. "Gas from a Burner" (1912), lines 15–18, cited by Levin, *Joyce*, 14–15.

13. Ibid., 7.

14. <He is banned there.>

15. <criticism>

16. Levin, *Joyce*, 134–35.

17. <bitterness and>

18. <alternately>

19. <extremely>

20. Levin, *Joyce*, 195.

21. T. S. Eliot, "The Approach to James Joyce," *Listener*, 14 October 1943, pp. 446–47.

[1]Eastern Service
Purple Network
Thursday, 23rd March 1944
1515-1530 GMT

SOME BOOKS

by

E. M. Forster

Last night there was a discussion of the Brains Trust type at the Churchill Club, on the subject of "Is the Novel dead." Before I come to the discussion, and whether the novel is dead, I should like to say something about the Churchill Club. This is a new institution which was founded last year, mainly by American initiative. Membership is for officers and men of the fighting forces, American, British and Dominion, and for the Women's Auxiliary Services, but since the premises of the Club are not large, the membership is limited, and I believe that those who want to join must supply some evidence of their cultural and intellectual interests. The idea, evidently, is to provide in the upheaval of wartime, a place where people who are likely to get on with each other can gather. I have been there occasionally as the guest of American and other friends, and very pleasant it is. The premises, though not large, are distinguished, for the Club is housed in part of the old buildings[2] near the Abbey. There is an exquisite staircase, 300 years old, the work of Inigo Jones, and one eats a tray meal or drinks coffee and smokes in rooms of beautiful proportions, adorned with their original fittings, and breathing the spirit of the English past. Does that make you jealous? Or does it irritate you? It might get you either way. Anyhow there was, in the Churchill Club last night, a discussion on "Is the Novel dead?"

Desmond MacCarthy - our leading literary critic - took the chair, and with him sat three people who have written novels: Rose Macaulay and myself, representing the older generation of writers, and Graham Greene, representing a younger. Evelyn Waugh and Philip Toynbee should have come too, but were prevented.[3] Questions were sent up by the audience, and we discussed these with an eye on the future of fiction. We were asked, for instance, whether biography wouldn't attract people away from novels, since there is increasing publicity about events. We didn't think it would, since biography tells or ought to tell the truth, and novels ought to be creative; two different lines, which shouldn't compete. Another questioner said that life was being daily made "more regimented restricted and dull by so called social progress", so wouldn't men turn more and more to novels for excitement and imaginative stimulus. This question muddled us rather for (i) Will life be regimented and dull? (ii) If it is, will the novelist, or for that matter the dramatist, be able to find any congenial subject matter? There were also some special questions: For instance, which is the greatest literary artist, Jane Austen, George Eliot, or Virginia Woolf? I said Jane Austen, because she had the completest control of her subject matter, whereas Virginia Woolf was often experimental and tentative, and George Eliot less an artist than a moralist. This led Desmond MacCarthy to discuss the nature of Virginia Woolf's talent - more of a poet than a novelist, he thought - and Graham Greene to put up a case for George Eliot's masterpiece, Middlemarch. A question on Proust followed. Didn't we think the influence of Proust bad. Some of us said 'no', others that he had no influence at all. Then there was an interesting intervention from the body of the hall by the novelist, Arthur Koestler, who was sitting there; I've spoken to you of Koestler and his striking book "Arrival and Departure".[4] He put it to us that indignation is the basic motive which causes a man to write fiction. We didn't agree. Indignation often makes people write good novels today, of course; but Trollope, Jane Austen, Henry James, even Dickens - surely indignation didn't set them going. By this time it was 9.0 p.m. and we had to clear out. We had decided that the novel isn't dead, and whether this be so or not, a thoughtful time had been had by all. The night was brilliantly clear and the inmates of the Churchill Club dispersed through the streets[5] under a sky of stars.

With this query in my mind - Is the Novel Dead? - I have been considering two recently published novels and I'll go on to talk about them. Here is "Sailor's Song" by James Hanley - as its title suggests, it's about the sea. Here is "Why Was I Killed" by Rex Warner - about the Unknown Warrior who returns to earth.[6] These books - what ever their individual vitality - do they represent any decay in the art of fiction?

Now if it's a novelist's job to describe individuals and tell a story, certainly neither Mr. Hanley nor Mr. Rex Warner are really doing their job. They are both of them more interested in something which might be called 'poetry', or - a better word perhaps - 'incantation'. They give us the feeling that they are evoking, standing over a tripod, scattering magic herbs, and human life, as they give it us, retains indeed its incidents and its personalities and its realism, but it comes to us wrapped up in a vision. We found that visionary quality in James Joyce, last month.[7] We scarcely ever find it in the classical novelists of the Victorian period, though it occurs in Victorian poetry. For instance, in Browning, and in the Victorian historian Carlyle. In fiction the spell, the incantation is almost new, and is becoming very common. The younger critics call it apocalyptic and the older critics shake their heads. What do you think?

Now this novel of James Hanley, "Sailor's Song" - there's a story in it, to be sure; it's about a man who can't keep away from the sea, any more than his father could, any more than his son will; the sea has got him, and dooms him to roughness and cold, to exploitation and unemployment, to disaster and death. But the story doesn't come out straightforwardly. It is more like the jumbled vision of someone who is being drowned, and that is what Mr. Hanley is trying to do - to convey the facts of a sailor's life out of their time-sequence and so make them more poignant, and to surround them with the magic of the sea. It is a remarkable book - sometimes it becomes monotonous and unbearable like the sea itself, but it will hold you to the bitter end. Here is a passage from it, describing a submarine; and notice that technique of incantation which began with Joyce and D. H. Lawrence and Virginia Woolf and is now so popular.

Deep below, oh very deep below, was something that had a date with this sea, and with this ship, and with all sailormen aboard her. Sort of fish, grey-black under the belly, grey-black over. Not like any fish you ever saw, this one had a brain brighter than anything you ever heard of. Call this fish iron, call it steel, little wheels inside its belly. . . . . It had a date with us. This thing was mouthless, was dumb, it made no noise as it swam, you couldn't hear, wouldn't know if she were about. But she knew if you were, her brighteye shine and fasten on smell of a ship, see it a long way off, feel all sailormen aboard her. This fish was new to a sea, this God's fright, but not to men, being a man's fish, made by men.[8]

This isn't a description of a submarine. It's an evocation which increases our terror of the monster, the steel-fish, the God's fright which has a date with men. And James Hanley keeps up this technique all through, even when he is speaking of the queues of the unemployed. There's a lot more I could say about this novel "Sailor's Song". I didn't strictly enjoy it, but it wasn't written to be enjoyed. It's a tragic spell binder.

The same is true of Mr. Rex Warner's last novel "Why was I Killed?" Here the actual writing is descriptive and sedate, but the conception is fantastic and out of the normal tradition. The spirit of a dead man, who has been killed in this war, finds itself in a cathedral, by the Unknown

Warrior's tomb. A priest who is coming down from the altar, can see the man, and they speak. A group of sightseers enter - a mixed company, including a conservative country gentleman, a cocky young working-man, a refugee professor, a member of the international brigade who fought in Spain, and a woman in deep mourning. To the sightseers the dead man is invisible. But he can touch their minds and he asks each of them the question "Why was I killed?" He wants particularly to have an explanation of the double vision which came at the instant of death. He saw - mutilation, shattered arms and legs, and at the same time a vast and glorious world of beauty and opportunity. If this is the ultimate human experience, how is it to be interpreted? The sight-seers speak and we learn much about their lives, which are cunningly interwoven, and, all warped or impoverished by the recurrent wars of our age. They are types rather than individuals - that is characteristic of the novel's development, and I didn't agree when someone said at the Churchill Club yesterday that "Why was I killed?" isn't a novel. Mr. Rex Warner makes the types credible and one of them - the canny working-man who wanted education as a boy but in the end cared for nothing but his wages and insured himself against everything and wouldn't even risk having a baby is a new type and devastatingly described. The man himself is not to blame - Mr. Rex Warner, who has deep humanity, makes that clear. The system is to blame - the system which creates the meanness of modern industrialism and the recurrence of modern war.

But none of the sight-seers, not even the fighter from Spain or the desolate woman can answer the dead man's question; why was he killed and why, at the instant of death and failure, did earthly life seem so worthwhile. The priest has his interpretation, with which the book closes. He returns to his altar, and the dead man goes towards the houses of men.

These two books, "Sailor's Song" and "Why was I killed?" made me feel that the novel isn't dead, but that it is unlikely to repeat its great triumphs of the nineteenth century - triumphs of character drawing and plot. It's becoming more fantastic, more meditative, and more like an incantation.

---

1. <NOT CHECKED WITH BROADCAST> Z. A. Bokhari signed off on the broadcast's security and policy clearance. EMF's proposal to talk about the Churchill Club debate ("Is the Novel Dead?") as well as two novels raised difficulties with the censor: "I can't get [the debate] into the original script which has to be with you on the morning of the 22nd, but maybe I could insert additions on the 23rd without upsetting Security: It has been possible to do this in the past" (EMF to Mrs. Haldane, 10 March 1944, E. M. Forster File 6, 1944 R CONT 1, BBC WAC).

2. <of Westminster School, close against>

3. Rose Macaulay, novelist and critic best known for satiric novels such as *Told By an Idiot* (1923), *Going Abroad* (1934), and *Towers of Trebizond* (1956); Philip Toynbee, author of three novels by 1944, including *The Savage Days* (1937) and *The Barricades* (1943).

4. See EMF's broadcast dated 27 January 1944.

5. <of Westminster>

6. James Hanley, *Sailor's Song* (London: Nicholson and Watson, 1943); Rex Warner, *Why Was I Killed? A Dramatic Dialogue* (London: John Lane, 1943). Hanley's novel was dedicated to EMF: "For E. M. Forster (A Salute to Integrity)."

7. See EMF's broadcast dated 24 February 1944.

8. Hanley, *Sailor's Song*, 50.

[1]As BROADCAST
Eastern Service
Purple Network
Tuesday, 11th April, 1944
1515-1530 GMT

SOME BOOKS

by

E.M. Forster

The first book on our list is Jane Austen's novel <u>Sense and Sensibility</u>. I[2] put it in because a dramatised version of it is to be broadcast to India.- the first instalment is next week - I won't describe the plot of Sense and Sensibility, for that[3] might spoil your pleasure in the broadcast, but a few words about the characters in the book may be acceptable, also a few words about Miss Austen herself, and the conditions under which she wrote. Think of her as a country clergyman's daughter, living quietly in southern England about 150 years ago. She is devoted to her father, her mother, her numerous brothers and sisters.[4] It's a happy and affectionate family, respectable, as befits the father's profession, but by no means dowdy or prim. The girls are fond of dancing, and visits to London, and dress. While not rich, they are comfortably off, and while not belonging to the aristocracy they have solid social contacts, mostly in the provinces. They are cheerful, and so self-contained that they tend to be satirical about outsiders, and to poke fun at them, thus becoming more cheerful than ever. Family life, to Jane Austen, is the flower of life, and that's one of the things[5] to be remembered when you are reading her novels, or listening to the forthcoming broadcast. You'll find a very happy family in <u>Sense and Sensibility</u> - the widowed Mrs. Dashwood, and her daughters Elinor and Marianne - not always happy in their fortunes, but happy in themselves, and fond of one another. The Dashwoods are the sort of people she approves - and by the way you'll notice that the Dashwoods are supposed to be poor, but all the same they keep three servants and have wine and dessert every evening. If that's poverty I could do with it myself, and it amusingly illustrates Jane Austen's economic outlook. She's not concerned with the really poor, any more than she is concerned, in the moral sphere, with the very wicked, or, in the physical sphere with disaster and death. She keeps to what she understands, to middle class comedy of a high type, to the little square of ivory as it has been called[6] - and that's why she is one of our great novelists.

Now let's think of her more precisely at the age of twenty-two, an inexperienced girl of course, but very much on the spot, chattering away in the Hampshire rectory, doing little charitable jobs, paying visits, thinking of husbands, and quizzing the outside world, which consists for her of other families of her own social standing, but families not always so amiable, families not always so genteel. Why shouldn't she put this sort of thing into the form of fiction, make fun of those other families or people like them and read it aloud at home of an evening? It will amuse her brothers and sisters.[7] So she writes a novel in the form of letters, and calls it Elinor and Marianne. Elinor is the personification of Sense, and much admired by her young creator; she calls her 'my Elinor'. Marianne, younger sister, unstable and romantic, but perhaps more lovable, personifies Sensibility. That's in 1797. Some years pass, and, having rewritten this early draft in narrative form, she publishes it in 1811 as Sense and Sensibility, the work you're going to hear broadcast. It's the first of the six novels upon which her[8] reputation rests. Remember, when you listen to it, that it was written to please the family circle, and that the more ridiculous or unpleasing characters in it - such as Mrs. Jennings, or Lucy Steele, or John Dashwood the girls' half-brother - must have evoked peals of laughter round the rectory fire.

That fire went out long ago. Jane Austen chronicles a social system that has completely passed away, in England and elsewhere. Today, families are smaller, the bonds uniting them are looser, when a rectory is warmed at all it is by central-heating, and when a rector's daughter has brothers in the Navy, she herself probably joins the Wrens. Miss Austen herself joined nothing. There was nothing for her to join. She didn't even, in modern[9] parlance, know that there was a war on. There was a war on. One of the greatest wars of English history was on - our[10] fight with Napoleon. This girl, this old maid as she became, lived through the terrific events that have been chronicled by Tolstoy and Thomas Hardy and Carlyle[11] - through the French Revolution, the overthrow of kingdoms, the invasion menace - greater than any we've had to face until[12] the other day - the retreat from Moscow, the crowning deliverance of Waterloo - she lived through it and wrote through it all, and it made no impression on her whatsoever. She does indeed notice the navy, because the Navy may mean prize money or promotion for her brothers or for some of her characters. But there her interest ends. She cared nothing for Napoleon. And Napoleon no doubt returned the compliment, cared nothing for her, and probably never heard her name.

This contrast between the writer, then when war was localised and standardised, and the writer today, when war is total, is a[13] striking contrast. Not all Jane Austen's contemporaries[14] stood as aloof as she did - Wordsworth, for instance, felt the Napoleonic wars deeply[15] - but they could keep out of the turmoil if they wanted to, without feeling self-conscious or guilty. Her interests remained domestic comedy, shades of conduct, moral and social nuances, the gay, the absurd, match-making, and sometimes tenderness and love. She did not care for public[16] affairs. On one occasion she rejected politely but firmly a suggestion that she should compose a historical romance, in honour of the House of Saxe Coburg. 'I could no more write a romance' she exclaims, 'than an epic poem. I must keep to my own style and go on in my own way.'[17] And she keeps to her square of ivory.

Sense and Sensibility, being the first of her efforts, isn't the best. It contains strong contrasts of character and some heightened scenes, and no doubt that has recommended it for dramatisation on the air. But it is rather immature; it lacks, well the brilliancy of Pride and Prejudice, or the moral profundity of Mansfield Park, or the supreme accomplishment of Emma. The morality in it is too much on the surface - the authoress tends to preach - and though the producers have wisely cut the preaching, there's one difficulty they can't do away with; the two heroes in the book are such bores, and the villain isn't any better. But you'll enjoy the two heroines, Elinor and Marianne - and they are charmingly played - and you'll like the vulgar and irrepressible Mrs. Jennings. I don't feel as a matter of fact that Mrs. Jennings is played quite vulgarly enough - she's much more obstreperous and boisterous on the printed page than she'll be on the air, much more a hangover from the eighteenth century; I always think of Mrs. Jennings as shouting. Still, you'll get fond of her, and when Elinor and Marianne are married - I won't say to whom - and the villain has been punished - I won't say how - then will you read the book itself, in a particular edition. I want you, if you possibly can, to get hold of the World's Classics edition of Sense and Sensibility, because there's an admirable preface to the novel in it, by Lord David Cecil. And this preface is a model of criticism. It brings out the merits of the book, which are great, and it analyses its considerable weaknesses. I've mentioned Lord David Cecil's work before when talking to India - he wrote a good study on Thomas Hardy for instance.[18] So procure Sense and Sensibility in the World's Classics if you can.[19]

Well, I ought to go on to other matters, but having started on Jane Austen I find it difficult to stop, I am so fond of her. She's English, I'm English, and my fondness for her may be rather a family affair. I may like her as I like the village green because I'm used to it, and when I set her on the vast curve of the world, and think of her being read in the tropics, and in the modern tropics - well, I wonder how she'll travel. Anyhow, please don't dismiss her as a spinster in a backwater. She's much more than that. She is a great artist.

The other two books on my list[20] are concerned with India.[21] One of them is a novel about India, the other is a book by an Indian, in fiction form. Before speaking of them, though I[22] have to mention with deep regret the death of two writers.[23] One died out in India, the Welsh poet and story-writer, Alun Lewis.[24] He is best known as a poet, but I appreciated most his short stories, and one of these, The Orange Grove[25] made a deep impression on me.[26] The scene of The Orange Grove was laid in Central India, in the very country where I[27] used to be so happy myself in distant times. Under the powerful pen of Alun Lewis, the country becomes sinister, the dark bungalow hostile, and the British officer who was the main character lost, utterly lost. Through the nightmare gleamed now and then the image of an orange grove, a place where you could grow your own stuff, and live decently, instead of wandering through murderous rubbish. The Orange Grove wasn't embodied, it wasn't even in India, it was the grove of a poet, but in the end when the young officer encounters some gypsies who carry away the corpse of his dead orderly for him, and depart, with friendly gestures, for some pasture, some well, the sense of futility, of misdirection, slips from him, and he achieves calm. This is a clumsy description, and I shouldn't have attempted it had I not just heard of Alun Lewis's death.[28]

And I've also just heard of the death of one of my own contemporaries, the novelist L.H. Myers.[29] And it's very fitting that homage should be paid to Myers by a broadcaster to India, for his most important work was round an Indian theme. He wrote four novels inspired by the court and the civilisation of the Emperor Akbar. They are scarcely historical novels, and he didn't offer them as such: "I have done what I liked with history and geography" he remarked.[30] But he found in sixteenth-century India, with its special contacts between Hindus and Moslems a fertile soil for his own subtle and philosophic talent, and he sought to express the problems of the twentieth century through that[31] remote medium. The names of Myers' Indian-inspired novels are: 'The Near and the Far', 'Prince Jali', 'The Root and the Flower' and 'The Pool of Vishnu'.[32] Of these four, The Root and the Flower is the best known, and when it came out here nine years ago it attracted a great deal of attention and won various literary prizes. Myers wrote other novels too, but this[33] Indian sequence is his main achievement.

The novel about India is Comedy in Chains by Denis Gray Stoll.[34] [35]This is vividly written,[36] the scene is laid in South India, it opens in a temple, and one of its characters is a dancing girl who is rescued from her slavery there by a young doctor. The novel deals with the troubles of recent years (1939 to 1941 is its period) and its sympathies are with the Congress point of view.[37] I was sometimes reminded when reading it of the work of an admirable Indian novelist Raja Rao:[38] one or two of its chapters have a rapt quality, you find in him, a quality as of an old village woman, chanting herself to sleep. For the most part the book proceeds straightforwardly, and though the title is Comedy in Chains the denouement is pretty tragic. Like most books on modern India Mr. Stoll's novel is political; indeed it's hard to see how anything non-political could at present be written about the country.

The last work to be mentioned is scarcely a novel, though it is cast in fiction form. It is called Life's Shadows, and it is by a Tamil writer, who writes under the pseudonym of Kumara Guru.[39] It deals with Hindu family life - but meditatively, and not as Jane Austen dealt with family life in England.[40] This work by Kumara Guru, it's in 2 volumes - it came to me from India. I was glad to receive it, and as I've said once before, I will always, when possible, mention in these talks books sent to me from your country. They may not always reach me, and they may in some cases be unsuitable - technical works, for instance, are unsuitable. But I'll be pleased to mention them whenever I can.[41]

---

1. <NOT CHECKED WITH> Z. A. Bokhari signed off on the broadcast's security and policy clearance.

2. <include it>

3. <would>

4. <, particularly to her sister Cassandra>

5. <you must>

6. By Austen herself, in a 16 December 1816 letter to her nephew, James Edward Austen.

7. <, particularly Cassandra>

8. <fame>

9. <phrase>

10. <struggle>

11. EMF alludes to Tolstoy's War and Peace (1865–1869), Hardy's The Dynasts (1904–1908), and Carlyle's The French Revolution (1837).

12. <1940>

13. <very remarkable one>

14. <were>

15. Wordsworth's responses to the war included The Prelude (1850) and several of his sonnets.

16. \<wants\>

17. Quoted in Guy Rawlence, *Great Lives* (London: Duckworth, 1934), 124.

18. Jane Austen, *Sense and Sensibility*, ed. Lord David Cecil, World's Classics series (London: Oxford University Press, 1931); Cecil, *Hardy, the Novelist: An Essay in Criticism* (London: Constable, 1942).

19. \<Interest in Jane Austen is well established in this country. Only the other day a book about her came out here entitled <u>Talking of Jane Austen</u>. It is the joint work of two contemporary novelists, Miss Sheila Kaye-Smith, and Miss G.B. Stern. It is an informal book, full of allusions and references, and it is intended for those who already know the six novels well. Lord David Cecil's introduction, on the other hand being more helpful for the beginner.\> Kaye-Smith and Stern, *Talking of Jane Austen* (London: Cassell and Co., 1943).

20. \<also have some reference to\>

21. \<though of a different character\>

22. \<wish\>

23. \<out in India - the death, on military service, of\>

24. Lewis's death (from a bullet in his own pistol) was viewed as suicide, especially by those who knew his susceptibility to depression; EMF was one of Lewis's favorite authors.

25. "The Orange Grove" first appeared in *Horizon*, December 1943.

26. \<when I read it in a magazine some time back\>

27. \<was\>

28. \<and of his death in India\> A handwritten note adds, "Myers Insert 7." The succeeding paragraph on Myers appears at the end of the script on the seventh page.

29. Leopold Hamilton Myers died 7 April 1944.

30. Preface to L. H. Myers, *The Near and the Far* (London: Jonathan Cape, 1940), 9.

31. \<distant\>

32. *The Near and the Far* was first published in 1929; *Prince Jali*, in 1931; *The Root and the Flower*, in 1935; and *The Pool of Vishnu*, in 1940 (all London: Cape). Myers entered the Bloomsbury circle after his first novel, *The Orissers*, was published in 1922; he satirized the group that included EMF, the Woolfs, and Lady Otteline Morrell in *The Root and the Flower*.

33. \<Emperor Akbar\>

34. *Comedy in Chains* (London: V. Gollancz, 1944).

35. \<It\>

36. \<its\>

37. The Indian Congress (founded in 1885) led the Indian national movement. When Great Britain without consultation declared India a belligerent nation on the side of the Allies in 1939, the Congress under Gandhi's leadership demanded to know whether Britain waged war on behalf of democracy or of imperialism. When the demand was set aside, the Congress made its cooperation dependent on a British commitment to Indian independence. After a preliminary campaign of civil disobedience, the Congress passed a December 1941 resolution expressing sympathy for war against Germany while maintaining that only a free citizenry could effectively defend India—at which point Gandhi, committed to nonviolence, resigned his office.

38. The first published novel of Raja Rao, *Kanthapura* (London: George Allen and Unwin, 1938), represented the impact of Gandhi's freedom movement on a remote village.

39. Chandrasekhar Subrhmanya Ayyar (pseud. Kumara Guru), *Life's Shadows*, 2 vols. (Bombay and Madras: D. B. Taraporevala Sons, 1938, 1943).

40. \<It shows how the old ways change under western impact, and it also - its main theme - shows how one member of a family can cast a shadow over another, sometimes unwittingly, Hence its title - Life's Shadows. The first volume deals with Brother, Wife, Son,

Friend, the second volume (recently published) with the shadow that may be cast by a daughter.>

41. A "15." next to the last line of the paragraph presumably indicates that EMF had reached his fifteen minutes allotted for the broadcast, hence the cancellation of these last two paragraphs of the script:

<Next month - or perhaps the month after - I have rather an ambitious talk in view. I want to give you some idea if I can of Professor Arnold Toynbee's great Study of History. It is a monumental work, and I am no historian, but unlike some monumental works it is beautifully written and reading it is a pleasure.

I'll end now by repeating the names of books referred to in the present talk. They are the World's Classics Edition of Jane Austen's Sense and Sensibility; Talking of Jane Austen by Sheila Kaye Smith and G.B. Stern; Comedy in Chains by Dennis Gray Stoll, and Life's Shadows by Kumara Guru - these last two dealing with modern India.>

[1]As BROADCAST
Eastern Service
Purple Network
Tuesday, 9th May, 1944
1515-1530 GMT

SOME BOOKS

by

E.M. Forster

I have just been away for a few days to the English Lakes. It is the first time for about two years that I have got clear of London and its neighbour-hood, and the sudden change from trolley-buses, queues, bombed areas, official posters, and alerts to wildness, silence, rocks, primroses, streams, and the leaping of thousands of lambs in the sunshine was very enjoyable. I felt that the Lakes and Nature are somehow more real than the city and the mechanical gadgets to which we attach the name of civilisation. I didn't feel this consciously. I was occupied at the moment in trying to get up a waterfall to a tarn or to tell the time by the sun, since I hadn't my watch. One doesn't, at the moment, say, "Yes, yes. This is reality". The con-viction comes afterwards. And it's now that I am back in the south again and the Lakes gleam remote in space that they seem to occupy more than their geographical[2] area, and to become, for England, a sacred mountain region like the Himalayas for India. They are our only sacred region. No gods have inhabited them, and they are meagre in legend. But they have extreme natural beauty and they have been the scene of one great psycho-logical experience. The name of the person who had that experience was William Wordsworth, and because he had it in surroundings of such solemnity and radiance, the district is glorified. Wordsworth without fine scenery, or scenery without the genius of Wordsworth wouldn't have done the trick. It is the powerful combination that counts. And today, thousands of people, feel as I do that the Lakes are more real than other places in the British Isles. A moment's reflection dispels that feeling: it is

300

quite illogical. But before that moment has come, before the emotions are disciplined, we too have had a psychological experience, we have guessed what Wordsworth felt and was trying to convey.

This very great, but not wholly attractive Englishman, is a difficult subject for an overseas broadcast, and I am not tackling Wordsworth in force. Indeed I scarcely thought of him while I was there, except on the last day when it rained and I couldn't climb Helvellyn. Now he looms up in my mind, and I am tempted to glance to and fro for a few minutes between him and the mountains he transfigured. How can I describe that 'looming up in the mind', so characteristic of his influence? Best in a passage out of one of his own poems that famous episode in the Prelude, where he recalls how, in boyhood, he rowed out one evening upon Esthwaite Water, and evoked a vision. I'll read the passage. In order to keep a straight course, the boy had fixed his eyes upon a crag, which bounded his horizon, and he was pulling away from it. The evening was calm, the moon shone, the grey sky was pointed with stars. The boat moved silently outward into the lake and then, unexpected yet inevitable, the vision came.

> "I dipped my oars into the silent lake,
> And, as I rose upon the stroke, my boat
> Went heaving through the water like a swan;
> When, from behind that craggy steep till then
> The horizon's bound, a huge peak, black and huge,
> As if with voluntary power instinct,
> Upreared its head. I struck and struck again,
> And growing still in stature the grim shape
> Towered up between me and the stars, and still,
> For so it seemed, with purpose of its own
> And measured motion like a living thing,
> Strode after me. With trembling oars I turned,
> And through the silent water stole my way
> Back to the covert of the willow tree;
> There in her mooring-place I left my bark, -
> And through the meadows homeward went, in grave
> And serious mood; but after I had seen
> That spectacle, for many days, my brain
> Worked with a dim and undetermined sense
> Of unknown modes of being; o'er my thoughts
> There hung a darkness, call it solitude
> Or blank desertion. No familiar shapes
> Remained, no pleasant images of trees,
> Of sea or sky, no colours of green fields;

But huge and mighty forms, that do not live
Like living men, moved slowly through the mind
By day, and were a trouble to my dreams."[3]

That is what Wordsworth found in the Lakes - boats, green fields, primroses, daffodils, lambs, country talk and such pleasant and familiar things, and behind those familiar things something looming up, the huge black peak of some mountain. Some mysterious and mighty form that troubled his dreams. And that too is what we can find in Wordsworth. He hands on what he discovers. He seems often to versify trifles and twaddle, he has defects of style and temper, but constantly when we do not expect it, he looms up. He fills our minds with his influence and even when the familiar horizon has returned we are left with that

dim and undetermined sense
Of unknown modes of being.
of which he speaks.

He is often referred to as a simple poet, and he wanted to be simple, and he maintained that the language of poetry is the same as the language of the common man. Actually he had an unusual equipment. He was no ordinary man and there is no counterpart to him in English literature. He has this power to loom up and obscure our horizon with inexpressible thoughts. And he secreted that power in the Lakes, as a boy. In that place, at that age, he had the intense psychological experience, which the twentieth century visitor encounters at a remove.

An experience is popularly supposed to be something which happens at once, in a click. It needn't. It may happen slowly, and everything about Wordsworth was slow. He moved slowly, he was stocky in build, stubborn and tenacious in character and often his verses creak. And this great influence that came to him from the mountains and lakes of his homeland arrived slowly, over a term of years. I understood this from my own little holiday last week. It seems appropriate to the scenery. You don't realise a mountain right away, click. You see it from this angle and that, one day and the next, under all lights, or through driving mist and cloud as on my last afternoon until it becomes a solid and living thing, with an existence of its own. I guess that's what happened to Wordsworth. He lived among the mountains from boyhood, with a receptivity most of us don't possess, until they sank into his soul.

As time went on he fitted his marvellous experience into a formula. We all tend to do that, we like to find meaning as well as mystery in what happens to us. We like to impose some sort of order, and Wordsworth had an orderly mind. The formula he found was Christian pantheism. He came to believe that nature, particularly in Lakeland, reveals God, and that our youthful impressions are intimations of immortality. Whether he was right I am not here to discuss, though I must point out that the vision I've quoted of the looming mountain does not fit into any soothing scheme, and comes near in spirit to the disquieting apparitions of D.H. Lawrence.[4]

If that quotation I made from the Prelude interested you, perhaps you'll read Wordsworth further. I'm assuming you don't read him much, because I assume you're not English, and there is no doubt that Wordsworth is not well known or well liked outside England. Of all our great poets he exports the worst, he will not travel, and that's what I meant earlier on when I said he was a[5] difficult subject for an overseas broadcast. He hasn't gone down on the European continent. Shakespeare - yes: Byron, Wilde, T.S. Eliot yes. Wordsworth no. And I imagine it to be the same in India. You read him[6] from a sense of duty, don't you, rather than with a feeling of affinity. Even his pantheism - supposing you to be a pantheist - doesn't quite accord with yours.

There are two reasons for this overseas unpopularity, and one of them is to Wordsworth's credit[7] and one against him. It is to his credit that he was passionately local. He belonged to his soil, not someone else's, to his rocks, not to the Himalayas, to his own sky and his own flowers. I can no more convey him to you in his native freshness than I could[8] post you the little bunch of wood-sorrel which I saw growing last Tuesday in the cleft beneath Angle Tarn, its pale lilac blossoms sprinkled by the water from the beck. Some things can't travel.

The other reason - and it is to his discredit - is that for all his visionary insight and moral earnestness he is not a sympathetic character. He came of tough middle class stock, he was cautious formal and respectable, and adopted, as his life went on, a gravely edifying tone. The French Revolution thrilled him in his youth, but he reacted from it till he held that all change is subversive and became upholder of the powers that be (I expect you know Browning's indignant poem on him when he became Poet Laureate: "Just for a handful of silver he left us").[9] Moreover a discovery has been made of late years that when in France[10] Wordsworth had an illegitimate daughter - he the proclaimer of an austere and rustic virtue. It has done his reputation harm with foreign critics, who find him a neat example of British hypocrisy, and shrug their shoulders cynically. On the whole he is not an attractive character, despite much solid merit, and here is the second reason why he does not export.

The best approach to him I think is through The Prelude, the great poem which enshrines the impressions of his youth. Here we come closest to his intense passion for rocks, lakes, mists, flowers, and for that which looms up behind them. Much has been written about the teaching of

Wordsworth, but what overwhelms me is not what he taught but what he felt, and I am thankful that any one of his sensitiveness should have been bred in scenery so exquisite and so eternal. The scenery survives. It promises permanence. The daffodils still dance beside Ullswater, descendants of those whom he saw, the cuckoo is still a wandering voice, the primrose gilds the bank of the river, the lambs run races, the thorns and juniper are carved into fantastic shapes by the upland wind. They prove emotionally that mechanism is not everything and will not triumph everywhere. Emotionally not logically, and perhaps 'prove' is the wrong word. But it is difficult to use a different word after a few days spent among them.

1. <NOT CHECKED WITH>
2. <size>
3. *The Prelude* (1850), 1.374–400.
4. See EMF's broadcast dated 16 April 1930, in which he attributes to Lawrence's fiction "the poetry that broods and flashes."
5. <tricky>
6. <with>
7. <the other>
8. <send>
9. EMF cites the opening line of Robert Browning's "The Lost Leader" (1845).
10. <he>

¹As BROADCAST
Eastern Service
Purple Network
Tuesday 24th October, 1944
1515-1530 GMT

SOME BOOKS

by

E.M. Forster

Here is another book about Tolstoy. And here is another book about Mr. Bernard Shaw, by himself. Here also is quite a crop of anniversaries, commemorations, and I will speak of them before I proceed to the two books. I don't know whether anniversaries do much good, and they certainly shouldn't be kept too solemnly. But they are useful as reminders that civilisation didn't begin to day or even last night, and that we have, whether we like it or not, a cultural past. Every now and then we think Hullo? exactly one hundred years ago so and so died. Or "I say! it's just five centuries since such and such a book was written." We are as it were nudged by a ghost, and perhaps we shudder or perhaps we go to lay a flower on a grave. I was certainly glad a couple of months back to be talking of the centenary of Edward Carpenter.²

This month is the centenary of the birth of Robert Bridges. May be you'll be having a special talk about Robert Bridges from someone qualified to speak on him. There ought to be one, for though I admire his poetry and his personality I can't celebrate him adequately. He was very much the poet's poet, and his metrical experiments appeal most to his fellow-craftsmen. He was, also, very much the English country gentleman, and through most of his life his views of society might be called rigid. But he had great generosity and great curiosity, and notable independence of spirit, and in his later days, when I had the honour of his acquaintance,³ he broke into new paths. His last long poem, <u>The Testament of Beauty</u>,⁴ is remarkable not only for its technique but for its attempt to embody in the poetic vision, the

305

results and the speculations of modern science. Robert Bridges, as you know, was Poet Laureate. Worthily and independently did he fill his post.

Then - also this month - is the tercentenary of the birth of William Penn, the quaker, and mystic, who suffered for his opinions in the 17th century, who fought for toleration, and who founded in America the colony of Pennsylvania. William Penn is not celebrated as an author, but he did write a number of books - No Cross no Crown[5] is the title of one of them and a significant title, - and he ought to be commemorated because he displayed the fair mindedness of the English character.

Now for another tercentenary. The year that William Penn was born - that is to say 1644 - Milton issued his Areopagitica. This pamphlet - the most famous of his prose works - is a plea for the freedom of the press and of printing generally, and Milton's argument is roughly that punishment afterwards is preferable to censorship beforehand; as a lover of liberty and as a creative artist he dreaded the censorship, not only for what it may suppress but for its psychological effect upon the writer. He thought it better that illegal books should be published and bad books should be published, rather than that all books should be submitted before publication to a government official. What is illegal, he thought, can be prosecuted, and what is bad will be forgotten. The modern world - that is to say the world of modern warfare - has taken a different view, and Milton must be glad that he is not living at this hour.[6] The Areopagitica is indeed an explosive work, still controversial because it is still alive, and its tercentenary is being celebrated over here - well, very variedly, and sometimes rather gingerly. I've been particularly interested in a conference held by the P.E.N. club - an international organisation of writers of which you may have heard - there are centres of the P.E.N. at Bombay and at Calcutta. Last August, the P.E.N. convened a five days meeting over here to commemorate the Areopagitica and to discuss the place of spiritual and economic value in the future of mankind.[7] There was much interesting, learned and courageous talk, but what sticks in my mind is that during those five days the liberation of France started. We had met in the French Institute - a fine modern building and we were the recipients of French hospitality. It was overwhelming when the news began to come through: we had a sense of the persistence of freedom and of the victory - though it be an intermittent victory - of the light. Milton might have been glad to have been living at that hour.

Well this doesn't exhaust my list of commemorations and anniversaries. Now one more. This month - October the 10th to be precise - the National Gallery celebrated the fifth year of its concerts, and has brought out a booklet about them.[8] The National Gallery concerts are a wonderful enterprise, and they were started by the energy and genius of one person - the pianist Dame Myra Hess.[9] When the war began, all entertainments were shut down, and culture was officially at an end. Myra Hess wondered whether this need be, she approached the director of the National Gallery and arranged to give a lunch hour concert there on Tuesday October 10th 1939. She played Scarlatti Bach Beethoven Schubert etc. She expected a couple of hundred people at most. Over a thousand turned up, and from that day to this, Mondays to Fridays regularly, the concerts have continued, the entrance fee is 1/-, over 1,300 programmes of chamber music have been performed, and about 100,000 people have attended every year, and £10,000 have been given from the profits to the Musicians Benevolent Fund. Bombs have fallen, the concerts have had to go underground, but they have never stopped, and they are to me one of the most heartening events during these unglamourous years - more heartening than anything in literature - and a proof that the English do like good music. For these haven't been popular concerts in the sense of playing down to people. They have given the best classical stuff - yet day after day the great central hall of the National Gallery has been crowded out. All this is described in the commemorative booklet. There's a complete list of the performers and the works performed - which includes several series of masterpieces - for instance all the Beethoven string quartets and all the Mozart piano concertos -, and there are photographs of the crowds on the Gallery Entrance and at the canteen, and of the performances. Music isn't my province but I wanted to mention this five year commemoration, for the reason that culture is indivisible, and that if the visual arts (represented by the National Gallery) have given hospitality to the art of sound, the art of words, which I am supposed to represent, has a right to celebrate the happy union. The chief inspirer of the wonderful enterprise has been, let me repeat, Myra Hess.

But I must get on to those two books. The one on Tolstoy is by Janko Lavrin. He calls it An Approach to Tolstoy.[10] Professor Lavrin is Slovene by birth. He has written a previous book on Tolstoy, also on Ibsen and Dostoievsky.[11] His interest in literature is psychological. He regards each author as a case enclosing an inner harmony or disharmony out of which his books proceed. Tolstoy is a case of inner disharmony: all critics have realised the conflict within Tolstoy between the artist and the moralist, between the sensuous lover of life and the mystical condemner of life. You can even detect that conflict in an early story like The Cossacks, you can see it rather more plainly in War and Peace, still plainer in Anna Karenina, while in the later works like Ivan Ilyitch and Resurrection it becomes the theme of the story, and morality and mysticism are shown triumphant. I think we should all agree with this interpretation of Tolstoy - so far as it goes. But it goes such a little way. It doesn't make us enjoy him more, or even understand how he got his marvellous effects. It doesn't explain why he was a genius. And I think that Professor Lavrin takes this psychological method too seriously, and that he is an analyst rather than a literary critic. Also he has a theory, which I don't share, that the writer who is torn by an inner conflict must be handicapped as a writer. While respecting Tolstoy's greatness, he treats him too much as an august invalid who would have been even greater had he possessed sound health. Read his book <u>An Approach to Tolstoy</u> if you happen to come across it, and see whether you agree, and do consider in any case this very interesting question of the psychological approach to literature. What can it teach us? What can't it teach?

Now for Mr. Bernard Shaw! His book is called <u>Everybody's Political What's What</u>.[12] As its name suggests, it is an informal work, indeed it ranges from vivisection to architecture, and from anthropometry to gambling. All these subjects, and indeed all subjects, are politics in Mr. Shaw's eyes; that is to say they all concern the individual in his relation to society. Mr. Shaw's constant and serious aim is that we should become better citizens and that the state should give us the chance to be better citizens. Generally it doesn't. He has often expounded this before, and in <u>Everybody's Political What's What</u> he doesn't set out to say anything new. It is discursive and repetitive and when reading it I felt I was in the company of a lively and decent housekeeper who was turning out a cupboard. This and that appears in the well stocked recesses, the housekeeper, namely Mr. Shaw, comments acutely and holds up that or this to ridicule, and sometimes to admiration. Now he quotes Nietzsche's definition of a nation as "people who read the same newspapers". Now he is singing a hymn with the Salvation Army in the Albert Hall. Now he is explaining the difference between Nationalisation as the Capitalist understands it and as the Socialist understands it. Now he stands in the ruins of Baalbec. Now he is running away from Scotch children who throw stones at him and call him 'Beaver' because of his venerable beard. Now he is attacking the Soviet scientist Pavlov, and attacking him virulently; onslaughts on the science he believes to be false and harmful occupy much of the book; now he is shirking jury-service and canonisation and now explaining why he is half-educated. All that is in the cupboard, and much more. Shaw is our greatest living writer, but it hasn't the sustained merit of some of his works (e.g. The Intelligent Woman's Guide to Socialism) and it is best read on and off.

1. <NOT CHECKED WITH>

2. EMF's script, read on 29 August 1944, was republished after considerable revision in *Two Cheers*.

3. See Furbank, *A Life*, 2:55, 111.

4. Robert Bridges, *The Testament of Beauty: A Poem in Four Books* (Oxford: Clarendon Press, 1929). Bridges was poet laureate from 1913 until his death in 1930.

5. William Penn, *No cross, no crown: or several sober reasons against hat-honour, titular-respects, you to a single person, with the apparel and recreations of the times: being inconsistent with Scripture, reason, and practice, as well of the best heathens, as the holy men and women of all generations, and consequently fantastick, impertinent and sinfull: with sixty eight testimonies of the most famous persons of both former and latter ages for further confirmation: in defence of the poor despised Quakers, against the practice and objections of their adversaries* (London: Printed by Andrew Sowle, 1669).

6. EMF alludes to the opening line of Wordsworth's "London, 1802": "Milton! thou shouldst be living at this hour."

7. The conference met 22–26 August at the French Institute in South Kensington. EMF presided and gave an address (Furbank, *A Life*, 2:254–55), to which a *Listener* editorial responded on 31 August 1944 (p. 232). EMF also gave a Home Service talk on the tercentenary that was published in the *Listener* (7 December 1944, pp. 633–34) and then revised and included in *Two Cheers*.

8. *National Gallery Concerts in Aid of the Musicians Benevolent Fund, 10th October 1939–10th October 1944* (London: National Gallery, 1944).

9. See EMF's broadcast dated 6 January 1943.

10. Janko Lavrin, *Tolstoy: An Approach* (London: Methuen, 1944).

11. Lavrin, *Tolstoy, A Psycho-Critical Study* (London: W. Collins, 1924); *Ibsen and His Creation: A Psycho-Critical Study* (London: W. Collins Sons and Co., 1921); *Dostoevsky: A Study* (London: Methuen, 1943).

12. George Bernard Shaw, *Everybody's Political What's What?* (London: Constable, 1944).

[1]As BROADCAST   To be recorded from transmission
Eastern Service   SOX 42379
Purple Network
Tuesday 21st November, 1944
1445-1500 GMT
Reproductions: G.O.S. Thursday 23rd November - 0030-0045 GMT
            Pacific Sunday 26th November - 0730-0745 GMT
            African Sunday 26th November - 1745-1800 GMT
            N.A.S.[2] Monday 27th November - 0030-0045 GMT
            "   "   "   "   0415-0430 GMT

SOME BOOKS

by

E.M.Forster

The other day I went to Shakespeare's Richard III, with a party which included a boy of eleven.[3] The play had been arranged, for purposes of performance, into two acts, and when the first act was over, and the crooked Richard had wriggled himself to the throne, the little boy whispered to me "Is that all?" I said "No". He said "Oh good". Then came the second act, and when the final curtain fell with Richard dead upon Bosworth Field, he asked me the same question. Undeterred by the actors and actresses, who were bowing at us over the foot-lights, he whispered again "Is that all?" I said "Yes," He said "Oh dear."

These two comments of the child "Oh good" and "Oh dear", well indicate the nature of a chronicle play. "Oh good" we are glad it goes on. "Oh dear" we are sorry when it stops, but we can never be sure when it will stop. It is based on history, and history never stops. History has gone on without a curtain from the death of that King[4] to the present moment. And so the final curtain of the chronicle play has something arbitrary about it.[5] It is not like the play which is based on an individual - a play like Hamlet, for instance, which I've also been to lately, and will be talking about. Richard III dies, Henry VII[6] succeeds, and Shakespeare might have written a Henry VII had he chosen to do so. They are part of English history, and the host of minor characters, the nobles who are often so confusing to follow, suggest the continuity of England. Those Buckinghams, Warwicks, Gloucesters, Herefords, Norfolks, Lancasters - how one's head whirls with them, and how difficult it is, especially for a foreigner, to remember who is fighting against whom, and why. But if we think of them as the English counties,[7] so to say, vibrating in the background and supplying the scenery, then it doesn't matter[8] much when we get them mixed. I don't think that the little boy got his nobles in Richard III sorted out, and I know I didn't.[9] They were part of the background to history.

Kings are also part of the background, in the eyes of the modern historian; but that isn't how Shakespeare looks at kings. He turns the spot light on them. Sometimes the spot light wavers, as in the two great plays which he wrote about King Henry IV, or as in Henry VIII. At other times it shines steadily - upon Henry V the hero, or upon Richard III here. Decking them with the attributes of glory and power, seating them upon high thrones,[10] casting them into depths of misery - he keeps our attention on them, and prevents the chronicle play from becoming a muddle and a bore. I found it very interesting to compare Hamlet and Richard III from this point of view. The play of Hamlet belongs to Hamlet. When it is over, and flights of angels have sung him to his rest,[11] the curtain falls for ever and there is no more to say. But the play of Richard is a chronicle which doesn't specially belong to anybody. It is the Shakespearean spot light, pursuing the king, which gives it psychological intensity, if not dramatic[12] unity.

The King is marvellously acted by Laurence Olivier,[13] I had always thought of Mr. Olivier as doing handsome heroes, and it was a surprise and a pleasure to see his self-denying portrait of a villain. Think what Richard of Gloucester looks like - ill favoured, lame, hunchback, indeed a monster who was born into the world with feet foremost and his mouth full of teeth. Think what he does. Before the play starts, he has murdered King Henry VI and his son, and[14] under our eyes he marries that son's widow, the Lady Anne, and he murders his own brother Clarence, his nephews the little princes, his friend who has helped him to the throne, and the Lady Anne when she has served his ambition. His last night before the battle is peopled with ghosts who curse him and salute his adversary. His wickedness isn't the slow decline from nobility which characterises Macbeth. Nor is it the wickedness of Iago, which is varied by good fellowship and charm. He is wicked wicked wicked, and how is he to be presented on the stage without becoming a sort of golliwog.[15] Mr. Olivier triumphed. He convinced us that this horrible creature, whom everyone hates, is a human being. I think he did it by suggesting here and there, touches of madness. There is a moment when Richard, who has been posing piously between two bishops at a window, leaps and sprawls out of the window on to the pavement. The man's a maniac, you think. And Mr. Olivier also makes much of Richard's occasional hilarity. Hell can be fun. In the last scene after the ghosts have passed, there is a moment of introspection, a Hamlet moment, and Richard, as near to remorse as he can attain, sees what has been wrong with him: he has never succeeded in making contact with any one except himself.

> What! do I fear myself? there's none else by:
> Richard loves Richard: that is, I am I.
> Is there a murderer here? Yes, I am:
> Then fly: what! from myself? Great reason why:
> Lest I revenge. What! myself upon myself?
> Alack I love myself. Wherefore? for any good
> That I myself have done unto myself?
> Oh! no. alas! I rather hate myself
> For hateful deeds committed by myself
> I am a villain.[16]

That's the last word upon this odd character: he is twisted in on himself. Shakespeare didn't stress it, being on a chronicle job, but he knew that egoism alone makes unrelieved wickedness credible. The death of Richard was appalling he wriggled and twitched, and the feeling of relief in the audience was a tribute to the poet and his interpreters. Mr. Olivier had been adequately supported, and the spectacle lovely to look at. And Bosworth Field was after all one of the crucial battles in English history. It was a fight on a small scale, nothing distinguished it at the time from the skirmishes of the Wars of the Roses. But it did happen to establish, in the person of Henry VII, the dynasty of the Tudors, under whom Shakespeare flourished. And the victorious Henry declaimed with vigour and feeling the final lines:

> God if thy will be so
> Enrich the time to come with smooth fac'd peace
> With smiling plenty and fair prosperous days.[17]

A prayer echoed again by the audience. For the chronicle of history has not finished in this country yet. Nor in any country.

I have given so much space[18] to Richard III that I shall rather have to crowd Hamlet into a corner - not a position to which the Prince of Denmark is accustomed. This - the greatest of all plays in English - is being given with one of our best actors, John Gielgud, as Hamlet.[19] The producer, Mr. George Rylands, is new to London. He lives in Cambridge, where he is a Fellow of one of the colleges, and he has worked with the Cambridge Arts Theatre. I liked his production of Hamlet very much. He gives the play without cuts, and it gains enormously. Fortinbras and the healthy Norwegians come in at the end - as a rule the play ends with

Hamlet's death and the lovely words of Horatio. But the Norwegians should come in. Something has been rotten in the state of Denmark and their sunlit entry brings it out. And - do you remember when reading the play a little scene between Polonius and a very minor character named Reynaldo?[20] Reynaldo is going to Paris, where he is to see Polonius' son, give him some money, and make some discreet enquiries as to his moral conduct. I have never seen this scene acted before, and it makes extremely good[21] comic relief, both the old men being very funny - Polonius author- itative, worried, plump, Reynaldo with a glazed red face and staring eyes. Their colloquy on youth and its dangers was a scream. Excellent too were those other minor characters Rosencrantz and Guildenstern with their fake good-looks and their false bonhomie. I mention these little points to[22] indicate what a sensitive producer Mr. Rylands is. He has brought fresh- ness as well as scholarship to the London stage. John Gielgud as Hamlet is quiet, intelligent, dignified handsome - and I am sure that Hamlet was like that, and wasn't the hysterical undergraduate he's sometimes repre- sented as being. Hamlet thought: and Mr. Gielgud has that marvellous power of being able to convey the process of thinking. I don't know any other actor who can do it: he did it too in Macbeth.[23] He looked splendid and gave a beautiful performance - my only criticism being that it didn't move me very much emotionally. I found myself thinking too, and I am not quite clear whether I as well as Hamlet ought to be thinking while he is on the stage. I was excited by the action though - and what an exciting play it is, something always going on. If it was merely thoughtful, merely profound it wouldn't be the greatest play in English. As it is there's an alliance of external and internal which makes it unique.

The play isn't as good to look at as Richard III, the scenery and the dresses are dull. On the other hand the acting all round is better. I enjoyed both plays very much, and we are lucky to have two such actors as Mr. Olivier and Mr. Gielgud maintaining the glory of Shakespeare in the sixth year of a national war. Both plays are part of a repertory programme. Richard alternates with Ibsen and Shaw, Hamlet with Congreve and Somerset Maugham. There are other plays in London worth seeing - but for the purpose of this talk I have stuck to Shakespeare.

My next talk will be the last in the year, and I shall stick then to books about India.

---

1. <NOT CHECKED WITH>
2. G.O.S.: General Overseas Service; N.A.S.: North American Service.
3. Robin Buckingham, the son of Bob and May Buckingham, and EMF's godson (Furbank, A Life, 2:184 and personal communication).
4. <Richard III.>

5. EMF added accent marks above the first syllables of "final" and "curtain."

6. <reigns>

7. <as it were>

8. <so>

9. <I didn't turn a hair when I heard two of them were executed off.>

10. < - there is a marvellous scene of Richard on a throne>

11. 5.2.371.

12. <waiting>

13. Olivier opened at the New Theatre (now the Albery) on 13 September 1944.

14. <now>

15. "golliwog": "A name invented for a black-faced grotesquely dressed (male) doll with a shock of fuzzy hair" (*OED*).

16. *Richard III*, 5.3.182–91.

17. Ibid., 5.5.32–34.

18. <over>

19. The play opened at the Haymarket Theatre in October 1944.

20. *Hamlet*, 2.1.

21. <comedy>

22. <show you>

23. See EMF's broadcast dated 19 August 1942.

[1]As BROADCAST
Eastern Service
Purple Network
Friday 15th December, 1944
1445-1500 GMT
ENGLISH PROSE No. 11

THE SHORT STORY

by

E.M.Forster

Last week you had a talk from Mr. William Plomer, on the art of the Short Story.[2] He pointed out that because it is[3] short it will follow certain rules which do not apply to a long novel.[4] No one compels it to obey these rules, and they may not have been in the author's mind while he was writing. But you will find that, unless he respects them, you will be left with a dissatisfied feeling at the end.

This week's talk is a sort of footnote to that one. I want to discuss a couple of short stories by contemporary writers, and while I am doing this the art of the short story will probably get illustrated. [5]I want to speak of <u>The Salt of the Earth</u> by Rebecca West and <u>The Child of Queen Victoria</u>, by William Plomer himself.[6] <u>The Salt of the Earth</u> is about a crime and why it was perpetrated, it has a glittering detective quality, and takes place in middle class England; <u>The Child of Queen Victoria</u> takes place in romantic Africa, has little plot, and is a love story. They are both well written in styles appropriate to them, and the characters in them seem real.

The chief character in <u>The Salt of the Earth</u> is Alice Pemberton, a perfect woman. Perfect? We shall see. Alice, who is happily married, has been paying a visit to her mother when the story opens, (since she hasn't been very well, something gastric), and it is a shock to her, and indeed to the reader, that her mother seems rather relieved when the visit ends.[7] Alice is intelligent, humourous, helpful, kind, and excellent at reorganising other people's lives and explaining to them where they[8] have gone wrong. Why

315

wasn't the old lady more grateful? However, she is going back to her own lovely home, and to Jimmy, her adoring husband. She arrives sooner than she is expected, and since Jimmy isn't back she calls upon her sister, and upon her brother, who are neighbours. What a contrast! their houses are in a muddle, her sister lies on an untidy sofa - her brother, she is rudely denied access to him by his family. She puts all to rights as best she can, then returns, and has an interview with her cook. I'll read that interview with the cook for it illustrates the malice of Rebecca West's art, and her bitter comedy.

'What are we having for dinner, cook?'

[']Artichoke soup, cod, saddle of mutton, apple dumpling and welsh rabbit.'

'Oh cook', said Alice, 'what a dreadful dinner! So dull and so heavy! You really shouldn't give the master dinners like that just because you think I'm going to be out of the way.'

'I wouldn't do no such thing,' answered cook with her colour rising. 'The master ordered this very dinner, I ain't nothing to do with it 'cept cook it as best I can.'

'I can't think he really wanted this awful dinner', said Alice. 'Are you sure you haven't made a mistake? Such things have been known to happen, Cook. We're none of us perfect. Do you remember when you sent up a <u>rice</u> pudding at a dinner party when I ordered <u>ice</u> pudding? That was funny. Fortunately they were all very nice about it. Oh don't be offended, Cook. We all make mistakes sometimes.'

'We do Mum', said Cook.

'But do remember not to do this sort of thing. The times when you should show initiative, you never do . . It's heartbreaking, Cook' she repeated 'Yes it's simply heart breaking . . Oh, and by the way, are you sure that there's none of the copper pans that need recoppering?'

'Quite sure, Mum![']

'That can't be it, then. You know, my mother's doctor thought that my attacks might have been not gastric at all, but due to irritant poisoning. And the only way we could think that I could have been poisoned was through some of the copper vessels having worn out. I can't think of any other way, can you Cook?'

'No mum, I can't. If you was a lady with a nagging tongue, always finding fault with everything, and making trouble where there's only kindness meant, then I suppose we might all be wanting to drop poison into your food. But you aren't like that, are you mum?'

Alice's heart nearly stopped. Cook's face was bland, but her tone was unmistakably insolent. What was the reason for this madness that afflicted one and all of the servant class?[']9

And what is the reason that no one really appreciates her? Her mother doesn't. Her sister and brother don't, although her own aim has been to help them and to correct their mistakes. Why is it? Thank God, there is Jimmy her husband, who loves her.

But when Jimmy returns, they pass a painful evening. He actually criticises her. He is affectionate, gentle and charming as always. 'Poor little Alice' he calls her, but he implores her not to interfere so much with other people's lives. 'I don't interfere' she wails. 'It is only that I know best'. 'You are the salt of the earth' he says solemnly, 'but no one likes even the salt of the earth when it is rubbed into their wounds.' The happiness of the servants, of her family, yes even his own happiness depends upon her stopping herself from being the salt of the earth. He warns her, loverlike, and she half promises. Then she withdraws her promise; she must do what she thinks right, and cook comes in with her evening cup of chocolate. Jimmy, the silly fellow, is agitated by the argument and is rolling about in his hand a phial of powder which she had found in his dressing-gown. She turns after cook, to give some final instructions, comes back, and drinks the chocolate. It has a bitter flavour. Mists rise before her eyes, pains gripe her, she collapses, her husband carries her on to the bed and says again 'Poor little Alice'. The salt of the earth is - arsenic. He has poisoned her.

This brilliant and grim story is perfect in its way. Miss Rebecca West has done exactly what she wanted to do and I cannot imagine any one doing it better. It is a masterpiece. The characters are appropriate to the action and the action never ceases moving to its astounding yet inevitable end. But it is not the only sort of short story, and, much as I admire it, I pass now to something nearer to my heart.

The Child of Queen Victoria by William Plomer has no plot to speak of, and I can describe its action in a single sentence. A youth fresh from an English public school falls in love, out in South Africa with a native girl and she loves him, but she is drowned. That is all. It is the setting which transforms. The incident, which might be told cynically or too sentimentally, is set amidst tenderness and grandeur. Frant - that is the youth's name - has come out to learn trading in a native reserve. The owner of the store is a coarse-grained Scotsman, who regards the inhabitants of the country as beneath contempt, though not always beneath familiarity. With him and with his scrawny wife Frant has to live, cut off from other white society. Frant is a good fellow, intelligent, hard working, honest, civilised, polite, but half asleep emotionally. The native Africans who come to the store to buy the European rubbish which is pushed at them like him, and one of them sums him up as nickname "The Child of Queen Victoria". There is criticism in the nickname. There is also respect and affection. "My advice is don't stand any cheek from any nigger" is the Scotsman's comment when he hears of it.[10] Frant keeps quietly on his way, liking and humouring his customers, learning their language, and responding to the magic of the scenery. Even the interior of the store fascinates him - and in describing it William Plomer doubtless draws upon personal experience for he has related in his autobiography <u>Double Lives</u>[11] how he[12] once worked in a store in Zululand. And then the inevitable happens. Frant, who has great capacities for living, meets a magnificent African girl, and realises the existence of life. I'll quote.

> She had moved now, and the diffused radiance reflected from the sunburnt hill-top outside shone full upon her through the open door. Her hair was dressed in a cylinder on the crown of her head, stained with red ochre, and stuck with a long bone pin, at the broad end of which was a minute incised design; she wore no ornament but a flat necklace of very small blue beads and a few thin bangles and anklets of silver and copper wire. She was dressed in a single piece of dark red stuff which was supported by her firm and pointed young breasts, and fastened under her arms . . .[13]

What shall the Child of Queen Victoria do? This girl torments his imagination. Then desire turns into something more profound. She comes back after many days with a present for him - a snakeskin, the skin of a fifteen-foot python which she has killed with her hoe in a maize field. She loves him. Offspring of a warrior race, she brings it as an offering to a hero. What is he to do? He cannot marry her. He disdains a vulgar intrigue. His doubts remain, but his loneliness has vanished.

> In the evening he nailed up the skin on the walls of his bedroom. It was so long that it took up the whole of two sides. And very late before putting out his light, he lay in bed looking at it. Like a banner it hung there to celebrate the intensity of his happiness: it hung like a trophy - the skin of the dragon of his misery, killed by Seraphina as she hoed her father's field of maize.[14]

Finally he decides to go and see her - to go not with any sophisticated plan in his head, but simply, like the primitive people whom he has learnt to admire. Twice he sets out for her kraal, which lies far beneath in a valley, and each time he is stopped by Fate. The first time a young man meets him, bounding up the hill, and tells him that the girl is away. The next time - the tropic rain has started. It is wild on the uplands, but they[15] have only felt the edge of the storm. Out of the gathering darkness an old native rushes up crying 'Child of the Queen! What are you doing here? Where are you going? Child! My child, Look!' and drags him to the edge of the table land.[16] Frant looks. In the place of the kraal and the little maize fields there is nothing but a gigantic swirl of greyish water. The river came down like a wall. The houses, the people - all are drowned.[17]

It was easy for me to describe <u>The Salt of the Earth</u> for it goes with a snap, but a story like <u>The Child of Queen Victoria</u> has to be left to your imagination and your own reading. Delicacy, nobility, tragic power: civilisations colliding: and human beings now magnified by their vast African surroundings, and now[18] shrinking to the size of an insect or a flower. I don't know what the moral of the story is, and I should be surprised if William Plomer had one. He is concerned to rouse our sense of beauty and to touch our hearts.

1. <NOT CHECKED WITH>

2. For more on Plomer, see EMF's broadcast dated 27 January 1944.

3. EMF added an accent mark above "is."

4. <It must have a point. And it will probably observe the unities of place and of time.>

5. <Their names are>

6. Rebecca West, "The Salt of the Earth," in *The Harsh Voice: Four Short Novels* (London: Jonathan Cape, 1935), 179–250; William Plomer, "The Child of Queen Victoria," in *The Child of Queen Victoria and Other Stories* (London: Jonathan Cape, 1933), 13–76. For more on West's work, see EMF's broadcast dated 27 May 1942.

7. EMF added accent marks above the first syllables of "rather," "relieved," and "visit" and above "ends" in this sentence.

8. EMF added an accent mark above "they."

9. West, "Salt of the Earth," 205–8.

10. Plomer, "Child of Queen Victoria," 36.

11. Plomer, *Double Lives: An Autobiography* (London: Jonathan Cape, 1943).

12. EMF added an accent mark above "he."

13. Plomer, "Child of Queen Victoria," 38–39.

14. Ibid., 54.

15. EMF added an accent mark above "they."

16. Plomer, "Child of Queen Victoria," 74.

17. <¶Something in Frant urged him to leave the old man and run down the hill and plunge into those maddened waters and lose himself, but something stronger told him that he must return to the store, to the trader, to the making of a livelihood, to the fashioning of a way of life, and to a python skin nailed to a wall like a banner, with two large holes in it, cut by a girl with a hoe. . . .> (Plomer, "Child of Queen Victoria," 76).

18. EMF added accent marks above both instances of "now" in this sentence.

As[1] CHECKED WITH BROADCAST   To be recorded from transmission
Eastern Service   SLO 66780
Purple Network
Tuesday 19th December, 1944
1445-1500 GMT
Reproductions: G.O.S. Thursday 21st December 1944 - 0030-0045 GMT
            Pacific Sunday 24th December - 0730-0745 GMT
            African Sunday 24th December - 1745-1800 GMT
            N.A.S. Monday 25th December - 0030-0045 GMT
              "   "   "   "   0415-0430 GMT

SOME BOOKS

by

E.M. Forster

Several books on India have lately come my way - religious, political, humorous; books of all sorts except two. The two sorts which don't come my way, and don't appear to get published any more, are books by globe trotters and complacent books. The globe trotter still visits India, but he has to pretend that he is not trotting: he proceeds with weighty steps and a furrowed brow. And the complacent book of the "all's well with our Raj" type, with elephants and Koh-i-Noors[2] on its dust-jacket, seems to have vanished altogether.

[3]The first work to be mentioned,[4] is a new translation of the Bhagavad-Gita. It comes from America, and it is the joint work of Swami Prabhavananda and of Christopher Isherwood.[5] Christopher Isherwood is a brilliant up to date novelist; you may know his novel about pre-war Berlin "Mr. Norris changes Trains"; and he has collaborated in plays with W.H. Auden.[6] He has for many years now lived in America, and seems to be turning from fiction to psychology and to mysticism. Being extremely intelligent, he does not suppose that India has any monopoly in mystic goods, but he does realise that certain Indians, particularly in the past, have speculated in the religious direction, and that the Bhagavad Gita is the supreme monument of that adventure. He believes that it deals with

our troubles today, and he is quite right. He thinks it will solve them, and here I don't know. Collaborating with Swami Prabhavananda, a Sanskrit scholar, he has produced a translation which is more than readable: it is exciting. He keeps up the spiritual pressure as it were, partly through his command of English and partly through the[7] happy device of translating in a variety of styles. Some of the passages are in prose, others in verse. The transitions[8] are arbitrary since the whole of the original is in verse, but they do represent its emotional variety and make the reader's heart beat. The Gita, he points out, is so many things: a piece out of an Indian epic: a technical exposition of Vedanta philosophy: a mystic utterance about God: and, fourthly and lastly, a Gospel, where God, our friend, tells us bothered individuals what we ought to do. It reaches high out of our vision, it reaches down to small practical things: to how I should do this broadcast for instance. And it gives the small practical man a bit of advice; he should act, he should do his bit, but he should renounce the fruits of action. If he achieves that he will come, by his appropriate[9] path, to the same goal as the saint. Knowledge and action are really one, and the followers of action will meet the seekers after knowledge in the long run.

I mustn't however stray into expounding the Bhagavad Gita - it's a task for which I'm unqualified. I'm just recommending you (if you don't know Sanskrit) this lucid and civilised translation by Prabhavananda and Isherwood. 'The Song of God' is its subtitle. And there's an introduction to it by Aldous Huxley.

Another Indian religious book I want to mention is the Kusti Prayers and their exposition by Miss Pilloo Nanavutty, who is a member of the Parsi community in Bombay.[10] The Avestan text of the prayers is printed on one side, and the English translation opposite. Reading the Kusti prayers immediately after the Bhagavad Gita, I am struck by their dualism, their insistence on the conflict between good and evil. Miss Nanavutty adds a helpful footnote on the symbolic nature of the prayers. This tiny volume was published in India, and I would like to take the opportunity of saying what particular pleasure it gives me to mention books from India in these broadcasts. They make me feel less isolated. I can't undertake to mention them, but whenever they are suitable, I will. Only yesterday I had another book from your country - of a very different character from Miss Nanavutty's, for it is humourous colloquial journalism, and it bears the gay title of Onions and Opinions. The author's name is N.G. Jog, and he reprints various light articles which he contributed to newspapers in Bombay and Calcutta. Mr. Jog writes rather in the style of our Robert Lynd (Y.Y.).[11]

But I must proceed to books on a subject which is neither humourous or light, namely politics. Here is <u>The People of India</u> by Kumar Goshal,

<u>Verdict on India</u> by Beverley Nichols, <u>British Soldier in India</u>, being the let-
ters of Clive Branson, and <u>Nine Drawings</u> of the Indian Famine by the caricaturist Vicky, with a preface by Mulk Raj Anand.[12] The attitudes of these
writers vary, I will try to describe them dispassionately. Mr. Kumar
Goshal[13] lives in America and addresses an American public. He is well
informed and writes well. He is anti-British, not interested in the
Moslems, pro-Hindu, nationalist, and favourable to Congress - to
Congress in its popular and socialist aspect, that's to say. Mr. Beverley
Nichols, an English journalist, is critical of the British, hostile to the
Hindus, and to Congress, which he regards as a purely Hindu body, and
favourable to the Moslem league and to Pakistan. He eulogises Mr.
Jinnah,[14] whom he met, denounces Mr. Gandhi, whom he didn't meet, is
most severe on the Indian arts, and dismisses the Vina as an 'off colour
guitar.' Clive Branson - the late Clive Branson I have to say - for he was
killed in Burma - he was an artist by profession, and a communist politically; what struck him in India was the poverty; anti-British, anti
Congress, and anti Moslem League too I imagine; pro-food and economic
reconstruction on communist lines. With him may be classed the left-wing
caricaturist, Vicky. To them, hunger not communal division is the basic
problem.

That should roughly indicate to you the character of these four political
books. I want to say a word about the most remarkable of them, Clive
Branson's <u>British Soldier in India</u>. Mr. Beverley Nichols wields the readier
pen and supplies plenty of emotional warmth, but India, one feels is
merely a new subject on his long list, for he is the globe trotter who pretends he isn't trotting. Clive Branson, on the other hand, found something
special in the place which moved him deeply and responded to him. He
had no advantages, no introductions, he was only a Tommy,[15] but he
instantly made friends with the Indians who came in his way, and entered
into their lives. He was a rigid Marxist, who belonged to his Party. He was
also a sincere and warm hearted fellow, and when reading these letters to
his wife I felt that India would have continued to move him, even when
he grew old. Here is a typical[16] passage; the[17] vision of[18] poverty reinforced
by the eye of the artist.

"I have just got back from a swim - it was lovely. It is of course piping hot - a cruel sun that makes the earth sand-dry even within a few
yards of the water's edge; and the green, long leaves of the young sugar
cane glint like bayonets. But oh, the ghastly poverty of the Indian people! Wherever one goes it is the same thing. Little clumps, sometimes
village size, of broken stone walls, sacking, bits of tin, corrugated iron
roofing propped against a wall, and matting, called "home" by millions
of human beings. In the middle, or nearby, a temple or a church, and far

away in the cities the swine who live wealthily."[19]
'British Soldier in India' is a moving book, whatever you think of its political and economic creed. Clive Branson cared about India and would have
continued to care; whereas Mr. Beverley Nichols,[20] may probably never
give the place another thought.

That makes eight books in all, and this talk too much of a book list. I'll
conclude by going back to the translation of the Bhagavad Gita and quoting a verse passage. Shri Krishna is speaking, the divine charioteer,
instructing Arjuna[21] who is everyman on the nature of the universe before
they go into battle

> There is a fig tree
> In ancient story
> The giant Aswatha,
> The everlasting
> Rooted in heaven,
> Its branches earthward:
> Each of its leaves
> Is a song of the Vedas,
> And he who knows it
> Knows all the Vedas.
>
> Downward and upward
> Its branches bending
> Are fed by the gunas,
> The buds it puts forth
> Are the things of the senses,
> Roots it has also
> Reaching downwards
> Into this world,
> The roots of man's action.
> What its form is,
> Its end beginning,
> Its very nature,
> Can never be known here.[22]

In this passage the complexity of the universe, of which India is a fraction,
gets indicated. The roots of man's action in the earth and the roots up in
heaven both nourish this puzzling tree.

---

1. Though "As" has been inserted above "NOT CHECKED WITH BROADCAST," no
words have been canceled. A handwritten "As Broadcast" follows the list of reproductions.
EMF timed the broadcast carefully. At the top of page 4 (of 5) of the typescript he wrote
"2'/1 to go"—that is, two minutes, one second.

2. Koh-i-noor: the famous Indian diamond transferred to the British Crown jewels when the Punjab was annexed in 1849.

3. <Of the works>

4. <the most important>

5. *Bhagavad-Gita: The Song of God,* trans. Swami Prabhavananda and Christopher Isherwood (Hollywood: Marcel Rodd Co., 1944). EMF added an accent mark above the first syllable of "Prabhavananda" and a dividing line before "nanda," both presumably to guide pronunciation.

6. *Mr. Norris Changes Trains* (London: L. and Virginia Woolf at the Hogarth Press, 1935). Among the plays on which Isherwood and Auden collaborated was *The Dog Beneath the Skin; or, Where is Francis? A Play in Three Acts* (London: Faber and Faber, 1935).

7. <ingenious>

8. EMF added an accent mark above the second syllable of "transitions."

9. <faith>

10. Piloo Nanavutty, trans., *Kusti Prayers* [Zoroastrian] (India, 1944); no copy has been located. EMF added an accent mark over the second "a" in Nanavutty in the first two mentions of the name.

11. Narayan Gopal Jog, *Onions and Opinions* (Bombay: Thacker and Co., 1944). Robert Lynd provided a preface to Jog's book. Lynd himself wrote under the pseudonym "Y.Y.," as his 1941 book acknowledged: *Life's Little Oddities,* by Robert Lynd (Y.Y.) (London: J. M. Dent and Sons, 1941).

12. Kumar Goshal, *The People of India* (New York: Sheridan House, 1944); Beverley Nichols, *Verdict on India* (London: Cape, 1944); Clive Branson, *The British Soldier in India: The Letters of C. Branson* (London: Communist Party, 1944); *9 Drawings by Vicky* [scenes of the Indian famine with accompanying text] (London: Modern Literature, [1944]). Branson was killed in action in 1944. "Vicky" was the pseudonym of cartoonist Victor Weisz.

13. EMF added an accent mark above the first syllable of "Goshal."

14. Muhammad Ali Jinnah, a constitutional lawyer by training, was head of the Muslim League and the founder of Pakistan, though he originally supported the Indian Congress and Hindu-Muslim unity. For more information, see S. M. Burke and Salim Al-Din Quraishi, *The British Raj in India: An Historical Review* (Oxford: Oxford University Press, 1995), 343–49. For additional details of the Indian Congress, see EMF's broadcast dated 11 April 1944, n. 35.

15. An ordinary soldier (as in the Kipling poem of the same name).

16. <and terrible>

17. <appalling>

18. <famine>

19. Branson, *British Soldier in India,* 37.

20. <his verdict delivered, will>

21. EMF added an accent mark above the initial "A" of "Arjuna."

22. *Bhagavad-Gita,* trans. Prabhavananda and Isherwood, 147–48. EMF added accent marks above the initial "A" of "Aswatha" and the first syllable of "gunas."

[1]As BROADCAST
Eastern Service
Purple Network
Tuesday 13th February, 1945
1515-1530 GMT
Reproductions: G.O.S. - 15.2.45 - 0030-0045 GMT
              Pacific - 18.2.45 - 0730-0745 GMT
              African - 18.2.45 - 1745-1800 GMT
              N.A.S. - 19.2.45 - 0030-0045 GMT
                               0415-0430 GMT

To be recorded from
transmission

SOME BOOKS

by

E.M.Forster

Books about the war are the subject of today's talk. I never find[2] such books easy to discuss partly because they are remote from my own experiences. I haven't so far been injured in the war myself, or lost any of my property, indeed the nearest I have come to danger was last year when I was feeding some chickens in the country, and a shell burst up in the sky. Fragments of shrapnel whizzed through the bushes and stuck into the lawn, but they didn't hit me, or the chickens, and that was that. When I compare[3] such raw experience with those of others, I feel ill equipped. Peoples' sufferings, bodily and mental, their heroism, even their brutality - it's something I don't know about. I've had to pick up passive courage during the last six years, like most civilians, and to put up with things and not get fussed. But the active courage which takes the initiative and is heroic - [4]that's beyond me, and the three books I'm discussing today are full of it.

I am also rather put off war books for another reason. Too many of them are semi-novels, worked-up diaries, records where names and places are changed for security reasons. We are not sure whether we are getting at the facts. And we want facts if it's only about me and the chickens. There has been too much propaganda, too much presentation. The historian of the future, whose aim is presumably truth, will have an awful job when he starts sorting things out. And of the war books I've been reading lately, by far the best is the work of the war correspondent to the Daily Express, Mr. Alan Moorehead, who doesn't set out to make any particular impression, and succeeds in making a deep one. I have also been interested by a semi-novel about Spanish prisons, another about the French resistance movement.[5] But it's Mr. Moorehead's book I want to emphasise.

He calls it <u>African Trilogy</u>.[6] It is actually three books bound together as one, and it is a personal account of our three years struggle against the Axis in North Africa. There are excursions to the Sudan and Abyssinia, Crete, Syria, and Persia, India during the Cripps mission,[7] but the main scene is the African coast, from Cairo to Algiers. What a scene - 2,000 miles long. And what a subject! The Italian threat to Egypt, its repulse, the arrival of Rommel and the Germans, Tobruk, Alamein, the arrival of the Americans, Tunis, victory. Mr. Moorehead gives a clear account of the military operations, and - so far as he knows them - of the political intrigues, but what attracts me is his human outlook - human without being soppy - and the excellence of his writing, which is vivid without being picturesque. I don't know whether you are like me, and have grown to mistrust the picturesque report. One reads it the first time, and it seems good, one reads it a second time and the goodness has evaporated. But listen to a couple of quotations from African Trilogy.[8] Here is our capture of Tobruk in January 1941.

> [9]Inside the town fires blazed. Shops, homes, offices, were torn up and their furniture and household goods strewn across the roads. Walking through it, I felt suddenly sickened at the destruction and the uselessness and the waste. At this moment of success, I found only an unreasoning sense of futility. The courage of the night before had been turned so quickly to decay. And now the noise and the rushing and the light had gone, one walked through the streets kicking aside broken deckchairs and suits of clothes, and pot-plants, and children's toys. A soldier was frying eggs on the counter of the National Bank. A new fire leapt up in a furniture store house in the night, and the wine from the vats next door spilled across the road. Stray cats swarmed over the rubbish. In the bay a ship kept burning steadily. By its light the wounded were being carried down to the docks.[10]

In this description there is a touch of T.E. Lawrence's Seven Pillars,[11] though I don't suggest there is any resemblance between the style of the works. Lawrence too could observe little things at great moments, and could detect futility at the heart of victory. I know he would have understood the very end of the book, where the German and Allied soldiers in

Tunis after the surrender stand together looking at one another with listless and passionless curiosity. "The struggle had gone on so long. It had been so bitter. So many men had died. There was nothing more to say."[12]

Here's a quotation in lighter vein. Tunis is being captured.[13]

Hundreds of Germans were walking in the streets, some with their girl friends. Hundreds more were sitting drinking aperitifs in a big pavement cafe. No one had warned them the British were near.[14] Now suddenly, like a vision from the sky, appeared three British armoured cars. The Germans rose from their seats and stared. The Tommies stared back. There was not much they could do. Three armoured cars could not handle all these prisoners. In the hairdressing saloon next door more Germans struggled out of the chairs, and, with white sheets round their necks and lather on their faces, stood gaping. The three armoured cars turned back for reinforcements.[15]

Mr. Moorehead's attitude to our German and Italian enemies is notable. Though he is often scathing about their mental make up, he never abuses them mechanically, or makes the ridiculous mistake of calling them sub-human. Another good mark I'd give him is for his feeling for scenery, both cultivated and desert. African Trilogy is a book to get hold of, and, as Lord Wavell says in his foreword, it will be very valuable to future historians. It isn't itself history, for there must be much that Mr. Moorehead doesn't know about the campaigns, and much that he knows and mustn't reveal. It is, rather, a collection of materials, made by a civilised journalist who has learnt the great art of keeping himself in the background.

I have also been reading a book by another journalist. It is about Spain, or rather the interior of Spanish prisons, where the writer, much to his surprise, spent several months during 1941 and 1942. He is a Belgian, and his name, D'Ydewalle, is so difficult to catch that I'll spell it. D'YDEWALLE. An Interlude in Spain by Charles D'Ydewalle.[16] Arrested at the instance of the Gestapo, he was first in a Model Prison at Barcelona, and then at a huge camp in the interior.[17] The atmosphere was human, the relation between prisoners and warders was pleasant - indeed at a turn of fortune's wheel the prisoners might well become warders and vice versa. Comforts could be bought and were shared. There was a sense of comradeship. On the[18] other hand, most of the prisoners had never been charged with any crime, they were liable to torture, and they were constantly being executed. Death, death, seemed the Spanish government's only solution of its difficulties.

I entered the Model Prison (writes Mr. D'Ydewalle) in the company of three stocky little British soldiers, from the Buffs and the Gordon Highlanders. I pointed out to them the long line of our unhappy neighbours, and said: "Those are the men condemned to death". They smiled an unbelieving smile. The second time they suspected me of an ill timed joke. But one day, confronted by a particularly dismal array of mattresses, they were compelled to accept the evidence. They shook their heads in horror: and the oldest of them merely muttered "Well England's good enough for me".[19]

That anecdote shows that he has grasped the British character anyway, and most of the book is pretty convincing, though at times - especially towards the end - I feel that the writer is working his prison inmates up into a series of short stories, and that I am not getting the facts. I never had that feeling with Mr. Moorehead. <u>Interlude in Spain</u> is remarkable though, because it is an indictment of General Franco's government by a writer who is not on the Left. Mr. D'Ydewalle is a monarchist and a devout Catholic; I have been told that he fought on General Franco's side in the Civil War; he certainly has no sympathy whatever with republicans or communism, that makes his denunciation of the present regime the more impressive.

From Spain to France. Here lastly is a book about the French underground resistance movement. <u>Army of Shadows</u> by Joseph Kessel.[20] It gives me the impression of fiction based upon facts, though the author claims in the preface that there is no fiction in it at all.[21] Whether all the events described in it, "happened" or not, it is a terrible book, full not only of heroism but of the hardness which must be acquired by people who are fighting for a cause; all, all must be given up for the sake of France.

> On our side we kill kill kill. The French were not prepared, not disposed to kill. Their temperament, their climate, their country, the state of civilisation they had reached turned them away from bloodshed.[22] Now the Frenchman kills to protect his home, his daily bread, his loved ones, his honour. He kills every day. He kills the German, the German's accomplice, the traitor, the informer. He kills for a reason and he kills by reflex.[23]

There are many thrills and coincidences in <u>Army of Shadows</u>, including an escape from a firing squad, and an encounter, on a secret adventure, between a young man and his elder brother whom he has always regarded as a muff, but who turns out to be the head of the whole resistance movement. The burthen of Mr. Kessel's story is 'Kill - kill to free France' just as the burthen of that Spanish prison was 'Kill - kill to keep Spain safe.' One closes them both with a mixture of admiration, envy and deep depression. How marvellous the human race is! And how disgusting. One thinks of Mr. Moorehead's book on Africa where at the end the German and Allied soldiers are left standing opposite each other, exhausted, too tired to destroy any more.

1. <NOT CHECKED WITH> Handwritten numbers in the margins note the elapsed time throughout the script; several cancellations appear to be the result of time limits.

2. <them easy>

3. <this>

4. <it is>

5. <and a third about the British merchant navy>

6. *African Trilogy: Comprising Mediterranean Front, A Year of Battle, The End in Africa: A Personal Account of the Three Years' Struggle Against the Axis in the Middle East and North Africa, 1940–3*, foreword by Field-Marshal Viscount Wavell (London: H. Hamilton, 1944).

7. On the Cripps Mission, see EMF's broadcast dated 18 July 1943.

8. <Mr. Moorehead gets home as a journalist should, and abounds in telling phrases, but there is something in the quality of his observation and the temper of his mind which makes the phrase stay.>

9. <Sickness, death and wounding enveloped Tobruk.>

10. Moorehead, *African Trilogy*, 90–91.

11. T. E. Lawrence, *Seven Pillars of Wisdom: A Triumph* (London: Jonathan Cape, 1926).

12. Ibid., 580.

13. <and everyone is agape. ¶Meanwhile another patrol of armoured cars had taken the right fork, the Rue de Londres, down to the centre of the town. They took the city entirely unawares.>

14. <The attack had gone so quickly that here in the town there had been no indication that the Axis line was broken.>

15. Moorehead, *African Trilogy*, 563.

16. Charles d'Ydewalle, *An Interlude in Spain*, trans. Eric Sutton (London: Macmillan, 1944).

17. <Let me summarise the good side and the bad side of the experiences. On the good side>

18. <bad side>

19. D'Ydewalle, *Interlude in Spain*, 46–47.

20. Joseph Kessel, *Army of Shadows*, trans. Haakon Chevalier (London: Cresset Press, 1944).

21. <only the disguises and shufflings of places and people needed for reasons of security>

22. <I remember how difficult it was for me, in the first period of the resistance, to contemplate murder in cold blood, ambush, planned assassination. And how difficult it was to recruit people for this. No question of any such repugnance now. Primitive man has reappeared in France.>

23. <I would not say the French people have grown hard, but their edge has been sharpened.> Both the canceled and the quoted sentences are from Kessel, *Army of Shadows*, 89.

[1]As BROADCAST   To be recorded from transmission
Eastern Service
Purple Network
Tuesday 10th April, 1945
1515-1530 GMT
Reproductions: G.O.S. - 12.4.45 - 0030-0045 GMT
                    Pacific - 15.4.45 - 0730-0745 GMT
                    African - 15.4.45 - 1745-1800 GMT
                    N.A.S. - 16.4.45 - 0030-0045 GMT
                               0415-0430 GMT

SOME BOOKS

by

E.M.Forster

I am sorry I couldn't be here last month. But I hear that William Plomer spoke in my place,[2] and you will have been well served. I am very glad to be back. I shall begin by speaking of a remarkable film which is running in London - Shakespeare's Henry V.[3]

Now Henry V is a play I used to dislike. I hated the mixture in it of sanctimoniousness and swank. I hated the hero, attacking France for reasons of family honour, and then telling the French it was their fault if they got hurt. I hated his treatment of Falstaff[4] who had loved him - Falstaff left to die, because we must be respectable now, we must be constructive. I hated his cad's courtship of the French princess at the end. He reminded me too vividly of a hero out of Kipling, and I longed to see, rising beyond the brassy horizons of Agincourt, the figure of Joan of Arc, presenting true patriotism in place of false.

But when I saw the film the other day,[5] I was troubled by no such scruples and gave myself up to a very different interpretation.[6]

It begins by floating us over Shakespeare's London, and we wobble slowly down into a little round building.[7] This is the Globe Theatre. An Elizabethan audience is gathering, and Henry V is being performed on the[8] open air stage. It is not impressive, the actors have nowhere to dress, and little to dress in, the noises off are done wrong, and we sympathise with the dilemma of the opening chorus when it asks

> Can this cockpit hold
> The vasty fields of France? or may we cram
> Within this wooden O the very casques
> That did affright the air at Agincourt?[9]

It cannot, they can't be got in, we are exhorted to use our imagination to supply the want! The earlier scenes of the film take place on this cramped stage. When we embark for France there is an exciting change. The Globe Theatre vanishes, the Chorus sails out of sight into the clouds and we are amongst vast landscapes, luxuriant colours, and ample deeds. The battle of Agincourt, the scenes in the French Palace, are marvelous: they are not quite realistic: there is a touch of tapestry in them, and of the mediaeval[10] missal. It is so splendid and so enjoyable that one doesn't stop to consider whether the King is behaving as an enlightened young man should. There he is, in the person of Mr. Laurence Olivier, handsome, energetic, and impulsive, and whatever he wants must be right. Even his dubious love scene is a success and Katharine marries the enemy of her country without a qualm. At the end, we are back in the Globe Theatre again, the stage is cramped, the princess is played by a boy, and floating up into the air, we see, once more, Shakespeare's little London. What would he have thought of it all? I am sure he would have been gratified. He would have felt that the film did carry out some of his hints, and remove some of his fetters. He wouldn't have felt all the producers claim, for they take up the line that the Bard has waited for celluloid to come in to his own. That's nonsense. Shakespeare's 'own' is always the world of the spectator's imagination - and we must bring our imaginations to the movies just as our ancestors had to bring theirs to the Globe Theatre. Technique will never do that trick. When the French king mutters in his terror

> And he is bred out of that bloody strain
> That haunted us on our familiar paths[11]

it is a terror which imagination must expand. And when Henry finds the boys murdered in his camp and cries in his generous wrath

> I was not angry, since I came to France
> Until this instant[12]

it is our imagination which must speed him as he rides to vengeance.[13]

But I must get on to the books - a new novel by Aldous Huxley, a new volume of poems by W.H.Auden. They too, it happens have connections with Shakespeare, though not with the pageantry of Henry V.

The Huxley novel is called <u>Time must have a Stop</u>.[14] People sometimes complain that Mr. Huxley is too much interested in ideas and in satire to be a real novelist, and if you define a real novelist as one whose deepest interest is in individuals, this is true. Jane Austen, George Eliot, Arnold Bennett, Tolstoy, Proust - they are really novelists in a sense in which Huxley isn't. However much they may reach out to other themes, their start is the individual, and their genius is concentrated on making him seem real. Huxley is after something different. Take the title <u>Time must have a Stop</u>. What does it mean? It comes from the speech of the dying Hotspur in Henry IV

> But thought's the slave of life and life's time's fool,
> And time, that takes survey of all the world,
> Must have a stop.[15]

He means that unless we can stop time, unless we can get rid of the tyranny of the past and the future and live in the moment we shall never realise eternity. What a theme for a work of fiction, you will say! How unsuitable! But he does turn out a brilliant readable book. The scene is in pre-war England and Italy. Some of the characters practice pleasure, others social reform, none are satisfied. [16]Take the intelligent voluptuary, Eustace Barnack. He has married money, inherits a villa in Florence loves food and wine and cigars and improper jokes, and to a lesser extent literature and art. Such a harmless life, and, to his young nephew Sebastian such an attractive one. Then suddenly, and in agony, Eustace dies, and the novel, which has hitherto been realistic and sardonic, introduces the mystic element which characterises Aldous Huxley's later work. Eustace dies, but he remains alive as consciousness, he participates at a seance which tries to communicate with him, and observes with amusement the medium getting all his messages wrong. He is tormented by his horrible frivolous memories, and by his visions of what will happen in Europe when the war starts. He knows he is vile and that the world's vile. And above him glares the white pure light of eternity, which he can enter as soon as he chooses to drop his personality or what he mistakes for such, as soon as he gives up memory and exists in the moment. Time must have a stop. He refuses. Even after death time shall go on. Restless and degraded entangled in his snippety sensual past, he planes above the action, which is now concerned with the fortunes of his nephew Sebastian. To Sebastian, on earth, the same choice is presented, and though Sebastian is often absurd and selfish lustful and cruel he chooses right, we are given to understand, he sets out on the true way.

That is the[17] philosophic content of the book, and I wanted to summarise it because it is what is important to the author, and because it gives the book its peculiar taste. Don't imagine though that the whole thing is seances and disquisitions. For most of the time you will be amused - or disgusted, for Aldous Huxley is remorseless when he describes physical suffering. He has indeed a notable lack of tenderness - the tenderness which blurs our sense of fact and perhaps our sense of the spiritual but which certainly enables us to get on with one another while we remain under the dominion of time. I don't think his experiences of earthly life at all resemble my own or most men's. Are they like yours?

Now to pass on from this novel which isn't really a novel to W.H.Auden's new book of poems. Are they really poems? The lyrical and even the rhetorical element is slight, and they are very difficult to understand. The title is For the Time Being.[18] The first section is a commentary on Shakespeare's Tempest and the second is a Christmas[19] meditation. What strikes me here, as in Huxley, is the philosophic seriousness.[20] To both these men, the material world won't do. Pleasure doesn't pay, social reform isn't enough. Auden wittily presents Herod as a social reformer who is horrified by the irregularity of a divine birth in his dominions and sees only too clearly what the results will be unless he calls in the military promptly. To Auden something else is needed - something which protests if it is only Caliban protesting against Prospero. In the Christian section of the book, that which protests is the Way, the Truth, the Life: We are in mysticism again.

You should read For the Time Being if you already admire and understand Auden's work. It is not a book to begin on - you had better begin with the volumes called Look Stranger or The Orators,[21] or with one of the plays, and there you will follow more easily the workings of his unusual mind. He is off-hand, subtle, facetious, dignified, profound - a rare make up. I'll read you the last stanza of the Preface to the Tempest section, with its Shakespearean references: some of his quality gets into it.

> Well, who in his own backyard
> Has not opened his heart to the smiling
> Secret he cannot quote?
> Which goes to show that the Bard
> Was sober when he wrote
> That this world of fact we love
> Is unsubstantial stuff:
> All the rest is silence
> On the other side of the wall:
> And the silence ripeness,
> And the ripeness all.[22]

References here not only to the Tempest, but to Hamlet and to Lear. My talk ends, as it began, with Shakespeare, in whom are included the rousing pageantry of the films, and also disquiet, discontent and the faith that ripeness is all, and the ripeness silent.

1. <NOT CHECKED WITH>

2. <and since he is one of the most intelligent critics of our time, and also the most humane and civilised in his outlook,>

3. *Henry V* (1944), directed by Laurence Olivier, starring Laurence Olivier with Renée Asherson as Princess Katharine.

4. <the philosopher>

5. <with Laurence Olivier in the title role,>

6. <and was completely carried away.> EMF's exuberance over a film closely allied to World War II propaganda represents a departure from his usual attitudes toward propaganda as well as toward Shakespeare's play.

7. <open to the air>

8. <Elizabethan>

9. *Henry V*, prologue, lines 11–14.

10. <mind>

11. *Henry V*, 2.4.51–52.

12. Ibid., 4.7.58–59.

13. <¶The acting is admirable. Mr. Laurence Olivier looks gallant but not too classy - and that's the way to put that King across: the tough young Englishman who can be a bit of a lad when he has the time, and who can give and take as an equal when he talks to the men he commands. He has been fighting all his life. Don't you criticise him, you poor little liberal. And Falstaff, his eternal critic - he is touchingly played by Mr. George Robey. Falstaff, you will remember, doesn't appear in this play - he dies off - but a scene in King Henry IV, where he does appear, has been cleverly utilised. And the Princess Katharine - she was delicious, and so intelligent and sensitive beneath her formality. What a lucky chap! Mind you see the film when it gets out to you.>

14. Aldous Huxley, *Time Must Have a Stop* (New York and London: Harper and Brothers, 1944).

15. *Henry IV, Part I*, 5.5.81–83.

16. <The chief character is an>

17. <prophetic>

18. W. H. Auden, *For the Time Being* (London: Faber and Faber, 1945).

19. <Oratorio>

20. <though there is a gruff compassion in Auden which brings him nearer to my heart>

21. Auden, *Look, Stranger!* (London: Faber and Faber, 1936); *The Orators: An English Study* (London: Faber and Faber, 1932; 2d ed., 1934).

22. Auden, *For the Time Being*, 8.

[1]As BROADCAST
Eastern Service
Purple Network
Wed 9th May, 1945[2]
1245-1300 GMT

<u>SOME BOOKS</u>

by

<u>E.M.Forster</u>

Reproductions: G.O.S. 10.5.45 - 0030-0045 GMT
                Pacific 13.5.45 - 0730-0745 GMT
                African 13.5.45 - 1745-1800 GMT
                N.A.S. 14.5.45 - 0030-0045 GMT
                              0415-0430 GMT

What is the use of Art? There's a nasty one. Well, if I had to answer the question in a single sentence I think I'd say "Art is useful. Because it presents us with order in a disorderly world". It is the only thing on earth we know of which has internal harmony, and[3] much to man's credit that he has practised it. I don't think you can defend art because it amuses or because it educates - although amusement and education are both of them desirable - and[4] talk about beauty[5] gets so vague. But you can defend art because it succeeds where politics and social effort have hitherto failed: success in creating order. Poems plays statues films - they have, when successful, an internal harmony, which arises out of their construction and isn't imposed on them from outside.

Why do I go off like this on the subject of Art? Because I have been reading the autobiography of Sir Osbert Sitwell and at the beginning he makes a remark which delighted and comforted me. He says:

Men die, even the most evil, and stupidity perishes as much as grace. By its nature, the triumph can be but temporary of ape over man. Between them Art is and always has been the dividing line.[6]

Apes differ from men not because men make bombs and apes can't, not because men are allowed to broadcast and apes mayn't, but because man, unlike the ape, dreams of internal order, and succeeds in embodying it in works of art. Here's the dividing line. The dream has led us out of animal darkness, and if we reject it we shall return to the darkness. That's my belief anyway, and Osbert Sitwell shares it. He believes that Art is useful, eternally so, and, in his complex nature, this is his guiding faith.

It is a complex book. The title indicates as much. It is <u>Left Hand - Right Hand</u> - the left hand, according to the palmists, containing the lines which are incised on us at birth, whereas the right hand has been modified by our actions and environment. This volume - it is first of a series - is mostly[7] occupied with the world into which Osbert Sitwell was born and with his ancestry.

Now the Sitwells are aristocrats. Sir Osbert is a fifth baronet, and on his mother's side his descent is even more distinguished: his grandfather was Earl of Londesborough, his great grandfather Duke of Beaufort and so on. He, his sister, Miss Edith Sitwell, and their brother Sacheverell are aristocrats who have wanted to write and have descended into an arena which is mainly occupied by the middle classes. In the past, the aristocrats have on the whole not wanted to write: they have patronised art, they have commanded it, they have shown discrimination and good taste, but they have seldom sought distinction as creative artists. "The Sitwells" as one conveniently calls them are an exception to this. They have wanted to come down and make things or if you prefer it to go up and make things. They have not been content to command. And in <u>Left Hand - Right Hand</u> Osbert Sitwell shows them starting as children on this fascinating expedition.

Their father, Sir George Sitwell, did not start. Sir George, a powerful and extraordinary character brilliantly[8] described, remained the patron, the connoisseur, the commander. Confident that he was always right, and that he knew people[']s business better than they did he interfered with artists and told them how to do their jobs. He interfered for instance with the painter Sargent whom he had commissioned to do a family group, and Osbert Sitwell devotes the last chapter of the book to the incident. It is a very witty chapter and a very sensitive one; it traces the line which divides people who want to give orders from people who want to do things. I think it could only have been written by a man who had had experiences both sides of that line by the aristocrat who has desired to create. <u>Left Hand - Right Hand</u>: you now see the point of the title clearly.

Here is the[9] incident in brief. Sir George Sitwell possessed a charming eighteenth century group of his ancestors. He decided he would have a group to balance it, depicting himself, his wife,[10] and the three children. It was one of many decisions. We find him writing to his agent

'I feel now equal to paying for a large portrait group, and wish you would ask your artist friend whom he recommends. I also wish to buy two pieces of land behind the butchers shop. What is to be done about buying a billiard table?[']'[11]

The billiard table and the land behind the butchers were simple matters. The portrait group led to unexpected complications. Sargent was the artist finally selected, the most fashionable painter of the day, who could make his sitters look as if they were old masters and at the same time[12] modern. Sir George determined to be painted among his possessions up in Derbyshire. Sargent would only paint in his own London studio. Here was a problem! It was solved by Sir George bringing his possessions up to London with him. A war was on, but it was only the South African War, and he[13] transported a panel of priceless Brussels tapestry (thirty feet by twenty) a large and exquisite[14] table, designed by Robert Adam, a silver racing cup, his wife, his three children, toys for the children to play with, a pug dog they were expected to fondle, though it snapped at them, and even then he forgot the china. All arrived in time at Sargent's studio. Sir George wore riding kit (though he seldom rode), he made his wife wear evening dress and a hat, he made his daughter wear scarlet, he made the children offer the pug a biscuit, and the picture started. The Boer war proceeded. Ladysmith fell, nobody took any notice.[15] As the picture[16] matured Sir George became increasingly dictatorial, contradicting the painter, starting theories, getting them accepted, withdrawing them after acceptance. At times Sargent fell into a rage and rushed about the studio like a bull. When this happened, Sir George was delighted "for according to his code, a show of temperament was expected of every artist - who ought indeed to be goaded daily by the patron until he give it, that being part of the contract, as it were, existing between them, and a guarantee that the work would be of the highest quality."[17] Finally the work was finished, the children could escape from the floor and the companionship of the dreaded pug, everything and everyone went back to Derbyshire and there, in the noble house which Sir Osbert now owns, the picture can still be seen.[18] His estimate of its aesthetic value is temperate. He regards it chiefly as a period piece. It was painted in 1900. With the new century different standards came in, and we shall hear of them in a future volume.

I have spoken about this Sargent group chapter partly because it is so entertaining partly because it so well illustrates the contrast between the aristocratic outlook and the creative outlook. The Sitwells are not only fine writers. They are also descendants of a masterful stock, accustomed to social priority. They bring an unusual equipment to literature. Osbert

Sitwell is aware of this, and he writes about his origins as simply as middle class or working class writers write or should write about theirs. He is never snobbish or flustered. He did come from certain ancestors and he realises that their blood runs in his own, and influences his reactions.

Some of the most charming passages deal with a servant, Henry Moat, who came as a footman to the family, rose to be a butler, often gave notice, was often given it, and remained on and off for 43 years. Not at all the dear old butler but robust original and audacious, with a respect for learning and a latent sense of poetry. Listen to these extracts from a letter of his to Osbert Sitwell after the latter had grown up: the reference to Ginger by the way is to no less a person than Sir George Sitwell himself.

Hotel Bristol, Berlin. 1929

Dear Captain Osbert,

We have been traveling a good deal in Germany and very interesting it is Sir George taking me and sometimes Miss Fowler to see the Castles Palaces Museums and Pubs. We have become well known in Germany, Ginger visiting the above places over and over again and giving the attendants a hell of a time so that when we enter a door and they see him they scatter like scalded cats some through doors some through windows and others up the chimneys one fat old woman wanted to take his umbrella from him and then commenced a vigourous tug of war result the fragments of the umbrella has been sent to the Castle to be put away in the armoury . . . But joking apart Sir George is very good to me and took Miss Fowler and me to Potsdam. Very interesting. The palace and gardens are truly beautiful . . . There was also a beautiful globe of World in the Kaiser's study, and I showed Sir G. where you was in Spain.

Now dear Master Osbert, take great care of yourself. We leave here this Wednesday, then Her Ladyship departs direct for Florence and GRS and self for Verona. I remain your obedient servant Henry Moat.[19]

This letter indicates the freshness and width of the book. There's a sort of social lavishness about it which is most attractive.

It's the book of a man who feels himself in the saddle. And with this self confidence Osbert Sitwell combines sensibility, humaneness, and the desire to write well. The strands of the aristocrat, who wants to lead, and the artist who wants to create are finely combined. In Sir George his father they were not combined. Sir George wanted only to lead - to teach Sargent how to paint a picture until he had him bellowing over the studio to teach German custodians their job until he got his umbrella broken. I'll repeat the name 'Left Hand - Right Hand'. An admirable book.

Here I would like[20] to leave books altogether, and to say a word in conclusion about a concert which was given last Friday in the National Gallery which I enjoyed immensely. As you probably know, there have been concerts there almost daily since the beginning of the war, but this one was unique because it was devoted to Indian music. It was organized by Dr. Narayana Menon who spoke a few words of introduction.[21] Dr. Menon played the veena, and the other musicians were distinguished westerners, using western instruments, and the aim of the concert was to show that Indian music can thus be transcribed and interpreted [by] the west. Among the items were some north Indian vocal music, arranged for the unaccompanied violin, some songs of Tagore, adapted for flute veena and harpsichord, and a traditional south Indian melody, in which flute oboe violin harpsichord and veena all took part. There was an enormous audience, most of whom can never before have heard a note of Indian music, either adapted or unadapted, there was sincere applause, and Dr. Menon has every reason to congratulate himself on the enterprise. Purists might complain and I am a bit of a purist myself about Indian music, although so ignorant of it. I do prefer it unwesternised. But I do see that it needs publicity in the west, and that a brilliant and attractive concert in the National Gallery, by eminent artists is[22] an appropriate way of procuring that.

1. <NOT CHECKED WITH>

2. Though the typed heading gives "Tuesday 8th May, 1945" as the broadcast date, "Tuesday 8th" has been canceled and "Wed 9th" inserted by hand to the left. Similarly, the typed "1515-1530 GMT" has been canceled and replaced by "1245-1300."

3. <it is immensely>

4. <if you start> talk<ing>

5. <that is>

6. *Left Hand, Right Hand! An Autobiography* (London: Macmillan and Co., 1945), viii.

7. <left hand for it is>

8. The placement of "brilliantly," handwritten at the bottom of the page, is conjectural.

9. <story, or part of it>

10. <Lady Ida>

11. Sitwell, *Left Hand, Right Hand!* 213. EMF omits the reference to the artist friend, D. S. MacColl.

12. <up to date>

13. <carted along>

14. <piece of furniture>

15. British troops failed to repel Boer attackers on 30 October 1899 and retreated to Ladysmith, which was besieged by Boer forces until British reinforcements arrived on 28 February 1900.

16. <went on>

17. Sitwell, *Left Hand, Right Hand!* 222.

18. The family portrait remains at Renishaw Hall in Derbyshire today.

19. Sitwell, *Left Hand, Right Hand!* 95–96.

20. <to pause. I can't do so - there isn't the time - but I want to leave <u>Left Hand - Right Hand</u>, with strong recommendation, and>

21. Menon, who earned a Ph.D. in English from the University of Edinburgh, worked for BBC during World War II and was introduced to EMF by Orwell; he was a musician as well as a literary scholar (see Menon, "E. M. Forster: A Tribute," in *E. M. Forster: A Tribute,* ed. K. Natwar-Singh [New York: Harcourt, Brace and World, 1964], 13–14).

22. <the best>

CHECKED WITH B'CAST   Producer: SUNDAY WILSHIN
EASTERN SERVICE - PURPLE NETWORK.
WEDNESDAY, 20th JUNE 1945.
1515-1530 GMT.
O.S.2.
"THE WRITTEN WORD" No.19. - 'The Development of Criticism' No.12

'MATTHEW ARNOLD'

By

E.M. FORSTER

Matthew Arnold is a poet who believed in poetry and said so. All poets believe in poetry or they would not produce it, but few of them say so, few of them proclaim and expound in prose the importance of poetry and of creative literature generally. He did that. And here is one reason why we must attend to him as a critic. We must listen to him with great respect because he knows about literature from the inside. He has helped to make it. And even when he is ponderous and facetious in his criticism[1] I always read him with a thrill and the famous phrases he uses - such as 'sweetness and light' or 'culture and anarchy' or 'poetry is a criticism of life'[2] - they come[3] with the authority of a creative artist. He is not mouthing them from a professorial chair or jotting them down at a desk in the education office, though he did in fact occupy both those uninspiring positions.[4] He is a poet who believes in poetry and says so. Every now and then in English history we have these poets who are also eminent as critics. Dryden is one example. Coleridge another, and in our own day Mr. T. S. Eliot is perhaps a third. But Matthew Arnold is to my mind, the pick of this little bunch, partly because I like his opinions, partly because he had a keen sense of the century in which he lived, and a shrewd premonition of what was coming after it.

'Sweetness and light'. 'Culture or anarchy'. 'Poetry is a criticism of life'. I want to say something about these[5] phrases. But before I run off on them, let me remind you of Matthew Arnold's dates. Born 1822. Son of a great

341

headmaster of Rugby,[6] educated at Oxford and very much educated - Greek, Latin, French, German - became inspector of elementary schools, lectured in America and at home. Died 1888. But the date most relevant to this particular broadcast is - 1865. For then it was that his most important critical work came out: his Essays in Criticism.[7] His poems are far more important, but we are not listening to them this afternoon. We are listening to him saying in prose why he believed in poetry and why literature in general is worth while. He said it best in Essays in Criticism, and that is the book of his you should try to get hold of. Although it was published eighty years ago it may make you sit up. It starts with two chapters on general themes. The first is called 'The function of criticism at the present time'. And if you are inclined to be impatient about criticism,[8] read that chapter: it will make you think. The second chapter is on 'The literary influence of academies', and if you are inclined to say 'We don't want academies[9] - we do things our own way' - then read that chapter: it may again make you think.[10] And then follow eight other chapters dealing with particular writers. None of these writers are English, and some of them are unfamiliar. But Matthew Arnold[11] seizes the spiritual meaning of each and relates them to the critical thesis he has laid down at the start. We feel, as we close Essays in Criticism, that civilisation is a <u>unity</u>, and that the uniters are the poets and those akin to poetry, whenever and wherever they lived, and however little they may have been recognised by the world.

[12]I'll go back now to the famous phrases which are scattered throughout Matthew Arnold's prose works and will first tackle 'Poetry is a criticism of life'.

What Matthew Arnold disliked in life, in the social life of nineteenth century England, was its sectarianism. People were energetic, able, sincere, but they would collect into groups, attach labels to themselves and live in and for the group. I'm a Tory. I'm a Radical. I believe in vaccination. I don't. I'm a Bible Christian. I'm a Supernumerary Bible Christian. And so on. He detested the self-complacency and the acridity so prevalent inside groups. And he saw through the spurious fairmindedness,[13] which leads the Tory to say to the Radical, 'Well, I suppose everyone has the right to his own opinion', and the Radical to make the same remark to the Tory, after which each goes his way[14] chanting 'I'm a Tory' or 'I'm a Radical' as before. This isn't fairmindedness at all: it's just a defence gadget. Matthew Arnold, in his dislike of the group spirit, spotted a real defect in Victorian democracy, and he asked himself what was to be done. He had not to ask long. The remedy he found was criticism - criticism which is disinterested, and doesn't side with this group or that. He admitted that groups and clashes of opinion must exist in a community - he wasn't a muff - but he saw too (and here we are getting to poetry) - that there is a point in human development where groups and clashes can be regarded from outside. The intellect can do this a little. But still more effective is the poetic intelligence, which has no need to argue. If you write good poetry, which few of us do, or appreciate it, which many of us can, you get into a state of mind where a new view of daily life is possible. And that is what he means by his phrase 'Poetry is a criticism of life'. It doesn't say 'Vote Radical' or 'Vote Tory'. It rearranges.

You will probably see by now what it was that people objected to in Matthew Arnold as a prose writer. They complained that he was superior. And I think that he was guilty in his weaker moments of looking down on his fellow beings, Olympian, as though he were a god. But he atoned for it,[15] by the passion and the persistency of his upward flights. He wanted to know and to make known what is greatest in human achievement. Being literary, he desired to make literature known.[16] He was immensely excited that writers of the[17] stature of Homer, Dante, Shakespeare and Goethe should have existed on this little earth, this Tory-versus-Radical earth, and by all his intelligence, by all the poetry which he too possessed, he strove to make them real, and to raise us all towards their stature. Sometimes he even made them into touchstones - rather a questionable device this. At other times, and more soundly, he used those great poets as the supreme examples of his conception of culture; he felt that they had realised their complete humanity, which is what we must each of us do in our smaller spheres.

That word 'culture' it introduces us to another of the famous phrases 'culture or anarchy'.[18] I must discuss it for a moment. Today, many people might prefer anarchy to culture, for the reason that the word 'culture' has had an unfortunate history. It soon turned into 'cultchaw' and symbolised affectation. Then, in the last war, the Germans made it odious as 'kultur'. And recently it has done itself further harm in that awful phrase 'cultural platform', which always suggests to me that the platform is covered with bacteria. No wonder people suspect culture when it has been so misused. But in Matthew Arnold's day it[19] meant getting to know what is best in human achievements, and trying to pass it on. It meant a belief in standards and a willingness to submit, in certain ways, to discipline. Anarchy meant not merely the dropping of bombs by people unauthorised to do so by their governments, but also spiritual bombing, mental violence, ill-considered blame and even ill-considered praise. Anarchy meant eccentricity. And one of his complaints against his countrymen was that they were eccentric and didn't desire to be anything else. They didn't want to be better informed or urbane, or to know what is great in human achievement. They didn't want culture. And he flung at them another of his famous accusations: Philistines. The Philistine is the sort of person who says 'I know what I know and I like what I like and that's the kind of chap I am'. And Matthew Arnold, a Victorian David, slung his pebble bang in the middle of Goliath's forehead.

What of 'sweetnesss and light'. Where do they come in? I never feel this phrase a very happy one. Arnold took it from Swift,[20] and applied it to express the gifts conferred on us by great literature. It misses out, I think, the excitement in literature. There's not only sweetness and light in it; there's fire.[21] He didn't want to keep sweetness and light for himself though. He had a strong social conscience, and believed that the human heritage must touch the many before it can be perfected in the few. He stipulates, though, that this sweetness and light which we hand out must be genuine. He did not, in other words, believe in giving the public what it wants or is supposed to want. He realised that if this is done there will soon be nothing left in the world worth wanting.

If you want to go further into Arnold's criticism,[22] there's a good book on him by an American, Lionel Trilling.[23] And do anyhow get hold of Essays in Criticism, mentioned earlier in the talk. My talk, by the way, may have left you in doubt whether Arnold himself was a Tory or a Radical. I am very glad that you should feel doubtful, and he too would be glad. For the whole aim of his criticism was to get into a position where the clashes of parties and classes[24] get into perspective and where the mountain heights which their dust obscures can be seen.

It is time you heard some of his own words. Here is part of the famous passage when he eulogises Oxford - a city which had[25] often irritated him.

"And yet steeped in sentiment as she lies, spreading her gardens to the moonlight, and whispering from her towers the last enchantments of the Middle Ages, who will deny that Oxford, by her ineffable charm, keeps ever calling us nearer to the true goal of all of us[26] . . . . . Adorable dreamer, whose heart has been so romantic, who hast given thyself so prodigally to sides and to heroes not mine, only never to the Philistines! Home of lost causes and forsaken beliefs and unpopular names and impossible loyalties! What examples could ever so inspire us to keep down the Philistine in ourselves?[27] (She will forgive me if I have unwittingly drawn upon her a shot or two aimed at her unworthy son. . . for she is generous, and the cause in which I fight is, after all, hers.) Apparitions of a day, what is our puny warfare against the Philistines, compared with the warfare which this queen of romance has been waging against them for centuries and will wage after we are gone?"[28]

You will find this passage in[29] Essays in Criticism. And you may reflect with sadness that Oxford today, stuffed with organisations, and throttled with industrialism, seems already to have falsified the prophecy of her son.

1. < - and he sometimes is - >

2. <which is the most famous of them all - these phrases>

3. <to me dressed in authority,>

4. Arnold was professor of poetry at Oxford from 1857 to 1867, and from 1851 to 1886 he served as a school inspector.

5. <three famous>

6. Thomas Arnold (1795–1842), who inspired the memorable portrait of Rugby by Thomas Hughes in *Tom Brown's Schooldays.*

7. Arnold, *Essays in Criticism* (1865; rpt. Oxford: Humphrey Milford, Oxford University Press, 1914). Most of the essays had previously been published in periodicals.

8. <and to dismiss it as academic>

9. <(in England) - we leave that sort of thing to the French>

10. <And these two opening chapters of generalisation are>

11. <, in every case,>

12. <That's all I can say about Essays in Criticism.>

13. fairminded <men>ness

14. <shouting>

15. <in my judgement>

16. <That was the positive side of his criticism.>

17. <calibre>

18. <: it is actually the title of one of his books> EMF refers to *Culture and Anarchy* (London: Smith, Elder and Co., 1869).

19. <was guiltless of these overtones.>

20. <who had wittily used it about the bees - they give us sweetness through honey, candles through wax> Swift borrowed from Aesop's comments about the bees (representing the ancients) in "Battle of the Books."

21. <, and he handled fire cautiously>

22. <and Arnold generally,>

23. Lionel Trilling, *Matthew Arnold* (New York: W. W. Norton and Co.; London: George Allen and Unwin, 1939). Trilling also wrote *E. M. Forster* (Norfolk, Conn.: New Directions, 1943; London: Hogarth Press, 1944).

24. < become - not unimportant but>

25. <sometimes> As Park Honan notes, "Oxford threatened to fine him for giving too *few* talks [as professor of poetry], and many tutors noted his ignorance" (*Matthew Arnold: A Life* [New York: McGraw-Hill, 1981], 292).

26. <to the ideal, to perfection>

27. <what teacher could ever so save us from that bondage to which we are all prone?>

28. Preface to *Essays in Criticism,* 7–8.

29. <the preface to>

[1]As BROADCAST
Eastern Service
Purple Network
Tuesday 3rd July, 1945
1515-1530 GMT

To be recorded from
transmission - DOX 52074

Reproductions: General Overseas Service - 5.7.45 - 0230-0245 DBST
African Service - 8.7.45 - 1945-2000 DBST
North American Service - 0230-0245 DBST

SOME BOOKS

by

E.M. Forster

I speak in a state of excitement, which I want to push overseas at you if I can. I have just been for the second time to an opera by a young English composer, Benjamin Britten. It seems to me a great work, both musically and emotionally, and I would like to devote this talk to it.[2]

Britten's opera is called Peter Grimes, and it is inspired by a poem of Crabbe![3] Crabbe, who lived about 150 years ago, was a very peculiar writer. He was by profession a clergyman, and he composed narrative poems on the lines of Pope, but the result wasn't like Pope, nor like a clergyman either. The poems are grim, melancholy and sardonic, with touches of tenderness, and they are impregnated with the flavour of the sea. The sea? Yes, but what sea? Not the great ocean of romance, but the work-a-day sea, out of which poor men have to get a living by catching fish; the sea which laps and sometimes bangs on the shingle of a mean little East Coast town. That is Crabbe's world.[4] He understood it and has interpreted it. He has left us a number of sketches of the inhabitants of the[5] town - the Borough he calls it - the feeble clergyman, the[6] domineering lawyer, the landlady of the riotous pub and her so called nieces, the[7] gentle schoolmistress and so on: and the most powerful of these sketches deals with Peter Grimes, a fisherman, who murdered his apprentices.

I'll begin by quoting Crabbe's poem, then I'll go on to the presentation of Grimes in the opera.

In the poem, Grimes had hated his father, a good pious old man, and
>'When the father in his Bible read
>He in contempt and anger left the shed.
>"It is the word of life" the parent cried
>"This is the life itself" the boy replied.[']

and took to drink. [8]On his father's death, he became fisherman, poacher, outlaw:

>But no success could please his cruel soul
>He longed for one to trouble and control
>He wanted some obedient boy to stand
>And bear the blow of his outrageous hand.

and he gets a work house brat from London and ill treats him. The townsmen notice this, but they are too hard and too poor for compassion.

>'None put the question 'Peter dost thou give
>The boy his food? What man, the lad must live'.
>None reasoned thus and some, on hearing cries,
>Said calmly 'Grimes is at his exercise'.

And at last the boy dies. How? Oh in bed apparently. Another boy is procured and dies out fishing. How? Oh he fell into the well where the catch was kept. And a third. Oh he was drowned. Peter is now forbidden[9] to employ any more apprentices, and since none of his townsmen will help him, has to fish alone. Here begins the magic and the horror of the poem. He takes his boat into the mud of the estuary, does nothing, day after day, and is gradually haunted not only by the murdered boys but by his own father. They rise from the tide-way they compel him, and finally drive him mad.[10] In the hospital, to the terrified attendants, he recounts the progressive apparition - the ghostly boys pale with mischief, while his father

>scoop'd the flood
>And there came flame about him mixed with blood,
>He bade me stoop and look upon the place
>Then flung the red, hot liquor in my face.

He expires in terror.

>He dropped exhausted, and appear'd at rest
>Till the strong foe the vital powers possessed.
>Then with an inward, broken voice he cried,
>'Again they come' and muttered as he died.[11]

So much for Peter Grimes the poem. Now for Peter Grimes the opera. Benjamin Britten and his librettist Montagu Slater have made notable changes in the story, which I will discuss if I have time.[12]

The curtain rises at once, on the town hall, where Peter Grimes is being examined as to the death of his last apprentice. Public opinion is against him, but the gentle schoolmistress, Ellen Orford, intervenes in his favour, and he is given the benefit of the doubt. This scene is[13] powerful, and distinct, and of the nature of a prologue. An orchestral interlude follows, and here it was I began to feel that this may be one of the greatest operas of our time. For the interlude suggested the sea, the work-a-day sea, lapping against the little boats in the harbour, and when the curtain went up again on the public place of the Borough, the music persisted behind the fishermen and women, going on as usual with their lives. The atmosphere was set. People pass. Auntie, the landlady, peeps out of her pub. A well to do lady hovers about trying to get some laudanum, to which she is an addict. And Peter Grimes is working alone.[14] No one will help him since the scene in court. But Ellen Orford, the schoolmistress, pities him and uses her influence to procure him - one more boy. This time, surely, there will be no scandal. And Peter is determined, this time, to make good, and to marry Ellen. He is presented to us in the opera as a Byronic character, misunderstood, sensitive; whereas Crabbe presented him just as a sadist.

The next scene is inside the pub. The sea music has thickened to storm. But inside is jollity, drunkenness, the nieces, a fight, and in a corner the respectable lady who has come in for her laudanum, and chants very funnily 'This is no place for me . . this is no place for me.' The musical complication is tremendous, we are in a whirl of human sounds, and each time the door of the pub opens the whirlwind of the storm rushes in and joins them. Grimes arrives. Silence. He sings - not in Crabbe's words: these are seldom used - a mysterious monologue about the stars and the irrevocability of fate. Everyone feels a bit uncomfortable. Come along let's sing a catch says Auntie, and off we all go with great gusto

> Old Joe has gone fishing and
> Young Joe has gone fishing and
> You know has gone fishing and
> Found them in a shoal.[15]

The music is immensely complicated and[16] yet it's direct. Grimes interrupts the catch and there is a choral tussle with the orchestra throwing its weight about wildly. The door opens once more. Ellen arrives with the new apprentice, a terrified and silent child, and Grimes takes him out home into the storm, 'Home' shouts everyone derisively, and with a crash and a roar the amazing scene closes.

This first act seems to me one of the greatest things I have seen on the operatic stage. The two other acts didn't excite me so much, and their departures from the narrative and the atmosphere of Crabbe were not always explicable.[17] Charming[18] however was the beginning of Act II, where Ellen sat with the boy outside the church, and tried to make him talk: while the music of the service intervenes. She discovers a bruise on him. It has begun again, the ill-treatment: Grimes is at his exercise. She pleads with Grimes they quarrel, he goes off with the boy, public opinion is worked up, and a crowd of citizens[19] depart for Grimes' hut to find out what if anything is[20] amiss. In the hut, he and the boy are discovered alone.[21] He makes the boy go over the cliff to get the boat ready. The boy falls,[22] shrieks - the one sound he ever makes - [23]and dies. The citizens arrive to find the hut empty. In Act III we are back at the public square. An enormous man-hunt starts, indeed cries of Grimes Grimes Peter Grimes - now loud now distant - punctuate all the act. Grimes is never caught, he slinks back in the fog, almost mad, and he is advised by a friend to scuttle his boat, row her out, and drown. The stage is now dark, and there is a queer moment when the characters no longer sing but speak. It is a deliberate anti-climax.[24] He goes out to commit suicide in the most undramatic way possible, and no one bothers about him any more.

Then the day dawns and the sea music from the beginning of the opera returns - the work-a-day sea - and once more life starts on its hard course for the little town. The nieces come out of the pub eating bread and jam. The clergyman goes to early service. The fishermen go to work. And they sing - this time in the solid words of Crabbe - they sing against the lovely broken arpeggios of the eternal theme.

> To those who pass the Borough, sounds betray
> The cold beginning of another day
> And houses sleeping by the waterside
> Wake to the measured ripple of the tide,
> Or measured cadence of the lads who tow
> Some entered hoy to fix her in her row,
> Or hollow sound that from the passing bell
> To some departed spirit bids farewell.
> In ceaseless motion comes and goes the tide . . .[25]

And slowly very slowly the curtain falls.

You'll notice, looking back at the poem, that the opera, besides romanticising the character of Grimes and omitting his father, has made no use of the apparitions, or of the death bed scene. - two items which strike one as dramatic. I suppose they weren't what the composer wanted for his music or for his effects, and anyhow he knows his business better than I do, and has created a work of very great importance, excitement and beauty. I can't think of any literary work of the last six years comparable to it. It was splendidly sung and produced at the opera house of Sadlers Wells.

1. <NOT CHECKED WITH>

2. <An opera is of course not unconnected with books. Of all musical forms it is the most closely allied with literature. It employs words, it requires a plot, it often goes in for character-drawing like a novel, and it often aims at atmospheric effects that are also the province of

lyric poetry. Some people like opera because it has these connections with books, and praise it for being universal, while others denounce it for being mixed and impure. In either case it is not unsuitable for a book talk.

Benjamin>

3. *Peter Grimes* debuted on 7 June 1945 at Sadler's Wells Theatre in London. As Furbank notes (*A Life*, 2:281), Britten was led to compose the opera by reading EMF's published broadcast on Crabbe (see "George Crabbe: The Poet and the Man," *Listener*, 29 May 1941, pp. 769–70). "Peter Grimes" is part of Crabbe's epistolary poem *The Borough* (1810).

4. In this and the prior sentence of the script, EMF added accent marks above "Not," "bangs," "East," "Coast," "town," and "That."

5. <little>

6. <grasping>

7. <sweet but ineffective>

8. <When his father died>

9. <by the mayor>

10. EMF added "they compel him" by hand but omitted to cancel the phrase "to meet him" that followed.

11. EMF quotes in succession lines 16–19, 53–56, 73–74, 77–78, 356–59, 372–75. See "Letter XXII. Peter Grimes," *The Borough*, in George Crabbe, *Poems*, ed. Adolphus William Ward, 3 vols. (Cambridge: Cambridge University Press, 1905–1907), 1:492–501.

12. A journalist, poet, novelist, and scriptwriter, Montagu Slater (1902–1956) was also a left-wing activist. Benjamin Britten had written music to accompany Slater's narration of the documentary film *Coal Face* (1935) and drama *Stay Down Miner* (1936) prior to their collaboration on *Peter Grimes*. Slater's libretto, which he published separately as *Peter Grimes and Other Poems* (London: Bodley Head, 1946), enlarged the role of the community and of minor characters such as Ellen in Britten's opera.

13. <very>

14. In this and the prior two sentences, EMF added accent marks above the first syllables of "Auntie" and "Peter," the second syllable of "about," and "Grimes."

15. *Peter Grimes Vocal Score*, music by Benjamin Britten, words by Montagu Slater, vocal score by Erwin Stein (London: Boosey and Hawkes, 1945), 126–27, 147.

16. <I would like to mention in passing the union of complication and directness in Benjamin Britten's music>

17. <Still, I enjoyed them, and musicians say their power will grow.>

18. <certainly>

19. <go off to>

20. <afoot>

21. <Grimes bullies and appeals for understanding and bullies again, and receives no answer.>

22. <and with a>

23. <he>

24. <Grimes>

25. *Peter Grimes Vocal Score*, 372–77; Crabbe, "Letter I. General Description," *The Borough*, lines 290–94, in *Poems*, 1:292).

[1]As BROADCAST   To be recorded from trans.
Eastern Service
Purple Network
Tuesday 31st July, 1945
1515-1530 GMT
Reproductions: African Service - 5.8.45 - 1845-1900 BST
                North American Service - 5.8.45 - 0130 & 0515 BST

SOME BOOKS

by

E.M.Forster

The death of a French writer, Paul Valéry, occurred in Paris earlier in the month,[2] and since I try to report to you on continental literature as well as English, I want to mention him. Valery[3] was a poet and a man of letters. He was highly esteemed in France, and by writers outside France, but he was too fastidious, too subtle and difficult to get a wide reputation.[4] He was not obscure for the sake of obscurity, he would gladly have been lucid and simple, but he did not happen to see life in those terms. And what an honest writer has to do - what Valery did - is to express life as he sees it, and not as it is reported to him. He was a very independent man, for all his modesty, he took his own line, and it is characteristic of him that though he was not[5] a collaborationist, during the German occupation of his country, he should all the same have had some courteous words to say on the subject of Marshal Petain.[6]

I opened one of his prose[7] books before preparing this talk to see if I could find a sentence or two which would give you the flavour of Valery. The book is called An Evening with M. Teste - M. Teste being an imaginary character into whom the author puts his own philosophy. Well, the very first sentence is illuminating "La bêtise n'est pas mon fort."[8] Stupidity is not my strong point. No it wasn't. Valery was never never stupid. If he had been stupid sometimes, he would no doubt have been more in touch with the rest of us, who are stupid so frequently. That was his limitation.

Remember on the other hand what limitations are ours, and how much we lose by our failure to follow the action of a superior mind.

Here's another quotation from M. Teste, a few pages further on, he says, with his gentle irony: "I am very sorry to offend people who love the light. Nothing attracts me more than clarity. But unfortunately I can scarcely ever find it. - I whisper that into your ear: don't hand it on. Yes, clarity is a rare experience for me, it is indeed unknown to me in the world of thought, and I only find it in the relation of the diamond to the mass of the globe."[9]
There again you get Valery's intelligence, his honesty, and his fastidiousness. He won't say things are O.K. when he finds them complex. As for his poems, the best known and the easiest is La Cimitiere Marin - the cemetery by the sea: of which there is an English translation.[10] He has been called the T.S.Eliot of France, and that does give a rough idea of him. But a rough one. He had not Mr. Eliot's preoccupation with religion and sin. Nor do I expect that Mr. Eliot will be found with a volume of Voltaire by his sick bed as Valery was. I only met him once - about ten years ago in Paris at a committee of intellectuals of which he was President.[11] Here again he was difficult - difficult to follow, difficult even to hear. Exquisite phrases got lost in his thick moustache. But I realised his distinction, his integrity, and his shy friendliness. He might be and he was superior. But he did not condescend. He is a loss to his country and to his language, and if you have studied that language you will have realised that he was in the tradition of the French symbolists, of Baudelaire and Mallarmé. He is also a loss to humanism.

France being in our minds, here is a book by a Frenchman.[12] It is written in English, and it is about England. Its title is <u>The English Way</u> and the author's name is Pierre Maillaud.[13] M. Maillaud is a journalist. He has lived for many years over here, first as correspondent to a news-agency, and during the war he broadcast five days a week on the French service of the BBC, and helped to encourage the resistance movement after the collapse of 1940. He knows England well - so well that he can even handle her dialects, and in The English Way he gives a picture of her normal life and a description[14] of her political problems, internal and external, during the 30s. The picture of her normal life did not interest me so much, but then I do find most foreign observers (with the exception of Karel Capek[15]) unsatisfactory on this subject: they dish it up all right, but it gets wrong through being on a dish. The best part - and, the larger part of M. Maillaud's book deals with politics - here he is precise - and provocative. He is what is known as a realist. What is the use of a League of Nations which has no power to enforce its decisions? What is the use of imposing sanctions on Italy at the time of her Abyssinian adventure, and then refusing to implement those decisions by practical means?[16] What is the use of a gentleman's agreement with Hitler when he was a gangster, or of a business deal with him when he wasn't a business-man and didn't want to deal? M. Maillaud criticises English moral uplift and idealism - tendencies not bad in themselves, but sometimes startling in their repercussions and precipitating the idealist into war. He is also realistic on the delicate subject of the Commonwealth of Nations. The dominion governments,[17] being far away from European affairs, failed to interpret them or to realise the Nazi menace or the peril of France; and English policy had to hold back until the dominions understood, and were willing to come in. And this leads him to ask us whether, after the war is over,[18] England is going to stay in the European system, or to become part of the Commonwealth. There is much to say on either side. England is linked to Europe geographically and by two thousand years of history. She is linked to her dominions by a common language and by a common conception of law.[19] Which system shall she remain in? M. Maillaud has no doubt. The European. And this is also the opinion of Mr. Raymond Mortimer, who writes a trenchant introduction to the book. Mr. Mortimer says "No Englishman is likely to underrate the sacrifices made by the Dominions in the common cause: but many of us feel, though we rarely express, alarm at the possibility of England, once the war is won, being again drawn out of the European orbit by the gravitational force of the British Commonwealth".[20] There is a problem for you to think over, and if you want my opinion I think that England will belong in a muddled way to both systems. The result may be confusing, it will lack clarity, but I believe, with Paul Valery, that clarity is seldom to be found in human affairs, and that politicians are too fond of simplifying.

The other book I have been reading is a novel - the last instalment of a long work by the German Thomas Mann. It's about the patriarch Joseph. The first volume was called The Tales of Jacob the next The Young Joseph - it told of the coat of many colours, and the pit - then came Joseph in Egypt with the episode of Potiphar's wife, and here, finally is Joseph the Provider.[21] The story keeps close to the Old Testament narrative: the dreams of the chief butler and the chief baker; Pharaoh's dream of the fat and lean kine; Joseph's rise to power owing to his interpretation of the dreams; the arrival of his brothers seeking corn in Egypt; their return with Benjamin; the recognition, the reconciliation, the arrival of the aged Jacob to end his days under the protection of his son; the blessing of Jacob, his death - it all passes before us as it does in the pages of Genesis,[22] but the atmosphere through which we view it is different, and is peculiar. I didn't at first like the atmosphere.[23] Then I saw rather better what he was up to. He was trying to reinterpret the story in the light of modern knowledge and modern needs.[24] Take Pharaoh - the one who dreams about the fat and lean kine. Mann identifies him with that remarkable king Akhenaton, who has been called the first individualist in history, who was a pacifist, who tried to start a new monotheistic religion. And he finds in the famine which enveloped the world the explanation of Akhenaton's safety. Although he was a pacifist, no one attacked him, because there was corn in the granaries of Egypt and nowhere else, and people wanted to buy it and couldn't make war on him, because they were starving. The book is a novel, not a work of learning, and Mann is not obliged to prove that the identification with Akhenaton is correct. He uses it as a device to increase the interest in his story. It's an example of his use of modern knowledge.[25] And then - modern needs.[26] He finds in the story a symbol of human progress, of advancement towards perfection, of an alliance between God and man. In the early days human sacrifice was prevalent and proper. Abraham nearly killed Isaac. Then - somehow or other - it went out of fashion, and Joseph represents a further move towards the humane. He forgave his brethren who had thrown him into the pit. He realised what God, by that time, wanted. Thomas Mann is a great anti-Nazi, and he explains the recent[27] war as our failure to understand the immediate wishes of God. Into these profound speculations I do not myself follow him, but I can see how deep and rich the book is, and how the off-hand half-joking way in which the story is told does make the reader think, and link up Genesis with his own troubles. Thomas Mann believes that there is a pattern in life - a pattern which becomes clearer when we look into the past where the beginnings of it were traced. And the past is not just the facts of history. It includes the myths which have been deposited by the human spirit. The Story of Joseph is such a myth, it took his fancy and he has worked on it without considering whether it is or isn't historical. He is an old man now - 70 this very year - and it is an impressive conclusion to his work. I wonder - as so often - whether you'll be able to get hold of it. And I would like to mention a collection of his stories, which has come out in Everyman's edition, and so may be obtainable.[28] Stories and Episodes by Thomas Mann it is called.[29]

So this talk has been a European one. I have spoken of two great writers - Paul Valery the Frenchman who has died, and Thomas Mann the German, who was driven by his own countrymen[30] into exile. And I have mentioned the book of a French journalist, Pierre Maillaud, who argues that it is with Europe rather than with her far-away dominions, that England should be connected in the future.

1. <NOT CHECKED WITH>

2. 20 July 1945.

3. EMF inserted the cue "(spell)" here after "Valery" and later in the script after "Maillaud."

4. <'Difficult' is the word which constantly occurs to one, a word to be uttered with respect, for h> EMF added an accent mark above the first syllable of "difficult" in the sentence prior to the canceled passage.

5. EMF added an accent mark above "not."

6. Pétain headed the Vichy government during Hitler's occupation of France. When Pétain was inducted into the French Academy after World War I, Valéry termed him "the spirit of the resistance" (Glorney Bolton, *Pétain* [London: George Allen and Unwin, 1957], 95).

7. <works>

8. Paul Valéry, *Monsieur Teste: Nouvelle Édition Augmentée de Fragments Inédits* (Paris: Gallimard, 1946), 15.

9. EMF translates the following passage: "je suis désespéré d'affliger ces amateurs de lumière. Rien ne m'attire que la clarté. Hélas, ami de moi! je vous assure que je n'en trouve presque point. Je mets ceci dans votre oreille toute proche. N'allez point le répandre. Gardez excessivement mon secret. Oui, la clarté pour moi est si peu commune que je n'en vois sur toute l'étendue du monde, —et singulièrement du monde pensant et écrivant, —que dans la proportion du diamant à la masse de la planète" (ibid., 88).

10. The verse translation by C. Day Lewis was completed in 1945 though not published until 1946 (London: Martin Secker and Warburg).

11. Valéry and Gilbert Murray alternately presided at "The Immediate Future of Literature," sponsored by the League of Nations Committee for Intellectual Co-operation, July 1937 (see Furbank, *A Life*, 2:221). EMF added an accent mark above the first syllable of "difficult" in the sentence that follows.

12. EMF added an accent mark above the first syllable of "Frenchman."

13. Pierre Maillaud, *The English Way* (London: Oxford University Press, 1945). See Asa Briggs, *The History of Broadcasting in the United Kingdom*, 5 vols. (London: Oxford University Press, 1961–1995), 3:246–49, for the details of Maillaud's BBC broadcasts to France.

14. EMF added accent marks above the first syllables of "picture" and "description" and above "picture" in the following sentence.

15. Capek's *Letters from England* was first published in 1925 (London: G. Bles).

16. The League of Nations imposed sanctions on Italy for annexing Abyssinia in the war of 1935–1936, but member nations did not uniformly uphold them.

17. EMF added accent marks above the first syllables of "dominion" and "governments."

18. <we are>

19. In this and the prior two sentences EMF added accent marks above the first syllables of "either" and "Europe" and the second syllable of "dominions."

20. Maillaud, *The English Way*, 5.

21. *Joseph and His Brethren*, trans. H. T. Lowe-Porter (London: Martin Secker, 1945), which gathered into one volume prior novels in the series—*The Tales of Jacob* (1934), *The Young Joseph* (1935), *Joseph in Egypt* (1938)—plus the concluding installment, *Joseph the Provider* (1945).

22. Genesis 30–50.

23. <I thought that Thomas Mann was merely distending the lovely story, or - worse still - was guying it, and was poking fun at it, his rather Teutonic <<feud>> fun.>

24. EMF added accent marks above the first syllables of "knowledge" and both instances

of "modern" and above "needs." In the following sentences he added an accent mark above the third syllable of Akhenaton ("Akhenáton").

25. EMF added accent marks above the first syllable of "modern" in this and the next sentence, above the first syllable of "knowledge," and above "needs."

26. <He is concerned to find>

27. <catastrophes>

28. <That is Tony Kroger - a lovely little work, and more successful artistically than the cumbersome Joseph epic.>

29. <is the exact title of the volume. There are several stories - including the famous Death in Venice - and at the end are some extracts from the Joseph stuff.> Thomas Mann, *Stories and Episodes*, trans. H. T. Lowe-Porter (London: J. M. Dent and Sons, 1940).

30. <to take refuge in America>

[1]CHECKED WITH BROADCAST
EASTERN SERVICE - PURPLE NETWORK
WEDNESDAY, 3rd JULY 1946.
1435-1450 GMT.
Produced by John Arlott.[2]

Pre-rec.: 1.7.46
Rec. No.: SOX.72331
Duration: 14'20"

"SOME BOOKS"

By

E. M. Forster

Since last I spoke here I have visited India. I had a very happy time, meeting old friends, and making some new ones, and perhaps I'm talking now to some one who showed me hospitality and kindness. I know that India to-day is not a pleasure garden, still less is it a fun fair, and I was conscious all the time of political tensions and economic tragedy. Nevertheless, the country did bring me personal happiness. It always does, it always will, and I want to say 'thank you'.[3]

I returned from it by air. Behind me, in a boat, followed a number of books by Indian writers, which I had acquired during my travels.[4] We have all arrived safely, and I propose to devote my talk to-day to some of these books. I'll concentrate on books from Bengal. I had never been to[5] Bengal before, and my visit was deplorably short - nine days in Calcutta and one memorable day at Santiniketan[6] - but I managed to meet a few Bengali writers and artists and to realise their cultural importance and some of their problems. A superficial view is better than no view. A blind[7] uncle is better than none, as a Bengali proverb says, and with imperfect vision and imperfect pronunciation I begin.

The book I've enjoyed most is a novel by Saratchandra Chatterji. I'd never read Saratchandra before, he's quite unknown over here, despite his high reputation with you. This novel - called The Deliverance in its English translation,- gave me great pleasure after the first few pages.[8] These were extremely difficult, because the subject is a Hindu joint-family, a form of social life unfamiliar to the west. A swarm of children are romping on a lady's bed, she suffering from malaria. Are they her children? Whose wife is she? Other ladies come in with cups of milk for the invalid. Who are their husbands? When I had sorted the relationships out, and realised that the word 'brother' sometimes meant 'cousin', and the word 'mother' 'daughter', I got on with The Deliverance very well. It is the sort of novel I like, for it is about individuals and it is a comedy which recognises sadness. The ladies quarrel, the husbands are too busy practising at the bar to take much notice. The ladies quarrel, the children fight inside the vegetarian kitchen, the ladies quarrel worse and make it up and regroup, and quarrel again. Will the Hindu joint-family stand the strain? It won't and the end is a law suit. Saratchandra, if I understand him rightly, is not greatly interested in the social fabric. It is for him a framework for the individual just as the British unjointed family is a framework for the individuals of Jane Austen. His chief character - the malarial lady - is touchingly portrayed. She is not clever, she is not even[9] equable, but she is very very nice. She is tricked by a cunning sister-in-law, into making trouble, and into expelling from the household the woman whom she has always loved. The atmosphere is feminine. Occasionally, the husbands take notice, and try to remember which child is where, and who ought to have done what. But the women dominate, and the sad muddle is seen through their eyes.

I have also read a novel of Tarashankar Banerji, called (in its English translation) Epoch's End.[10] In this book the social fabric is all important, and the individuals only casually sketched; one might almost say 'shot' for the effect is rather that of a film. The action of Epoch's End takes place in Calcutta, during the tragic winter of 1942-43. Famine and squalor and profiteering, bags of rice in the godowns,[11] while the poor starve outside, and[12] sell their women folk . . . . . and then the wrath from Heaven upon all the bombs of the Japanese. That is the general picture, and more particularly we are concerned with an old Brahmin family which has gone rotten and with the one untainted member of it, the hero. He comes through, he makes good, he will help to inaugurate the new age, and to overthrow the capitalism in which he almost acquiesced. It is a documentary novel with a purpose, and belongs to a class of fiction which originated in Russia, and has now spread over the world. It does not reach or desire to reach any high artistic level, but it is sincere and warm-hearted. Tarashankar Banerji is a member of the Progressive Writers Association.[13] His best work, I believe, is in his stories of country life, and these have not been translated into English yet.

I have several volumes of short stories - it is a form of art that evidently interests Bengal. Here is Tales of Four Friends by Pramatha Chaudhuri.[14] This is a brief symposium on the subject of womanhood. The treatment is fantastic and slight and also somewhat cynical. The scene is set in a Calcutta Club, during a storm; the four friends are held up by it, and agree to exchange their experiences to while away the time, and the result owes something to Boccaccio; and something to the Tales of Hoffmann. One of the ladies concerned was a lunatic, another was a thief, another was a neurotic, the last and most amiable was a ghost, and all four of them were English. None of them have come my way, I hasten to add, though I have encountered the English weather which Pramatha Chaudhuri brilliantly describes - when 'half the rain comes down from above and half from below, and the trees become limp and the roads slushy, and Englishmen feel like committing murder, so it is no wonder that Indians feel like committing suicide.'[15] The weather moves, in various phases, through all four stories, against it the women vibrate in their varying moods, and in the last story it clears for the presentation of the gracious ghost.

And here are two anthologies: Stories of Rural Bengal, edited by Sanjay Bhattacharya, and Best Stories of Modern Bengal (Volume 2), edited by D. K. Gupta.[16] It is not easy to review anthologies, but you should read both these, if you have not done so already. How can I generalise about them? They are interested in womanhood - and this seems characteristic of[17] Bengali literature. And they are interested in the collision between the old order and the new - the old order being orthodox Hinduism, with its various social implications, and the new order having two aspects. The humanitarian and the industrial. There is the same collision in English literature,[18] but our religion is less traditional and less hieratic, and our humanitarianism and industrialism have impinged more gradually. It is the suddenness of the break-up which is exciting the Bengali writers. I would instance two touching stories. One of them comes in Stories of Rural Bengal. It is called At the Confluence, it is by Premendra Mitra, and it tells of the linking of a pious Brahmin lady with a prostitute child. The other story comes in Best Stories of Modern Bengal. It is called Mercy. The author is K. P. Chatterjee, and it tells how a hardened cynical doctor has pity upon a deformed girl who is being exhibited as a freak at a fun-fair, and puts her tenderly to death.

Before I leave fiction there is the last novel of Tagore to be mentioned, translated as Farewell my Friend.[19] I shan't discuss it, because the translator - whom I had the pleasure of meeting - isn't entirely satisfied with his version and may be revising it. The novel is half-poetic, half-mocking in its tone, and to translate it from the highly stylised Bengali into English that shall be neither stilted nor flat must be a difficult task. Tagore, in the past, hasn't been well served by translators, even when he himself has been one of them. His poems in particular have come to us bloodless and vague, drained of their original richness. I think, indeed, that the presentation - or

rather the re-presentation - of this great man to the West is worth considering by his compatriots, and I sympathetically suggest to them that fortissimo praises are not wise and have been overdone. I encountered them
sometimes in India, and on one occasion - not in Bengal - I was[20] invited
almost to worship one of Tagore's pictures and to accept him as a great
pictorial artist, the equal of William Blake. Less reverence and more
detachment are necessary if Tagore is to come into his own.

Turning from creative work to critical, here are studies of two well-
known men of letters - Aminya Chakravarti and Dilip Kumar Roy, and a
book on Indian music by D. P. Mukerji, and a book on the Bengali painter
Jamini Roy by Bhishnu Dey and John Irwin (who is an Englishman).[21] The
book on music I will leave aside - perhaps it will teach me something: at
present I enjoy Indian music, and sometimes even know whether it is
good or not, but don't understand it and can't discuss it. And I'll also leave
aside the art book, which did help me to understand Jamini Roy, a small
exhibition of whose paintings has been on show in London.[22] A word on
the two literary works. Amiya Chakravarti publishes Modern Tendencies
in English Literature - studies on Yeats, Eliot, Spender, Day Lewis and
Auden, together with reflections on the increasing scope of contemporary
poetry, which can now sing about railway trains - a subject which
Wordsworth did indeed touch in one of his sonnets, but very gingerly.[23] It
is a sensible and sensitive volume, full of first hand observation and wisdom. Listen to its opening sentence: "Beware of those who rebel against
the fine arts in the name of power." How I agree! and how I mistrust the
people who say 'This is no time for art.' It is always the time for art. On
the same page Amiya Chakravarti says "Great poetry cannot be produced
under any sort of dictatorship."[24] Here, I would like to agree but can't; for
the inconvenient names of Virgil and Racine occur to me - they produced
their masterpieces under dictators and were content to do so. The question, like so many, is a complicated one - the truth being, I think, that
Freedom and Art can't do without one another in the long run, but occasionally part company.

Dilip Kumar Roy's book "Among the Great" expands a series of conversations which he has had with Romain Rolland, Gandhi, Bertrand
Russell, Tagore and Sri Aurobindo - a third of the book being devoted to
the last named.[25] The section about Bertrand Russell is interesting and
provocative, since, being a materialist, he only just comes into the author's
canons of greatness, and he is the occasion for some lively interchange.

That concludes my talk about Books from Bengal.[26] I also brought back
books from other parts of India, and perhaps these may be the subject of
a future talk. Next month, though, I expect to be talking about conditions
here, or in Europe.

1. <NOT> A canceled, handwritten note at the upper right reads, "Miss Plagle [?], / The Listener, / Langham Hotel." The significance of the notation is unclear.

2. John Arlott was a poet as well as a BBC producer, broadcaster, and cricket authority (*Listener*, 12 September 1946, p. 354; Lago, *A Literary Life*, 98). As EMF wrote to Arlott on 27 May 1946, "I have about 30 books from India here. Shall some of these be the subject of my first talk? . . . I would like to make the talks for India, with India alone in my mind" (private collection of Elizabeth MacLeod Walls).

3. See Furbank, *A Life*, 2:259–63, for an account of EMF's trip; he left England on 5 October 1945 to attend the All-India P.E.N. conference at Jaipur. EMF kept a diary of this trip that is now in the Archives at King's College, Cambridge. The travel journal records his grief for his friend Syed Ross Masood, who had died in 1937 and whose grave EMF visited during this trip. Flying back to England, EMF seemed especially philosophical about India as a symbol of hope in a world emerging from war: "O Lovely World, teach others to expound you as I have not been able to do! O untroubled spaces, seldom looked upon by men's eyes . . . clouds on the Mediterranean, which will keep moving when I have passed, then deserts in Arabia which I flew over on my way out. . . . You remain pure" (Indian Journal, 28 December 1945, King's College, Cambridge, Archive).

4. EMF also brought back a number of manuscripts, as Francis Watson commented in the *Listener*: "I doubt whether his sixty-five pounds of airways luggage can take in the manuscripts he has been offered by a host of eager young men—and women" ("What Is Indo-English?" 29 November 1945, p. 624).

5. <this part of India>

6. The school (Santiniketan) founded by Rabindraneth Tagore; see Lago, *Tagore*, 32–37; Lago, *"India's Prisoner": A Biography of Edward John Thompson, 1886–1946*, 150, 184; Furbank, *A Life*, 2:262.

7. <writer's>

8. Sarat Chandra Chatterji, *The Deliverance*, trans. Dilip Kumar Roy, revised by Sri Aurobindo, foreword by Rabindranath Tagore (Bombay: Nalanda Publications; N. M. Tripathi, 1944).

9. <agreeable>

10. Tarasankar Banerjee, *Epoch's End*, trans. Hirendranath Mookherjee (Calcutta: Mitralaya, 1945[?]).

11. godown: "A warehouse or store for goods, in India and other parts of Eastern Asia" (*OED*).

12. <prostitute>

13. The first All India Progressive Writers Association conference convened in Lahore in 1936; thereafter it became increasingly associated with Marxist politics and literary theory.

14. Pramatha Chaudhuri, *Tales of Four Friends*, trans. Indira Devi Chaudhurani (Calcutta: Published for Visva-Bharati by P. Sen, 1944).

15. Ibid., 25. EMF revises considerably the passage from which he quotes: "the trees, catching the infection, all become limp, and the roads all become slushy with mud. It seems as if half the rainy weather comes down from above, and the other half rises up from below; and between the two of them they make a dismal, dirty and disgusting mess all over the sky. . . . Englishmen say they feel like committing murder on such days."

16. Premendra Mitra et al., eds., *Stories of Rural Bengal*, trans. Karali Kanta Biswas (Calcutta: Purvasa, 1944); Dilip K. Gupta, ed., *Best Stories of Modern Bengal*, vol. 2, trans. Nilima Devi (Calcutta: Signet Press, 1945).

17. <most>

18. <I know,>

19. Rabindranath Tagore, *Farewell, My Friend: A Novel,* trans. K. R. Kripalani (London: New India Pub. Co., 1946).

20. <asked>

21. Amiya Chandra Chakravarty, *Modern Tendencies in English Literature* (Calcutta: D. M. Roy, [n.d.]); Dilip Kumar Roy, *Among the Great* (Bombay: N. M. Tripathi, 1945); Dhurjati Prasad Mukerji, *Indian Music: An Introduction* (Poona: Kutub, 1945); Bishnu Dey and John Irwin, *Jamini Roy* (Calcutta: Indian Society of Oriental Art, 1944).

22. Francis Watson reviewed the exhibition at the Arcade Gallery in the *Listener* (9 May 1946, p. 620), noting that EMF opened the show on 25 April.

23. "On the Projected Kendal and Windermere Railway," first published in the 16 October 1844 *Morning Post,* then reprinted in 1845.

24. Page citation unavailable.

25. Sri Aurobindo was a linguist, political activist, and yogic philosopher.

26. < - none of which, by the way, was by a Moslem>

¹CHECKED WITH B'CAST
EASTERN SERVICE
PURPLE NETWORK
WEDNESDAY, 31st JULY, 1946
1435-1450 GMT

PRODUCTION BY: Sunday Wilshin
(Rm. 218 O.S.)
REC. from TRANS. on DOX 73228
DURATION: 13/20"

"SOME BOOKS"

by -

E.M. FORSTER

The chief event in the world of letters has been the ninetieth birthday of Mr. Bernard Shaw last Friday.[2] He has received congratulations from the multitudes of people whom he has amused and helped and stimulated and irritated, and he is probably enjoying the homage of the irritable most. What a run he has had for his money. What a dance he has led us, and what a profitable dance. This great English writer who isn't one, this great Irishman who wouldn't live in Ireland - how can we thank him for his gaiety, his seriousness, his courage, his uniqueness, his humanity? There never was anyone like him, nor would he wish there to be. At one time - it was many years ago - his style was rather cramped by a school of disciples called Shavians, and as Lord Acton once said one can forgive anything to the founder of a school except the school.[3] But the Shavians have[4] vanished, and Shaw himself did all he could to blow them away - chiefly by turning upon himself or his supposed self in his plays, and making Shavianism ridiculous. What is his greatest work? Saint Joan, including the Epilogue,[5] and I make this dogmatic remark in order to stir up strife amongst listeners, for it would never do to celebrate Shaw in an atmosphere of peace - perfect peace. Is there a good book about him? There is. It is that biography by Hesketh Pearson.[6] It is brilliantly written, amusing[7] intelligent, and it brings out the goodness and greatness of his heart - a point which critics have sometimes missed, and which Shaw himself has not been anxious for them to perceive. If you want to pay homage to

363

Bernard Shaw, and don't know how to begin, get hold of Hesketh Pearson's book and appropriate remarks will immediately occur to you.

[8]Another recent literary event that calls for comment,[9] is the Congress of the International P.E.N. which took place in June in Stockholm. You may remember the P.E.N. Congress last year at Jaipur. That was an Indian Congress, convened by the Indian Centre, whereas the Stockholm Congress was international and the first of its type to be held since the war ended.[10] It was an exciting affair for writers from all over Europe and elsewhere were again able to meet and exchange views. I couldn't go myself, but Mr. Ould the secretary went - he and I were both at Jaipur - and Mr. Ould has[11] shown me[12] the forthcoming report.[13] Socially the Congress was delightful and Swedish hospitality generous. But there were some sharp conflicts of opinion in the meeting, notably over the establishment of a Black List.

Should there be - do you think there ought to be - a Black List of writers who have collaborated with the enemy during the past war, or indeed have behaved at all suspiciously? The President of the Dutch P.E.N. proposed that such a list should be made, not indeed for publication, but for secret transmission between the various P.E.N. centres, so that undesirable writers could not usurp a position in another country. The proposal was vehemently opposed by Mr. Ould. He said that it was most dangerous and contrary to the spirit of the P.E.N., that it would lead to fruitless and pernicious recrimination, and that there would be no end to the bad feeling created. He also pointed [out] that each centre had tests of admission, and also machinery by which it could expel members who did not live up to their obligations, and wasn't that enough? The Congress thought it wasn't, for when the Dutch proposal for a Black List was put to the vote it was carried by a large majority - seventeen in favour and six against, and three abstentions. So the various P.E.N. centres can now prepare black lists if they desire to do so. The seventeen in favour were all members of European countries which had been occupied by the Nazis during the war, and had suffered from informers. The six against and the three abstentions belonged to countries that had not been so occupied - such as the United States of America, Great Britain, China. It was a vote of the unfortunate against the fortunate. Not that we in England can be called fortunate with our V.1's, V.2's[14] and the rest of it, but we hadn't to undergo psychological misery like Holland or France and that[15] seems to be the dividing line. I know that I should have voted <u>against</u> the Black List, I am glad the Indian delegate voted against it, and I am certain those who voted for it were ill-advised, still I understand their[16] mentality. There was a certain amount of[17] private denunciation, and I believe that in our instance the same person was denouncer and denounced - which neatly supports Mr. Ould's argument.

As for the other motions before the Congress, there was a message of greeting to the writers of the U.S.S.R. which was passed after discussion. Russia declines any connection with the P.E.N. There was a protest against the suppression of free-speech in Spain and the barring there of the Catalan Basque and Galician languages, and there was a general resolution which I will quote in full:

"To rekindle the hope in Mankind, which these dark years of terror have almost extinguished, be it resolved by the International P.E.N. Club that each and all will do their utmost, with that great power of the written word, to dispel race, class and national hatreds, and champion the ideals of one humanity living in peace in one world."

So much for the Stockholm Conference. Now I return to England, and take you down to a little village in Sussex called Glyndebourne where the new opera of Benjamin Britten is being performed. The name of the opera is The Rape of Lucretia.[18] Britten's first opera, Peter Grimes, was based on a poem by George Crabbe, and depicted the grim, dour life in an English fishing town, with its economic injustice and crowd cruelty. In The Rape of Lucretia he has taken an incident from ancient Roman History - the story of the wicked tyrant Tarquin who steals away from the camp and assaults the chaste and beautiful wife of his general. Lucretia will not survive her shame. She summons her husband, tells him of Tarquin's infamy, and stabs herself, and as a result of the crime the tyrants are expelled and Rome becomes free. The treatment of this story by Benjamin Britten and by his librettist, Mr. Duncan, is[19] unusual. In the front of the stage are two commentators, a man and a woman, who represent the wisdom of the ages, and view the story from outside time. Musically they belong, but they do not intervene in the[20] drama. They are Christian, and this story of antique virtue and vice is presented as a prefiguration of the passion and sacrifice of Christ, of love betrayed again and immolated on the altar of man's lust. The last words recall the audience to Christ "It is He, it is He . . ." and the words are echoed touchingly and skilfully by the instruments of the orchestra, one after another, until the music dies into silence, the final sound being a major third. The Christian motive is also indicated subtly by Mr. John Piper in his decor. He has designed a drop-curtain before the bed chamber of Lucretia which is at first sight merely a sumptuous chaos of blots and webs. As the music requires, lights play on the fabric and outlines are defined, and we dimly discern the Godhead enthroned above the confusion of this world with the souls of the righteous in his hand.

I did not like the Christianisation of the story. It seemed arbitrary and cranky, and I found myself jibbing much as I should if The Rape of Lucretia was interpreted in terms of orthodox Marxism as no doubt it could be. However as long as one was content to look and listen and not to think or reflect the tendentiousness did not signify. What Britten really cares about of course is the music, and he has probably been content to accept a religious framework for this opera as he accepted an economic framework for Peter Grimes. What ravishing music it is. It pleases at the first hearing, and yet it[21] has immense reserves. The opera had an immediate success. It is going to London and European productions are already arranged.[22]

Glyndebourne I'd like to add is the home of a wealthy amateur who has done much for music in this country, and has built a small private theatre. The lovely scenery, the long bare downs, the stretches of rich green plains, the formal gardens where the audience stroll in the interval, the large barn where they can partake of an exquisite dinner - all make[23] Glyndebourne a paradise, a paradise into which the serpent of snobbery has sometimes crept. Here is opera for the rich - no denying that - and before the war a good many people went to listen to their own voices rather than to that of Mozart, and to gaze at one another's clothes in preference to the view. Today things are simpler, if not cheaper, and the smarti boots element less aggressive. I went down with two Indian friends, both of whom are musicians.[24] The Rape of Lucretia might be described as a chamber-opera, since the orchestra contains twelve instruments only - only twelve, but each is a soloist. The small Glyndebourne Theatre was perfect for such a work, it was a perfect performance, and we enjoyed ourselves greatly.

1. <NOT>

2. 26 July 1946.

3. EMF had attended Lord Acton's lectures as an undergraduate at Cambridge (Furbank, *A Life*, 1:55–56).

4. <dispersed>

5. [George] Bernard Shaw, *Saint Joan: A Chronicle Play in Six Scenes and an Epilogue* (London: Constable and Co., 1924).

6. Hesketh Pearson, *Bernard Shaw, His Life and Personality* (London: Collins, 1942).

7. <and>

8. <There's>

9. <and that>

10. The Stockholm conference opened on 4 June 1946. For the 1945 P.E.N. conference in Jaipur, see the General Introduction as well as EMF's broadcast of 3 July 1946.

11. <allowed>

12. <to see his>

13. Hermon Ould, a dramatist, was secretary of the International P.E.N. and in 1945 edited *Freedom of Expression: A Symposium Based on the Conference Called by the London Centre of the International P.E.N. to Commemorate the Tercentenary of the Publication of Milton's Areopagitica, 22–26th August, 1944* (London: Hutchinson International Authors, 1945).

14. German missiles fired at England were called V.1's and V.2's from the German abbreviation "V," for *Vergeltungswaffe* or "reprisal weapon" (*OED*).

15. <was>

16. <morality>

17. <whispering>

18. *The Rape of Lucretia* debuted on 12 July 1946 at Glyndebourne.

19. <original and strange>

20. <action>

21. <grows>

22. After the opera was broadcast on the Third Programme, Eric Blom reviewed it in the 3 October 1946 *Listener* (p. 453) and noted adverse critical reaction to the libretto; see also Humphrey Carpenter, *Benjamin Britten: A Biography* (New York: Charles Scribner's Sons, 1992), 238–39.

23. <the place>

24. Unidentified, but see the reference to Narayana Menon and other Indian musicians in EMF's 9 May 1945 broadcast.

[1]CHECKED WITH BROADCAST   Pre-rec.: 21.8.46
EASTERN SERVICE - PURPLE NETWORK   Rec. No.: DOX.74248
WEDNESDAY, 28th AUGUST 1946.   Duration: 13'20"
1435-1450 GMT.
Repros.: AFRICAN - 1st September - 1745 GMT
        NORTH AMERICAN - 2nd/3rd September - 0000 GMT
        G.O.S. - 3/4th September - 2330 GMT.

"SOME BOOKS"

By

E. M. Forster

Anything I have to say this month must be overshadowed by the death of H.G. Wells.[2] A great figure in world literature has been removed, and if he[3] seemed smaller of late years it is because the world has absorbed his ideas but has neglected his warnings. He prophecied, right back at the beginning of the century, what would come upon us if we didn't unite, if we didn't control the applications of science, and if we weren't reasonable. What do I see in to-day's newspapers - the same which announce his death? [4]Trouble at your side of the world, trouble at mine, trouble in Palestine and South Africa, strikes, protests, bans, black markets and black lists, global menaces, like the atom, and little local nuisances like[5] the dirty ice cream that is now being sold in the London streets. This doesn't look like unity, or control, or reasonableness, and Wells died conscious that his advice had been ignored, and convinced that humanity was doomed. He was a terrific individualist, however he might urge cooperation upon others, he wouldn't work with people - witness his quarrel with the Fabians and the Sidney Webbs[6] - and he could not realise that humanity might be saved by paths beyond his vision. If he had realised it, he wouldn't have been H.G. Wells.

In his last years he grew old. All of us, as we grow old, become tiresome in different ways, and the particular form his tiresomeness took - truculence and petulance - annoyed people and blotted his copy-book. Old men cause less offence when they dodder. Wells never doddered. He was too vital[7] to do that. I like a remark of his which has been quoted in the newspaper. A friend had been talking to him[8] when he was ill, and noticed that he wasn't attending. "Don't interrupt me. Can't you see I'm busy dying?" said Wells.[9] He was busy to the bitter end. And though the remark hasn't the moral grandeur or the beauty of Goethe's "Light, more light", I shall always think of the two together.[10] They both express the determination of the human spirit to understand.

I didn't know him well - liked him enormously when we did meet, and he was always charming to me. I remember being on a platform in the early thirties with him, to protest against the Incitement to Disaffection Bill.[11] Wells - always naughty - seized the opportunity to attack the Soviet Union, a topic which had nothing whatever to do with our objective, and which threatened to disrupt our audience. He never could resist bringing out a peashooter and having a pot. It was part of his eternal boyishness. I remember, too - not so long ago - him calling after me in his squeaky voice "Still in your ivory tower?" "Still on your private roundabout" I might have retorted, but did not think of it till now. His contempt for the ivory tower, and indeed for all that might be dubbed art, was characteristic. Consider how, in his wonderful Outline of History,[12] he only mentions Dante once, and only in a footnote and only as a founder of the modern Italian language. That is all that the Divine Comedy, the supreme achievement of mediaeval Christianity and perhaps of European civilisation, meant to H.G.

Thinking of him quickly, as one does after a death - one recalls most vividly his ideas, ideas on biology, astronomy, planning, sex, education, maps, money, or whatever it was that entered his fertile and public brain. He popularised ideas. He caught hold of thousands of men and women whom the schools and academies have missed, and made them think, or anyhow follow his thoughts. But ideas were only a fragment of his vast equipment. He was also a rich and human novelist who could create individuals and make us care about them and laugh[13] and a fantasist who used his knowledge of science to produce the macabre.[14] When he is seen in perspective, his fiction will loom large. And perhaps it is as an artist that his impatient and generous spirit will be best remembered.[15]

It is curious to turn from him to the two books which I had been thinking about when I heard of his death - Milk of Paradise by Forrest Reid, and The Scarlet Tree, which is the second volume of the autobiography of Sir Osbert Sitwell.[16] For they are both of them protests against the Wellsian outlook. They attempt to view life not in terms of social construction. And they offer very little advice. Mr. Forrest Reid believes in gentleness and quietness, and in taking a personal line which may or mayn't appeal to other people. And Sir Osbert Sitwell, though he has moved much in the world and has noted its vagaries, does so as an amazed spectator. Turning to these two books, I say, one has to readjust, to refocus, and to listen in Mr. Reid's case, to music that is ethereal.

> Weave a circle round him thrice
> And close your eyes in holy dread
> For he on honey dew hath fed
> And drunk the milk of Paradise.[17]

These words of Coleridge provide him with his title: <u>The Milk of Paradise</u>. And his book is[18] about poems which he has enjoyed.[19] We feel, when reading, that he is not trying to convert. He has had pleasure which he would like to share, and if it is incommunicable - very well! Nor is his attitude critical, but, owing to his sincerity, it is more impressive than most criticism. He makes us think of the poem instead of the apparatus which the critic employs. He helps us to enter into the creative spirit which inspired the poet as he was writing, and for my own part I like such a guide.

I wonder how much you know of Forrest Reid's work. It hasn't had adequate recognition. He has always lived in Northern Ireland, kept away from cliques, and remained completely indifferent to fashion. Though gentle, he is anything but yielding, and I can think of no writer more certain of himself. His main achievement has been in fiction. But he has interpreted also, written monographs on Yeats and De la Mare and on the wood-cut illustrators of the Sixties. <u>The Milk of Paradise</u> belongs to the interpretative class.[20] Chatterton, William Blake, Wordsworth and Coleridge, of course, Edgar Allan Poe, Sydney Dobell, John Clare, William Allingham, Thomas Hardy - here are some of the writers, great and small, who appeal to[21] him, and who didn't, I feel sure, appeal to H.G. Wells.[22]

Yet I must qualify this. Wells had imagination, and he had a feeling for the intangible. A good example of this feeling is that lovely short story, <u>The Door in the Wall</u>.[23] The hero, you may remember, passes a door in a wall when he is a boy: he would like to push it open and have a look, but he's[24] hurrying to sit for an exam and he can't find it again afterwards. Repeatedly through life he passes the door, but he's on his way to get a job, or to be married: there's never the time. Finally he sets out to keep an appointment which would have proved disastrous for him, though he didn't realise it. He never arrives. Search is made. His body is found at the bottom of a builder's excavation into which he had fallen through opening a door in a wall. In this story, and elsewhere, Wells proves himself no materialist. But he is far away from the brooding poetical mysticism of Forrest Reid.[25]

He is also far away from Sir Osbert Sitwell, to whose fascinating auto-biography I must now turn. The Scarlet Tree is a second instalment. It takes the writer from the age of eight to the age of eighteen, and it takes the reader down many paths and into many countries.[26] You may remem-ber my mentioning the first volume last year. That had a wonderful climax to it: the description of the painting of the Sitwell family group by Sargent.[27] There is nothing equivalent to this in The Scarlet Tree, but there is the same brilliancy and gaiety, the same passion for civilisation and for aesthetic distinction, the same power of evoking people, scenery, and architecture. Schools (how Sir Osbert detests schools and sport!), holidays with the aristocracy (shootin' and fishin' variety), holidays with the aris-tocracy (religious variety), playing upon the pianola, the Camoora[28] at Naples, a monkey who swallows an old lady's wig, the butler who remarks "You'll cop it, Master Osbert, when the Great White Chief sees you": varied are the pleasures which are provided. I will quote a specimen passage, a cheerful fantastic passage which shows how the writer[29] ele-vates a school-boy rag into a piece of literature. Osbert Sitwell is at Eton, and is attending what is known at Eton as 'Absence': that is to say, a roll call where the boys prove they are not absent by being present. Absence, he tells us, is held in an enclosure, called Cannon Yard, containing an old cannon from the Crimea.

"There had gone to Eton the same day as myself a young Scottish chieftain - a wild, rather unsociable, though jolly boy, who liked to roam by himself. If, however, a row of any kind broke out, he would materi-alise in an amazingly short time, and, throwing himself into the thick of it, become the very centre of the storm . . . On this occasion of which I am writing, he seemed to have been out of trouble for some days . . . But suddenly, during Absence on a Saturday afternoon, when a good many ox-eyed parents were listlessly wandering about outside the railings, there was a vast explosion from the Cannon, accompanied by a long, spluttering, popping fizzle, an apocalyptic rushing of flame, wind and soot, and a discharge of such miscellaneous objects as unwanted but-tons of all sorts, and old boots and toothbrushes. Stars and whorls of fire seared the air: hats were blown from heads in every direction, and even the mortar-board of the officiating master was lifted from his head and dashed to the ground. And for some minutes the air remained dark, as after a volcanic eruption, with falling lumps of hard, appar-ently cindery matter and pieces of charred paper. Through the railings, the blackened, hatless faces of parents gazed in wondering dismay . . . The Scot had contrived it, to enliven a dull mid-term. Having hoarded a great many fireworks he had then acquired some black-powder, a compound of charcoal and saltpetre, had set himself, with the aid only of his native ingenuity and application, to prepare for us this pleasant surprise."[30]

That is a specimen of The Scarlet Tree, and other excellent and more serious scenes are to be found. The name, by the way, is fanciful, and refers to the belief of the ancient anatomists that the blood forms a growing tree inside the human body, a belief, I need hardly add, which is not countenanced by H.G. Wells.

1. <NOT>

2. Wells died on 13 August 1946.

3. <bulked>

4. <Maladjustment>

5. <the London gas strikes, or>

6. Wells's quarrel with Bernard Shaw and the Webbs, long-standing members of the Fabian Society, resulted from his affairs with Rosamund Bland (daughter of Hubert Bland and E. Nesbit, fellow Fabians) and Amber Reeves, and from his unflattering portrait of the Webbs in The New Machiavelli, published in 1911.

7. <, too curious>

8. <in his last illness>

9. New York Times, 14 August 1946, p. 1.

10. <in the future>. George Henry Lewes gives a less idealized rendition of Goethe's dying words, noting the gradual incoherence of Goethe's thoughts: "His speech was becoming less and less distinct. The last words audible were: More light!" (The Life of Goethe, 2d ed. [1864; rpt. New York: Frederick Ungar, 1965], 563).

11. The Incitement to Disaffection Bill of 1934 replaced the Mutiny Act of 1797 and, in its proposed form, would have substantially increased the government's power to prosecute seditious acts (see Furbank, A Life, 2:188).

12. Wells's Outline of History was first issued in twenty-four parts, November 1919–November 1920, then in a number of editions.

13. < - Kipps, Mr. Polly, Mr. Lewisham, the Pondereros, [sic] Mr. Britling. And he was also a>

14. <: The Island of Dr. Moreau, The Time Machine, The First Men in the Moon, The War of the Worlds. His best fiction belongs to his earlier period, so we forget it.>

15. <Perhaps - though this homage would irritate him most - he will be classed a great man. How he mistrusted great men! How mischievous he is about them!>

16. Forrest Reid, The Milk of Paradise; Some Thoughts on Poetry (London: Faber and Faber, 1946); Osbert Sitwell, The Scarlet Tree, being the second volume of Left Hand, Right Hand! An Autobiography (London: Macmillan and Co., 1946).

17. EMF quotes the last four lines of "Kubla Khan."

18. <a series of short talks>

19. <, poems all of them belonging to the Romantic Movement>

20. <It is full of quotations - some of them new to me, and even when they are familiar he makes them sound new. I discovered myself reading Lucy Gray as if for the first time. Poetry, he holds, must have mixtures of heaven and earth in it; it may be playful, but it must convey more than it says. If it doesn't, it is prose - or Pope.>

21. <Mr. Forrest Reid>

22. The eighteenth-century poet Thomas Chatterton committed suicide at age seventeen

when he faced starvation; Sydney Dobell authored the "Spasmodic" epic *Balder* (1854); the Anglo-Irish William Allingham, whose posthumously published *Diary* (1907) chronicled his friendship with Tennyson, was also known for his lyrics, his ballads, and an epic entitled *Lawrence Bloomfield in Ireland* (1862–1863).

23. *The Door in the Wall, and Other Stories* (London: Grant Richards, 1911).

24. <too busy>

25. Compare EMF's fantastical story "The Other Side of the Hedge" in *The Celestial Omnibus and Other Stories* (London: Sidgwick and Jackson, 1941), in which a nameless protagonist is—quite literally—trudging along the road of life. The road itself is dusty, but otherwise unremarkable. Dry brown hedges line the stretch of road that apparently leads nowhere at all. In a desperate attempt to experience something new, the protagonist deviates from the road, falls into a hedge, and emerges through to the "other side"—an astonishing and lush paradise filled with individuals doing as they please and answering to no one. Though on the surface "The Other Side of the Hedge" seems to champion a socialistic worldview in which fruitless competition and drudgery are eschewed in favor of communal happiness, EMF maintains a decidedly enigmatic tone throughout the story. The protagonist is at once lured and repelled by the bland joy he encounters on the other side of the hedge. He finds himself longing for "life, with its struggles and victories, with its failures and hatreds, with its deep moral meaning and its unknown goal!" (52). The story suggests EMF's own ambivalence about the vague promises of idealistic social systems as well as their counterpart: imperialistic democracies grounded in injustice and dominated by those who embrace competition. The story ends by reifying the promise of the new world, however. The protagonist encounters his brother, whom he had abandoned on the road of life in order to be a more competitive walker, living in banal happiness on the other side of the hedge.

26. <, full of detours and disquisitions>

27. See EMF's broadcast of 9 May 1945.

28. Camorra: "A secret society of lawless malcontents in Naples and Neapolitan cities" (*OED*).

29. <builds up his material, and>

30. Sitwell, *The Scarlet Tree*, 275–76. A number of passages in the excerpt were canceled from the original script, presumably because of time limits: chieftain < - it is remarkable how much character the young of that stock appear to maintain in spite of the prevalent tendency towards uniformity - ,>; if any kind broke out, he would, <although one so seldom met him otherwise,> materialise; the officiating master < - by some mischance the same whom a few weeks before I had laid low with my pea shooter - >; fireworks <which he had bought just before Guy Fawkes Day. Catherine-wheels, rockets, squibs, Roman candles and many other joys once common on that now forgotten festival,> he had then; saltpetre, <in those days to be obtained at shops, it being used for smoking-out wasps' nests, and, having collected anything else that he thought might come in handy,> had set himself; surprise. <But none of us could ever understand how he had been able to put in as much work on the job as plainly he must have done, without it being detected. He owned up to his crime in a most imperturbable manner, as if proud - as well he might be! - of what he had achieved . . . Many years later, it came as no surprise to hear that his career in the army, during the 1914-1918 war, had been most distinguished, and his men would follow him wherever he led, and that his ingenuity and gallant conduct had earned him many awards and mentions in despatches.>

EMF's comment about the passage was also excised: <Notice the quick fluid movement of the prose and occasional heightening of the effect by skilful exaggeration.>

[1]CHECKED WITH BROADCAST   Pre-rec. 19.11.46

EASTERN SERVICE - PURPLE NETWORK   Rec. No.: DOX.48894

WEDNESDAY, 20th NOVEMBER 1946.   Duration: 13'50"

1505-1520 GMT.

Produced by John Arlott[2]

Reproductions: G.O.S. - Tues./Wed. 26/27th November - 2330-2345 GMT
    N. AMERICAN - Mon./Tues. 25/26th November - 0000-0045 GMT

"SOME BOOKS"

By

E. M. Forster

Few important books have appeared lately - few anyhow have come my way. Perhaps the world is in too agitated a state for events to be recorded, or for the still more difficult feat of creation. In the region of affairs we really do not know what is happening. Iron curtains fall on every side, not always through political censorship, but because of the mechanism of the age. And in the region of the spirit there is doubt and withdrawal and mistrust of the cries of the planners, plan they never so loudly, and this doubt and withdrawal impairs artistic work at the source and prevents visions from taking an external form, to profit or delight mankind. That the world will always be so agitated and wretched and muddled, I do not believe. We have struck a bad patch. We shall come through. Calm and confidence will return. But they will not return in my day nor perhaps in yours. Pessimism for the immediate future, anyhow, seems reasonable. One's own experiences suggest it, it is supported in every column of the news, and by the subtler testimony of books. The books I have come across lately all express the prevailing uneasiness. They are tentative and parenthetic. The authors[3] cannot know what is happening around - and how should they when the secret services don't know. Nor have they the impulse to embody an inner vision.

A book which has interested me - and you should read it - is Stephen

Spender's <u>European Witness</u>.[4] This is a very high class piece of journalism. Mr. Spender was sent to Germany officially last year to find out what had happened to German culture as a result of the war. The old Germany, which gave us Goethe and Beethoven - did it survive to any extent? The later Germany which produced Wagner, Nietzsche and indeed, Thomas Mann - what remained of that? And the latest Germany of all - Hitler's and Goebbels' - was it still alive,[5] no more than scotched, and ready to strike as soon as the Allies quarrelled? Stephen Spender was well qualified for such an enquiry with his knowledge of the language and literature, his interest in poetry and art, his interest in politics, and - for he is a novelist as well as a poet - his interest in the discrepancies of human nature. And he has produced a most readable report - with some fictional touches. He does not pretend to offer more. Yet despite its merits <u>European Witness</u> leaves a confused impression, the trouble being that which I indicated.[6] Uncertainty and agitation. The writer cannot be sure what is happening either in Germany or in himself. Given every official facility, he can note this phenomenon or that. But what is the general tendency of phenomena and what would he have that tendency be? Some of the Professors are Nazis, at heart, no doubt of it. Away with them. Yet here is he himself eating at a single meal as much food as must last a Professor, Nazi or otherwise, for a week, and he feels remorse. Again, he can rebuke an old German woman who says mournfully 'Poor Germany' by retorting 'Poor Norway, poor Poland, poor Holland, poor Greece!' But when he retired to his own comfortable quarters and meets an A.T.S.[7] girl at a dinner party, he is tempted to be even more scathing about the A.T.S. girl. Listen to his account of her:

"She looked specially smart in her neat uniform, with her hair done in such a way that it looked pressed and moulded over her head as if it were part of her uniform. There was a metallic gleam about her coiffure which strengthened this impression. This girl was well made up with large cold shining eyes impooled in lashes like the feelers of an insect, and with a determined painted mouth, through which she uttered decisive and stupid remarks in an extremely refined accent."[8]

The waspishness of this account is typical, and the author so often buries his sting in the unexpectant contours of the British, that the book might be called 'Occupational Witness' instead of 'European Witness'. The dinner party, he adds, did not go well. One is not surprised, and nothing does go well. The conquerors, like the conquered, are uneasy, are full of malaise. And in a more serious passage he indicates why this is happening. Germany is in decay, and it is not mere national decay: it is the decay of part of the human race, and can infect other human beings, who come in contact with it.[9] I have seen nothing of post-war Europe, except from the air, but the observers who come back from it all confirm Mr. Spender: they too have felt the breath of decay. Some return frivolous or hard or resolved to forget. The better sort try to diagnose the disease and prevent it from spreading: the best sort of all add to this a conviction that the human race is one, diseased or sound.

In part of the book Mr. Spender visits France. The descriptions here are less poignant. But he states with force the problem which he thinks confronts that country. It is this: can France retain the cultural values which have made her famous in history - the fusion of sensuous and spiritual experience which has been her great contribution to western civilisation. When I was in India last year at Jaipur,[10] there was a little exhibition of French printed books. They delighted me, not only by their taste and charm, but as a reminder that France was carrying on. Can she carry on - in this particular way? Mr. Spender doubts it. Nicely printed books are a luxury. They represent so much off war-effort or peace-reconstruction.[11] Fresh from the obvious horrors of Germany, he feels France too is part of a ruined Europe.

The book closes back in Germany, with its uncertain intellectual movement, and its blends of resentment and falseness and its stark misery which only the A.T.S. girl and her sort can ignore. Sensitive rather than dynamic, Mr. Spender does not come to any clear-cut conclusion. He is often irritable, sometimes he is captious. But he has a clear conception of a diseased area which no iron curtains will segregate from the rest of the world.

Do Germany or Europe matter to you, in India? With your great troubles, is it worth your while spending time on troubles so far away? I have discussed this with Indians, and I found in some cases reluctance and resentment at being asked to consider the distant misery - in one or two cases there was even suspicion, as if Europe was a red herring. God knows you have enough on your hands, and God also knows that the troubles of India have often been ignored by the west. So you can retort by indifference if you choose, and nobody will blame you. Still, I recommend you Mr. Spender's book as a timely reminder that humanity is one and that disease cannot be localised.

The next book, The Cult of Power by Rex Warner[12] also deals with contemporary malaise. Its title reminded me of those words of the great historian, Lord Acton, which are so often quoted, and which cannot be too often quoted: "All power corrupts" wrote Lord Acton. "Absolute power corrupts absolutely. All great men are bad."[13] I like pondering over these sentences, and I rather hoped to find an examination of them in Mr. Rex Warner's book. It is, however, a collection of essays, The Cult of Power itself occupying only a dozen pages. His thesis is that when the individual revolts against his surroundings, the results are often good, for revolt is the seed of progress. But when the revolt is only self-assertion it is against the nature of man and of society, it will become more and more outrageous in order to preserve itself, and it will tragically fail. For the rebel cannot be a leader, though Hitler thought he could, and though a very different personality - D. H. Lawrence - believed in such leaders['] life and in the dark aristocracy of the blood. I wish that Mr. Rex Warner had worked out in greater detail his conception of the two stages of rebellion - the beneficial and the disastrous - and that he had defined "the nature of man and of society" of which he speaks as if it were something absolute, which we challenge at our peril. But he passes on to other themes - there are essays on Dickens, Dostoevsky, Aeschylus. There is a religious undercurrent in his thought and that tendency to allegory which occurs in his novels. You may remember <u>Why was I killed?</u>, about which I broadcast, and <u>The Wild Goose Chase</u> and <u>The Aerodrome</u>.[14] He is of this generation - uneasy, questing - . Many years have passed since the four square Liberalism of Lord Acton, there has been economic upheaval and psychological uncertainty, and it is natural that the two men should discuss the Cult of Power in a different way.

When I was a young man, I went to Acton's lectures. It was at Cambridge, and since I happen to be in Cambridge now, my mind goes back to them. I had the sense to know that they were remarkable, and some of the things he said have remained with me through life. Humped up, bald, bearded, he said 'Every villain is followed by a sophist with a sponge.' He also said - and now he is going to shock you "Democracy means payment by the rich and government of the poor."[15] For though he was a liberal and a champion of liberty, he lived before the great economic overturn and the acuter stirrings of the social conscience. He was also a European - he had Italian and Austrian blood in him as well as English, and he was European in his sympathies and in his learning. Where is Europe to-day? What are Naples and Vienna like? Or Berlin? Mr. Spender has told us. If the ghost of the great historian could walk, what would it find now in the haunts congenial to it? What surmises would it indulge in for their future? It is not a good thing to mourn all the time, but I believe in a little mourning - it humanises us, it gives us perspective. And I desire to conclude this talk on our present uneasiness with a tear for the vanished past Lord Acton embodied, vanished for ever into the dignity of a tomb.

1. <NOT>
2. See note 2 for the 3 July 1946 broadcast.
3. <don't>

4. Stephen Spender, *European Witness* (London: Hamish Hamilton, 1946).

5. <although>

6. <at the beginning of this talk>

7. A.T.S. is the Auxiliary Territorial Service, a division of the army open to women.

8. Spender, *European Witness*, 83.

9. <"And all the time, behind London, Paris, Prague, Athens, are those shadows, those ghosts, the destroyed towns of Germany, which are also the part of the soul of Europe which has collapsed visibly into chaos and disintegration. Their ruin is not just their ruins, it is also pestilence, the epidemic of despair spreading over and already deep-rooted within Europe, the black foreshadowing of the gulf which already exists in us - the gulf which we can still refuse."> Ibid., 97.

10. See the General Introduction as well as EMF's broadcast of 3 July 1946.

11. <And he remarks: ¶"Beyond the frontiers of France there are countries reduced to a condition where they [*sic*] way of life which makes French cultural values possible has been completely destroyed. And the question is whether it has not been destroyed in France also."> Spender, *European Witness*, 111.

12. Rex Warner, *The Cult of Power: Essays* (London: John Lane, 1946).

13. Lord Acton, April 1887 letter to Bishop Mandell Creighton. EMF slightly misquotes Acton: "Great men are almost always bad men, even when they exercise influence and not authority." *Life and Letters of Mandell Creighton*, ed. Louise Creighton, 2 vols. (London and New York: Longmans, Green, 1904), 1:372.

14. *The Wild Goose Chase: A Novel* (London: Boriswood, 1937); *The Aerodrome: A Love Story* (London: John Lane, 1941); *Why Was I Killed?* (London: John Lane, 1943). EMF broadcast on the last title on 23 March 1944.

15. EMF slightly misquotes Acton's originals: "The strong man with the dagger is followed by the weaker man with the sponge. First, the criminal who slays; then the sophist who defends the slayer"; "There is no doubt that he held fast to the doctrine of equality, which means government by the poor and payment by the rich." Lord Acton, *Lectures on the French Revolution* (1910; rpt. Kitchener, Ontario: Batoche Books, 1999), 78, 243.

NOT CHECKED WITH BROADCAST

Produced by John Arlott
Room 219, 200 O.S.

Pre-rec.: 14.1.47 - Ram. 2.
Rec. No.: DOX.81443
Duration (without anncts.):

"SOME BOOKS"

By

E. M. Forster

Transmission:
EASTERN SERVICE: WEDNESDAY, 15th JANUARY 1947: 1505-1520 GMT
Repros.:
G.O.S.: Tues./Wed. 21/22nd JANUARY - 2330-2345 GMT
N. AMERICAN: Mon./Tues. 20/21st January - 0000-0015 GMT.

ANNOUNCER:
This is London Calling in the Eastern Service of the B.B.C. SOME BOOKS.
Here is another talk in this series of monthly book talks, given once again
by Mr. E. M. Forster.

MR. FORSTER:
 Bertrand Russell's <u>History of Western Philosophy</u>[1] will concern us today. It is a long book (over nine hundred pages), and it is a learned book.
To broadcast about it adequately, I ought to be both a philosopher and a
historian, and I am neither. It is also an amusing book, full of wit, unexpected comparisons, apt turns of phrase, and it is brilliantly written. I like
being amused. And I like the companionship of a first-class mind which is
not ashamed to be gay. I find that companionship in Bertrand Russell, and
am encouraged by it to talk to you. Can I give you, in the course of the
next ten minutes, any idea of this important and fascinating work? I will
have[2] a try.
 This <u>History of Western Philosophy</u> might almost have been called History of Western Philosophers. That is to say, Russell's method is biographical.

379

He approaches thought through the thinkers. He starts with Thales, a Greek who lived in Asia Minor two thousand five hundred years ago, and passes through Plato and Aristotle to the Epicureans and Stoics and Plotinus. That constitutes the first division of his work: Ancient Philosophy. Catholic Philosophy follows, beginning with the rise of Christianity, and passing through St. Augustine and the Dark Ages and St. Thomas Aquinas to the decay of the Papacy and the Reformation. With the Reformation, the third and final section of the book begins: Modern Philosophy. The great names come crowding: Machiavelli, Thomas More, Descartes, Spinoza, Leibnitz, Locke, Hume, Rousseau, Kant, Hegel, Schopenhauer, Nietszche, Karl Marx, Bergson, William James - here are some of them. And the pageant - if philosophers can march in a pageant - concludes by Bertrand Russell stating his own attitude in a chapter entitled The Philosophy of Logical Analysis. All through, he has handled his material through lives and not through problems. For instance, he has not considered the development of determinism, and free will as a subject. He has introduced it incidentally into his account of the men who have been interested in it, such as St. Augustine, Spinoza, and Bergson. Men are always more interesting than their interests, anyhow to me, and here is one reason why the book, despite its seriousness and erudition, is likely to sell. I hope it will.[3] It is an admirable work, and a humane one. No one can read it without being struck by the nobility of the human spirit. I have said it is an entertaining book, it is also an inspiring one. It makes the reader want to draw his little sword and do something in the secular battle of his race against dullness and evil. Did you happen to see a review of the book in the Times Literary Supplement entitled 'A Philosopher of Melancholy'? When I saw that review I could only say to myself 'Well, well. How different reviewers are!' For to me, the message[4] is[5] Hopefulness.

Let Russell himself speak for a moment. I will read you a passage in which he considers together the three sections I've mentioned: Ancient Philosophy, Catholic Philosophy and Modern Philosophy and surmises what the Modern has to do.

"The Ancient[6] world found an end to anarchy in the Roman Empire, but the Roman Empire was a brute fact, not an idea. The Catholic world sought an end to anarchy in the Church, which was[7] an idea, but was never adequately embodied in fact. Neither the ancient nor the mediaeval[8] solution was satisfactory - the one because it could not be idealised, the other because it could not be actualised. The modern world, at present, seems to be moving towards a solution like that of antiquity: a social order imposed by force, representing the will of the powerful rather than the hopes of common men. The problem of a durable and satisfactory social order can only be solved by combining the solidity of the Roman Empire with the idealism[9] of St. Augustine's City of God. To achieve this, a new philosophy will be needed."[10]

That is an able synthesis, and it puts one on one's toes. What's to be done? What[11] power[12] has thought? The human mind, despite imperfections and lesions, and inhibitions, is not negligible. It can work for good and can accomplish something in this[13] crisis of the human race.

You'll have noticed the phrase above "durable and satisfactory social order." This reminds me that I haven't yet given you the full title of the book. It's a History of Western Philosophy and its "Connection with Political and Social Circumstances from the Earliest Times to the present Day." The philosophers are considered in relation to their environment, and when the environment is unfamiliar, as in the Mediaeval period, Russell presents it more fully. Much of the book is social history, enlivened by anecdotes, and this is the easier part to read, and I enjoyed it most. When he really gets down to philosophy, the reading gets much tougher, and I wish you better going than I had through the chapters on Aristotle, and the windowless monads of Leibnitz. Just as one thinks "Oh this book's no good for me, I'm too stupid", something acceptable comes along, an account of Byron perhaps or St. Augustine's interesting theory of time, or a resumé of famous[14] works that one always wants to read without having read them, like More's <u>Utopia</u>, or the <u>Forged Donations of Constantine</u> - and then one cheers up and thinks "Well, I'm not such a fool after all, I don't dislike thought." Russell's main purpose, I believe, is to promote such an attitude in the reader. He has written a popular book containing some difficult technical sections, which we can skip and to which we may be tempted to return.[15]

Now what were these philosophers like personally? The man in the street is curious to know. They have been at it for 2,500 years now in the west and even longer[16] in the east. Have they made better jobs of their lives than ordinary men? Russell is so far pessimistic as to think that their reaction to a crisis will be purely instinctive; all of them, from Thales onwards, would yelp if they sat[17] on a tin-tack. He thinks too that physical torture, as scientifically applied by the Nazis, can disintegrate the noblest mind. As regards the[18] question of conduct, no general answer seems forthcoming. Socrates behaved nobly, so did Sir Thomas More, Erasmus was a coward, Rousseau a cad, and so on. A point to remember, I think, is that men do not pursue wisdom in order to become good. They pursue it in order to enlarge the human horizon, which enlargement should improve us all in the long run. Meanwhile the results on character[19] cannot be calculated. Here the philosopher differs from the religious, who does pursue a certain course in order to become good, and whose mind failure or success has a direct connection with his aims.

Philosophy,[20] Russell thinks, lies between religion and science. It is a sort of No Man's Land, exposed to attacks from both sides. Like theology, it speculates on matters about which we haven't so far any definite knowledge. Like science, it rejects authority and appeals to reason. What's the good of it? the common man may ask. It's good for two reasons. One of them is the historical - [21]circumstances and theories are always[22] interacting and have to be studied. And secondly, there is a more personal answer. It teaches us to live without certainty and yet without being paralysed by hesitation, and that Russell thinks, it can still do for those who study it. Some day, perhaps, science will discover and explain everything. Some day, perhaps, the assertions of theology will be proven. If either of these events occur, the speculations of philosophy will cease, and No Man's Land disappear.

Such, as far as I can generalise, are the essentials of this book. The approach is biographical. There is a triple division into Ancient, Mediaeval and Modern, and there are two underlying beliefs, namely that philosophy explains history, and that it helps us to be strong without being cocksure. It certainly is a remarkable product of the human mind, though not in my judgment remarkable as art. Here it is set out in a form that is partly comprehensible to the outsider. If you are in the habit of cracking jokes at its expense, you'll find them cracked by Russell, and quite as brightly. What you won't find is[23] sneers, the feeling of superiority in which too many outsiders indulge when they are in the presence of what they don't understand.

I've a minute or two left, so here are some more points I've noted. Russell is awfully good at administering unexpected shocks which bring us up against the problems of our own day, when we thought we were safely tucked away in the past. Discussing the Middle Ages for instance, he notes the increasing power of the Church, and adds: "The Church, therefore, was in a very strong position in opposing royal divorces and irregular marriages. In England it lost this position under Henry VIII, but recovered it under Edward VIII."[24] The last six words contain the sting. Edward VIII? Does he dare to comment on the late abdication, and on the[25] line adopted over it by the Archbishop of Canterbury? Yes he does, he insists on correlating the present and the past. You may disagree with the comment, but it has made you jump.

Another point is the vigour with which he criticises great names, such as Plato and Aristotle, and the sympathetic generosity which brings to the front names which are obscured to-day. Among the latter I'd instance Boethius and John the Scot. Boethius who lived in Italy in the sixth century after Christ, is a singular figure. He was a Christian, but his book, The Consolation of Philosophy, is pagan in tone. He was a Prime Minister, but he fell inexplicably from power. "There is no trace in him"[26] writes Russell, "of the superstition or morbidness of the age, no obsession with sin, no excessive straining after the unattainable. There is perfect philosophic calm - so much that if the book had been written in prosperity it might have been called smug. Written when it was, in prison, under sentence of death, it is as admirable as the last moments of Socrates."[27] To John the Scot, of whom I had scarcely heard, a whole chapter is given. He was an Irishman who lived in the ninth century, was a scholar, knew Greek, travelled in France, attacked intellectual problems with freshness and originality, believed in reason, and questioned Authority - much of which applies to Bertrand Russell himself.

1. Bertrand Russell, *A History of Western Philosophy and Its Connection with Political and Social Circumstances from the Earliest Times to the Present Day* (New York: Simon and Schuster, 1945).

2. <to>

3. <It strikes me as>

4. <contained>

5. <one of>

6. EMF added an accent mark above "Ancient."

7. EMF added accent marks above "Catholic" and "was."

8. EMF added accent marks above "ancient" and "mediaeval" in this sentence and "modern" in the next.

9. EMF added accent marks above "solidity" and "idealism."

10. Russell, *A History of Western Philosophy*, 494–95.

11. <is the>

12. <of>

13. <physical>

14. <books>

15. <And he stresses the interaction between men's circumstances and their thoughts.>

16. <at it>

17. <down>

18. <general>

19. <are incalculable>

20. <he>

21. <I have already indicated:>

22. <interesting>

23. <the>

24. Russell, *A History of Western Philosophy*, 395–96.

25.

26. Russell's text does not include "in him"; presumably EMF added this specificity to provide clarity for his listeners.

27. Russell, *A History of Western Philosophy*, 371.

[1]CHECKED WITH BROADCAST   Produced by John Arlott
Pre-rec.: 11.2.47 - Mixer 2   Room 219, 200 Oxford St.
Rec. No.: DOX 83508
Duration (without anncts.): 13'50"

"SOME BOOKS"

By

E.M. FORSTER

Transmission:
EASTERN SERVICE: WEDNESDAY, 12th FEBRUARY 1947: 1505-1520 GMT
Repros.:
G.O.S.: Tues./Wed. 18/19th FEBRUARY - 2330-2345 GMT
N. AMERICAN: Mon./Tues. 17/18th FEBRUARY - 000-0015 GMT.

ANNOUNCER:
This is London calling in the Eastern Service of the BBC. SOME BOOKS. Here is another book talk in our monthly series, given once again by Mr. E.M. Forster.

MR. FORSTER:
I have here a new book on Italy, a new book on France, and a reprint of an old book. I shall concentrate on the old book,[2] since it is the more important. It is a long short story by the American novelist Hermann Melville, and it is called Billy Budd. We know Hermann Melville best as the author of Moby Dick - that amazing novel about whaling and the pursuit of a whale which is evil.[3] The whale is killed but its pursuer perishes with it. There is no novel like Moby Dick in literature;[4] nor can there be a short story like Billy Budd.[5] The name suggests comedy, commonness almost and indeed the hero is only an illiterate young sailor. But here, as in Moby Dick, Melville hunts after the mystery of evil.

He wrote Billy Budd in 1891 when he was seventy years old and his genius seemed to have expired. He took immense pains with it; as though

384

it was his last message to the world; but it never got printed in his life time; and only appeared in the collected edition of his works.[6] There, it lay amongst a lot of unreadable rubbish. For Melville is a writer who often misses his stroke. Critics got to know of it and to admire it. I remember first reading it in a library where I wasn't allowed to take it away for fear of breaking the set. That's why the present reprint is so important. It puts a curious masterpiece within the reach of the general public.

A curious masterpiece, but a simple story. A tale of the sea. The scene is laid in the British Navy, a hundred and fifty years ago shortly after the mutiny of the Nore.[7] Billy Budd incurs the dislike of a petty officer, Claggart, is wrongfully accused by him of mutinous intention, and in his horror and rage strikes him dead in the presence of their commander Captain Vere. That is all the story, but Melville significantly calls it an "inside narrative" and peers deeply into human motives and the working of fate. Billy, though just a rough[8] simple chap is amazingly handsome and since his good looks go with a good heart and good spirits and good health he is popular with his mates and indeed worshipped by them - not that he notices that, being unsophisticated. He is perfect - except for one blemish: a stammer or stutter which overcomes him when he is upset. "A striking instance" remarks Melville that "the arch interpreter, the envious marplot of Eden, still has more or less to do with every human consign- ment to this planet of earth. In every case, one way or another, he is sure to slip in his little card as much as to remind us - I too have a hand here."[9] 'Arch-interpreter' by the way is an odd expression to use of the devil.[10] Why not Arch-fiend? But no: arch-interpreter. Melville's mind is full of such oddness. And the stutter with which he handicaps Billy not only pre- vents[11] the young[12] sailor from being a plaster saint, too good to be true, but has a symbolic value. Everywhere evil has some hold.

Claggart, the adversary, is wholly evil. As soon as Billy comes on board he recognises in him his opposite who must be destroyed. Melville's analysis of Claggart is remarkable. He lists him as an example of Natural Depravity which contains no alloy of the Brute, is not mercenary, sordid or sensual, is indeed without vices or small sins. But deep down Claggart is a maniac,[13] and one whose lunacy is not continuous but occasional, and therefore the more dangerous. Outwardly he is an efficient and dignified petty officer, disliked rather than detested, and with a sagacious and sound judgement which he directs, as soon as Billy crosses his path, to the furtherance of insanity. Apparently friendly to the lad, who spills some soup across the deck,[14] he only reprimands him with 'handsomely done my lad. And handsome is as handsome did it, too[!]'[15] But he determines after that trivial encounter to destroy him, moved it would seem by reluc- tant love as well as by hate. He sets his subordinates to vex Billy secretly, he tries to tempt him through one of them to mutiny. All failing, he accuses him to the Captain.

The Captain is amazed. And in Captain Vere, the third of this unusual trio, Meville portrays a man who despite his education, understands. Yes, despite education. For the depths of human nature, he thought, are not revealed by study or books or even by experience and are sometimes obscured by them. Knowingness[16] never helps us to know. But Captain Vere, though conversant[17] with the world, has not lost his natural insight and he <u>knows</u> that Claggart is evil, Billy good. "You have but noted his fair cheek your honour" insinuates Claggart. "A mantrap may be under his ruddy-tipped daisies".[18] The Captain is contemptuous of the charge and summons both men to his cabin to examine it.

Then the catastrophe occurs. Billy, absolutely innocent, is utterly unprepared for the charge. The shock makes him speechless. Then the terrifying paralysing stammer, the diabolical inhibition starts. "The next instant, quick as the flame from a discharged cannon at night, his right arm shot out, and Claggart dropped to the deck".[19] He is dead. Evil is dead. But the avenging angel, the glorious athletic youth must die too.

The closing scenes, the visit of the surgeon, the drum head court, Billy's arraignment and condemnation, his final interview with Captain Vere (none other being present), the visit of the bewildered chaplain, the hanging from the yard arm, form a sequence of events which are poignantly human and also have an overtone, a halo which takes us into a region where thought fails, and events are in progress which cannot be put into words. Melville writes:

"The hull, deliberately recovering from the periodic roll to leeward, was just regaining an even keel, when the last signal, the preconcerted dumb one, was given. At the same moment it chanced that the vapouring cloud fleece hanging low was shot through with a soft glory as of the fleece of the Lamb of God seen in mystic vision, and simultaneously therewith, watched by the wedged mass of upturned faces, Billy ascended; and ascending took the full rose of the dawn.

"As the pinioned figure arrived at the yardend, to the wonder of all, no motion was apparent save that created by the slow roll of the hull, in moderate weather so majestic in a great ship heavy cannoned."[20]

Melville in this story shows what he most admires in human nature: natural goodness,[21] barbarian innocence, "unworldly servers of the world" is a phrase in one of his poems. And he also shows that this innocence is not safe in a civilisation like ours, where a man must practice a "ruled undemonstrative distrustfulness" in order to defend himself against traps. This 'ruled undemonstrative distrustfulness' is[22] not confined to business men, but exists everywhere. We all exercise it. I know I do, and I should be surprised if you, who are listening to me, didn't. All we can do (and Melville gives us this hint) is to exercise it consciously, as Captain Vere did.[23] It is unconscious distrustfulness that corrodes the heart and destroys the heart's insight, and prevents it from saluting goodness.

I hope I have said enough to commend this[24] unusual story, but must add a word of caution. The style is often clumsy and dowdy. Wonderful phrases leap out, the sum total is overwhelming, but if you judge young Billy by what he says and by much that is said of him, you'll think him an incredible stick. A little patience in reading is desireable, and a little humility, and the[25] short introduction to this edition by William Plomer[26] will put you in the proper mood.

To turn from these imaginative flights of genius to the two other books on my list means a heavy drop, especially when one of the books is about Queen Victoria. I recommend it though; it's title is <u>A Distant Summer</u>.[27] The author is Miss Edith Saunders.[28] It is about the visit of the Queen and the Prince Consort to France in 1855, and about all the expensive entertainments provided for them by their host, the Emperor Napoleon III.[29] <u>A Distant Summer</u> covers one week in time - a week of Parisian sunshine and happiness, Queen Victoria delighted, Albert sedately pleased. Napoleon III ebullient and humane, Empress Eugenie not jealous - nor has she cause to be - of the queen. Nothing but joy. But towards the end Bismarck appears as a guest - Bismarck who fifteen years later was to destroy the nineteenth-century dream, shatter the Western European symmetry and initiate that age in which we are struggling now.[30] Here again - as in the profound work of Melville - what is valid is goodness. The Prince Consort, who wants to serve the world, is contrasted with Napoleon III, who wants to exploit it.

The third book is the war diary of an Englishwoman who is married to an Italian nobleman, and it gives us an inside view of the Italian countryside during the years 1943 and 1944. It too is humane, civilised and courageous and the later entries are exciting. War in Val d'Orcia it is called,[31] the Orcia being one of the rivers of Tuscany, where the writer's estate lies. Her name is Marchesa Iris Origo.[32] She and her husband[33] risked their lives helping British prisoners of war and partisans.[34] But she describes it all quietly, as if it was part of the day's work and she returns to her ruined home with the conviction that the land will be ploughed again and blossom, and that hope is in the air.

1. <NOT>
2. <first>
3. < - not absolutely evil perhaps, but evil beyond the comprehension or control of man.>

4. <and I don't think there can>

5. EMF added accent marks above "Billy" and "Budd."

6. <about thirty years after his death.>

7. The May 1797 mutiny against living conditions at Nore, a naval shipyard in the Thames Estuary, was led by former officer Richard Parker; the mutiny was swiftly put down and its leaders hanged.

8. <merry>

9. Herman Melville, *Billy Budd*, ed. William Plomer (Luton: Leagrave Press, 1946), 28.

10. <Arch-fiend is more obvious.>

11. <that>

12. <man>

13. EMF added an accent mark about the first syllable of "maniac."

14. <and is only reprimanded>

15. Melville, *Billy Budd*, 51.

16. <men>

17. EMF added an accent mark above the second syllable of "conversant."

18. Melville, *Billy Budd*, 77.

19. Ibid., 83.

20. Ibid., 113. EMF altered Melville's "vapoury fleece" to "vapouring cloud fleece."

21. <athletic>

22. <most obvious in>

23. EMF added accent marks above the first syllables of "consciously" in this sentence and "unconscious" in the next.

24. <remarkable>

25. <there is a>

26. <, which>

27. Edith Saunders, *A Distant Summer* (London: S. Low, Marston, 1947).

28. <It's the sort of book which might be trivial, for>

29. <It is not trivial for it has historical sense, it describes pleasure sympathetically and attractively, and it is a very good shape. The shape of a book matters more than one realises.>

30. <Bismarck gives the book shape and raises it from a chronicle of banquets and balls into a work of art. And in the background subtly indicated by Miss Saunders is the Crimean War.>

31. Marchesa Iris Origo, *War in Val d'Orcia* (London: Jonathan Cape, 1947).

32. <She is anti-fascist, anti-Axis, and pro-Italian, and as an Italian she longs for peace.> EMF inserted cues into the script to spell out "Orcia" and "Origo" for listeners.

33. <risk>

34. <and she made a perilous journey in the June of 1944 taking her children and the others on foot through what was really the front line.>

Pre-rec.: 11.3.47
Rec. No.: DOX 84186
Dur.

Produced by John Arlott
219, Oxford Street

"SOME BOOKS"

By

E.M. Forster

Transmission:
EASTERN SERVICE: WEDNESDAY, 12th MARCH, 1947: 1505-1520 GMT

Repros.:
G.O.S.: Tues./Wed. 18/19th FEBRUARY - 2330-2345 GMT
N.AMERICAN: Mon./Tues. 17'18th FEBRUARY - 0000-0015 GMT.

ANNOUNCER:

This is London calling in the Eastern Service of the BBC. SOME BOOKS. Here is another book talk in our monthly series, given once again by Mr. E.M. Forster.

MR. FORSTER:

Here's a book called "The Writer's Responsibility", and here's another called Democracy and the Arts.[1] Both, as you will judge from their titles, discuss a problem of immediate interest to us: namely the relation of the artist to the community into which he is born. The artist is not an ordinary man - if he were the position would be simpler. He is extraordinary.[2] He[3] is specially sensitive, and in most cases[4] specially trained. Leonardo da Vinci, Goethe and Beethoven for instance are not ordinary, and even if you take three artists of lesser calibre - Sir Joshua Reynolds in painting, Leigh Hunt[5] in literature, Mendelssohn in music occur to me in passing - they too are not ordinary, they occupy a special position.

Yet these great people don't and can't exist outside the community. They have to eat,[6] they often fall in love and produce children who have to be educated, they utilise the public services. How are they to be fitted in? One solution is for the community to say to the artist "Give us what we want, and we'll give you what you want." That's state-controlled art, and it suits some artists. Others don't like it, and they say "No. [7]Not the community. We'll produce what we want, irrespective of its suitability". That's art for art's sake, and the community[8] doesn't always appreciate it.

In practice there is usually a compromise. And the two little books I've mentioned realise this in their different ways. One of them, The Writer's Responsibility, is by an American Mr. J. Donald Adams. Mr. Adams has been for the last twenty years the editor of the New York Times Book Review and so has had a good opportunity of surveying the American literary scene. He is mostly concerned with novels, which, as he rightly says, are particularly sensitive to the spirit of their time. He finds in American fiction at the beginning of the century a complacency which sprang from ignorance of life. This was followed by self-criticism and disillusion, and he discusses in detail the work of Theodore Dreiser and his influence - Dreiser whose novels certainly suggested that all was not beautiful in the American garden. The twenties and thirties of this century were unsatisfactory, Mr. Adams thinks, because they contributed nothing positive; they pricked holes in the old complacency (like Sinclair Lewis) or indulged in private fantasies (like James Branch Cabell[9]) or played about frivolously like Scott Fitzgerald. They weren't constructive, they didn't help the community as a whole. Today, he thinks, literature at all events in America has taken a turn for the better. It has been purified and steadied by the second world war. It is turning towards affirmation and away from the preferences of the self-appointed few. It will confirm, as Dunkirk did, the dignity of man.[10] Belonging as I do to the[11] dubious twenties, I do not altogether follow Mr. Adams in his optimism. It is too much like uplift. I am always suspicious of phrases like "self-appointed," and wonder whether the new complacency which he heralds will prove to be better-grounded than the old which he condemns. He subordinates the artist to the community too much for my taste. Still, he is never extreme or dogmatic. He does not believe the novelists and others ought to preach, even on a text handed out to them by the State. And he gives a most readable account of contemporary American fiction. Dreiser, Hemingway, Faulkner, Steinbeck; and other names less known to me like James Farrell and Elizabeth Madox Roberts,[12] and Thomas Wolfe. Possibly you in India are in closer touch with literary America than are we in Great Britain. Here we certainly don't know as much as we should. We haven't the curiosity about American writers which we extend to the French. It is a serious demerit, and Mr. Adams helps us to correct it.

The second book which I've mentioned - Democracy and the Arts - also bears on this problem of the Artist and the Community. The author is - of all people - Rupert Brooke.[13] I say 'of all people' because Rupert Brooke is usually regarded as a poet, a half mythical figure who died young and was buried on a Greek island. Brooke was[14] a great deal more than that. He was intensely interested in his surroundings. He became a Socialist, he joined the Fabian Society, he was a friend and contemporary at Cambridge of the present Chancellor of the Exchequer[15] and thirty-seven years ago at Cambridge he wrote this paper on Art and Democracy, now printed for the first time. It is a remarkable paper. It has the vigour and aggressiveness of youth in it, the cockiness appropriate to a high-spirited boy; and that one might expect. It has also - and this makes it remarkable[16] - a prophetic quality. It foresees, in 1910, the problem of the artist and the community which confronts us today. And it offers practical solutions which are still worth considering.

Rupert Brooke asserts that Art is important and that the people who have produced it hitherto have either had private means or been supported by patrons. All that is disappearing in the economic revolution which he foresaw and welcomed, and, in the future, if the community doesn't subsidise Art there won't be any. Art, he insists, is a full-time job, you can't do it in your spare moments, and he ridicules William Morris' idea that a man ought to compose poetry while he is working at a loom. Don't mix up Art and Crafts he cries, "It is so easy to do so, and it is tempting to slide from the keen edge of Art into the byways, the pursuits that don't disturb." And don't talk rubbish about Art expressing the soul of the community. "The community hasn't got a soul. You can't voice the soul of the community any more than you can blow its nose."[17] Art is and always will be an individual and unique affair.

Now the community may not have a soul or a nose, but it may be said to have a pocket. It can subsidise. And the latter half of Rupert Brooke's paper discusses why it is worth its while to pay for Art and how the payment can be made. Worth-while, because in the long run the fineness (not the refinement) of Art can enter into many men's lives, and delight can be widespread. He emphasises the difference between fineness and refinement - the latter[18] is only appreciated by cultured cliques, and is unimportant. And he has no illusion that most people are going to care even for fineness yet. "The first generation of universal education has not given us a nation of art lovers. Nor will the second. Nor the third. We must face the problem that public demand isn't going to settle it" That's frank. And franker still is his admission that Art has to be supported by people who don't understand it. They often pretend they do. They lie. But they are necessary. "Concerts, one hears, are hard enough to get up at Cambridge as it is. If only those who cared for the music went, they would be impossible. The Arts are built up on a crowd of prattlers, dilettanti, wits and pseudo-cultured. It is worth while."[19]

Then he discusses how this queer product, which at present only a few people care for, can be protected until everyone cares for it and he works out a system of subsidy. He suggests a committee of about thirty to advise a Cabinet Minister,[20] and the endowment for life of two hundred musicians and as many painters, sculptors, poets and prose writers. They are to be given £500 a year each (these are 1910 prices you must remember) at a cost to the treasury of half a million, and if anyone wants to realise the insignificance of half a million let him consider modern expenditure on armaments. The subsidised artists won't be required to show results - the wastage resulting from their idleness or their dissipation will be negligible. But they will not be allowed to fritter away their time by teaching or criticising. If they do want an alternative to creation, let them be given something disgusting to do, like cleaning sewers.

Those are the chief points in this remarkable pamphlet. Of course it is written extravagantly and provocatively. The young man is throwing his weight about and teasing socialists and non-socialists alike. But it should not be dismissed as an undergraduate's squib. There is wisdom in it which Dr. Hugh Dalton, who heard it then in those far off days, might profit by now. It does face up to the problem of the artist and the community. It realises that most people don't care for good literature, music and painting. It looks forward to a day when they will[21] care for them. Meanwhile the state will have to do something. I like it better than Mr. Donald Adams' book - both are hopeful, but I prefer the quality of Brooke's[22] hopefulness. And it comes to me, with a curious shock, that I have been preparing this broadcast for you at Cambridge within a few yards of the very room where he once read his paper to the University Fabian Society. So little space divides us. So many years. Had Brooke lived, I am not sure that he would have increased his reputation as a poet. But he would certainly have become a live wire in public affairs, and an energetic and enlightened administrator. He had the necessary mixture of toughness and idealism.[23]

CLOSING ANNOUNCEMENT: That was Mr. E.M. Forster speaking in the series SOME BOOKS.

The next programme in this series on April 9th, that is in a month's time, will be given by Mr. Daniel George.[24]

1. James Donald Adams, *The Writer's Responsibility* (London: Secker and Warburg, 1946); Rupert Brooke, *Democracy and the Arts* (London: Rupert Hart-Davis, 1946).
2. EMF added accent marks above the first two syllables of "extraordinary."
3. <has special sensitiveness>
4. <special training which differentiates him>

5. <Byron>

6. <, for instance,>

7. <Damn>

8. EMF added an accent mark above "community."

9. James Branch Cabell (1879–1958), Virginia novelist best known for his eighteen-volume *The Biography of the Life of Manuel* (1927–1930).

10. From 26 May to 4 June 1940, 338,000 Allied troops were evacuated from the French port of Dunkirk under fire, some in civilian vessels, after the failure of an invasion intended to stop Hitler's advance. Despite this disastrous defeat, Winston Churchill rallied the nation in a 4 June 1940 address to the House of Commons, saluting the heroic rescue of so many and vowing that Britain would fight Germany in Europe as well as on the beaches and fields at home and never surrender.

11. <regrettable>

12. James T. Farrell (1904–1979), Irish American writer best known for his Studs Lonigan novels; Elizabeth Madox Roberts (1881–1941), novelist and poet, best known for *The Great Meadow* (1930), inspired by her pioneer ancestors' travels into Kentucky with Daniel Boone.

13. Furbank notes the skepticism in EMF's response to Brooke, whom he knew (*A Life*, 2:18–19).

14. <that. But he was>

15. Dr. Hugh Dalton (1887–1962), mentioned later in the broadcast, was chancellor of the exchequer from 1945 to 1947.

16. EMF added accent marks above "youth" and "that" in the prior sentence and the second syllable of "remarkable."

17. Brooke, *Democracy and the Arts*, 5, 6.

18. <being>

19. Ibid., 11, 27.

20. <to endow>

21. EMF added an accent mark above "will."

22. EMF added an accent mark above "Brooke's."

23. EMF wrote the final sentence and "enlightened administrator" of the prior sentence, typed on p. 6 of his script, at the bottom of p. 5, presumably so that he could finish his delivery without turning the page.

24. Pseudonym of David George Bunting, minor author and anthologist.

AS RECORDED   Producer: Robin Russell
DOX 91441.   213 O.S.
Dur: 3'18"
Rec. 5.8.47.

"MESSAGE TO INDIA"

by

E.M. FORSTER

TRANSMISSION: Eastern Service; Friday, 15th August, 1947; 1615-1630 GMT[1]

Today, the country I have known as India enters the past and becomes part of history. A new period opens, and my various Indian friends are now citizens of the new India or of Pakistan. You must excuse me if I begin with my friends. They are much in my mind on this momentous occasion. It is nearly forty years since I met, here in England, the late Syed Ross Masood. But for Masood I should never have come to your part of the world. And but for another friend, the late Maharajah of Dewas Senior, I might never have returned to it. I mention these two names to indicate my position. The tie that has bound me in the past is affection. And today, with the future dawning, I think with love of those who are gone, and I wish the beloved ones who remain happiness and strength and peace.

After my friends, I think of my fellow authors. A writer by profession, I want to send a word of good will to Indian writers. May they interpret their ways to us, and may they interpret us to ourselves, thus increasing our sense of life. But I wish they were better paid. Here is my advice on this point: Indian writers must organise; otherwise they will be exploited. It is for them to decide what form the organisation or organisations should take, but some kind of Society of Authors seems necessary. I hope too that the new governments who today come into being will realise the importance of literature, more fully than has been done in the West.

After writing, I think of the visual arts, especially painting. I have seen and enjoyed some modern work, at Santineketan[2] and in Calcutta, and while I was preparing this broadcast in my London flat, there hung above me on the wall, looking at me as it were and maybe inspiring me, a picture by the contemporary painter Jamini Roy - a fine picture and a valued gift.[3] May the visual arts prosper. Good luck to your architecture! Good luck to your films! And may you preserve and extend your ancient heritage of music. May you also preserve your antiquities - the marvellous buildings of the past scattered all over the sub-continent, many of them in a disastrous state of repair. Here again is work for the governments to be.

I dwell on these topics because they are too seldom dwelt on. I know that your urgent problems are still economic and political, and others with more authority than myself will be referring to them. But culture counts too, by culture in the long run is a community judged, and it is part of my duty today to greet it in the new India and in Pakistan, and to wish it well.

1. See the General Introduction for details about EMF's invitation to broadcast on the occasion of Indian independence.

2. On the school founded by Tagore, see note 6 for the 3 July 1946 broadcast.

3. See Furbank, *A Life*, 2:261, and Francis Watson, "The Case of Jamini Roy" (*Listener*, 9 May 1946, p. 620), an illustrated review of Roy's London exhibition at the Arcade Gallery, which EMF opened.

Producer: Rex Moortoot,
Room 802, Bush

As Broadcast
Pre-recorded: 10.3.48
No: DIO 25640
Duration of talk and reading: 15'05"

IT'S GOOD ENGLISH

by

E.M. FORSTER.

Biographies[1]

TRANSMISSION:
ENGLISH PROGRAMME
FAR EASTERN SERVICE   Tuesday, 13th April 1948

It's Good English! This is a weekly programme in which the speaker selects one of his favourite passages of English writing and talks about it - gives his reasons why he thinks it is good English.[2] Today the well-known writer, E.M. Forster, has selected a passage from the Biography of George Crabbe, written by his son.

THE PASSAGE IS READ BY JOHN MORRIS

MR. FORSTER:

You are going to hear an extract from a biography of which I am extremely fond: it is the biography of the poet, George Crabbe, written by his son.[3] Crabbe himself is familiar to you, and he has become still better known of late owing to the opera of Peter Grimes, which is founded on one of his poems.[4] His son is not well known, and but for this life of his father would be forgotten. It is one of those natural books which appear occasionally in literature. The writer has not been trained professionally, he isn't smart, and his sentences sometimes go clumsy. But he loves his subject, namely his father - that is one thing; he loves the country where he and his father before him were brought up - that is another thing; and, thirdly, he has an eye and an ear which are sensitive, so that he can bring the father and the countryside before us vividly.

In the passage to be read the poet himself doesn't appear. It is about local life, and a word of introduction may be helpful. The scene is East Anglia, where the family belonged. The particular county is Suffolk, which is today still agricultural and little touched by industrialism. The particular village is Parham, a very quiet place lost in the heart of Suffolk. And the particular spot to be considered in Parham is a substantial house, half manor-house, half farm, and it belongs to Mr. Tovell, the poet's uncle by marriage. They go to pay him a visit there in a gig, father and son, and the son, writing in after years, recalls the visit with excitement and affection. His age at the time was six, he was dressed for the first time as a grown-up little boy, and he was dressed in scarlet. They arrive, he enters and we enter with him. The date is 1791, and the month - months are more permanent than years - is September.

EXTRACT FROM "THE LIFE OF GEORGE CRABBE"
BY HIS SON.
JOHN MORRIS:

On entering the house, there was nothing at first sight to remind one of the farm: a spacious hall, paved with black and white marble - at one extremity a very handsome drawing-room, and at the other a fine old staircase of black oak, polished till it was as slippery as ice, and having a chime-clock and a barrel-organ on its landing-places. But this drawing-room, a corresponding dining parlour, and a handsome sleeping apartment up stairs, were all tabooed ground, and made use of on great and solemn occasions only - such as rent days, and an occasional visit with which Mr. Tovell was honoured by a neighbouring peer. At all other times the family and their visitors lived entirely in the old-fashioned kitchen along with the servants. My great-uncle occupied an arm-chair, or, in attacks of gout, a couch on one side of a large open chimney. Mrs. Tovell sat at a small table, on which, in the evening, stood one small candle, in an iron candlestick, plying her needle by the feeble glimmer, surrounded by her maids, all busy at the same employment; but in winter a noble block of wood, sometimes the whole circumference of a pollard, threw its comfortable warmth and cheerful blaze over the apartment.

At a very early hour in the morning, the alarum called the maids, and their mistress also; and if the former were tardy, a louder alarum, and more formidable, was heard chiding the delay - not that scolding was peculiar to any occasion, it regularly ran on through all the day, like bells on harness, in spiriting the work, whether it were done ill or well. After the important business of the dairy, and a hasty breakfast, their respective employments were again resumed; that which the mistress took for her especial privilege being the scrubbing of the floors of the state apartments. A new servant, ignorant of her presumption, was found one morning on her knees, hard at work on the floor of one of these preserves, and was thus addressed by her mistress: "<u>You</u> wash such floors as these? Give me the brush this instant, and troop to the scullery and wash that, madam! . . . As true as G—d's in heaven, here comes Lord Rochford, to call on Mr. Tovell. - Here, take my mantle (a blue woolen apron), and I'll go to the door!"

If the sacred apartments had not been opened, the family dined on this wise: the heads seated in the kitchen at an old table; the farm-men standing in the adjoining scullery, door open - the female servants at a side table, called a <u>bouter</u>; with the principals, at the table, perchance some travelling rat-catcher, or tinker, or farrier, or an occasional gardener in his shirt-sleeves, his face probably streaming with perspiration.[5]

E.M. FORSTER:

Yes, the writer has entered Mr. Tovell's house at Parham and we have entered with him. We really are there, and that is the chief reason why the passage you have just heard is good English. It has done its job. It has taken us, without pretentiousness or fuss, into the heart of a house, into a corner of a vanished rural community. The writer is simple and sincere, he is remembering facts affectionately and accurately, his heart has gone out to the past, his memory recalls the details in it, and so without being literary he has achieved one of the aims of literature, namely shared his emotional experiences with the reader. You know how sometimes when you are reading a book, and maybe it's quite a good book, you feel "Yes, I'm sure it's good, but somehow I'm not there. The author's there, but I'm not there. He hasn't succeeded in taking me with him. I wonder why." The answer is either that the author couldn't make things vivid, or that he was self-conscious, and more interested in himself than in what he described. Suppose in the above passage the writer had been self-conscious. He would have continually visualised himself at Parham as the little boy in scarlet whom he only incidentally refers to. He would have described the little boy skipping up the stairs or sitting by the hearth, or saying this or that to his uncle or aunt, and his effects would have become strained and inacceptable; he would have been calling us into himself, instead of away with himself to the past. We shouldn't have reached the past. We get straight there, thanks to his integrity. He is not self-conscious. Nor is he dull. (A writer may have integrity, and yet be a crashing bore.) He is sensitive as well as sincere. He has eyes and ears that register. There is another passage - I wish there was time for you to hear it also - which is lyric, and into which nightingales and glow-worms enter. He can take us into the lanes and coppices at night when he chooses, as well as into that solid old house. It has gone, that old house, I am sorry to say. I was near Parham a couple of years ago, and hoped to visit it. But it had gone. And the life it had sheltered vanished even in young Crabbe's day, when Mr. Tovell died.

This then is my main point about the passage. It is good English because it does its job. It sets out to describe a house in Suffolk and the life led there, and it lets nothing get in the way, with the result that we actually see the rat-catcher sitting down at the hospitable board, or the presumptuous servant rising from her knees and retiring to scrub the scullery. And it succeeds because the writer wasn't thinking about himself, because he had eyes and ears and a good memory, and because he had thoroughly enjoyed himself as a child.

I'll add two notes, analysing some minor effects, but I want to emphasise that the writer did not achieve these effects deliberately. They arrived because he was keen on his subject.

In the first sentence: "a spacious hall paved with black and white marble - at one extremity a very handsome drawing-room, and at the other a fine old staircase of black oak". These words are in themselves not interesting. They are a bit of a bore. They suggest ye olde English interior, beloved of Washington Irvine,[6] and what ho the wassail bowl. But the sentence goes on ". . . a fine old staircase of black oak, polished till it was as slippery as ice, and having a chime-clock and a barrel organ on its landing places." The slipperiness, the clock, and the organ reassure. They are what the writer observed. He was there. And so we are there.

Take another sentence: "Mrs. Tovell sat at a small table, on which, in the evening, stood one small candle, in an iron candlestick, plying her needle by the feeble glimmer." Experiment with that sentence by removing the words "in an iron candlestick" and you will find that most of its magic disappears. The iron candlestick is the little piece of extra observation that does the trick. The writer, without thinking the problem out, put it in, and clamps the old lady and her attendants into our imagination. There they sit, 150 years later, still plying their antique chores, and there in its iron candlestick, their one small candle burns.

There is one small etymological difficulty in the extract - namely the word 'bouter', which does not occur elsewhere in English literature. 'Bouter' is a dialect word and apparently means outside - the side table at which the female servants sat. Otherwise the extract runs straightforwardly. There are no aesthetic subtleties to discuss, no intellectual arguments to follow. We are concentrated on the subject, the old house, and this being so, you should want to know what happened to the old house when Mr. Tovell died. For he did die, the very next year.

Well, he left Parham to the Crabbes. Everything became theirs - farm, servants, slippery black staircase, barrel-organ, chime-clock - and full of joy and expectation they moved in. The poet - who was a clergyman - gave up his living in Leicestershire, and prepared to play the substantial yeoman, and his little son, and future biographer, cried "Here we are - here we are, little Willy and all", as they descended from their chaise and took possession of their property.[7]

Alas! The magic had passed. As soon as they owned Parham it turned to dust and ashes in their hands. The poet could not run the estate, or roister with his neighbours; his politics were suspect, his wife a nervous invalid, old Mrs. Tovell remained alive, weeping, and Mr. Tovell's sister, an acidulated spinster, stayed near, criticising all that the new owners did and complaining that things were not what they were used to be. Nor were they, and the biography here presents to us in its unobtrusive fashion a profound truth. For Parham died when old Mr. Tovell died. His heirs belonged to a different tradition, and with the best will in the world and with enthusiasm and love they could not carry on. In after years, when the little boy grew up and looked back, it was his romantic arrival there as a guest that remained important, not the futile period of his possession. There is, in all our lives, a difference between what we really own and what we own legally. Title deeds and legacies cannot confer what the spirit withholds. He really owned his visit to Parham, not the house itself. That visit became his lasting possession, and, thanks to him, we possess it too.

1. Handwritten addition (not EMF's).

2. The series ran from 13 April 1948 to 9 January 1949; other series broadcasters included Desmond MacCarthy, Hesketh Pearson, Lord David Cecil, and C. Day Lewis.

3. EMF wrote the introduction to *The Life of George Crabbe, by His Son* (London: Oxford University Press, 1932), vii–xix. There he characterizes the account of the "Tovells in all their glory" as "brilliant" (xii).

4. See EMF's broadcast dated 3 July 1945.

5. Crabbe, *Life*, 136–38.

6. EMF refers to Washington Irving. Much of *The Sketch Book of Geoffrey Crayon, Gent.* (first published in England in 1820) concerns historic English scenes.

7. Crabbe, *Life*, 144. Willy was, as the biography explains, Crabbe's "seventh and youngest child" (144 n. 1).

As Recorded:

Producer: John Morris,
Bush House

Pre-recorded 12.00 - 12.30 2.1.49
Disc. No: DBU 25141
Duration: 10'50''[1]

I SPEAK FOR MYSELF

by

E. M. FORSTER

TRANSMISSION:
ENGLISH PROGRAMME   1200 GMT
FAR EASTERN SERVICE   Tuesday, 11th January, 1949

LEAD-IN: This is the first of a new series of talks under the title "I Speak
for Myself" in which people distinguished in various walks
of life will tell you of some of the things that have exercised
them or influenced them at one time or another. We are very
happy that Mr. E.M. Forster, perhaps the most distinguished
living writer, has consented to give the opening talk in the
series. He has just celebrated his seventieth birthday and the
British press during the past week has had much to say about
the unique position he enjoys in the literary world. He does
not often broadcast and we are particularly fortunate to get
him to come to the microphone at the present time. Many listeners will probably have read "A Passage to India", his best-
known novel, and if so they will not need to be reminded that
Mr. Forster has long been greatly interested in the East.

E.M. FORSTER:
    I try to speak for myself. It is impossible to speak for someone else - one
cannot get inside another person's skin - and it is dangerous to speak on
behalf of a group or community, though most of us do that at times. A man

is only safe and straight when he realises he is an individual and speaks for himself. He is then fulfilling the purpose for which he was born into this troublesome and difficult world. No doubt the world was always difficult, but it can never have been so full of movements as it is today - so full of appeals to the individual to sink his individuality and allow some organisation or movement to speak for him. It is[2] even put before him as a duty. In my view it is a dereliction of duty. I imagine[3] a Last Judgement in which we shall be asked not only "What did you say?" but "Did you say anything at all?" It will not profit us at that hour to indicate[4] that the party or organisation to which we adhered had constant access to the microphone. We shall be judged by what we ourselves have said. In the end, as in the beginning, is the Word.

"Speaking for oneself" is a phrase which must not[5] be interpreted too crudely. It does not[6] mean clucking like a hen or even singing like a lark. It means - amongst other things - the power to realise that other people also speak. I am[7] holding forth now, I have got at the microphone for the moment, and my voice, much distorted by atmospherics, is offering itself overseas. Part of my job is to remember that you too speak, that you too are an individual. I can't know what you're like[8] - your upbringing and your mother tongue are probably different from my own, and your experience of life may well be deeper - but I do know that you are a person who can answer back if he chooses, and that if I assert my personality properly I shall assert yours. Myself, I am an Englishman, middle-class, aged 70, and of literary education and proclivities, and you - you may be Chinese, working-class, scientifically educated, and aged 17. Or you may be Japanese, Malay and so on. What possible link can there be between us? Well, just this one. We both of us can speak for ourselves, and if we speak properly can listen.[9] We know we are individuals - that's a start - and if we ever met should have that much basis for intercourse. It is no great importance my being English and so on, and - with all respect to you - it is no great importance your being Chinese or whatever it is.[10] What matters is our common humanity - and I intend those[11] words not in a vague sentimental way but as a truth which has to be utilised each[12] time two human beings meet. As one goes about,[13] one takes too much for granted, one gets blunted and blurred, and I don't think[14] the cinema or the newspapers or the wireless, or other modern gadgets, are helpful in sharpening us up. They promote passive acceptance of the world instead of increased wonder. What does sharpen us is talking personally, with its correlative, listening. Talking and listening do get the human race on a little and help it towards the tolerance which is requisite for its existence, and towards the love which is the reason for its existence.

I speak for myself, then, in the belief that by so doing I emphasise your right to speak for yourself, and our joint duty to listen to one another. That being agreed, I[15] pass on.

A subject[16] I've been thinking about today is the employment of leisure, particularly leisure under industrialism. The world, whether peaceful or warlike, is likely to become more industrialised during the next century, and it is hard for some of us to realise what this means. A few people will find their work interesting and varied, as work often has been in the past, but they will only be a tiny aristocracy of labour, they will[17] have special jobs. The vast majority will find it dull, or at best[18] colourless. They will[19] be directed to specialise on some insignificant mechanical detail, and will have to go on[20] year after year. The factory, with its routine, will replace the open air with its variety of the seasons. I know a girl who worked in a factory through[21] the last war, and her job was to stamp out of pieces of metal, the little pointers which were to go on the dials on time-bombs. She was not[22] concerned with the dials themselves, nor with the bombs. It was stamp a pointer, stamp a pointer, stamp a pointer. At first she was worried by the work, then she was bored by it, and finally she didn't notice it.[23] Phrases like the 'joy of work' and the 'glory of work' and the 'creativeness of work', which may have been appropriate during the 19th century, could have no meaning[24] for this child of the 20th century, and any suggestion that she was, or ought to be, an artist in her small way, would[25] have made her guffaw. Why should she use up anything good in her on stamp-a-pointer, stamp-a-pointer?[26] To do so would be suicide of the spirit. All that is good in the average industrial worker, all that is spiritual or creative, has to be reserved for the leisure period. Leisure is important, not because it rests us from having stamped pointers, or strengthens us to stamp more pointers, but because, in leisure and in leisure only, the proper activity of our race can now be continued. Some people still try to keep romantic over work, and to pretend that it can be made interesting. I don't believe it can be[27] - except for a very small minority. The analogy between work and craftsmanship must be dropped, and imagination[28] concentrated upon leisure, upon the holidays. You, to whom I'm talking, may not[29] be as industrialised as we are over here, and industrialism may be on the wane. But there are no present signs of it,[30] and I am anxious that we should shake ourselves out of our conventional respect towards work, admit[31] that it is a soul-scarifying nuisance, that leisure alone can have merit, and then be very careful how we spend our leisure.

You will[32] find plenty of people who are anxious to spend your leisure for you. They will[33] shepherd you into clubs, youth organisations and so on, and tempt you with instructional films. This may be all right, but sometimes there is an ulterior motive, so keep your eyes open, and if the instructional film seems to be instructing you on the sanctity of work, keep them very wide open. The true purpose of leisure is to wake you up to the wonder of the universe into which you have[34] been born, and to some understanding of it, and to help you to speak for yourself, and to listen to others when they speak. That[35] achieved, you are a real individual, you are a human being, you are safe, you can go into a factory if you have to and stamp as many pointers as you like[36] without bothering.

Last year I heard our present Minister of Education,[37] Mr. Tomlinson, make a speech at a prize-giving at a technical school. He[38] was admirable. There were three reasons for education he said: to make a living, to help other people, and to understand and enjoy the world, and he emphasised the third reason as the essential one. Mr. Tomlinson had worked as a lad in a Lancashire cotton mill he told us: he had[39] always liked reading and on one occasion he had let the looms stop because he was thinking about Hamlet. His overseer, who like him was paid by the piece, was naturally outraged. "I'll 'Amlet you", he shouted, "I'll teach you about 'Amlet." But Hamlet had already been learnt. That strange and profound truth that the world is marvellous, that there are two sides to a question, that we must all speak for ourselves, had already sunk into the boy's mind.
EW[40]   (114 lines)

1. EMF's departures from the written script, preserved in the National Sound Archive (NSA) recording of this talk, are given below.

2. NSA: "It's"

3. NSA: "I can imagine"

4. NSA: "if we indicate." The familiar reading cue of the first word of the next page at the bottom of a given page appears throughout this script, beginning with "constant."

5. NSA: "mustn't"

6. NSA: "doesn't"

7. NSA: "I'm"

8. The rest of this and the next two sentences were cut from the broadcast though not from the script. NSA: "I can't know what you're like. What possible link can there be between us?"

9. NSA: "We can both of us speak for ourselves, and if we're speaking properly, we can listen."

10. NSA: "It's" rather than "it is" in the first two instances.

11. NSA: "these"

12. NSA: "every"

13. NSA: "around"

14. NSA: "think that"

15. NSA: "I'll"

16. NSA: "Now a subject"

17. NSA: "they'll"

18. NSA: "at the best"

19. NSA: "They'll"

20. NSA: "on at it"

21. NSA: "throughout"

22. NSA: "wasn't"

23. NSA: "didn't notice it. She just went on."

24. NSA: "meaning whatever"

25. NSA: "would very rightly"

26. NSA: EMF added a third "stamp-a-pointer" to the end of the sentence.

27. NSA: "I don't believe it *can*"

28. NSA: "imagination must be concentrated"

29. NSA: "mayn't"

30. NSA: "that"

31. NSA: "work, that we should admit"

32. NSA: "Now you'll"

33. NSA: "They'll"

34. NSA: "you've"

35. NSA: "Thus"

36. NSA: "have to"

37. NSA: "Education over here."

38. NSA: "Mr. Tomlinson" EMF refers to the Honorable George Tomlinson, Labour minister of education, 1947–1951.

39. NSA: "he'd"

40. Unidentified.

Rehearsal:	1.00-1.30
Record:	1.30-2.00
Studio:	Mixer 2
NO:	DOX 58756
Recorded:	15.6.51

Production by: T. Cooper
412 O.S.

<u>SATURDAY REVIEW</u>[1]

TRANSMISSION: 16TH JUNE 1951: 1320-1350 GMT

BAND ONE [ANNOUNCER]:
Dox 58756

This week the Festival of Britain[2] has blossomed out in several more places up and down the country. At the east coast village of Aldeburgh, the home of the composer Benjamin Britten, the programme has naturally been predominantly musical. On the Monday morning the Apollo Society[3] presented another of those programmes wedding poetry and chamber music which are quite a new feature of cultural life in England to-day. Just over a week ago in London a similar entertainment was given with participation of Cecil Day-Lewis the poet, who is also a superb reader of verse, Dame Edith Evans the actress, and John Hunt, the pianist. As an example of the contents of these programmes I would mention that at the London recital extracts from Alexander Pope's Moral Essays were grouped with Mozart's Phantasie in D. Minor, and Wordsworth's Immortality Ode was read between the first and third movements of a Beethoven Sonata. It's an interesting experiment, though, at first sight, the association of some of the poetry and music seems to be largely a matter of personal taste or idiosyncrasy.

Up in York, the revival, after many centuries, of the famous York cycle of medieval plays depicting events from biblical history has won unanimous praise from the dramatic critics. At another cathedral city, Salisbury, a new play by the well-known dramatist Ronald Duncan, based on a pious legend, has been performed with success.[4] An amusing comment on the contemporary scene is given in a new revue being presented at the little

Lyric Theatre out at Hammersmith.[5] There all our national weaknesses and follies are exposed to derision, and everyone enjoys it. Best of all is Noel Coward's song 'Don't Make Fun of the Festival' sung by two gloomy English couples in mackintoshes and holding up umbrellas, their noses red with cold, grimly proclaiming that it's the duty of every Englishman to be happy and gay this Festival summer.

Besides many important exhibition[s] of paintings, mostly by French nineteenth century artists, there is also to be a seen a collection of works by well-known people who paint for pleasure. It includes works by royal duchesses, field marshals, film stars, politicians, actors and newspaper proprietors. The works are to be sold for charity, and should fetch good prices, if only for their value as curios.[6]

BAND THREE [ANNOUNCER]:

Dox 58756

Meanwhile the sleepy seaside village of Aldeburgh between the marshes and the sea, has woken from its summer slumbers for the brief fortnight of its annual Festival of the Arts.[7] Amongst those taking part in the Festival has been the distinguished novelist, Mr. E.M. Forster. We had hoped that he could speak personally of the Aldeburgh Festival, but he's unfortunately broken his ankle[8] and has not been able to come up to London, so that to-night his talk is being read by Robert Finnigan.[9] Here is Mr. E.M. Forster's account of the Aldeburgh Festival:

FINIGAN: The fourth Aldeburgh Festival of Music and the Arts began with a peal of bells from the church tower, and this was so impressive and is so characteristic that I want to begin here too. There are six bells and the ringers played on them for three hours, the sounds floating out in the summer evening over the estuary and the marshes and the sea. How different this summer scene is to the wild winter storms that prevail along these shores and which keep the Aldeburgh Lifeboatmen constantly on the alert. The bellringers played what is technically known as a Spliced Peal of Surprise Minor in 5040 changes. I can't explain that in detail, but I stood for a time in the nave of the church and saw the ringers at work on their Surprise Minor and heard the curious noise half cry half cough, which their leader made when a change in sequence was due. This bell-ringing by hand - instead of by machine - is typically English, and the Aldeburgh Festival is English: not international, Not British, but English.

It was started by a Suffolk composer, Benjamin Britten. He has a house in the place, close to the beach; which rises on a ridge of shingle above the level of the village street; and out of this protective ridge - this rampart of shingle rises a flag-staff flying the pretty flag of the Festival - dark blue and light blue, and across it runs a stave of music from Britten's best

known opera, "Peter Grimes". Another of his operas, "Albert Herring", is
being performed now, and the action of both these operas is set in the
neighbourhood of Aldeburgh. Britten is also giving his Cantata, "St.
Nicholas",[10] and has produced an opera by the 17th century English composer Purcell, on the subject of Dido and Aeneas. Unaccompanied choruses
or Madrigals will be sung on a lake nearby. Handel's oratorio of Jeptha,
which he was encouraged to compose by King George III, has already
been given in the Aldeburgh Church, and from the top of its tower on the
last day of the festival hymns will be sung by the choir, to [end] the Festival as the bells began it.

Yes: it's an English affair which draws sustenance from local soil, and is
freshened by the breezes of the North Sea. There's a fishing exhibition to
take another example, which a young Aldeburgh fisherman has helped to
arrange.[11] And another exhibition, of Suffolk topography, and a bird film
about the Avocet. And together with this English stuff are some exquisite
foreign importations. Some songs by Brahms, an evening devoted to the
music of Verdi, and the Concerto for violin and viola by Mozart. It's all
most enjoyable, and the weather has been English too - perhaps almost too
much so: the sunshine has been interrupted by thunderstorms and by
scud - scud being the local fog which sometimes drifts in from the sea: it
only penetrates a few miles inland, but Aldeburgh lies well within its range.

The Festival is popular in the town - flags are flying, little tubs of gera-
niums cling to the electric light standards. And there are over a hundred
local guarantors. Unfortunately the seats are expensive, especially for the
operas: they are bound to be expensive - the Festival couldn't otherwise be
run at all - but this means that only the wealthier people can attend. Most
of the audience drive in from outside or are stopping at the hotels. This is,
I think, the problem that faces Aldeburgh and other flourishing centres of
regional culture. They can express the local spirit and common local
enthusiasm. But they can't count on local attendance, because they must
charge high: if they don't they fail. There is here something rotten in the
stage of England. How is it to be remedied? State subsidies is the only
answer that occurs to me. What do you think?[12]

1. Part of a Saturday Review series.

2. The five-month Festival of Britain was held to provide a postwar "tonic to the nation"
and to demonstrate, in the words of Lord Ramsdem, chair of the first official committee,
"the recovery of the United Kingdom from the effects of War in the moral, spiritual, and
material fields." See Asa Briggs, "Exhibiting the Nation," *History Today* 50.1 (January 2000):
16–25.

3. The Apollo Society Ltd, incorporated on 11 June 1947, was a philanthropic organization founded to advance education through drama, dance, instrumental and choral music, and other art forms. Peggy Ashcroft and C. Day Lewis were among the founding subscribers. Our thanks to Elizabeth Pridmore, King's College Archives, for providing details.

4. Ronald Duncan (1914–1982) wrote *Our Lady's Tumbler*, a religious verse play first performed specifically for the Festival of Britain at Salisbury Cathedral on 5 June 1951.

5. *The Lyric Revue* (an H. M. Tennent production, with music by Michael Flanders and Donald Swann), opened on 24 May 1951. The skits included *"Peter Pan* as Mr. Tennessee Williams might rewrite it; *Cinderella* revised by Freud" (*Times*, 25 May 1951, p. 2).

6. We omit portions of the broadcast by James Laver, director of the Prints Department, Victoria and Albert Museum, about the exhibition entitled "Splendid Occasion," and by the Maharaj Kumari Indira of Kapurthala about the Ascot Races.

7. The Aldeburgh Festival, founded in 1948, is closely associated with composer Benjamin Britten, who moved to Aldeburgh in 1947.

8. See Furbank, *A Life*, 2:286.

9. Most likely this was R(obert) J(ames) Finigan, a staff announcer with the Overseas Programme Operations (Presentation) during the early 1950s. The script first refers to him as "Finnigan," then as "Finigan." Our thanks to Trish Hayes, BBC WAC, for details on Finigan.

10. The cantata, with libretto by Eric Crozier, debuted on 5 June 1948, the first day of the inaugural Aldeburgh Festival. EMF was present and discussed the performance in his talk on 20 June 1948, published in the *Listener*, 8 July 1948, pp. 1011, 1013.

11. Perhaps Bill Burrell, the fisherman whom Furbank describes as "a handsome and good-natured young man"; EMF occasionally visited Burrell and his wife in subsequent years (Furbank, *A Life*, 2:285).

12. The broadcast concluded with remarks by Mrs. Sylvia Matheson about the Covent Garden flower show earlier in the week.

[1]CHECKED IN TALKS DEPARTMENT WITH 'AS BROADCAST' SCRIPT
Producer: P. H. Newby

Fifth Anniversary of the Third Programme - by E.M. Forster

Disc No: MTLO 10680
Transmission: Saturday, 29th September, 1951. 7.45 - 8.20 p.m.
Repeat: CMDLO Monday, 1st October, 1951. 9.45 - 10.20 p.m.
25'50"   THIRD PROGRAMME

The Third Programme couldn't exist apart from the Home Service and the Light Programme. It is inseparable from them, and that point must be made before attempting any eulogy of it. It is also supplementary to them. It came into existence last, and is the youngest and[2] maybe the trickiest cherub of the air. It does or should do the unexpected. It does[3] what the other two programmes don't do, and if it doesn't do things it is because they already do them. It is exclusive and is meant to be exclusive for the reason that the important matters it excludes are dealt with elsewhere. Realisation of this would save many a critic of it from much bad temper.

But do critics want to be saved from bad temper? Ah! This is a painful subject to which I may have to return. Meanwhile let us contemplate this aerial trio: Home, Light, Third.

The Home I always visualise as the Father of a Family, whose main interests are politics and sport, but he is very fair minded, likes music and is anxious[4] that[5] all his listeners should have something[6] to enjoy, provided they are not criminals or cranks. The Light I visualise as an eternal debutante, always swinging down the dance, though this view of her is[7] too simple: she too dabbles in politics and wrestles with sport, moreover she can handle the arts also, as in her excellent "Music in Miniature". Still on the whole she is the gladgirl. She is also the dominant partner. She commands a far larger public than the Home.[8] How do I visualise the Third? Janus-faced,[9] two faces, one of them gazing with tranquility into the past, the other with ardour into the future. One of them reflects, the other explores. One of them is old perhaps and the other young, though of this age-division I am not sure. I only know that the Third is not directly concerned with the present, with passing fashion, passing events, passing hopes and fears.[10] It does not give the News and it should[11] avoid news-commentaries. It deals with the present of course - everything must - but it tries to enrich the present rather than describe it: that in a single sentence is its function. It[12] wants us to lead fuller lives through the past out of which the human race has come, and through the future into which it is going. The backward look at achievements, the forward look at possibilities: the double vision of Janus.

Talking about it to it ought to be an easy job. One addresses the converted presumably.[13] I speak to a Third Programme audience. Though do I? Is there such a thing? "Audience" suggests a lecture room or a theatre, which it is impossible to[14] enter or quit unobtrusively. My audience, if I have one, can arrive or depart unobserved, it can come in off other wave lengths or retreat to them or switch off altogether. One cannot generalise about it as one could about the audiences of the past, who were confined to a room or a theatre or a concert hall or a church. The extreme fluidity of broadcasting still puzzles me and sometimes paralyses. One person talks to a microphone, other people[15] switch on or off. Addressing them is not such an easy job after all.

[16]To start off - I don't intend[17] to make lists of broadcasts which I have liked or have not liked, nor shall I refer to any particular broadcast. There seems no[18] propriety in doing this when the occasion is an anniversary talk. The Third has been going for five years now, its place in British Broadcasting and indeed in World Broadcasting has become evident. It has made enemies and friends, and counting myself[19] as a friend, I want to say why on general grounds I think it so important.

I have already said that it tries to enrich the present rather than to describe it. It is concerned on the whole with things that[20] are not immediately useful - with art, literature, and music, with philosophic speculation and non-practical religion and unapplied science.[21] All these things may come in useful sometime, they may pay, and I believe some of them will, but there is a latent paradox: if we pursue them <u>because</u> they are going to pay, we never catch them, we never possess them, they elude us like the gold at the bottom of the rainbow, which while we are pursuing, the rainbow[22] itself vanishes, and we lose its beauty. To enjoy and to understand the world - that is what the Third has, for the last five years, been helping us to do. Other agencies have helped of course - [23]but by reason of its backing by a powerful corporation it is outstandingly important. Everyone understands and enjoys the world a little; it is a natural tendency in us, but other tendencies combine to check it. We need outside help, reassurance, sign-posts, reminders, and Broadcasting, or one side of it, has done this. It has helped something living in us to keep alive. It has reminded us, in its graver moments, that life won't last and that for this very reason there are things more important than[24] success or power. To put it in another way, the Third has been educational.

As soon as one mentions the word education, the experts enter,[25] and I know that those who are responsible for the Third, and more particularly for its talks, have thought a good deal about its educational side. To what extent should it specialise? Should it instruct or stimulate or both? What is its relation to our numerous Universities, to the W.E.A.,[26] study groups, etc? Problems such as these.[27] Without entering into them, I venture to assert that Third Programme talks should not be too easy, they shouldn't spoon feed, they should require us to make an effort. Spoon feeding in the long run teaches us nothing but the shape of the spoon. The contents come to taste all alike, jam and powder's just the same, and we cannot understand the world or even enjoy it as soon as this deplorable monotony has been established. Effort, and the will to experience and experiment must come in, above all the individual must learn that it is his own job to occupy his heritage. Scientific gadgets like broadcasting can't do it for him. The kind clever people inside Broadcasting House can't do it for him. He is alone and always will be - a creature to be helped and reassured, but not to be superseded. On its educational side the Third[28] appreciates this. Janus-like, gazing this way at the past, and that way at the future, it appreciates the limitations of broadcasting, better perhaps than do its less introspective colleagues the Home and the Light. That broadcasting should realise how little broadcasting can do is very important. It must not be beguiled by its engineers.

It is always helpful to see our problems from a distance, and I should like to quote at this point an address of Signor Alberto Mantelli. He is the President[29] of the Italian Broadcasting and he here inaugurates the Italian Third Programme - il Terzo Programma - for our Third Programme is I am glad to say not unique, though it can claim to have been[30] a pioneer: Signor Mantelli speaks of the need of differentiation: the undifferentiated programme, which tries to please everyone, is indeterminate in its impact. He finds, as had previous researchers, that three programmes at present respond best to the need[31] of a contemporary society. And he goes on to discuss the problems of culture and adult education with which a Third is particularly concerned.[32]

"Culture, as understood by the Third Programme, goes beyond what might be called humanist culture, and includes the statement and treatment of the multitudinous problems which touch contemporary man so closely. Even when these problems seem fairly straight forward there is always some aspect in which the practical motif crosses with the idealistic and has a human value which puts it on the level of spiritual interests, from which the Third Programme cannot be separated except at the cost of an isolation from life."

Believing as I do that it is the job of a Third Programme to enrich the present rather than to describe it, I don't agree with Signor Mantelli entirely. He opens the door too easily to "actualities" and reportage. Let us have such things but not here.[33] I would prefer to keep to the humanist culture he finds too narrow. But how well he indicates the complexity, the spiritual criss-cross, and how I agree with him when he says further on that erudition is not culture, only one of its instruments. Let the Third be difficult. Let it even dare to be dry. But don't let it be undigested or indigestible.

The Terzo Programma of Italy is as far as I know our only parallel. This is regrettable, but not surprising, considering the state of the world. A Third would be out of place in a Totalitarian State. Nor, on the other hand, is it compatible with commercial broadcasting. We have reason to be proud[34] of our achievement. Some would even maintain it has upheld our prestige abroad.[35] I doubt this. I care too much for art and literature and thought to get interested in the prestige they[36] convey, and I believe that most listeners whether at home or abroad care for them for their own sakes, and that this is the only way to care for them. It is anyhow absurd to suppose that our efforts on the Third or elsewhere influence world-opinion, for the sad and simple reason that World opinion no longer exists. Politicians still invoke it at times, but it is a bubble which burst soon after the first world war. More solid if less sonorous[37] is the praise of the Third sometimes voiced by individuals. An Australian student, new to this side of the globe says that nothing, not even the architecture, has impressed him like the Third. Two Canadian students tune in night after night, very critical, but they listen. A friend from the country calls it "one of the finest instruments for extra mural activity ever invented" gaily adding "if people don't listen, that's no reason for feeling you are wrong. The majority is always in the wrong. (Who said that?)".[38] These scraps from my own experience may indicate how lively if sporadic, is the Third's appeal.

Sporadic. This leads on to[39] an important point. It is impossible to justify the Third on a quantitative basis. Most listeners are not interested in it, and why should they be? It doesn't offer what they want. They aren't[40] hostile - except when[41] popular journalists work them up. But they are indifferent, and reasonably so.[42] Last year I was talking to an East Anglian fisherman, a middle-aged man[43] and we got on the subject of music. I said I liked it. He replied[44] "I can sum music up for you in one word: No Good". He spoke without[45] any bitterness. He was just giving his opinion good temperedly and firmly, as opinions ought to be given. But that one word "No good" summed up music for him and Third Programme stuff generally, and it sums them up for many[46] other decent and intelligent people, and for most people. I believe that the Third Programme audience will increase, partly because of better transmission, partly because more and more listeners will experiment and[47] be interested and pleased. But unless the structure of our society is transformed, it will always be a minority programme. It cannot be defended quantitatively. To the vast majority it must always remain 'No good', and this must be faced by its[48] admirers.

Facing it, I always get rather worried when the ingenious organisation known as Audience Research - Listener Research it used to be called[49] - turns its attention on to the Third. Listener Research may be able to show how many people listen to any given item, but it only deals with numbers, it cannot register <u>how</u> people listen.[50] To switch on is enough. Now when people switch on to the Third, it is probable that they attend: they don't use it to talk against in a pub or as background music while using a vacuum cleaner. They are listening properly, but their attention, their intelligent concentration, their varied reactions, don't and can't get on to the graph. The other day I encountered an Audience Researcher myself - a rather sad-faced young lady, dressed in spinach green. She[51] explained her mission, and asked (very courteously) whether I had listened in yesterday. I had to say "No". She said "Did you listen to the News? That would do". I had to say "No". She said "Oh dear!" I then said, rather pertly,[52] "Do you wish I had listened in?" She drew herself up at that and said "Oh no, certainly not, not at all. One keeps strictly to the facts". She passed on in search of more facts, but the facts she found could have nothing to do with quality, and the Third can only be justified by quality - the quality of what it provides, the quality of the reactions to it. Quality is everywhere imperilled in contemporary life. Those who value it, as I do, are in[53] a vulnerable position. We form as it were an aristocracy in the midst of a democracy, and we belong and desire to belong to the democracy.[54] These conflicting loyalties cannot always be reconciled. They can be in British Broadcasting more easily than elsewhere, for the reasons that there are three programmes: Home, Light and Third.[55]

Returning to Audience Research, I note that Mr. Harold Nicolson shared my anxieties about it when, in 1948, he broadcast on the second anniversary of the Third as I do on its fifth anniversary. This is what he said:

"The Chairman, the Governors, the Director-General, the Board of Management, the planners, the controllers, the producers, and even the announcers of the BBC will all assure you - and in perfect sincerity - that they never for one moment allow Listener Research to affect their policy or judgment. That is not true. Imperceptibly, this temperature chart seeps into their subconscious and influences their morale."[56]

I have myself[57] seen examples of this "seeping" as Mr. Nicolson calls it. On one occasion someone who was connected with the BBC[58] asked me whether the continuance of the Third could be justified in view of the smallness of its audience. I said it was justified. He then asked me whether[59] it ought to go on if the audiences became even smaller. I said it ought still to go on - for the reasons I've just been giving you. Perhaps his questions were[60] what is termed routine, but they disquieted me, nor (though this is a smaller matter) have I liked certain signs of popularisation which at one time appeared. I remember some concerts of light music: excellent in themselves, but the Third was not the place for them - they ought to have gone on the Home or the Light. Audience Research may have its value, but it is deplorable should it result in discrediting the Third, or in watering it down. To quote Mr. Nicolson again "The rulers of the BBC must not allow themselves for one moment to become even subconsciously influenced by this marking system".[61] As far as I know, the rulers in question stand firm. They believe in the Third and[62] will uphold it. Good. Still, eternal vigilance is the price of culture[63] and it is as well to be watchful.

"That is all very well" you may say, "but there is another price we are asked to pay - the price of our licences. What about that pound? Why should so much of it go on what we don't want?" So much of it? The relatively small cost of the Third should be remembered in connection with this complaint.[64] It costs about one & fourpence out of every pound license. The cost for last year was £828,000. For a public service it is grotesquely small.[65] When looking at it, I think of another figure which once happened to catch my eye in the Times[66] - a figure which represented complete waste. The War Office (stated an official report[67]) had spent £1,777,000, on a storage-depot in East Africa, abandoned it, and did not intend to use it again. £1,777,000 - that is to say nearly a million more than the annual cost of the Third, all thrown away in East Africa, and yet as far as I know there was no public comment, no one batted an eyelid.[68] The charge of extravagance and of unnecessary expenditure is reserved for our modest - our very modest - cultural efforts, in the Third in the Arts Council, and elsewhere. They are sniped at,[69] they are fair game. We are told that we cannot afford them[70] and that in the national interest they should be[71] curtailed. Whatever the inner history of that East African storage-depot may have been, it is very significant as a symbol.[72] It is worth remembering.

Most criticism of the Third comes from humourous or sarcastic columns in the daily press. They are often clever, but are inspired by what might be called conscientious bad temper. The writer[73] feels it is his duty to be irritated, perhaps is even employed to be so. I don't mean that the picking to pieces in which he indulges is morally wrong. Indeed I believe that all truths, whether religious or scientific or aesthetic ought to be picked to pieces at times in a serious way. It is a human duty. But I do dislike the idle brilliance of the professional carper, who picks to pieces out of habit. It can't be answered, because it[74] keeps slipping underground. Here is an example - not to be sure a brilliant[75] one. The critic said that the only items in the Third which were of interest to the ordinary man were the talks and the operas, and then held up for special censure an evening which included[76] a complete performance of the Meistersingers. By the time[77] he concluded his attack he had forgotten how it started. In the early days of the Third niggling denigration of this sort must have been a worry. It is less important today - the fifth birthday. The Third stands strong through its own record, its integrity, and the support of the Higher Broadcasting Command. It cannot stand on the results of Audience Research and I hope it will never attempt to do so nor point out that its public is after all not as small as might have been expected. "Non tali auxilio nec defensoribus istis"[78] if I may quote an obsolete language with a discredited accent.[79]

My eulogy, if that is the right name for it, now nears its close. Some listeners may feel that I have been too little laudatory, and that this was an occasion for celebrating the specific achievements of the last five years. I was anxious though not to view the Third as an isolated project, but in relation to broadcasting in general, and to a still wider problem: the problem[80] of value, the problem of maintaining and extending aristocracy in the midst of democracy. It is a terrific problem,[81] with which the modern world has scarcely coped. Anxious,[82] when it isn't killing people, to feed and house them properly, it has assumed[83] that values will look after themselves, or that what "the people" want will be ipso facto culture. It ignores the pioneer, the exceptional, the disinterested scientist, the meditative thinker, the difficult artist, or it contemptuously dismisses them as 'superior'. One trusts that they are superior. They are certainly the types who have helped the human race out of the darkness in the past. And if they vanish now, if they dissolve into the modern world's universal grey, what is to happen to the human race in the future? Into what final darkness will it disappear?

The Third Programme grapples with this question I think. It was easy enough for - well for Louis XIV for instance - to grapple with it. Louis XIV could support the plays of Racine in Paris, while down on the coast people like my East Anglian fisherman were starving. The social conscience has changed all that. And British Broadcasting is trying to do what must be done if we are to carry on adequately: to promote incompatibles: aristocracy in the midst of democracy: and has devoted a small part of its resources to the establishment of the Third. Perhaps one day everyone will want to listen to Racine.[84] I don't think so, and I don't at the bottom of my heart hope so. I don't take to[85] the idea of civilisation being too tidy. Racine and music and so on delight and sustain me, I couldn't bear up without them, and yet I like[86] hearing that one word "No good".

1. <NOT> On 19 September 1951 EMF telegraphed to P. H. Newby, "London preferably at Mr Buckinghams Shepherd Bush" (E. M. Forster File 9A, 1949–1951 R CONT 1, BBC WAC); he recorded this broadcast at the home of Bob Buckingham, 129 Wendell Road, on 27 September. Throughout the recording one can hear external sounds: children's voices during the first two paragraphs, traffic noise during the fourth, fifth, twelfth, and final paragraphs; a particularly noisy truck driving past the residence in the seventh and tenth paragraphs; a clock striking at the end of the twelfth paragraph; horses' hooves clopping in the thirteenth paragraph; and the whistling of a passerby and voices outside the house in the last two paragraphs. With the more intrusive noises, EMF's voice rises to mask and counteract them.

Given below are variants between EMF's manuscript and typescript that illuminate his composition process for broadcasts as well as variants between his script and actual broadcast delivery that illuminate his broadcast style. EMF's tendency to favor contractions over formal constructions in oral delivery is evident throughout the recording (see note 40 below, however).

2. MS: <perhaps>
3. MS: <things>
4. NSA: "he's very fair minded, he likes music and he is anxious"
5. MS: <every one>
6. MS: <of every thing>
7. MS: <of course superficial>
8. This and the prior sentence were not in the MS or the first draft of the script.
9. NSA: "And how do I visualise the Third? Well, as Janus-faced"
10. <Very rightly,>
11. MS: <not give>
12. MS: <helps>
13. NSA: "Talking about it ought to be an easy job. One's addressing the converted presumably."
14. MS: <go into or>
15. MS: <may have tuned in and may>
16. MS: <In talking about it, one thing I'll avoid>
17. MS: <to refer to any particular broadcast, in particular, or>
18. MS: <advantage>
19. <among the latter>
20. MS: <don't pay>
21. NSA: "not immediately useful—art, literature, and music, philanthropic speculation, non-practical religion and unapplied science."
22. MS: <itself fades>
23. MS: <it hasn't and I hope never will have a cultural monopoly - >
24. MS: <reputation>

25. NSA: "Now as soon as the word education is mentioned, the experts come in"

26. W.E.A. is the Workers' Educational Association; see Briggs, *History of Broadcasting*, 2:218–22, for the complex relationship between the BBC Talks Department and the W.E.A. in the late 1920s.

27. NSA: "Problems like this."

28. MS: <accepts> appreciates this, <I think>.

29. NSA: "I'd like to quote at this point to quote an address of Signor Alberto Mantelli. Signor Mantelli is the President. . . ." A 5 September 1951 letter from Harman Grisewood, controller, Third Programme, to EMF provided statistics on the audience share the Third attracted and enclosed "a booklet which the Italians produced when they started their Third Programme in October 1950. As you see, it pretty closely follows our own policy" (E. M. Forster File 9A, 1949–1951 R CONT 1, BBC WAC).

30. MS: <first in the field>

31. NSA: "structure"

32. NSA: "concerned. Here are his words:"

33. NSA: "Let's have such things by all means, but not here."

34. NSA: "very proud"

35. NSA: "And some people would even maintain it has even upheld our prestige abroad."

36. MS: <<<give>> confer>

37. MS: spectacular (deleted by EMF in the script, then restored in the *Listener* version of the talk published on 4 October 1951, pp. 539–41).

38. EMF's respondents are unknown. "Who said that?": most likely Henrik Ibsen in *Enemy of the People*, act 4: "The majority is never right. Never, I tell you!"

39. MS: <a painful but>

40. NSA: "are not"

41. MS: <a few professional critics work them up and <<pretend>> tell them they are being looked down on des>

42. MS: <They just let it go by. The other day>

43. In 1950 EMF was in Aldeburgh recuperating from prostate surgery and collaborating with Benjamin Britten on the opera *Billy Budd*. EMF and Britten often went sailing with the young fisherman Bill Burrell; presumably the middle-aged informant EMF quotes was a friend or colleague of Burrell's (see Furbank, *A Life*, 2:285).

44. MS: <the stuff. He said>

45. MS: <the least severity>

46. MS: <others, indeed for the vast majority "No good.">

47. MS: find <they do not mind it after all. like it.>

48. MS <defenders>

49. The Listener Research Unit was established in 1936 and changed its name to Audience Research in 1950 to reflect the inclusion of television.

50. NSA: "Audience Research may be able to show how many people listen to any good item, but it only deals with numbers, it can't register how people listen." As noted in the General Introduction, both EMF's "Fifth Anniversary" broadcast and T. S. Eliot's 1953 lecture, "The Three Voices of Poetry," reached only 0.2 percent of the U.K. adult population.

51. <stopped me,>

52. MS: <<<"Are you sorry I didn't listen?">> "Are you sorry I didn't listen in?" This rather disconcerted her and she said>

53. <an awkward>

54. MS: <I am not saying that it can be done but But it's easier to do it>

55. NSA: "there are these three programmes: the Home, the Light and the Third."

56. Harold Nicolson, "Birthday of the Third Programme," *Listener*, 7 October 1948, p. 527. Nicolson (1886–1968), diplomat, biographer, member of Parliament (1935–1945), and literary critic, contributed regular broadcasts to the BBC beginning in the 1930s entitled "People and Things" and, later, "The Last Week." In 1942 Nicolson became a member of the BBC Board of Governors. Harmon Grisewood's 18 May 1951 letter to EMF transmitted the text of Nicolson's 26 September 1948 broadcast on the second anniversary of the Third (E. M. Forster File 9A, 1949–1951 R CONT 1, BBC WAC).

57. NSA: "myself you know"

58. <, and more influentially connected with it than I like to think,>

59. MS: <whether I thought>

60. <merely formal>

61. Nicolson, "Birthday of the Third Programme," 527.

62. MS: <are determined to uphold it>

63. MS: <in these days, and, as it is of freedom,>

64. <The Third costs rather more than one twelfth of the BBC's total expenditure - about one shilling and tenpence of every pound spent in other words. The stated figure for the Third is £828,000.>

65. NSA: "And for a public service that is grotesquely small."

66. <earlier in the year>

67. <of May 22nd>

68. MS: <It is worth remembering this.>

69. MS: <in the popular press>

70. NSA: "afford them at a time of crisis"

71. MS: <kept down>

72. MS: <It shows what can be put across and what can't.>

73. <of Hecate's column or what ever it is called>

74. NSA: "he"

75. NSA: "very brilliant"

76. NSA: "presented"

77. NSA: "You see by the time"

78. These are the words spoken in the *Aeneid* (2.677–78) by Hecuba to Priam as he attempts to arm himself while Troy is being sacked ("The time is past / For help like this, for this kind of defending," Robert Fitzgerald translation). EMF's MS and script erroneously give "anxilio" rather than "auxilio." We thank A. A. Markley and his colleague for assistance with the Latin quotation and source.

79. <After which I must stop. My final word shall be my opening sentence, for it has been in my mind all along. Here it is: The Third Programme could not exist apart from the Home Service and the Light Programme.> The last two paragraphs of the script are on a separate page labeled "ADDITION."

80. NSA: "problem namely"

81. NSA: "It's a difficult problem"

82. NSA: "The modern world is anxious"

83. NSA: "and so it is assumed"

84. NSA: "the plays of Racine."

85. NSA: "I don't like"

86. NSA: "enjoy"

[1]AS RECORDED COPY

PRODUCER P. H. NEWBY

<u>SAMUEL BUTLER</u> - Talk No. 1.[2]

by

<u>.E.M. FORSTER</u>

Recording Date: Thursday 29th May - SLO 3011
Transmission Date: Sunday 8th June 1952 8.50 - 9.10 p.m.
THIRD
Repeat: Weds. 11th June 11.0 - 11.20 p.m.

DURATION 20'5"

Samuel Butler influenced me a great deal, so it is perhaps appropriate that I should be talking about his legacy. He, Jane Austen, and Marcel Proust are the three authors who have helped me most over my writing, and he did more than either of the other two to help me to look at life the way I do.

What is that way? It is[3] the undogmatic way.[4] I will come back to it. But I wanted at the start to raise my hat personally to this remarkable man and to thank him. I mayn't be so polite to him later on, nor would he wish me to be; he resented deference.

Butler was himself particularly interested in the question of legacy of influence and I can imagine him listening in this evening, from his some-what cynical limbo.[5] It is always appearing in his speculations. He believed that a man's real influence is exerted only after his death, that it is then that he really begins to live, that the great man - like Shakespeare - then enters into his immortality, and that we small men have a temporary immortality in the hearts of our friends and in the recollections of us that survive. We shall be forgotten - and the great men will be forgotten some day, for great things are compounded of small, and the time comes when they too must perish. But there is for all of us this extension: we are wrong in assuming that our earthly activities end in the grave. We may be

420

remembered inaccurately: witness the sad example of Mr. Higgs, who escaped from EREWHON in a balloon[6] and revisited that country to dis-cover that he had founded a new religion and was being worshiped as a sungod. Things became very awkward for Mr. Higgs. But accurately or inaccurately we shall be remembered.

The idea of earthly immortality is not original. It occurs in the ancients, it is familiar to the Renaissance. What's interesting is the passion with which Butler grasped it, and the cleverness with which he twisted it into a philosophy. The most famous of his sonnets handles it - I'll read it.

> Not on sad Stygian shore, nor in clear sheen
> Of far Elysian plain shall we meet those
> Among the dead whose pupils we have been,
> Nor those great shades whom we have held as foes;
> No meadow of Asphodel our feet shall tread,
> Nor shall we look each other in the face
> To love or hate each other being dead.
> Hoping some praise, or fearing some disgrace.
> We shall not argue saying "Twas thus" or "Thus",
> Our argument's whole drift we shall forget;
> Who's right, who's wrong, t'will all be one to us:
> We shall not ever know that we have met.
> Yet meet we shall and part, and meet again
> Where dead men meet, on lips of living men.[7]

To be mentioned by living men - for instance by ourselves - that is what Samuel Butler desired. He is sometimes rather conceited and self-conscious about it, sometimes rather pathetic, and I doubt whether the great creative artists have had this desire very strongly. They have been too anxious to get on with their jobs. Butler was always wondering what effect he would have on the future. Would the critics - whom he despised - praise him[8] for the wrong reasons? He would hate that. Would decent people whom he admired - the healthy, handsome, well-dressed people[9] - caricature him and make fun of him? He shouldn't mind that at all. What he dreaded was oblivion, and being no fool - he knew that he would be forgotten some day: as shall we all.

For the first quarter of this century his reputation was high, and con-firmed his hopes of posthumous life. THE WAY OF ALL FLESH was pub-lished by his executor soon after his death.[10] It made a great sensation and reawakened interest in EREWHON. To me, and to many others, he quickly became a commanding figure, and with varying ability we inter-preted him and preached his gospel. Somewhere about 1910 I read a paper on him to a local literary society in a London suburb.[11] The secretary of the society tried to stop me. She said her committee did not seem to have heard of Butler, and would I read about Bernard Shaw instead. I refused. I said it would be Butler or nothing, and got my way. Her committee did hear of him and so it went on. A novel I wrote contained a reference to him, and gained me a welcome letter from his representative and friend, Henry Festing Jones.[12] This led to personal friendship, and to contact with what may be called the Butler[13] cult. And in 1914 I had actually signed a contract to write a book about my hero when the first world-war intervened.

It was[14] Bernard Shaw, already famous himself, who mainly spread Butler's fame. He had spotted him right back in 1887, when he reviewed LUCK AND CUNNING,[15] and after his death made constant[16] references. In the preface to Major Barbara, Shaw writes:

"It drives one almost to despair of English literature when one sees so extraordinary a study of English life as Butler's posthumous WAY OF ALL FLESH making so little impression that when, some years later, I produce plays in which Butler's extraordinarily fresh, free and future-piercing suggestions have an obvious share, I am met with nothing but vague cacklings about Ibsen and Nietzsche."[17]

He praises Butler's attitude to money, to crime, to disease, and to religion, and once, at an EREWHON dinner, I heard him speak on the subject of Butler and the life-force. I don't remember the speech precisely: it had an after-dinner quality, although Shaw was teetotal - something rather vague about the bad behaviour of the human-race, and the danger of a new form of life whisking down the chimney and taking charge, if we continued to misbehave. But I recall his respect and his enthusiasm, Butler certainly influenced him.[18] He has also influenced a writer of a different type: Sir Desmond MacCarthy, who has charmingly recorded a boyhood meeting.[19]

So by the time of the first world-war, Butler had acquired a considerable reputation. He was constantly on the "lips of living men," and his reputation held good during the twenties. During the thirties it began to sag. The second world-war[20] obscured him, and I am not going to pretend to you that he is influential today. He is not. The young don't discuss him. EREWHON is still read, and the notebooks, but they don't get talked about. The vicarious immortality for which his soul yearned is ended, is anyhow in abeyance.

It is my duty to offer some explanation of this. But I would like to say in passing I don't consider the subject of influence a very important one. A man's influence, the ups and downs of his reputation: it's all right to discuss such minor matters and we are now discussing them, but what really matters is a man's work: is it good, or is it bad? - Apart from the accidents of fashion or time. This talk of mine is only indirectly concerned with the quality of Butler's work - That will be dealt with directly in other broadcasts in this series.[21]

Now of late years Butler has been exposed both to responsible criticism and to bad-tempered attacks. The criticism - and it alone concerns us - is unfavourable to his achievements as a scientist and as a scholar and as an aesthetic interpreter. In these directions he has no influence today, nor is he likely to regain any. Few will support him in his controversy with Darwin, or will uphold the views of Lamarck, as he did, or will agree the Odyssey was written by a lady who lived in the West of Sicily, or that Gaudenzio Ferrari was an important painter or Tabachetti a great sculptor,[22] and[23] not many will consent to exalt Handel to the heights with him, and to debar Beethoven to the corresponding depths. His research is too one sided, his judgements too whimsical and arbitrary. One often feels that he adopted them in the first place in order to tease someone, and then forgot they had been intended as a joke. On one small point he has struck lucky: he assigned a very early date to some of Shakespeare's Sonnets, and modern scholarship inclines to the same view. Otherwise he fails. Nor - to turn to creative matters - has he left any legacy either as a painter or as a musician. His pictures are not looked at; his cantata, Narcissus, is never performed.

He has partly gone out of favour because he was a critic of society, and the society he criticised has passed away. He grew up under Victorianism, he was nearly strangled by it and had to fight against it and only saved his soul by escaping to New Zealand. A[24] critical study on him, by Mr. P.N. Furbank,[25] suggests that the fight nearly killed him spiritually, and though he conquered he always carried the scars of conflict. That's probably correct and it helps to explain Butler's obsession on the subject of family life. As you know he didn't get on with his parents and THE WAY OF ALL FLESH is largely autobiographical. Ernest Pontifex, its hero, is a dead sort of character to whom several living things happen; he is lowered into the hell of a Victorian rectory as Butler remembered it, he writhes under the paternal lash, he is[26] stifled by the maternal embrace: he[27] saved his soul alive, but at the cost of mistaking an honest girl for a prostitute, and going to prison in consequence. Part of the novel is interesting, part of it has become a bore, because the type of tyranny it criticises no longer exists. We can't share the author's assumption. We are now sentimental over Victorianism - admiring its good side, and condemning its bad side because we have not had to suffer from it. In particular we don't[28] want to abuse family life: indeed many of us are anxious to preserve it as a bulwark against the overmastering fussiness of the State. Today it is the State that bullies: the State that[29] stifles: not Papa and Mamma.

Butler is also out of date over money. He is more interesting and original over money than over the family, but here too, he is describing a vanished society. Today, money is still powerful, but not as it was in Victorian

times. Today, no one in Great Britain can amass a fortune unless he is prepared to do so dishonestly. The honest man, who makes a truthful income
tax return, can never become wealthy for he will be relieved of his gains
by super-tax. In Butler's day it was different. It was possible to become
rich honestly, that is to say in accordance with the law and with public
opinion. The rich could get richer if they were clever, and the poor
depended on the rich. Butler accepted this state of affairs with complacency: like his hero Ernest he had himself both made and lost money, and
he is always intelligent and suggestive about it. But it is a state of affairs
that has passed away. He did not foresee the Welfare State and has little to
say to those who are entangled in its coils. He belonged to the jungle of
free enterprise. What he has to teach us here is the general lesson of clarity: it is a good thing to get clear about one's economic position. It's dangerous, very dangerous, to pretend that money does not exist, or to
dismiss it as vulgar as people did when I was young.

It is also good to get clear about crime and about disease. He has left us
a legacy here. In EREWHON he reversed their positions, with the happi-
est results. Crime, in that topsy-turvy land, is an object for sympathy, and
it can be cured. Disease is sinful, and is punishable, sometimes by death.
The fantasy is profound and fruitful, and, in serious form, it has entered
into thoughts of responsible people today. And another[30] fancy - the idea
machines may take charge of the human race and may subdue it - has also
taken root. His genius though not poetic, was lively and adventurous: he
was always sending it out on new errands and making it handle unpropi-
tious material. Sometimes the results were unimportant. At other times
they were exciting and helpful. If Butler hadn't lived, many of us would
now be a little deader than we are, a little less aware of the tricks and traps
in life, and of our own obliviousness.

His value, indeed resides not in his rightness over this or that, not in his
happy hits, not even in the frequent excellence of his prose and verse, but
in the quality of his mind. He had an independent mind. He might
indulge in private prejudices, but he never bowed to the prejudices of others, he suspected authority, he took nothing on trust, and he had no use
for dogmas.

Here is his legacy, and his is of particular value to us today. The world
of 1952 is so ugly and frightening that men take refuge blindly in anything
that may shelter them. Some turn to communist dogma others to ecclesi-
astical: creeds spiritually opposed but alike in this, that they offer the individual shelter at the price of his unquestioning obedience to authority.
This tendency is not new in history it has often shown itself when society
is sick: it happened in the 14th Century for instance, after the Black Death,
it happened along the coast of North Africa when the Roman Empire

broke. It has achieved substantial results, but it has not advanced the human spirit.

Voltaire, in his large way, knew this: he built a church to God but wrote "écrasez l'infame".[31] Butler, in his smaller way, knew it too: he has left us the little fable of the Musical Banks,[32] and though anything but an Atheist he protested at being bullied or snubbed into the acceptance of the supernatural against his will. He stands for the undogmatic[33] outlook, for tolerance, good temper, good taste, empiricism, and reasonableness. Well aware that reason is fallible, he held that we should be reasonable as long as we can, and should not plunge into mysticism because problems are difficult, or in obedience to the command of a priest or a commissar. There will always be mystery in the universe, perhaps there always should be mystery, but it is for the free spirit of man to reduce the mysteriousness and extend the frontiers of the known. Human pride will have a fall every now and then, and obscurantists will cry "There! I told you so! Next time you'll listen to me." But, all being well, human pride will scramble up[34] once more and will wipe off the dust and the blood and go forward. Butler's main legacy therefore is this: he upheld, in his particular limited[35] cranky way, the human spirit, and for this, fifty years after his death, let us thank him.

Let me end on another note and with reference to a very different sort of legacy: to the odds and ends he left behind him: manuscripts, letters, to or from him, pictures, personal bric-a-brac, mantelpiece ornaments, his passport, a kettle-holder made for him by[36] Miss Savage, mementoes from Sicily or elsewhere and so on. These were all preserved, with humorous piety, by his friend and my friend, Festing Jones. I used to see them in his hospitable house in Maida Vale.[37] Butler's best picture, Family Prayers, hung in the spare room there. It was a harmless cult - and I have known many worse ones - and it rested on affection rather than on awe. Festing Jones wanted to give it the chance to continue, so he arranged that the various objects should be divided between two institutions. Some of them have gone to St. John's College, Cambridge, (Butler's old college), others to Williams College, Williamstown, Massachusetts. I visited the Cambridge collection lately and sat for an hour where it is housed. It was a lovely morning. In the sunlight outside, ignoring the Butler legacy passed the people whom he admired and called the Nice People and tried to depict in such characters as Towneley and George - people who were healthy and happy and young and instinctive, and who would, he hoped, make fun of him when he was gone.

. . . .

1. <NOT CHECKED BY TALKS DEPARTMENT WITH>

2. Talks by Graham Hough and Philip Toynbee succeeded EMF's inaugural talk in the series, which marked the fiftieth anniversary of Butler's death. All three broadcasts were reprinted as essays in the *Listener*, EMF's on 12 June 1952 (pp. 955–56).

3. < - speaking roughly - >

4. EMF added accent marks above the first syllable of "undogmatic" and above "way."

5. The paragraph originally read, "I can imagine <Butler> him listening in this evening, from his somewhat cynical limbo. <For he> Butler was himself particularly interested in the question of legacy of influence." For the broadcast EMF reversed these sentences, then restored the original order in the *Listener*.

6. An incident in *Erewhon*, Butler's novel of 1872 (revised in 1901).

7. EMF added several accent marks in the sonnet, for example, above "those," "great," and "shades" in line 4 and "dead," "men," and "meet" in line 14. The sonnet, composed in Butler's notebook in 1898, was published first in the 4 January 1902 *Athenaeum* and then in successive editions of the notebooks. EMF's transcription slightly alters occasional words, punctuation marks, and capitalization in the original (*The Note-books of Samuel Butler* [1926; rpt. London and New York: AMS Press, 1968], 427).

8. EMF added an accent mark above "him."

9. <like Towneley> Towneley exemplifies physical and social grace as well as freedom from cant in *The Way of All Flesh* (1903).

10. After Butler's death in 1902, his executor, R. A. Streatfeild (1866–1919), oversaw the 1903 publication of *The Way of All Flesh* (London: Grant Richards).

11. EMF's lecture entitled "Samuel Butler 1835–1902" was delivered to the Weybridge Literary Society in December 1913 (King's College, Cambridge, Archive).

12. *A Room with a View*, chapter 12. For EMF's friendship with Jones, Butler's biographer and friend, see Furbank, *A Life*, 2:3–4.

13. <tradition>

14. <, of course,>

15. *Luck and Cunning* was a critique of Darwin and an endorsement of design.

16. <enthusiastic>

17. Shaw, "Preface to Major Barbara: First Aid to Critics," in *Major Barbara: In Three Acts* (London: Constable and Co., 1912), 161.

18. EMF added an accent mark above "him."

19. Sir Desmond MacCarthy, "Samuel Butler," in *Criticism* (London: Putnam, 1932), 3–4.

20. <did him no good>

21. <, and I refer you to them.>

22. Butler discussed both Gaudenzio Ferrari (c. 1470–1546), an Italian painter of the Piedmontese School, and the sculptor Tabachetti in *Ex Voto: An Account of the Sacro Monte or New Jerusalem at Varallo-Sesia. With Some Notice of Tabachetti's Remaining Work at the Sanctuary of Crea* (London: Trübner and Co., 1888).

23. <very few>

24. <recent>

25. Furbank, *Samuel Butler, 1835–1902* (Cambridge: Cambridge University Press, 1948).

26. <strangled>

27. <sang>

28. <care>

29. <strangles>

30. <fantasy>

31. *Écrasez l'infame*: "crush the infamous," in this case, superstition. EMF's script reads "écrasez l'infane."

32. In *Erewhon* banks are accorded the ritual and music customarily associated with churches (chapter 15).

33. <view of life>

34. <again>

35. Word omitted from the *Listener.*

36. <his friend> For details of Miss Savage, see Furbank, *Samuel Butler,* 74–81.

37. <They are now divided between to institutions: St. John's College, Cambridge, (Butler's old College) and Williams College,>

[1]AS RECORDED COPY   PRODUCER: P. H. NEWBY

'THE PELICAN HISTORY OF ART - THE ART AND ARCHITECTURE OF INDIA'

REVIEW BY E.M. FORSTER

RECORDING DATE: Friday 24th July 1953.   SLO 33130
TRANSMISSION: THIRD   Sunday 6th September 1953. 9.30 - 9.50 p.m.
REPEAT: 7th September. 11.30 - 11.55 p.m.[2]   DURATION: 20'07"

Exactly one hundred and ten years ago, Lord Macaulay made a speech in the House of Commons. I want to begin[3] by reading you some of Lord Macaulay's remarks:

"The great majority of the population of India consists of idolators, blindly attached to doctrines and rites which[4] are in the highest degree pernicious.[5] The Brahminical religion is so absurd that it necessarily debases every mind which receives it as truth: and with this absurd mythology is bound up an absurd system of physics, an absurd geography, an absurd astronomy. Nor is this form of Paganism more favourable to art than to science.[6] Through the whole Hindu Pantheon you will look in vain for anything resembling those beautiful and majestic forms which stood in the shrines of Ancient Greece. All is hideous, and grotesque and ignoble. As this superstition is of all superstitions the most irrational and of all superstitions the most inelegant, so it is of all superstitions the most immoral."[7]

Thus spoke Lord Macaulay, together with much else, in the year 1843. We are now in 1953,[8] and here is a large and learned book[9] about the "inelegant superstitions" he so forcibly condemned, containing no less than 190 plates in which the inelegancies are illustrated, and numerous ground plans and elevations of the idolatrous temples that so roused his ire. It is true that few of the illustrations resemble the shrines of Ancient Greece.

He was right there. But it does so happen that Greece and India are different places, seeking different[10] goals, which trifling fact escaped him. Macaulay was a great man and when a subject was congenial to him he could be sensitive as well as forcible. But he was not good at making the preliminary imaginative jump; he never thought of learning from India, he only thought of improving her, and since Indian art did not strike him as improving, it had to be destroyed.

A good deal of it was destroyed; and the residue was insulted; only in my own life time has it been recognised as a precious possession of the whole human race, and its presentation and classification attempted, and aesthetic appreciation accorded to it. Indian Art isn't easy - one can't pretend that about it - it seldom[11] appeals right away to the Westerner, or else he catches on to it and then falls off it and has to try again: this has been my[12] experience, and here is one of my reasons for being grateful to Professor Rowland for this book - it's a helpful book. He's an American - at Harvard.[13]

I will try to summarise its contents to you. In doing so, I will use as few Indian words as possible. Indian words make a broadcast difficult to follow, also I am likely to mispronounce them.

The curtain rises over 4,000 years ago. The scene is the valley of the Indus. Here the remains of two great cities have been excavated. Their discovery caused great excitement, but we discovered very little about them. We don't know who planned them or what gods they worshipped. We can't decipher their script. They seem to have been trading cities[14] connecting on to Mesopotamia and they may have originated the Indian civilisation[15] we know. They flourished for over a thousand years and then vanished. Perhaps they were swallowed up by the sands, perhaps they were destroyed by invaders from the north. We don't know. The curtain falls. Those two cities on the Indus form, so to speak, the prelude to our drama.

The next scene takes place much later, about 400 B.C. As the curtain rises again, we see that the invaders from the north have established themselves and are practising a religion[16] akin to Hinduism. When it has[17] fully risen we witness the establishment of Buddhism. And now the main drama begins. The connection between Hinduism and Buddhism is complicated.[18] They are not rival sects - nothing so clear cut as that. They both started in India and you can still see there - I have seen it and have picked a leaf[19] - you can still see there a descendant of the sacred tree under which Buddha sat when he attained enlightenment. They both taught, or usually taught, that this life is an illusion, and they both sometimes emphasised and sometimes[20] ignored the unity of God. And both of them were entangled in local folk-lore. You can't draw any definite line between Buddhism and Hinduism.[21] Their real point of issue is social: they took up different attitudes towards the caste-system. Buddhism condemned caste and[22] so it exported easily and became a missionary religion abroad. Hinduism was rooted in caste, and it tended to stay at home.

[23]Professor Rowland is enthusiastic about Buddhism, and much of his book - almost a quarter of it - is occupied in following Buddhist exports outside India. He follows them north to Afghanistan and Turkestan, eastward to Nepal, southward to Ceylon and Java, Burma and Siam.[24] My own interests are passionately Indian[25] so I shall confine myself more strictly than he does to the Indian sub-continent.[26]

Buddhism, I was saying, developed there about 400 years before Christ, when Ancient Greece was powerful. In time it produced two schools of art - one of them was a Greco-Indian or Roman-Indian school up by the Northern frontier. The other was a native Indian school further south, on the banks of the Ganges. The two sprang up under the same dynasty. The northern school used to be greatly praised by critics, especially by those who inherited Lord Macaulay's attitude, and felt that Indian Art which had been influenced by Greece or Rome[27] would not be as bad as art which was merely Indian. That was the attitude of Kipling; you may remember his[28] account - a charming account - of the statues which Kim saw in the Wonder House at Lahore:[29] they were Greco-Indian statues[30] and I am not decrying them, and while I was[31] thinking about this talk, I had a photograph of one of them stuck up to look at. But the southern stuff, the art which developed by the banks of the Ganges is preferred by modern[32] critics, and Professor Rowland gives good reasons for the preference. If you would like to see some of this stuff in London you can do so on the main-staircase of the British Museum. You will find there some reliefs from a great Buddhist shrine.

And now drop the curtain again: I am sorry to keep on with this curtain but I cannot manage without it: it helps to arrest the sense of flux which paralyses us when we contemplate through so many centuries a civilisation that is always flowing: it imposes upon India the semblance of form. Drop the curtain again I say, and raise it about the year 400 A.D.: about the time when the Roman Empire is falling to pieces, that's to say. What do you see now?

You see Indian art at its highest. You see the beginning of the famous Gupta period. It was so called after one of the dynasties which reigned during it. I will read what Professor Rowland says on the subject.

"Seldom in the history of peoples do we find a period in which the national genius is so fully and typically expressed in all the arts as in Gupta India.[33] The Gupta period may well be described as a 'classic' in the sense of the word describing a norm or degree of perfection never established before or since, and in the perfect balance and harmony of all elements, stylistic and iconographic - elements inseparable in importance."[34]

- - -

He proceeds to describe and to illustrate some of the masterpieces of that period - the caves, hollowed out into churches for the congregational worship of Buddha. The isolated statues of Buddha - for it is the religion that still dominates. Hinduism persists and the two Indian gods who are most worshipped today - Siva and Krishna, - receive their shrines.[35]

Somewhere about the year 800 - my figures are very rough: I pick on 800 because it was the year when Charlemagne was crowned in Rome and started for that tiny place, Europe, the Holy Roman Empire; - somewhere about 800 the Gupta civilisation came to an end and its curtain falls. Our next scene - and it will be our[36] final scene - contains our major surprise. Buddhism has disappeared, Hinduism, dormant through so many centuries, becomes rampant and prevails. It had already modified Buddhism, and[37] complicated it. Now it manages to expel it, the caste system is re-affirmed, the elaborate Hindu temples arise with their towers that are not quite spires, their spires that just fail to be towers, their mushrooms and sun hats, their gateways and gates, their colonnades, platforms and court-yards, their writhing sculpture and the sculpture is sometimes[38] indecent.[39] All is being prepared for the displeasure of Lord Macaulay. And minds more sympathetic to India than his, minds less aggressively western, have also recoiled from the Hindu temple and regretted the expulsion of Buddhism. The late Lowes Dickinson had such a mind. My first visit to India was in his company, and I remember how he used to cower away from those huge architectural masses, those pullulating forms as if a wind blew off them which might wither the soul.[40] This wasn't the Parthenon at Athens, no it most certainly wasn't and those gods with six arms or a hundred heads and blue faces were far from the gods of Greece.

I got easier with the Indian temple as soon as I realised or rather as soon as I was taught that there often exists inside its complexity a tiny cavity, a central cell, where the individual may be alone with his god. There is a temple-group in the middle of India, once well known to me, which adopts this arrangement. The exterior of each temple represents the world-mountain, the Himalayas, its topmost-summit (the Everest of later days) is crowned by the sun, and round its flanks runs all the complexity of life - people dying, dancing, fighting, loving and creatures who are not human at all, or even earthly. That is the exterior. The interior is small, simple. It is only a cell[41] where the worshipper[42] can for a moment face what he believes. He worships at the heart of the world mountain, inside the external complexity. And he is alone. Hinduism, unlike Christianity and Buddhism and Islam, does not invite him to meet god congregationally; and this commends it to me.

The name of this temple-group is the Khajraho group. There are twenty temples standing out of an original eighty-five and all of them are deserted. They rise like mountains of buff in the jungle. They were built[43] shortly before William the Conqueror was born. They belong, according to Professor Rowland's classification, to the final period of Indian art - the period which began when Buddhism was driven from the land of its birth, and which peters out amongst the nineteenth century Rajput miniatures.

I ought at this point to allude to the 190 illustrations already mentioned. They are rather a disappointment. They have been intelligently selected, they range widely, some of them come off, but they don't on the whole give an adequate idea of the marvellous architecture and sculpture of India. "What could?" you may say and you are right. But photographs of the same subjects, which I bought out there, are certainly less inadequate. I have been doing some comparing and[44] my photographs win. Possibly the method of reproduction is at fault, I don't know, but here is a weakness in an otherwise admirable work, and[45] I hope it may be remedied in future volumes of the series.

So much for my summary. I fear I have lugged you rather than led you through the book, omitting much and patting into shape much that was amorphous. I haven't discussed any of the non-Indian chapters, and one of them - about Cambodia - I haven't even mentioned. Instead of these remote exports, I would rather have heard more about monuments[46] native to the Indian soil: more about the Elephanta caves, for instance: they are dismissed in under two pages. However, that is a personal preference. Moslem art is naturally[47] omitted: it is a separate subject.[48] But just in passing, just in order to emphasise the complexity of India, I would like to mention that Hindu and Moslem art do occasionally blend there. One example is the work of the Emperor Akbar. Another - a striking one - is the architecture of Ahmedabad, where the mosques, though correct ritually, are compounded in the Hindu style and waver aesthetically into temples. And there is a third example in a Moslem tomb outside Golcanda, in the south. Eating my lunch there[49] - one does or did eat one's lunch at Moslem tombs: it was part of their graciousness and courtesy - I could admire two styles of architecture, on a single little building. I like to record these blendings[50] of Moslem and Hindu though they may not be congenial to contemporary politicians. The past is never as cut and dried as the present would like it to be. And the present, with its[51] insistence on purity and its fanatical faith in the racial or religious 100% needs a reminder of this.

There are a few minutes left and I'll spend them in reminiscing about one of the monuments which I have seen and enjoyed. I'll choose the Elephanta Caves - just mentioned. They are well known, being on an island near Bombay, and listeners who have seen them may think that 'enjoyment' is the wrong word to employ. Certainly nothing more solemn, more remote from the pleasures of daily life can be imagined. I would not picnic in an Elephanta Cave. I last went there on a steamy December after-noon,[52] nearly eight years ago.[53] The waters of the harbour were calm, and close to the island they[54] became shallow and muddy. A mangrove swamp was starting. "Up to no good" is always one's reaction when mangrove swamps are mentioned, but they are not sinister to look at. Their bright lit-tle green[55] noses pushed up on either side of the slippery landing stage. There was a climb up a couple of hundred feet, through brushwood, ticket taking, and close ahead, over a level space, the chief cave. It showed as a dark gash in the cliff wall. It has been terribly damaged. The Portuguese when they discovered it in the sixteenth century did what they could to destroy the shrine. They too[56] despised the religion and art of India. The cave is dedicated to Siva.[57] Enormous sculptures of him loom, and the light, filtering into the main chamber from several directions, picks out his limbs unexpectedly or illuminates the magnificent giants who guard his[58] shrine. Above is the living rock, supported by pillars hewn out of it, and meriting the title of living for vegetation springs from its cracks. Elephanta is not one of those caves into which one penetrates;[59] exchanging light for darkness steadily. It is broad, it doesn't dig far into the mountain, and one's impulse is to wander in and out of it through the various gaps, always finding new effects and unexpected drama. The eight giants round the sacred sentry box[60] impressed me most. They weren't doing anything, as Siva was in the niches at the side. They weren't dancing on the world or treading down demons, or slaughtering or getting married against a background of air-born imps. They were merely guarding the symbol of generation and they had[61] guarded it for a thousand years. Elsewhere Siva predominated. He was everywhere. He was the male sex and the female also, all life came from him and returned to him. I like the idea - grave scholars have entertained it - that his wife got tired of this, that constant unity with the deity bored her and that on one of the Elephanta reliefs she is depicted as losing her temper.

I don't remember much else about that[62] gracious and enviable day - only the haziness and the stillness outside and a road which curved left round the hill towards some other caves.[63] Our small party had the good luck[64] to be on Elephanta alone, and no doubt that has recommended it to me. It is certainly unique. I have regretted that Professor Rowland has not said more about it, but what he does say is stimulating, and I will end by quoting.[65]

"The colossal panels of Elephanta suggest spectacular presentations on a stage,[66] their dramatic effectiveness enhanced by the bold conception in terms of light and shade. Probably such a resemblance to the unreal world of the theatre[67] is not entirely accidental; for in Indian art, as in Indian philosophy, all life, even the life of the gods, is an illusion or play set against the background of eternity."[68]

1. <NOT CHECKED BY TALKS DEPARTMENT WITH>

2. <10.35 - 11.15 p.m.>

3. <my talk on Indian Art>

4. <, considered merely with reference to the temporal interests of mankind,>

5. EMF added accent marks above "highest" and "pernicious" and deleted the following: <In no part of the world has a religion ever existed more unfavourable to the moral and intellectual health of our race.>

6. EMF added an accent mark above "art" in this sentence and above the second syllable of the third and fourth instances of "absurd" in the prior sentence.

7. Thomas Babington Macaulay, "The Gates of Somnauth" (9 March 1843), in *Speeches by Lord Macaulay with His Minute on Indian Education*, ed. G. M. Young (London: Humphrey Milford, Oxford University Press, 1935), 202–3.

8. EMF added accent marks above "9" and "5."

9. Benjamin Rowland, *The Art and Architecture of India: Buddhist, Hindu, Jain*, Pelican History of Art series (London: Penguin Books, 1953).

10. <gods>

11. <makes an instinctive>

12. EMF added an accent mark above "my."

13. <¶Its full title is THE ART AND ARCHITECTURE OF INDIA: BUDDHIST, HINDU, JAIN: it is published in the Pelican series - an extremely thick Pelican, it's [*sic*] author is an American at Harvard.> EMF wrote to John Morris on 25 May 1953, "I should like to do the Penguin Indian Art Book for the Third, especially if I may keep it" (*Selected Letters*, ed. Lago and Furbank, 2:251).

14. <with connections with>

15. <with which we are familiar.>

16. <recognisable as>

17. <half>

18. <and raises all sorts of problems for the art historian>

19. EMF's 29 January 1913 letter to his mother reports having plucked two leaves "from the sacred Pipul Tree at Boddh Gaya," one of which he encloses for her (*Selected Letters*, ed. Lago and Furbank, 1:183).

20. <neglected>

21. <, either metaphysical or mythological>

22. <consequently>

23. <Much of Professor Rowland's book>

24. <He doesn't follow them as far as China: no doubt he had to stop somewhere, and since my>

25. <I shouldn't have minded him stopping sooner and confining himself>

26. <¶Let us return to it now.>

27. <must be better than>

28. <charming>

29. The statues figure importantly in chapter 1 of Kipling's *Kim*.

30. <of Buddha>

31. <writing out this script> The *Listener* (10 September 1953, pp. 419–21) cut EMF's reference to thinking about the talk and the photograph he "stuck up to look at."

32. *Listener:* "more detached"

33. <Here was florescence and fulfilment after a long period of grandual [*sic*] development, a like sophistication and complete assurance in expression in music, literature, the drama, and the plastic arts.>

34. Rowland, *Art and Architecture*, 129–30.

35. <My own experience of Indian religion has <<concentrated in>> led me to the cult of Krishna - Krishna the cowboy - and I was pleased to find that that amiable deity of the Mild East had established himself so long ago.>

36. <last>

37. <made it>

38. <improper>

39. *Listener:* "obscene"

40. For details of EMF's travels with Lowes Dickinson, see Furbank, *A Life*, 1:215–37.

41. <which>

42. <may circumambulate, and where he>

43. <about the year one thousand - >

44. <mine>

45. <perhaps>

46. <which belong>

47. <ruled out>

48. <and no doubt it will be treated elsewhere>

49. See Furbank, *A Life*, 1:252.

50. *Listener:* "bastards"

51. <stern><priggish>

52. <seven or>

53. EMF refers to his 1945 trip to India at the invitation of All-India P.E.N. (Furbank, *A Life*, 2:259–63).

54. <were>

55. <spikes>

56. <detested>

57. Siva: the third deity in the Hindu triad associated both with generation and destruction.

58. <central>

59. EMF added an accent mark the first syllable of "penetrates."

60. <pleased>

61. <been doing so>

62. <agreeable>

63. <which I have never visited.>

64. <to visit the island>

65. <him:>

66. EMF added an accent mark above "stage."

67. EMF added an accent mark above the first syllable of "theatre."

68. <¶Thus far have we travelled from Lord Macaulay.> EMF's quotation is from Rowland, *Art and Architecture*, 188.

¹'AS BROADCAST' SCRIPT
Producer: P. H. Newby

"THE MINT" by <u>T. E. Lawrence</u>
Reviewed by <u>E.M. FORSTER</u>
Published by Jonathan Cape at 17/6d.[2]

Rehearsal: Friday, 11th February 1955:   3.45 p.m.
Recording: "   "   "   "   5.15 - 5.45 p.m.
Transmission: Monday, 14th February 1955:   9.15 - 9.35 p.m.
Repeat: Sunday, 20th February 1955:   10.55 - 11.15 p.m.
Recording No: SLO 72516   THIRD PROGRAMME
Duration: 21'37"   <u>N.B.</u> Approx. 700 words' quotation - F.D.

I saw a good deal of T. E. Lawrence while he was writing <u>The Mint</u>.[3] He was not in the Air Force[4] at the time - he had been driven out of it by a newspaper stunt and was hiding away amongst the Tanks instead - but he managed to get back there and on April the 16th, 1928, he wrote to me from Karachi, referring to "some notes on life in the ranks . . . crude unsparing faithful stuff; very metallic and uncomfortable." These notes turned into <u>The Mint</u>, I read it in typescript. Letters passed between us and later on we talked,[5] and later still, after his death, I was lent a copy of the privately printed edition. So I have been in and out of[6] the book from its early days and in that way I am well qualified to talk about it.

In another way I'm ill qualified. I know nothing whatsoever of the life it describes. I have known servicemen of course - at Lawrence's own retreat of Clouds Hill, for instance, where I met friends of his with whom I still keep in touch. But I've always known them off duty, I've never seen them at work, still less worked with them.[7] I've never shared any of Lawrence's experiences so I cannot interpret them except by guessing at them and I cannot check his statements. Is he telling the truth? He didn't always, and he will always bewilder those excellent people who identify telling the truth[8] with being true. True he was, but he loved fantasy and leg pulling and covering up his own tracks, and he threw up a great deal of verbal dust, which bewilders the earnest researcher.

Why ever did he join up? Well may you ask. Why break off a brilliant career and plunge into the squalor of an R.A.F. depôt when nobody wanted him to, when indeed a good many officials were inconvenienced by his insistence? Why exchange comfort and distinction for fatigues and the square? It was partly[9] the desire to abase himself, to crash from the heights of commanding to the depths of obedience, it was partly the desire to hide, partly the itch for adventure.[10] But believing him, as I do, to be true, I believe there was a deeper motive than these. He joined up[11] because he wanted to get into touch with people, and felt he could only do this by doing the work they did, and by sharing their lives. He is very difficult to understand and probably didn't understand himself, but throughout his complexities there is one constant quality - namely, compassion. It showed itself in little things, in ordinary kindnesses - such as I and most of his friends experienced. It showed itself also in the deeper, the literal sense, of the word compassion; in his desire to share experience with people and if necessary to suffer with them.[12]

[13]The Mint's a good book - better technically than the straddling <u>Seven Pillars</u>. It is soundly constructed: three sections which connect with one another to make a coherent whole. The first two sections deal with the Uxbridge depot, the third with the Cadet College at Cranwell in Lincolnshire, to which he was posted as an aircraftsman. The atmosphere of the three sections varies but there is always the idea of training: one might paraphrase them as The Misery of not[14] being trained, The Misery of being trained, and The joy of having been trained. The conceptions of training and of loyalty dominate <u>The Mint</u>.[15] Per ardua ad astra.[16] Or as one of his own mates put it Per ardua ad asbestos. For loyalty changes its[17] objective. At the Depot it is the loyalty of the down-trodden trainees to one another, it is the fellowship of the Insulted and Injured. In the third section[18] it is loyalty to the air, and to the R.A.F. whom he regards as its sole conqueror. I will try to think about this later on. Just now, whatever the ethical appropriateness here of training and of loyalty, we may agree that they bind the book together excellently and make it a well made book.

It is also a well written book. Lawrence's style, though slow-moving and mannered, can convey a great variety of actions and attitudes, scenery and scenes, to do which is[19] a main function of style. He can do you a repartee, a rough house, a sprained ankle, a garbage bin, the slow passing across windows of the moon, troops in church, himself at Marlborough House, bird cries,[20] bacon and eggs, and can capture for you one after other the impressions that have impinged upon his unusual mind. He only fails[21] when he tries to examine the workings of that mind, when he becomes introspective-or even merely philosophic. Then the slow motion of the style generates stickiness and its mannerisms crack into self-consciousness, and he conveys nothing to us except that he is a good deal worried, which we have already guessed. There are not many of these introspective passages in <u>The Mint</u>. If there were more its compactness might suffer. It is made up of 69 vivid short chapters, each easy to read and all geared into the general scheme of training and of loyalty. It is the work of a man who had much to put across and knew how to put it.

Before I go further I'd like to emphasise that the general edition now on sale is almost exactly the same as the original privately printed edition of 1936. I didn't think it would be. I thought there would be bowdlerizing and cuts, especially in view of the book prosecutions which have been so prevalent lately. One scatological passage has been omitted, so have "the coarse words automatic in barrack-room speech" (there are about half a dozen such words and nearly every one knows what they are.) And there are some slight textual variants, due to collation of manuscripts. That's all. Otherwise it is exactly the same as the original edition, and the editor his brother (Professor A. W. Lawrence) and the publishers (Messrs. Cape) are to be congratulated on it. They have also issued a small unexpurgated edition for subscribers.

And now[22] to tackle the Uxbridge Depot. Here's a grim story. The misery experienced there, both before and during training, could have been avoided, he thinks. It was caused[23] by the officers being too few and too aloof and the N.C.O.'s being too numerous and too uncontrolled. Having too little to do, they fall upon the hapless recruits and put them through the mill, dealing out punishments and fatigues indiscriminately and sometimes reducing them to nervous pulp. A chapter about a garbage cart - to give it a bowdlerized name - passes belief, and even more fantastic are some sacks, full of grease and maggots, which the recruits have to boil up and get clean for the butcher, the result being a stinking soup which had to be thrown away, sacks and all. There's a morning's work for the Royal Air Force! And when they pass from the chaos of not being trained to the rigours of being trained, they encounter the same wastage and cynicism, plus physical distress: they encounter Stiffy, the drill adjutant, an exguardsman who is incapable of seeing anything beyond drill, punishments,[24] drill. The portrait of Stiffy is delicately drawn and there is a clever turn at the end of it when he makes an ingratiating speech to his victims as they are leaving and[25] advertises himself as not such a bad fellow after all: whereupon they despise him.

Professor Lawrence in his introduction says that his brother did not write <u>The Mint</u> as propaganda for alleviating recruits' hardships. It is clear, however, that he thought they should be alleviated and that unless they were alleviated R.A.F. morale would suffer. Here's the passage where he expresses this view.[26]

They have put us into maudlin fear,[27] to moral abasement. A littler longer . . . and we're hospital cases. Five have slunk there already; or rather three have slunk and two decent lads were carried in.

I have been before at depots and have seen or overseen the training of many men, but this our treatment is rank cruelty. While my mouth is yet hot with it I want to record that some of those who day by day exercise their authority upon us, do it in the lust of cruelty. There is a glitter in their faces when we sob for breath . . . which betrays that we are being hurt not for our own good but to gratify a passion.[28] Alone of the hut, I've energy at this moment to protest . . . I am not frightened of our instructors, nor of their over-driving. To comprehend why we are their victims is to rise above them. Yet despite my background of achievement and understanding, despite my willingness . . . that the R.A.F. should bray me and remould me after its pattern: still I want to cry out that this our long-drawn punishing can subserve neither beauty nor use.[29]

Such was his opinion. The R.A.F., like other organisations, evidently believed in breaking down individuals so that it might build them up again in more serviceable shapes: before the metal could be minted it had to be melted. If you want an extreme example of such breaking down and building up, read Orwell's 1984: there you get The Mint in excelsis. Whether the Uxbridge depot went too far in its breaking down process as Lawrence thought, whether Depots today are different, I do not know, though some of you may. I'll turn[30] to the pleasanter side of his picture: to Hut 4, to the mutual loyalty of the recruits who were being broken. He shared a hut with 50 others who came from different places and classes. In three days all were friendly and (as he shrewdly observes) never became any friendlier. What they wanted from personal relationships was solidarity, mutual support against the over harsh[31] discipline of training, and as soon as they got it they felt safe. The N.C.O. in charge of the hut was decent, and when they were not too exhausted by P.T. - oh the noise they made.[32]

The key of Hut 4 remains laughter;[33] the laughter of shallow water. Everywhere there is the noise of games, tricks, back chat, advices, helps, councils, confidences, complaints: and laughs behind the gravest of these. The noise is infernal. Our jazz band is very posh of its kind, because Madden leads it with his mandoline. He is supported by two coal-pans, the fire buckets, five tissued combs, two shovels, the stove doors, fire[34] boiler lids and vocal incidents. The louder it is the louder they sing, the more they leap about their beds, strike half-arm balances, do hand-springs and neck-rolls, or wrestle doggily over the floors and iron-bound boxes. There's hardly a night without its mirthful accident of blood letting.[35]

There's plenty of this gay and good tempered stuff in The Mint. Much of it's lively reading, "Give him a gob of your toffology" they cry, when they want him to answer the sergeant back.[36] And he gives it.[37] And the sergeant's struck dumb.[38]

Outside these contrary[39] principles of the Square and the Hut, Discipline and Loyalty, stands Church Parade, professing to reconcile them and to represent the[40] principle of Love. Lawrence watched its efforts[41] with detachment. A bare over restored fourteenth century church gave him convenient opportunities for reflection.

Worship seemed due from us on so sunny a morning.[42] So perforce I heard another unreal service and again its misapplication stung me, preached as it was over the serried ranks of those healthy irks I knew from the skins upward. Now they were alike - dressed and all singing "The King of Love my Shepherd Is" with the voice and the pagan enjoyment of their every day blasphemy. Nor did their minds see any contradiction between their worship and their life. Neither their clean words nor their dirty words had any significance. Words were like our boots, dirty on the fields, clean indoors; a daily convention, no index of the fellows' minds. They had not learned to speak. The blind padre was still labouring to draw a response from the dumb. The truckling humility of his general confession, his tremendous pretence of absolution, jarred across the congregation - as stridently as would one of our oaths across a hushed church. Simply there was no contact between these worlds.[43]

There is much else to[44] discuss in the Uxbridge sections. But we must move in - as did he.[45]

Here's a cheerful account of him as he leaves the Depot and starts his journey[46] to Cranwell.

At the station gate they threw on my shoulders (knocking my cap off) the kit bag of all my spare goods: only eighty more pounds. The trip slowly convinced me that this military equipment was not designed for peace-time trains. I had become too wide to advance frontally through any carriage door. In each queue or press I jabbed the next man with a buckle in the mouth, or browned the next woman with my equipment's clay. The old lady next me in the Underground wore a flippant skirt, all doo-dahs. My scabbard[47] enlarged one of these. She rose up and went, more fretted even than the skirt. I bulged with relief into her extra space, but my water-bottle tilted nose-down on the arm rest, and filled the vacant seat with a secret lake.[48]

This third section of The Mint - the one I've labeled The Joy of having been trained - is a complete contrast to its predecessors and is intended to contrast.[49] It shows the positive idealistic side of the R.A.F., it celebrates its conquest of the air, and it is foreshadowed by a quaint barrack room eulogy of Lord Trenchard. Pleasant airy reading it makes; full of summer sun and Lincolnshire wind, and huge hangars where officers and men cooperate, full too of common sense and informality and service loyalty to a common cause, and the trustfulness of men who have all been[50] trained and can consequently trust each other. There's no longer the split between loyalty and training that made Uxbridge so tragic and so fascinating. All in accord. At the end there is a thrilling set-piece in honour of speed:[51] he on his motor bike, his Boanerges, races a Bristol Fighter, close above him in the air. The last words of all are "Everywhere a relationship: no loneliness any more".[52] Relationship is <u>through</u> the R.A.F. - not the relationship a civilian calls 'personal'.

I was never easy about this third section and sometimes discussed it with him.[53] I told him that he might have been happy at Cranwell but he had not succeeded in communicating his happiness to me, that he had plunged me into a sort of comforting bath water where I sat contented and surprised but not convinced that I was being cleansed. I wanted something more detergent than bath water after Hell. I also complained that he was being fair minded and had thought it his duty to emphasise the pleasanter side of the R.A.F. before laying down his pen. Against this he defended himself mildly. As regards happiness we agreed that it is of all emotions the most difficult to convey, and that perhaps he had been happy although he had not said so.[54]

Re-reading this third part today I still feel dissatisfied although it contains some[55] brilliant chapters. It is too[56] insipid a conclusion for such a serious work. Moreover time has been unkind to it. The conquest of the air, for which he romantically yearned, has been all too thoroughly achieved. From sixty to seventy countries are now flying about in the stuff and some of[57] them own hydrogen bombs. Romance must look further afield than the air - or perhaps nearer at home in the unexplored tracts of the heart. And the eulogy of speed rings unacceptably when one thinks of the nature of his death.[58] Per ardua ad asbestos.

I sometimes speculate whether he will ever become a national hero. He has few of our national characteristics but that is no obstacle. He is not more alien to our stodginess than Nelson was to the stodgy court of George III. He nearly made the hero grade in the early twenties amid the splendours of his Arabian victories,[59] and again in the mid thirties after his dramatic death. Then oblivion and criticism thickened and now he is in the limelight again[60] and once more the subject of a newspaper stunt.[61] I don't expect the Press will be further interested in him. That part's over. But he had mystery about him, and power, and the power to inspire affection and to create legends, and there are moments when I see him, smiling rather wryly, in[62] the British Valhalla, at the same time glad and not glad to be there.

---

1. <NOT CHECKED IN TALKS DEPARTMENT WITH>

2. The publishing details for *The Mint* are inserted by a hand other than EMF's; P. H. Newby's vetting signature also appears at the top along with three handwritten notations: "Repeat Announcement Attached," "Speaker's Copy," and "N.B. Approx. 700 words' quotation - F.D."

3. <so in one way I am a suitable person to broadcast about it this evening>

4. <when we first met> As the NSA recording of this broadcast reveals, EMF preferred contractions (wasn't, I'll, etc.) to more formal constructions in performing his script. Other variants between the script and EMF's oral delivery are noted below.

5. NSA: "We wrote to each other, and later on talked"

6. <The Mint>

7. <He worked with them, and he believed that was the only way in which they could be understood. worked with them. Never having>

8. <and>

9. NSA: "Well, it was partly"

10. NSA: "and it was partly the desire to hide, and partly the itch for adventure."

11. NSA: "He really joined up"

12. <When he broke off his brilliant career and plunged himself into the squalor of an R.A.F. depot, when he exchanged comfort and distinction for fatigues and the square, it was partly the desire to abase himself, I know, and it was partly the itch for adventure. But deeper than either of these motives - very deep - was the hope that if he worked with people he might come to understand them and share their lives. Never having had his experiences, I have to broadcast about them as it were, from the outside. I cannot interpret them, nor can I check his statements. In this way I'm ill qualified to hold forth. All I can do is to talk about his book as a book.> This canceled passage originally opened page 2 of the script; EMF inserted a new page 1A, beginning, "I've never shared any of Lawrence's experiences" (see above).

13. <It is>

14. EMF added an accent mark above "not."

15. <Through strivings to the stars.>

16. <as the lofty Air Force motto puts it.>

17. <direction>

18. NSA: "third, final section"

19. <the>

20. NSA: "beautiful bird cries"

21. NSA: "He only fails I think"

22. NSA: "Well and now"

23. NSA: "It was caused, according to him,"

24. <and>

25. <wants them to think he is>

26. NSA: "Here's the passage where he expresses this view - I've cut it a little."

27. NSA: "They have put us into maudlin fear, he says"

28. <I do not know if all see this; our hut is full of innocents . . . But they know that there is more in this severity than training. Lawful discipline would not have scared them into the present funk, which with exactness of adjective they call piddling . . . Another week and the R.A.F. will have confirmed the coward in every one of us.>

29. *The Mint* (London: Jonathan Cape, 1955), 102–3. EMF omitted remarks on the tormentors' sexual excitement ("sob for breath; and evident through their clothes is that tautening of the muscles (and once the actual rise of sexual excitement) which betrays. . .") and Lawrence's judgments upon himself: "Am I overdone, emotional? Is it only the impact of strenuous conditions upon a frame unfitted by nature and its career for present hardship?" (102); "If time has made me more worn than them, also it has made me deeper. . . . these fellows' feelings, because of their youngness, seem like shallops on a river. . . . Whereas to root out one of my thoughts - what upstirring of mud, what rending of fibre in the darkness!" (102–3); "despite my willingness (quickened by a profound dissatisfaction with what I am) that the R.A.F. should bray me" (103).

30. NSA: "I'll turn, with pleasure"

31. <hard>

32. NSA: "when the young men were not too exhausted by P.T.—well, oh the noise they made."

33. NSA: "laughter, Lawrence says,"

34. NSA: "five er fire" (Lawrence's text actually reads "five locker lids")

35. Lawrence, *The Mint*, 133. A slight laugh is audible on the NSA recording as EMF recounts the men's frenetic handsprings and wrestling.

36. Ibid., 117.

37. <Another sergeants' clash.>

38. NSA: "And the sergeant collapses and is struck dumb."

39. <tendencies>

40. <tenderness>

41. NSA: "effects"

42. NSA: "so sunny a morning, he records."

43. Lawrence, *The Mint*, 92–93.

44. <discover>

45. NSA: "There's much else I could discuss about the Uxbridge sections but it's time to move on, and he moved on in time."

46. NSA: "joyous journey"

47. <chafe> The *Listener* (17 February 1955, pp. 279–80) restores "scabbard chafe," an error for Lawrence's "scabbard chape" (*The Mint*, 166) — a "metal plate or mounting of a scabbard or sheath" (*OED*).

48. Lawrence, *The Mint*, 166–67. A slight laugh is audible in the NSA recording when EMF mentions the secret lake.

49. EMF added accent marks above the first syllable of the first "contrast" and the second syllable of the second "contrast" (emphases audible in the NSA recording).

50. <through the depot and can>

51. NSA: "Loyalty and training are in accordance. And at the end Lawrence provides a thrilling set-piece in honour of speed:"

52. Lawrence, *The Mint*, 206.

53. NSA: "Now I never was easy about this third section and sometimes I discussed it with him."

54. NSA: "hadn't really managed to say so."

55. <fine>

56. <boyish a>

57. <our>

58. Lawrence died in a motorcycle accident (see Furbank, *A Life*, 2:207).

59. *Listener*, NSA: "reputation"

60. NSA: "Then oblivion and criticism moved in and now he's in the limelight again"

61. In the preface to her 1955 biography of Lawrence, Flora Armitage explains that T. E. Lawrence was illegitimate, a fact quietly disclosed by Thomas Jones in *A Diary with Letters, 1931–1950*, issued in October 1954 by Oxford University Press. At the beginning of 1955, in advance of his 1955 biography of Lawrence, Richard Aldington leaked the fact of Lawrence's illegitimacy to the newspapers as if it were a "sensational coup" (Armitage, *The Desert and the Stars: A Biography of Lawrence of Arabia* [New York: Henry Holt and Co., 1955], vii–viii). Armitage quotes EMF's broadcast on *The Mint* in her preface, dated July 1955 (viii).

62. <our>

¹CHECKED IN TALKS DEPARTMENT WITH "AS BROADCAST" SCRIPT

Producer: Leonie John

"GOLDSWORTHY LOWES DICKINSON"
Talk by E.M. Forster

Transmission:	Friday, 5th October, 1956: 8.50 - 9.20 p.m.
	THIRD PROGRAMME
Recording:	Friday, 28th September, 1956: 4.15 - 5.15 p.m.
Rehearsal:	from 3.15 p.m.
Studio:	3D
Tape No:	TLO 13521

Goldsworthy Lowes Dickinson was born on August the 6th 1862. (For I want to preface this talk with a brief account of his life. It was not a dramatic life. So let us get it out of the way). He was born, then, of cultivated middle class stock. His father was a portrait painter of note. His mother had a connection with a well-known firm of publishers.² The marriage of his parents was a happy one, and with one brother and three sisters he passed a very happy childhood. "Goldie" they called him. He went on to a preparatory school and to Charterhouse, at both of which institutions he was uniformly miserable. Not until Cambridge did the clouds begin to break and the mists to rise, and the possibility of living and of helping others to live dawn. King's, the college to which he went, just suited him,³ but mainly because there is a tradition there which he did all he could to promote: that of easy intercourse between old and young. Dons at King's don't live in one box and students in another. Anyhow they needn't unless they want to.

He read Classics,⁴ left the University and turned his attention to political studies. He also tried to work with his hands on a cooperative farm, also tried to be a doctor. These⁵ attempts were abortive but are symptomatic. He was trying to give away what he was beginning to receive, and to help his fellow creatures. A more appropriate avenue was opened in 1887 when King's made him a Fellow, he⁶ went into residence there and began a career of teaching in Cambridge and London. Subjects: Political History, analysis of constitutions, that sort of thing. He also wrote books.

He also travelled: to Europe constantly, twice to America and once to India and the Far East. I went with him[7] to India.

And then came the 1914 war.

It's impossible to convey to a younger generation what 1914 felt like. It was such a <u>surprise</u>. That word is a feeble one, yet I can think of none more appropriate. It certainly gave Dickinson a surprise that lasted him for the rest of his life. He knew the war was coming or might be coming, he was prepared for it intellectually, but he could not foretell his emotions. His feelings are best conveyed by an analogy: they resembled the feelings which arise when a promise has been broken by a person whom one loves. One knows all the time that the promise will not be kept, perhaps cannot be kept, yet the shock is none the less mortal. In 1914 civilisation broke its promise to him, and he never felt sure of it again.

Not that he collapsed or despaired.[8] His old values held firm. In the very first fortnight of the war he jotted down on a half-sheet of note-paper a scheme for a League of Nations which should prevent future wars. The phrase 'League of Nations' did not exist then, but he had earlier than any-one the idea.[9] For the next fifteen years he was concerned with the incep-tion and the organisation of the League, did propaganda for it in America and elsewhere, and constantly attended at Geneva when it took up its quarters in that city.[10] His great work <u>The International Anarchy</u>,[11] where the war's origins are analysed, dates from now.[12] Its importance must be emphasised - especially to those who still assume that a don does not[13] trouble himself with outside affairs.

During the last years of his life he had a respite from anxiety. He had done what he could[14] and he sat back. He was in Cambridge again and found it as congenial and charming as ever and a place where the old could still learn from the young. And the young seemed to be learning from him.[15] Then he fell ill. An operation was advised and[16] apparently succeeded, and when I saw him in the hospital he was cheerfully planning for the future. But on the following day he died - August the 3rd 1932. He was three days under the age of seventy.

So much for the life of Goldsworthy Lowes Dickinson.

What of his work?

He was a prolific writer. His complete Bibliography totals nearly 400 items. Most of these are newspaper articles or letters or translations, but there are over twenty books, from which I must now choose.[17] I need only mention in passing <u>A Modern Symposium</u>,[18] for you will hear that broad-cast tomorrow: when listening to it you should note the progress in it from the politicians, with whom it starts, to the visionaries with whom it con-cludes; from the first speakers who are obviously the nineteenth century Lord Salisbury, Gladstone and Disraeli, down to the last speaker who is said to be George Meredith. And be sure not to miss the poet, the most unusual poet, who is modelled upon Dickinson's friend and my friend, R.C. Trevelyan.[19]

The International Anarchy stands at the head of a group of war books. The Modern Symposium stands at the head of a little group of Dialogues. At the head of a little Greek group stands the Greek View of Life, to which I must now refer.[20]

I must be brief, because I am saving up my time for two other books - the Letters from John Chinaman and The Magic Flute. The Greek View of Life was published in 1896, and it exploded the fallacy that only those who know Greek can know Greece. It has run into about twenty editions, and must have introduced thousands of young men and women to an inheritance they were in danger of neglecting. The Ancients are Modern. That was Dickinson's contention. They are modern, firstly, because many of their political and social problems have been ours, and have been expressed, particularly in Athens, with a lucidity beyond our power. Our passions colour our judgments - and are bound to, or we shouldn't be alive. Ancient Greece has the advantage of being remote from us in time. It can be studied dispassionately. And it has a further advantage. It is not just a convenient laboratory for the social scientist. The joy of living and the greatness of existence are also to be found there.[21] It is the greatest literature the western world has produced. It has one disadvantage. It can only be read by people who have sweated at the language for years, and they often cannot read it as well as they pretend. Translations are therefore imperative. The Greek View of Life might be called an introduction to translations. It is an attempt to show the non-expert the character and environment of hidden treasures, and to leave him amongst them. If Dickinson were alive today - which for many reasons he would not wish to be - he would anyhow be cheered by the excellence of popular translations from the Greek: T.E. Lawrence's Odyssey and Mr. Rex Warner's Thucydides are two that come to my mind.[22]

From Greece let us hasten to China.

Letters from John Chinaman came out, quietly enough, in 1901. It purports to be addressed by a Chinese official to an English friend, and it describes the charm and the sanity of Chinese civilisation, and the approaching threat to it from the economic imperialism of the West, and its possible vengeance on[23] the West. It appeared anonymously[24] but was rightly assumed by English readers to be by an Englishman. In America it had a more dramatic reception, which shall be described in Dickinson's own words.

It penetrated to America, and there everybody seems to have accepted naively its Chinese origin. It was attributed to the then Chinese ambassador; and Mr. Bryan, the famous politician, thought it worth while to write a special reply to it, in which he observed, among other things, that clearly the writer had never seen the inside of a Christian home. Before publishing his book he ascertained that the author was really an Englishman and he said as much in his preface. But he thought his book none the less worth publishing, and it is not for me to dispute that it may have been.[25]

If only a politician will speak strongly for or against a book that book will certainly sell, and good Mr. Bryan sold <u>John Chinaman</u> like hot cakes. We today - reading the book after the excitement is over, and after the prophecies contained in it have been but confusedly fulfilled - read it for the sureness of its touch, the exquisiteness of its style, and the truth of its feeling. It is the loveliest of his works - too smooth maybe for some tastes and bearing[26] little relation to the China of today. To the China of his[27] day it was germane. Eleven years after writing it, he visited the country, and was not disappointed. "China is much as I imagined it", he wrote to me from Pekin in 1913. "I thought I was idealising, but I doubt it".[28] He may have been idealising. He certainly experienced the emotion of love. There was some deep[29] affinity. When he got old and felt the draughts he used to wear a little Chinese cap - or rather a series of caps for he kept losing them - made out of black silk with a tiny red button on the top. Foreign trimmings do not as a rule suit the Britisher but his were appropriate. They suited him.[30]

Since I have mentioned this cap, I will allude to the physiognomy beneath it. Here is what he looked like[31] in his later days. Clean-shaven; features strongly marked; spectacles; the complexion not good; the head bowed a little forward from the shoulders when he walked, though the shoulders themselves, like the body generally, were shapely and strong. The hands - to proceed with this inventory - were large. The clothes erred on the dowdy side - dark blue serges, shirts of indistinction, podgy ties. Thus caparisoned, he did not present a commanding figure, but there was about him a most[32] commanding charm. Charm, in most men and nearly all women, is a decoration. It genuinely belongs to them, as a good complexion may, but it lies on the surface and can vanish. Charm in Lowes Dickinson was structural. It penetrated and upheld everything he did, it remained into old age. It conferred on him a beauty which cannot be given that rather patronising label of "spiritual", a beauty which, though it had nothing to do with handsomeness, did belong to the physical, so that his presence was appropriate amidst gorgeous scenery or exquisite flowers.

And now for <u>The Magic Flute</u>.

This remarkable little fantasy came out in 1920, shortly after the first world war had ended. It recalls the opera of Mozart, and it adapts for its own purposes the libretto that Mozart set to music. The Queen of the Night stands for instinct: she dwells on the other side of Mind, in the dark, creating while she sleeps. She is Queen of the Night, but not of the heavenly bodies, whom she hates because of their brightness and their order. Sarastro stands for reason - and for something else: what else Sarastro stands for we shall one day see. Pamina, their daughter, is the world's desire. Tamino, in quest of Pamina, is Every Youth; his ardour and his nobility are matured by experience until he reaches the goal and understands the nature of the goal. For it is not what[33] Tamino first supposed it would be. He passes through the Fires of agony and the Waters of doubt to no ordinary consummation. The mystic side of Dickinson has taken charge. It also inspires[34] two profound and profoundly moving episodes that he has introduced into the Mozartian story: the episode of the Hermitage of Jesus and the episode of the Lotus Lake of Buddha.

The story opens with the Queen of the Night persuading Tamino to rescue her daughter who, she declares, is imprisoned by Sarastro in his castle; untrue: Pamina remains with Sarastro of her own will. The foolish enterprise turns into a war - not with Sarastro, who will not use force and cannot be touched by force, but between the deluded peoples of the earth. It is the[35] war through which Dickinson had himself just passed.[36] Tamino fights, kills his enemy, and then it is revealed to him through the power of Sarastro, that he has killed his friend. He leaves the battle-field and preaches peace - to find that the civilisation he trusted has betrayed him, he is thrown into prison and into fire, and through the fire the spirit of Pamina leads him - she and the music of his own flute, which, unknown to him, had once played in the castle of Sarastro.

The allegory then gathers strength. The war section is the weakest in the book: Dickinson stood too near to the horrors he was trying to exorcise. It is when Tamino has passed the test of the Fire, and is approaching the test of[37] the waters of doubt - that the author's genius finds scope. Tamino has been purged of selfishness. He desires Pamina no longer for himself but for the whole world.[38] He seeks her and knows that he cannot find her unless he finds truth. With[39] truth as his aim he sets out for the desert.

At the very edge of the desert is a house surrounded by a garden, and over the garden gate a man is leaning - an elderly man with an ironical mouth and kindly eyes. It is Candide - Voltaire's Candide. They take to each other and Tamino stays with him for a time and helps him cultivate his garden. Candide - ever since his mistress Cunegonde left him to run a brothel on the Bosphorus - has known few inconveniences. He is intelligent, humane, considerate, gay, he has no pains, no pleasures, no desires, no philosophy, no interest in Truth. He is a congenial companion except in one respect: Tamino cannot mention Pamina to him, for he would only take her for another Cunegonde. So he has to continue his journey into the desert.

Candide accompanies him a little way into it - partly through friendliness, partly because the road passes a ruined building, called the Hermitage of Jesus, which he is curious to visit. Not that he is interested in antiquities, but there is an odd rumour that Jesus has returned there and he should like to verify this. They are overtaken by another traveller, a handsome and agreeable man.[40] He also has heard the rumour and is bound for the Hermitage. He adds "I have a special interest, for I met Jesus here once before. My name is Satan." Candide is delighted to meet Satan, and cries "So you are visiting the scene of your discomfiture". Satan answers "No - that has been misrepresented: the scene of my triumph. I offered Jesus in this wilderness the three things which could alone have made his mission a success - imposture, science and empire. He rejected them all, and so showed himself a failure, as I intended he should". This leads to an interesting talk and Candide shrewdly asks why he took the trouble to tempt.[41] Satan's answer brings us up against one of Dickinson's profound beliefs: his belief in some unity that exists beneath Good and Evil. "I acted under orders" he answers. "I don't know why they were given, or who gave them. But apparently I executed them satisfactorily, for I have just been ordered to tempt Jesus again".[42]

By this time they have reached the Hermitage and find quite a company there. A Spanish Jesuit, a French abbé of the modernist type, a Scottish Presbyterian and a Russian priest have all heard the rumour and have come to meet Jesus. They have been waiting for several days and their relations have become strained. Satan and Candide establish a pleasanter atmosphere, they all sit round the fire, with the darkness and the sounds of the wilderness at their backs, and each of them explains in turn the bearing of this new event (if indeed it has occurred) on his particular creed. The Jesuit begins. In a thoughtful and brilliant speech he expounds the importance of the Church, which "took up the truth revealed by Jesus, interpreted it to the intelligence of mankind, and applied it to their institutions".[43] And he warns his hearers not to confuse the Jesus of Eternity, whose revelation was absolute and final, with the Jesus of Time, who visited the world nearly 2000 years ago, and who - if indeed he is returning to it - will find much to bewilder him and will need the expert guidance of his own Church.

Tamino is impressed, but becomes aware of the sounds of the desert and of something - or is it someone? - who stands outside the circle of their fire. The same sensation recurs during the address of the second speaker, the French abbé, who explains the doctrine of Progressive Revelation and informs the irritated Jesuit that the heresies of one generation are the orthodoxies of the next. [44]Brilliant eyes fix Tamino - set in the night and brighter than the stars - and a possibility enters his mind. Then the Russian priest speaks - most touchingly, for the Jesus he waits for will not belong to the clever or the influential or the advanced, but to the poor. And again the gaze beckoning out of the night, the possibility becoming a certainty. Finally the Scottish Presbyterian speaks. He has some sharp words for Candide, whom he understandably mistrusts, and the Jesus he expects is or should be hard, for hardness is what this backsliding generation needs. They are not fit for the Sermon on the Mount. Tamino he characterises as "a nice laddie," who must go back to his work, accept the teaching of his own Church, and expect to find it true when he is old enough to understand.

Tamino does not hear this sound advice. For the possibility has become a certainty and without speech he speaks to Jesus.

"Lord was your gospel true or false?"

"True and false".

"What was true in it?"

"Love one another. Forgive your enemies."

"What was false?"

"The scourge of small cords and the coming on clouds to judge the world."

"Are any of the Churches your Church?"

"None."

"How can I belong to your Church?"

"By following me. By following Truth in Love."

"How shall I find Truth?"

This last remark he makes aloud and the Presbyterian answers tartly "I have already told you Truth is found". None of the Churches have been aware of Jesus and Satan says "It must have been some hallucination". But Satan has seen him and has to admit it, adding "He is more impracticable than ever. I shall not even trouble to tempt him. Fortunately these gentlemen have me to direct them, and between us, I daresay, we shall build a tolerable church against anarchy".[45]

Tamino then realises that Satan is Fraud, that the church he hopes to build is for the worship of the Golden Calf; and he hates him.

The next stage of his quest for Truth is the Lotus Lake of Buddha. This is a solemn and exquisite place, inspired by what Dickinson has seen in China and Tamino at first mistakes it for the Castle of Sarastro. But it is a monastery whose inmates follow the quest of Eternity, and he himself, since he follows Pamina, is a child of Time. He undergoes the discipline of the monastery.[46] He[47] meditates in a wood lost in meditation, and preparing to pass into the final, the eighth stage, from which there is no return -

and then a traveller came through the wood, thieves set on him and left
him for dead. He called for help but Tamino could not give it, he was too
far away, and by the time he returned to the body the man was dead, and
he saw in his eyes that look of the man on the battlefield, who had been
both his enemy and his friend. He went back to the monastery. In the setting sun, one of the statues of Buddha glowed, and Tamino held with it a
voiceless colloquy, such as he had in the Hermitage of Jesus.

"Lord Buddha, was your gospel true?"

"True and False."

"What was true in it?"

"Selflessness and Love."

"What false?"

"Flight from Life."[48]

The light fades from the statue, to illumine the lotus buds on the lake, and
they flower into the face of Pamina. He must go back to life. And having
passed the Waters of Doubt with the help of her spirit and the music of his
flute, he enters the Castle of Sarastro.

This, the climax of the book, is rather unsatisfactory:[49] too much has to
be worked in. The décor is again Mozartian: Tamino has passed the tests,
and is initiated into the Order of Truth.[50] Who else has been admitted into
the Order? Amongst the Greeks, Socrates and Aristotle, but not Plato.[51]
Why not? Because Plato fell back in the end under the dominion of the
Queen of Night; he came to prefer religion to reason, authority to liberty,
and the state to the individual. And these are the three great heresies[52]
which no-one holding can remain a member of the Order. The same bar
excludes Dante, the greatest of poets,[53] but the builder of a prison, and to
the Castle of Sarastro none come but freemen. One more question: is
Candide here? The answer is no; Candide almost qualifies but he lacks the
one thing needful: the Sacred Fire.

With this reference to the Sacred Fire my attempt to recall Lowes
Dickinson draws to its close. You see the importance of the reference:
Dickinson believes in reason but is not a rationalist. He believes also in the
Sacred Fire, and the fusion of these two beliefs is attempted in his concep-
tion of Sarastro. How can they be fused? How can water and fire combine?
Certainly not in the material world. But when we consider the complexi-
ties of the human spirit fusion becomes, if not possible, at all events com-
prehensible.

I have used the phrase "to recall Lowes Dickinson" and I fear it is an apt
one, for I do not think he is much read or much talked about today - not
even in King's College Cambridge, the tiny corner of the world which
once contained him. I am sorry about this, not for his sake, but because he
has so much to offer. He challenges the materialism of our age. He also

challenges the religiosity, the revivalism, the insistence on sin that are so often[54] offered as correctives to materialism. In place of those false goods and gods he offers the human spirit which tries to follow reason, knows that reason sometimes fails, yet when it does fail does not scuttle to take refuge in authority. Add to this his belief that it is through poetry and through music that man comes closest to the Sacred Fire, and his claim to be remembered is confirmed.

He has also a tangible memorial. When you are in London, and if you are in the neighbourhood of Kensington, go and look at Edwardes Square. It is a charming square to the south of Kensington High Street. No.11 Edwardes Square is the house where Dickinson's sisters lived, and where he lived when he was in town. A plaque has been put up to him on the house. It describes him as a writer and a humanist, and the word humanist also describes Sarastro.[55]

1. <NOT>
2. <He had one>
3. <partly because of its architectural and scenic beauty,>
4. <took a good degree,>
5. <latter>
6. <started to live>
7. <as far as>
8. <or ceased to believe in love or the imagination or reason, or in the necessity for work. On the contrary.>
9. <, and when others took the idea up he worked it out with them.>
10. For more on Dickinson's devotion to the league and his efforts on its behalf, see EMF's biography, *Goldsworthy Lowes Dickinson* (London: Edward Arnold, 1934).
11. Goldsworthy Lowes Dickinson, *The International Anarchy* (London: Allen and Unwin, 1926).
12. <I shall not have time to talk about <u>The International Anarchy</u>, nor have I the competence, but>
13. <concern>
14. <over the League of Nations>
15. <His love of music - I've never mentioned that - could be gratified, his studies in Goethe extended.>
16. <appeared to have worked>
17. <The formidable <u>International Anarchy</u> has already been mentioned. And>
18. *A Modern Symposium* (London: George Allen and Unwin, 1905). As an 8 June 1956 letter from John Morris to EMF indicated, the original plan was to present *A Modern Symposium* on the same night as EMF's broadcast, with EMF's talk serving as an introduction; both features were part of a festival week celebrating the tenth anniversary of the Third Programme (E. M. Forster File 10a, 1955–1957 R CONT 1, BBC WAC). The *Listener* cut EMF's reference to the following night's dramatization and the rest of the paragraph, adding an asterisk after "I need only mention in passing <u>A Modern Symposium</u>" that directed readers to a note at the bottom of the page: "This talk was given on October 5 as an introduction to

a shortened version of Lowes Dickinson's *A Modern Symposium* which was broadcast on October 6" (EMF, "A Great Humanist," *Listener,* 11 October 1956, p. 545).

19. <(I suppose I <<ought not>> it is risky to suggest that one can progress from a politician to a visionary or a poet but it is progress that Dickinson himself regarded as essential.)> R. C. Trevelyan, older brother of the historian G. M. Trevelyan, had known EMF distantly in Cambridge. For their relationship and Trevelyan's poetic ambitions, see Furbank, *A Life,* 1:112–13.

20. Dickinson, *The Greek View of Life* (London: Methuen, 1896).

21. <Greek literature combines beauty and depth, wisdom and wit, gaiety and insight, speculation and ecstasy, carnality and spirit; it has variety; it has constructional power;>

22. T. E. Lawrence, trans., *The Odyssey of Homer* (London: Oxford University Press, 1934); Rex Warner, trans., *History of the Peloponnesian War* (Harmondsworth, England: Penguin, 1954).

23. EMF added an accent mark above "on."

24. <and was taken>

25. See EMF, *Goldsworthy Lowes Dickinson,* 143. It is not clear, either in his biography of Dickinson or in the BBC talk, from which source EMF quoted.

26. <no>

27. EMF added an accent mark above "his."

28. For the complete letter, see EMF, *Goldsworthy Lowes Dickinson,* 147–49.

29. EMF added an accent mark above "deep."

30. <I remember too how he once amused an audience by saying "I am speaking to you about China - not because I know anything about the subject nor because I once visited the country, but because in a previous existence I actually was a Chinaman". So perhaps Mr. Bryan may have been right in denying him the <<interior>> inside of a Christian home.>

31. <when I knew him>

32. <compelling>

33. <he>

34. <the>

35. <first world>

36. <, and the causes of which, political and psychological, he had elsewhere examined>

37. <the Water ->

38. <, over whom she must reign as queen>

39. <that>

40. <on horseback>

41. <when he wanted to fail>

42. Goldsworthy Lowes Dickinson, *The Magic Flute: A Fantasia* (London: Allen and Unwin, 1928), 79–80. For EMF's earlier remarks on *The Magic Flute,* see his broadcast dated 10 October 1932.

43. Lowes Dickinson, *The Magic Flute,* 86.

44. <Once again>

45. Lowes Dickinson, *The Magic Flute,* 97–99.

46. <, since it may lead to Truth, and he passes through seven stages of initiation, each with its own reward. By the time he reaches the seventh stage, he is aware of nothing and his soul <<was>> is like nothing, it <<was>> is a state beyond peace, and he would have been glad to remain in it for ever.>

47. <sat> (restored in the *Listener*)

48. Lowes Dickinson, *The Magic Flute,* 107–8.

49. < - like the beginning, but for a different reason>

50. <He is welcomed by someone who is the dying soldier and the murdered traveller, and the enemy-friend, and they gaze together into the past and the future.>

51. *Listener:* "Who else has been admitted into the Order? Not Plato."

52. EMF added accent marks above "three," "great," and the beginning of "heresies."

53. <l'altissimo poeta,> (the highest poet). The *Listener* dropped the reference to Dante.

54. <and so unwisely>

55. <The Magic Flute, John Chinaman and A Modern Symposium are all in print, The Greek View of Life will be reprinted shortly. There is, furthermore, a biography of Lowes Dickinson by myself.>

Duration = 21'23"
[1]'AS BROADCAST' SCRIPT

                                    Producer: P.H. Newby
[2]RECOLLECTIONS OF NASSENHEIDE
by <u>E.M. Forster</u>
Recording: Friday, 28th November 1958 5.00 - 5.45 p.m. 3C.
Number: Third 72581
Duration:
Transmission: Sunday, 28th December 1958 [3]9.05 - 9.30 p.m.
<u>Germany</u>   THIRD PROGRAMME

Please open this book on page 128.[4] There you will see a photograph of me. I am a slim youth, for the photograph is over half a century old, and I am standing beside another and more solid young man. His name is Herr[5] Steinweg and he is a German tutor. I am an English tutor. In front of us sit two governesses, in white blouses, white aprons, long thick skirts and stout boots. One of them is German - Fraulein Backe - the other French: Mademoiselle Auger de Balben. And the photograph is entitled "The teaching staff at Nassenheide in 1905". There we are in the garden, in the pre-war summer sunshine, the sunshine that expected shadow but had no conception of disintegration. And there behind us lies Nassenheide, supposed to be a Schloss,[6] but really a charming low grey country house, in the depths of Pomerania. Somewhere inside it, or perhaps in her summer-house, writing one of her novels, is our employer, the <u>Countess von Arnim</u>,[7] and somewhere else again must be our three little pupils.

Let me explain how I got out there.[8] I wanted to learn some German, and do some writing and a Cambridge friend put me in touch with his aunt. She was English (born in Australia actually) and she had married an aristocratic Pomeranian landowner. She was furthermore a well known and gifted authoress, who wrote under the name of Elizabeth. Her 'Elizabeth and her German Garden' was widely read, and her three eldest girls, had become household words in many a British household. I am not talking about her books, but[9] they are much neglected to-day, and I hope that this excellent biography of her will bring them back to prominence. I was one of a series of tutors - Hugh Walpole[10] himself was to succeed me -

456

and I was to pick up in exchange what German I could. At first I feared I should not get the job, for I met none of her requirements - refused to come permanently, could not give all my time, couldn't teach mathematics or anything except English. But the more difficulties I raised the warmer grew Elizabeth's letters. She begged me to come when I liked and as I liked. She trusted I shouldn't find Nassenheide dull, and she asked me to be so good as to bring her from London a packet of orris root.

My arrival occurred on the 4th of April 1905. Never shall I forget it. I took the express from Berlin to Stettin, and there had to change into the light railway for Nassenheide. When I arrived there it was dark. We drew up in the middle of a farmyard. Heaps of manure, with water between them, could be seen in the light that fell from the carriage windows, but of the Countess von Arnim not a sign. The guard shouted. There was no reply. He got off the train and plunged[11] into the night, presently re-emerging with a farm labourer who was to carry my bag and show me where the Schloss was. Heavy luggage remained in the manure. We slipped and splashed through an atmosphere now heavily charged with romance, and in God's good time came to the long low building I was presently to know under sunlight. The bell pealed, a hound bayed, and a half-dressed underservant unlocked the hall door and asked me what I wanted. I replied "I want to live here". The hall was white and vaulted and decorated with the heads of birds and small animals, and with admonitory mottoes in black paint. The hound continued to bay. Presently the German tutor was aroused, the cordial and intelligent Herr Steinweg, who explained that I had not been expected so soon. He showed me my room, also my bed, but I could not occupy the latter for the reason that the out-going English tutor had not yet vacated it. It was settled that I had better sleep in the nobler part of the house, in the best spare room itself. The cold was appalling in the spare room,[12] the wall paper excruciatingly pink and green, the sound of a pump from the farm yard where my luggage lay was ceaseless and ghostly. Came the dawn and came breakfast, and with it all possible kindness from my colleagues. And presently I stood in the presence of the Countess herself.

Elizabeth of the German Garden proved to be small and graceful, vivid and vivacious. She was also capricious and a merciless tease. The discomforts of my arrival seemed to have lowered me in her opinion:[13] indeed I lost all the ground I had gained through refusing to come. Glancing up at my tired and peaked face, she said in her rather grating voice "How d'ye do Mr. Forster. We confused you with the new housemaid . . . Can you teach the children do you think? They are very difficult . . . oh yes Mr. Forster very difficult, they'll laugh at you, you know. You'll have to be stern or it'll end as it did with Mr. Stokoe." I gave her the packet of orris root, which she accepted as only her due, and the interview ended. Subsequently our relations became pleasant[14] and she told me that she had nearly sent me straight back to England[15] there and then, since I was wearing a particularly ugly tie. I do not believe her. I was not. She had no respect for what may be called the lower forms of truth. Then we spoke of some friends of hers whom I had met in Dresden. "They don't like me" she said. I replied "So I saw".[16] This made her think.[17]

So[18] my arrival was on the tough side. Still all went well,[19] and all around us stretched the German countryside, which is my main theme. When I began to look about me I was filled with delight. The German Garden itself, about which Elizabeth had so amusingly written,[20] did not make much impression. Later in the summer some flowers - mainly pansies, tulips, roses,[21] salpiglossis - came into bloom, and there were endless lupins which the Count was drilling for agricultural purposes. But there was nothing of a show and Nassenheide appeared[22] to be surrounded by paddocks and shrubberies. The garden merged into the park which was sylvan in character, and had a field in it over whose long grass at the end of July, a canopy of butterflies kept waving.

It was the country, the flat agricultural surround, that so ravished me. When I arrived in April the air was ugly and came from the east. A few kingcups were out along the edges of the dykes, also some willow-catkins, no leaves. The lanes and the paths were of black sand. The sky lead. The chaussée,[23] white and embanked, divided the desolate fields, cranes flew overhead, crying Ho Hee Toe, Ho Hee[24] Toe as if they were declining the Greek definite article. Then they shrieked and ceased, as if it was too difficult.[25] Storks followed the cranes. Over the immense dark plough galloped the deer to disappear into the cliffs of a forest. Presently the spring broke, slow, thematic, teutonic, the birch trees forming the main melody. You cannot imagine the radiance that descended upon that flat iron-coloured land in May. The birches lined the dykes and strayed into the fields, mistletoe hung from them, some of them formed an islet in the midst of a field of rye, joined to the edge by a birchen isthmus. I would go[26] to this islet on warm afternoons with my German grammar, at first the rye was low, later on it hid the galloping deer. Herr Steinweg and I, both friendly to Nature, took many short walks and he recited poetry.[27] Sometimes we got[28] into the forests. There was a track not far from the house that covered undulating ground and had not been planted too regularly and one evening the light flooded a gallery through it with golden beer upon whose substance a solitary leaf floated motionless. By chance I was myself also full of beer, and encountering the miraculous leaf I thought it might be an illusion. But I pointed it out to Steinweg, who was the soul of sobriety, and he saw it too, which proves its existence doesn't it?

Steinweg and I had our rooms at the end of the long low annexe that ran[29] from the main building. I[30] had a little room which got the morning sun so that I could sit in my bath and be shone upon. He[31] had a larger room where we harmoniously breakfasted, usually upon plovers' eggs. He had a passion for cleanliness, and would daily lift off the lid of the tea-pot to see whether it was coated, as had happened on one occasion, with jam, and it was owing to him that our stoves generally burnt, and that ashes did not sift too thickly over our possessions. He was a delightful companion, always cheerful and considerate and most intelligent from the theological point of view. I only shocked him once, and if I tell you how I shall shock you: I let out to him that I thought telephone wires were hollow and that one spoke down them! He could not imagine such mental incompetence any more than you can and he was silent and cold for a little time afterwards. His pleasant temper, his good sense, and his slight inclination to autocracy made him the natural leader of us menials, and it is to him that the Teaching Staff at Nassenheide owed its most agreeable summer. Later on he became a Pastor in the Lutheran Church. We kept in touch, he came to stay[32] with me in England indeed our friendship actually[33] survived two world wars.

The third member of our quartet was the French lady Mademoiselle Auger de Balben, a charming and childlike soul. Externally she looked a termagant, and well suited for[34] the post of guarding little girls: she always sat in the schoolroom when Steinweg or I taught them. But her nutcracker-face, specs, grey locks, and rounded shoulders accompanied a delightful personality. She was always helping someone or making something - making I can't remember what: paper boxes inside which you found a filigree rabbit or a pig made out of shavings: that gives the idea.[35] I kept for many years the papier-maché snake that she gave me when I left Nassenheide, together with its inscription "C'est le grand serpent Boa, quand il mord ceux qu'il mord sont morts".[36] (Herr Steinweg - he gave me Faust). She was almost totally uneducated and had read fewer books and acquired less information than I should have thought possible. "If I had been educated I might have become a famous woman like Madame de Sevigne",[37] she once remarked gaily. She could however play upon the zither and once when her bracelet caught in the strings of that unusual instrument and fixed her to it immovably, it took the combined efforts of her colleagues and her pupils to set her free. Every one loved her.[38] So did all animals and like a character in a book she would catch them, catch wild animals from the wood and birds in[39] the garden, pet them for a little and let them go. I don't know what became of her.

Fraulein Backe - often called Teppi - was less happily placed. The Countess had recently made her housekeeper as well as German governess and she was overworked. The rest of us were probably under-worked. I was certainly. My teaching duties were only an hour a day. I had abundant leisure[40] for my German and my writing and was most considerately treated if I asked for leave. But Fraulein Backe was always on the run. The Countess called Teppi at all places and hours. The children leapt[41] on her back. The Count stormed because she hadn't provided potatoes, it was to her that Steinweg complained of the jam in our tea pot, the servants cheeked her. She had not asked life to be thus. She was a tall sentimental maiden and it was her secret ambition to 'live in art'. She sang when allowed to do so but so out of tune that permission was seldom accorded. Mademoiselle's zither was preferred. She loved discussing operas, particularly Strauss' Salome, and would dramatise its tenser moments. At times she would attempt fantasy, appearing as an Easter Hare in the garden amidst piles of coloured eggs, or giving at the Schiller centenary a comic performance of Der Alte Moor[42] which was not thought[43] amusing. Dumb devotion bound her to the Countess and the family: her other passion was for the Inspector of Forests, a large taciturn handsome married man; she would become lyrical about the stillness and beauty of his life in the woods. I met her again a few years later, during an amusing caravan tour which the Countess organised in Kent, and recently[44] I had news of her death. It seems that her devotion persisted and that she remained the mainstay of the family through the tensions and tragedies that were to befall them. She died greatly beloved. Sometimes I apply the epitaph of Housman to her - the one about 'the brisk fond lackey to fetch and carry, the true, sick-hearted slave',[45] but it does not really apply for Fraulein Backe has had the reward of gratitude even in this life.

So there we are in that photograph, the four of us immortalised.[46] I do not intend to stray outside it and speak of our pupils, delightful and original and easy as they were, or of their mother, delightful and original and occasionally difficult though she was. I am not reviewing this Biography[47] only reminiscing round the pages in it I know best. [48]I'll keep to Nassenheide, and to a couple of extracts from[49] my Journal[50] there.[51]

May 28, 1905.   A 12 hours expedition to the Oder Berge.[52] (Herr Steinweg, Fraulein, Mademoiselle, self, 3 girls.) Straggling villages full of people who looked fairly happy. But never a comfortable effect, in spite of cleanliness and flowers. The roads are so broad and sandy, the houses are set so aimlessly in their surroundings, and there is no attempt to conceal or group the outhouses.[53] A very pleasant day has happened too recently to write about it. The hills had a mountain stream running down them although they were only 300 feet high. The woods were full of bicyclists' paths.

We had a second lunch and played skittles with a most rickety return-gallery for the balls, and saw a black bull[54] calf, a very clean scullery, and a tall lady-artist in flowing white piquet. Then through woods of spindly[55] oaks to Falkendorf, where I saw two most beautiful things: bathers running naked under sun-pierced foliage, and a most enormous beech, standing in the village like a god. A villager was proud of it. More woods with lilies-of-the-valley in them, and close to this house two lovers asleep by the road, face downwards, their arms over each other. They looked as ugly and ill-shaped as humanity can be, but I merely felt grateful.

The seven of us all came back safe from the great Oder Berge outing, although Fraulein Backe got 'bubbles' on her feet.[56] When I wrote Howards End I brought in the Oder Berge and other[57] Pomeranian recollections.

The next extract is more meditative; and covers ground already indicated.[58]

July 14.   At 8.00 this evening the east and zenith were full of huge saffron clouds. The moon showing at times between them. In the west the sun setting in clear sky with a few golden bars[59] above it. The light from the trees fell marvellously on the moving hay carts and on the shoeless Poles. Would also remember the sun of last Sunday, into whose light we ascended in the dip ups of the birch woods. After beer it looked like a stream of beer, and its last reflections, together with those of the crescent-moon, were reflected in the Thur See.[60] The magic change - I noted yesterday - comes at 6.15, now. Everything turns bright and coloured.[61] Back from picnic with children. Smeared with blaubeeren,[62] butter, milk coffee, dust and gooseberries.

It is curious that Germany, a country which I do not know well or instinctively embrace, should twice have seduced me through her country side. I have described the first occasion. The second was half a century later[63] when I stayed in a remote hamlet in Franconia. The scenery was more scenic than in Pomerania. There were swelling green hills rising into wood-lands. There were picturesque castles and distant views. But the two districts[64] resembled each other in their vastness and openness and in their freedom from industrialism. They were free from smoke and wires, and masts and placards, and they were full of living air: they remind me of what our own countryside used to be before it was ruined. The tragedy of England is that she is too small to become a modern state and yet to retain her freshness. The freshness has to go. Even when there is a

National Park it has to be mucked up. Germany is anyhow larger, and thanks to her superior size she may preserve the rural heritage that smaller national units have had to scrap - the heritage which I used to see from my own doorstep in Hertfordshire when I was a child, and which has failed to outlast me.

1. <NOT CHECKED IN TALKS DEPARTMENT WITH> The talk's duration was added by hand at the top of the script. The broadcast was published as an essay in the 1 January 1959 *Listener* (pp. 12–14), immediately following the publication of a television interview of EMF in honor of his eightieth birthday (pp. 11–12); both articles were illustrated with photographs.

2. <ELIZABETH OF THE GERMAN GARDEN by Leslie de Charms>

3. <9.10 - 9.40 p.m.>

4. Leslie de Charms, *Elizabeth of the German Garden: A Biography* (London: Heinemann, 1958).

5. EMF added an accent mark above "Herr."

6. Schloss: castle.

7. Born Mary Annette Beauchamp in Sydney, Australia, on 31 August 1866, the Countess von Arnim was best known during her lifetime for *Elizabeth and Her German Garden* (1898).

8. NSA: "I must explain how I got out there."

9. <I must say in passing that>

10. For EMF's earlier comments on Walpole, see his broadcasts dated 4 July 1941 and 10 December 1941.

11. NSA: "and kindly plunged"

12. NSA: "the best spare room"

13. NSA: "esteem"

14. *Listener:* "easy"

15. NSA: "she told me gaily that she'd nearly sent me straight back to England"

16. <which made her sit up>

17. *Listener:* "This gave her a jump."

18. NSA: "Yes"

19. NSA: "Still all turned out well"

20. NSA: "amusingly and brilliantly written"

21. NSA: "Later in the summer flowers—pansies, tulips, roses"

22. NSA: "really appeared"

23. Chaussée: causeway.

24. EMF added accent marks above each repetition of "Hee."

25. NSA: "as if finding the definite article too difficult"

26. NSA: "go out"

27. NSA: "Herr Steinweg and I, both very friendly to Nature, took many short walks together and he often recited poetry."

28. NSA: "got out"

29. NSA: "ran out"

30. EMF added an accent mark above "I."

31. EMF added an accent mark above "He."

32. NSA: "stop"

33. Word omitted from the *Listener.*

34. <her>
35. NSA: "that gives the sort of idea"
36. Translation: It is the great serpent Boa; when he bites, those he bites die.
37. See the 19 December 1932 broadcast, note 18.
38. *Listener:* "She could run like the wind. Everyone loved her."
39. NSA: "out of"
40. NSA: "My teaching duties only took an hour a day and I had abundant leisure"
41. NSA: "jumped"
42. Der Alte Moor: The weak old father, Count Maximilian Von Moor, in Friedrich Schiller's late-eighteenth-century tragedy *The Robbers*. One of the count's sons turns robber while the other vindictively schemes against his brother and the father whose wealth and lands he covets.
43. <funny>
44. NSA: "quite recently"
45. Epitaph: A. E. Housman, "XXIII 'Crossing alone the nighted ferry,'" lines 5–6, in *More Poems* (London: Jonathan Cape, 1936).
46. The script inadvertently leaves uncanceled "in that photograph" following "immortalised" despite EMF's handwritten shift of the phrase to earlier in the sentence.
47. <. I am>
48. <Let us>
49. <the>
50. <I kept>
51. NSA: "I'll keep to Nassenheide, and now I'll read a couple of extracts from the Journal I kept out there."
52. Oder Berge: Oder Mountains, so called from the Oder River.
53. NSA: "The roads so broad and sandy, the houses set so aimlessly in their surroundings, and there's no attempt to conceal or group the outhouses."
54. EMF added an accent mark above "bull."
55. EMF added an accent mark above the first syllable of "spindly."
56. NSA: "The seven of us all got back safe from that great Oder Berge outing, although Fraulein Backe afterwards got 'bubbles' on her feet."
57. NSA: "various other"
58. NSA: "Now for my second extract from the journal—it's more meditative; and it covers ground that I've already indicated."
59. EMF added an accent mark above "bars."
60. Thur See: a lake.
61. NSA: "Everything at that moment turns bright and coloured."
62. Blaubeeren: blueberries.
63. NSA: "And the second came not long ago, half a century later"
64. <were linked together by>

Index

BBC: British Broadcasting Corporation
EMF: Edward Morgan "E. M." Forster